Praise for Best Places® Guidebooks

"Best Places *are the best regional restaurant and guide books in America.*"
—THE SEATTLE TIMES

"Best Places *covers must-see portions of the West Coast with style and authority. In-the-know locals offer thorough info on restaurants, lodgings, and the sights.*"
—NATIONAL GEOGRAPHIC TRAVELER

"*Travelers swear by the recommendations in the* Best Places *guidebooks.*"
—SUNSET MAGAZINE

"*Known for their frank yet chatty tone.*"
—PUBLISHERS WEEKLY

"*For travel collections covering the Northwest, the* Best Places *series takes precedence over all similar guides.*"
—BOOKLIST

"*Not only the best travel guide in the region, but maybe one of the most definitive guides in the country, which many look forward to with the anticipation usually sparked by a best-selling novel. A browser's delight,* Best Places Northwest *should be chained to dashboards throughout the Northwest.*"
—THE OREGONIAN

"*Visitors to Washington, Oregon, and British Columbia would do well to pick up* Best Places Northwest *for an exhaustive review of food and lodging in the region. . . . An indispensable glove-compartment companion.*"
—TRAVEL AND LEISURE

TRUST THE LOCALS

The original insider's guides, written by local experts

EVERY PLACE STAR-RATED & RECOMMENDED

★★★★ The very best in the city

★★★ Distinguished; many outstanding features

★★ Excellent; some wonderful qualities

★ A good place

HELPFUL ICONS

Watch for these quick-reference symbols throughout the book:

 FAMILY FUN

 GOOD VALUE

 ROMANTIC

 EDITORS' CHOICE

BEST PLACES®
PORTLAND

The Locals' Guide to the Best Restaurants,
Lodgings, Sights, Shopping, and More!

Edited by
ELIZABETH LOPEMAN

EDITION

SASQUATCH BOOKS
SEATTLE

Printed in the United States of America
Published by Sasquatch Books
Distributed by PGW/Perseus

Eighth edition
15 14 13 12 11 10   9 8 7 6 5 4 3 2 1

ISBN-10: 1-57061-624-8
ISBN-13: 978-1-57061-624-2
ISSN: 1095-9742

Project editor: Rachelle Longé
Cover photograph: Kenny & Zuke's Delicatessen by Rob Casey
Cover design: Rosebud Eustace
Interior design and composition: Scott Taylor/FILTER/Talent
Maps: Lisa Brower/GreenEye Design
Indexer: Michael Ferreira

SPECIAL SALES

Best Places guidebooks are available at special discounts on bulk purchases for
corporate, club, or organization sales promotions, premiums, and gifts. For
more information, contact your local bookseller or Special Sales, Best Places
Guidebooks, 119 South Main Street, Suite 400, Seattle, Washington 98104,
800/775-0817.

SASQUATCH BOOKS

119 South Main Street, Suite 400
Seattle, WA 98104
206/467-4300
www.sasquatchbooks.com
custserv@sasquatchbooks.com

CONTENTS

CONTENTS

Introduction and Acknowledgments

If great empires grow out of well-fed people, Portland might soon rule the world. The food scene in Portland is so exquisite and booming, it's been discussed repeatedly and at length by the *New York Times*, *Gourmet*, *Food & Wine*, and numerous other national publications. The community supports its chefs, who in return proudly support their farmers, the result being truly imaginative and, more important, delicious things to eat everywhere you go.

Starting with such inspired creations in their bellies, Portlanders have been especially productive in the last decade, and exponentially so in the last three or four years, at building the city they want to live in. Within an hour of Portland are opportunities to hike, bike, ski, surf, and kayak or canoe, but Portlanders also cherish their time out of the weather, and from that has come a quite serious coffee culture, an ever-evolving and boundary-pushing music scene, and world-class arts for stalwart appreciators and contributors. With the marriage of the Museum of Contemporary Craft and Pacific Northwest College of Art, we'll likely see an even more impressive explosion of visual arts in the near future, much like the city has experienced recently with theater arts. The strength of literary arts in Portland is quite probably only second to New York in terms of participation per capita. Literary readings and events take place literally every evening, and there is frequently more than one. Portland is a truly fantastic city with wonderfully unique shopping opportunities, especially agreeable public transportation, and exceedingly comfortable hotel accommodations. We'll be happy to show you around!

This book could not have been possible without the following contributors:

Elianna Bar-El
Lizzy Caston
Joan Cirillo
Visnja Clayton
Dana Cuellar
Mollie Firestone
Alton Garcia
Ava Hegedus
Trevor Hill
Miranda Rake
Terry Richard
Andrea Slonecker
Mike Thelin

Special thanks to Terence Maikels and Rachelle Longé at Sasquatch Books; Bette Sinclair, Dina Nishioka, Melissa Broussard, and Lisa Hill; and John Gottberg, Dan Leif, Lota LaMontagne, and Paige Powell.

—*Elizabeth Lopeman*

About Best Places® Guidebooks

People trust us. Best Places guidebooks, which have been published continuously since 1975, represent one of the most respected regional travel series in the country. Our reviewers know their territory and seek out the very best a city or region has to offer. We are able to provide tough, candid reports about places that have rested too long on their laurels, and to delight in new places that deserve recognition. We describe the true strengths, foibles, and unique characteristics of each establishment listed.

Best Places Portland is written by and for locals, and is therefore coveted by travelers. It's written for people who live here and who enjoy exploring the city's bounty and its out-of-the-way places of high character and individualism. It is these very characteristics that make *Best Places Portland* ideal for tourists, too. The best places in and around the city are the ones that denizens favor: independently owned establishments of good value, touched with local history, run by lively individuals, and graced with natural beauty. With this eighth edition of *Best Places Portland*, travelers will find the information they need: where to go and when; what to order; which rooms to request (and which to avoid); where the best music, art, nightlife, shopping, and other attractions are; and how to find the city's hidden secrets.

How to Use This Book

This book is divided into ten chapters covering a wide range of establishments, destinations, and activities in and around Portland. All evaluations are based on reports from local and traveling inspectors. Final judgments are made by the editors. **EVERY PLACE FEATURED IN THIS BOOK IS RECOMMENDED.**

STAR RATINGS *(for Top 200 Restaurants and Lodgings only)* Restaurants and lodgings are rated on a scale of one to four stars (with half stars in between), based on uniqueness, loyalty of local clientele, performance measured against the establishment's goals, excellence of cooking, cleanliness, value, and professionalism of service. Reviews are listed alphabetically, and every place is recommended.

★★★★	The very best in the region
★★★	Distinguished; many outstanding features
★★	Excellent; some wonderful qualities
★	A good place
UNRATED	New or undergoing major changes

(For more on how we rate places, see "Best Places Star Ratings" on page x.)

PRICE RANGE *(for Top 200 Restaurants and Lodgings only)* Prices for restaurants are based primarily on dinner for two, including dessert, tax, and tip (no alcohol). Prices for lodgings are based on peak season rates for one night's lodging for two people (i.e., double occupancy). Peak season is typically Memorial Day to

BEST PLACES® STAR RATINGS

Any travel guide that rates establishments is inherently subjective—and Best Places is no exception. We rely on our professional experience, yes, but also on a gut feeling. And, occasionally, we even give in to a soft spot for a favorite neighborhood hangout. Our star-rating system is not simply a checklist; it's judgmental, critical, sometimes fickle, and highly personal.

For each new edition, we send local food and travel experts out to review restaurants and lodgings and then rate them on a scale of one to four, based on uniqueness, loyalty of local clientele, performance measured against the establishment's goals, excellence of cooking, cleanliness, value, and professionalism of service. That doesn't mean a one-star establishment isn't worth dining or sleeping at—far from it. When we say that all the places listed in our books are recommended, we mean it. That one-star pizza joint may be just the ticket for the end of a whirlwind day of shopping with the kids. But if you're planning something more special, the star ratings can help you choose an eatery or hotel

Labor Day; off-season rates vary but can sometimes be significantly less. Call ahead to verify, as all prices are subject to change.

$$$$ Very expensive (more than $125 for dinner for two; more than $250 for one night's lodging for two)

$$$ Expensive (between $85 and $125 for dinner for two; between $150 and $250 for one night's lodging for two)

$$ Moderate (between $35 and $85 for dinner for two; between $85 and $150 for one night's lodging for two)

$ Inexpensive (less than $35 for dinner for two; less than $85 for one night's lodging for two)

RESERVATIONS *(for Top 200 Restaurants only)* We've used one of the following terms for our reservations policy: reservations required, reservations recommended, no reservations. "No reservations" means either reservations are not necessary or are not accepted.

PARKING *(for Top 200 Restaurants and Lodgings only)* We've indicated a variety of options for parking in the facts lines at the end of each review as appropriate.

that will wow your new clients or be a stunning, romantic place to celebrate an anniversary or impress a first date.

We award four-star ratings sparingly, reserving them for what we consider truly the best. And once an establishment has earned our highest rating, everyone's expectations seem to rise. Readers often write us letters specifically to point out the faults in four-star establishments. With changes in chefs, management, styles, and trends, it's always easier to get knocked off the pedestal than to ascend it. Three-star establishments, on the other hand, seem to generate healthy praise. They exhibit outstanding qualities, and we get lots of love letters about them. The difference between two and three stars can sometimes be a very fine line. Two-star establishments are doing a good, solid job and gaining attention, while one-star places are often dependable spots that have been around forever.

The restaurants and lodgings described in *Best Places Portland* have earned their stars from hard work and good service (and good food). They're proud to be included in this book—look for our Best Places sticker in their windows. And we're proud to honor them in this, the eighth edition of *Best Places Portland*.

ADDRESSES AND PHONE NUMBERS Every attempt has been made to provide accurate information on an establishment's location and phone number, but it's always a good idea to call ahead and confirm. For establishments with two or more locations, we try to provide information on the original or most recommended branches.

CHECKS AND CREDIT CARDS Many establishments that accept checks also require a major credit card for identification. Note that some places accept only local checks. Credit cards are abbreviated in this book as follows: American Express (AE), Carte Blanche (CB), Diners Club (DC), Discover (DIS), Japanese credit card (JCB), MasterCard (MC), Visa (V).

E-MAIL AND WEB SITE ADDRESSES Web sites or e-mail addresses for establishments have been included where available. Please note that the Web is a fluid and evolving medium, and that Web pages are often "under construction"—or, as with all time-sensitive information, may no longer be valid.

MAP INDICATORS The letter-and-number codes appearing at the end of most listings refer to coordinates on the fold-out map included in the front of the book. Single letters (for example, F7) refer to the downtown Portland map; double letters (FF7) refer to the Greater Portland map on the flip side. If an establishment does not have a map code listed, its location falls beyond the boundaries of these maps (for example, Oregon Wine Country locations).

HELPFUL ICONS Watch for these quick-reference symbols throughout the book:

 FAMILY FUN Places that are fun, easy, and great for kids.

 GOOD VALUE While not necessarily cheap, these places offer a good deal within the context of the area.

 ROMANTIC These spots offer candlelight, atmosphere, intimacy, or other romantic qualities—kisses and proposals are encouraged!

 EDITORS' CHOICE These are places that are unique and special to the city, such as a restaurant owned by a beloved local chef or a tourist attraction recognized around the globe.

 Appears after listings for establishments that have wheelchair-accessible facilities.

INDEXES In addition to a general index at the back of the book, there are six specialized indexes: restaurants are indexed by star rating, neighborhood, and features at the beginning of the Restaurants chapter; hotels are indexed by star rating at the beginning of the Lodgings chapter; and nightspots are indexed by neighborhood and feature at the beginning of the Nightlife chapter.

PLANNING A TRIP

PLANNING A TRIP

How to Get Here

BY PLANE

PORTLAND INTERNATIONAL AIRPORT, or **PDX** (7000 NE Airport Wy; 503/460-4234 or 877/739-4636; www.flypdx.com; map:DD4), is served by most major U.S. airlines and some foreign carriers, with excellent connections from points around the Pacific Northwest and beyond. Allow at least 30 minutes—more during rush hours—to get between the airport and downtown by car.

The **TRI-MET** (503/238-7433; www.trimet.org) MAX Red Line, an extension of eastside light-rail service, takes about 40 minutes during peak hours and about 55 during off-peak hours to make the trip between Pioneer Courthouse Square and Tri-Met's terminal near the baggage claim at PDX. Check online or call to get exact times. Cost is $2.30. There are several intermediate bus-transfer stations for visitors staying on Portland's east side.

All major **CAR RENTAL** companies operate from the airport. **TAXIS** and **SHUTTLES** are readily available on the lower deck; after picking up your baggage, cross the first roadway, which is reserved for passenger pickup, and proceed to the commercial roadway. Expect to pay about $30 for the trip downtown.

PARKING (877/PDX-INFO) at PDX comes in three flavors, and where you park probably depends on how long you'll be there. The Economy Lot ($10 per day, $60 per week; served by a free shuttle) is a good bet for extended parking. Close to the terminal, the Long-Term Lot ($16 per day) is designed for parking over a one- to three-day period; the Parking Garage, or short-term parking ($3 per hour, $24 per day), is best for quick trips. Parking for the disabled in all lots is $10 per day and $3 per hour. Call ahead to check space availability in any lot.

BY BUS

Near Union Station, just north of Old Town, is the **GREYHOUND** station (550 NW 6th Ave, River District; 503/243-2357 or 800/231-2222; www.greyhound.com; map:M4), which has a complete schedule of buses each day. Both the train station and the bus station are within walking distance of the downtown core known as "Fareless Square," where you can ride MAX trains or Tri-Met buses for free and catch MAX and Tri-Met into downtown and beyond, to most suburbs in the metropolitan area.

BY TRAIN

AMTRAK (503/273-4866 recorded arrival and departure times, or 800/872-7245 reservations; www.amtrak.com) operates out of the lovely Union Station (800 NW 6th Ave, River District; map:N4), just north of downtown Portland; look for "Go By Train" written in neon on the prominent clock tower. Built in 1896 from brick, stucco, and sandstone in an Italian Renaissance style, Union Station memorializes the bygone era of the great railways. Trains come from and head for points north, east, and south daily.

BY CAR

Most drivers come into Portland via either **INTERSTATE 5**, which runs north-south between Canada and Mexico, or **INTERSTATE 84**, which extends west into Portland through the Columbia Gorge. **US HIGHWAY 26** links Portland to the Oregon Coast via Hillsboro (west) and to central Oregon via Mount Hood (east).

    INTERSTATE 205 is a 36-mile, semibeltway route through Portland's east side that loops off I-5 between Tualatin (12 miles south of downtown) and north Vancouver, Washington (16 miles north). It passes near Lake Oswego, West Linn, Oregon City, and Milwaukie, among other towns. **INTERSTATE 405** is a 3-mile-long alternative route to I-5 that skirts the western edge of downtown. Rush hours in Portland can mean standstill traffic on all highways, but if you arrive midday (after 9am but before 3pm) or after 7pm, you should have clear sailing into town.

When to Visit

Portland is in bloom—culturally speaking—year-round. When to visit is strictly a matter of preference, but knowing a few constants can make planning a trip a little bit easier.

WEATHER

Unless you don't mind getting soaked—and many natives own neither slicker nor umbrella—bring something water-resistant no matter what the season. Portland skies are ever changing. The common denominator is precipitation, but all the rain does pay off: Portland boasts close proximity to fabulous skiing on Mount Hood, lush year-round parks, and a temperate clime that makes it OK to have hot chocolate or ice cream pretty much any time of year.

    Outside of snow on the nearby mountains, frozen, fluffy white flakes are generally not welcomed. Children's peals of "No school!" may seem premature when only a trace of snow is visible, but they know that the City of Roses is a city that closes when snow falls. Still, snow rarely lasts long on city streets (not because plows remove it, but because it simply melts), so enjoy the dusted evergreens while you can. If you visit in winter, be prepared for bus delays and traffic snarls on those rare occasions when snow falls.

    Portland's true summer runs from July to early October, so sun worshippers should time their trips accordingly. Bring the shades and—gasp!—sunscreen. Allergy sufferers will find May and June the toughest going, but they can still enjoy the fulsome beauty of Bridgetown's gardens. Early spring is redolent with its magnolia, cherry, and plum blossoms; June's end sees the full explosion of Portland's famous International Rose Test Garden.

AVERAGE TEMPERATURE AND PRECIPITATION BY MONTH

Month	Daily Maximum Temp. (degrees F)	Daily Minimum Temp. (degrees F)	Monthly Precipitation (inches)
JANUARY	45.6	34.2	5.07
FEBRUARY	50.3	35.9	4.18
MARCH	55.7	38.6	3.71
APRIL	60.5	41.9	2.64
MAY	66.7	47.5	2.38
JUNE	72.7	52.6	1.59
JULY	79.3	56.9	0.72
AUGUST	79.7	57.3	0.93
SEPTEMBER	74.6	52.5	1.65
OCTOBER	63.3	45.2	2.88
NOVEMBER	51.8	39.8	5.61
DECEMBER	45.4	35.0	5.71

Source: U.S. National Oceanic and Atmospheric Administration

TIME

Portland is on Pacific Standard Time (PST), which is 3 hours behind New York City, 2 hours behind Chicago, 1 hour behind Denver, 1 hour ahead of Anchorage, and 2 hours ahead of Honolulu. Portland is 17 hours behind Tokyo and 8 hours behind London. Daylight saving time begins in early March and ends in early November.

WHAT TO BRING

The Portland fashion aesthetic is ever evolving—with a solid representation of the hipster, punk, and rockabilly variety—but most locals aren't too picky (much to the dismay of some bigger-city transplants). Here's the rule of thumb for tourists: dress for comfort—good walking shoes are a must. Men may want to pack a jacket for dinner, but it won't be required anywhere; women, as usual, have more choices: dresses, skirts, or pants are all fine, and you should know that many people—though not everyone—will be wearing jeans, T-shirts, and Nikes (or the equivalent) no matter what day of the week it is (or what line of work they're in). If you want to draw attention, dress with polish or dress Miami Beach; to blend in, think fleece and cotton.

Essentials for all seasons include a water-resistant shell; comfortable, water-resistant shoes; sunglasses (rain or shine); lip balm; and a wardrobe geared toward layering. Summer days are often cool in the mornings and evenings, so pack a jacket, even in August.

General Costs

Visitors are often surprised to find that Oregon has no sales tax (hence higher income and property taxes than many states), making it a shoppers' paradise—and ensuring that there's always a tax revolt in the works. Portland's economy is driven by a broad base of services and industries. Manufacturing includes machinery, electronics, metals, transportation equipment, and lumber and wood products, and there are some 1,000 high-tech companies in the metro area, the largest of which is Intel. Among other large companies in the Portland area, a few internationally known names stand out, including Nike, Columbia Sportswear, and Tektronix.

It's a buyer's market in the luxury-hotel trade in downtown Portland, at least until the demand catches up to the supply. In the past few years, a number of downtown hotels, large and small, have opened for business, and now there are too many to fill on a regular basis. Inquire about special rates and packages; you might find a bargain, or at least a set of amenities (maybe a shopper's package or a romance package), that will make your hotel stay memorable.

Prices at Portland restaurants may be above the national average, but for visitors who are used to eating out in San Francisco or Seattle (Portland's closest big-city neighbors), dining in the City of Roses may seem like a bargain.

AVERAGE COSTS FOR LODGING AND FOOD

Double room

INEXPENSIVE	**$45–$85**
MODERATE	**$85–$150**
EXPENSIVE	**$150 AND UP**

Lunch for one (including beverage and tip)

INEXPENSIVE	**$6–$12**
MODERATE	**$12–$20**
EXPENSIVE	**$20 AND UP**

Beverages

12-OUNCE HOUSE COFFEE	**$1.50**
PINT OF MICROBREW	**$3.75**
GLASS OF WINE	**$6–$10**

Other common items

MOVIE TICKET	**$9**
TAXI	**$2.50 PICKUP; $2.30 PER MILE**
ROCK SHOW (LOCAL ACTS)	**$10–$20**
ADMISSION TO OREGON ZOO	**$6.75–$9.75**

Tips for Special Travelers

FAMILIES WITH CHILDREN

If you think your child has ingested something toxic, call the **POISON CENTER** (800/222-1222). To report child abuse, call the **CHILD ABUSE HOTLINE** (800/422-4453). For other emergencies, dial 9-1-1. **LEGACY EMANUEL HOSPITAL AND HEALTH CENTER** (2801 N Gantenbein Ave, North Portland; 503/413-2200; map:FF6) has an excellent children's facility; **LEGACY GOOD SAMARITAN HOSPITAL AND MEDICAL CENTER** (1015 NW 22nd Ave; 503/413-7711; map:GG7) in Northwest Portland is close to the downtown center. Another close-in hospital is the **PROVIDENCE ST. VINCENT HOSPITAL** (9205 SW Barnes Rd, West Hills; 503/216-1234; map:HH6), and the **PORTLAND CLINIC** (800 SW 13th Ave; 503/221-0161; map:H1) is in the heart of downtown.

Most major hotels can arrange for babysitters if notified in advance. The **NORTHWEST NANNIES INSTITUTE** (503/245-5288) places course graduates for live-in or daily care throughout the metro area. **CARE GIVERS PLACEMENT AGENCY** (503/244-6370) also matches families with daily or overnight nannies. **METRO CHILD CARE RESOURCE AND REFERRAL** (503/253-5000) offers free information on day-care services in the tricounty area.

Many young families move to Portland with the idea that it is a great place to raise children—and they're right. Not surprisingly, there is plenty to do here for children of all ages. **THE CHILDREN'S MUSEUM** (4015 SW Canyon Rd, Washington Park; 503/223-6500; www.portlandcm.org; map: HH7), opposite the zoo in Washington Park, is a local philanthropic success story. Check out the climbing structure and the waterworks. Both the **OREGON ZOO** (4001 SW Canyon Rd, Washington Park; 503/226-1561; www. oregonzoo.org; map:HH7) and OMSI, the **OREGON MUSEUM OF SCIENCE AND INDUSTRY** (1945 SE Water Ave, Southeast; 503/797-4000; www.omsi. org; map:HH6), are top-notch family standbys.

For an up-to-date overview of possibilities, check out the activity calendars in *Metro Parent* magazine (503/460-2774; www.metro-parent.com) and *Portland Family* magazine (503/906-7952; www.portlandfamily.com). These free publications can be found at coffee shops and newsstands. When copies are scarce, try **FINNEGAN'S TOYS AND GIFTS** (922 SW Yamhill St, Downtown; 503/221-0306; map:H2) or **RICH'S CIGAR STORE** (820 SW Alder St, Downtown; 503/228-1700; map:I3).

For a copy of the **OFFICIAL OREGON KIDS TRAVEL GUIDE**, call the state tourism commission or visit the Web site (800/547-7842; www.travel oregon.com).

Watch for this icon throughout the book: 👫 . It indicates places and activities that are great for families.

SENIORS

In Multnomah County, the **AGING SERVICES DEPARTMENT** operates a **SENIOR HELPLINE** (503/988-3646), which assists seniors with information about health services, low-income housing, recreation, transportation, legal services, volunteer programs, and other matters. Washington County also has an **AGING SERVICES DEPARTMENT** (503/640-3489); its counterpart in Clackamas County is **AGING AND DISABILITY SERVICES** (503/655-8640).

Senior citizens and people with disabilities receive free transportation with the cost of the activity when participating in activities sponsored by the **PORTLAND CITY PARKS PROGRAM FOR DISABLED CITIZENS AND SENIOR LEISURE** (503/823-4328).

PEOPLE WITH DISABILITIES

Public transportation in Portland, on Tri-Met buses and MAX trains, is wheelchair accessible. Press the blue button outside the MAX doors for ramp access. The doors will remain shut longer than the doors for foot traffic, but don't panic—the beeping sound means that the ramp is being lowered.

INDEPENDENT LIVING RESOURCES (503/232-7411) assists people of various disabilities. The **ARC OF MULTNOMAH COUNTY** (503/223-7279) offers services for people with developmental disabilities, including in-home and center-based respite care. Call well in advance to take advantage of this service. **TRIPS INC. SPECIAL ADVENTURES** (800/686-1013; www.tripsinc.com) has provided chaperoned excursions for people with developmental disabilities since 1991. Many of these Trips Inc. adventures are out-of-state, but check with the office for in-state camping and rodeo offerings.

The **OREGON TELECOMMUNICATIONS RELAY SERVICE** (800/735-1232 or TTY 800/735-2900) is a relay service providing full telephone accessibility to people who are deaf or hearing- or speech-impaired.

WOMEN

Portland is a relatively tranquil place, but as in most cities, women travelers should take extra safety precautions at night. The **WOMEN'S CRISIS LINE** number is 503/235-5333. For health and reproductive services, call **PLANNED PARENTHOOD** (503/775-0861 or 503/288-8826).

GAYS AND LESBIANS

Portland residents pride themselves on tolerance and open-mindedness, and thus Portland is a city with a healthy gay and lesbian scene. The **PORTLAND OREGON VISITORS ASSOCIATION** (877/678-5263) publishes its *GLBT Portland Guide* as a resource for gay, lesbian, bisexual, and transgendered visitors and includes a link on its Web site (www.travelportland.com). Visitors can also pick up a copy of the widely available tabloid newspaper *Just Out* (503/236-1252; www.justout.com), a free bimonthly source for gay news, arts, and community events.

HAVE DOG WILL TRAVEL

Rated one of the most dog-friendly cities in the country, Portland has more than 136,000 canines, according to *Dog Fancy* magazine. The city sure loves its pooches, as evidenced by its numerous dog parks, day-care options, and boutiques, as well as dog-friendly hotels and restaurants.

If your dog has an emergency, call **DOVE LEWIS EMERGENCY ANIMAL HOSPITAL** (1945 NW Pettygrove St, Northwest; 503/228-7281; www.dovelewis. org; map:GG7). It has trained staff on call 24 hours.

First on Fido's "To Do" list might be to visit one of the many dog parks or dog-friendly trails. The Web site www.portlandonline.com/parks lists 32 off-leash dog parks (some are fenced). Among them are **BRENTWOOD PARK** (6799 SE 62nd Ave, Southeast), **GABRIEL PARK** (SW 45th Ave and Vermont St, Maplewood), **NORMANDALE PARK** (NE 57th Ave and Halsey St, Northeast), and **WALLACE PARK** (NW 25th Ave and Raleigh St, Northwest). Numerous dog-friendly trails can be found in and around the city; pick up *A Bark in the Park: The 45 Best Places to Hike with Your Dog in the Portland, Oregon Region*, by Lisa Johnson, at Powell's or any bookstore for further information.

Many Portland hotels accept dogs, some with a fee. If you're staying in the heart of the city, options include **HOTEL MONACO**, **HOTEL LUCIA**, and **HOTEL DELUXE**; **THE NINES** takes as many as two dogs up to 80 pounds each (see reviews in the Lodgings chapter). Ask in advance about the hotel's pet fee, which can range up to $75. Check www.dogfriendly.com for more information.

Fido can also have his own resort lodging by day or night. **HOWLIDAY INN** (940 SE Madison St, Downtown; 503/230-1050) allows your dog access to a rooftop patio. **IT'S A DOG'S LIFE** (8709 N Lombard St, North Portland; 503/286-2688) provides plenty of supervised playtime—interspersed with nap and snack

For a complete list of gay-friendly businesses, pick up a copy of *Portland's Gay & Lesbian Community Yellow Pages*. The free directory is published annually and can be found at most coffee shops and the like. To scope out the city before arriving, visit its Web site (www.pdxgayyellowpages.com). The **GAY RESOURCE CONNECTION** operates an AIDS/STD hotline (800/777-2437) and will provide referrals for both services and activities.

PET OWNERS

See "Have Dog Will Travel."

times. **URBAN FAUNA** (338 NW 6th Ave, Chinatown; 503/223-4602) has a dog-grooming studio and offers obedience classes. **VIRGINIA WOOF** (1520 W Burnside St, Downtown; 503/224-5455) has more than 3,300 square feet of play space; the staff is trained in basic animal first aid. **WAG THE DOG** (2410 SE 50th Ave at Division St, Southeast; 503/238-0737), which has 5,000 square feet of play space, considers its services to be doggy therapy.

Your dog will deserve a treat or two while in Portland, and luckily, downtown and various neighborhoods have delectable doggie munchies. **GREEN DOG PET SUPPLY** (4605 NE Fremont St, Beaumont Village; 503/528-1800) features an array of organic treats that are good for your dog and the earth. The **LEXIDOG BOUTIQUE AND SOCIAL CLUB** (6767 SW Macadam Ave, Johns Landing, 503/245-4363; 416 NW 10th Ave, Pearl District, 503/243-6200) offers high-end fashionable accessories, tasty treats, and even birthday parties with frosted cakes. **HEALTHY PETS**, with three locations (1402A SE 39th Ave, Hawthorne, 503/236-8036; 2224 NE Alberta St, Alberta, 503/249-6571; 7642 SW Capitol Hwy, Multnomah Village, 503/222-2686), specializes in pet foods with no chemical preservatives, meat by-products, or artificial colors. They also carry herbal remedies and canine supplements. **SALTY'S DOG SHOP** (3741 N Mississippi Ave, Northeast, 503/249-1432; 8119 SE Stark St, Montavilla, 503/445-9449) has so many toys and treats that dog owners will be as intrigued as their pets.

For an offbeat experience, you can tap into Fido's psyche (or that of any other pet) with pet psychic Faye Pietrokowsky at **INNER DESIGN** (510 SW 3rd Ave, Ste 418, Downtown; 503/221-2123). All you need is your pet's name and a photo (if you have it with you), and she communicates with the animal—even those that have passed on—for an entertaining, if not informative, session.

—Alexandra Arch and Elizabeth Lopeman

FOREIGN VISITORS

Some tour companies will provide a translator if they know in advance which language is needed, or you can inquire through **TRAVEL PORTLAND** (800/962-3700). Currency can be exchanged at any main bank branch or at **TRAVELEX AMERICA** (503/281-3045), located at Portland International Airport across from the United Airlines ticket counter. Ask about commission charges, or call 800/CURRENCY.

For general visa information, contact **U.S. CITIZENSHIP AND IMMIGRATION SERVICES** (511 NW Broadway, Room 117, Downtown; 800/375-5283; www.uscis.gov; map:L4). Oregon is home to a number of foreign consulates, some large, some small, and most of them are in Portland. Visitors from around the globe can contact their local consulates.

BARBADOS, 10202 SE 32nd Ave, Ste 601, Milwaukie; 503/659-0283

BELGIUM, 2812 NW Imperial Terrace, Hillside; 503/228-0465

CYPRUS, 1130 SW Morrison St, Ste 510, Downtown; 503/248-0500

CZECH REPUBLIC, 10260 SW Greenburg Rd, Ste 560, Tigard; 503/293-9545

DENMARK, 888 SW 5th Ave, Downtown; 503/802-2131

FINLAND, 2730 SW Cedar Hills Blvd, Beaverton; 503/526-0391

FRANCE, PO Box 751, Portland 97201; 503/725-5298

GERMANY, 200 SW Market St, Ste 1695, Downtown; 503/222-0490

ITALY, 4507-A SE Milwaukie Blvd, Brooklyn; 503/287-2578

JAPAN, 1300 SW 5th Ave, Ste 2700, Downtown; 503/221-1811

LITHUANIA, 1 Produce Row/333 SE 2nd Ave, Inner Southeast; 503/234-5000

MALAYSIA, 7497 SW Aloma Wy, Ste 6, Garden Home; 503/246-0707

MEXICO, 1234 SW Morrison St, Downtown; 503/274-1442

NETHERLANDS, 520 SW Yamhill St, Ste 600, Downtown; 503/222-7957

NORWAY, 4380 SW Macadam Ave, Ste 120, Johns Landing; 503/228-8828

PANAMA, 829 N Russell St, Albina; 503/284-1189

SWEDEN, 111 SW 5th Ave, Ste 2900, Downtown; 503/227-0634

THAILAND, 121 SW Salmon St, Ste 1430, Downtown; 503/221-0440

UNITED KINGDOM, 520 SW Yamhill St, Downtown; 503/227-5669

WEB INFORMATION

The best general-interest Web sites include those for **TRAVEL PORTLAND** (www.travelportland.com) and the **PORTLAND CHAMBER OF COMMERCE** (www.portlandalliance.com). The **CITY OF PORTLAND**'s own Web site (www.portlandonline.com) has links to a variety of urban requirements. For information on **LOCAL MICROBREWERIES**, see www.oregonbeer.com; for **LOCAL WINERIES**, head to www.oregonwine.com; and for a **LOCAL FOOD-IES' CALENDAR**, go to the Web site for **NORTHWEST PALATE MAGAZINE** (www.nwpalate.com). For the *Oregonian*'s calendar of events, visit the site for **OREGON LIVE** (www.oregonlive.com), and for *Willamette Week*'s calendar of events, see www.wweek.com. Finally, to check **CURRENT WEATHER CONDITIONS**, visit www.koinlocal6.com/weather.

LAY OF THE CITY

LAY OF THE CITY

Orientation

The mighty **COLUMBIA RIVER** and the oft-bridged **WILLAMETTE RIVER** set the blueprint for Portland. In fact, natural landmarks eliminate the need for a compass, at least when skies are clear. **MOUNT HOOD** marks the east like a glistening guardian, and the verdant green West Hills mark, appropriately, the west. To the north, visible from many parts of the city, is Washington's volcanic **MOUNT ST. HELENS**, whose top from this perspective appears flat.

The Willamette (pronounced "wil-LAM-it") enters town from the south, cleaving Portland's west side from its east. Burnside Street separates north from south. The light-rail, known as MAX, runs basically east-west. Each quarter of town has its own flavor, and new cultural environments are always emerging.

PIONEER COURTHOUSE SQUARE, Portland's public red-bricked plaza, marks central downtown. Most of the bricks are engraved with names of donors who helped create what some call Portland's living room. Portlanders gather here for lunch, people-watching (the Square attracts many young alternative folk), and various events. SW Broadway, which skirts the west side of the Square, is downtown's aorta, and many of the major city hotels are located either on this thoroughfare or within a few blocks east or west.

The Square, shadowed on the east by its namesake 1860s courthouse, is only six blocks from the banks of the Willamette, where **GOV. TOM MCCALL WATERFRONT PARK** stretches riverside for more than a mile. Extending north from the South Waterfront to the Steel Bridge, and passing beneath three other bridges en route, the grassy strip replaced a four-lane expressway. Beneath the west end of the Burnside Bridge, it passes Portland's **SATURDAY MARKET**, which is as busy on Sunday as it is the day before. There's plenty to see, hear, and smell as artisans hawk their wares and steamy ethnic foods make mouths water.

PGE PARK (formerly Civic Stadium), home of minor-league baseball and college football, is about 12 blocks west of Pioneer Courthouse Square, a five-minute MAX ride. The **ROSE GARDEN** (aka the Rose Quarter), home of the Portland Trail Blazers pro basketball team and a major concert venue, is a 15-minute MAX ride to the east. The ultramodern **OREGON CONVENTION CENTER**, its twin towers a city landmark, is but a few blocks walk from the Rose Garden.

Across Burnside Street from PGE Park is Portland's trendy **NORTHWEST NEIGHBORHOOD**. Though it's divided by the I-405 corridor, shoppers along NW 23rd Avenue ("Nob Hill") and gallery-goers in the **PEARL DISTRICT** (between 9th and 15th aves) find getting around as easy as A-B-C, 1-2-3. The north-south avenues march westward in numerical order, and the east-west streets (Burnside through Wilson; Ankeny is south of Burnside) are helpfully named in alphabetical order.

The northernmost reaches of the neighborhood, at the end of NW Thurman Street, mark the beginning of 5,000-acre **FOREST PARK**, which cloaks much of the West Hills. Forest Park's 23-mile Wildwood Trail extends south to **WASHING-TON PARK**, climbing the hills immediately west of downtown (beginning just 1 mile from Broadway). Washington Park includes several of Portland's best-known visitor attractions, including the **OREGON ZOO**, the **INTERNATIONAL ROSE TEST GARDEN**, and the **JAPANESE GARDEN**.

The newest westside neighborhood, the **SOUTH WATERFRONT**, also called the River Blocks, is just south of downtown along the Willamette River. Its beacon, easily accessed via the Portland Streetcar (see Getting Around in this chapter), is a gleaming silver aerial tram that travels to the **OREGON HEALTH SCIENCES UNIVERSITY** facility on **MARQUAM HILL**. The South Waterfront is the largest example of environmentally sound urban planning in the country. Eat at one of the riverside restaurants in the area, and take a walk or a tram ride here.

On the east side of the river, Grand Avenue northbound and Martin Luther King Jr Boulevard southbound are speedy through streets that parallel I-5. With few exceptions, however, eastside neighborhoods have an east-west orientation, perhaps reflecting sprawl from downtown toward Mount Hood. The eastside business focus is still the **LLOYD CENTER** (south of Broadway between NE 9th and 15th aves), built in 1960 as the nation's first indoor shopping mall. The **IRVING-TON** and **ALAMEDA** districts, northeast of the Lloyd Center, are known for their many gracious and well-kept older homes.

Elsewhere in **NORTHEAST PORTLAND**, an economic upswing has come from both external gentrification and community-based business development. North Mississippi Avenue has filled in with hip boutiques, restaurants, and one of the city's best breweries, **AMNESIA BREWING**. In the residential Northeast neighborhoods, pedestrians have the best luck exploring NE Alberta and Fremont streets, as well as Broadway.

SOUTHEAST PORTLAND is the city's hippest area, sort of like what Berkeley is to San Francisco. Sections of **SE HAWTHORNE BOULEVARD** and **SE BELMONT STREET**, the **LAURELHURST** district near 28th and Burnside, and the **CLINTON STREET** neighborhood at SE 25th Avenue are good bets for food-and-wine aficionados, bargain-hunting moviegoers, thrift-store devotees, and shoppers of all persuasions. **MOUNT TABOR PARK** marks the eastern edge of the hip Southeast. A view of downtown from the top and the endless staircases that mark the back entrance make this park a popular spot for runners and relaxers alike.

A couple of quirky neighborhoods worth noting are south of the downtown core. The adjacent **SELLWOOD** and **MORELAND** districts, with great dining and antiquing, are along SE Milwaukie Avenue, south of Bybee Boulevard, and along SE 13th Avenue. The **MULTNOMAH VILLAGE** neighborhood winds along SW Capitol Highway at SW 35th Avenue.

Beyond Portland's urban boundaries, suburbs and bedroom communities spread in all directions. Directly south—up the north-flowing Willamette River via SR 43 (SW Macadam Ave) through the Johns Landing neighborhood—are the towns of **LAKE OSWEGO** (7 miles), **WEST LINN** (12 miles), and **OREGON CITY** (13 miles). Moving west around the clock face are **TUALATIN** (12 miles) at 7 o'clock, **TIGARD** (9 miles) at 8 o'clock, and **BEAVERTON** (8 miles), home to the Nike empire, at 9 o'clock. **HILLSBORO** (15 miles) is at 10 o'clock.

PORTLAND'S BRIDGES

Portland has its great art museum. It has its history museum, its interactive science museum, its children's and maritime and forestry museums. But the city also has the most remarkable open-air museum—a collection of full-scale movable bridges, all of them in daily use—that you'll see anywhere.

This "museum" includes 10 highway bridges that span the Willamette River within the city, 2 more south to Oregon City, and another 2 crossing the Columbia River between Portland and Vancouver, Washington. There are also railroad bridges.

The collection features all three basic bridge types (arch, suspension, and truss), all three movable span types (swing, vertical lift, and bascule, or seesaw), bridges that are close to one another (eight within 3 miles of one another), and midtown bridges with short and safe pedestrian approaches.

From north to south, Portland's highway bridges are the St. Johns (built in 1931), Fremont (1973), Broadway (1913), Steel (1912), Burnside (1926), Morrison (1958), Hawthorne (1910), Marquam (1966), Ross Island (1926), and Sellwood (1925).

The Willamette Valley's only suspension bridge, the **ST. JOHNS BRIDGE** (6.6 miles north of Burnside St), is rumored to have been a model for the Golden Gate, built in San Francisco six years later. When this impressive, cathedral-like bridge opened to great fanfare, biplanes flew beneath its twin towers en route to the now-defunct Swan Island airport. Today the city landmark welcomes marine traffic traveling upriver to Portland.

The **FREMONT BRIDGE** (1.3 miles north of Burnside St) is the world's longest tied arch bridge (1,255 feet)—which means it has no in-water pier supports in the main channel. The 902-foot midspan of this three-span bridge was built off-site and assembled on Swan Island, a mile downstream. Engineers from around the

MILWAUKIE (6 miles) and **CLACKAMAS** (10 miles) are to the southeast, at around 5 o'clock. **GRESHAM** (12 miles) and **TROUTDALE** (14 miles) are due east, at 3 o'clock. And due north, spreading along the opposite bank of the Columbia River from about 11 to 2 o'clock, is the burgeoning Washington city of **VANCOUVER**.

Visitor Information

People have been moving to Portland at such a clip that sometimes it seems as if there's been another homesteading act. A good place to start, for both visitors and new Oregonians, is the **TRAVEL PORTLAND VISITOR INFORMATION CENTER** world watched as its 6,000 tons were raised 175 feet above the river at a rate of 7 feet per hour.

The **BROADWAY BRIDGE** (0.7 mile north of Burnside St) was the world's longest double-leaf drawbridge when it opened and is still considered the single outstanding example of the Rall-type bascule span: its hinged lift-span leaves glide backward and upward on wheels along steel tracks.

The **STEEL BRIDGE** (0.3 mile north of Burnside St) is the only vertical-lift bridge in the world with twin decks capable of independent movement. The lower rail deck, normally kept in raised position, moves independently of the upper deck, which carries cars, pedestrians, bicycles, and the MAX light-rail. It is Portland's shortest bridge, at 211 feet.

The city-center **BURNSIDE BRIDGE** is best known locally as the site of the Saturday Market, which operates weekends (except January and February) under its west end. Above its west end is the revered "Made in Oregon" neon sign; until 1998, it advertised White Stag sportswear. A double-leaf bascule drawbridge like the Broadway and Morrison bridges, the Burnside replaced an earlier (1894) truss bridge.

The **MORRISON BRIDGE** (0.4 mile south of Burnside St) opened in 1958 to replace Portland's first river bridge, an 1887 toll bridge that charged 15 cents for a horse, buggy, and driver. With its concrete and steel pile foundations, open-grating steel deck, and double-leaf trunnion bascule, this minimalist bridge was considered cutting-edge modern architecture five decades ago.

The **HAWTHORNE BRIDGE** (0.7 mile south of Burnside St) predates (by two years) the Steel Bridge as the world's oldest vertical-lift bridge still in full operation. Its open steel gratings, which "sing" as vehicles cross, replaced a wooden deck in 1945.

Closing the last gap in the Mexico-to-Canada interstate freeway system when

(503/275-8355 or 877/678-5263; www.travelportland.com; map:H3), located on the lower west side of Pioneer Courthouse Square (701 SW 6th Ave). It's open daily (Mon–Fri 8:30am–5:30pm, Sat 10am–4pm, Sun 10am–2pm). Here, shelves are well stocked with brochures in English; ask about foreign-language guides to the area. Inside the center, visitors can surf the Web site and purchase discounted tickets to events happening that day. The main office of Travel Portland is nearby (1000 SW Broadway, 23rd floor, Downtown; 800/962-3700). If you're planning a convention, you might want to look into the **OREGON CONVENTION CENTER** (take their virtual tour at www.oregoncc.org).

Maintained in cooperation with the *Oregonian* newspaper, **OREGON LIVE** (www.oregonlive.com) lets Web surfers stay up-to-date with local news stories it opened in 1966, the **MARQUAM BRIDGE** (1.1 miles south of Burnside St) is a double-deck cantilever truss. It was designed for "simplicity and economy of design," its engineers told a public disenchanted with its utilitarian, "Erector Set" appearance. The Marquam does not allow pedestrian access.

Pedestrians have always used the **ROSS ISLAND BRIDGE** (2.6 miles south of Burnside St), the first downtown bridge built without streetcar tracks. Today, this cantilever-truss span—designed by Gustav Lindenthal, who also created New York's Queensboro Bridge—is Portland's most heavily traveled nonfreeway bridge, serving the city's sprawling southeast neighborhoods. Ross Island, where bald eagles and great blue herons nest, is just south of the bridge.

For 40 years before construction of the **SELLWOOD BRIDGE** (4.1 miles south of Burnside St), Portlanders depended upon the Spokane Street Ferry to take them across the Willamette River to the Oaks Amusement Park. The narrow (two-lane) Sellwood, a four-span continuous-deck truss design, was Portland's first fixed-span vehicle bridge.

Of Portland's other bridges, two are contemporary spans on I-205: the sleek **ABERNETHY BRIDGE** (1970) near Oregon City and the 600-foot **GLENN L. JACKSON MEMORIAL BRIDGE** (1982) across the Columbia River, named for Oregon's longtime State Highway Commission chairman. The **INTERSTATE BRIDGE** on I-5 between Portland and Vancouver replaced an interstate ferry when it was built in 1917; its second (southbound) span didn't open until 1958.

Conde McCullough, famed for his Oregon Coast bridges, designed the **OREGON CITY BRIDGE** in 1922. This 745-foot arch bridge features fluted Art Deco main piers and hammered inset panels. Just north, on the Clackamas River, McCullough's **MCLOUGHLIN BRIDGE** has been rated the most beautiful steel bridge of its kind in the United States.

—John Gottberg

and arts coverage. The **CITYSEARCH** Web site (www.portland.citysearch.com) offers food and music reviews. Find out more about the **CITY OF PORTLAND**—everything from which parks have dog runs to how city government is run—at www.portlandonline.com. Finally, the **PORTLAND CHAMBER OF COMMERCE** (220 SW Market St, Ste 1770, Downtown; 503/228-9411; www.portlandalliance.com; map:H2) can answer questions about conducting business in Portland.

For statewide tourism information, contact the **OREGON STATE TOURISM DIVISION** (800/547-7842; www.traveloregon.com).

Getting Around

BY BUS OR MAX

TRI-MET (503/238-RIDE [7433]; www.trimet.org) operates both the **CITY BUS SYSTEM** and the sleek **METROPOLITAN AREA EXPRESS (MAX)** trains, as well as the **PORTLAND STREETCAR**; tickets for the three systems are interchangeable. All vehicles are wheelchair accessible. Almost all the Tri-Met lines run through the **PORTLAND TRANSIT MALL** (SW 5th and 6th aves, Downtown); MAX lines also cross through downtown, extending east to Gresham and west to Hillsboro, and a new line takes riders south along I-205.

Buses run north across Burnside all the way to the Tri-Met North Terminal, just past the Greyhound station and across the street from Union Station. The North Terminal is the first stop on the transit mall and serves as a place for bus drivers to park while they take a break and wait to complete their schedule.

Travelers in the downtown area can ride buses or MAX for free anywhere in the 330-block **FARELESS SQUARE**. The square extends from I-405 on the south and west to NW Irving Street on the north; to the east, it crosses the Willamette River to the Rose Quarter and the Lloyd Center.

Fares outside the square are $2 for travel in two zones (from downtown to residential areas within the metropolitan area) and $2.30 for three zones (necessary for travel from downtown to most parts of Tigard, Beaverton, Gresham, Milwaukie, Lake Oswego, and the airport). Youth tickets are $1.50 per ride, and as many as three children age 6 and younger can ride free with a fare-paying customer. All-day tickets are $4.75. Honored citizens—those over 65 or the disabled—can catch a bus for 95 cents per ride or pay $26 for a monthly pass. Tickets can be purchased on the bus (exact change only) or at MAX stops. **TRI-MET'S CUSTOMER ASSISTANCE OFFICE** (weekdays 8:30am–5:30pm) is in the middle of Pioneer Courthouse Square, in the center of downtown. This is the place for face-to-face route information or ticket purchases. MAX trains run on the honor system; that is, MAX drivers never check fares. However, Tri-Met inspectors do frequently request proof of fare payment on buses and MAX, and passengers who haven't paid are fined or cited in district court.

The **MAX LIGHT-RAIL SYSTEM** travels on 52 miles of track throughout Portland and goes all the way to Portland Airport. Airport travelers may board the **RED LINE** downtown or transfer at several stations en route.

MAX's original **BLUE LINE** starts from Hillsboro in the west and winds through Beaverton, making its first Portland stop at the Oregon Zoo. From there it stops in the Goose Hollow neighborhood at SW Salmon Street and 18th Avenue, passes through downtown and Old Town, crosses the Steel Bridge, and continues on the east side, swinging by the Oregon Convention Center and the Lloyd Center before making its way along I-84, then east beside Burnside Street, to Gresham. And a new **GREEN LINE** starting at Portland State University on 5th Avenue stops at Union Station (the Portland

---

HIGHER EDUCATION

Portland is a young city, so it makes sense that it's an educational hub. With a dozen four-year schools and numerous additional junior colleges and technical schools, its institutions of higher learning offer something for everyone.

PORTLAND STATE UNIVERSITY (724 SW Harrison St; 503/725-3000; www.pdx.edu; map:E1), Oregon's urban university, straddles the south end of downtown's South Park Blocks and has an especially strong and nationally renowned public-affairs school.

In North Portland, the **UNIVERSITY OF PORTLAND** (5000 N Willamette Blvd; 503/943-7911; www.up.edu; map:EE8) was founded in 1901 by the Roman Catholic archbishop of Oregon and remains a Catholic university. Architect Pietro Belluschi, better known for the Portland Art Museum (1932), designed the handsome Chapel of Christ the Teacher in 1986.

Nationally renowned for its academic rigor and free-thinking student body, **REED COLLEGE** (3203 SE Woodstock Blvd, Eastmoreland; 503/771-1112; www.reed.edu; map:II5) is located in Southeast Portland. At the Cooley Art Gallery in the Hauser Memorial Library (just east of Eliot Circle off SE Woodstock Blvd),

---

Amtrak station) and extends south through East Portland roughly along 92nd Avenue to Clackamas Mall, with numerous stops along the way.

Glass-covered stations along the way provide schedule information and ticket machines. The comfortable trains run every 15 minutes at most hours of the day—more frequently during rush hour—every day of the week. Trains are generally spacious during non-rush-hour times, but they get packed (although not quite as badly as in New York or Tokyo) during the morning and evening commute.

Of the 20 stops between downtown and Hillsboro, 9 have parking lots, with room for a total of 3,700 vehicles. Hang on to your transfer and check out the public art at these stations. Architects, artists, and engineers collaborated to create individual identities for each station. Art brochures are available on MAX trains and buses.

Established in 2004, the 5.8-mile **YELLOW LINE** runs between downtown and North Portland's Multnomah County Expo Center. The route, mainly along N Interstate Avenue, has added nine new stops.

You can take your bike on the bus or train. All Tri-Met buses and MAX trains are outfitted with bike racks; a good-for-life bike pass costs $5.

BY STREETCAR AND TROLLEY

The **PORTLAND STREETCAR** (www.portlandstreetcar.org) whisks travelers from Portland State University through the downtown core, into the Pearl major touring exhibitions share gallery space with a permanent collection of 19th- and 20th-century American and European masters.

LEWIS AND CLARK COLLEGE (0615 SW Palatine Hill Rd, Riverdale; 503/768-7000; www.lclark.edu; map:JJ6), founded in 1867, is Portland's oldest; a liberal arts school known for its international programs, it is located off SW Terwilliger Boulevard. The acclaimed **NORTHWESTERN SCHOOL OF LAW**, founded in 1884, merged with Lewis and Clark in 1965.

Specialized four-year institutions include **OREGON HEALTH SCIENCES UNIVERSITY** (3181 SW Sam Jackson Park Rd, Marquam Hill; 503/494-8311; www.ohsu.edu; map:HH6), **OREGON GRADUATE INSTITUTE OF SCIENCE AND TECHNOLOGY** (20000 NW Walker Rd, Beaverton; 503/748-1121; www.ogi.edu/csee), **PACIFIC NORTHWEST COLLEGE OF ART** (1241 NW Johnson St, Pearl District; 503/226-4391; www.pnca.edu; map:M2), and **OREGON COLLEGE OF ART AND CRAFT** (8245 SW Barnes Rd, West Slope; 503/297-5544; www.ocac.edu; map:HH9). Near Portland are **PACIFIC UNIVERSITY** (2043 College Wy, Forest Grove; 503/357-6151; www.pacificu.edu) and **MARYLHURST UNIVERSITY** (17600 SW Pacific Hwy, Lake Oswego; 503/636-8141; www.marylhurst.edu; map:NN5).

District, and up to NW 23rd Avenue at Northrup Street. Book lovers appreciate the stop in front of Powell's City of Books, but there are plenty of other intriguing stops along the way. A new extension loops through the South Waterfront district, where it links up to Portland's aerial tram.

Streetcars run seven days a week (Mon–Thurs 5:30am–11:30pm, Fri 5:30am–11:45pm, Sat 7:15am–11:45pm, Sun 7:15am–10:30pm). On weekdays, cars arrive every 12 minutes between 9:30am and 5pm, and after 5pm and before 9:30am the trains run every 14–20 minutes. Saturday cars arrive every 12 minutes (11am–8pm) with morning and evening service every 15–20 minutes. Sunday service is every 15–20 minutes. Fares are the same as Tri-Met's—in other words, free within Fareless Square, $2 for adults, $1.50 for youths, and 95 cents for honored citizens beyond NW Irving Street and South Waterfront.

Another option is the oak-paneled and brass-belled **VINTAGE TROLLEY** (503/323-7363). Operating March through December, four of these circa-1900-style vehicles follow the MAX line from the Lloyd Center to the downtown turnaround at SW 11th Avenue and back. Top speed is 35 miles an hour, and (best of all!) rides are free. The round-trip takes about 40 minutes, and trolleys run about a half hour apart, Sundays only, from noon until 6pm. You can also ride the trolleys on the Portland Streetcar routes, Saturday and Sunday only, from 10am–6pm.

BY CAR

Although Portland is relatively easy to navigate using mass transit, you may want a car for driving to wineries or to the Columbia River Gorge or Oregon City. Most major **RENTAL CAR** companies have offices at the airport; some have locations throughout the metro area. Here are some downtown agents: **AVIS** (330 SW Washington St; 503/227-0220), **DOLLAR** (132 NW Broadway; 503/228-3540), **ENTERPRISE** (445 SW Pine St; 503/275-5359), **HERTZ** (1605 SW Naito Pkwy; 503/223-1234), and **THRIFTY** (632 SW Pine St; 503/227-6587). If you're an AAA member, you can pick up free maps and route advice at **AAA OREGON** (600 SW Market Ave, Downtown; 503/222-6734; map:E2); if not, try **TRAVEL PORTLAND** (503/275-8355; map:H3).

The best bet for **PARKING** downtown is in one of the seven **SMARTPARK GARAGES**; many merchants will validate your parking ticket for one or two hours of free parking with a minimum purchase of $25. You can find these garages at SW First Avenue and Jefferson Street, SW Fourth Avenue and Yamhill Street, SW Third Avenue and Alder Street, SW 10th Avenue and Yamhill Street, SW Naito Parkway and Davis Street, under O'Bryant Square (at SW Park Avenue and Stark Street), and in the Pearl District between NW Station Way and NW Lovejoy Street. Of course, many other parking garages exist downtown, but their rates are usually higher for short-term use.

In most of downtown Portland and north to Union Station, solar-powered **SMARTMETERS** have replaced traditional parking meters for street parking. A single meter collects payment (by coin or credit/debit card) for multiple parking spaces, typically one side of a block, returning a stick-on receipt that is fastened to the inner car window. Rates vary but are reasonable compared with other major cities.

Driving in Portland is not difficult once you figure out the woven pattern of one-way streets downtown (although beware of the tangle beneath the Morrison Bridge's west entrance). Here's a warning about crossing town: The drawbridges open frequently for Willamette River traffic. Always expect a delay so you won't be surprised when there is one.

BY TAXI

Though you may be able to flag a taxi in Portland, it's most advisable here to call ahead. Your options include **BROADWAY CAB** (503/227-1234), **GREEN CAB** (503/234-1414), **PORTLAND TAXI** (503/256-5400), **RADIO CAB** (503/227-1212), and **SASSY'S CAB** (503/656-7065). All five companies charge identical pickup and per-mile rates, so let cab availability be your guide. If you're headed to the airport, expect to pay $30–$35.

BY BICYCLE

Bicycling magazine has ranked Portland as the number-one city in the United States for two-wheelers. New bike lanes are still being added to the city streets, and even the police operate a cadre of bike patrollers. Most of Portland is flat enough that it can be enjoyed by bike, and there are bike racks in most MAX light-rail cars, so feel free to go for it, even if you aren't an ironman or -woman.

For bike-centric maps of the city, visit the **BICYCLE TRANSPORTATION ALLIANCE** (233 NW 5th Ave, Downtown; 503/226-0676). The BTA is a great source for bike advocacy and up-to-date cycling information.

Essentials

BANKS

The usual major West Coast institutions can be found downtown. Most offer money exchange services but will cash personal checks only for account holders. Call for branch locations and hours: **BANK OF AMERICA** (503/279-3445), **BANK OF THE WEST** (503/224-7066), **KEY BANK** (503/323-6767), **US BANK** (503/872-2657), **CHASE** (503/238-3100), and **WELLS FARGO** (800/411-4932).

COMPUTER RENTALS AND REPAIRS

SMART SOURCE (15075 SW Koll Pkwy #G, Beaverton; 503/443-3833; www.bit-by-bit.com; map:NN9) is a well-established, nationwide rental service that will rent you an IBM-compatible PC and even deliver and set it up for you anywhere in the Portland metro area. They also lease laptops and some Macs, as well as peripheral equipment. Twenty-four-hour service is available. For repairs, the **PORTLAND MAC STORE** (700 NE Multnomah St, Irvington; 503/238-1200; map:GG5) and **COM TEK** (1135 SW Alder St, Downtown; 503/227-1190; map:J2) are two of many places to take ailing Macs or PCs.

DRY CLEANERS, TAILORS, AND LAUNDROMATS

Many hotels offer dry cleaning and laundry services, or they can direct you to the closest place that does. One of the most convenient dry cleaners in the downtown area is **BEE TAILORS AND CLEANERS** (1026 SW Salmon St; 503/227-1144; www.beecleaners.com; map:G2), open weekdays and Saturday mornings. Bee offers curbside service; just honk. Or try **LEVINE'S DRY-CLEANING**, with several branches downtown; the main location is at 2086 W Burnside Street (503/223-7221; map:GG6). Near the Oregon Convention Center, **NEW CHINA LAUNDRY AND DRY CLEANERS** (105 NE 8th Ave, Downtown; 503/239-4100; map:GG6) offers delivery service. Many self-service laundries are tucked into neighborhood commercial centers or located in strip malls, so you can do your errands while your clothes wash.

GROCERY STORES

Grocery shoppers in Portland have many choices: **FRED MEYER**, the most central of which is just off Burnside Street near PGE Park (100 NW 20th Ave, Downtown; 503/273-2004; map:GG7), has for many years been the local favorite. Others prefer the upscale feel of **ZUPAN'S** (2340 W Burnside St,

21

Northwest, 503/497-1088, www.zupans.com, map:HH7; 3301 SE Belmont St, Belmont, 503/239-3720, map:HH5; and other locations). For a healthier selection, there's **WHOLE FOODS** (1210 NW Couch St, Pearl District, 503/525-4343, map:HH6; 3535 NE 15th Ave, Fremont, 503/288-3414, map: FF5; and other locations) and **NEW SEASONS** (1954 SE Division St, Clinton; 503/445-2888; www.newseasonsmarket.com; map:II5). For variety, there's **QFC** (7525 SW Barnes Rd, West Haven; 503/203-0027; map:HH9; and other locations). Portlanders also love **TRADER JOE'S** (2122 NW Glisan St, Northwest, 971/544-0788, map:GG6; 4715 SE 39th Ave, Hollywood, map:GG5; and other locations) for staples and affordable imported foods.

HOSPITAL AND MEDICAL/DENTAL SERVICES

Several hospitals provide physician referrals, including **ADVENTIST MEDICAL CENTER** (10123 SE Market St, Russellville; 503/256-4000; map:GG2) and **EASTMORELAND HOSPITAL** (2900 SE Steele St, Eastmoreland; 503/234-0411; map:II4). **PROVIDENCE PORTLAND MEDICAL CENTER** (4805 NE Glisan St, Laurelhurst; 503/215-1111; map:GG4) and **PROVIDENCE ST. VINCENT MEDICAL CENTER** (9205 SW Barnes Rd, West Hills; 503/216-1234; map:HH9) share a referral line (503/216-6595). **LEGACY HEALTH SYSTEM**, whose local facilities include both **EMANUEL HOSPITAL AND HEALTH CENTER** (2801 N Gantenbein Ave, North Portland; 503/413-2200; map:FF6) and **GOOD SAMARITAN HOSPITAL AND MEDICAL CENTER** (1015 NW 22nd Ave, Northwest; 503/413-7711; map:GG7), also has a physician referral line (503/335-3500). The **MULTNOMAH DENTAL SOCIETY** (503/513-5010) provides emergency and routine referral service at no charge.

LEGAL SERVICES

The **OREGON STATE BAR LAWYER REFERRAL SERVICE** (5200 SW Meadows Rd, Lake Oswego; 503/684-3763; map:LL8) has offered referrals since 1971. Expect to pay $35 for an initial office consultation, after which you'll be charged the firm's normal hourly rates. A reduced-fee program is available.

LOST PETS

If you see a stray or any animal in need of help, or if you've lost your furry travel companion, call **MULTNOMAH COUNTY ANIMAL CONTROL** (503/988-7387) or the nonprofit **OREGON HUMANE SOCIETY** (503/285-7722). For emergency medical care for your pet, call the highly respected **DOVE LEWIS EMERGENCY ANIMAL HOSPITAL**, which has a Nob Hill clinic (1945 NW Pettygrove St; 503/228-7281; map:GG7) and two branches, Eastside and Aloha (Beaverton area).

PHARMACIES

National giant **RITE AID** has numerous locations in Portland, including downtown (622 SW Alder St; 503/226-6791; map:I3); call 800/748-3243 to find the one nearest you. Ditto **WALGREENS** (800/925-4733), which has

24-hour prescription service at three stores; the Belmont store is closest to downtown (940 SE 39th Ave; 503/238-6053; map:HH5). For a full-service pharmacy that also stocks a wide selection of supplements, herbs, homeopathic remedies, and various other natural alternatives, go to **PHARMACA** (13 NW 23rd Pl, Northwest; 503/226-6213; map:GG7). Several grocery stores (Fred Meyer, Safeway) contain pharmacies also. For downtown-area delivery, go to **CENTRAL DRUG CO.** (538 SW 4th Ave; 503/226-2222; map:H5).

PHOTOGRAPHY EQUIPMENT AND SERVICES

Most area **FEDEX KINKO'S** stores (950 NW 23rd Ave, Northwest, 503/222-4133, map:GG6; 1400 SW 5th Ave, Ste 110, Southwest, 503/223-2056, map:F3; and other locations) have digital photo kiosks. Most **FRED MEYER** stores also have digital kiosks and can develop traditional film as well. For special treatment, helpful staff, and custom orders, head for **SHUTTERBUG** (501 SW Broadway at Washington St, Downtown; 503/227-3456; map:I3), where you'll find digital photo kiosks; all color film development is done on-site. For a full selection of the newest photography equipment, **CAMERA WORLD** (400 SW 6th Ave, Downtown; 503/205-5900; map:I4) is the spot.

POLICE AND SAFETY

In serious, life-threatening emergencies, dial 9-1-1. In nonemergency situations, dial 503/823-4636 for **PORTLAND POLICE INFORMATION,** or 503/823-3333 to make a report. Unlike many American cities, Portland is generally safe for walking day and night; but if you're out after dark, let common sense be your guide: know your destination. And don't leave your valuables in the car at any time.

POST OFFICES

Two full-service post offices are located in the downtown core. The **MAIN OFFICE** (open Mon–Fri 7am–6:30pm, Sat 8:30am–5pm) is at 715 NW Hoyt Street (map:M4). **UNIVERSITY STATION** (open Mon–Fri 7am–6pm, Sat 10am–3pm) is at 1505 SW Sixth Avenue (map:E2), just blocks from Portland State University. Call 800/275-8777 to locate additional branches.

PUBLIC RESTROOMS

The big news in Portland public restrooms is the **PORTLAND LOO** (www.portlandonline.com/water/loo). Located between 5th and 6th avenues on Glisan Street, it uses solar power to run water and power flushes. More loos are in the works, and the city of Portland hopes to market them to other cities! The most centrally located public restrooms downtown are those in **PIONEER COURTHOUSE SQUARE** (701 SW 6th Ave; map:H3), near the Tri-Met office. The lobby opens at 8:30am and closes at 5pm weekdays and is open during the afternoon on weekends (hours vary). Farther south, public restrooms are in the **CLAY STREET PARKING GARAGE** (map:E3) between SW Third

PLACES OF WORSHIP

Like any major city, Portland has sanctuaries for people of all faiths. Many long-established churches are grouped downtown, which allows these historical structures to be easily visited in a pleasant walking tour.

Start at the oldest, an 1883 Carpenter Gothic edifice known only as **THE OLD CHURCH** (1422 SW 11th Ave; 503/222-2031; www.oldchurch.org). Saved from the wrecking ball in 1970 and no longer used for regular services, the church is the site of meetings, performances, weddings, and other events.

Two blocks east on the South Park Blocks, the **SIXTH CHURCH OF CHRIST, SCIENTIST** (1331 SW Park Ave; 503/227-6024) features elaborate Byzantine/Art Deco exterior brickwork typical of the Depression era (1932) in which it was built. Next door, a castlelike stone tower rises above **ST. JAMES LUTHERAN CHURCH** (1315 SW Park Ave; 503/227-2439; www.stjameslutheranportland. org). The Gothic Revival structure dates from 1910, although its 1891 Pioneer Chapel is contained within the church.

Across the South Park Blocks is the **FIRST CHRISTIAN CHURCH** (1315 SW Broadway; 503/228-9211; www.firstchristianpdx.com), on this site since 1890 (the current structure dates from 1922). This church has a brick exterior embellished with glazed terra-cotta, a semicircular brick stairway, Doric portico columns, and a collection of Povey stained-glass windows. Just north, next to the Portland Center for the Performing Arts, is the **FIRST CONGREGATIONAL CHURCH** (1137 SW Broadway; 503/228-7219). Built in 1889–95, it is an impressive Venetian Gothic building modeled after Boston's Old South Church. It has a dramatic 175-foot latticed bell tower and is often used for literary arts lectures.

Four other important churches are on the west side of downtown. **FIRST**

and Fourth avenues. Restrooms are also available at **PIONEER PLACE** and in **MAJOR DEPARTMENT STORES** such as Macy's and Nordstrom.

Local Resources

BOOKSTORES

POWELL'S CITY OF BOOKS (NW 10th Ave and W Burnside St, Downtown; 503/228-4651; www.powells.com; map:J2) is the nation's largest independent bookseller and has become a must-see for many visitors as well as remaining a local favorite. Occupying an entire block, Powell's has color-coded rooms and free maps to the store to help bookworms find their way around. Specialty satellite stores buttress the million-plus volumes.

UNITED METHODIST CHURCH (SW 18th Ave and Jefferson St; 503/228-3195; www.fumcpdx.org) adjoins the UMC Center, which serves the Oregon-Idaho region. One of the largest U.S. Unitarian Universalist congregations makes its home at **FIRST UNITARIAN CHURCH** (1011 SW 12th Ave at Main St; 503/228-6389; www.firstunitarianportland.org), built in 1924. **FIRST BAPTIST CHURCH** (909 SW 11th Ave; 503/228-7465; www.fbc-portland.org), known as the White Temple, was built in 1892–94. **FIRST PRESBYTERIAN CHURCH** (1200 SW Alder St; 503/228-7331; www.fpcpdx.org) was built in 1890.

Among other churches outside of downtown is **ST. PHILIP NERI CATHOLIC CHURCH** (SE 18th Ave and SE Division St; 503/231-4955), where classical concerts are sometimes performed. **ST. MARY'S CATHEDRAL** (1716 NW Davis St, Nob Hill; 503/228-4397) is just a few blocks from the massive **TEMPLE BETH ISRAEL** (1972 NW Flanders St, Nob Hill; 503/222-1069). This reform congregation was founded in 1858; the temple was built in 1926–28.

On the east side, the immense **HOLY TRINITY GREEK ORTHODOX CHURCH** (3131 NE Glisan St, Laurelhurst; 503/234-0468; www.goholytrinity.org) hosts a lavish festival each October. **TRINITY EPISCOPAL CATHEDRAL** (147 NW 19th St, Northwest; 503/790-2877; www.trinity-episcopal.org), the hub of the Oregon diocese, is not far from the Pearl District and downtown. Covering a full city block, **ALL SAINTS EPISCOPAL CHURCH** (4033 SE Woodstock Blvd, Southeast; 503/777-3829) is a Portland landmark. At the **DHARMA RAIN ZEN CENTER** (2539 SE Madison St; 503/239-4846; www.dharma-rain.org), disciples of Soto Zen meditate and study Buddhist teachings. **MASJID AL-HIJRAH** (7007 NE Martin Luther King Jr Blvd; 503/281-7691) is Portland's Muslim center.

—John Gottberg

ANNIE BLOOM'S BOOKS (7834 SW Capitol Hwy, Multnomah Village; 503/246-0053; www.annieblooms.com; map:JJ7) is a friendly, cozy shop with a kind and helpful staff, and **BROADWAY BOOKS** (1714 NE Broadway, Irvington; 503/284-1726; www.broadwaybooks.net; map:GG5) is a long-standing establishment that features frequent author readings and events. See the Shopping chapter for more listings.

BROADCAST MEDIA

KBOO radio is a true labor of love for each of its hundreds of volunteers. The station has been on the air since 1975, and visitors find it a great way to tap into Portland's vibrant, eclectic communities. Tune into Iranian music, local newshounds, ditties from Holland, or local hip-hop megastars. Pick up a schedule at the station (20 SE 8th Ave, Buckman; 503/231-8032; map:GG5) and listen your way to Portland's epicenter. The city does, of course, offer standard radio and TV fare. Headbangers and those fond of honky-tonks will soon find their homes on the dial; cable-access scholars and soap-opera junkies can get comfy on the couch. Here's a basic rundown:

RADIO STATIONS

750 AM	KXL	NEWS
1150 AM	KKGT	SPANISH TALK
1190 AM	KEX	TALK, NEWS, SPORTS
1410 AM	KBNP	BUSINESS
89.1 FM	KMHD	JAZZ
90.7 FM	KBOO	ECLECTIC
91.5 FM	KOPB	NATIONAL PUBLIC RADIO
92.3 FM	KGON	CLASSIC ROCK
94.7 FM	KNRK	NEW/ALTERNATIVE ROCK
95.5 FM	KXJM	DANCE/ROCK
97.1 FM	KKSN	OLDIES
98.7 FM	KUPL	COUNTRY
99.5 FM	KWJJ	COUNTRY
100.3 FM	KKRZ	TOP 40
101.1 FM	KUFO	NEW/ALTERNATIVE ROCK
103.3 FM	KKCW	ADULT CONTEMPORARY
105.1 FM	KRSK	ADULT CONTEMPORARY
106.7 FM	KKJZ	SMOOTH JAZZ

TELEVISION STATIONS

2	KATU	ABC
6	KOIN	CBS
8	KGW	NBC
10	KOPB	PBS
12	KPTV	FOX
32	KRCW	CW
49	KPDX	MYTV (FOX)

INTERNET ACCESS

All **MULTNOMAH COUNTY LIBRARY** branches have Internet access. Another place to get online is at **TRAVEL PORTLAND** (Pioneer Courthouse Square, Downtown; 503/275-8355; www.travelportland.com; map:H3). Most **COFFEE SHOPS** in Portland offer wi-fi service, or you can pay for Internet time by the minute at any **FEDEX KINKO'S** outlet.

NEWSPAPERS AND PERIODICALS

The lone daily in Portland, the *Oregonian* (503/221-8327), has been published since 1850 and reigns as the king of print journalism in the city. Call the newspaper's telephone information service (800/555-8355) to hear everything from lottery results to movie schedules. The *Oregonian* doesn't maintain its own Web site, but you can glean much of what's in the paper from www.oregonlive.com. The useful arts-and-entertainment section, *A&E*, appears on Fridays.

The *Oregonian* is joined on Tuesdays and Fridays by the news feature–oriented *Portland Tribune* (503/226-6397; www.portlandtribune.com), available free from racks throughout the city. The *Tribune* has been honored as the nation's best nondaily newspaper with a circulation exceeding 10,000. *Cue* is its Friday calendar section.

Willamette Week (503/243-2122; www.wweek.com) is Portland's alternative newsweekly. Thought-provoking, irreverent, and often controversial, it covers politics, the arts, and civic matters; it appears on Wednesdays and is distributed free.

The *Portland Mercury* (503/294-0840; www.portlandmercury.com) is a very alternative, free weekly aimed more at the 18 to 35 crowd, with a focus on the local music scene; appearing each Thursday, it also offers alternative arts and limited news coverage. *Just Out* (503/236-1252; www.justout.com), Portland's free gay and lesbian newspaper, is published on the first and third Friday of each month.

Portland businesspeople are devotees of the *Daily Journal of Commerce* (503/226-1311; www.djc-or.com) and the weekly *Portland Business Journal* (503/274-8733; www.bizjournals.com/portland).

The *Columbian* (503/224-0654; www.columbian.com) is the daily paper in Vancouver, Washington. Many of Portland's other suburbs have newspapers of their own. They include the *Beaverton Valley Times* (weekly), *Canby Herald* (biweekly), *Forest Grove News-Times* (weekly), *Gresham Outlook* (biweekly), *Hillsboro Argus* (biweekly), *Lake Oswego Review* (weekly), the *Newberg Graphic* (biweekly), the *Sandy Post* (weekly), the *Tigard/Tualatin/Sherwood Times* (weekly), and *West Linn Tidings* (weekly).

Portland Monthly (503/222-5144; www.portlandmonthlymag.com) is a handsome, glossy magazine with a cutting-edge style. Feature articles focus on personalities and the Portland lifestyle.

PUBLIC LIBRARIES

The **MULTNOMAH COUNTY LIBRARY** (www.multcolib.org) has 15 branches throughout the city, with movie, tape, and book borrowing, plus other services. The library sponsors a variety of films, lectures, and programs for children. Portlanders are exceedingly proud of their **CENTRAL LIBRARY** (801 SW 10th Ave, Downtown; 503/248-5123; map:H1), which was completely remodeled in the mid-1990s; in 1998 voters also approved funds for upgrading many branch libraries. Cardholders are entitled to one hour of Internet access per day; visitors can obtain a 24-hour card for Internet use.

Clackamas County has 10 city libraries and 3 county libraries. Call individual branches for hours and events. The **BEAVERTON CITY LIBRARY** (12375 SW 5th Ave, Beaverton; 503/644-2197; map:II9), Washington County's biggest, is available for use by citizens in Washington, Multnomah, or

Clackamas counties and is open seven days a week. Although Washington County's 11 libraries are individual nonbranch entities, they all share databases.

Important Telephone Numbers

EMERGENCY: POLICE, FIRE, AMBULANCE	911
DIRECTORY ASSISTANCE	411
AAA (AUTOMOBILE ASSOCIATION OF AMERICA) OREGON	503/222-6734
AIDS HOTLINE	503/223-AIDS
ALCOHOLICS ANONYMOUS	503/223-8569
AMERICAN RED CROSS	503/528-5848
ANIMAL CONTROL	503/988-7387
AUTO IMPOUND	503/823-0044
BETTER BUSINESS BUREAU	503/226-3981
BIRTH AND DEATH RECORDS (OREGON VITAL RECORDS)	503/731-4095
BLOOD DONATION (RED CROSS)	503/284-4040
CHAMBER OF COMMERCE	503/228-9411
CHILD ABUSE HOTLINE (NATIONAL)	800/422-4453
CITY OF PORTLAND (GENERAL INFORMATION)	503/823-4000
COAST GUARD	503/240-9310
CONSUMER COMPLAINTS	503/229-5576
ENVIRONMENTAL PROTECTION AGENCY	503/326-3250
FEDERAL BUREAU OF INFORMATION (FBI)	503/224-4181
HEALTH INFORMATION AND REFERRAL	503/248-3816
HUMANE SOCIETY (LOST PETS)	503/285-7722
IMMIGRATION AND CITIZENSHIP (INFORMATION)	800/375-5283
INTERNAL REVENUE SERVICE	800/829-1040
MARRIAGE LICENSES	503/988-5027
OREGON DEPARTMENT OF REVENUE	800/356-4222
OREGON STATE TOURISM	800/547-7842
PARKS AND RECREATION INFORMATION	503/823-PLAY
PASSPORTS	503/988-4508
PERMIT CENTER INFORMATION	503/823-7310
PLANNED PARENTHOOD	503/775-0861, 503/288-8826
POISON CONTROL CENTER	503/494-8968, 800/222-1222
POLICE (NONEMERGENCY)	503/823-3333
POSTAL SERVICE INFORMATION	800/ASK-USPS
POWER OUTAGES (24 HOURS)	503/464-7777, 800/544-1795

RECYCLING INFORMATION	503/823-7202
ROAD CONDITIONS	503/588-2941, 800/977-6368
STATE PATROL (MON–FRI)	503/731-3020
SUICIDE AND MENTAL HEALTH CRISIS	503/215-7082
TICKETMASTER	503/224-4400
TRI-MET	503/238-RIDE (7433)
VISITOR INFORMATION	503/275-8355
VOTER INFORMATION	503/988-3720
WOMEN'S CRISIS LINE (SEXUAL ASSAULT, DOMESTIC VIOLENCE)	503/235-5333

RESTAURANTS

RESTAURANTS

Restaurants by Star Rating

★★★★
Castagna
Clarklewis
The Heathman
   Restaurant and Bar
Le Pigeon
Paley's Place
23 Hoyt

★★★½
Beast
Carlyle
Fenouil
Higgins
The Joel Palmer House
Morton's of Chicago:
   The Steakhouse

★★★
Andina
Bluehour
Carafe
Clyde Common
DOC
El Gaucho
Giorgio's
Gracie's
Hiroshi
Laurelhurst Market
London Grill
McCormick & Schmick's
   Seafood Restaurant
Murata
Nel Centro
Nick's Italian Café
Nostrana
Park Kitchen

Plainfield's Mayur
Pok Pok and Whiskey
   Soda Lounge
Saucebox
Sel Gris
Simpatica Dining Hall
Ten 01
Toast
Toro Bravo
Urban Farmer
Veritable Quandary
Wildwood
Wong's King Sea-
   food Restaurant

★★★½
Acadia
Alba Osteria & Enoteca
Apizza Scholls
Beaker and Flask
Belly
BeWon Korean Restaurant
Broder
Bugatti's Ristorante
   Italiano
East India Company
Huber's
Hudson's Bar & Grill
Ichiban
Lauro Kitchen
Lemongrass Thai
Lincoln Restaurant
Lucca
Lucy's Table
Meiji-En Japanese
   Restaurant
Mother's Bistro & Bar

Navarre
¡Oba!
Pazzo Ristorante
Piazza Italia
Portland City Grill
Red Hills Provincial Dining
Red Star Tavern &
   Roast House
Ristorante Fratelli
Ruth's Chris Steak House
Serratto
Sinju
3 Doors Down Café
Tina's
Ya Hala

★★
Alexis
Autentica
Belly Timber
Bernie's Southern Bistro
Biwa
Bombay Cricket
   Club Restaurant
BridgePort Alehouse
BridgePort Brewpub
Bunk Sandwiches
Café Castagna
Caffe Allora
Caffe Mingo
Clarke's
Daily Cafe
Departure
Deschutes Brewery
   & Public House
Doug Fir Lounge
Dundee Bistro

Eleni's Estiatorio
Eleni's Philoxenia
Esparza's Tex-Mex Café
The Farm Café
Gilt Club
Gino's Restaurant and Bar
Harborside
Holden's Bistro
India House
Jake's Famous Crawfish
Jake's Grill
James John Café
Jo Bar and Rotisserie
Kame
Karam
Kenny & Zuke's
    Delicatessen
Ken's Artisan
    Bakery & Café
Ken's Artisan Pizza
Le Bouchon
Le Happy
Lolo
Lovely Hula Hands
Masu
Nicholas' Restaurant
Noble Rot
Otto's Sausage Kitchen
Pambiche
Papa Haydn
Patanegra
Ping
The RingSide
RingSide East
Roots
Saburo's
Saint Honoré Boulangerie
Salty's on the Columbia
Savoy Tavern & Bistro
Screen Door
Siam Society

Southpark Seafood
    Grill and Wine Bar
Syun Izakaya
Tabla
Tanuki
Thai Peacock Restaurant
Three Square Grill
Trébol
Tucci
Typhoon!
Vindalho
Zell's: An American Café

★★☆

Al-Amir
Beaches Restaurant & Bar
Blueplate Lunch Counter
    & Soda Fountain
Bread and Ink Cafe
Campbell's Bar-B-Q
Clay's Smokehouse
Corbett Fish House
Country Cat
Dove Vivi
Elephants Delicatessen
Everett Street Bistro
Fa Fa Gourmet
Flying Elephants
    at Fox Tower
Gravy
Hands On Café
Hash
Henry's 12th Street Tavern
Hopworks Urban
    Brewery
Horn of Africa
J & M Café
John Street Café
Kenny & Zuke's
    SandwichWorks
La Calaca Comelona
La Petite Provence
Marrakesh

Milo's City Café
Mint
Montage
Nuestra Cocina
Perry's on Fremont
Pine State Biscuits
Podnah's Pit BBQ
Russell Street Bar-B-Que
Sweet Basil Thai
Three Degrees Waterfront
    Bar & Grill
Tin Shed Garden Cafe
Tokyo Restaurant

★

Baan Thai
Bar Mingo
Bastas Trattoria
Bijou Café
Blossoming Lotus
Burgerville
Byways
Cactus Ya Ya
Caldera
Cha!
Cha! Cha! Cha!
    Mexican Taqueria
Dan and Louis' Oyster Bar
Delta Cafe and Bar
Dots Cafe
Edelweiss Sausage
    & Delicatessen
Fat City Cafe
Fire on the Mountain
Flying Elephants at
    Kruse Way
Fujin
Good Taste
Grand Central
    Baking Company
Habibi
Hakatamon
Half and Half

33

Hot Lips Pizza
Hot Pot City
Hunan
Justa Pasta
Kornblatt's Delicatessen
Little Italy's Trattoria
Little Red Bike Café
Marco's Café &
  Espresso Bar

McCormick's Fish
  House and Bar
Meat Cheese Bread
Mekong Grill
Noho's Hawaiian Café
Original Pancake House
Pho Van
Por Qué No?
Queen of Sheba

The Restaurant at the
  Historic Reserve
Silk
Swagat
Vista Spring Café
Wu's Open Kitchen
Yakuza
Yoko's Japanese
  Restaurant and
  Sushi Bar

Restaurants by Neighborhood

ALAMEDA
Acadia
Perry's on Fremont

ALBERTA
Bernie's Southern Bistro
Lolo
Podnah's Pit BBQ
Siam Society
Tin Shed Garden Cafe

ALBINA
Mint

BEAVERTON
Hakatamon
McCormick's Fish
  House and Bar
Swagat

BELMONT
La Calaca Comelona
Pine State Biscuits

BROOKLYN
Edelweiss Sausage &
  Delicatessen

**BROUGHTON
BEACH**
Salty's on the Columbia

BUCKMAN
Beaker and Flask
Bunk Sandwiches
Doug Fir Lounge
The Farm Café
Fire on the Mountain
Lemongrass Thai
Meat Cheese Bread
Nostrana
Simpatica Dining Hall
Zell's: An American Café

BURLINGAME
Original Pancake House

CAMAS
Roots

CHINATOWN
Gilt Club
Good Taste
Ping

CLINTON
Broder
Dots Cafe
Noho's Hawaiian Café
Savoy Tavern & Bistro
Vindalho

CONCORDIA
Autentica
Beast
Yakuza

DIVISION
Clay's Smokehouse
Lauro Kitchen
Nuestra Cocina

DOWNTOWN
Baan Thai
Blueplate Lunch Counter
  & Soda Fountain
Carafe
Clyde Common
Departure
East India Company
El Gaucho
Flying Elephants
  at Fox Tower
Gracie's
Habibi
Half and Half
The Heathman Restaurant
  and Bar
Higgins
Hot Pot City
Huber's
Hunan

India House
Jake's Famous Crawfish
Jake's Grill
Karam
Kenny & Zuke's
  Delicatessen
London Grill
Masu
McCormick & Schmick's
  Seafood Restaurant
Morton's of Chicago:
  The Steakhouse
Mother's Bistro & Bar
Murata
Nel Centro
Pazzo Ristorante
Portland City Grill
Red Star Tavern &
  Roast House
Ruth's Chris Steak House
Saucebox
Southpark Seafood
  Grill and Wine Bar
Thai Peacock Restaurant
Typhoon!
Urban Farmer
Veritable Quandary

FREMONT
Lucca
Perry's on Fremont

GLENDOVEER
RingSide East

HAWTHORNE
Apizza Scholls
Belly Timber
Bombay Cricket
  Club Restaurant
Bread and Ink Cafe
BridgePort Alehouse
Café Castagna
Castagna

Fujin
Por Qué No?
Sel Gris
3 Doors Down Café

HILLSBORO
Swagat
Syun Izakaya
Tokyo Restaurant

HILLSDALE
Alba Osteria & Enoteca
Three Square Grill

INNER SOUTHEAST
Biwa
Clarklewis
Daily Cafe
J & M Café
Le Pigeon
Montage
Nicholas' Restaurant
Noble Rot

IRVINGTON
Grand Central
  Baking Company
Milo's City Café
Sweet Basil Thai

JOHNS LANDING
Corbett Fish House

LAKE OSWEGO
Clarke's
Flying Elephants
  at Kruse Way
Tucci
Wu's Open Kitchen

LAURELHURST
Dove Vivi
Esparza's Tex-Mex Café
Ken's Artisan Pizza
Laurelhurst Market

Navarre
Pambiche
Tabla

MISSISSIPPI
Gravy
Lovely Hula Hands
Por Qué No?

MONTAVILLA
Country Cat
Pho Van
Ya Hala

MULTNOMAH VILLAGE
Fat City Cafe
Marco's Café &
  Espresso Bar

MURRAY HILL
Ichiban

NORTHEAST
Belly
Horn of Africa
Lincoln Restaurant
Meiji-En Japanese
  Restaurant
Queen of Sheba
Russell Street Bar-B-Que
Toro Bravo

NORTH PORTLAND
DOC
Fire on the Mountain
Little Red Bike Café
Trébol

NORTHWEST
Bar Mingo
Bastas Trattoria
BeWon Korean Restaurant
Caffe Mingo
Carlyle

Cha!
Elephants Delicatessen
Jo Bar and Rotisserie
Justa Pasta
Kenny & Zuke's
   SandwichWorks
Ken's Artisan
   Bakery & Café
Kornblatt's Delicatessen
Le Happy
Lucy's Table
Marrakesh
Paley's Place
Papa Haydn
Patanegra
The RingSide
Saint Honoré Boulangerie
Serratto
Swagat
Sweet Basil Thai
Tanuki
23 Hoyt
Typhoon!
Wildwood

OLD TOWN
Al-Amir
Alexis
Bijou Café
Dan and Louis' Oyster Bar

OREGON CITY
Bugatti's Ristorante
   Italiano

PEARL DISTRICT
Andina
Blossoming Lotus
Bluehour
BridgePort Brewpub
Byways Cafe
Caffe Allora

Cha! Cha! Cha!
   Mexican Taqueria
Daily Cafe
Deschutes Brewery
   and Public House
Eleni's Philoxenia
Everett Street Bistro
Fenouil
Giorgio's
Henry's 12th Street Tavern
Hiroshi
Holden's Bistro
Hot Lips Pizza
Le Bouchon
¡Oba!
Park Kitchen
Piazza Italia
Ristorante Fratelli
Silk
Sinju
Ten 01

PORTLAND HEIGHTS
Plainfield's Mayur
Vista Spring Café

RICHMOND
La Petite Provence
Pok Pok and Whiskey
   Soda Lounge

RIVERPLACE
Harborside

SAINT JOHNS
James John Café
John Street Café

SELLWOOD
Eleni's Estiatorio
Gino's Restaurant and Bar
Hash
Mekong Grill

SOUTHEAST
Caldera
Campbell's Bar-B-Q
Hopworks Urban
   Brewery
Screen Door
Toast
Wong's King
   Seafood Restaurant
Yoko's Japanese
   Restaurant and
   Sushi Bar

SOUTH WATERFRONT
Daily Cafe
Three Degrees
   Waterfront Bar & Grill

TIGARD
Sinju

VANCOUVER, WA
Beaches Restaurant & Bar
Burgerville
Cactus Ya Ya
Fa Fa Gourmet
Hudson's Bar & Grill
Little Italy's Trattoria
The Restaurant at the
   Historic Reserve

WEST LINN
Bugatti's Ristorante
   Italiano

WESTMORELAND
Papa Haydn
Saburo's

WEST SLOPE
Hands On Café

WINE COUNTRY
Dundee Bistro
The Joel Palmer House
Kame

Nick's Italian Café
Red Hills Provincial Dining
Tina's

WOODSTOCK
Delta Cafe and Bar
Otto's Sausage Kitchen

Restaurants by Food and Other Features

AMERICAN
Beaches Restaurant & Bar
Bluehour
Blueplate Lunch Counter
  & Soda Fountain
Bunk Sandwiches
Burgerville
Byways Cafe
Café Castagna
Carlyle
Clyde Common
Country Cat
Daily Cafe
Dots Cafe
El Gaucho
Fat City Cafe
Henry's 12th Street Tavern
Huber's
J & M Café
Jake's Grill
Jo Bar and Rotisserie
John Street Café
Marco's Café &
  Espresso Bar
Meat Cheese Bread
Milo's City Café
Mint
Mother's Bistro & Bar
Papa Haydn
Perry's on Fremont
Portland City Grill
Red Star Tavern &
  Roast House

The Restaurant at the
  Historic Reserve
Ruth's Chris Steak House
Savoy Tavern & Bistro
Three Square Grill
23 Hoyt
Zell's: An American Café

BAKERIES
Grand Central Baking
  Company
Hands On Café
Ken's Artisan Bakery
  & Café
La Petite Provence
Pazzoria Bakery and Cafe
Saint Honoré Boulangerie

BARBECUE
Campbell's Bar-B-Q
Clay's Smokehouse
Good Taste
Podnah's Pit BBQ
Russell Street Bar-B-Que
Thai Peacock Restaurant

BENTO
Tokyo Restaurant

BREAKFAST
Bijou Café
Blossoming Lotus
Bread and Ink Cafe
Broder
Bunk Sandwiches
Byways Cafe

Caffe Allora
Daily Cafe
Everett Street Bistro
The Farm Café
Fat City Cafe
Gracie's
Grand Central Baking
  Company
Gravy
Half and Half
Hands On Café
Hash
The Heathman
  Restaurant and Bar
Hudson's Bar & Grill
J & M Café
Jake's Grill
James John Café
John Street Café
Kenny and Zuke's
  Delicatessen
Kenny and Zuke's
  SandwichWorks
Ken's Artisan
  Bakery & Café
Kornblatt's Delicatessen
Little Red Bike Café
London Grill
Marco's Café &
  Espresso Bar
Meat Cheese Bread
Milo's City Café
Mother's Bistro & Bar
Original Pancake House

Pambiche
Pazzoria
Red Star Tavern &
    Roast House
Rose's Deli & Bakery
Saint Honoré Boulangerie
Three Degrees Waterfront
    Bar & Grill
Tin Shed Garden Cafe
Typhoon! (Downtown)
Urban Farmer
Zell's: An American Café

BRUNCH
Autentica
Bastas Trattoria
Beast
Belly
Belly Timber
Bluehour
Bread and Ink Cafe
Broder
Country Cat
Daily Cafe
Fenouil
Hands On Café
The Heathman Restaurant
James John Café
Jo Bar and Rotisserie
La Petite Provence
London Grill
Papa Haydn
Red Star Tavern &
    Roast House
Roots
Salty's on the Columbia
Screen Door
Simpatica Dining Hall
Three Square Grill
Toast
Urban Farmer
Veritable Quandary

BURGERS
Beaches Restaurant & Bar
Bijou Café
Bread and Ink Cafe
BridgePort Alehouse
BridgePort Brewpub
Burgerville
Byways Cafe
Café Castagna
Carafe
Clyde Common
Country Cat
Daily Cafe
Deschutes Brewery
    and Public House
Dots Cafe
Doug Fir
Elephants Delicatessen
Everett Street Bistro
Fat City Cafe
Gilt Club
Henry's 12th Street Tavern
Higgins
Holden's Bistro
Hopworks Urban
    Brewery
Jo Bar and Rotisserie
Lauro Kitchen
London Grill
Lovely Hula Hands
Marco's Café &
    Espresso Bar
Mint
Mother's Bistro & Bar
Perry's on Fremont
Red Star Tavern &
    Roast House
The RingSide
RingSide East
Savoy Tavern & Bistro
Three Square Grill
Tin Shed Garden Cafe

23 Hoyt
Vista Spring Café
Wildwood
Yakuza
Zell's: An American Café

CAJUN/CREOLE
Acadia
Delta Cafe and Bar
Montage
Perry's on Fremont
Russell Street Bar-B-Que

CARIBBEAN
Mint
¡Oba!

CHINESE
Fa Fa Gourmet
Fujin
Good Taste
Hot Pot City
Hunan
Wong's King Sea-
    food Restaurant
Wu's Open Kitchen

COCKTAIL LOUNGE
Andina
Bar Mingo
Bastas Trattoria
Belly Timber
Bluehour
Carlyle
Clarklewis
Country Cat
Dots Cafe
East India Company
Elephants Delicatessen
El Gaucho
Fenouil
Gilt Club
Gino's Restaurant and Bar
Harborside

The Heathman Restaurant and Bar
Holden's Bistro
Huber's
Hudson's Bar & Grill
Jake's Famous Crawfish
Jake's Grill
La Calaca Comelona
Masu
Mint
Montage
Morton's of Chicago: The Steakhouse
Mother's Bistro & Bar
¡Oba!
Park Kitchen
Pazzo Ristorante
Perry's on Fremont
Portland City Grill
The RingSide
RingSide East
Saucebox
Siam Society
Silk
Ten 01
23 Hoyt
Typhoon! (Downtown)
Urban Farmer
Veritable Quandary
Whiskey Soda Lounge
Wildwood
Yakuza

CONTINENTAL
Bluehour
Castagna
Clarke's
Gilt Club
Gracie's
Holden's Bistro
London Grill
Red Hills Provincial Dining

CREPES
Le Happy
Original Pancake House

CUBAN
¡Oba!
Pambiche

DELICATESSEN
Edelweiss Sausage & Delicatessen
Elephants Delicatessen
Flying Elephants at Fox Tower
Flying Elephants at Kruse Way
Kenny and Zuke's Delicatessen
Kornblatt's Delicatessen
Otto's Sausage Kitchen

DESSERTS (EXCEPTIONAL)
Bread and Ink Cafe
Bugatti's Ristorante Italiano
Carlyle
Clarke's
Daily Cafe
Dan and Louis' Oyster Bar
Dundee Bistro
Hands On Café
The Heathman Restaurant and Bar
Higgins
Jake's Famous Crawfish
Le Happy
Le Pigeon
Lovely Hula Hands
Marco's Café & Espresso Bar
Paley's Place
Pambiche
Papa Haydn

Park Kitchen
Red Star Tavern
Roots
Screen Door
Sel Gris
Tucci
Urban Farmer
Wildwood

DIM SUM
Wong's King Seafood Restaurant

EAST AFRICAN/ ETHIOPIAN
Horn of Africa
Queen of Sheba

ECLECTIC
Daily Cafe
Hands On Café
Holden's Bistro
Marco's Café & Espresso Bar
Mother's Bistro & Bar
Simpatica Dining Hall
Tucci

EDITORS' CHOICE
Apizza Scholls
Belly
Bijou Café
Biwa
Bluehour
Bunk Sandwiches
Byways Cafe
Clarklewis
Clyde Common
Dots Café
Doug Fir Lounge
Elephants Delicatessen
Flying Elephants at Fox Tower
Flying Elephants at Kruse Way

The Farm Café
Gracie's
Half and Half
Hands On Café
The Heathman Restaurant
 and Bar
Higgins
India House
J & M Café
Jake's Famous Crawfish
Lauro Kitchen
Le Pigeon
Little Red Bike Café
London Grill
Meat Cheese Bread
Montage
Navarre
Nick's Italian Café
Nostrana
Paley's Place
Park Kitchen
Pine State Biscuits
Plainfield's Mayur
Pok Pok Whiskey
 Soda Lounge
Por Qué No?
The Restaurant at the
 Historic Reserve
The RingSide
RingSide East
Roots
Saint Honoré Boulangerie
Simpatica Dining Hall
Southpark Seafood
 Grill and Wine Bar
Thai Peacock Restaurant
Tina's
Toro Bravo
Veritable Quandary
Vindalho
Wildwood
Ya Hala
Yasuka

FAMILY
Alexis
Beaches Restaurant & Bar
Bijou Café
Bread and Ink Cafe
Burgerville
Dan and Louis' Oyster Bar
Fat City Cafe
Gino's Restaurant and Bar
Grand Central Baking
 Company
Harborside
Hot Lips Pizza
Ken's Artisan Bakery
 & Café
Ken's Artisan Pizza
Little Italy's Trattoria
McCormick & Schmick's
 Seafood Restaurant
McCormick's Fish
 House and Bar
Mother's Bistro & Bar
Original Pancake House
Perry's on Fremont
Piazza Italia
Swagat
Sweet Basil Thai
Three Square Grill
Toast
Vista Spring Café
Wu's Open Kitchen
Zell's: An American Café

FIREPLACE
Fenouil
The Heathman Restaurant
 and Bar
Hudson's Bar & Grill
Jake's Famous Crawfish
The Joel Palmer House
¡Oba!
Plainfield's Mayur
Red Hills Provincial Dining

The RingSide
Tina's

FRENCH
Carafe
Carlyle
Everett Street Bistro
Fenouil
The Heathman Restaurant
 and Bar
Le Bouchon
Le Pigeon
Paley's Place
Saint Honoré Boulangerie
Sel Gris
Tabla

GERMAN
Edelweiss Sausage
 & Delicatessen

GOOD VALUE
Alexis
Bastas Trattoria
BeWon Korean Restaurant
Blue Plate Lunch Counter
 & Soda Fountain
Burgerville
Byways Cafe
Caldera
Cha!
Cha! Cha! Cha! Mexican
 Taqueria
Corbett Fish House
Dan and Louis' Oyster Bar
Delta Cafe and Bar
Dots Cafe
Fa Fa Gourmet
Fire on the Mountain
Fujin
Gino's Restaurant and Bar
Good Taste
Henry's 12th Street Tavern
Horn of Africa

Hot Pot City
Justa Pasta
Kame
Le Bouchon
Nicholas' Restaurant
Original Pancake House
Pambiche
Pho Van
Pine State Biscuits
The RingSide
RingSide East
Saburo's
Swagat
Thai Peacock Restaurant
Tin Shed Garden Cafe
Tokyo Restaurant
Vista Spring Café
Wong's King Seafood
  Restaurant
Ya Hala
Yoko's Japanese Restau-
  rant and Sushi Bar

GOURMET TAKEOUT

Edelweiss Sausage
  & Delicatessen
Elephants Delicatessen
Flying Elephants
  at Fox Tower
Flying Elephants
  at Kruse Way
Lorenzo's

GREEK

Alexis
Eleni's Estiatorio
Eleni's Philoxenia

HAWAIIAN

Noho's Hawaiian Café

HISTORIC BUILDING

Al-Amir
Biwa

Blueplate Lunch Counter
  & Soda Fountain
Bunk Sandwiches
Clyde Common
Dan and Louis' Oyster Bar
Jake's Famous Crawfish
Jake's Grill
The Joel Palmer House
Marco's Café &
  Espresso Bar
McCormick & Schmick's
  Seafood Restaurant
Nick's Italian Café
Plainfield's Mayur
Red Hills Provincial Dining
The Restaurant at the
  Historic Reserve
Siam Society
Syun Izakaya

INDIAN

Bombay Cricket
  Club Restaurant
East India Company
India House
Plainfield's Mayur
Swagat
Vindalho

ITALIAN

Alba Osteria & Enoteca
Bar Mingo
Bastas Trattoria
Bugatti's Ristorante
  Italiano
Caffe Allora
Caffe Mingo
DOC
Fratelli
Gino's Restaurant and Bar
Giorgio's
Justa Pasta
Little Italy's Trattoria
Lorenzo's

Lucca
Nick's Italian Café
Nostrana
Pazzo Ristorante
Piazza Italia
Ristorante Fratelli
Serratto
Tabla
Tucci

JAPANESE

Biwa
Hakatamon
Hiroshi
Ichiban
Kame
Masu
Meiji-En Japanese
  Restaurant
Murata
Saburo's
Sinju
Syun Izakaya
Tanuki
Tokyo Restaurant
Yakuza
Yoko's Japanese Restaurant
  and Sushi Bar

JEWISH

Kenny and Zuke's
  Delicatessen
Kornblatt's Delicatessen
Mother's Bistro & Bar

KOREAN

BeWon Korean Restaurant
Biwa

LATE NIGHT

Clyde Common
Delta Cafe and Bar
Dots Cafe
El Gaucho

Gilt Club
Holden's Bistro
Le Happy
Montage
Pazzo Ristorante
Saucebox

LATIN AMERICAN
Andina
¡Oba!
Pambiche

MEDITERRANEAN
Clyde Common
Lauro Kitchen
Lucy's Table
Nicolas' Restaurant
Serratto
Southpark Seafood
  Grill and Wine Bar
Tabla
3 Doors Down Café
23 Hoyt
Ya Hala

MEXICAN
Autentica
Cha!
Cha! Cha! Cha! Mexican
  Taqueria
Esparza's Tex-Mex Café
La Calaca Comelona
Nuestra Cocina
Por Qué No?
Trébol

MIDDLE EASTERN
Abou Karim
Al-Amir
Bombay Cricket
  Club Restaurant
Habibi
Karam
Nicholas' Restaurant

Tabla
Ya Hala

MILKSHAKES
Bijou Café
Blueplate Lunch Counter
  & Soda Fountain
Burgerville
Byways Cafe
Elephants Delicatessen
Fat City Cafe
Mother's Bistro & Bar
Vista Spring Café

MOROCCAN
Marrakesh
Tabla

NORTHWEST
Beast
Belly
Belly Timber
Bluehour
Carlyle
Castagna
Clarklewis
Clyde Common
Dundee Bistro
The Farm Café
Hands On Café
The Heathman Restaurant
  and Bar
Higgins
Hudson's Bar & Grill
Jakes Grill
Lucy's Table
Noble Rot
Paley's Place
Park Kitchen
Pazzo Ristorante
Red Star Tavern &
  Roast House
Roots
Serratto

Simpatica Dining Hall
Ten 01
Three Degrees Waterfront
  Bar & Grill
Tina's
Toast
Urban Farmer
Veritable Quandary
Wildwood

ONION RINGS
Burgerville
Byways Cafe
Doug Fir
Hudson's Bar & Grill
Lincoln
Red Star Tavern &
  Roast House
The RingSide
RingSide East
Three Degrees Waterfront
  Bar & Grill
Wildwood

OUTDOOR DINING
Apizza Scholls
Autentica
Bastas Trattoria
Blossoming Lotus
Bluehour
Bugatti's Ristorante
  Italiano
Caffe Mingo
Castagna
Cha!
Dundee Bistro
Elephants Delicatessen
Everett Street Bistro
Fenouil
Flying Elephants
Hands On Café
Harborside
India House
Jo Bar

Justa Pasta
La Calaca Comelona
Noble Rot
Noho's Hawaiian Café
Paley's Place
Pambiche
Perry's on Fremont
Por Qué No?
Red Hills Provincial Dining
Saint Honore
Serratto
Southpark Seafood
Grill and Wine Bar
Sweet Basil Thai
Thai Peacock Restaurant
Tin Shed Garden Cafe
Tucci
Typhoon! (Northwest)
Veritable Quandary
Wildwood
Yakuza

OYSTERS
Acadia
Andina
Bar Mingo
Bluehour
Bread and Ink Cafe
Clay's Smokehouse
Corbett Fish House
Dan and Louis' Oyster Bar
El Gaucho
Harborside
Higgins
Jake's Famous Crawfish
Jo Bar and Rotisserie
McCormick & Schmick's
Seafood Restaurant
McCormick's Fish
House and Bar
Montage
Red Hills Provincial Dining

Red Star Tavern &
Roast House
Salty's on the Columbia
Ten 01
Three Degrees Waterfront
Bar & Grill

PAN-ASIAN
Ping
Pok Pok and Whiskey
Soda Lounge
Saucebox
Siam Society

PERUVIAN
Andina

PIZZA
Apizza Scholls
Beaches Restaurant & Bar
BridgePort Alehouse
BridgePort Brewpub
Bugatti's Ristorante
Italiano
Café Castagna
Dove Vivi
Dundee Bistro
Elephants Delicatessen
Flying Elephants at
Fox Tower
Flying Elephants at
Kruse Way
Henry's 12th Street Tavern
Hopworks Urban
Brewery
Hot Lips Pizza
Jo Bar and Rotisserie
Ken's Artisan Pizza
Lauro Kitchen
Little Italy's Trattoria
Lucca
Nicholas' Restaurant
Nick's Italian Café
Nostrana

Pazzo Ristorante
Serratto
Tucci
Vista Spring Café
Wildwood

PRIVATE ROOMS
¡Oba!
Pazzo Ristorante
Serratto
Simpatica Dining Hall

ROMANTIC
Acadia
Bastas Trattoria
Bluehour
Caffe Allora
Carlyle
Castagna
DOC
East India Company
El Gaucho
The Farm Café
Fenouil
Gilt Club
Giorgio's
Higgins
Hudson's Bar & Grill
The Joel Palmer House
Le Happy
Lovely Hula Hands
Lucy's Table
Marrakesh
Mint
¡Oba!
Papa Haydn
Portland City Grill
Red Hills Provincial Dining
Ristorante Fratelli
Saucebox
Sel Gris
Serratto
Siam Society

Silk
Sinju
Tabla
Ten 01
23 Hoyt
Wildwood

SEAFOOD

Acadia
Andina
Bluehour
Castagna
Cha!
Clarke's
Clyde Common
Corbett Fish House
Dan and Louis' Oyster Bar
Dundee Bistro
El Gaucho
The Farm Café
Harborside
Higgins
Jake's Famous Crawfish
Jake's Grill
Jo Bar and Rotisserie
Lauro Kitchen
McCormick & Schmick's
   Seafood Restaurant
McCormick's Fish
   House and Bar
Mint
¡Oba!
Paley's Place
Papa Haydn
Perry's on Fremont
Ping
Ristorante Fratelli
Roots
Salty's on the Columbia
Saucebox
Screen Door
Sel Gris

Southpark Seafood
   Grill and Wine Bar
Three Degrees Waterfront
   Bar & Grill
Typhoon!
Wong's King Seafood
   Restaurant
Wu's Open Kitchen
Yoko's Japanese Restaurant
   and Sushi Bar
Yuki Japanese Restaurant
Urban Farmer

SOUP/SALAD/ SANDWICH

Bijou Café
Blueplate Lunch Counter
   & Soda Fountain
Bread and Ink Café
BridgePort Alehouse
BridgePort Brewpub
Bunk Sandwiches
Byways Cafe
Café Castagna
Caffe Allora
Daily Cafe
Dots Cafe
Edelweiss Sausage
   & Delicatessen
Elephants Delicatessen
Everett Street Bistro
The Farm Café
Fat City Cafe
Flying Elephants at
   Fox Tower
Flying Elephants at
   Kruse Way
Grand Central Baking
   Company
Half and Half
Hands On Café
Henry's 12th Street Tavern
J & M Café

Jakes Grill
John Street Café
Kenny and Zuke's
   Delicatessen
Kenny and Zuke's
   SandwichWorks
Ken's Artisan Bakery
   & Café
Kornblatt's Delicatessen
Le Petite Provence
Marco's Café &
   Espresso Bar
Meat Cheese Bread
Milo's City Café
Mother's Bistro & Bar
Otto's Sausage Kitchen
Papa Haydn
Saint Honoré Boulangerie
Serratto
Three Degrees Waterfront
   Bar & Grill
Three Square Grill
Tin Shed Garden Cafe
Vista Spring Café
Zell's: An American Café

SOUTHERN/ SOUL FOOD

Bernie's Southern Bistro
Delta Cafe and Bar
Montage
Pine State Biscuits
Podnah's Pit BBQ
Russell Street Bar-B-Que
Screen Door
Three Square Grill

SOUTHWESTERN

Cactus Ya Ya
Esparza's Tex-Mex Café

SPANISH

Lolo
Patanegra

Tabla
Toro Bravo

STEAK HOUSES

El Gaucho
Jake's Grill
Morton's of Chicago:
    The Steakhouse
Portland City Grill
The RingSide
RingSide East
Ruth's Chris Steak House
Urban Farmer

SUSHI

Hakatomon
Hiroshi
Ichiban
Kame
Masu
Meiji-En Japanese
    Restaurant
Murata
Portland City Grill
Saburo's
Sinju
Syun Izakaya
Tanuki
Tokyo Restaurant
Yakuza
Yoko's Japanese Restaurant
    and Sushi Bar

TAPAS/SMALL PLATES

Andina
Colosso
Lolo
Navarre
¡Oba!
Park Kitchen
Patanegra

Southpark Seafood
    Grill and Wine Bar
Tanuki
Toro Bravo

THAI

Baan Thai
Lemongrass Thai
Ping
Pok Pok and Whiskey
    Soda Lounge
Siam Society
Sweet Basil Thai
Thai Peacock Restaurant
Typhoon!

UNIQUELY PORTLAND

Bijou Café
Bluehour
Byways Cafe
Clarklewis
Clyde Common
Dots Cafe
The Farm Café
Hands On Café
Higgins
Jake's Famous Crawfish
J & M Café
John Street Café
Little Red Bike Café
London Grill
Lovely Hula Hands
Mother's Bistro & Bar
Nick's Italian Café
Original Pancake House
Paley's Place
Pine State Biscuits
Podnah's Pit BBQ
Pok Pok and Whiskey
    Soda Lounge
The RingSide
RingSide East

Roots
Simpatica Dining Hall
Southpark Seafood
    Grill and Wine Bar
Thai Peacock Restaurant
Veritable Quandary
Vindalho
Wildwood
Ya Hala
Yasuka

VEGETARIAN/ VEGAN

Blossoming Lotus
Bombay Cricket
    Club Restaurant
Byways Cafe
Cha!
Cha! Cha! Cha!
    Mexican Taqueria
Daily Cafe
Dots Cafe
The Farm Café
Fire on the Mountain
Habibi
Higgins
Horn of Africa
Hot Lips Pizza
India House
Le Happy
Lucy's Table
Nicholas' Restaurant
¡Oba!
Queen of Sheba
Ristorante Fratelli
Swagat
Tin Shed Garden Cafe
Vindalho

VIETNAMESE

Mekong Grill
Pho Van
Silk

VIEW	WINE BAR	
Beaches Restaurant & Bar	Alba Osteria & Enoteca	Navarre
Elephant's Delicatessen	Café Castagna	Nick's Italian Café
Harborside	Caffe Allora	Noble Rot
The Heathman	Dundee Bistro	Nostrana
Restaurant and Bar	The Joel Palmer House	Paley's Place
Noble Rot	Ken's Artisan	Serratto
Portland City Grill	Bakery & Café	Southpark Seafood
Salty's on the Columbia	Le Bouchon	Grill and Wine Bar
Three Degrees	Lincoln Restaurant	Tabla
Waterfront Bar & Grill	Lucy's Table	Ten 01
		Tina's

Top 200 Restaurants

Acadia / ★★★

1303 NE FREMONT ST, ALAMEDA; 503/249-5001

At Acadia chef Adam Higgs blends seasonal Northwest products with distinctive seafood imported from the Louisiana Gulf Coast. A marriage of Cajun and Creole, the dishes are reminiscent of what you'd find in the French Quarter. Oysters en brochette with creole rémoulade are a staple starter, but for an extraordinary offering, go for the snapping turtle soup garnished with a white-truffle deviled egg. Crawfish étouffée, a New Orleans classic, is amped up with a delicacy not commonly found in these parts: soft-shell crab with a tempura-like batter. Tip-top service in the candlelight-bathed dining room completes the winsome experience. **COME HERE FOR A TASTE OF THE BAYOU.** *$$–$$$; AE, DIS, MC, V; no checks; lunch Wed, dinner every day; full bar; reservations recommended; www.creolapdx.com; street parking; map:FF5.* &

Al-Amir / ★★

223 SW STARK ST, OLD TOWN; 503/274-0010

Housed in the historic Bishop's House—an 1879 Gothic confection that is one of Portland's most charming architectural oddities—Al-Amir is the elder statesman of local Middle Eastern restaurants. Stepping into the somber, stained-glass chamber is an immersive experience, as you're greeted by spicy scents of Lebanese cooking and soft-spoken and gracious servers. Ambience, gentility, and attention to detail set the place apart—care is taken with every dish from a simple *ful mudammas* (marinated fava bean salad) to the elaborately seasoned and prepared *kharouf muhammar* (roasted lamb with a cucumber-yogurt sauce). The house tea is an intoxicating mixture of black tea, mint, anise, and cardamom. **COME HERE FOR A GRACIOUS MIDDLE EASTERN DINING EXPERIENCE.** *$$; AE, DIS, MC, V; no checks; lunch Mon–Fri, dinner every day; full bar; reservations recommended; www.alamir portland.com; street parking; map:I5.* &

Alba Osteria & Enoteca / ★★★☆

6440 SW CAPITOL HWY, HILLSDALE; 503/977-3045

When a vacation to the Italian Alps is out of the question, the next best thing is Alba. This charming 48-seat jewel brings the best of the small Piedmontese osterias to Portland. Antipasti such as salt cod, potato, and chicory *insalata di baccalà* shine, while Alba's signature velvety Parmesan-coated egg noodle *tajarin* (pasta), with its earthy bite of morel and porcini mushrooms, is a standout. Hearty entrées echo the region's mountain roots, with offerings such as *costine di maiale*—slow-roasted pork ribs and sausage with red cabbage and beans—or the tender *tagliata* flatiron steak with fresh horseradish and salsify fries. Friendly service, an outstanding Italian-focused wine list, and a romantic *enoteca*, or wine bar, make Alba a perfect pick. **COME HERE FOR EUROPEAN SOPHISTICATION MARRIED WITH THE BOUNTY OF OREGON.** *$$–$$$; AE, DIS, MC, V; no checks; dinner Tues–Sat; full bar; reservations recommended; www.albaosteria.com; self parking; map:JJ7.* &

Alexis / ★★

215 W BURNSIDE ST, OLD TOWN; 503/224-8577

Whitewashed walls, blue-and-white-checkered tablecloths, and shouts of "Opa!" transport this family-run institution from gritty Burnside Street to a seaside taverna near Athens. Warm and welcoming, Alexis gives equal attention to large groups and cozy romantic couples alike. Beloved Greek staples such as golden, crunchy fried calamari with garlicky tzatziki, tender grilled lamb souvlaki, freshly made spinach-feta spanakopita, and eggplant moussaka are solid choices that come in generous portions. *Saganaki* (kasseri cheese doused with ouzo and set ablaze tableside) adds to the festivities. Try the bright cured olives and creamy feta—the Alexis family imports them directly from Greece. The $16.95-per-person family-style dinner option is a bargain. **COME HERE FOR AN AUTHENTIC GREEK EXPERIENCE.** *$$; AE, DC, MC, V; no checks; lunch, dinner Mon–Sat (belly dancers Fri–Sat in evenings); full bar; reservations necessary for 10 or more; www.alexisfoods.com; street parking; map:K6.*

Andina / ★★★

1314 NW GLISAN ST, PEARL DISTRICT; 503/228-9535

Andina highlights the inventiveness of Novo Peruvian food. Owner Doris Rodriguez de Platt creates a sophisticated atmosphere while gathering some of the most talented chefs from Lima and beyond. Expect delights such as the Pulpo a La Oliva (octopus in endive leaves with a bright olive sauce), or one of the many outstanding rotating seafood ceviches such as prawns with green mango and passion fruit. Even humble potato cakes become something special here with the inclusion of key lime juice and fillings such as the Mixta Nikkei: spicy tuna, crab, and crispy shrimp. The refreshing signature Pisco Sour, made with Peruvian grape brandy, fresh lime, sugar, and whipped egg whites, is textbook. Adding to the appeal are generous happy hour specials, live music, and food portions that come in three sizes for all appetites and budgets. **COME HERE FOR A TASTE OF PERU.** *$$–$$$; AE, DIS, MC, V; local checks only; lunch, dinner Mon–Sat; full bar; reservations recommended; www. andinarestaurant.com; street parking; map:M1.* &

Apizza Scholls / ★★☆

4741 SE HAWTHORNE BLVD, HAWTHORNE; 503/233-1286

Apizza Scholls has transformed the humble event of pizza eating into a special occasion at its upper Hawthorne hideaway. Portland's pizza-loving populace travels from all over the city and beyond to endure at times an hour-long wait for perfect pies that live up to their deservedly inflated reputation. What separates this pizza parlor from nearly every other is a heavenly dough made only once a day and fermented slowly, resulting in a crust so complex it's at once creamy, chewy, and echoing with crunch. The kitchen makes only so much dough: if it runs out on a busy night, the restaurant closes early—though that doesn't happen too often. Pies include the peasant Apizza Margo'rita, a take on the simple cheese pizza, with fresh garlic and chopped basil, and white pies such as the Tartufo Bianco's combo of pecorino Romano, truffle oil, and sea salt. The Caesar salad with whole romaine leaves and rustic croutons holds cult status in Portland. Few wines top $25 on the short and ample wine list, and the European beer selection is heavenly. Apizza Scholls is also home to some of the most authentically delicious cannoli in town. **COME HERE FOR SOME OF THE BEST PIZZA PIE IN PORTLAND.** *$; MC, V; local checks only; dinner Tues–Sun; beer and wine; reservations for 8–12 (only 1 accepted per night); www.apizzascholls.com; street parking; map:HH4.* &

Autentica / ★★

5507 NE 30TH AVE, CONCORDIA; 503/287-7555

Autentica features light and fresh small plates; slow-cooked meats in savory, complex sauces; and seafood specialties from owner Oswaldo Bibiano's native state of Guerrero, Mexico. Trained in some of Portland's finest restaurants, Bibiano produces starters such as Mexican blue crab and watercress salad or spicy octopus cocktail that share the bill with the more humble, rustic menudo. Locally sourced beef, chicken, and pork manifest themselves in many forms, whether a richly flavored Guerrero-style mole or in traditional enchiladas and tortas. For lunch, savor cactus leaves stuffed with tomatoes, onions, rosemary, and young requesón cheese, or choose authentic tacos and quesadillas. Chilaquiles and the house Bloody Mary pair perfectly for brunch. Autentica opens its doors to a breezy backyard patio during the summer, where Bibiano and company grill meat and chicken to order. **COME HERE FOR INVENTIVE MEXICAN SOUL FOOD FOR BRUNCH, LUNCH, OR DINNER.** *$$; MC, V; no checks; lunch, dinner Tues–Sun, brunch Sat–Sun; full bar; reservations recommended; www.autenticaportland.com; street parking; map:FF4.* &

Baan Thai / ★

1924 SW BROADWAY, DOWNTOWN; 503/224-5155

With its standing-room-only lunch rushes and warrenlike floor plan, this popular Thai cafe near Portland State University has the appearance of a well-loved hangout serving up wholesome rice and noodle dishes to famished college kids. And while it's true the menu offers such standards as chicken satay and pad thai, you'll be rewarded for venturing into less-trodden territory. Crispy catfish stir-fried with basil and lemon leaf is multitextured and complex in flavor, while a trout salad with julienned fruit provides surprising refreshment after a bout with the spicy rice and noodle dishes. Don't miss the Volcano Chicken, a house specialty that involves a whole game hen, spicy barbecue sauce, and dancing live flames. **COME HERE FOR ADVENTUROUS THAI CUISINE.** *$$; MC, V; no checks; lunch, dinner Mon–Sat; beer and wine; no reservations; street parking; map:D1.* ♿

Bastas Trattoria / ★

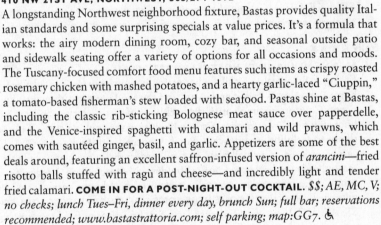

410 NW 21ST AVE, NORTHWEST; 503/274-1572

A longstanding Northwest neighborhood fixture, Bastas provides quality Italian standards and some surprising specials at value prices. It's a formula that works: the airy modern dining room, cozy bar, and seasonal outside patio and sidewalk seating offer a variety of options for all occasions and moods. The Tuscany-focused comfort food menu features such items as crispy roasted rosemary chicken with mashed potatoes, and a hearty garlic-laced "Ciuppin," a tomato-based fisherman's stew loaded with seafood. Pastas shine at Bastas, including the classic rib-sticking Bolognese meat sauce over papperdelle, and the Venice-inspired spaghetti with calamari and wild prawns, which comes with sautéed ginger, basil, and garlic. Appetizers are some of the best deals around, featuring an excellent saffron-infused version of *arancini*—fried risotto balls stuffed with ragù and cheese—and incredibly light and tender fried calamari. **COME IN FOR A POST-NIGHT-OUT COCKTAIL.** *$$; AE, MC, V; no checks; lunch Tues–Fri, dinner every day, brunch Sun; full bar; reservations recommended; www.bastastrattoria.com; self parking; map:GG7.* ♿

Beaker and Flask / ★★★

727 SE WASHINGTON ST, INNER SOUTHEAST; 503/235-8180

With a keen eye focused on creating exceptional food, such as pan-seared black cod served with mussels, chorizo, fennel, and green beans, Beaker and Flask might almost make you forget about the creative mixology going on at the bar. Once the bartender at Clyde Common, Kevin Ludwig branched out and opened up this close-in eastside establishment that fashions creative drinks to accompany a menu featuring fresh local ingredients. Drinks to try might be the Dock Ellis—a concoction of rye whiskey, limoncello, Dolin Blanc, cynar, and bitters—or the Broken Shark, with gin, Averna, grapefruit juice, and wormwood. There's a drink for almost any palate as well as a good wine list and six beers on draft. **COME HERE FOR TRULY CREATIVE DRINKS.**

$$–$$$; V, MC; no checks; dinner every day; full bar; reservations recommended; www.beakerandflask.com; street parking; map:HH5.

Beast / ★★★½

5425 NE 30TH AVE, CONCORDIA; 503/841-6968
Owner Naomi Pomeroy's notoriety has elevated Beast to a restaurant on the entire nation's radar. The nontraditional dining experience offers five- or six-course prix fixe dinners (and Sunday brunch), with "substitutions politely declined," and a minimal, mostly French wine list to pair with the "ghetto French" cuisine. All seating is communal. One particular dinner in midspring began with a petite bouillabaisse, followed by Pomeroy's signature charcuterie plate. The main event, a medium-rare slice of roasted New York steak, farmers market–fresh asparagus, and smashed potatoes with green garlic, showcased the restaurant's local-seasonal philosophy. A palate-cleansing green salad made way for two rich courses: the first, a selection of artisanal cheeses; the second, a decadent chocolate-and-caramel tartlet. **COME HERE FOR SHARED TABLES AND THOUGHTFULLY PLANNED DAILY MENUS.** *$$$$; AE, DIS, MC, V; no checks; dinner Wed–Sat, brunch Sun; beer and wine; reservations recommended; www.beastpdx.com; street parking; map:EE5.* ♿

Belly / ★★★

3500 NE MLK JR BLVD; NORTHEAST; 503/249-9764
Eating at Belly feels a bit like what eating in your own home might be like if home were always bright and clean, and the food perfectly, thoughtfully prepared. Comforting simplicity is the backbone of this operation, and it is down-home but not down-market. Seasonally driven, the cooking comes right from the heart—skillful and delicate. Potato gnocchi with house-smoked salmon can be ordered as a small plate or a full order; the burgers are available any season, as is the barbecued pork shoulder with peach glaze. Veggies are seasonal and always prepared with an inspired Northwest enthusiasm. Don't miss the killer desserts. **COME HERE FOR PACIFIC NORTHWEST SOUL FOOD.** *$$; AE, MC, V; no checks; dinner Tues–Sat, brunch Sun; full bar; reservations recommended; www.bellyrestaurant.com; self parking; map:FF6.* ♿

Belly Timber / ★★

3257 SE HAWTHORNE BLVD, HAWTHORNE; 503/235-3277
"Belly timber" is Victorian slang for food of all sorts, and at this restored Victorian-turned-restaurant, consideration and ambition are the passwords. Right from the get-go, chef David Siegel's concise seasonal menu displays his preference for pure, diverse flavors. Your baguette and butter comes with sprinkles of two house-made salts, coriander and beet, and fennel seed; a plate of his charcuterie may follow, accompanied by his own mustards. A risotto of nettles, asparagus, and ricotta salata is a fine next course; it's light and verdant—springtime on a plate. Other entrées include a crisp, seared lingcod with fennel and saffron broth, and a grilled hanger steak presented with white beans and shallot french fries. The talents of the bar match those

of the kitchen here: a Vodka Collins with applewood-smoked New Deal Vodka heads an inventive cocktail menu. **COME HERE FOR A CREATIVE FARE WITH A GENEROUS SELECTION OF MEAT AND SEAFOOD.** *$$$; MC, V; dinner Tues–Sun, brunch Sat–Sun; full bar; reservations recommended; www.belly timberrestaurant.com; street parking; map:HH6.*

Bernie's Southern Bistro / ★★

2904 NE ALBERTA ST, ALBERTA; 503/282-9864

Start a conversation about your favorite fried chicken in Portland, and the subject of Bernie's Southern Bistro is bound to arise. While purists are often bothered that Bernie's buttermilk-marinated fried fowl arrives at the table deboned, this simple tweak hasn't stopped the restaurant's signature dish from becoming a ritual favorite among the nontraditionalists of the Alberta 'hood and beyond. The menu is a roster of Southern jewels, from the spicy blackened catfish sweetly kissed by bourbon–brown butter sauce to the chicken-fried steak in milkshake-thick gravy on a pile of buttery mashed potatoes. Bernie's is not afraid to veer off the beaten path with the likes of thick Carlton Farms pork chops with a rhubarb pan jus over sweet potato gratin and minced peas. The kitchen also has a light hand with the fryer, and its cornmeal-crusted fried oysters, fried okra, and fried pickles are perfect. As well, there are several entrée-sized salads and, come winter, marvelous gumbo. Bernie's happy hour is also among the finest. **COME HERE FOR THE HOUSE-MADE CORN BREAD AND HONEY BUTTER.** *$$; AE, DIS, MC, V; no checks; dinner Tues–Sun; full bar; reservations recommended; street parking; map:FF5.* &

BeWon Korean Restaurant / ★★★⯪

1203 NW 23RD AVE, NORTHWEST; 503/464-9222

By virtue of meticulous cookery and presentation, and the knowledgeable servers' patient explanations, BeWon is a white-tablecloth take on authentic Korean cuisine. The prix fixe Han Jung Shik is a seven-course extravaganza that approximates a traditional Korean meal for an unbelievably reasonable $24.95, or $39.95 with wine pairings. Main courses, such as *galbi* (marinated beef short ribs) and *daeji bulgogi* (sliced pork in spicy red pepper paste), are also available à la carte, and come with a vivid parade of accompanying side dishes called *banchan*: nine tiny ramekins hold such specialties as dried squid in hot pepper sauce, both spicy and mild kimchee, crab griddle cakes, pickled daikon radish, and marinated taro root. Lunch is served Fridays only with a reduced menu and prices. **COME HERE FOR THE HAN JUNG SHIK SEVEN-COURSE DINNER WITH WINE PAIRINGS.** *$$; AE, DIS, MC, V; no checks; lunch Fri, dinner Mon–Sat; beer and wine; reservations recommended; www. bewonrestaurant.com; street parking; map:GG7.* &

Bijou Café / ★

132 SW 3RD AVE, OLD TOWN; 503/222-3187

For over 25 years, this bright, casual downtown spot has provided everyone from local politicos to families with a high quality wake-up. The crispy on the outside, creamy on the inside potatoes are legendary. Freshly squeezed juices, locally sourced Willapa Bay oyster or halibut hashes, thick pancakes with real maple or marionberry syrups, and one of the best French rolled omelets around—made with free-range, farm-fresh eggs—highlight the commitment to quality. Despite the focus on breakfast, lunch offerings are just as good—the organic Painted Hills beef burger is juicy and substantial, while the Japanese soba noodle salad with julienned vegetables is perfect for lighter appetites. As one of the early adopters of "seasonal and local" eating, the Bijou has grown into a Portland classic, with traditional offerings and updated modern touches. **COME HERE FOR BREAKFAST POTATOES.** *$–$$; MC, V; local checks only; breakfast every day, lunch Mon–Fri; beer and wine; no reservations; street parking; map:J5.* &

Biwa / ★★

213 SE 9TH AVE, INNER SOUTHEAST; 503/239-8830

As one of the few *izakaya* restaurants in Portland, Biwa creates terrific renditions of small-plate foods meant to be shared and served with drinks, among them, spicy fresh vinegared mackerel, and the Korean-influenced *yukke* (ginger-sesame seasoned beef tartare) and crispy-tender pan-fried vegetable *chijimi* cakes. The *yakimono* (grilled skewers) are extensive: miso scallops, simple roasted shiitake mushrooms with sea salt, and melt-in-your-mouth marinated chicken hearts are standouts. Biwa also specializes in noodles; the house-made ramen noodles are addictively soothing, served in a light chicken and soy-based broth or in a deeply intense pork base with a choice of add-ons such as egg or a wonderful fatty *chasyu* (barbecued pork). As is *izakaya* tradition, Biwa offers a large sake selection, beers from all over, and inventive Asian-influenced cocktails. Sit at the bar to watch the high-energy cooks in action. Open late. **COME HERE FOR RAMEN AND UDON AND JAPANESE SKEWERS.** *$$; AE, MC, V; local checks only; dinner every day; full bar; reservations for 6 or more; www.biwarestaurant.com; street parking; map:HH5.*

Blossoming Lotus / ★

925 NW DAVIS ST, PEARL DISTRICT; 503/228-0048

For a city blessed with vegetarian-friendly restaurants, Portland doesn't have that many meat-free restaurants. Enter Blossoming Lotus. Located within Yoga Pearl, Blossoming Lotus provides healthy breakfast, lunch, and dinner options to anyone interested in tasty high-quality and highly satisfying foods. Live and raw dishes are a specialty here with such menu items as the Buckwheat Granola, which is rich with walnuts, pumpkin, and hemp seeds, and the "Live Pasta," with zucchini ribbon pasta, basil pesto, and cashew cheese. The cashew hummus or a fresh-squeezed juice or smoothie makes a flavorful and substantial snack. One of the wrap sandwiches, such as the maple-smoked tempeh, is enough to keep you going for an afternoon. Other offerings include a chunky miso soup filled with veggies and seaweed; spicy black bean chili; and brown rice or noodle bowls with toppings such as quinoa, in-season vegetables, and such aromatic sauces as Curried Indian Bowl

or Thai Peanut. **COME HERE FOR A VARIETY OF DELICIOUS RAW DISHES.** *$;
AE, DIS, MC, V; local checks only; breakfast, lunch, dinner every day; beer and
wine; reservations for 6 or more; www.blpdx.com; street parking; map:K3.* &

Bluehour / ★★★

250 NW 13TH AVE, PEARL DISTRICT; 503/226-3394
Restaurateur Bruce Carey has set the standard for Portland dining, elevat-
ing the city from a culinary backwater in the 1980s to one of the finer food
cities in the country today. Bluehour has long been a gem among Portland
eateries. Under New York–born, Italian-American chef Kenny Giambalvo,
Bluehour's fare is as American as European. Start with a selection from the
well-appointed cheese cart. Try the signature gnocchi: velvety, cheesy cushions with a salty kick and hint of black truffle. The risotto touts ever-changing
accents such as wild sturgeon, sweet red peppers, and fresh basil. Bluehour's
signature sea scallops are thinly veiled in bacon and served with changing
seasonal accompaniments such as celery root purée and caper dressing. Giambalvo molds complex flavors into an edible harmony. **COME HERE FOR GLAM-
OUR; COME BACK FOR GREAT FOOD.** *$$$; AE, DC, MC, V; no checks; lunch
Mon–Fri, dinner Tues–Sat, brunch Sun; full bar; reservations recommended;
www.bluehouronline.com; valet and street parking; map:L1.* &

Blueplate Lunch Counter & Soda Fountain / ★★☆

308 SW WASHINGTON ST, DOWNTOWN; 503/295-2583
Buried in one of the ground-level storefront nooks of the historic Dekum
Building, Blueplate is a downtown diner and soda fountain dishing out
old-fashioned American food, sundaes, shakes, and creative soda concoc-
tions. Alongside such standbys as grilled-cheese sandwiches and house-made
tomato soup, there are three rotating items for lunch: an entrée-sized salad,
a daily sandwich, and the namesake blue-plate special. Blueplate is home to
one of the only in-house soda fountains in Portland, featuring the likes of
chocolate Coke; the Hawaiian Sunset, a strawberry soda with pineapple and
coconut; and the Chai Bomb. Skip dessert and reach into the jars of penny
candy near the register—just like in Mayberry. Blueplate serves French-press
coffee, and with a free wi-fi connection, it's not a bad place to spend a rainy
afternoon. **COME HERE FOR THE BLUE-PLATE SPECIAL.** *$; DIS, MC, V; no
checks; lunch Mon–Fri; no alcohol; no reservations; www.eatatblueplate.com;
street parking; map:H5.* &

Bombay Cricket Club Restaurant / ★★

1925 SE HAWTHORNE BLVD, HAWTHORNE; 503/231-0740
This lively little restaurant on Hawthorne serves familiar and darn-good
Indian food—curries, vindaloo, tandoori, biryani—plus a small selection
of Middle Eastern dishes. All the while, the TV at the tiny bar broadcasts
recorded cricket matches. If cricket is not your thing, never mind; once
you've tasted your first mango margarita and dipped a samosa into the tangy
tamarind chutney, you'll find yourself distracted. The condiments that usually

accompany an Indian meal—mango chutney, yogurt raita, and dal—must be ordered separately. The dozen-or-so tables are often packed, and you should make a reservation well in advance. **COME HERE FOR THE AWESOME NAAN.** *$$; AE, DIS, MC, V; no checks; dinner every day; full bar; reservations recommended; www.bombaycricketclubrestaurant.com; street parking; map:HH5.*

Bread and Ink Cafe / ★★☆

3610 SE HAWTHORNE BLVD, HAWTHORNE; 503/239-4756

There's more to the beloved Bread and Ink than its blintzes. This homey, light-filled bistro in the heart of the funky Hawthorne District serves a marvelous Jamaican jerk-chicken sandwich, grilled black-bean cakes, and panfried oysters with chipotle-lime aioli for lunch. At dinner, you can't go wrong with the chèvre, arugula, and hazelnut salad; risotto primavera; or pork tenderloin with fresh rosemary, garlic, and white wine. Regulars rave about the oversize hamburger, with house-made condiments to do it justice, and the impressive baked desserts, including a legendary cassata. Intriguing framed line drawings on the walls, crayons by request, and huge windows onto Hawthorne are more reasons the place has become a neighborhood landmark. Enjoy their blintzes—delicately crisped squares of dough, enfolding a lemony ricotta—with Bread and Ink's raspberry jam. **COME HERE FOR THE BLINTZES.** *$$; AE, DIS, MC, V; checks OK; breakfast, lunch, dinner Mon–Sat, brunch Sun; beer and wine; no reservations; www.breadandinkcafe. com; street parking; map:HH5.* &

BridgePort Brewpub / ★★
BridgePort Alehouse / ★★

1313 NW MARSHALL ST, PEARL DISTRICT; 503/241-3612
3632 SE HAWTHORNE BLVD, HAWTHORNE; 503/233-6540

As the oldest craft brewery in the state of Oregon, BridgePort is a must for any beer lover. With its flagship gastropub located right in the middle of the trendy Pearl District, the fully functional brewery is buzzing night and day with thirsty locals and visitors alike. Stop by in the morning for a cup of coffee and a delicious slice of house-baked bread or come by for a midday snack of fresh-out-of-the-oven pretzels with ESB mustard and BridgePort's irresistable Blackstrap Stout cheddar spread. Dinner finds the brewpub rather full, but with three seating options there's always room for more. With the same menu as the brewpub, the alehouse has a slightly more neighborhood pub feel. Both dining rooms are a slightly more formal affair—cozy, mellow, and much more family friendly. Wherever you sit, bring a group of good friends and a healthy appetite, as you'll want to try everything on the well-thought-out menu. Juicy, tangy, with just a touch of smoke, the house-smoked pulled pork sandwich is not to be missed. Fries are serviceable, but if it's carbs you're looking for, opt instead for pizza, which the gang at Bridgeport has been slinging since it first opened back in 1984. **COME HERE FOR A TASTE OF OREGON'S BEER HISTORY.** *$$; AE, MC, V; no checks; breakfast, lunch, dinner every day; reservations recommended; www.bridgeportbrew.com; self parking; map:O1; map:HH5.* &

Broder / ★★☆

2508 SE CLINTON ST, CLINTON; 503/736-3333

The Swedes don't eat what we call breakfast. They might, though, if they had Broder—Peter Bro's homage to Scandinavian food. The morning menu is served all day and features baked eggs with a choice of potato pancake, sautéed greens, or roasted tomato. Also on the menu are *bords*: collections of sweet and savory bites that include excellent house-cured gravlax, Swedish farmer cheese, rye crisps, and lingonberry jam. Not to be missed are the *aebleskiver*: small, spherical Danish pancakes served with a trio of lemon curd, maple syrup, and jam. This is not your usual gut-busting breakfast; instead of a gigantic omelet, Broder serves up baked scrambles of such varieties as smoked trout and red onion, or wild mushroom and caramelized onion. A spicy aquavit Bloody Mary completes maybe the best brunch in town. **COME HERE FOR THE AEBLESKIVER.** *$$; MC, V; no checks; breakfast, lunch every day, dinner Thurs–Sun; full bar; no reservations; street parking; www.broderpdx.com; map II5.* &

Bugatti's Ristorante Italiano / ★★☆

18740 WILLAMETTE DR, WEST LINN; 503/636-9555
334 WARNER MILNE RD, OREGON CITY; 503/722-8222

Lydia Bugatti's endearing Italian restaurant in West Linn features fine Italian wines at affordable prices, a friendly and attentive staff, and a seasonally changing menu. Anytime, watch for rigatoni carbonara and spaghetti frutti di mare. Regulars also love the *pasta della casa*: fettucine with cremini mushrooms and artichoke hearts in a creamy tomato sauce. On the entrée side, you might find a grilled chicken risotto or veal with shallots and grilled asparagus. Save room for dazzling desserts, such as the cloudlike tiramisu or the melt-in-your-mouth cannoli. The well-dressed yet simple dining room is quite large, but reservations are a good idea: it's a popular place, especially when the outdoor patio is open. The new Oregon City restaurant, strong in pastas and pizza, fills a void in that town's dining scene. **COME HERE FOR THE PASTA DELLA CASA.** *$$; MC, V; local checks only; dinner every day; beer and wine; reservations recommended; street parking; map:OO5; map:QQ3.* &

Bunk Sandwiches / ★★

621 SE MORRISON ST, BUCKMAN; 503/477-9515

A recent influx of chef-driven sandwich shops has taken over the Portland lunch scene, and Bunk is king. Lines form early at this incredibly popular breakfast and lunch spot in inner Southeast Portland that is owned by "sandwich aficionados" Tommy Habetz and Nick Woods. The duo has spread their fine-dining backgrounds between two slices of bread, creating such gourmet wonders as bone marrow and snails on toast. With offerings like the pork belly Reuben, Roman-style tripe with pecorino, and tongue on rye with onions and spicy mustard, it's unclear whether they're going for the ultimate sandwich experience or just pure shock value. Though the menu changes daily, the devourable meatball Parmigiano hero is a standard, as well as the

ROCK-STAR CHEFS

Portland chefs are bursting onto the food scene like rock stars and shaping the city's indie restaurant culture with inventive cuisine and innovatively designed spaces. National food magazines and the *New York Times* can't stop writing about them; devoted fans pack their convivial dining spaces, marked by open kitchens and communal tables; and their cooking consistently puts them on the nation's best chef and restaurant lists. Mostly thirty-somethings, they're the new generation of the city's restaurant chef-owners, and their eateries carry brassy names like Bunk, Beast, and Pok Pok.

Youngest of the pack is Gabriel Rucker, nominated in 2009 for the prestigious James Beard Rising Star Chef award. The 28-year-old describes his restaurant, **LE PIGEON**, as a "fun bistro." The pigeon tattoos on his right arm inspired his restaurant's name, but his celebrated genius drives his recipes. He has a knack for transforming the familiar by cooking what he calls "layered food." The result? Signature dishes such as beef cheek bourguignonne and whimsical delights such as profiteroles filled with foie gras ice cream, drizzled with caramel sauce and sea salt.

A few blocks away, master butcher Benjamin Dyer has delighted diners at **SIMPATICA DINING HALL**. Defining the city's supper club movement, Dyer and his partners serve handcrafted, locally sourced communal Friday and Saturday supper and weekend brunch in a simple, congenial space. Their house-made bacon and charcuterie, savory crepes, and fried chicken and waffles are legendary. He broke new culinary ground with the opening of **LAURELHURST MARKET**, the city's first

breakfast hard roll filled with bacon, egg, and cheese. **COME HERE FOR THE BEST SANDWICH YOU WILL EVER EAT.** $; *DIS, MC, V; no checks; breakfast, lunch Mon–Sat; beer only; no reservations; www.bunksandwiches.com; street parking; map:HH6.* &

Burgerville / ★

307 E MILL PLAIN BLVD, VANCOUVER WA
(AND BRANCHES); 360/693-8801

An Oregon and Washington institution, Burgerville proves that fast food need not be bad food. Quality reigns here, with a deep commitment to the regional food economy through locally and sustainably farmed, fished, and ranched foods. Locals look forward to yearly seasonal treats such as Walla Walla onion rings in the spring, marionberry milkshakes in the summer, and sweet potato fries in the winter months. Halibut fish-and-chips are crispy and magically grease free. Even the juicy signature burgers feature Country Natural Beef and Oregon Tillamook cheddar cheese. Nine outlets in Portland; the butcher shop/restaurant near the stone Laurelhurst Gates on Burnside.

John Gorham, Dyer's former partner, in 2007 converted a turn-of-the-20th-century building next to the Wonder Ballroom on NE Russell into a bustling haven for Spanish-inspired fare and tapas. At **TORO BRAVO**, the affable, tattooed Gorham reigns from an open kitchen over a red-walled, hopping dining room. Gorham has redefined tapas with such dishes as house-smoked *coppa*, house-cured salt cod fritters, and at once traditional and innovative paellas.

Another seasoned chef, Andy Ricker, is reinventing Asian small plates and reju-venating the city's Chinatown with **PING** (Thai for "grilled"), opened in 2008. Portland's resident expert on Southeast Asian street food, Ricker serves up small plates of grilled skewers, noodles, and such authentic dishes as house-made steamed *bao* (bun) with sweet shredded pork.

Ricker has translated street finds from his extensive Southeast Asian travels to menus there and at his first restaurant, **POK POK** (which in Thai means the sound of a pestle striking mortar), across town. The casual eatery, specializing in street food from the Thai region, spills out from a house to include a take-out shack with outdoor seating.

Pok Pok screams "hip," but Naomi Pomeroy's **BEAST** whispers relaxed refine-ment with a dinner party feel. At Beast, her tiny restaurant off NE Killingsworth Street, Pomeroy quietly serves six-course, French-inspired prix-fixe dinners and Sunday brunch from a central island. Twenty-four diners enjoy a 2½-hour meal at two communal tables in a candlelit room, listening to Edith Piaf or possibly The Rolling Stones.

closest to downtown is the Rose Quarter location (1135 NE Martin Luther King Jr Blvd, near Lloyd Center; 503/235-6858; map:N9). **COME HERE FOR RESPONSIBLE FAST FOOD**. *$; MC, V; checks OK; lunch, dinner every day; no alcohol; no reservations; www.burgerville.com; self parking.* &

Byways Cafe / ★

1212 NW GLISAN ST, PEARL DISTRICT; 503/221-0011
A quintessential no-frills breakfast and lunch joint, tucked into the heart of the often glitzy Pearl District. Basic and classic dishes in generous portions, such as a Frisbee-sized Denver omelet or a heap of velvety biscuits and gravy, sit alongside signature items like Meg's Vegetarian Mountain Hash with salsa and cheese, or decadent buttery Amaretto French Toast. Lunch features a variety of burgers (including a wonderful turkey version), sandwiches such as a chicken salad with Granny Smith apples, and a popular thick-as-a-fist Reuben. Sides such as fries, onion rings, and entrée-sized Cobb or chef salads round out the offerings. A local favorite; expect long waits on the weekends.

The restaurant's name and controversial ad (depicting an aproned Pomeroy in a field caressing a dead 50-pound suckling pig) leave no doubt about the focus here. Pork, meat, and charcuterie (including a celebrated foie gras bonbon) are the cornerstones of a changing weekly meal that often ends with salted caramel ice cream.

Across town, in the Park Blocks off Burnside, Scott Dolich showcases the best of the area's bounty at **PARK KITCHEN**. He calls it an "upscale tavern . . . a good meeting and greeting place." Dolich has been nominated twice for a James Beard Best Northwest Chef award and, like Pomeroy and Rucker, was named a *Food & Wine* Best New Chef. Active with the Portland Farmers Market, he rotates dishes by season and serves such signature staples as flank steak salad and vegan chickpea fries with squash ketchup.

Finally, when it comes to lunch, Tommy Habetz reigns over the city's sandwich explosion. A former sous chef for Mario Batali, Habetz in 2008 opened **BUNK**, an East Coast–style sandwich joint on the East Side near the Morrison Street Bridge. The breakfast and lunch crowd squeeze into the miniscule storefront with its open grill, counter, and cramped tables. Lines stretch down the block as customers wait for a pork belly Reuben or Oregon albacore tuna melt.

With fresh produce from the Willamette Valley and an exceptionally creative sensibility, Portland has become a haven for foodies, and with rock-star chefs like these, it's no wonder it's now a celebrated dining destination.

—Joan Cirillo

COME HERE FOR THE BREAKFAST-ON-THE-ROAD VIBE. *$; DIS, MC, V; no checks; breakfast every day, lunch Tues–Sat; no alcohol; no reservations; www.bywayscafe.com; self parking; map:M2.* &

Caffe Allora / ★★

504 NW 9TH AVE, PEARL DISTRICT; 503/445-4612

It's uncanny how sitting at one of Allora's tiny tables can instantly transport you to Italy. You smell the heady vapor of strong espresso in the air and the fresh, pungent aromas of oak, olive leaves, and chopped garlic. Allora is both espresso bar and *enoteca*, paying equal tribute to *caffé* and vino. Such traditional small plates as *bresaola* (thinly sliced cured beef, arugula, and shaved Parmesan) and *prosciutto e melone* are handsomely prepared and presented as light accompaniments. Panini and bruschetta are available with a variety of pungent accompaniments—chunked tuna, speck, sautéed peppers, sliced pears, fresh mozzarella. **COME HERE FOR TRUE ITALIAN AMBIENCE.** *$$; MC, V; no checks; breakfast, lunch, dinner Mon–Sat; beer and wine; dinner reservations recommended; street parking; map:M3.* &

Caffe Mingo / ★★
Bar Mingo / ★

807 NW 21ST AVE, NORTHWEST; 503/226-4646
811 NW 21ST AVE, NORTHWEST; 503/445-4646

Caffe Mingo has been a popular choice for over a decade for those seeking simple but beautifully prepared Italian cuisine in intimate surrounds. Yet the popularity of this tiny space has also been its downfall—a packed standing-room bar, crowded seating, and long waits were the bane of hungry diners. So in 2008, when a larger space two doors down opened, Caffe Mingo expanded into Bar Mingo. Caffe Mingo remains solid for both antipasti and entrées; signature dishes such as the Spiedini di Gamberi (seasoned shrimp and croutons threaded on skewers), buttery gnocchi alla Romana, and the Agnello Brasato (braised SuDan Farms lamb shank with cannellini beans, braised greens, and a spicy mint sauce) are all as good as ever. **COME HERE FOR FULL-FLAVORED SEASONAL DISHES.**

Bar Mingo is larger, with more elbow room at the bar and table seating, but dishes are meant to be shared in smaller portions. Still, this "bar" offers enough to make it an easy dinner option or predinner snack before your table is ready at Caffe Mingo. Antipasti are a choice of mix-and-match as a single option for $8 or ordered in groups of three for $21; they include raw oysters *crudo*, artisanal cheeses and meats, chicken livers with marsala wine, and *polpettine*—lamb meatballs in tomato sauce flavored with oregano and mint. Bar Mingo's cocktails, such as the classic Bellini and Negroni, are perfect. **COME HERE FOR THE COCKTAILS.** *$$; AE, DC, DIS, MC, V; no checks; dinner every day; beer and wine (Caffe Mingo), full bar (Bar Mingo); reservations recommended; www.caffemingonw.com; www.barmingonw.com; street parking; map:GG7.* &

Caldera / ★

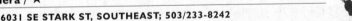

6031 SE STARK ST, SOUTHEAST; 503/233-8242

Housed in the 1910 Graham Pharmacy building high on the shoulder of Mount Tabor, serene and homey Caldera rests on a slumbering volcano. A beautiful varnished bar (left over from the apothecary days) gives the small dining room a seasoned gravitas, while ample patio seating lets large parties dine in the flickering light of tiki torches. The menu is a mix of home cooking's greatest hits, with echoes of exotic locales thrown in. Ingredients as daring as papaya-rubbed pork (in the Caribbean salad) feel right at home alongside beef stroganoff—a savory platter of wide, fluttery egg noodles, strips of stewed beef, and mushroom gravy. The affordable prices make the comfort food here that much more comforting. **COME HERE FOR AN ERUPTION OF SOLID HOME COOKING.** *$–$$; AE, DIS, MC, V; no checks; dinner Tues–Sun; full bar; reservations recommended; www.calderapublichouse.com street parking; map:HH4.* &

Campbell's Bar-B-Q / ★★☆

8701 SE POWELL BLVD, SOUTHEAST; 503/777-9795

Come into this little house along Powell Boulevard and inhale deeply to get more of a barbecue hit in one breath than some places provide in a rack of ribs. The dining area is quaint, the servers are cheerful and efficient, and side dishes (especially potato salad and corn bread) are inviting. But what packs the place is an exuberant vision of barbecue. Pork and beef ribs, slathered with one or all of four sauces (including a smoky brown-sugar sauce), are messy and satisfying. Plenty of other options include smoked turkey, barbecued chicken, beef brisket, and link sausage. Campbell's sauce has zip; as they might say in the heart of barbecue country, this is right good Q. A space is available for parties, though some people claim any meal here is a party, and the party's never over until they've run out of peach cobbler and sweet-potato pie. **COME HERE FOR MARVELOUSLY SLOPPY BARBECUE.** *$–$$; AE, MC, V; no checks; lunch, dinner Tues–Sat; no alcohol; no reservations; www.campbellsbbq.com; street parking; map:II3.* &

Carafe / ★★★

200 SW MARKET ST, DOWNTOWN; 503/248-0004

Located across from Keller Auditorium on the south end of downtown, Carafe is abuzz before the show. Come after 7:30pm on show nights to get a table. With checkered cafe chairs, a thorough Franco-centric wine list, and native Parisian chef Pascal Sauton's elegant bistro classics, Carafe will impress for business or pleasure. Start with Sauton's tender baked escargots with hazelnut-parsley butter or the steak tartare kissed by Dijon mustard, onions, and capers—it's the best in Portland. On to the classic *frisée au lardon*, before settling into Carafe's wintertime favorite: savory cassoulet of tomato-stewed white beans, duck confit, pork belly, and lamb baked with bread crumbs. Or try the seared hanger steak with creamy béarnaise and crisp *frites* on the Parisian-esque patio in the summer. For a casual cafe lunch, Carafe's sensational freshly ground Oregon Country Beef burger is offered with a choice of cheese, bacon, or a fried egg on a Ken's Artisan bun. **COME HERE FOR AN AUTHENTIC FRENCH BISTRO EXPERIENCE.** *$$; AE, DIS, MC, V; no checks; lunch Mon–Fri, dinner Mon–Sat (dinner only Tues–Sat in winter); full bar; reservations recommended; www.carafebistro.com; valet and self parking; map:D4.* &

Carlyle / ★★★☆

1632 NW THURMAN ST, NORTHWEST; 503/595-1782

A culinary oasis in industrial Portland's gritty heart, Carlyle imparts French style to New American cuisine while holding itself accountable to Portland's garden-driven farm-to-table ethos—the results are precise yet compelling. Its high, airy ceilings are elegantly augmented by deep, warm colors and dark wood. That sophistication is shared by the cuisine, with such dishes as perfectly roasted Sonoma duck breast with salsify confit and black trumpet mushrooms, or pan-seared foie gras accompanied by sultana grape purée, caramelized cipollini onions, and *saba*. Carlyle's seasonal offerings may bring vegetarian options such as spring nettle tortellini tossed with mascarpone, morels, and shaved Parmigiano. With impeccably rich desserts like a chocolate framboise pyramid perfect for sharing, Carlyle delivers a sultry, sweet ending. **COME HERE ON A DATE.** *$$$; AE, DIS, MC, V; no checks; dinner Mon–Sat; full bar; reservations recommended; www.carlylerestaurant.com; street parking; map:GG7.* &

Castagna / ★★★★
Café Castagna / ★★

1752 SE HAWTHORNE BLVD, HAWTHORNE; 503/231-7373
1758 SE HAWTHORNE BLVD, HAWTHORNE; 503/231-9959

Castagna's top-brass food and elegant dining room ooze an understated luxury fit for special-occasion dining. The menu reflects this refinement and sophistication; flavors are clean and balanced with an emphasis on Pacific Northwest–European inspirations. Starters seduce in the form of plump sautéed sea scallops with fennel, blood orange, and chervil, or fried veal sweetbreads with radish and egg mimosa salad. Dishes such as meticulously prepared Muscovy duck legs braised in Seville orange juice with polenta and crispy *speck*-cabbage rolls highlight the kitchen's talents. **COME HERE FOR THE SCALLOPS.**

Café Castagna, the casual cousin next door, offers the same attention to detail and quality in a more buttoned-down package. Some claim the Café Castagna burger as the best in town; with its prime, perfectly seasoned and cooked meat; crispy yet tender bun; and choice of melting artisan cheese, it's hard to argue. Crackling thin-crust pizzas are quite good, as are crisp salads with flawless fresh vegetables and lettuces, inspired seasonal soups, and such substantial rustic entrées as the braised pork cheeks with sage—all are bistro classics with an upscale twist. **COME HERE FOR THE BURGERS.** *$$$; $$; AE, MC, V; checks OK; lunch Tues–Sat (Café Castagna), dinner Wed–Sat (Castagna), dinner every day (Café Castagna); full bar; reservations recommended (Castagna); www.castagnarestaurant.com; street parking; map:HH5.* &

Cha! Cha! Cha! Mexican Taqueria / ★
Cha! / ★

1208 NW GLISAN ST, PEARL DISTRICT (AND BRANCHES); 503/221-2111
305 NW 21ST AVE, NORTHWEST; 503/295-4077

Portland is a city of many taco trucks, but few provide food as good and as fresh as the plump offerings purveyed at area chain Cha! Cha! Cha! Mexican Taqueria. From its primo Pearl District outpost, Cha! Cha! Cha! pushes plenty of hand-rolled options: burritos, tacos, tortas, and salads with juicy grilled strips of carne asada, spicy pork carnitas, chicken, and fish, with the usual edible accoutrements of rice, beans, cheese, and veggies. Ask for a burrito "wet," and for a measly buck, they'll bath it in spicy red enchilada sauce and finish it with pico de gallo, sour cream, and sharp house-made guacamole. And then there's Cha!, the empire's upscale taqueria, offering nearly all of the above plus easy-sipping margaritas and such bold traditional offerings as seafood-stuffed poblano peppers and Dungeness crab enchiladas drenched in garlic–white wine sauce. Few Portland patios offer better al fresco dining and people-watching than Cha!'s covered deck on 21st Avenue. It's just too bad the neighborhood requires Cha! to pack in its tables by 10pm. But shed no tears: the bar stays open late. **COME HERE FOR GIGANTIC BURRITOS.** *$; $$; AE, MC, V; no checks; lunch, dinner every day; no alcohol (Cha! Cha! Cha!), full bar (Cha!); no reservations; www.chaportland.com; street parking; map:M2; map:GG7.* &

Clarke's / ★★

455 2ND ST, LAKE OSWEGO; 503/636-2667
Transplanting himself from downtown Portland, where he produced an alluring menu at Toulouse, British-born Jonathan Clarke has scored a solid hit in Lake Oswego, where upscale dining has been a sometime thing. Clarke's is a serious, skillful restaurant, and its proprietor has a sure sense of what to do with dishes such as braised lamb shank, Alaskan razor clams, and fresh fish. Presentations are particularly interesting—try the Hawaiian blue king prawns grilled with a mango-jalapeño-lime sauce—complementing the contemporary grace and soft lighting of the restaurant (if you don't look out the window at the parking lot). Desserts are equally inspired, including the peach upside-down cake with caramel and ginger ice cream. Happy hours, daily from 4:30 to 6pm, are a local hit. **COME HERE FOR THE LOBSTER-AND-SHRIMP RISOTTO.** *$$; AE, DIS, MC, V; checks OK; dinner every day; full bar; reservations recommended; www.clarkesrestaurant.net; street parking; map:MM6.* &

Clarklewis / ★★★★

1001 SE WATER AVE, INNER SOUTHEAST; 503/235-2294
Headed up by chef Dolan Lane, this minimally adorned eatery tucked into industrial Portland's underbelly is a trusted favorite of locals. Such dishes as grilled Monterey Bay calamari with wild greens, crushed Castelvetrano olives, and Meyer lemon illustrate this eatery's ethos of fresh and seasonal above all. House-made pasta, including tagliarini with white shrimp and chile, or tagliatelle with Cattail Creek lamb ragù, remain incredible. Simplicity reigns, as evident by the butter-braised halibut and fava beans, braised pork leg with pancetta and mustard greens, and pan-roasted chinook salmon with spring onions and butter-stewed morels. **COME HERE FOR AN ICONIC PORTLAND MEAL.** *$$$; AE, DIS, MC, V; no checks; dinner Tues–Sat; full bar; reservations recommended; www.clarklewispdx.com; street parking; map:F8.* &

Clay's Smokehouse / ★★½

2932 SE DIVISION ST, DIVISION; 503/235-4755
Named for chef-owner Michael Slyman's son, Clay's is an outpost of South Carolina hospitality. Barbecue is the name of the game and nearly everything on the extensive menu sees a little time in the smoker. Jump right in with a plate of cold-smoked oysters, salmon, and catfish, or a big bowl of bean-and-smoked-vegetable chili. Most options are simple and straightforward, with

such choices as the spare rib platter or the smoked quarter chicken, both accompanied by plenty of home fries and slaw. Indecisive eaters can taste a little of everything with the combo platter, which features ribs, chicken, and hot links. The menu has a large number of veggie options; try the open-face grilled vegetable sandwich or the lovely corn-and-barley salad topped off with smoked tomato salsa and yet more grilled vegetables. Desserts are as down-home as they come, made by Clay's grandma herself. **COME HERE FOR A TASTE OF SOUTH CAROLINA RIGHT HERE IN THE PACIFIC NORTHWEST.** *$; AE, DIS, MC, V; no checks; lunch, dinner Wed–Sun; no reservations; beer and wine; www.clayssmokehouse.ypguides.net; street parking; map:II5.*

Clyde Common / ★★★

1014 SW STARK ST, DOWNTOWN; 503/228-3333
This high-energy newcomer in the hip Ace Hotel crosses a boisterous European brasserie with a New American menu. A large zinc bar is the center of the action and offers some of the best artisan cocktails in the city, alongside whimsical snacks such as popcorn topped with smoky-hot *pimentón* pepper powder or crispy breaded lamb "tenders." At the communal table dining (smaller tables are available upstairs), the theme continues: olive-oil-poached octopus, potato, chorizo, and frisée salad with "ink" vinaigrette highlights the kitchen's commitment to quality, and the pappardelle with wild nettle pesto, walnuts, and grana padano cheese is comforting and sophisticated all at once. Sides, such as the black lentil salad with cold-smoked shrimp, are simply memorable. Always surprising and one of a kind, Clyde Common is an easy, but unique Portland experience. **COME HERE FOR EXCELLENT COCKTAILS, SOPHISTICATED FOOD, AND HIPSTERS.** *$$; AE, DIS, MC, V; no checks; lunch Mon–Fri, dinner every day; full bar; reservations for 6 or more, 12 or more served family-style; www.clydecommon.com; street parking; map:J2.* &

Corbett Fish House / ★★☆

5901 SW CORBETT AVE, JOHNS LANDING; 503/246-4434
All smiles, long braids swinging, and knee socks pulled high, the waitresses at Corbett Fish House seem like they were plucked from the Midwest. They deliver imperial pints in a flash and tell you truthfully that the Pilsner Urquell isn't running well on a given night. They feature five fried-fish platters ranging from chile-fried catfish to coveted walleye, a lake perch seldom found at West Coast restaurants. Rather than overcooking seafood in heavy batter, Corbett uses light breading and flash fries its fish, rendering a delicate flavor and nongreasy texture. Sides include wasabi-spiked coleslaw and the "World's Greatest Fries"—long, lean, and crispy, they certainly come close. **COME HERE FOR THE FRIED WALLEYE PLATTER.** *$–$$; AE, DIS, MC, V; no checks; lunch, dinner every day; full bar; no reservations; www.corbettfishhouse.com; street parking; map:II6.* &

Country Cat / ★★☆

7937 SE STARK ST, MONTAVILLA; 503/408-1414

Four miles from the city center, longtime Wildwood chef Adam Sappington riffs on classic American fare and delivers solid comfort food. Upon arrival at this Montavilla outpost near Mount Tabor, head straight to the bar to sample Country Cat's house-cured beef jerky with original bourbon-spiked cocktail concoctions. Once you're seated, friendly servers offer such favorites as fried chicken, bathed in a spunky Tabasco vinaigrette that's superb. The sticky-sweet, hickory-smoked duck leg is some of the best use of mallard parts in the city, and Country Cat's Heritage Burger has found its place among PDX's ground-beef elite. Perhaps Country Cat's most iconic dish is the Whole Hog—pork bellies, shoulders, and chops atop the best white grits this side of the Mason-Dixon line. Arrive hungry; you'll leave stuffed. Dessert includes baked-to-order seasonal pies of cherry or rhubarb. **COME HERE FOR THE DUCK LEG.** *$$; AE, MC, V; no checks; dinner every day, brunch Sat–Sun; full bar; reservations for 4 or more; www.thecountrycat.net; street parking; map:HH3.* &

Daily Cafe / ★★

902 NW 13TH AVE, PEARL DISTRICT; 503/242-1916
1100 SE GRAND AVE (REJUVENATION), INNER SOUTHEAST; 503/234-8189
3335 SW BOND AVE (OHSU CENTER FOR HEALTH AND HEALING), SOUTH WATERFRONT; 503/228-3080

It's hard to say which is the best meal at Daily Cafe. Is it the multicourse Sunday brunch with appetizer-size blintzes, colorful scrambles, and hedonistic French toast? Would it be the supremely fresh dinner entrées such as blue-cheese-and-leek soufflé and porter-braised venison? Or even lunch, with several quiches, melty panini, salads, pizzettas, and wonderful cookies? All day long, the Daily turns out creative, seasonal treats in three hip, tasteful settings without pretension. Dinner in particular presents some intriguing plates. A half-pound burger, made with Sauvie Island beef, is served with optional cheddar, Swiss, or blue cheese. Leave room for chocolate *pot de crème* with beignets—yum. The Daily's original location inside Rejuvenation offers the same great breakfast and lunch, but no dinner or Sunday brunch. **COME HERE FOR GOOD SANDWICHES AND COOKIES.** *$–$$; MC, V; no checks; breakfast, lunch every day, dinner Wed–Sat, brunch Sun (Pearl District); beer and wine (Pearl District), no alcohol (Inner Southeast and South Waterfront); reservations for 6 or more (Pearl District); map:N1; map:F9.* &

Dan and Louis' Oyster Bar / ★

208 SW ANKENY ST, OLD TOWN; 503/227-5906

Tourists who visited Portland before the advent of the automobile came to this Old Town establishment for seafood. Among the place's charms are value ($15.95 for the classic oyster fry) and its coffee and pie (the marionberry is wonderful). With a greater number of grilled fish items to complement traditional deep-fried and stewed entrées, the Oyster Bar's cuisine has improved in recent years; service is friendly, if not especially swift. The decor is family friendly, with a lot to look at, from plates on the walls to maritime bric-a-brac everywhere; you get the feeling the Wachsmuth family has held their restaurant together through thick and thin for almost a century, serving up oyster stew every single day. **COME HERE FOR (WHAT ELSE?) THE OYSTERS.** *$$; AE, DC, DIS, JCB, MC, V; local checks only; lunch, dinner every day; full bar; reservations recommended; www.danandlouis.com; street parking; map:J6.* &

Delta Cafe and Bar / ★
4607 SE WOODSTOCK BLVD, WOODSTOCK; 503/771-3101
This funky storefront has been providing nearby Reed College students with specialties from below the Mason-Dixon line for years. Its hush puppies, fried okra, greens, and fritters are pure South. Down-home fried chicken, cornmeal-crusted catfish, and the "White Trash Meatloaf" with rich chicken gravy is soul food for some, while such Creole and Cajun specialties as the crawfish etouffée and mahogany-dark gumbo are a nod to all things Louisiana. Those feeling less peckish can simply choose three sides to make any kind of meal they want. Drinks such as Lynchburg lemonade with Jack Daniels and the garlic-infused Bloody Mary pack a punch. Waits can be long, service can be harried, but order the 40-ounce PBR served in a champagne bucket and kick back. The living is easy at the Delta. **COME HERE TO KICK BACK.** *$; no credit cards; checks OK; lunch Sat–Sun, dinner every day; full bar; no reservations; www.deltacafeandbar.com; street parking; map:JJ4.* &

Departure / ★★
525 SW MORRISON ST, DOWNTOWN; 503/802-5370
From the tippy top of the historic Meier and Frank building, the creative Asian cuisine at Departure can be enjoyed from a large rooftop deck or expansive windows with stunning views of the West Hills or the Willamette River. The yacht/spaceship–inspired interior assures you're en route to someplace different. Fresh sushi, an extensive sake list, and creative dishes mean the food is as good as the view. Small plates make it easy to try a number of flavors. Start with Hamachi sashimi with white truffle oil and fleur de sel or Hawaiian king prawn dumplings before trying a chicken skewer with spicy yuzu and cilantro, or a skirt steak skewer and elephant garlic chips. The panko-crusted Kobe meatballs with foie gras are divine, while the sea scallops with pea tendrils and citrus vinaigrette shouldn't be missed. The coconut panna cotta is a wonderful treat for dessert. The bar gets very crowded on weekend nights and is a great place for people-watching over a drink. **COME HERE FOR A VIEW AND SAKE.** *$$–$$$; AE, DIS, MC, V; no checks; dinner Tues–Sun; full bar; reservations recommended; www.departureportland.com; valet parking; map:H4.* &

Deschutes Brewery & Public House / ★★
210 NW 11TH AVE, PEARL DISTRICT; 503/296-4906
Portland is chockablock with brewpubs, but one of the best is this airy restaurant serving a variety of dishes worthy of a return trip. To go with one of its excellent beers, have a nice thick burger made with freshly ground beef. It

arrives at your table cooked exactly as ordered—rare means rare at Deschutes. The burger is accompanied by real, double-fried french fries, made with hand-cut Idaho potatoes. Or order the fragrant venison-and-bean chili or the Buffalo wings doused with a zingy hot sauce. This pub puts real effort into its dishes, serving a changing lineup of house-made charcuterie. Duck prosciutto or a Grilled Sausage of the Moment is served with stone-ground ale mustard, pickled vegetables, and goat cheese flatbread. The servers will offer you wet naps, but don't bother with them; just lick your tasty pub-food fingers. **COME HERE FOR DESCHUTES BEER PAIRED WITH THOUGHTFUL PUB FOOD.** *$$; AE, DC, MC, V; no checks; dinner every day; beer and wine; reservations for 8 or more; www.deschutesbrewery.com; street parking; map:L2.* &

DOC / ★★★

5519 NE 30TH AVE, NORTH PORTLAND; 503/946-8592

Because you'll walk through the door into a small two-cook kitchen, DOC lets you know right away what you're getting into: expect total sensory takeover. Four candles glow on every one of the seven tables, and black chandeliers drip their sepia light over the elegant, intimate dining room, coaxing diners out of daily stress and into pure pleasure. Chef Greg Perrault does right by Oregon's bounty, working closely with small farms to get his hands on only the most pure, most intriguing ingredients. Though small, the menu dazzles with such dishes as the house-made gnocchi, pan-fried and served with rich, buttery gigas mushrooms and green garlic. Chilled parsnip buttermilk soup is a revelation, at once rich and unbelievably fresh. Having difficulty choosing between the gently seared chinook salmon with puréed leeks or the luscious razor clam risotto with brussel sprout shoots and seasoned with miniscule choppings of black olive? Have both; at $50, the tasting menu is a real steal. Wine pairings are a must; there is no glass list, but trust DOC to bring you just the thing. **COME HERE FOR A ROMANTIC FEAST THAT FEEDS BOTH BODY AND SOUL.** *$$$; AE, MC, V; no checks; dinner Tues–Sat; full bar; reservations recommended; www.docpdx.com; street parking; map:EE5.* &

Dots Cafe / ★

2521 SE CLINTON ST, CLINTON; 503/235-0203

Dots is Dots is Dots. As long as Portland has a hipster intelligentsia, it will have Dots. A dark box of a nouveau diner, Dots is adored for its cheap, proven, veggie-friendly menu and its established cool. Velvet wallpaper, off-beat ephemera, and an ever-hopping bar provide the vibe, and it's all backed by a dependable menu. Looking for a quick, inexpensive lunch or dinner? Dig into a Ms. Bunny's Gardenburger with cream cheese and alfalfa sprouts or a gooey grilled cheese with soup. Want a bite after a night of carousing? Count on Dots to serve food long after other restaurants have been put to bed. Pay close attention to the fries, honored as an entire menu category here: cheese fries, bacon-cheddar fries, fries with spicy tofu sauce. Portions are very generous; a small plate will feed several. Tried-and-true desserts include devil's food cake. **COME HERE TO EXPERIENCE A TRUE-BLUE PORTLAND HIPSTER**

HANGOUT. *$; no credit cards; checks OK; lunch, dinner every day; full bar; no reservations; street parking; map:II5.* &

Doug Fir Lounge / ★★

830 E BURNSIDE ST, BUCKMAN; 503/231-9663
A one-stop fun spot, Doug Fir Lounge is all style. Designed by the Portland-based architecture firm SkyLab, the interior's chic interpretation of a truck stop diner with a log cabin motif shines in the restaurant, the lounge, and the downstairs state-of-the-art music venue. The menu is fit for a hungry lumberjack, with breakfast served from 7am daily, then lunch, happy hour, and dinner through midnight (until 2:15am on Fridays and Saturdays). The Fir Burger is a build-your-own version, with options of beef, buffalo, chicken, or black beans—all pair perfectly with thick-cut tempura onion rings. Hardy classics, like "Grandma's" meatloaf, are juxtaposed with crunchy pan-fried trout and soda-pop-marinated wild boar ribs on the dinner menu. Lunch is a condensed version of the dinner service with the addition of sandwiches. And for breakfast, the French Connection substitutes croissants for a buttery, battered start to the day. **COME HERE BEFORE ATTENDING A SHOW DOWNSTAIRS.** *$$; AE, DIS, MC, V; no checks; breakfast, lunch, dinner every day; full bar; no reservations; www.dougfirlounge.com; street parking; map:HH6.* &

Dove Vivi / ★★☆

2727 NE GLISAN ST, LAURELHURST; 503/239-4444
Portlanders can't seem to agree how best to describe the cornmeal-crust pizza that is the specialty at Dove Vivi. Deep-dish? Not really. Crisp? Sort of—more like sturdy. Must have? Everyone seems to agree on that one. Owners Gavin and Delane were inspired by the pizza at San Francisco's now-defunct Vicolo and have worked hard to perfect the dough made from olive oil and local cornmeal that is the base for their creative whims. Featuring 10 daily pizzas, as well as 2 vegan options and 3 specials of the day, all available by the slice, this comfortable, family-friendly spot pleases even the pickiest of eaters. House-smoked-ham pizza with mozzarella and roasted pears is a surprise hit. Always on the menu, the ever-popular corn pizza is gooey with both mozzarella and smoked mozzarella, studded with sweet corn and tangy balsamic-roasted onions. Such eclectic sides as kale salad with lemon and pecorino are a refreshing complement to all the cheesy goodness. **COME HERE FOR CORNMEAL-CRUST PIZZA AND INNOVATIVE TOPPINGS.** *$; DIS, MC, V; no checks; dinner every day; beer and wine; no reservations; www.dovevivi pizza.com; self parking; map:HH5.*

East India Company / ★★☆

821 SW 11TH AVE, DOWNTOWN; 503/227-8815
Elegant and sophisticated, this downtown Indian hot spot is quite a departure from its counterparts around Portland. Service can be slow, but relax, it's worth the wait, as every last thing is made to order. Cocktails such as the Rangpur Chill—fresh cucumber and Indian green chiles muddled with

Tanqueray Rangpur gin—are a refreshing complement to the heat and richness of the food. *Tandoori khumbi*, succulent marinated mushrooms that have been kissed by the tandoor oven, or the classic *samosa chaat*, with heady spiced potatoes and a crispy shell, work their magic, preparing your tastebuds for what's to come. Though it's hard to go wrong with any entrée, East India Company is perhaps best known for its *murgh makhani*, or butter chicken, a creamy, tomatoey delight. Patrons would no doubt lick the bowl if it weren't for generous baskets of chewy and addictive *lachha paratha*, a sort of naan-meets-croissant, ideal for lapping up every last drop. Saffron-infused syrup surrounds a pistachio-crowned doughnut—the perfect end to a transporting meal. **COME HERE FOR AN ELEGANT TASTE OF INDIA.** *$$$; AE, MC, V; no checks; lunch, dinner Mon–Sat; full bar; reservations recommended; www.eastindiacopdx.com; street parking; map:H2.* &

Edelweiss Sausage & Delicatessen / ★

3119 SE 12TH AVE, BROOKLYN; 503/238-4411

Just a perfect bratwurst's throw from busy Powell Boulevard, this cramped old-world enclave feels as if it's been airlifted straight from Bavaria. Because Edelweiss does its house-made sausage so right, the store is predictably packed with Northern European transplants, speaking their native tongues and queuing up for good sandwiches, authentic German deli items, and imported beer and wine. A few tiny tables clustered in the corner offer a worthy vantage point to enjoy it all. Edelweiss doubles as a European market with a great selection of imported European chocolates, cheeses, and other items difficult to find in the United States. **COME HERE FOR AUTHENTIC GERMAN-STYLE SAUSAGE.** *$; MC, V; checks OK; breakfast, lunch, dinner Mon–Sat; beer and wine; no reservations; www.edelweissdeli.com; self parking; map:II5.* &

Eleni's Philoxenia / ★★
Eleni's Estiatorio / ★★

112 NW 9TH AVE, PEARL DISTRICT; 503/227-2158
7712 SE 13TH AVE, SELLWOOD; 503/230-2165

Both of these restaurants showcase the best of Greek cuisine; owner Eleni Touhouliotis hails from Crete, but her recipes won't show up at other Greek restaurants in Portland. Both locations have an extensive, shared menu. Start with the Exochiki Salata, a traditional salad of ripe tomatoes, onion, cucumber, scallions, and peppers. The leg of lamb, served over ziti and topped with pungent Greek cheeses, and the rabbit, rubbed with orange, rosemary, and garlic and braised with tomatoes and baby onions, are standouts. The real attraction at Philoxenia is the 30 or so small sharable plates—from traditional tzatziki to spinach in many forms, baked feta cheese in filo dough with ouzo and honey, and beef meatballs—that easily make a colorful meal. Both Eleni's locations are well suited for large groups. **COME HERE FOR AUTHENTIC GREEK FOOD.** *$$; AE, DIS, MC, V; no checks; dinner Tues–Sat; full bar; reservations recommended; www.elenisrestaurant.com; street parking; map: K3; map:JJ6.* &

Elephants Delicatessen / ★★☆
Flying Elephants at Fox Tower / ★★☆
Flying Elephants at Kruse Way / ★

115 NW 22ND AVE, NORTHWEST; 503/299-6304
812 SW PARK AVE, DOWNTOWN; 503/546-3166
5885 SW MEADOWS RD, LAKE OSWEGO; 503/620-2444

A Portland institution, Elephants in recent years has taken a bar-and-grill approach with more-generous seating, outdoors and in. In addition to a small, well-appointed bar, it offers excellent hamburgers, fish-and-chips, and killer Reuben sandwiches. Elephants also makes pizzas fired in a wood-burning oven. To take out or eat in, choose from a smorgasbord of offerings, from Mama Leone's Chicken Soup to an array of colorful salads in the deli case. Its sisters, two Flying Elephants locations, cater to the business and movie crowd with a smaller selection of the same fine fare and a few tables and chairs. **COME HERE FOR TOMATO-ORANGE SOUP AND SOURDOUGH BREAD.** *$$; AE, MC, V; checks OK; breakfast, lunch, dinner every day (Delicatessen, Fox Tower), breakfast, lunch Mon–Fri (Kruse Way); full bar (Elephants), beer and wine (Fox Tower, Kruse Way); no reservations; www.elephantsdeli. com; self parking (Delicatessen, Kruse Way), street parking (Fox Tower); map: HH7; map:H2; map:MM7.* ᶜ

El Gaucho / ★★★

319 SW BROADWAY, DOWNTOWN; 503/227-8794

Those with easy sticker shock, beware: high-priced opulence reigns supreme at El Gaucho, with its swank dining room, überprofessional service, and the highest-quality steaks around. You'll pay dearly, but the experience is worth it. Steaks are the focus; you'll find your perfect match in the highest-quality aged Angus—be it a buttery filet mignon, a hearty prime rib with bordelaise sauce, or the over-the-top Steak El Gaucho, "baseball cut" and served with lobster medallions. Such classic starters as oysters Rockefeller, crab cakes, and large, sweet diver scallops show that El Gaucho also has a deft hand with seafood. Sides like roasted sweet corn with chipotle butter and grilled portobello mushrooms keep the menu from being stuck in 1950. Do save room for dessert; the bananas Foster and cherries jubilee are made tableside with flair. There's also an outstanding wine list, with an international focus. **COME HERE FOR THE STEAK.** *$$$$; AE, DC, MC, V; no checks; dinner every day; full bar; reservations recommended; www.elgaucho.com; valet parking; map:J3.* ᶜ

Esparza's Tex-Mex Café / ★★

2725 SE ANKENY ST, LAURELHURST; 503/234-7909

People may wonder how a Tex-Mex restaurant has become a landmark in Portland—but the surprise doesn't survive the first visit, nor certainly the first smoked beef-brisket taco. By then, new visitors have already been seduced by this eatery straight outta San Antone—replete with stellar jukebox, Mexican marionettes creepily dangling from the ceiling, and an exhaustive array of

69

tequilas. Servers will help you choose the right tequila to match the hearty Cowboy Tacos—filled with thick slabs of smoked sirloin, barbecue sauce, guacamole, and pico de gallo—or the Uvalde, a smoked-lamb enchilada. Portions are meaty and as big as the great outdoors. If you can manage an appetizer, go for *nopalitos*, a tasty cactus dish. Augmented by daily specials, the menu has quite a reach, from red snapper (smothered with sautéed peppers and tomatoes) to smoked pork loin (stuffed with spiced buffalo). Unusual meats—such as buffalo tongue in tacos—also crop up. **COME HERE FOR BORDER KITSCH AND VARIETY MEATS.** *$$; AE, DC, DIS, MC, V; no checks; lunch, dinner Mon–Sat; full bar; reservations recommended; street parking; map:HH5.* &

Everett Street Bistro / ★★

1140 NW EVERETT ST, PEARL DISTRICT; 503/467-4990
With a European-inspired bistro menu, Everett Street serves three meals daily in Francophone-lite environs. Whether you order a panini or an Everett Street Benedict with Dungeness crab, the breakfast menu is reliably good and runs late into the afternoon every day. Charcuterie and cheese plates can be ordered for a first course for lunch or dinner. A selection of salads, soups, quiches, deli sandwiches, and panini are good lunch options, or have a burger *avec pommes frites*. Dinner shares many of the lunch items, with the addition of such entrées as chicken Marbella, roasted salmon, and the classic steak au poivre. The desserts and baked goods are divine with an espresso. **COME HERE FOR A LATE BREAKFAST.** *$$–$$$; AE, MC, V; no checks; breakfast, lunch every day, dinner Tues–Sun; full bar; reservations recommended; www. everettstreetbistro.com; street parking; map:L2.* &

The Farm Café / ★★

10 SE 7TH AVE, BUCKMAN; 503/736-3276
The Farm is a petite, decidedly urban Victorian cottage set back from bustling E Burnside—not by a pasture, but by a parking lot. The house's moody interior has been dressed up with salvage from the neighboring Viscount Ballroom. The emphasis on fresh Northwest produce (almost all ingredients are supplied by area growers) makes for a light and lovely menu. Entrées are evenly divided between seafood and vegetarian, with breaded tofu a frequent special. A favorite is Dungeness crab risotto with Rogue Creamery's Smokey Blue cheese. Desserts are limited, but a molten chocolate soufflé and a mascarpone cheesecake are fine options. **COME HERE FOR STRAIGHT-FROM-THE-FARM PRODUCE.** *$$; MC, V; checks OK; dinner every day; full bar; no reservations; www.thefarmcafe.net; self parking; map:HH6.* &

Fat City Cafe / ★

7820 SW CAPITOL HWY, MULTNOMAH VILLAGE; 503/245-5457
Diners in general are fading bits of American culinary history, and this particular one has its own place in Portland's past: it's where Mayor Bud Clark (a regular even now, years after he left office) fired his police chief back in

1987. Inside is the classic narrow layout of booths and a counter, with walls covered in street and traffic signs. The menu is exactly what you'd expect. For breakfast, there are monster stacks of pancakes, eggs every which way, and legendary hash browns; for lunch, substantial burgers, great sandwiches, and marvelous milkshakes. The name has less to do with any geographic location than with how you're going to feel after you've eaten here. There's no such thing as a small meal at Fat City. **COME HERE TO FILL UP YOUR TANK.** *$; DIS, MC, V; no checks; breakfast, lunch, dinner every day; full bar after 5pm; no reservations; www.fatcitycafe.net; self parking; map:JJ7.* &

Fenouil / ★★★⯪

900 NW 11TH AVE, PEARL DISTRICT; 503/525-2225

Whether you're dining on the large patio overlooking Pearl centerpiece Jamison Square or in the truly stunning two-level dining room accented in stone and white, with numerous fireplaces, few restaurants in Portland have more class than Fenouil. This modern French bistro is one sexy character, and its fare lives up to its appearance—be prepared to pay. Start with house-smoked salmon, crème fraîche, and arugula on olive ciabatta, or the more decadent *foie gras poêlé* on toasted brioche with kumquat confit, bourbon gastrique, and bee pollen. This marriage of the bold and the delicate continues with Fenouil's signature dish of seared scallops resting on a pillow of creamy green potatoes (colored and faintly flavored from watercress oil), with crispy bacon, leek fondue, and two sauces: verjus-butter and a balsamic reduction. Enjoy such cocktails as the Fenouil 75 or Le Viêt Nam with the Hamburger Parisien and truffled *pommes frites* in the lounge. The restaurant's Sunday brunch is an indulgent affair. **COME HERE FOR A SPECIAL OCCASION OR A BUSINESS LUNCH.** *$$$$; AE, DIS, MC, V; no checks; lunch Mon–Sat, dinner every day, brunch Sun; full bar; reservations recommended; www.fenouilin thepearl.com; street parking; map:N2.* &

Fire on the Mountain / ★

4225 N INTERSTATE AVE, NORTH PORTLAND; 503/280-9464
1708 E BURNSIDE ST, BUCKMAN; 503/230-9464

Fire on the Mountain (named for a popular Grateful Dead tune), makes chicken wings in batches of 6 up to 250 at a time. Fried to a perfect crisp but never overcooked; coated in a sticky, tangy sauce; and served with the classic pairing of blue cheese dressing and celery, these buffalo wings hold their own in mild, medium, hot, or extra hot. Other sauces include sweet BBQ, Jamaican Jerk, and buffalo lime cilantro. Vegetarians will delight in the Portland Wings—soy protein nuggets that are as tender and tasty as their meat counterparts. Fire on the Mountain's menu also includes a variety of sandwiches, salads, and special entrées such as fish-and-chips and a spicy peanut pasta. **COME HERE FOR THE WINGS.** *$; MC, V; no checks; lunch, dinner every day; beer and wine; no reservations; www.portlandwings.com; street parking; map:FF6.* &

Fujin / ★

3549 SE HAWTHORNE BLVD, HAWTHORNE; 503/231-3753

Here's a little neighborhood treasure that refuses to let you go broke, assisting the wealth and prosperity (*fujin*) that its name promises. In this simple but comfortable storefront with its tile floor, Formica tables, and a small Taoist altar at the rear, the friendly Kevin Chan and his family have been serving superb Szechuan, Mandarin, and Hunan cuisine since 1989. Chan's specialty is "pepper-salted" seafood, which you're more likely to find on the specials board than on the regular menu. There are many good things here, such as Fujin's chicken trio: smaller-size portions of General Tso's, Snow White (steamed with carrots, snow peas, and water chestnuts), and tangy lemon chicken with rice. It's still enough to provide you with leftovers for tomorrow's lunch. **COME HERE FOR THE LUNCH SPECIALS.** *$; DIS, MC, V; no checks; lunch Mon–Sat, dinner every day; beer and wine; no reservations; street parking; map:HH5.* &

Gilt Club / ★★

306 NW BROADWAY, CHINATOWN; 503/222-4458

Inside its low-lit, red-hued walls, accented by gilded picture frames and light fixtures, the Gilt Club feels a lot more like New Orleans than Portland. This late-night hideaway offers full dinners until the wee hours and fills a niche as a sophisticated oasis that distracts from its rough Old Town surroundings. The cuisine includes the likes of foie gras torchon wonderfully adulterated by sweet cherry compote and slightly toasted homemade brioche, plus hand-cut *pommes frites* with a splash of peppery, garlic-infused olive oil. Gilt's Caesar salad, with just the right balance of lemon, garlic, and anchovy, is the perfect prelude to the ground Angus burger with caramelized onions, thick bacon, melted *tartufo* (truffled cheese), and garlic aioli. Lamb chops are nestled on a bed of garlic spaetzle and huckleberry jus; an earthy, seasonal wild mushroom risotto is finished with marscarpone. **COME HERE FOR LATE-NIGHT ROMANCE.** *$$; AE, DIS, MC, V; no checks; dinner Mon–Sat; full bar; reservations recommended; www.giltclub.com; street parking; map:L4.* &

Gino's Restaurant and Bar / ★★

8051 SE 13TH AVE, SELLWOOD; 503/233-4613

Anyone who's eaten at Gino's has a favorite dish. It could be the beautifully flavored clams steamed in a white-wine-and-butter sauce revved by chile and fish broth or the perfect Caesar salad served family-style. Perhaps it's Grandma Jean's meaty pasta; over-the-top cioppino; Gino's classic, caper-studded chicken marsala; or a prime Painted Hills steak specially cut for Gino's. Whichever dish you claim, it keeps you coming back for more. The casual, airy restaurant exudes neighborly warmth and offers terrific value. The kitchen rounds out the list of perennial favorites with seasonal specials such as braised lamb shoulder with bucatini or a winsome stew of butternut squash, Chioggia beets, carrots, and parsnips laid over white polenta. The place can get crowded, but you can eat at the adjoining Leipzig Tavern, which boasts a gorgeous mahogany bar, cozy booths, Guinness on tap, and full dinner service from Gino's. **COME HERE FOR THE UNPRETENTIOUS CHARM.** *$$–$$$; MC, V; checks OK; dinner every day; full bar; reservations recommended; www.ginossellwood.com; street parking; map:KK5.* &

Giorgio's / ★★★

1131 NW HOYT ST, PEARL DISTRICT; 503/221-1888

Some restaurants scream; Giorgio's quietly seduces. In the high-end European tradition, this little rectangular space tucked away in the heart of the Pearl is tasteful yet understated, with neutral tones, black-and-white-tiled floors, and glittering, gold-framed mirrors. The seasonal menu, chock-full of Northwest ingredients, points the compass to Northern Italy, which makes sense; owner Giorgio Kawas's family is from Emilia-Romagna. Simple but perfectly prepared items, such as a watercress salad with marinated feta, blood oranges, and Marcona almonds, are pure harmony, while the hand-chopped steak tartare with salsify "alla Romano" and Parmigiano-Reggiano cheese shows the kitchen's quiet confidence. House-made pastas triumph here. Expect light surprises like the celery root–stuffed ravioli with black trumpet mushrooms and a beet-Dijon reduction, or a hearty pappardelle with earthy boar ragù. Other memorable items include the crispy black bass seared with lemon-artichoke purée, nettles, and shaved sunchokes, or a tender slow-roasted guinea hen with grilled eggplant, baby basmati rice, and a carrot-cumin reduction. **COME HERE FOR THE HOUSE-MADE PASTA.** *$$–$$$; AE, MC, V; no checks; lunch Tues–Fri, dinner Tues–Sat; full bar; reservations recommended; www.giorgiospdx.com; street parking; map:M2.* &

Good Taste / ★

18 NW 4TH AVE, CHINATOWN; 503/223-3838

You'll be lured into the restaurant by the caramel-brown, glistening Peking duck and pork ribs hanging in the window, but once inside, Good Taste has close to zero ambience. Don't be deterred. Specializing in excellent noodles and authentic Cantonese barbecue in the heart of Chinatown, Good Taste will land you in hog heaven. Meat is on the pedestal here, and whether it's a mountain of stellar shrimp-studded, ground-pork wontons, the crispy roasted pork atop glorious house-made egg noodles, or the superb Peking duck, Good Taste is one of the last bastions of superb meat-centric ethnic cuisine in Portland's once-thriving Chinatown. As well, Good Taste's daily assortment of steamed greens includes bok choy and gai lan (Chinese broccoli) bathed in savory garlic sauce, which makes for one of downtown's healthiest lunchtime diversions. The congee—Chinese rice porridge—served here is the perfect hangover cure. **COME HERE FOR WONTON SOUP AND PEKING DUCK.** *$; MC, V; no checks; lunch, dinner every day; no alcohol; no reservations; street parking; map:K5.* &

Gracie's / ★★★

1239 SW BROADWAY, DOWNTOWN; 503/222-2171

As one of Portland's grand hotel dining rooms, Gracie's comes with a rich heritage and was regularly visited by James Beard when he returned to his hometown from New York. A keystone at the Hotel deLuxe (see review in the Lodgings chapter), Gracie's sparkling classic interior still flows like a 1940s Fred Astaire musical. Beard would be thrilled: this is sophisticated, classic American dining, now focusing on Oregon's bountiful locally produced foods. Brunch here is a civilized white-tablecloth affair with a signature Dungeness crab Benedict served on Oregon Bay shrimp cakes, Crispy Bread Pudding French Toast, and smoked salmon or beef hash. Lunches bring together West Hills society matrons alongside hotel guests and business lunchers for the hearty Cascade Cobb Salad, featuring Oregon's award-winning Rogue Creamery blue cheese; seasonal soups such as creamy spring asparagus or autumn harvest corn chowder; and a wonderful pork loin sandwich with local cheddar cheese and apple chutney. Grab a pre- or postdinner drink in the straight-outta-the-'50s Driftwood Room (see review under Music, Clubs, and Lounges in the Nightlife chapter) next door. You can almost see the brat pack chumming around in the background. **COME HERE FOR OLD-HOLLYWOOD NOSTALGIA.** *$$–$$$; AE, DC, DIS, MC, V; no checks; breakfast, lunch Mon–Fri, dinner every day, brunch Sat–Sun; full bar; reservations recommended; www.graciesdining.com; valet parking; map:HH6.* ♿

Grand Central Baking Company / ★

1444 NE WEIDLER ST, IRVINGTON (AND BRANCHES); 503/288-1614

Grand Central was one of the first bakeries to bring European-style artisan breads to Portland, and they set a high bar. From its signature Como Italian loaf to its rustic baguette, this is bread with flavor—crispy, crumbed crusts and soft toothsome insides make a wonderful foundation for one of their perfect sandwiches. The sack lunch, which includes a bag of chips, pickle wedge, and cookie along with a sandwich, is a bargain at only $1 more than a solo sandwich. The "Tosti" grilled panini are legendary. Try the capered tuna and cheddar on sourdough or the oozing ham and cheese on rye. With table seating, patios, and wine and beer, Grand Central isn't just for grab-and-go. Sweet treats include a variety of excellent pastries such as a decadent triple-chocolate cookie, sweet jam-filled biscuit "Jammers," seasonal fruit tarts and pies, and some of the best cakes around. Branches on Fremont St (714 N Fremont St; 503/546-5311), in the Hawthorne District (2230 SE Hawthorne Blvd; 503/232-0575; map:HH6), Multnomah Village (3425 SW Multnomah Blvd; 503/977-2024; map:II7), Sellwood (7987 SE 13th Ave; 503/546-3036; map:KK5), and Northwest Portland (2249 NW York St; 503/808-9860; map:GG7) sell the same delicious breads, pastries, and sandwiches, with limited seating. **COME HERE FOR EUROPEAN-STYLE BREADS.** *$; AE, MC, V; local checks only; breakfast, lunch, dinner every day; no alcohol; no reservations; www.grandcentralbakery.com; street parking; map:GG5.*

Gravy / ★★☆

3957 N MISSISSIPPI AVE, MISSISSIPPI; 503/287-8800

Flocks of breakfast-loving Portlanders have been keeping Gravy buzzing since the day it opened. In a town where everyone's must-have meal is brunch and everyone has a favorite, Gravy is a contender for the crown. Weekend mornings, savvy locals make their way through the crowd that's always busting out the door to get their names on the waitlist. Have a cup of coffee and enjoy the excellent N Mississippi people-watching until you get your spot. Or watch the delicious food fly by and start daydreaming; the namesake biscuits and gravy are mountainous and even available in a vegetarian incarnation (this is Portland, after all), and egg dishes such as spinach, feta, and mushroom scramble are generous and tasty, if not particularly innovative. Fluffy sweet potato pancakes are tasty with sour cream and applesauce on the side. Breakfast is still pretty popular when lunch hits, but for sandwich lovers, there are plenty of worthy selections. **COME HERE TO EXPERIENCE PORTLAND BRUNCH IN ALL ITS HIPSTER GLORY.** *$; AE, MC, V; no checks; breakfast, lunch every day; no alcohol; no reservations; street parking; map:FF6.* &

Habibi / ★

1012 SW MORRISON ST, DOWNTOWN; 503/274-0628

Why 90 percent of Middle Eastern restaurants in America boast nearly identical menu items is a modern dining mystery, but Habibi is different. Sure, it doles out first-rate renditions of all the usual suspects: zesty hummus, garlicky baba ghanoush, tangy tzatziki, and crispy-fried pods of falafel, but its additional offerings go well beyond the norm. Gigantic steam-filled pillows of baked-to-order pita bread precede starters such as *lebney*—a Lebanese yogurt-cheese served with fresh mint, kalamata olives, and tomatoes—and mains such as *ful mudammas*—fava beans simmered with lemon and cumin. Habibi's divine casserole of artichoke hearts and rice is as healthy as it is delicious. The vegan mezes include *majadra*, a casserole of rice, lentils, and sweet stewed onions. Sharing is encouraged, as these gigantic Middle Eastern sampler plates nearly feed two hungry people, and you'll want to save room for Habibi's baklava and creamy rice pudding with coconut and pistachios. **COME HERE FOR LEBANESE FOOD SERVED IN LARGE PORTIONS.** *$; MC, V; checks OK; lunch, dinner every day; beer and wine; no reservations; www.habibirestaurantpdx.com; street parking; map:I2.* &

Hakatamon / ★

10500 SW BEAVERTON-HILLSDALE HWY, BEAVERTON; 503/641-4613

Japan is filled with hidden gems such as Hakatamon—little suburban locales that look generic but provide wonderful quality cooking at value prices. Wedged next to the popular Asian supermarket Uwajimaya, Hakatamon pushes out better-than-average versions of tempura, sushi, and donburi rice bowls with such toppings as *oyako* (chicken and egg), or fried *katsu* pork cutlets smothered in curry. House-made udon and ramen noodles in addictive soy-seafood or rich pork broths are a signature and perfect for Oregon's often cold and drizzly climate, while specialties such as seasoned Hawaiian marinated tuna poke are wonderful any time of the year. Bustling and busy, this isn't a kimono fantasy version of Japanese dining, but it's simply good, authentic, everyday fare. **COME HERE FOR THE RICE BOWLS.** *$; AE, MC, V; no checks; lunch, dinner every day; beer and wine; no reservations; self parking; map:JJ7.* &

Half and Half / ★

923 SW OAK ST, DOWNTOWN; 503/222-4495

With red vinyl upholstery and a hip crew serving up the goods, Half and Half is a Portland essential just a stone's throw from Powell's City of Books. It serves local Stumptown coffee and locally made doughnuts or homemade granola for breakfast. The lunch menu indulges in experimental cuisine, artistically reflecting the rainy-town aesthetic with items like the Glendale, featuring arugula, turkey breast, kumquats, cucumber, and Swiss. The tuna melts and grilled cheese are made with Italian-style bread from Grand Central Baking Company. **COME HERE FOR LUNCH OR AN EARLY DINNER.** *$; MC, V; checks OK; breakfast, lunch Mon–Sat; beer; no reservations; street parking; map:J3.* &

Hands On Café / ★★☆

8245 SW BARNES RD, WEST SLOPE; 503/297-1480

If only every institution of higher learning had a cafeteria like this one! The campus of the Oregon College of Art and Craft may seem an unlikely place to sit down to dazzling baked goods—from scones to stunning, ever-changing desserts—but the ovens here produce items every ounce as artful as those from the kilns next door. With its small, open kitchen and informal aura, the cluttered cafe feels a bit like a home-economics classroom, but it opens out onto a welcoming patio near a grove of trees and white azaleas. The eclectic lunch and early-dinner menus change daily but can include anything from simple vegetable curry to pasta salad with capers to a cabbage roll stuffed with ground veal. Popular Sunday brunches are inspired by regional specialties from New Orleans to Peru. Pumpkin bread and bowls of strawberries sprinkled with candied ginger will keep you busy while you wait for the main course. **COME HERE FOR BAKED GOODS ON THE GARDEN PATIO.** *$; no credit cards; checks OK; lunch Mon–Fri, dinner Mon–Thurs, brunch Sun; no alcohol; reservations recommended; self parking; map:HH9.* &

Hash / ★★☆

8728 SE 17TH AVE, SELLWOOD; 503/239-3966

Hash opened in 2008, filling the void of breakfast spots in the Sellwood neighborhood. The owners formerly cooked at Sel Gris, and that artistic presentation shows up on their breakfast and lunch plates. They take pride in sourcing local produce and sustainably raised meat and eggs, and everything from the Canadian bacon to the hot sauce to the breads are made in-house. As the name suggests, the signature dish is hash, and you'll find two meat and two vegetarian options that rotate seasonally, served perfectly formed on the plate and topped with eggs cooked to your liking. The standard, corned beef hash, is a sure bet. For those with a sweet tooth, there are aebleskivers, Danish pancakes with a crisp exterior and moist, cakey interior, complemented by a trio of sauces. At lunch, the grilled cheese, on Hash's delectable brioche, is heavenly rich, with house-cured pancetta and artisan cheeses such as taleggio. **COME HERE FOR CORNED BEEF HASH.** *$; DIS, MC, V; no checks; breakfast, lunch Tues–Sun; beer and wine (and Bloody Marys); no reservations; www. hashrestaurant.com; self parking; map:KK6.* &

The Heathman Restaurant and Bar / ★★★★

1001 SW BROADWAY, DOWNTOWN; 503/241-4100
When chef Philippe Boulot came to Portland over 20 years ago to head up the Heathman, the city had less than a handful of choices in upscale international quality dining. Even though times have changed and Portlanders are now spoiled for choice, the Heathman continues to be an impressive destination for inspired Northwest food with spirited Gallic undertones. Boulot holds a James Beard Award of Excellence, and it shows. His kitchen is consistently creative and precise, highlighting an unsurpassed attention to detail. Wild Sturgeon Vallee d'Auge with potato risotto, beet tartare, and apple glaze is an homage to Oregon's bounty, while the leg of lamb cooked for seven hours, or the roasted quail and braised pork belly with mascarpone polenta, French beans, roasted shallots, and sherry vinaigrette are pure Europe. *Wine Spectator* gave the Heathman an award of excellence in 2008. Breakfast and lunch are less costly, but just as stellar. Desserts are rich and comforting and include a brandied apricot bread pudding with caramel sauce, or a local-fruit pear-blackberry cobbler with ice cream. Each Christmas season the Heathman offers a traditional high tea in the swanky Tea Court, but make reservations early (September), as this is a very popular destination. The Heathman's lounge offers more-casual nibbles and classic cocktails. **COME HERE FOR TOP-TIER FRENCH-INSPIRED NORTHWEST CUISINE.** *$$$; AE, DC, DIS, MC, V; checks OK; breakfast, lunch, dinner every day; full bar; reservations recommended; www.heathmanhotel.com; valet and street parking; map:G2.* &

Henry's 12th Street Tavern / ★★

10 NW 12TH AVE, PEARL DISTRICT; 503/227-5320
Perennially packed with young professionals and college coeds, Henry's Tavern is the Henry Weinhard's brewery resurrected as the place where pretty, young Portlanders go to mingle. The cavernous restaurant and billiard hall is a sleek playhouse that's forever filled to the baseball-cap brim. Henry's most attractive attribute, however, is the more than 100 rotating beer selections that pour from its chrome-plated taps. The bar counter has a moat of ice built right into its granite surface to keep your brew cold. Choices include domestic brews, handcrafted ales from every corner of the world, and 10 Belgian selections to wash down gigantic burgers, monstrous California rolls, gorgonzola cheese fries, and other cheap happy-hour items seven days a week. The adjacent dining room sports such American favorites as meat loaf and mashed potatoes, tender pot roast, and superb steaks, alongside wood-fired pizzas, entrée-size salads that

easily feed two, family-size sandwiches, piles of pasta, and several tasty Asian selections, including the popular orange chicken. As Henry's portions are huge, sharing is encouraged. **COME HERE TO FRATERNIZE WITH THE COEDS.** *$$; AE, DIS, MC, V; no checks; lunch, dinner every day; full bar; reservations recommended; www.henrystavern.com; street parking; map:K3.* &

Higgins / ★★★⯪

1239 SW BROADWAY, DOWNTOWN; 503/222-9070

Greg Higgins remains one of Portland's biggest champions of local and sustainable dining. Having opened his upscale dining room and separate casual bistro near Portland State University in 1994, he continues to win accolades and national acclaim for such menu items as the house-made charcuterie plate with Italian DOC-worthy salami and prosciutto served with homemade pickles; garden-fresh salads popping with local hazelnuts and blue cheese; and creamy squash lasagne with wild Oregon chanterelle mushrooms. Entrées can range from the light beauty of citrus-crusted Alaskan halibut with couscous, roasted cauliflower, and a saffron-ginger beurre blanc to an incredibly rich Tuscan-inspired "whole pig" plate featuring fennel sausage, braised pork belly, ribs, and crépinette with black kale and cranberry bean stew. The lower-priced Higgins Bistro next door has a huge selection of obscure local and imported beers, while the cuisine shines all on its own. Some consider its signature organic sirloin burger the best in town, while the baked oysters with nettle pesto and garlic bread crumbs are bistro refinement. Higgins might not be the newest, biggest, or most showy of the bunch, but it continues to prove that commitment to quality never goes out of style. Excellent Northwest-focused wine list. **COME HERE FOR THE CHARCUTERIE.** *$$–$$$; AE, DC, DIS, MC, V; local checks only; lunch Mon–Fri, dinner every day; full bar; reservations recommended; www.higgins.ypguides.net; street parking; map:G2.* &

Hiroshi / ★★★

926 NW 10TH AVE, PEARL DISTRICT; 503/619-0580

Hiroshi has elevated its standards so high that, after one meal at this sushi-centric restaurant, it can be difficult to eat raw fish anywhere else in town. Fortunately for the competition, Hiroshi's prices are also elevated—placing this destination restaurant under the special-occasions category. Where else in Portland will you find an appetizer of squid and mountain yam topped with caviar? Tiny, crispy, cute-as-a-button handmade eel croquettes? Monkfish liver and sturgeon roe laced with earthy truffle vinaigrette? Less extravagant but no less memorable is a tower of tuna slightly torched to order, then tossed in ever-so-slightly spiced chile-miso glaze. At Hiroshi, details make the difference, and even the simplest items shine. Take the soft-shell crab roll in rice paper for an extra dimension of texture, an extraordinarily velvety California roll, or striped bass nigiri slightly kissed by sweet ponzu. **COME HERE FOR THE BEST SUSHI IN PORTLAND.** *$$–$$$; AE, DIS, MC, V; no checks; lunch Tues–Fri, dinner Mon–Sat; beer and wine; reservations recommended; street parking; map:M3.* &

Holden's Bistro / ★★

524 NW 14TH AVE, PEARL DISTRICT; 503/916-0099

Holden's used to be the kind of place where you could walk in dripping with rain, grab a section of the *New York Times*, and happily ensconce yourself at a booth, satisfying sandwich in hand. This Pearl District nosh spot has souped up its menu and its image, venturing a tricky transition from rough-hewn breakfast-and-lunch counter to nighttime bar and bistro. The cuisine—a little bit Asian, a little bit homegrown, and a little bit continental—offers an interesting range of well-articulated flavors and textures. The specialties are gourmet fried chicken and spicy shrimp tacos. Ahi tuna with slaw is also very good. The Bima Burger, a yummy, hearty half-pounder, is made even better accompanied by the highly addictive fries. Seasonal specials, deft cocktails made with fresh-squeezed juices, and late dining hours on Friday and Saturday add up to one fab destination for the nocturnal set. **COME HERE FOR THE FRIED CHICKEN AND DELICIOUS DRINKS WITH FRESH-SQUEEZED JUICES.** *$–$$; AE, DIS, MC, V; local checks only; dinner Mon–Sat; full bar; reservations recommended; www.holdensbistro.com; street parking; map:M1.* &

Hopworks Urban Brewery / ★★☆

2944 SE POWELL BLVD, SOUTHEAST; 503/232-4677

Calling itself "Portland's only Eco-Brewpub," Hopworks Urban Brewery serves up all things sustainable and organic, from terrific beer to wood-fired pizzas. Make like a regular and ride your bike over to HUB for a pint of the lemony and refreshing Crosstown Pale Ale. Or, for something that packs more of a punch, opt instead for the Survival Stout, a heady brew of seven grains finished with—count them—15 pounds of local favorite Stumptown Coffee's Hairbender blend. Soak up all that organic goodness you've imbibed with a killer half-pound Cascade Natural burger, served on a Tillamook cheddar and onion roll and grilled to charcoal perfection. Not to worry, the menu also abounds with veggie options such as the Vegisaurus, a mouthful of a sandwich that towers with seasoned tofu, lettuce, tomato, cucumbers, pepperoncini, kalamata olives, feta, and provolone topped with sun-dried tomato pesto and vinaigrette. **COME HERE TO SAVE THE WORLD, ONE PINT AT A TIME.** *$; AE, MC, V; no checks; lunch, dinner every day; beer and wine; no reservations; www.hopworksbeer.com; street parking; map:II5.* &

Horn of Africa / ★★☆

5237 NE MARTIN LUTHER KING JR BLVD, NORTHEAST; 503/331-9844

At this friendly storefront cafe, proprietors Mohamed and Khadija Yousuf serve authentic fare from all the countries surrounding the Horn of Africa. Seating and lighting are utilitarian, but the Horn serves a meal as warm and well balanced as if it came from a family kitchen. The finger-food platter of vegetarian *hoe-dra*—collards, navy beans, basmati rice, and lentil salad—lies fanned on a bed of cabbage with all the colorful diversity of a nutrition diagram. Poultryvores should try *luukun habasha*, a chicken dish seasoned with garlic, paprika, and, like most things on the menu, "African spices." Scoop it up with a spongy bread known as *biddeena*. A mango lassi will make all this health go down easier. The meal finishes with good and good-for-you gobs of fried dough, gratis, on the same tray as the check. **COME HERE FOR DELICIOUS EAST AFRICAN HOME COOKING.** *$; MC, V; checks OK; lunch Tues–Fri, dinner Tues–Sun; no alcohol; no reservations; www.hornofafrica.net; street parking; map:FF6.* &

Hot Lips Pizza / ★

721 NW 9TH AVE, PEARL DISTRICT; 503/595-2342
633 SW 19TH AVE, NORTHWEST; 503/517-9354
5440 NE 33RD AVE, NORTHEAST; 503/445-1020
2211 SE HAWTHORNE BLVD, HAWTHORNE; 503/234-9999
1909 SW 6TH AVE, DOWNTOWN; 503/224-0311

A Northwest standard since 1984, Hot Lips's many locations have mastered what has to be a unique "Oregon Style" pie. With a toothsome-tender crust that is neither East Coast thin nor Chicago deep, each pizza is loaded with creative meat, vegetarian, and vegan toppings. The owners have a deep commitment to sustainable business practices and food—including sourcing from local farms and innovations such as the electric delivery cars and heating the building with the ovens. Standards such as pepperoni or cheese hold their own, while combos include such high-quality ingredients as tangy feta and goat cheeses, roasted eggplant or squash slices, buttery whole cloves of garlic, and seasonal combos like the local Carlton Farms bacon, sliced potatoes, and cheddar. Stores offer take-out or no-frills sit-down dining, whole pies, or a wide variety of slices. Silician, or focaccia-style, pies are also available. Hearty calzones and bread sticks, along with generously portioned salads and Hot Lips's own signature sodas in such flavors as berry and pear, make for one unique Portland pizzeria experience. **COME HERE FOR A DIVINE SLICE OF PIZZA.** *$; AE, DIS, MC, V; no checks; lunch, dinner every day; beer and wine; no reservations; www.hotlipspizza.com; street parking; map:K3; map:GG6; map:FF5; map:H6; map:E1.* &

Hot Pot City / ★

1975 SW IST AVE, DOWNTOWN NEAR PSU; 503/224-6696

A make-your-own, all-you-can-eat Asian noodle soup bar is the best way to describe this popular gem crowded with college students, Asian families, and local office workers. The clean and bright room features a long counter with individual heating elements and group tables. For around $8 at lunch or $13 at dinner, diners chose from eight different broths—ranging from a hot-and-sour Thai to the intensely chile-infused Ma-La, and even a nutty peanut sauce version. Then the fun begins. Diners go to the "salad bar" and load up on everything from rice stick noodles to pea tip greens, mushrooms, and sliced yams to different types of tofu. Meats are outstanding and beautifully presented: paper-thin sliced beef, ginger-marinated boneless chicken thighs, and meatballs are standouts. Seafood such as shrimp, squid, and white fish are available, and the fried, stuffed wontons make flavorful soup dumplings. Vegetarian and vegan friendly. **COME HERE FOR HOT POT FUN.** *$; MC, V; no checks; lunch, dinner every day; no alcohol; no reservations; street parking; map:E4.* &

Huber's / ★★☆

411 SW 3RD AVE, DOWNTOWN; 503/228-5686
A bastion of old Portland charm, Huber's has been dishing up American classics to hungry patrons since 1879. Turkey dinner with all the trimmings is the house specialty, served up 365 days a year, alongside such other old-school favorites as shrimp Louie, fresh trout amandine, and a generous 8-ounce filet mignon with red wine butter. Ask any local where to grab an after-dinner drink, and Spanish coffee at Huber's undoubtedly comes up. A dazzling fire show ensues when you place your order as bow-tied waiters mix the beverage tableside, slinging bottles of Kahlúa and triple sec, not to mention that essential flaming pour of 151 to finish things off. One is a great idea—two can be dangerous. Happy hour (daily from 4:30–6pm and 9:30–close), with budget options ranging from a quite tasty burger to a refreshing shrimp cocktail, is unbeatable and not to be missed. **COME HERE FOR A TASTE OF OLD PORTLAND.** *$$; AE, DC, DIS, MC, V; no checks; lunch Mon–Sat, dinner every day; full bar; reservations recommended; www.hubers.com; street parking; map:I4.*

Hunan / ★

515 SW BROADWAY, DOWNTOWN; 503/224-8063
There's finer, fancier Chinese food in town, but downtown veteran Hunan has a traditional panache that's tough to beat. On a rainy day, the dim lighting, plush banquettes, and eerie aquarium tanks make you feel like you're dining in an underwater cave. Cuisine from Hunan province is typically spicier than other Chinese food, and Portland's own Hunan doesn't disappoint. Indulge in a lip-smackingly sweet General Tso's chicken, Lake T'ung T'ing shrimp dumplings in hot oil, or fried pot stickers—but don't miss the relatively simple dishes like sautéed green beans or hot-and-sour soup. Piping-hot Chinese tea (complimentary, with endless refills) warms the cockles before you head back out into the cold. **COME HERE FOR CLASSIC HUNAN CUISINE.** *$$; AE, MC, V; no checks; lunch, dinner every day; full bar; reservations recommended; street parking; map:I3.* &

Ichiban / ★★☆

13599 NW CORNELL RD, MURRAY HILL; 503/641-0331
If you go to Ichiban because you've heard about the great sushi, pause a minute before ordering. You're likely to see a hot bowl of codfish soup with udon noodles or a fried soft-shell crab leave the kitchen. Don't hesitate if this sight is enough to prompt you to discard your salmon sashimi regime. *Unagi* donburi—a rice bowl topped with barbecued fresh-water eel and *yamagobo* (pickled burdock root)—is outstanding. However, you've heard right—the sushi bar here is among the best in town. Perfectly fresh fish, tender yet chewy rice, and a charming, entertaining chef all make a lunch or dinner at Ichiban

something to put on your to-do list. A new roll or two are always available. But the story here is not restricted to the usual; come to Ichiban to get something you've never had before. Don't worry; you'll have an appetite for that California roll another day. **COME HERE FOR UDON AND FRESH SUSHI.** *$$; AE, MC, V; no checks; lunch Mon–Fri, dinner Mon–Sat; beer and wine; reservations for 6 or more; self parking; map:GG9.* &

India House / ★★

1038 SW MORRISON ST, DOWNTOWN; 503/274-1017
The tandoori chicken here could draw people right off the light-rail trains that run by the door, and the crispy pakoras could make them miss the next train. With a wide selection of curries from vegetarian to lamb and warm, heavenly chapatis, India House is delightful. All spices and rice are imported from India. Some Portland Indian restaurants may be more elaborate and formal, but this storefront has consistently and skillfully maintained its place near the top of the list. Service and quality are excellent. Finish with a cup of hot chai tea. The lunch buffet has attracted a solid, happy constituency for years. Dishes from north and south India, including tandoor-roasted specials, make weekend dinner a crowded, festive affair. Bring a group to adequately sample the generous menu. **COME HERE FOR THE TANDOORI CHICKEN.** *$$; AE, DC, DIS, MC, V; no checks; lunch Mon–Sat, dinner every day; beer and wine; reservations recommended; street parking; map:I2.* &

J & M Café / ★★☆

537 SE ASH ST, INNER SOUTHEAST; 503/230-0463
The crowded Portland brunch scene with its wait for tables can be a trial, but J & M is worth the wait. Plus, you can pour yourself a bottomless cup of local Stumptown Coffee to keep you pleasantly occupied, and you'll need the time to make your mind up about what to order. As you watch the nicely portioned breakfasts come by, you're sure to deliberate: a cornmeal Belgian waffle covered with sautéed apples, a roasted eggplant-and-egg scramble, or crab cakes with hollandaise sauce? You could have a simple breakfast of eggs and toast, too. Whatever you choose, get a small side of the sautéed potatoes. They come with skins on, crispy on the outside and nice and mealy inside—with no hint of the greasy spoon. There are a ton of breakfast choices in Puddletown, but J & M is worth a visit for its creative and well-made fare. **COME HERE FOR A BREAKFAST-EATER'S BREAKFAST.** *$$; no credit cards; local checks only; breakfast, lunch every day; no alcohol; no reservations; street parking; map:HH6.* &

Jake's Famous Crawfish / ★★

401 SW 12TH AVE, DOWNTOWN; 503/226-1419
With a 113-year history, Jake's remains both a local and tourist favorite. Fish and seafood are taken seriously here, from the full-page "catch of the day" specials to the claim, "If it isn't fresh, it isn't on the menu." In-season Dungeness crab, a variety of fresh oysters, and such specialties as regional

Quinault razor clams and chinook salmon are seasonal draws. With menu items prepared in ways old (brook trout amandine) and new (seared yellowfin tuna with Asian cucumber salad), Jake's provides something for all tastes and most budgets, even offering a variety of steaks and vegetable pastas for the fish adverse. Desserts are worth a visit on their own; try the dense chocolate truffle cake and an outstanding three-berry cobbler served with local Tillamook ice cream. A hopping bar scene with a bargain happy hour and an Oregon-focused wine list make Jake's a perennial favorite for all occasions. **COME HERE FOR OLD-SCHOOL NORTHWEST DINING.** *$$; AE, DC, DIS, MC, V; no checks; lunch Mon–Fri, dinner every day; full bar; reservations recommended; valet and street parking; map:J2.* ₺

Jake's Grill / ★★

611 SW 10TH AVE, DOWNTOWN; 503/241-2100
Like the original Jake's Famous Crawfish, right around the corner, Jake's Grill features quality fresh seafood but is also a hard-working classic hotel restaurant (it's located inside the Governor Hotel; see review in the Lodgings chapter) with everything from better-than-average steaks, burgers, and pastas to entrée-sized salads and soups—there are over 100 different items on the menu, not including specials. It's easy to feel comforted here, though, with such menu items as club sandwiches, chowders, and prime rib—complete with baked potato and steamed broccoli. Jake's knows its meats, with over 10 different cuts of steak and juicy double-fist lamb chops. Desserts are of the gooey chocolate cake, cobbler, and bread pudding variety. The turn-of-the-20th-century high-ceilinged architecture, cozy nooks, and boisterous bar draw hotel guests, ladies who lunch, serious business dinners, and family birthday parties. Jake's Grill is simply an egalitarian, upscale Portland classic. **COME HERE FOR THE MAHOGANY-AND-BRASS-RAIL ATMOSPHERE.** *$$–$$$; AE, DC, MC, V; no checks; breakfast, lunch, dinner every day; full bar; reservations recommended; www.jakesgrill.com; valet and street parking; map:I2.* ₺

James John Café / ★★

8527 N LOMBARD, SAINT JOHNS; 503/285-4930
James John Café is more than the neighborhood coffee shop. Opened a few years ago by former Paley's Place bar maven Suzanne Bozarth, the cafe transforms into a sultry supper club by night. Each Friday and Saturday the crew puts together a menu of seasonal offerings on par with Portland's finest restaurants; every other Saturday you can make reservations for a four-course prix-fixe dinner incorporating locally grown produce and meats into a sophisticated menu. On Sundays, a full-service brunch is offered with such classics as eggs Benedict, featuring house-cured Canadian bacon; homemade biscuits and gravy; and roast beef hash with perfectly poached eggs and braised greens. **COME HERE FOR SATURDAY-NIGHT DINNER.** *$–$$; MC, V; no checks; breakfast, lunch Tues–Sun, dinner Fri–Sat, brunch Sun; full bar; reservations recommended; street parking; map:EE9.* ₺

Jo Bar and Rotisserie / ★★

715 NW 23RD AVE, NORTHWEST; 503/222-0048

Owned by the popular Papa Haydn's folks just down the street, Jo has a bustling French bistro vibe coupled with a quintessential Northwest culinary sensibility. Rotisserie is the focus here, with crackling-skinned chickens, ducks, juicy pork loins, and a succulent wood-fired leg of lamb. The signature Jo Burger with brie is worth a trip across town for, while crisp-fired pizzas and a substantial ahi tuna niçoise salad add to the appeal. Brunch is a serious affair that steers away from standard eggy scrambles; look for salsa-laden fried chilaquiles, vegetable frittatas, and tender, thick brioche French toast. Cocktail specials, made with fresh fruit juices and house-infused liquors, are wonderful anytime of the day or night. **COME HERE FOR THE JO BURGER WITH BRIE.** *$$; AE, MC, V; no checks; lunch Mon–Sat, dinner every day, brunch Sun; full bar; reservations recommended; www.papahaydn.com; street parking; map:GG7.* ♿

John Street Café / ★½

8338 N LOMBARD ST, SAINT JOHNS; 503/247-1066

With its sunny disposition and lack of airs, this cafe has established firm roots in its North Portland neighborhood. Co-owner Marie Noehren tends the kitchen as her partner-husband Jamie stays out front, serving dense banana bread with omelets of cheese, beans, guacamole, and salsa. The cuisine follows no culinary themes. It's straightforward and nicely done without too much fuss. On weekends, regulars know to order the corned beef hash for breakfast. Other days, lightly scrambled eggs with chives, brie, and oven-roasted potatoes, or plate-covering pancakes with currants and hazelnuts or apples, answer morning needs. At lunch, the kitchen stretches a bit, offering blackened snapper on a bun, linguine with shrimp in an aromatic tomato-leek broth, and a Reuben that is among the best in town. Desserts are often limited to cookies and lemon cheesecake. **COME HERE FOR A REUBEN SANDWICH.** *$; MC, V; local checks only; breakfast, lunch Wed–Sun; beer and wine; no reservations; street parking; map:EE9.* ♿

Justa Pasta / ★

1336 NW 19TH AVE, NORTHWEST; 503/243-2249

Starting off as a wholesaler of fresh pasta to a handful of Portland establishments, Justa Pasta is now also a full-fledged restaurant that offers good value for families in the Northwest neighborhood. The unassuming eatery is busy at lunchtime, presenting Caesar salads and bowls of three-cheese ravioli with marinara, served with perfect timing. Patrons can enjoy their Pearl Bakery baguette with olive oil and balsamic vinegar and a two-course lunch, and still get out in 45 minutes. Dinner is sleepier, serving daily special lasagnes and pastas. Day and night, several types of pasta and ravioli are available with sauces ranging from woodsy sautéed mushroom and garlic to creamy Alfredo. The menu changes with the seasons, but if you get too attached to that Swiss chard–ricotta ravioli, you can always buy a pound of it to go, along with a container of Justa's nutty pesto. Beer, affordable wine, and outrageous layer cakes complete the dining experience. **COME HERE FOR RESTRAINED PASTA DISHES AT ROCK-BOTTOM PRICES.** *$; AE, DIS, MC, V; checks OK; lunch Mon–Fri, dinner every day; beer and wine; reservations for 6 or more; www.justapasta.com; street parking; map:GG7.* ♿

Karam / ★★

316 SW STARK ST, DOWNTOWN; 503/223-0830

The first sign that you're in for a great meal at Karam is when you get some of their pita bread—its aroma is bread perfume. Hot and puffy, it has a tender crumb and a just-from-the-oven crust. Most of the traditional Lebanese appetizer dishes appear; the difference is that under chef Emelin Karam's hand, such familiar dishes as hummus, falafel, and tabouleh become new again—they're fresher and more carefully seasoned than the usual fare. *Kibbee saneeyeh*, a national dish of Lebanon, is a crisp orb of beef-stuffed bulgur. Try some *fatte*—grilled lamb served atop a layered stack of bread, roasted eggplant, chickpeas, and pine nuts. Goat simmered in red wine, with a flavor somewhere between veal and lamb, shows a French influence. Lebanese cuisine is very well known in Portland, yet after a look at Karam's menu, you realize that you've barely skimmed the surface. **COME HERE FOR SERIOUS LEBANESE CUISINE.** *$$; AE, DIS, MC, V; no checks; lunch, dinner Mon–Sat; no alcohol; reservations recommended; karamrestaurant.com; street parking; map:I5.* ♿

Kenny & Zuke's Delicatessen / ★★
Kenny & Zuke's SandwichWorks / ★☆

1038 SW STARK ST, DOWNTOWN; 503/222-3354
2376 NW THURMAN ST, NORTHWEST; 503/954-1737

Portland's answer to an authentic New York–style Jewish deli, Kenny & Zuke's is located in a large, light-filled space on the ground floor of the hipster-esque Ace Hotel (see review in the Lodgings chapter). Thick-cut pastrami piled high between slices of rye bread attracts the masses, but on Wednesdays, heart-stopping chicken soaked in buttermilk and fried in duck fat is all the rage. Such traditional Jewish delicacies as potato latkes, cheese blintzes, and noodle kugel make for appropriate sides. Bagels and bialys are boiled and baked in-house and smeared with cream cheese and lox with appropriate accoutrements. Opened in early 2009, the SandwichWorks offshoot serves cafe meals of meatball heros, hot dogs, soups, and salads with less opulent verve. **COME HERE FOR THE PASTRAMI.** *$; DIS, MC, V; no checks; breakfast, lunch, dinner every day (Delicatessen), breakfast Sat–Sun, lunch, dinner every day (SandwichWorks); beer and wine; no reservations; www.kennyandzukes.com; street parking; map:J2; map:GG7.* ♿

Ken's Artisan Pizza / ★★
Ken's Artisan Bakery & Café / ★★

304 SE 28TH AVE, LAURELHURST; 503/517-9951
338 NW 21ST AVE, NORTHWEST; 503/248-2202

Few moments were quite as influential in Portland dining as one morning in November 2001, when a former techie named Ken Forkish started selling his storied loaves of bread and other baked treats from his new bakery on Northwest 21st. The 2006 debut of Forkish's pizza restaurant was no different. Ken's crafts peerless pies and has hour-long waits on weekend nights to prove it. As with his loaves, pizza making to Forkish is a combination of hard chemistry and true love. It manifests itself in a thin, smoky crust with a lean layer of tomato sauce and such ingredients as fresh mozzarella cheese, spicy soppressata, house-made fennel sausage, pancetta, and local arugula. A garlicky Caesar salad is the perfect preamble to pizza. For dessert, you won't go wrong with hearth-fired peach crisp with blueberry ice cream or brown sugar–plum cake. **COME HERE FOR REAL ITALIAN OVEN-FIRED PIZZA.**

Ken sold his first pizza at the bakery in 2005, and he still offers them there on Monday evenings. Other times, bread lovers come for rustic levain-style loaves or dense walnut *campagne*. The croissants are the best in town. Simple French-inspired sandwiches and soups and yummy fruit tarts and macaroons are available at lunchtime. **COME HERE FOR COFFEE AND A CROISSANT, AND TAKE HOME A BAGUETTE.** *$; MC, V; checks OK; dinner Tues–Sat (Pizza), breakfast, lunch every day, dinner Mon (Bakery); beer and wine; no reservations; www.kensartisan.com; street parking; map:GG7; map:HH5.* &

Kornblatt's Delicatessen / ★

628 NW 23RD AVE, NORTHWEST; 503/242-0055

Although Kornblatt's is no longer the only outpost of New York–style deli-love this West Coast city has, it *is* the first. Though perhaps not up to high Manhattan standards, the inclusive menu—long for such a small deli—covers many Jewish soul-food choices: chopped liver, smoked fish, knishes, matzo ball soup, bagels, kosher franks, and cheesecake. A breakfast your mother could love—cream cheese–tomato omelet, home-fried potatoes, and bagels—carries you all day, and the fat pastrami on rye, sided by sauerkraut and macaroni salad, feeds two. Mirrored walls, baskets of bagels, and a deli case raise the ambience beyond a typical sandwich shop. **COME HERE FOR PASTRAMI ON RYE.** *$–$$; MC, V; checks OK; breakfast, lunch, dinner every day; beer and wine; no reservations; street parking; map:GG7.* &

La Calaca Comelona / ★★

2304 SE BELMONT ST, BELMONT; 503/239-9675

La Calaca's encyclopedic menu doesn't exactly ease dinnertime decision making, but it's tough to go wrong here. Enjoy one of the restaurant's excellent mojitos or the Batachan, a concoction of rum, lime, and pineapple juice, and enjoy a summer evening on one of the best patios around. La Calaca straddles the gap between taqueria and upscale restaurant with excellent tacos, tortas, quesadillas, and tostadas, alongside traditional soups, citrusy ceviche, and the fish empanada: a large, homemade corn tortilla stuffed to the brim with red snapper and fresh vegetables, served with a watercress salad and white rice. Specialties such as *mole en pipián*—a medium-hot green mole with pasilla and serrano chiles, hunks of chicken, and fresh pumpkin seed—are just delicate enough for summer dining. The *puerco con chile negro* is a better winter option: grilled pork loin and mushrooms in smoky-black chile sauce with grilled almonds. **COME HERE FOR THE HOUSE-MADE CORN TORTILLAS.** *$–$$; AE, DC, DIS, MC, V; no checks; dinner Mon–Sat; full bar; reservations recommended; www.lacalacacomelona.com; self parking; map:HH5.*

La Petite Provence / ★★☆

4832 SE DIVISION ST, RICHMOND; 503/233-1121

Portland has no shortage of bakeries, but not all are created equal. An offshoot of the original Provence bakery and bistro in Lake Oswego, La Petite Provence is one part restaurant and one part bakery counter, serving French-inspired entrées alongside all the original creations that put its big-sister bakery on Portland's culinary map. Such standbys as its famous lemon-poppyseed scones, moist and crispy-topped coffee cake, and chocolate-chip cookies share the stage with fussier selections like brioche, blueberry *papillons*, and croissants of many flavors: ham and cheese, almond, chocolate, and apricot. Brunch is decidedly the main event, with omelets, eggs Benedict served on a croissant with crispy potato cakes, and smoked-salmon hash. The house-specialty oatmeal redefines the humble porridge in a delicious rendition of rolled oats with brown sugar, sliced mango, and coconut milk. Entrée salads and sandwiches dominate the lunch hour. **COME HERE FOR BAKED GOODS; STAY FOR BRUNCH.** *$; AE, DIS, MC, V; no checks; breakfast until 2pm, lunch every day; no alcohol; no reservations; www.provence-portland. com; street parking; map:HH4.*

Laurelhurst Market / ★★★

3155 E BURNSIDE STREET, LAURELHURST; 503/206-3099

The crew from Simpatica Dining Hall—Ben Dyer, Jason Owens, and Dave Kreifels—have extended their reach to another fine dining endeavor with Laurelhurst Market. The restaurant serves dinner and features somewhat less common cuts of meat such as bone-in New York strip steak and double-cut pork chops cooked according to diner's specifications. Their crispy veal sweetbreads served with mushrooms, olives, and artichokes are light, flavorful morsels, while the roasted marrow bones with toast tips are a satisfying indulgence. Their salad greens and squash are sourced from local farms when in season, and the fresh-cut fries and ratatouille are not to be forgotten. The house-made charcuterie is also available during the day at the butcher counter, where generous sandwiches are served for lunchtime patrons from 10am to 7pm. **COME HERE FOR CRISPY VEAL SWEETBREADS AND STEAKS.** *$$–$$$; AE, DIS, MC, V; local checks only; dinner Wed–Mon; full bar; reservations recommended for 6 or more; www.laurelhurstmarket.com; map:HH5.* &

Lauro Kitchen / ★★★⯪

3377 SE DIVISION ST, DIVISION; 503/239-7000
Chef-owner David Machado has a terrific formula for his SE Division anchor: a casual upscale atmosphere with neighborhood prices, plus a sunny pan-Mediterranean focus. Menu items include outstanding versions of Spanish seafood paella, Moroccan chicken tagine with butternut squash and pistachio couscous, and a Provençal red wine–braised beef daube with polenta. Signature desserts include the Pudim, Portuguese port flan, and a puckery-sweet lemon tart with crème Chantilly, blood orange syrup, and candied citrus. Those seeking stateside fare will find it in the excellent Lauro burger with dry, aged Jack cheese and fries, and in the wood-fired pizzas. The dining room is loud, the bar is tiny, and the waits can be long, but those who stick around are rewarded with some of the best dining in Portland in a festive atmosphere. **COME HERE FOR GOURMET FARE AND NEIGHBORHOOD FUN.** *$$; AE, DC, MC, V; no checks; lunch Tues–Sat, dinner every day; full bar; reservations recommended; www.laurokitchen.com; self parking; map:II5.* &

Le Bouchon / ★★

517 NW 14TH AVE, PEARL DISTRICT; 503/248-2193
Elegant? *Non.* Pretentious? *Non.* Fine French dining? *Oui.* Here is a Left Bank bistro that is perfectly compatible with the Northwest lifestyle. The emphasis is on charm, not intimidation. Classically trained chef Claude Musquin holds forth in the kitchen while his ebullient wife, Monique, controls the dining room with a warm *"Bonjour!"* and a nod approving your wine selection. The intimate space—with closely staged tables, banquette seating, and a bar—demands tête-à-tête, but the dinner buzz adds authenticity. Musquin excels in French country and traditional bistro fare, and his wonderful sauces—Provençal, bourguignonne, and *deux vinaigres*, among others—are a highlight of dining here. Dishes prepared *à la minute* include a salmon draped in fresh dill sauce with potatoes au gratin. Classic French onion soup, baked in a crock, requires a spoon to break through a perfect cheese crust to reach rich broth and onions. After your escargot, lamb chops, and *grand-mère*'s noodles, you won't forgive yourself if you haven't left room for a dense white- and dark-chocolate mousse in a martini glass. **COME HERE IF YOU CAN'T AFFORD TO GO TO FRANCE.** *$$; AE, DIS, MC, V; no checks; lunch Tues–Fri, dinner Tues–Sat; full bar; reservations recommended; street parking; map:M1.* &

Le Happy / ★★

1011 NW 16TH AVE, NORTHWEST; 503/226-1258
Wedged between a real-estate office and a karaoke tavern is this closet-sized crêperie. With its cheerful red door and lace curtains, Le Happy seems out of place in the somewhat rundown neighborhood formerly known as Slabtown. Yet its cozy interior and a view of the streetcar yard below I-405's underbelly exert an off-kilter allure perfectly in sync with area businesses. The menu is mainly crepes—savory and sweet—but also includes terrific salads (don't miss the spicy steak salad) and a lone steak. Many crepes—such as Ma Provence,

a mix of roasted chicken, garlic, tomato, Gruyère, and goat cheese—are hearty enough for a regular entrée. Even meatless crepes are filling. The Oeuf Deluxe, with a poached egg exposed and glistening at the crepe's center, and Faux Vegan, a double whammy of chèvre and crème fraîche with spinach and cremini mushroom sauce, are especially good. Don't leave without ordering a dessert such as the Belle-Hélène, which folds a poached pear, chocolate, toasted almonds, and whipped cream into a delicate vanilla crepe. **COME HERE FOR THE OFFBEAT LOCALE AND EXPERT CREPES**. *$–$$; MC, V; no checks; dinner Mon–Sat; full bar; no reservations; www.lehappy.com; street parking; map:GG7.* &

Lemongrass Thai / ★★★

1705 NE COUCH ST, BUCKMAN; 503/231-5780
Shelly Siripatrapa's Lemongrass is nestled in a sweet, subdued Victorian house in leafy Buckman, where she prepares and serves much of the food herself. The zesty noodle dishes and be-still-my-heart curries (an impressive array of yellow, red, and green, available with chicken, prawns, and other proteins) have a spiciness scale that runs from 1 to 20—but even the most intrepid, Thai-philic westerner will probably be comfortable with a 3. Besides the spice, Lemongrass cuisine is notable for its emphasis on crisp textures and the heady scents of Thai herbs and spices: grassy basil and cilantro, aromatic Kaffir lime leaves and lemongrass, potent red chiles, tart slivers of lime. Because of the skeletal staff, service can be very slow, but patient diners still pour in for the crispy-chewy salad rolls, the creamy tom yum soup, and the palate-scorching Thai Noodle (known in some circles as pad thai). **COME HERE FOR THE SINUS-CLEARING CURRIES**. *$$; no credit cards; checks OK; lunch Tues–Fri, dinner Tues–Sat; beer and wine; no reservations; street parking; map:HH5.*

Le Pigeon / ★★★★

738 E BURNSIDE ST, INNER SOUTHEAST; 503/546-8796
This "bad boy" French bistro might feature heavily tattooed chefs and a rock-and-roll East Burnside locale, but the food is pure haute gourmet. In 2007 chef Gabriel Rucker was named one of the "Best New Chefs " by *Food & Wine* magazine, for an outstanding version of richer-than-sin pork belly with butter-poached prawns and creamed corn. This is strong, confident cooking that always honors classic techniques and local seasonal ingredients. Le Pigeon is not afraid of offal and pâtés, and knows how to handle them, creating memorable dishes such as pork tongue with pickled mushrooms and spicy aioli; sweetbreads with grapes, pancetta, and truffles; and the one-of-a-kind foie gras peanut butter and jelly sandwich. The menu changes daily, but the apricot corn bread topped with maple ice cream is a perennial dessert favorite. Although service is professional and friendly, don't expect special treatment here—the menu is clear: "Substitutions politely declined." **COME HERE FOR EXQUISITE FARE AND JUST A LITTLE EDGE**. *$$$; MC, V; no checks; dinner every day; full bar; reservations recommended; www.lepigeon. com; self parking; map:HH5.* &

Lincoln Restaurant / ★★★

3808 N WILLIAMS AVE, NO. 127, NORTHEAST; 503/288-6200

While brainstorming names for their North Williams dinner house, married owners Jenn Louis (chef) and David Welch (maître d') discussed the idea of an honest restaurant. They wanted a casual eatery where guests could read the menu and know exactly what they were going to get. Their idea is successfully executed in such dishes as light lemon and thyme fritters with bright yellow aioli, and baked eggs with cream and buttery-rich Castelvetrano olives. A main course of hanger steak with blue cheese butter and onion rings, while a bit basic, will appease the most finicky eater, while black cod with celeriac purée, roasted rapini, and grilled lemon butter satisfies an adventurous palate. The open kitchen overlooks a modern log cabin dining room, with a spacious bar serving happy hour specials. **COME HERE FOR "HONEST" BISTRO FARE.** *$$–$$$; AE, MC, V; no checks; dinner Tues–Sat; full bar; reservations recommended; www.lincolnpdx.com; street parking; map:FF5.* ♿

Little Red Bike Café / ★

4823 N LOMBARD ST, NORTH PORTLAND; 503/289-0120

Some things are too good to share. But the secret is out; this miniscule, more coffee shop than cafe deep in the heart of North Portland just happens to serve some of the best breakfasts in town. When we say "miniscule," we mean it: there are six small tables and a few window counter seats, so expect a wait or just order to go from the "bike-through window" up front. The satisfying breakfast sandwiches are simple but creative, made with quality local ingredients. Take the ZooBomb, for example. It's an oozing concoction of fried egg, caramelized onions, pepper Jack, and aioli on a ciabatta roll. Specials such as the mac-and-cheese and tuna melt make this a terrific lunch spot, too. Sweet treats are twists on the classics: house-made ice creams such as the Cap'n Crunch Milkshake or the grapefruit champagne sorbet are pure whimsy, while cupcakes and cookies like the "devil's chocolate" shortbread go well with one of the artisan coffee drinks featuring local microroasted Courier coffee. The chocolate bread pudding is outrageous and made with day-old chocolate croissants. Worth riding a bike across town for. **COME HERE FOR PURE PORTLAND STYLE.** *$; MC, V; local checks only; breakfast, lunch Tues–Sun; no alcohol; no reservations; www.littleredbikecafe.com; street parking; map:EE8.* ♿

Lolo / ★★

2940 NE ALBERTA ST, ALBERTA; 503/288-3400

Lolo is a whimsical mingling of Spain's best regional cuisines, while Italian-born owner Giorgio Kawas, who also owns Giorgio's (see review in this chapter), adds his own inspirations based on seasonal Oregon offerings. Small plates rule the roost; expect tasty nibbles such as *jamón serrano* and Manchego cheese croquettes; a refreshing Andalusian white gazpacho made from almonds and grapes; and straight-from-Basque-country sautéed prawns with garlic, chiles, and white wine. The tender sautéed octopus is a standout and changes throughout the seasons; a recent version featured shaved celery, farga olives, and piquillo pepper confit. Even simple *albondigas* (meatballs) or freshly made potato chips with sea salt are elevated here. Desserts, including traditional churros (fried pastries with thick dark chocolate for dipping), are authentic and decadent. **COME HERE FOR ALBERTA-STYLE SPANISH.** *$$; AE, DC, MC, V; no checks; dinner Tues–Sun; full bar; no reservations; www.lolopdx.com; street parking; map:FF5.* &

London Grill / ★★★

309 SW BROADWAY (BENSON HOTEL), DOWNTOWN; 503/295-4110
This place has been a Portland institution since before software, jogging, or even Mark Hatfield: definitely a 20th-century classic. Inside the stately Benson Hotel (see review in the Lodgings chapter), deep seats and rococo chandeliers speak to a traditional idea of what a power restaurant should be, and much of the menu harks back to that ideal. Entrées include Dungeness crab cakes with Kaffir lime leaves and lemongrass sauce, pan-seared Muscovy duck on plantain mash, and scallop-crusted halibut with beet couscous. London Grill has deeply loyal fans, high-quality ingredients, and (occasionally) a harpist. The service is highly professional, although it seems fewer dishes now involve tableside preparation. The long wine list is especially strong on French bottlings. **COME HERE FOR CLASSIC CONTINENTAL CUISINE AND PAMPERED SERVICE.** *$$$; AE, DC, DIS, MC, V; checks OK; breakfast, lunch, dinner every day, brunch Sun; full bar; reservations recommended; www.bensonhotel.com; valet and self parking; map:J4.* &

Lovely Hula Hands / ★★

4057 N MISSISSIPPI AVE, MISSISSIPPI; 503/445-9910
Lovely Hula Hands is a creative place where you can trust the swarms of foodie regulars in the Mississippi 'hood who swear by its incredibly inventive fare. Its first location was so popular when it debuted in 2003, it moved to larger digs just four years later and remains the top dining spot along North Portland's hippest stretch of pavement. Starters like green garlic soup or arugula with roasted rhubarb and goat cheese show that this innovative kitchen likes to pair seasonal freshness with deeper and bolder flavors. Pan-seared halibut is served with saffron-braised leeks. The grilled Cascade Natural rib eye wears a dollop of gorgonzola butter alongside sautéed greens and a potato cake. This restaurant also has a serious burger following: a third of a pound of ground chuck with bacon, cheddar, and caramelized onions served on a brioche bun in an environment this romantic deserves attention. **COME HERE FOR THE BURGER.** *$$; MC, V; no checks; dinner Tues–Sun; full bar; no reservations; www.lovelyhulahands.com; street parking; map:FF5.* &

Lucca / ★★½

3449 NE 24TH AVE, FREMONT; 503/287-7372
Italian restaurants in Portland are installing wood-fired ovens at a furious pace; however, they're usually strictly used for pizza. Not at Lucca. Chef Lissa Kane's oven produces roasted wild mushrooms, baked orecchiette with

house sausage, a roasted tomato conserve, and nearly all of Lucca's vegetables. The stellar pizzas from the oven are thin-crusted and topped—not overwhelmed—with a changing array of local meats, cheeses, and vegetables. A nice choice would be the Funghi: studded with porcini, misted with a hint of truffle oil, and bearing a golden-yolked egg at its center. For a main course, try a grilled pork chop married perfectly to a side of tender fennel. Chef Kane handles her ingredients with a light and direct touch. **COME HERE FOR GREAT WOOD-FIRED-OVEN ITALIAN MEALS.** *$$; AE, MC, V; no checks; dinner Tues–Sun, brunch Sun; full bar; reservations recommended; luccapdx. com/index.html; self parking; map:FF5.* &

Lucy's Table / ★★☆

704 NW 21ST AVE, NORTHWEST; 503/226-6126
A staple on Northwest 21st Avenue, Lucy's Table may change ownership, but it never strays from its stable concept. Loyal patrons come back time and again for their signature dish: goat cheese ravioli in brown butter sauce garnished with pecorino and crispy fried shallots. The well-established menu veers from pomegranate-glazed baby-back pork ribs and wild boar ravioli to a delicious vegetarian meat loaf that reeks gorgeously of wild mushrooms, but seafood and fish entrées change seasonally. The risotto is always a good bet, with vibrant combinations like beets, braised greens, and beautifully seared sea scallops. Don't leave without trying the flourless chocolate cake. Lucy's stocks an impressive and reasonably priced cellar of local and imported wines. A bustling happy hour presents several menu items for half the price, or sit in the richly hued dining room for a romantic evening for two. **COME HERE FOR THE GOAT CHEESE RAVIOLI.** *$$; AE, DC, MC, V; checks OK; dinner Mon–Sat; full bar; reservations recommended; www.lucystable. com; valet and street parking; map:GG7.* &

Marco's Café & Espresso Bar / ★

7910 SW 35TH AVE, MULTNOMAH VILLAGE; 503/245-0199
The Multnomah Village neighborhood is such a gem: a kid-size cluster of streets lined with bars, toy shops, bakeries, and this friendly diner. Marco's serves excellent lunches and dinners, but breakfast is the main event; expect to wait for a table on the busy weekends. Faithful standbys like cheese omelets or scrambles have a light touch, and the delicious brioche French toast with seasonal fruit and real maple syrup is a worthy glucose rush. From quiche lorraine to Texas-style nachos, lunch offerings are all over the map, including entrée-size salads and nearly 20 sandwich options, but the quality is always excellent, and generous portions won't leave you hungry. Marco's always does a great burger, and its ever-changing nighttime menu is pure comfort, from great homemade meat loaf with mashed potatoes and mushroom gravy to pork tenderloin prepared according to the seasons. Marco's roster of 10 or so desserts includes its famous bread pudding that's worth a try—or two. **COME HERE TO FILL UP.** *$$; AE, DC, DIS, MC, V; local checks only; breakfast, lunch every day, dinner Mon–Sat; beer and wine; no reservations; www.marcoscafe.com; self parking; map:JJ7.* &

Marrakesh / ★★☆

1201 NW 21ST AVE, NORTHWEST; 503/248-9442

Step into Marrakesh and take a magic carpet ride to a place where low lights reveal tapestried walls and yards of fabric drape tentlike from the ceiling. The appeal at this Moroccan restaurant is in the atmosphere and drama of the evening. Get comfortable on a cushion at a knee-high dining table: you're here for five courses. The meal begins with a finger-washing ceremony and ends with a sprinkling of orange water over your hands. In between, you eat without benefit of utensils (unless you order couscous, in which case you might wangle a fork). The first course is a cumin and coriander lentil soup; next comes an eggplant salad. The sweetened *b'stilla royale* (chicken pie) paves the way for your entrée—maybe lamb *m'rouzia* (with onions, raisins, and honey sauce) or braised hare in a rich cumin and paprika garlic sauce. The easiest way to sample the fare is to go with three friends and order the Royale Feast. **COME HERE FOR THE EXOTIC ATMOSPHERE.** *$$; AE, DC, DIS, MC, V; checks OK; dinner every day; beer and wine; reservations recommended; www.marakeshportland.com; street parking; map:GG7.* ♿

Masu / ★★

406 SW 13TH AVE, DOWNTOWN; 503/221-6278

Masu's downtown location is a fashionable stop with high, wood-beamed ceilings augmented by modern touches in the shell of an old brick office building built in 1923. A deep sake menu accompanies the full gamut of entrées, noodles, and sushi rolls. The udon noodle soup with tempura-fried vegetables and shrimp is a superb diversion on a rainy evening. There may be no other Japanese restaurant in Portland that serves grilled rack of lamb and fingerling potato hash with baby bok choy and oyster sauce. Of course, sushi is the real star at Masu, with the usual run of *maki* and *nigiri* in addition to creative specialty rolls, such as the 13th Avenue, with tempura shrimp, roasted red pepper, and avocado, topped with tuna and a mango salsa. The Death by Sushi roll is a combo of *unagi*, avocado, salmon, cream cheese, and tempura-fried crab. **COME HERE FOR SUSHI IN A SEXY SETTING.** *$$–$$$; AE, DIS, MC, V; no checks; dinner every day; full bar; reservations recommended; www.masusushi.com; street parking; map:J1.* ♿

McCormick & Schmick's Seafood Restaurant / ★★★
Harborside / ★★
McCormick's Fish House and Bar / ★

235 SW 1ST AVE, DOWNTOWN; 503/224-7522
0309 SW MONTGOMERY ST, RIVERPLACE; 503/220-1865
9945 SW BEAVERTON-HILLSDALE HWY, BEAVERTON; 503/643-1322

The homegrown McCormick & Schmick's enterprises now feature restaurants in several states and the local historic landmarks Jake's Famous Crawfish and Jake's Grill (see reviews in this chapter) here in Portland. Yet the formula of upscale clubby dining rooms and updated American classics with a focus on the large daily "fresh list" of seafood choices make this chain a successful choice for all kinds of dining events and moods. Here they take seafood seriously; each daily offering lists the location where it was procured: Beaufort, South Carolina, swordfish; Buhl, Idaho, rainbow trout; Cape Cod Wellfleet oysters. Preparations come simple or elaborate, classic or with modern global touches. Salmon might be roasted on a cedar plank, while seabass might be served with miso broth and udon noodles. The international wine list and beers on tap encourage a brisk bar scene. McCormick & Schmick's Seafood Restaurant is in the restored 1886 Henry Failing Building; Harborside offers a luscious Willamette River view; and the suburban Fish House is an oasis on a busy road. **COME HERE FOR FRESH FISH IN TIMELESS SURROUNDINGS.** *$$–$$$; AE, DC, MC, V; no checks; lunch Mon–Sat, dinner every day; full bar; reservations recommended; www.mccormickandschmicks.com; street parking; map:I6; map:C5; map:JJ9.* &

Meat Cheese Bread / ★

1406 SE STARK ST, BUCKMAN; 503/234-1700

The humble sandwich becomes a piece of art here with creative combinations and the inclusion of artisan ingredients. This barebones establishment serves surprisingly sophisticated breakfasts, lunches, and early dinners, with a colorful chalkboard announcing the day's selections. Breakfast bets include a flawless breakfast burrito or a flank steak and egg sandwich that comes on a hearty house-made bun with blue cheese. Later in the day, Meat Cheese Bread offers cold or hot options far from the standard sack lunch. The vegetarian asparagus is layered with a soft-boiled egg, bacon relish, Parmesan, and aioli, while the BLB is a fun riff featuring thick Nueske's bacon, lettuce, and sweet heirloom roasted beets as a stand-in for out-of-season tomatoes. There's not much in the way of sides (a creamy carrot or tomato soup and a bag of chips, for example), and the cramped space can be a challenge, but for a satisfying meal on a roll, Meat Cheese Bread shows good gourmet food comes in many guises. **COME HERE FOR A DARNED GOOD SANDWICH.** *$; AE, DIS, MC, V; no checks; breakfast, lunch, dinner till 7pm Mon–Sat; beer and wine; no reservations; www.meatcheesebread.com; street parking; map:HH6.* &

Meiji-En Japanese Restaurant / ★★★

2226 NE BROADWAY, NORTHEAST; 503/284-6774

Soft lantern light fills Meiji-En with a tranquil glow, welcoming its patrons to relax and enjoy the lovely sushi that awaits them. Beautiful tatami rooms are plentiful and easy to snag, so feel free to request one from your server. Sushi is the standout hit in this neighborhood spot, from simple *tamago* (sweet egg omelet) or *hamachi* (pristine yellowtail) *nigiri* to over-the-top *maki*, or sushi rolls. Sacrilegious though it may be, not even sushi purists can resist the Las Vegas roll, a deliciously deep-fried abomination stuffed with shards of green onion, salmon, and gooey cream cheese. A spicy tuna–topped delight known as Meiji #1 features crunchy asparagus and fresh crab. The seaweed salad appetizer, with three different salads, including toothsome wakame and vinegar-doused red seaweed, is a welcome refreshment from all that rice. Dessert lovers can have their fix with the traditional matcha ice cream. **COME HERE FOR AN AUTHENTIC JAPANESE EXPERIENCE.** *$$; AE, DIS, MC, V; no checks; lunch, dinner Mon–Sat; beer and wine; reservations recommended; street parking; map:GG5.*

Mekong Grill / ★

7952 SE 13TH AVE; SELLWOOD; 503/808-9092

A welcome addition to the family-centered Sellwood neighborhood, Mekong provides grateful neighborhood residents with simple Vietnamese take-out meals, easy sit-down lunches, and casual come-as-you-are dinners. Nothing here will set you back more than $8, but the enticing menu has aromatic and healthy grilled dishes over jasmine rice or tender rice noodles with appropriate vegetable and herb condiments, and features such protein meals as honey lemongrass chicken, garlic shrimp, and sesame beef short ribs. Crispy egg rolls or soft salad rolls come in either meat or vegetarian versions, and a few Vietnamese salads (try the crunchy lotus root with pork and shrimp) add to the appeal. **COME HERE FOR A BRIGHT SPOT ALONG SELLWOOD'S ANTIQUE ROW.** *$; AE, DC, MC, V; no checks; lunch, dinner Mon–Sat; no alcohol; no reservations; www.mekonggrill.com; street parking; map:KK6.*

Milo's City Café / ★★☆

1325 NE BROADWAY, IRVINGTON; 503/288-6456

In a city blessed with great cafes, it can be a challenge for a restaurant to distinguish itself. This urbane contender along browsable NE Broadway is so popular for breakfast, fans demanded that a few select morning items be served all day. The lengthy early menu follows the crowd with multiple variations of egg scrambles, hash and eggs, and eggs Benedict (including pepper, bacon, and tomato). At noon, find a fine wilted-spinach salad, hot and cold sandwiches, pastas, and full meals such as pesto salmon with a potato crust and rice pilaf or apple brandy pork loin. An exposed industrial ceiling, sunny walls, black accents, bright light, and friendly bustle create daylight cheerfulness. Evenings turn softer as Milo's lures the morning crowd back for filet mignon, roast duck, rosemary chicken linguine, and an Oregon-Washington wine list at moderate prices. **COME HERE FOR A SANTA FE OMELET.** *$$; AE, MC, V; no checks; breakfast, lunch, dinner every day; full bar; reservations for dinner only; www.miloscitycafe.com; street parking; map:GG5.* ⅃

Mint / ★★☆

816 N RUSSELL ST, ALBINA; 503/284-5518

A beautiful bauble of a restaurant, Mint has brought understated chic to this old industrial neighborhood and turned into a hopping destination for the cocktail set. It's little wonder, given that owner Lucy Brennan is a master mixologist, turning out intelligent drinks that have the power to become instant classics. One such triumph is the blended avocado daiquiri, a supple surprise that is neither cloying nor heavy. Take a seat in this bold-hued restaurant, and your server will bring a bowl of toasted pepitas to stave off your hunger. The menu—American bistro-style with Latin and Mediterranean influences—features a fair amount of seafood and intense flavors. The Dungeness crab cakes come with a ginger-caper rémoulade and a roasted garlic–tomato sauce. Pan-fried snapper comes with a quinoa salad, red chile sauce, snow peas, and spring onions. A Cuban lamb burger offers a departure from the standard beef, turkey, and vegetable varieties—plus, it's topped with a mint *chimichurri* and served with sweet potato fries. In the adjoining sophisticated 820 Lounge, the cocktails don't have to compete with food for attention (see review in the Nightlife chapter). **COME HERE FOR FRESH FLAVORS AND CREATIVE COCKTAILS.** *$$; AE, MC, V; no checks; dinner every day; full bar; reservations recommended; www.mintand820.com; street parking; map:GG6.* ქ

Montage / ★ ★

301 SE MORRISON ST, INNER SOUTHEAST; 503/234-1324
Every night is Mardi Gras at Montage. Serious diners come early; later on you'll wait in line with an alternative crowd for a spot at one of the long and noisy tables. Until 2am (4am Fri–Sat), Montage serves up best sellers such as the Old Mac (glorified macaroni in garlic and heavy cream), blackened catfish, and jambalaya with your choice of six different proteins, including crawfish, alligator meat, and andouille sausage. Other dishes are both ambitious and unique—from spicy frog's legs to gator linguine to green eggs and Spam—and make up in visceral satisfaction what they lack in finesse. Finish your meal with a slice of Mud Pie or Butter Cake. Montage boasts an extensive wine list, and all bottles are half price on Mondays and Tuesdays. La Merde Lounge, located behind the restaurant and open every day, is a great place to start or end your evening, offering a distinctive list of fresh-pressed cocktails. It also serves the full Montage dinner menu Sunday through Thursday in a more intimate setting. Portland's definitively hip late-night hangout is also open for weekday lunches: you won't get the wee hours, but you will get the same unexpectedly good, cheap Southern cuisine. **COME HERE FOR THE PARTY.** *$–$$; MC, V; no checks; lunch Tues–Fri, dinner every day; full bar; no reservations; www.montageportland.com; street parking; map:G9.* ქ

Morton's of Chicago: The Steakhouse / ★ ★ ★ ★

213 SW CLAY ST, DOWNTOWN; 503/248-2100
Portland has several fine steak houses, but none carries the reputation of Morton's—and none has earned it more. Consistently outstanding food, compelling service, valet parking, and expense-account prices are earmarks of this establishment, whose 80 restaurants can be found in most major U.S. cities and abroad. Chances are you'll order a tender and juicy steak, of which there are several, including a house-specialty 24-ounce porterhouse and a 20-ounce New York sirloin. There are a few nonbeef entrées (lamb, chicken, and lobster)—wild Alaskan coho salmon is a specialty of Morton's restaurants in the Northwest—but this is a steak house. Everything is ordered à la carte, which means you'll pay extra for your house salad or enormous baked Idaho

potato. The short list of wines by the glass doesn't maintain the quality of the superb steak menu, but there are excellent choices by the bottle. **COME HERE FOR THE OUTSTANDING STEAKS AND TABLESIDE SERVICE.** *$$$$; AE, DC, MC, V; checks OK; dinner every day; full bar; reservations recommended; www.mortons.com; valet parking; map:E4.* &

Mother's Bistro & Bar / ★★☆

409 SW 2ND AVE, DOWNTOWN; 503/464-1122

This is the way your mother should have cooked but almost certainly didn't, unless you're closely related to proprietor Lisa Schroeder. After cooking in Paris and New York, Schroeder opened the most comfortable of comfort-food restaurants in Portland, offering the likes of matzo ball soup, pot roast, and chicken with dumplings. The place flies in H&H bagels from New York and cures its own smoked salmon. The substantial, three-meals-a-day menu is not only reassuring but also impressively skilled, and every month Schroeder focuses on a different ethnic cuisine, providing offbeat specials ranging from Italian to Moroccan Jewish. Portions are sized to put meat on your bones. The various rotating desserts include an oversized, three-person strawberry and rhubarb cobbler topped with sweet, crunchy toasted almonds and pecans. The Velvet Bar and Lounge adjoins Mother's on Stark Street; both old and new quarters are decorated in maternal memorabilia, from old advertisements to particularly heart-tugging prints and personal photos. Inviting, overstuffed furniture and a warm wooden bar outfit the lounge, which is a great under-the-radar place to swing by for after-dinner drinks and dessert. **COME HERE FOR FOOD JUST LIKE MOM USED TO MAKE.** *$$; AE, MC, V; no checks; breakfast, lunch Tues–Sun, dinner Tues–Sat; full bar; reservations recommended; www.mothersbistro.com; street parking; map:I5.* &

Murata / ★★★

200 SW MARKET ST, DOWNTOWN; 503/227-0080

One of the most traditional Japanese restaurants in Portland and one of the best, Murata flies in fish several times a week directly from Japan, while its traditional private tatami rooms, complete with mats (no shoes please!) and paper shoji screens, add to the authenticity. The sushi bar can be cramped by Western standards, but it's worth rubbing elbows for Chef Murata-san's 50 years of experience cutting flawless pieces of velvety *toro* (tuna belly), fresh-from-the-ocean sea urchin, and rare finds such as raw abalone in the shell or quivering monkfish liver. Tender Nova lox–like smoked salmon is made in-house and is one of a kind. Lunch is a no-nonsense affair featuring bento boxes, udon noodles, and donburi rice bowls (the fried pork *katsu* with egg is a standout). Dinner options are a bit more formal and best for sharing; the *nabemono* beef or seafood stew is cooked on an iron pot at the table. Murata is one of the few restaurants in Portland to serve the multicourse tasting menu of *kaiseki-ryori*; this traditional ceremony celebrates the seasons, and ingredients are chosen by the chef to become a symphony of elegance and serenity on the plate. This is not your run-of-the-mill teriyaki and tempura joint—expect higher prices and quality. **COME HERE FOR AUTHENTIC JAPANESE CUISINE.** *$$$; AE, DC, JCB, MC, V; no checks; lunch Mon–Fri, dinner Mon–Sat; beer and wine; reservations recommended; murata@teleport.com; street parking; map:E3.* &

Navarre / ★★⯪

10 NE 28TH AVE, LAURELHURST; 503/232-3555

Suffering from been-there, done-that syndrome? Try airy Navarre. The menu—its items and presentation—wakes you from the dining doldrums. Long and skinny, it's a checklist of about two dozen choices, loosely grouped into small plates, appetizers, salads, starches, cheeses, and entrées, though you won't see any headings as such. This menu simply reads: Mushrooms. Olives. Lentils and Beets. Bird. "Trout baked in parchment" is about as explicit as it gets. The diner's job is to craft a meal from as few or as many dishes (all are petite, tapas-size portions) as desired, marking items on the list and handing it to the waiter. For those accustomed to highly informative menus, ordering from Navarre's oblique list will be a leap of faith. But you will be richly rewarded for your daring. Don't miss chef-co-owner John Taboada's gorgeous pâtés, his quail *escabeche*, delicate crab crepes, lamb sausage, signature braised greens, perky fried-green tomatoes (in season), and *frico* (crispy-fried cheese). As befits a wine bar, the selection is flawlessly chosen, with 60 to 70 vintages by the glass. **COME HERE FOR THE REFRESHING MENU AND SIMPLE, EXPERT COOKING.** *$$; AE, MC, V; checks OK; lunch, dinner every day; beer and wine; reservations recommended for large groups; www.navarreportland.blogspot. com; street parking; map:HH5.*

Nel Centro / ★★★

1408 SW 6TH AVE, DOWNTOWN; 503/484-1099

Nel Centro, in Italian, means "in the center," which applies to David Machado's downtown restaurant in more ways than one. It's not only centrally located, but also in the center of the food scene. An inspired menu includes local favorites with a hearty provincial twist, such as roasted halibut with ratatouille and tapenade, or grilled Delmonico steak with porcini butter and potato gratin, but the Provençal roasted pork with tomato gratin and mostarda di frutta should not be passed over. With a broad and thoughtful selection of wines and a variety of creative pasta dishes, such as trenette with new potatoes, green beans, and basil pesto, Nel Centro is also a bit of a center for comfort food. On the premises of the Hotel Modera, Nel Centro serves breakfast, lunch, and Sunday brunch. Private dining rooms seat from 12 to 90 people. **COME HERE FOR COUNTRY ITALIAN DINING WITH A PORTLAND TWIST.** *$$–$$$; AE, MC, V; no checks; breakfast, lunch, dinner every day, brunch Sun; full bar; reservations recommended; www.nelcentro.com; map:E2.* &

Nicholas' Restaurant / ★★

318 SE GRAND AVE, INNER SOUTHEAST; 503/235-5123

Nicholas' Restaurant started slinging pizza and calzones in 1986, adding more adventurous Lebanese and Middle Eastern food as its customers grew curious.

Now, Nicholas and Linda Dibe are retired (mostly) and daughter Hilda runs the show. The restaurant features irresistible traditional Lebanese cuisine. At Nicholas' you'll find local indie rock stars lunching beside highbrow businesspeople and extended families. Despite two potential drawbacks—no alcohol served, no credit cards accepted—Nicholas' is packed noon and night simply because the food induces cravings for more. It's a dive, but one with character, and basics such as rich baba ghanoush, light and creamy hummus, and crisp falafel are reliably excellent. Mountainous meze platters come in three equally satisfying varieties: meaty, vegetarian, and vegan. Definitely try the Lebanese cheese pizza, which is nothing more than tangy mozzarella and sesame seeds on fresh dough, but it's absolutely addictive. **COME HERE FOR UNERRING LEBANESE FOOD.** *$; no credit cards; checks OK; lunch, dinner every day; no alcohol; reservations for large groups; www.nicholasrestaurant. com; street parking; map:HH6.*

Noble Rot / ★★

IIII E BURNSIDE ST, 4TH FLOOR, INNER SOUTHEAST; 503/236-1110
Noble Rot has found a new home perched atop a four-story, bright red, LEED-platinum building, in the former Rocket space. Reminiscent of a spaceship, with an excellent view of downtown, the new digs for this 2004 *Oregonian* Restaurant of the Year mark a total change from the intimate wine bar it once was. But the European menu and balanced wine list remain unchanged. Such signature dishes as the onion tart, Noble salad, and mac-and-cheese appear next to more-inventive plates like potato and black truffle pudding with warm asparagus salad, and grilled leg of lamb with green herb yogurt and chickpea fritters. Chef Leather Storrs's rooftop garden gives new meaning to farm-to-table: he and his staff grow the lettuce, herbs, onions, and other vegetables used in the restaurant's repertoire. **COME HERE FOR THE VIEW OF DOWNTOWN PORTLAND.** *$$; AE, MC, V; no checks; dinner Mon–Sat; full bar; reservations for 6 or more; www.noblerotpdx.com; street parking; map:J9.* &

Noho's Hawaiian Café / ★

2525 SE CLINTON ST, CLINTON; 503/233-5301
As anyone who has spent time in Hawaii can tell you, Noho's is "Shaka, brah!" That's to say, "It's awesome, brother!" A veritable beach hut with surfboards on the bright peach walls and '80s-era Hawaiian art, Noho's serves the truest da kine meals you're likely to find this side of Honolulu. Korean-cut short ribs, richly marinated in honey, garlic, and sesame, are sublime; Phil's Ono Chicken, bursting with flavors of sweet ginger and salty soy, is cooked until it pulls apart in tender shreds. Hawaii's famous slow-roasted kalua pig is offered on Fridays only. There's also Japanese-style *saimin*, a noodle soup beloved by kamaaina (longtime Hawaii residents). In Hawaii, "plate lunch" wagons serve "two-scoop rice" and macaroni salad with entrées. At Noho's you have the choice of this traditional plating, menehune (one scoop of rice and macaroni salad), or blalah (three scoops of rice and two scoops

of macaroni salad) for varied appetites. **COME HERE FOR THE TRADITIONAL HAWAIIAN PLATE LUNCH.** *$–$$; DIS, MC, V; no checks; lunch, dinner every day; no alcohol; no reservations; www.nohos.com; street parking; map:II5.* &

Nostrana / ★★★

1401 SE MORRISON ST, BUCKMAN; 503/234-2427

Nostrana is simple elegance, a friendly and airy oasis with ceilings as high as oak trees, excellent classic Italian fare, wood-fired pizzas, and perhaps the most satisfying salad in town. That this 2006 *Oregonian* Restaurant of the Year plays by the local rules of fresh and sustainable is no fluke: its founder and chef, Kathy Whims (2009 James Beard Award Finalist for Best Pacific Northwest Chef), practically wrote the book as co-owner and chef of the venerable Genoa for 20 years. Nostrana maintains Whims's magical touch. The excellent Nostrana salad pairs bitter radicchio with Parmigiano and rosemary-and-sage croutons in Caesar-style dressing. It's a perfect preamble to the pizzas, like the simple Margherita, a hand-shaped sphere of smoky crust with house-made mozzarella and tangy tomato and basil, finished with fresh arugula when available. The restaurant prepares excellent ravioli according to the seasons, and Gnocchi Thursday is a great day to dine: Nostrana's potato dumplings are practically weightless. At the opposite pole is the legendary bisteca Fiorentina, a tender porterhouse served medium rare that clocks in at more than 2 pounds and easily feeds a family. The panna cotta sets the standard. **COME HERE ON THURSDAYS FOR HOUSE-MADE GNOCCHI.** *$$; AE, MC, V; no checks; lunch Mon–Fri, dinner every day; full bar; reservations recommended; www.nostrana.com; self parking; map:HH6.* &

Nuestra Cocina / ★★☆

2135 SE DIVISION ST, DIVISION; 503/232-2135

This family-run restaurant, with regional Mexican cuisine, is among the handful of Portland eateries that have forever raised the standards of south-of-the-border fare. Nuestra Cocina achieves excellence by perfecting the basics, such as soft and slightly sweet corn tortillas made to order for shredded-pork tacos. The lasting tang of lime-tinged ceviche is offset just slightly by chiles and cilantro, a proper precursor to such main courses as a tender half chicken simmered in a spice-laden Oaxacan mole that's kissed ever so slightly by chiles and a gentle sprinkle of cinnamon. Enchiladas with seasonal fillings like acorn squash, Painted Hills beef tips with reticently spicy chipotle sauce, or white prawns with garlic and pasilla chiles are palate-perfect examples of the highly regional and abundant Mexican gastronomy. Here, you can sample the best Mexico has to offer without worrying about the water. **COME HERE FOR PORTLAND'S BEST TORTILLAS.** *$$; AE, DIS, MC, V; checks OK; dinner Tues–Sat; full bar; no reservations; www.nuestracocina.com; street parking; map:II5.* &

¡Oba! / ★★☆

555 NW 12TH AVE, PEARL DISTRICT; 503/228-6161

¡Oba! has two identities. There's ¡Oba! the restaurant—a subdued, serious dining room serving one Nuevo Latino concoction after another—and there's ¡Oba! the bar, a cavernous expanse where trendy clothes and high-pitched revelry rule. Chef Scott Neuman has rocked the city with his jazzy renditions since 1998, and he continues to please palates with Cuban pulled flank steak and crispy coconut prawns with jalapeño marmalade. ¡Oba!'s Caesar with roasted corn and Manchego cheese, as well as the macadamia-crusted Pacific swordfish, pan-seared with cilantro pesto, grilled tomatoes, and a sherry glaze, are definite highlights. ¡Oba! offers a special menu with vegetarian, dairy-free, wheat-free, and heart-healthy selections. If you don't mind loud, alcohol-embellished speech reverberating off the bar's apricot walls, visit the lounge to try some of the most alluring cocktails in town. A bumpin' bar scene ensures fashion gazing or eavesdropping, but the star attractions are the handcrafted drinks, such as the ¡Oba!-tini, made with tequila, Cointreau, and house-made sweet-and-sour mix, with a float of hibiscus flower water. The tapas menu comes in a close second. **COME HERE FOR OUTRAGEOUSLY FLAVORFUL FISH ENTRÉES.** *$$; AE, DC, MC, V; no checks; dinner every day; full bar; reservations recommended; www.obarestaurant.com; street parking; map:M2.* ♿

Original Pancake House / ★

8601 SW 24TH AVE, BURLINGAME; 503/246-9007

A family-style diner with a pedigree, in 1999 the Original Pancake House was designated as a landmark by the James Beard Foundation. Open since 1955, it continues to provide a variety of, you guessed it, pancakes as well as large omelets and other breakfast treats with all the fixings. The pancakes are indeed fantastic: flapjacks and blueberry varieties are fluffy and filling, while specialties such as the lemony, puffy, powdered sugar–coated Dutch babies; tender crepes (try the Danish Kijafa Cherry); and waffles are just as good. Some offerings are indeed original: the Tahitian Dream is a crepe stuffed with golden, ripe sliced bananas in sour cream and triple sec, sherry, and brandy. Topped with diced bananas in apricot sauce, it's like a breakfast sundae for adults. Expect a wait on the weekends; this is the de facto Portland brunch spot. **COME HERE FOR PANCAKES OF ALL KINDS.** *$; no credit cards; checks OK; breakfast, lunch Wed–Sun; no alcohol; no reservations; www.original pancakehouse.com; street parking; map:KK7.* ♿

Otto's Sausage Kitchen / ★★

4138 SE WOODSTOCK BLVD, WOODSTOCK; 503/771-6714

Civilized but leisurely, the Woodstock neighborhood is home to a few good foodie destinations along its perennially packed sidewalks. None are quite so long-lived or iconic as Otto's Sausage Kitchen. This meat- and wienie-focused lunch counter, delicatessen, and beer-and-bottle shop has been crafting the likes of headcheese, liverwurst, kielbasa, chorizo, Cajun sausage, and brat-wurst since 1926, when founder Otto Eichentopf opened shop. Otto is long gone, but his sausage kitchen is staffed by a fourth generation of Eichentopfs, and its meaty legacy continues. A perfect Reuben with house-cured corned beef and the Kitchen Sink sandwich, with its stack of pastrami, salami, summer sausage, Swiss cheese, smoked Muenster, and the works on a toasted French roll, still rule the street. In addition, Otto's purveys more than 160 labels of imported and domestic beer and an eclectic collection of new- and old-world wines. **COME HERE FOR SUPERB SAUSAGE.** *$; AE, DIS, MC, V; checks OK; lunch, dinner every day; beer and wine; no reservations; www.ottossausagekitchen.com; street parking; map:JJ4.*

Paley's Place / ★★★★

1204 NW 21ST AVE, NORTHWEST; 503/243-2403
In 1995 Vitaly and Kimberly Paley waltzed into town from New York City and swept diners off their feet, and Paley's continues to dazzle, warm, and thrill Portlanders. Kimberly is known to dance around the intimate, thoughtfully designed dining room the way she once did on national stages, closely watching everything her husband—a Russian-born former concert pianist—sends out from the kitchen. Together, they maintain an atmosphere as artful as the James Beard Award–winning, French-influenced Northwest cuisine Vitaly prepares from regional farmers' offerings. In spring, their seasonal menu might showcase fried razor clams with sweet and smoky potatoes, fresh chickpeas, fava beans, spring onions, and sauce gribiche. Other seasons might bring a salad of fennel twig–roasted rabbit with house bacon and fennel pollen aioli or quail stuffed with bacon, prunes, and chestnuts. Menus may change with the harvests, but the desserts are consistently impressive. From one of the city's best crème brûlées to the warm chocolate soufflé cake to house-made sorbets and ice creams, there's something to satisfy every sweet tooth. In summer, porch and sidewalk seating dramatically increase the size of the dining area. **COME HERE FOR A SYMPHONY OF UNFORGETTABLE FLAVORS.** *$$$; AE, MC, V; no checks; dinner every day; full bar; reservations recommended; www.paleysplace.net; street parking; map:GG7.* &

Pambiche / ★★

2811 NE GLISAN ST, LAURELHURST; 503/233-0511
To have experienced Pambiche without a crowd is to have dined here shortly after it first opened. It has only 10 tables and limited counter seating, so it's entirely common to wait for a table. Perhaps it's the otherworldly feel of this tiny storefront, tucked behind a huge colonnade and painted inside and out in bold colors, that makes it so popular. Or the friendly staff, whose conversation slips back and forth between English and Spanish. Maybe it's the lip-smacking taro-root fritters, *tostones*, grilled Cuban sandwiches, or *pollo criollo* (chicken stewed in a Creole sauce with fresh herbs and orange). Or possibly the large glasses of South American wines? And though it's most definitely the café con leche that attracts neighbors between mealtimes, it's the dessert case that makes the largest impression anytime, day or night. Classic tortes, cheesecakes, and tarts spilling over with tropical fruits, liqueurs, chocolate, and nuts

are a force unto themselves. **COME HERE FOR A MINI VACATION TO CUBA.**
*$–$$; MC, V; no checks; breakfast, lunch, dinner every day; beer and wine; no
reservations; www.pambiche.com; street parking; map:HH5.* &

Papa Haydn / ★★

701 NW 23RD AVE, NORTHWEST; 503/228-7317
5829 SE MILWAUKIE AVE, WESTMORELAND; 503/232-9440

At Papa Haydn, it's tough not to be impressed with the expansive pastry cases, in terms of sheer volume. Cakes, tortes, and tarts are towering architectural marvels as pretty as debutantes bedecked in tulle and chiffon. Cassata (Kahlúa-soaked sponge cake with chocolate-ricotta filling), chocolate-buttermilk Saint Moritz cake with coconut-pecan filling, and lemon Bavarian are just a sampling of the confections. As a prelude to the last course, Papa Haydn offers lunchtime salads and sandwiches (try the chicken club with avocado and sun-dried tomato mayonnaise), and daily dinner choices such as pan-seared diver scallops with summer sweet corn, local fava beans, and chicken livers with an arugula-watercress emulsion. Papa's has wonderfully savory pasta dishes, succulent grilled chicken breast marinated in apple brandy and mustard, and, for a heartier selection, steak frites. The Northwest Portland outpost extends across most of a block, incorporating Jo Bar and Rotisserie (see review in this chapter). The Westmoreland location is more low-key with a few menu variances, but don't think that's a way to avoid the lines—it carries most of the famed desserts. **COME HERE FOR GREAT PEOPLE-WATCHING.** *$$; AE, MC, V; no checks; lunch every day (Northwest), Mon–Sat (Westmoreland), dinner every day, brunch Sun; full bar (Northwest), beer and wine (Westmoreland); reservations for large groups; www.papahaydn.com; street parking; map:GG7; map:JJ5.*

Park Kitchen / ★★★

422 NW 8TH AVE, PEARL DISTRICT; 503/223-7282

This inviting eatery fronted along a tree-lined stretch of Portland's North Park Blocks got off to a quiet start, but under the leadership of owner Scott Dolich and chef David Padberg, it has emerged as one of Portland's top kitchens. Thoughtful wine selections are mindful of the highly seasonal menu; summer starters may include chilled cucumber soup with burnet, or freshly marinated anchovies with preserved lemons and fennel. Park Kitchen offers a great selection of small plates that you can happily graze on for a satisfying meal. Or indulge in the larger plates, which in the summer may include sliced duck breast, hominy and English peas, or halibut, chorizo, and large white beans. During winter, you may find a rich lamb cassoulet, Berkshire pork with pears and sauerkraut, or monkfish braised with wild mushrooms and pinot noir. You're sure to be delighted by the ever-changing menu, with its emphasis on local, fresh, and exciting ingredients. Park Kitchen is consistently noted as a top spot for cocktails, and rightly so. Plus, desserts such as rhubarb-cashew crisp with house-made coconut ice cream are proof that Park Kitchen is at the top of its game from start to finish. **COME HERE FOR PURE FLAVORS.** *$$–$$$;*

MC, V; *breakfast, lunch Tues–Fri, dinner Tues–Sat, brunch Sat–Sun; full bar; no reservations; www.parkkitchen.com; street parking; map:L3.* &

Patanegra / ★★

1818 NW 23RD PL, NORTHWEST; 503/227-7282

As authentic Spanish food goes, Patanegra is as real as it gets on this side of the pond. It sticks to a shared-plate format with many choices available in full or half rations, and chef-owner and Spanish native Ricardo Segura's culinary knowledge of Iberia delves deep. From its ground-pork meatballs wrapped in tart Idiazábal cheese and served with a perky tomato sauce to the *ensalada mixta* with white asparagus; from Portland's best paella to the tender boiled octopus with paprika, olive oil, and sea salt, Patanegra flaunts exactly the fare you'd find in Old Castile and its surrounding regions. With advance notice, Segura will prepare such Madrid mainstays as roast suckling pig or lamb for groups of 20 or more. Patanegra also sports an encyclopedic wine list of Iberia's best selections, not to mention the tastiest flan in PDX. **COME HERE FOR THE MOST AUTHENTIC SPANISH FOOD IN PORTLAND.** *$$–$$$; AE, DIS, MC, V; no checks; dinner Mon–Sat; full bar; reservations recommended for 4 or more; www.patanegra-restaurant.com; street parking; map:GG7.* &

Pazzo Ristorante / ★★★

627 SW WASHINGTON ST (HOTEL VINTAGE PLAZA), DOWNTOWN; 503/228-1515

Chef John Eisenhart has been called the "master of flavor" by his former boss, famous New York chef Mario Batali. Eisenhart is now in charge of the kitchen at Pazzo's, the house restaurant at the elegant Hotel Vintage Plaza (see review in the Lodgings chapter), making this Portland institution a don't-miss stop for foodies. Beautiful salads and entrées that abound with fresh produce and house-made pasta reflect the ideal of using organic or sustainably harvested products whenever available. Pazzo also features a beautiful selection of antipasti, with daily preparations of seasonal fish or prosciutto with melon. You might start with a pasta course of pappardelle chickpea with Willamette Valley lamb and mint ragout, then order the Alaskan halibut with carrots, cabbage, and prosciutto in shellfish Friulano broth. In the bistro-style bar, you can get gourmet pizzas from the brick oven. For a quick and reasonably priced breakfast or lunch, head next door to Pazzoria (621 SW Washington St; 503/228-1695) and grab a strong cup of coffee or gooey panini. **COME HERE FOR THE EVER-BUSTLING ATMOSPHERE.** *$$; AE, DC, DIS, JCB, MC, V; checks OK; breakfast, lunch, dinner every day; full bar; reservations recommended; www.pazzo.com; street parking; map:J4.* &

Perry's on Fremont / ★★

2401 NE FREMONT AVE, ALAMEDA; 503/287-3655

For more than 25 years, Bill and Anna Perry's eponymous restaurant has been a favorite stop in the Alameda neighborhood. Perry's fare isn't so much American as it is popular in America, featuring such classics as fish-and-chips, chicken enchiladas, eggplant lasagne, and chicken potpie. The Cajun Fisher-woman's Stew is a subtle, slow-cooked cioppino of salmon, prawns, catfish, and a school of other sea creatures. Although risotto and pasta entrées are priced comparably with the fresh seafood fillets and steaks, your money is better spent on the meatier choices, which arrive daintily accompanied by fresh sautéed vegetables and starchy whipped garlic potatoes. The large patio is a lovely place to enjoy happy hour and flashy house drinks. **COME HERE FOR THE CHEAP HAPPY HOUR SPECIALS.** *$$; AE, DIS, MC, V; no checks; lunch Sat, dinner Tues–Sat; full bar; reservations recommended; www.perrys onfremont.com; street parking; map:FF5.* &

Piazza Italia / ★★⯪

1129 NW JOHNSON ST, PEARL DISTRICT; 503/478-0619

Casual but special, Piazza Italia has an infectious spirit that is so strong it can sometimes trump the menu. You can hear *la dolce vita* in the clatter of Italian conversation, smell it in the aromas wafting from the kitchen, taste it in the house chianti, and see it in the grins on customers' faces. The most important authentic ingredient in Italia's winning equation isn't the fresh mortadella, the handcrafted Roman ceramics, or the Illy coffee: it's the Italians who run and frequent the place. The concise menu changes frequently, but some dishes are available year-round. *Squarciarella*, a prized family recipe of egg noodles with prosciutto, pepper, garlic, and oil, is Piazza's most popular dish. Pasta spe-cialties include the Roman classic, *bucatini all'amatriciana*, al dente noodles punctuated by a tomato sauce with pancetta, red wine, onions, and pecorino Romano. Bookend any meal with insalata Caprese (tomatoes, fresh mozza-rella, basil, and olive oil) and a cannoli, and you'll certainly go home happy. **COME HERE FOR AN AUTHENTIC ITALIAN EXPERIENCE.** *$$; DIS, MC, V; no checks; lunch, dinner every day; beer and wine; reservations recommended; www.piazzaportland.com; street parking; map:N2.* &

Pine State Biscuits / ★⯪

3640 SE BELMONT ST, BELMONT; 503/236-3346

New on the Belmont scene, next door to the Triple Nickel bar, a rocker hang-out, this 400-square-foot storefront restaurant serves fast-food, Southern-style buttermilk biscuits with a locally sourced, Portland twist. Pine State is the nickname for North Carolina, where owners Walt Alexander, Kevin Atchley, and Brian Snyder grew up. With only four small tables and five stools, there is no room to linger or bring a large group, and this makes it a perfect candidate for takeout and quick bites. There is counter service only, but the friendly staff is ready to accommodate any unmet needs or wishes. The prices are unbeatable, and the sandwiches extremely generous. The biscuits are doused with either sausage or mushroom gravy, and the sides include hash browns cooked in clarified butter or local organic grits. The $8 Reggie Deluxe was named one of the best sandwiches in the nation in March 2008 by *Esquire* magazine. This winner is a homemade biscuit filled with fried chicken, heritage bacon, local Tillamook cheddar, sausage gravy, and a fresh egg overeasy or scrambled. For vegetarians, the Moneyball sandwich is the best alternative, served with shiitake mushroom gravy and an egg of your choice. The bottomless cup of Stumptown coffee is served along with chocolate milk engineered by local chocolatier David Briggs. **COME HERE FOR A SOUTHERN-STYLE BREAKFAST SANDWICH.** *$; AE, DC, DIS, JCB, MC, V; checks OK; breakfast, brunch, lunch Tues–Sun; no alcohol; no reservations; www.pinestatebiscuits.com; street parking; map:HH5.* &

Ping / ★★

102 NW 4TH AVE, CHINATOWN; 503/229-7464

Opened in early 2009, Ping is a modern addition to Portland's Chinatown by Andy Ricker, the restaurateur behind foodie favorite Pok Pok (see review in this chapter). The Asian-style pub food here is meant to be shared; try the Laksa, a steaming bowl of noodles with tofu, chicken, prawns, cockles, boiled eggs, and bean sprouts mingling in a vibrant curry soup. Grilled items, such as the delectable quail eggs wrapped in bacon and slathered in spicy mayonnaise, make up a large part of the menu. Whether it's an inspired Asian libation from the cocktail list or a sweet-and-tart-fruit drinking vinegar mixed with soda water, beverages are a must. The restaurant boasts floor-to-ceiling windows, revealing vibrant Asian pop art–lined tables and white paper scrolls hanging from the ceiling over the open kitchen. **COME HERE FOR UNPREDICTABLE ASIAN-AMERICAN FARE.** *$$; AE, DIS, MC, V; no checks; dinner Mon–Sat; full bar; no reservations; www.pingpdx.com; street parking; map:K5.* &

Plainfield's Mayur / ★★★

852 SW 21ST AVE, PORTLAND HEIGHTS; 503/223-2995

Richard and Rehka Plainfield pioneered the Indian cuisine scene in Portland way back in 1977. Family members still tend the kitchen and oversee service in the restored 1901 Victorian home that houses Plainfield's and a pilates studio. Two small dining rooms set out linens and silver—although close inspection reveals the wrinkles and tarnish of an empire in decline. Yet the kitchen remains sharp. India's cultural and geographical diversity, stretching from the Himalayas in the north to the tropical south, provides inspiration for familiar pappadams and curries and for exotics such as duck in almond sauce with cheese-stuffed apricots, and vegetables braised in cardamom-nut sauce. Regulars rave about *bhel* salad, an Indian street food of fried lentils, spinach, potatoes, and tomatoes in a tamarind dressing. Plainfield's has assembled a credible wine list, and Richard will happily discuss the merits of a pinot or gewürztraminer with saag paneer. **COME HERE FOR FRIED LENTIL BALLS IN GINGER-CORIANDER-YOGURT SAUCE.** *$$; AE, DIS, MC, V; checks OK; dinner every day; full bar; reservations recommended; www.plainfields.com; self parking; map:HH7.* &

Podnah's Pit BBQ / ★★☆

1469 NE PRESCOTT ST, ALBERTA; 503/281-3700
More than a few times during Podnah's 2006 rookie season, its brisket, pork ribs, and chicken were so popular, the restaurant would occasionally close in the afternoon because it had run out of meat. This is no surprise to patrons of this tiny outpost for Texas-style barbecue in Northeast Portland; they are well acquainted with its seriously good, slow-cooked meats. As with any Texas barbecue, brisket is center stage; Podnah's is smoked slowly for up to 12 hours, resulting in tender and juicy beef that's unmatched in the city. The pork shoulder is smoked 2 hours longer, tossed with North Carolina–inspired vinegar-based red barbecue sauce, and served with potato salad, collard greens, homemade corn bread, or creamy coleslaw. The pork and lamb spareribs also have no rival citywide, and the slightly spicy red chili could vie for the blue ribbon at the Austin state fair. Podnah's also serves lunch, and more than a few downtown jobbers make the deep trek here during their noon hour. No meal is complete at Podnah's without a slice of pecan pie with a glob of whipping cream. **COME HERE FOR THE BRISKET.** *$$; MC, V; checks OK; lunch, dinner Tues–Sun; beer and wine; reservations recommended for 6 or more; www.podnahspit.com; street parking; map:FF6.* &

Pok Pok and Whiskey Soda Lounge / ★★★

3226 SE DIVISION ST, RICHMOND; 503/232-1387
Pok Pok forged a humble start in November 2005 when Andy Ricker, a former sous chef at Portland's legendary Zefiro, opened a food cart on Division Street and started selling lemongrass-stuffed game hens. Within a year, Pok Pok debuted a dining room next door called the Whiskey Soda Lounge. By 2007 Ricker's Thai restaurant added another floor and was named Restaurant of the Year by the *Oregonian*. At Pok Pok, you'll find dishes such as unforgettable spicy papaya salad with tamarind and dried shrimp, truly addicting fish-sauce chicken wings, and those great game hens, now the restaurant's signature item. Such creations as Kaeng Som Thaleh, a sour tamarind-spiked seafood curry, and Yam Samun Phrai, a ginger-heavy herb salad with betel leaf and ground pork, have made many Portland diners forget that any other Asian restaurants exist. Pok Pok also serves a pared-down lunch menu; despite its popularity, the tiny food cart that started it all still cranks out to-go orders for diners not willing to wait to get seated in the popular dining room. **COME HERE FOR IKE'S VIETNAMESE FISH SAUCE WINGS.** *$$; AE, MC, V; no checks; lunch Mon–Fri, dinner Mon–Sat; full bar; reservations recommended for 5 or more; www.pokpokpdx.com; street parking; map:HH5.* &

Por Qué No? / ★

3524 N MISSISSIPPI AVE, MISSISSIPPI; 503/467-4149
4635 SE HAWTHORNE BLVD, HAWTHORNE; 503/954-3138
A gourmet taqueria that honors the best from Baja to Oaxaca, with a few gringo Portland interpretations thrown in for fun. Based on the highest-quality ingredients, the fist-sized tacos are an elevated art form here. Take

the shredded Carlton Farms pork *tinga* with smoky pasilla chile sauce or the cornmeal-crusted snapper—everything is fresh and served on billowy house-made tortillas. The daily specials board is worth the deviation; the tamales, enchiladas, and stuffed chiles rellenos are far above the norm. Homemade *aguas frescas* such as in-season watermelon or hibiscus flower are bursting with flavor. Available sans alcohol, they can also be doctored into tequila-infused cocktails. Along with the excellent margaritas, sangria, and beers, they add to Por Qué No?'s terrific happy hour. The Mississippi neighborhood location is tiny, while the newer Hawthorne location has much more legroom. **COME HERE FOR FUNKY ATMOSPHERE AND AUTHENTIC MEXICAN FOOD.** *$; AE, MC, V; no checks; lunch, dinner every day, brunch Sun; margaritas, beer, and wine; no reservations; www.porquenotacos.com; street parking; map:FF6; map:HH4.* &

Portland City Grill / ★★⯪

111 SW 5TH AVE (UNICO US BANK TOWER, 30TH FLOOR), DOWNTOWN; 503/450-0030
Portland City Grill, an überhyped penthouse restaurant in the clouds, has a lodgelike interior with sweeping vistas of downtown and the Cascades. The dinner menu is bona fide corporate America, however, promising prime steaks, lobster, pork, veal, and lamb chops—and few surprises. The kitchen does spice things up with Asian and Hawaiian twists, but the results are miso, shiitake, and ponzu glazes instead of original dishes. The gorgeous steaks are luckily outstanding, and they really are cooked to your preference. If you love rare meat, the crew here listens, delivering a New York strip that is red and fleshy in the middle and pink throughout. The full sushi menu, incongruous though it may be, is a highlight. Daily happy hour specials (all night on Sundays) provide the incredible view for a fraction of the price. **COME HERE FOR THE VIEW.** *$$–$$$; AE, DIS, MC, V; no checks; lunch Mon–Fri, dinner every day; full bar; reservations recommended; www.portlandcitygrill.com; self parking; map:J4.* &

Queen of Sheba / ★

2413 NE MARTIN LUTHER KING JR BLVD, NORTHEAST; 503/287-6302
Portland isn't home to many Ethiopian eateries, but this African enclave on MLK does proper justice to a great cuisine defined by a colorful array of highly aromatic and savory dishes served atop *injera* bread. Such creations as lentil with okra; a tangy paste of chickpeas, mushrooms, and beef; or the unique Yedero Wet, a citrusy chicken leg that reeks beautifully of cardamom, turmeric, and chiles, topped with a hard-boiled egg, are all wonderful. Cocktails are as creative and perfumed as the fare, and few beverages are more refreshing than Queen of Sheba's ginger juice or spicy Ethiopian ice tea. With as many meatless dishes here as at most vegetarian restaurants, Queen of Sheba accommodates any diet. **COME HERE IF YOUR GROUP IS LARGE.** *$; MC, V; no checks; lunch Thurs–Sat, dinner every day; full bar; reservations recommended for 6 or more; www.queenofsheba.biz; street parking; map:GG6.* &

Red Star Tavern & Roast House / ★★⯪

503 SW ALDER ST (HOTEL MONACO), DOWNTOWN; 503/222-0005
Chef Tom Dunklin has all the tools: a brick oven and smoker, a huge wood-burning grill, and a rotisserie. With big windows on one of downtown Portland's busiest corners and a back-hallway link to the revamped Hotel Monaco (see review in the Lodgings chapter), he's also got a can't-miss clientele. The result is some of Portland's finest Northwest regional cuisine. You might start with Nootka Sound oysters or halibut ceviche, or a Kobe beef tartare with young arugula and Parmesan, studded with a quail egg. The prime beef fillet is served with a blue cheese glaze, beer-battered onion rings, and house-made Worcestershire. The whole roasted California striped bass is presented with pearl onions, asparagus, and horseradish broth. **COME HERE FOR FINELY CRAFTED REGIONAL AMERICAN COOKING.** *$$–$$$; AE, DC, DIS, JCB, MC, V; checks OK; breakfast, lunch, dinner every day, brunch Sat–Sun; full bar; reservations recommended; www.redstartavern.com; street parking; map:I4.* &

The RingSide / ★★
RingSide East / ★★

2165 W BURNSIDE ST, NORTHWEST; 503/223-1513
14021 NE GLISAN ST, GLENDOVEER; 503/255-0750
Some surveys rank the RingSide as one of the top 10 independent steak houses in the country, but nobody needed to tell Portlanders that. For more than six decades, this restaurant has staked out the territory here, and the only real question for most fans is, which cut: the New York, filet mignon, or prime rib? The steaks appear at the table in black cast-iron platters, preceded by the sound of sizzling. Against the designer starches of newer steak houses, the RingSide holds to the standards and doesn't charge extra. Starring on the side are plump, light, slightly salty onion rings (made with Walla Walla sweets) that single-handedly made the place famous. For those with an aversion to beef, there is well-reputed fried chicken and a great seafood Caesar. The dignified, black-jacketed, and bow-tied waiters are eminently professional, and the wine list is over 530 bottles deep—ideal if you're looking for something red to go with beef. Come before 5:45pm or after 9pm for a supper menu that offers soup or salad and a steak entrée for just $25. Lunch is served at the Glendoveer location only. **COME HERE FOR THE STEAKS.** *$$; AE, DC, DIS, MC, V; no checks; lunch Mon–Fri (RingSide East), dinner every day; full bar; reservations recommended; www.ringsidesteakhouse.com; valet parking; map:HH7; map:HH1.* &

Ristorante Fratelli / ★★⯪

1230 NW HOYT ST, PEARL DISTRICT; 503/241-8800

In the restaurant-saturated Pearl District, this Italian gem embraces the artsy spirit of First Thursday all month long with kitchen artistry worthy of the district's many galleries. A narrow entrance leads to the rear of a long dining room of rustic minimalist mood, its two-story ceilings and spare wooden tables and chairs illuminated by late-afternoon sun or candles. With a traditional four-course approach, Fratelli offers such starters as chicken-liver-mousse crostini with pickled vegetables or prosciutto-mozzarella roulade. Entrées include fish specials that rotate weekly, pork scaloppine with spinach carbonara, or seared Draper Valley Farms chicken with creamy polenta and mushroom jus. Fratelli is committed to working with local farmers, so there are plenty of vegetarian options. Service here is smart, the mostly Italian wine list impressive, and the location unbeatable. **COME HERE FOR FARM-FRESH ITALIAN COOKING.** *$$; AE, MC, V; no checks; dinner every day; full bar; reservations recommended; www.fratellicucina.com; street parking; map:M2.* &

Russell Street Bar-B-Que / ★★☆

325 NE RUSSELL ST, NORTHEAST; 503/528-8224

As the name suggests, Russell Street does barbecue, but that's not all. Southern and Cajun specialties share the bill with slow-cooked meat, starting with such appetizers as creamy Louisiana-style pan-fried shrimp, billowy sweet-corn hush puppies, pimiento cheese with toast, and twice-cooked french fries done right: in peanut oil. Russell Street also features a blue-plate special every day that may include Southern classics like blackened catfish, excellent fried chicken, or smoked-beef-and-pork meat loaf. Despite these delicious diversions, barbecue still takes center stage: pulled pork, baby-back ribs, smoked turkey, and beef brisket. There are also grilled shrimp skewers and salmon, and diners may choose any three of the barbecue selections and two sides on the Meatapalooza platter. Russell Street also smokes tofu, which pairs especially well with sides like mac-and-cheese, sweet baked beans, candied yams, and slowly braised Southern greens. Don't leave without trying the gooey brownie sundae with homemade caramel and fudge sauces, or the fried chocolate pies. **COME HERE FOR THE HUSH PUPPIES.** *$; AE, MC, V; no checks; lunch, dinner every day; beer and wine; no reservations; www.russellstreetbbq. com; street parking; map:GG6.*

Ruth's Chris Steak House / ★★★☆

309 SW 3RD AVE, DOWNTOWN; 503/221-4518

In spite of the variety of good things to eat in Portland, sometimes the occasion calls for a great steak, and Ruth's Chris doesn't let steak eaters down. Presented on bone-white china in an atmosphere of high-cholesterol reverence, the steaks—notably the steer-size porterhouse for two—are rich and beefy, with an alluring tenderness. For diners who just had a porterhouse lunch, there are sizable (and sizably priced) lobsters, and there's the chance to pick one that's alive—which is more than you can do with the steak. You'll be paying extra for everything else, but it's still worth exploring the various potato dishes and the creamed spinach. The space is massive, and so are the portions; you'll still be eating your dinner at tomorrow's lunch. **COME HERE FOR BIG BEEF.** *$$$; AE, DC, MC, V; no checks; dinner every day; full bar; reservations recommended; www.ruthschris.com; valet and self parking; map:I5.*

Saburo's / ★★

1667 SE BYBEE BLVD, WESTMORELAND; 503/236-4237
It might not be law enforcement, but rules are rules. When ex-policewoman Joyce Nakajima established the many precepts that would govern this eclectic Japanese spot, run by her and husband, Saburo, she posted them on the walls. For years, Portlanders have tolerated Saburo's with a loyalty that sometimes borders on idolatry. It's a patronage that defies gruff service—if you can even get anyone's attention—and a no-reservations policy that keeps fans loitering on the sidewalk, awaiting a seat at the sushi bar or a table in this shoebox-size space. Prices for exceptionally fresh sushi are rock bottom, and portions are larger than at more expensive sushi bars. Teriyaki and tempura dinners, curry udon soup, gyoza, and pork *katsudon* round out the inclusive menu. Saburo's tough reputation is part of its charm—and, by the way, it isn't foolproof. Servers do smile, and orders eventually find their way to diners. **COME HERE FOR NO-FRILLS, VALUE SUSHI.** *$–$$; AE, MC, V; no checks; dinner every day; beer and wine; no reservations; www.saburos.com; self parking; map:JJ5.* ⅋

Saint Honoré Boulangerie / ★★

2335 NW THURMAN ST, NORTHWEST; 503/445-4342
315 1ST ST, LAKE OSWEGO; 503/445-1379
With an exquisite selection of authentic French breads and pastries, Saint Honoré is a delightful, traditional *boulangerie* that might have been transplanted directly from France. Founder Dominique Geulin named it for the patron saint of bakers. A lovely and refreshing spot for lunch or a light dinner, it serves wonderful Caffè Umbria coffee and offers a mouthwatering selection of pastries, traditional salads such as lyonnaise and niçoise, quiches, soups, and sandwiches. Everything is carefully crafted; breads and pastries are made from Northwest-grown wheat, ground in-house by a "slow stone method," and baked in a clay oven made from bricks quarried in the Rhône Valley. Going to Saint Honoré is like taking a mini vacation. **COME HERE FOR A SLICE OF FRANCE.** *$; AE, MC, V; no checks; breakfast, lunch, dinner every day; beer and wine; no reservations; www.sainthonorebakery.com; street parking; map:GG7; map:NN6.* ⅋

Salty's on the Columbia / ★★

3839 NE MARINE DR, BROUGHTON BEACH; 503/288-4444
From floor-to-ceiling windows that look upon the Columbia River near Portland International Airport, you can see planes taking off and landing, boats traveling up- and downriver—and all you really care about is that big Dungeness crab on your plate. Come any evening for a feast of shellfish—mussels, clams, oysters, or shrimp—plus award-winning seafood chowder and regional wines to pair. Australian rock lobster tail and blackened salmon are popular entrées. Sunday brunch offers 50-odd temptations: crab and fresh oysters, of course, but also carved roasts, omelets to order, eggs Benedict, and a plethora of desserts. The atmosphere is conducive to dressing up, the staff is friendly, and the service excellent. And if you're not a seafood lover, you'll

also find hearty steaks on the menu. Legendary jazz drummer Mel Brown and his trio play here on Friday and Saturday nights. **COME HERE FOR BRUNCH AND A HUGE VARIETY OF SEAFOOD.** *$$; AE, DIS, MC, V; no checks; lunch, dinner every day, brunch Sunday; full bar; reservations recommended; www. saltys.com; street parking; map:DD4.*

Saucebox / ★★★

214 SW BROADWAY, DOWNTOWN; 503/241-3393

The hottest spot in Portland for pan-Asian cuisine also has a chic atmosphere, divinely inspired cocktails, and a DJ-driven, late-night scene. Bruce Carey's Saucebox might also be at the top of any private-party list. Like the ever-changing list of cocktails, the starters are exquisite creations. Try the Vietnamese Salad Rolls filled with rice noodles, napa cabbage, tofu, mango, and basil, served with delectable dipping sauces, or a grapefruit-avocado salad with coconut, shallots, mint, lime, and chopped peanuts. The *New York Times* called Saucebox's Javanese Salmon "as good as salmon gets." Other entrées include grilled Hawaiian swordfish accented with tamarind, lime, cilantro, and mint, and roasted Peking duck with lemongrass and fresh egg noodles. While you may be distracted by the stylish crowd (often including visiting celebs), the exquisite art and plate presentation warrant second glances. Saucebox takes on a clubbier feel after 10pm, when DJs turn up the juice and only a bar menu is offered. **COME HERE FOR CELEBRITY SIGHTINGS.** *$$; AE, MC, V; local checks only; dinner Tues–Sat; full bar; reservations recommended; www.saucebox.com; street parking; map:J4.* &

Savoy Tavern & Bistro / ★★

2500 SE CLINTON ST, CLINTON; 503/808-9999

Savoy is the polar opposite of La Cruda, the healthy Mexican restaurant that occupied this corner restaurant space until closing in 2005 to make way for Portland's first and only Wisconsin-inspired eatery. The heartland gets a proper nod here, starting with the Wisconsin tavern board—a rotating variety of cheese, cured meat, and crackers from America's little Sweden. Deep-fried cheese curds in pale-ale batter, perfect pork meatballs with pine nuts, and smoked trout with horseradish cream are edible representations of the Badger State on large oval platters. Mains include a memorable mac-and-cheese with white Wisconsin cheddar and a pinch of cayenne, grilled steak with curry butter, plus a fantastic burger served with the best fries in the Clinton 'hood. In August 2007, Savoy's owners expanded into the adjacent restaurant space, debuting Broder (see review in this chapter), a Scandinavian cafe with enormous open-faced sandwiches (smorgas) on dark bread. Don't leave without trying the roasted-potato salad, and save room for dessert. The panna cotta–like Swedish cream is as cute as it's delicious. **COME HERE FOR THE FRIED CHEESE CURDS.** *$$; MC, V; no checks; dinner every day; full bar; reservations recommended for 6 or more; street parking; map:II5.* &

Screen Door / ★★

2337 E BURNSIDE ST, SOUTHEAST; 503/542-0880

Screen Door serves Southern-inspired dinners six nights a week, but this destination eatery is all about its brunch. After a night that ends at last call, there's nothing better than Screen Door's signature fried chicken and waffles, lacquered with syrup and washed down with bottomless cups of Stumptown coffee. Get here early, or put your name on the waitlist—often 30 minutes or more for a table. Brunch items also include a cornmeal-crusted fried-oyster Benedict with crispy bacon and hollandaise, and a gloriously gooey Alabama pimiento cheese scramble. The fried chicken also appears on the dinner menu, as do hush puppies, Carolina pulled pork, crispy fried catfish, garlicky shrimp and grits, fried green tomatoes with rémoulade, and a ground-sirloin burger with cheddar and fries. Though portions are huge, dessert is a must. You'll find no equal to Screen Door's sweet pecan pie; real New Orleans bread pudding and luscious banana pudding with caramelized bananas are worth their weight in calories. **COME HERE FOR FRIED CHICKEN AND WAFFLES DURING THE LEGENDARY WEEKEND BRUNCH.** *$$; AE, DIS, MC, V; no checks; dinner Tues–Sun, brunch Sat–Sun; full bar; reservations recommended for 6 or more; www.screendoorrestaurant.com; street parking; map:HH5.* ♿

Sel Gris / ★★★

1852 SE HAWTHORNE BLVD, HAWTHORNE; 503/517-7770

Clearly, chef Daniel Mondok is a modern art devotee, as his plates at Sel Gris could be mistaken for edible masterpieces. As much meticulous attention to detail is paid to his sophisticated, yet cramped space as to the food coming out of the stagelike open kitchen. Both his crisp veal sweetbreads and his foie gras complemented by seasonal accoutrements have garnered a reputation of their own, though sometimes preparations are over-reaching. Lamb "Two Ways" positions a grilled rack next to braised shoulder for a sampling of textures and flavor. Peking duck breast studded with Szechuan peppercorns and salt-and-pepper calamari nod to Asian influences on the mostly French menu. Save room for dessert—the grand finale is quite possibly the main event, with swirls of sauce, spun sugar nests, and chocolate curls adorning the decadent tarte tatin and chèvre cheesecake. **COME HERE FOR THE ARTFUL PRESENTATIONS.** *$$$; AE, MC, V; local checks only; dinner Mon–Sat; full bar; reservations recommended; www.selgrisrestaurant.com; street parking; map:HH5.* ♿

Serratto / ★★☆

2112 NW KEARNEY ST, NORTHWEST; 503/221-1195

Serratto has a refined atmosphere. Outdoor sidewalk seating is great in summer, and anytime you're in the dining room you'll get excellent service, cuisine, and ambience under golden lighting. You might have to wait for a table, but the staff will deflect any impatience by handing you a glass of prosecco or something to nibble on. The Italian- and Mediterranean-inspired menu features fresh ingredients from the Northwest. Serratto's pan-seared sea scallops on white wine–braised fennel risotto, with chives and basil oil, are to die for.

For a more substantial appetite, the grilled Strawberry Mountain skirt steak with blue cheese butter, sautéed spinach, and *pommes frites* won't disappoint. The lunch menu includes sandwiches, pizzas, and great salads. The wine list covers a wide variety of bottles from Italy, France, Spain, and the Northwest. **COME HERE FOR THE WIDE-OPEN DESIGN AND SUBLIME CUISINE.** *$$–$$$; AE, DC, DIS, MC, V; no checks; lunch, dinner every day; full bar; reservations recommended; www.serratto.com; street parking; map:GG7.* &

Siam Society / ★★

2703 NE ALBERTA ST, ALBERTA; 503/922-3675

Had a James Beard–led French naval fleet conquered Thailand, Siam Society's fusion fare is what the cuisine might look like in Bangkok today. This Thai eatery employs old-world techniques in modern Asian cooking with top-notch Pacific Northwest ingredients. A case in point is the savory pulled-pork spring rolls using swine braised in Riesling and Oregon hazelnuts, alongside sweet potato fries tossed in white truffle oil. The warm vermicelli noodle salad is made better with sautéed oyster mushrooms, pork, and green beans beside roasted peanuts and fresh cilantro, while the vibrant and savory coconut- and lemongrass-spiked tom yum soup is as good as any in town. Mains like the spicy roasted pepper pizza or char-grilled steak veer slightly from the Thai-themed roster, but a slurp-worthy rendition of *phad kee mao*, or Thai "drunken" noodles, with basil, steak, and grilled peppers, brings it back home. Siam Society is housed in a brilliantly restored turn-of-the-20th-century building and provides a romantic and sophisticated atmosphere that few eateries in Portland match. **COME HERE FOR THE BEST OF EAST AND WEST.** *$$; MC, V; no checks; lunch Tues–Sat, dinner Tues–Sun; full bar; reservations recommended; www.siamsociety.com; street parking; map:FF5.* &

Silk / ★
Pho Van / ★

1012 NW GLISAN ST, PEARL DISTRICT; 503/248-2172
1919 SE 82ND AVE, MONTAVILLA (AND BRANCHES);
503/788-5244

These restaurants are owned by the same family but differ slightly. Silk is the slightly more upscale Pearl District destination, complete with swank, hip cocktail bar, while the Pho Van locations offer beautifully designed but still casual surrounds featuring some of the best Vietnamese food in town. At both, expect wonderfully fresh pho with the traditional accompaniments of aromatic basil leaves, crunchy sprouts, and chiles. Other specialties include "hand rolls" (*cuon*) meant for wrapping with herbs in lettuce leaves, such as *bò lá lot* (minced seasoned beef), minced shrimp and chicken wrapped around sugar cane, or grilled Vietnamese sausages with rice paper. Delightfully exotic salads include a traditional shredded banana blossom with chicken and grapefruit in a lime dressing. Pho Van's simple rice dishes and noodle bowls include a honey lemongrass chicken or grilled salmon in turmeric and are outstanding values under $10 each. Silk's fancier fare includes pork tenderloin slices caramelized in a garlic sauce and served with mushrooms in clay pot. Shaken beef chunks of filet mignon flash-seared and immediately tossed with watercress, onions, and tomatoes highlights Vietnam's French influences. **COME HERE FOR PHO.** *$$; AE (Silk), DIS (Silk), MC, V; no checks; lunch, dinner Mon–Sat (Silk), lunch, dinner every day (Pho Van); full bar (Silk), beer and wine (Pho Van); reservations recommended for 6 or more; www.phovanrestaurant.com; street parking (Silk), self parking (Pho Van); map:M2; map:HH3.*

Simpatica Dining Hall / ★★★

828 SE ASH ST, BUCKMAN; 503/235-1600

For a restaurant that's officially open only two nights a week and weekends for brunch, Simpatica has garnered quite a following since its debut in 2005. Sure, the venture also includes a sizable catering operation, but Simpatica's main event is its Friday and Saturday supper club that features four or more courses of seasonally appropriate fare and excellent charcuterie offerings. A sample spring dinner might include seared chicken livers with shaved asparagus and saba dressing, followed by potato gnocchi with arugula pesto and Parmigiano-Reggiano, and crisp fried Oregon razor clams with smoky house-cured bacon and braised lettuces; finished with panna cotta topped with dried cherry sauce and apple mint. There are only 50 spaces, so you'll need to book ahead. Simpatica's stellar weekend brunch is worth the wait for heaping plates of biscuits and gravy, eggs Benedict, sandwiches, and poached eggs with seasonal hash. **COME HERE FOR FLAVORS CRAFTED WITH GREAT ATTENTION TO DETAIL.** *$$–$$$; MC, V; checks OK; dinner Fri–Sat, brunch Sat–Sun; full bar; dinner reservations required, brunch reservations recommended for 8 or more; www.simpaticacatering.com; street parking; map:HH5.* &

Sinju / ★★⯪

1022 NW JOHNSON ST, PEARL DISTRICT; 503/223-6535
7339 SW BRIDGEPORT RD, TIGARD; 503/352-3815

Seated in breezy tatami rooms and sequestered alcoves; surrounded by orchids, potted bamboo, and trickling fountains, it's easy to forget the food at pretty Sinju. But the well-chosen trappings are not mere gloss masking mediocre meals; they amplify the ultrarefined Japanese food. Sinju prepares a full range of traditional items, from teriyaki to *maki*, but the restaurant keeps its list brief and focused, offering a few favorites and introducing diners to unfamiliar rolls. The colorful Rainbow Roll exceeds the norm here, and the veggie-packed California roll, with glistening salmon, albacore, and shrimp, exhibits Sinju's exquisite presentation. **COME HERE FOR DYNAMITE SASHIMI AND GORGEOUS PRESENTATION.** *$$; AE, DC, DIS, MC, V; no checks; lunch Mon–Fri, dinner every day; full bar; reservations recommended; www.sinju restaurant.com; street parking; map:N2; map:LL9.* &

AROUND THE WORLD WITH PORTLAND'S FOOD CARTS

They might look humble from the outside, but Portland's more than 190 food carts are a local secret for gourmet dining on a dime. From grouped "pods" on surface parking lots to wandering taco trucks, the carts offer such diverse foods as traditional dishes from Thailand, Sicilian street snacks, artisan pizzas, and off-beat treats like fried pies, Korean tacos, and Quebec's famous dish, *poutine*. Food carts are so well loved by locals that a "cart culture" has emerged around them—with interactive Web sites and on-the-ground guides. A cart meal can range from a simple, freshly made tamale for $1.25 to an elaborate, whole Italian grilled chicken dinner, including panzanella bread salad and a side dish, for $12. However, most carts are a bargain. Expect lunch in the $5 range.

The grouping on SW 9th and 10th avenues and Alder Street is one of the biggest. **NONG'S KHAO MAN GAI** serves a highly flavorful chicken-and-rice dish from Thailand, while neighboring **SAVOR SOUP HOUSE** offers a rotation of wonderful homemade seasonal soups. **AYBLA GRILL** is well known for their garlicky gyros, while other carts such as **NUMBER 1 BENTO**, **SAMURAI**, and **SAWASDEE** make tasty traditional Korean, Japanese, and Thai dishes, in that order. **ZIBA'S PITAS** is a standout: tender strudel dough, stuffed with savory meats or cheese and vegetables, is baked until golden; it's the specialty at Portland's only Bosnian cart. For dessert or an early morning wake-up, do hit **SPELLA CAFFE** for flawless roman-style espressos and cappuccinos. In the summer, Spella's *affogato* (gelato with a shot), is a refreshing treat.

Another downtown pod is at SW 5th Avenue and Stark Street. **TABOR** is famous for its "Snitzelwich" sandwiches and other Eastern European delights, such as chicken paprikash and spaetzle dumplings. **GIVE PIZZA A CHANCE** has terrific artisan pizzas with toppings like goat cheeese with carmelized onions, and even the sodas are made in-house. **LA JAROCHITA** is a little maroon-colored taco truck wedged between a row of other taco trucks. Stop here for large crispy tender Huaraches—thick griddled corn tortillas topped with meats, salsas, and

Southpark Seafood Grill and Wine Bar / ★★

901 SW SALMON ST, DOWNTOWN; 503/326-1300

Sometimes sexy starters outshine the main course. This is true at Southpark, the downtown Mediterranean- and North African–leaning restaurant known for its spirited wine list and European-style sidewalk seating. Here, there are some two dozen "small bites" that include exquisite warm dates stuffed with Marcona almonds and cloaked in ribbons of serrano ham. Piping-hot shrimps redolent of garlic are baked with creamy feta, tomatoes, and oregano. One vegetables—or one of the big-as-a-brick burritos. If it's a burger you're craving, try a third-pound charred Angus in many different forms at the **BRUNCH BOX**; they serve gourmet burgers at drive-through prices.

Across the river, a late-night cart scene (usually Wed–Sat from dusk until 2 or 3am) has emerged on the corner of SE 12th Avenue and Hawthorne Boulevard. This is where you'll find **POTATO CHAMPION**'s crispy fries served with all manner of sauces, from pesto mayonnaise to spicy rémoulade and *poutine*. From **BUBBA BERNIE**'s Cajun jambalaya to **WHIFFIES** Southern-style fried pies, this is an "only in Portland" festive scene of neighborhood residents and twenty-somethings looking for late-night nibbles. If you're lucky, there'll also be a DJ dance party or a bonfire to add to the vibe.

Other must-try carts are scattered about. If you are on Sellwood's "Antique Row" during the day, check out **GARDEN STATE** (SE 13th Ave and Lexington St) for flawless *arancini* (stuffed and fried saffron-flavored risotto balls), chickpea fries, and other Sicilian street snacks. And downriver, **FLAVOURSPOT** on N Mississippi Avenue and Fremont Street makes wonderful waffles with a twist—they are turned into waffle "burritos," complete with such fillings as thin-sliced Black Forest ham and melting smoked gouda or Nutella, whipped cream, and raspberry jam. Breakfast doesn't get any more decadent. The **GRILLED CHEESE GRILL** on NE Alberta Street and 11th Avenue comes complete with a big yellow school bus for a dining room. Try one of its many gourmet grilled sandwiches, or go all out with the Fat Elvis, a grilled PB&J with banana and bacon. There's even a roaming Korean taco truck—**KOIFUSION**, serving spicy chicken with kimchi slaw or bulgogi stuffed inside homemade corn tortillas.

For food cart updates, check www.foodcartsportland.com and consult a food cart map at www.speakeasy.org/~aeschright/maps. If you're interested in a Portland food cart tour, contact **TRAVEL PORTLAND** (www.travelportland.com; 503/275-8355 or 877/678-5263).

—Lizzy Caston

oft-featured soup is a seriously seductive purée of almonds and saffron. And steamed mussels with chunks of fennel sausage, blanketed by a fragrant anisette marinara, are some of the most unusual bivalves in town. For entrées, stick to seafood off the fresh list, as well as chicken tagine and that perennial favorite, butternut squash ravioli with sage and hazelnuts. Whatever your choice, you'll find an appropriate wine on Southpark's thorough list. **COME HERE FOR UNFORGETTABLE SMALL BITES AND THE FESTIVE WINE BAR.** *$$; AE, DC, DIS, MC, V; no checks; lunch, dinner every day; full bar; reservations recommended; www.southparkseafood.com; street parking; map:H2.* &

Swagat / ★

2074 NW LOVEJOY ST, NORTHWEST; 503/227-4300
4325 SW 109TH AVE, BEAVERTON; 503/626-3000
1340 NW ORENCO STATION PKWY, HILLSBORO; 503/844-3838

Swagat means "welcome" in the Hindi language, and that spirit rules at all three locations. Cozy, dark, and moody, Swagat in Portland feels more British colonial than post-independence India. The casual Beaverton location, in a small, renovated house and garage, is anything but stylish. But the cuisine is sensual, perfumed, and complexly spiced. Traditional curries, pakoras, biryanis, and vegetarian choices cover north and south India. The handmade rava masala dosas are served warm and are a delicious accompaniment for curry. The inclusive menu brings no surprises to those familiar with Indian cuisine and never ventures beyond expected dimensions. The lunch buffet is a good bargain at all three locations. **COME HERE FOR RAVA MASALA DOSA.** *$$; AE, DIS, MC, V, no checks; lunch, dinner every day; full bar (Portland), beer and wine (Beaverton, Hillsboro); no reservations; www.swagat.com; self parking; map:GG7; map:II9.* &

Sweet Basil Thai / ★★☆

3135 NE BROADWAY, IRVINGTON; 503/281-8337
1639 NW GLISAN ST, NORTHWEST; 503/473-8758

Part of the fun at Sweet Basil comes with looking before touching: behold the artfully arranged platters that whet your appetite just before you dig in. Pad thai, served on colorful dishes with chopsticks jutting out at jaunty angles and a spray of bean sprouts on the side, tastes as good as it looks, spiked with mild to wild heat per your request. Pumpkin tempura, another unique spin on a classic, comes with a lovely spicy plum sauce. Weather permitting, be sure to take advantage of the gorgeous deck at the Broadway location. **COME HERE FOR THAI FOOD THAT'S WELL ABOVE AVERAGE.** *$-$$; AE, DIS, MC, V; no checks; lunch Mon–Fri, dinner every day; full bar; reservations recommended; www.sweetbasilor.com; street parking; map:GG5; map:GG7.* &

Syun Izakaya / ★★

209 NE LINCOLN ST, HILLSBORO; 503/640-3131

This Japanese *izakaya* (pub) and sushi bar is a welcome addition to Hillsboro's quaint downtown area. Expats, techies from nearby Intel, locals, and Japanophiles from all over flock to this cozy basement space to nosh on impeccable sushi, slurp noodles, and pass around endless small plates of Japanese "tapas." This is food meant to go with sake; the 35-plus bottle selection is one of the most extensive in the region. While well-known items such as crispy tempura, billowy meat-stuffed gyoza, and yakitori (grilled skewers) are fantastic, it's the specials that are truly special at Syun. Octopus in kimchi sauce with cucumber, *okonomiyaki* (griddled vegetable cakes), and *kinoko bata* (mushrooms sautéed in butter) highlight the kitchen's talents. Flawless top-grade sushi and sashimi. **COME HERE FOR OCTOPUS IN KIMCHI SAUCE.**

$$; AE, DC, DIS, MC, V; no checks; lunch Mon–Fri, dinner every day; full bar; reservations recommended; www.syunizakaya.com; self parking. &

Tabla / ★★

200 NE 28TH AVE, LAURELHURST; 503/238-3777

A pioneer of pan-Mediterranean cuisine in Portland, Tabla has a rotating seasonal menu that nods to areas as diverse as Italy, Spain, and the Middle East. Chef Adam Berger continues this commitment but has recently shifted its focus from small plates to a more standard approach of appetizers, soups and salads, and entrée-size portions. Starters might include tuna ricotta fritters with arugula pesto and preserved lemons, or a wild mushroom soup with nettle flan and asparagus. Tabla still makes its well-loved house-made pastas; pork cheek ravioli with saffron, currants, and pistachios and the thick-cut chitara noodles with prosciutto, ramps, and lemon show the kitchen's talents. The wine list contains some wonderful Italian and Spanish finds. A neighborhood favorite, the pastas alone are worth driving across town for. **COME HERE FOR THE RAVIOLI.** *$$; AE, DC, DIS, MC, V; no checks; dinner Tues–Sun; full bar; reservations recommended; www.tabla-restaurant.com; self parking; map:HH5.* &

Tanuki / ★★

413 NW 21ST AVE, NORTHWEST; 503/241-7667

Tanuki opened in 2008 in a tiny space with four tables and a row of counter spots, none available for children. Owner Janis Martin explains that her spot is not just a restaurant, but a Japanese-style drinking establishment. It's true that on a visit to Tanuki, one is likely to consume some interesting and unusual foods—sea urchin roe, lotus root, chilled monkfish foie gras—but in Japan, the purpose of an *izakaya* such as this is to consume alcohol and food together. The menu is inexpensive and ever changing, utilizing fresh Northwest ingredients to carry out traditional Japanese and Korean preparations. Order *omakase*-style, and the chef will choose your menu based on the price that you set, or pick from the *kushiyaki* menu of flavorful skewers to pair with sake. **COME HERE FOR SAKE PAIRED WITH ASIAN SMALL PLATES.** *$$; MC, V (only one credit card per table); no checks; dinner Tues–Sat; beer and wine; no reservations; www.tanukipdx.com; street parking; map:GG7.* &

Ten 01 / ★★★

1001 NW COUCH ST, PEARL DISTRICT; 503/226-3463

Quietly sophisticated and romantic, Ten 01 has emerged as one of Portland's premier upscale destinations for modern Northwest cuisine, starting with the intimate bar. Some say Ten 01 has the best cocktails in town; it offers well-balanced, original drinks, using nothing but the highest-quality ingredients; the Pistache, for example, combines top-shelf Jamaican rum with lime and a house-made pistachio cordial. The food menu shows that in the right hands simple ingredients combine to create delicate and clean flavors; the *hamachi crudo* with sea beans and black olives pops on the tongue, while clams with smoky *speck* in a light pesto broth satisfy without being too heavy. The rotating menu is based on the seasons; summer might feature a fresh-from-the-fields corn chowder, while spring brings the first of the season's favas in a creamy risotto. Desserts here are wonderful and worthy of their own rotating menu. Olive oil beignets with dark chocolate sauce are as light as air, while an orange buttermilk crème brûlée is a new twist on a classic. **COME HERE FOR AN OUTSTANDING WINE LIST FEATURING RARE NORTHWEST FINDS.** *$$$; AE, DIS, MC, V; checks OK; lunch Mon–Sat, dinner every day; full bar; reservations recommended; www.ten-o1.com; valet and street parking; map:K3.* &

Thai Peacock Restaurant / ★★

219 SW NINTH AVE, DOWNTOWN; 503/228-2310
Thai Peacock is located on the corner of a quiet NYC West Village–type block just south of Burnside Street and Powell's. Large windows and sidewalk tables with bright orange umbrellas add to its distinctly Thai atmosphere. The sticky rice is true to its character and goes extremely well with the exquisite crispy, juicy Thai barbecued chicken, a dish large enough for two people. The Thai salad roll is nicely presented, served with peanut sauce, and does not disappoint. The tom yum soup is delicious, served with shrimp and fresh galangal, but the tom kah is even better. The som tum, or green papaya salad, is tossed with peanuts, tomatoes, and chiles, lending it spice and crunch. The pad thai outshines most old standby versions. For a final burst of flavor, the mango sticky rice dessert is sublime, especially with a scoop of coconut ice cream on the side. **COME HERE FOR THE THAI BARBECUE CHICKEN.** *$–$$; AE, DC, DIS, MC, V; checks OK; lunch, dinner every day; beer and wine; no reservations; www.thaipeacockrestaurant.com; street parking; map:J3.* &

Three Degrees Waterfront Bar & Grill / ★★

1510 SW HARBOR WY (RIVERPLACE HOTEL), SOUTH WATERFRONT; 503/228-3233
The elegant dining room in the RiverPlace Hotel (see review in the lodgings chapter) overlooks the Willamette River just a stone's throw from downtown. The cuisine here is creative Pacific Northwest. The dinner menu features choices from land and sea. From the land you might order grilled New York strip or pork porterhouse steaks, as well as roasted duck breast with sweet onion purée, fingerling potatoes, and glazed carrots with dried cherry relish. From the sea you may order grilled white prawns, salmon, or seared rare ahi with ginger-lime vinaigrette, pickled shitake, and bok choy served with edamame. You could also opt for a burger, a BLT or a "good ole grilled cheese." Desserts are creative, as are breakfasts: consider the Elvis French toast, with peanut butter, bananas, and bacon. **COME HERE FOR THE RIVER VIEWS.** *$$$; AE, DC, DIS, JCB, MC, V; no checks; breakfast, lunch, dinner every day; full bar; reservations recommended; www.threedegreesrestaurant.com; valet and self parking; map:D5.* &

3 Doors Down Café / ★★⯨

1429 SE 37TH AVE, HAWTHORNE; 503/236-6886
3 Doors Down has found a rhythm in its seasonally experimental fare. The likes of prosciutto-wrapped halibut served over Oregon morels, spring asparagus, and fingerling potatoes has become a house standard that attracts a loyal and appreciative following. It doesn't stop there. Take the Bibb lettuce salad with chives and smoked bacon in a light but creamy roasted garlic dressing, or thin bruschetta with sweet cherry tomatoes and fresh basil. Entrées rotate constantly but are always prepared beautifully and inventively. An informed staff will tell you what you want to know about the huge wine list, the food, and its preparation. Save room for dessert, perhaps banana cream pie or double-chocolate mousse cake. **COME HERE FOR COZY NEIGHBOR-HOOD DINING.** *$$; AE, MC, V; checks OK; dinner Tues–Sun; beer and wine; reservations recommended for 6 or more; www.3doorsdowncafe.com; street parking; map:HH5.*

Three Square Grill / ★★

6320 SW CAPITOL HWY, HILLSDALE; 503/244-4467
At this storefront in the Hillsdale Shopping Center, textured yellow walls set a sunny scene for a casual American bistro that's also an upscale cafe. Barbara and David Barber's Southern-focused menu also roams from coast to coast, ensuring abundant creativity. Local contemporary art, table linens, affable servers, and seasonal produce have drawn attention beyond the neighborhood. Just about everything is prepared from scratch: Carolina barbecued pork, pickles, fruit preserves, and buns. House-smoked salmon hash and fresh-squeezed orange juice shine at breakfast. Dinner can be light and casual (black bean chili and spinach salad) or more substantial (soy- and maple-glazed salmon over sticky rice with shrimp-cucumber salad). There are plenty of Southern sides—hush puppies, collard greens, fried okra—plus old-fashioned rice pudding to keep the regulars satisfied. **COME HERE FOR NEIGH-BORHOOD AMBIENCE.** *$$; MC, V; checks OK; dinner Tues–Sun, brunch Sat–Sun; beer and wine; reservations recommended; www.threesquare.com; street parking; map:JJ7.* &

Tin Shed Garden Cafe / ★★⯨

1438 NE ALBERTA ST, ALBERTA; 503/288-6966
Located in Portland's hip Alberta neighborhood, the Tin Shed serves fare that's creative, a little irreverent, and always satisfying. Most breakfast creations are old standbys with a gourmet twist for added flavor. A heavenly biscuit is paired with the brie, apple, and sausage scramble. Both the salmon burger and veggie burger are great lunch choices: the Tin Shed feeds vegetarians and carnivores alike. Seating in the outdoor courtyard beside the herb garden can't be beat on nice days; indoor seating with yummy soups and sandwiches is especially cozy on rainy days. At predictably busy times (weekend breakfasts and dinners), you'll probably have to wait for a seat, but it's worth it. The Tin Shed serves microbrews as well as inspired cocktail

concoctions. **COME HERE FOR HOUSE-MADE BISCUITS.** *$; DC, MC, V; no checks; breakfast, lunch, dinner every day; full bar; no reservations; www.tinshedgardencafe.com; street parking; map:FF5.* &

Toast / ★★★

5222 SE 52ND AVE, SOUTHEAST; 503/774-1020

Every neighborhood should have a restaurant like Toast. It's a modest place serving breakfast, lunch, and dinner in a straightforward, no-nonsense style. Chef-owner Donald Kotler eschews industrial food service ingredients for local produce, farm eggs, and meats from a number of area ranches. The green salad is a verdant, lightly dressed tangle of pea shoots, mâche, and sweet peas. The house-made gnocchi is sautéed with wild mushrooms from the Oregon Coast. In the mornings, try the breakfast sliders—scrambled eggs and sausage with a lemony hollandaise. Chef Kotler makes a variety of baked goods including a Pullman sandwich loaf, brioche buns, a berry-studded coffee cake, and crunchy, roasted granola. Toast brings fresh and local cuisine down to earth. **COME HERE TO GET THE BEST OF OREGON'S BOUNTY WITHOUT THE USUAL COST.** *$$; AE, DIS, MC, V; no checks; dinner Wed–Fri, brunch Wed–Sun; full bar; no reservations; www.toastpdx.com; self parking; map:JJ3.* &

Tokyo Restaurant / ★☆

2331 NW 185TH ST, HILLSBORO; 503/690-1891

Restaurants in Japan often specialize in one cuisine—noodles, sushi, one-pot stews—but on these shores, they mainly fall into the category of *nihon-ryori*: literally, assorted Japanese cuisines. In Hillsboro's Tanasbourne shopping center, this little blond-wood, shoji-screened *nihon-ryori* packs them in, especially at noon. Diners choose from a wide menu of Japanese classics. With no room for a sushi bar, the kitchen still prepares it to order: *unagi* (eel) and *ebi* (shrimp) *nigiri* sushi, salmon-skin and tempura rolls. Typical lunch plates—salmon teriyaki, ginger pork, chicken *katsu* served over rice—are generous and moderately priced, as are bento boxes and soba or udon bowls. Tokyo also serves ramen bowls as a full meal. Easily overlooked, this place merits attention. **COME HERE FOR YAKISOBA NOODLES.** *$$; AE, DIS, MC, V; no checks; lunch, dinner every day; beer and wine; no reservations; self parking.* &

Toro Bravo / ★★★

120 NE RUSSELL ST, NORTHEAST; 503/281-4464

Spain lives happily in Northeast Portland right next door to the Wonder Ballroom. Chef John Gorham prepares shareable small plates that prove why he's among the best chefs in Portland. Whether it's radicchio salad with Manchego vinaigrette, fried fresh anchovies with fennel and lemon, spicy *patatas bravas*, or the most flawless salt-cod fritters this side of Bilbao, Gorham crafts complex masterpieces out of a handful of ingredients, reinterpreting simple dishes into edible memories. From saffron-scented paella with spicy house-made sausage to Andalusian-style braised lamb with apricots and coriander to *jamón serrano*–wrapped chicken with *pisto Manchego*—a ratatouille of eggplant and tomato from La Mancha—Toro Bravo gives a shout-out to the Spanish map while staying true to superb Oregon ingredients. Be sure to save room for dessert, as Gorham's moist olive-oil cake with seasonal fruit compote is like an adult version of the humble Twinkie. Meanwhile, chocolate-covered almonds and molten chocolate cake both shine. **COME HERE FOR THE BEST TAPAS IN PORTLAND.** *$$–$$$; AE, DIS, MC, V; no checks; dinner every day; full bar; reservations for 7 or more; www.torobravopdx.com; street parking; map:GG6.* &

Trébol / ★★

4835 N ALBINA AVE, NORTH PORTLAND; 503/517-9347
This Mexican-influenced eatery keeps a low profile in North Portland, but its tasty fare is of a Pacific Northwest bent that reflects chef-owner Kenny Hill's six-plus years as sous chef at farm-to-table stalwart Higgins (see review in this chapter). Trébol's rotating menu boasts its share of winners, starting with excellent lingcod ceviche; manila clams spiked with serrano chiles and house-made chorizo; and a salad of mixed smoked jicama, fennel, and citrus with olive oil–poached albacore. The taco sampler is always a sure bet, with such fillings as wild boar, fish, and slow-braised beef. The enchiladas spell comfort food, vegetarian-style, with the likes of wilted chard, wild mushrooms, zucchini, and *queso fresco*—all lathered in a slightly spicy red chile sauce and topped with an over-easy egg. Hill braises his meat beautifully, but seafood options also impress. Save room for dessert: the caramel flan is brushed gently by hints of tequila, and nothing quite finishes off a symphony of authentic Mexican flavors like Trébol's sopaipillas drizzled with sweet organic honey. **COME HERE FOR THE CEVICHE.** *$$; AE, DIS, MC, V; no checks; dinner every day, brunch Sun; full bar; reservations recommended; www.trebolpdx.com; street parking; map:FF6.* &

Tucci / ★★

220 A AVE, LAKE OSWEGO; 503/697-3383
An elegant addition to downtown Lake Oswego's evolving pedestrian scene, Tucci is a chic trattoria whose copper-backed open kitchen gives it a rustic allure. A wood-burning stove produces sophisticated pizzas, like rock shrimp with Sicilian pesto, fontina, and caramelized onions; but chef Roberto Alarçon is at his best with elaborate entrées. Halibut is pan roasted and served with a basil vinaigrette. Filet mignon comes with wild mushrooms in a port reduction. Don't miss the antipasti: black mussels steamed in pinot grigio with oregano; sweet white anchovies with a roasted tomato sauce. The lunch menu has a nice selection of salads and panini; if the sun is shining, enjoy them on a pleasant outdoor patio. (Inside, tables are tightly clustered beneath a balloonlike chandelier.) A stunning menu of desserts and coffee drinks makes this an outstanding after-dinner stop as well. **COME HERE FOR WARM CHOCOLATE POLENTA CAKE ON THE PATIO.** *$$–$$$; AE, MC, V; no checks; dinner every day; full bar; reservations recommended; www.tucci.biz; street parking; map:MM6.* &

23 Hoyt / ★★★★

529 NW 23RD AVE, NORTHWEST; 503/445-7400

23 Hoyt is Bruce Carey's answer to a neighborhood bistro atmosphere with uncompromising flavors. Chef Aaron Barnett has done a beautiful job filling the shoes of Portland culinary legend Chris Israel, who originally opened 23 Hoyt. Coming from restaurants such as Vancouver BC's Lumiere and San Francisco's Myth, Barnett does a fantastic job striking a Portland balance of sophistication and casual comfort with such dishes as local halibut with sweet pea purée, asparagus, new potatoes, morels, and citrus vinaigrette. Happy hour at 23 Hoyt is one of the best with truffle-oiled popcorn, and the burgers are dependably among the best if you're not quite ready for grilled hanger steak with blue cheese–herb butter and fries. Desserts such as local rhubarb crisp with vanilla ice cream or five-layer chocolate cake with caramel swirl ice cream are always inspired. **COME HERE FOR SOPHISTICATION AND COMFORT.** *$$$; AE, DIS, MC, V; no checks; dinner Tues–Sat; full bar; reservations recommended; www.23hoyt.com; street parking; map:GG7.* &

Typhoon! / ★★

2310 NW EVERETT ST, NORTHWEST (AND BRANCHES); 503/243-7557
410 SW BROADWAY (HOTEL LUCIA), DOWNTOWN; 503/224-8385

Typhoon! is expanding into a small empire. The original Northwest Portland space has been joined by a larger and stylish downtown location in the elegant Hotel Lucia (see review in the Lodgings chapter), and by two new cafes in suburban Portland, two more in the Seattle area, and another in Bend. Notice by national food magazines can do that, and besides, Bo Kline is a deeply gifted chef. From openers of *miang kum* (spinach leaves filled with any of a half-dozen ingredients) and mouth-filling soups, the menu moves into a kaleidoscope of flavors. You can't go wrong with curries (especially the green curry), inspired seafood dishes (such as seasonally available rainbow trout wrapped in lettuce with peanuts and vegetables), and multiple pungent Thai noodle dishes. Try the King's Noodles to know why it's good to be the king. Scored into a checkerboard grid, a fried fish blossoms into a pinecone, and dishes with names like Fish on Fire and Superwild Shrimp turn out to be named exactly right. Typhoon! also offers 145 different teas—including one that goes for $35 a pot. A half block away, Bo's Restobar is a new cocktail-oriented venture that serves "food you'll never get in a bar and drinks you'll never get in a restaurant." If you're in the suburbs, consider visiting the Gresham (543 NW 12th St; 503/669-9995) or Beaverton (12600 SW Crescent St; 503/644-8010) restaurants. **COME HERE FOR THE NORTHWEST'S FINEST GOURMET THAI CUISINE.** *$$–$$$; AE, DC, MC, V; no checks; breakfast every day (Downtown), lunch Mon–Sat (Northwest), every day (Downtown), dinner every day; full bar; reservations recommended; www.typhoonrestaurants.com; street parking; map:GG7; map:J4.*

Urban Farmer / ★★★

525 SW MORRISON ST, DOWNTOWN; 503/222-4900

Sitting like a nest above eight floors of the Nines hotel (see review in the Lodgings chapter), and beneath a sky-lighted atrium, Urban Farmer is a little bit country, a little bit future bending, and quite chic. With a menu that emphasizes local, sustainably raised beef (giving you the choice between corn- or grass-fed), local poultry, a splendid array of locally produced cheeses, and house-made charcuterie, you'll start to understand the "Farmer" in the name. As well, Northwest Dungeness crab finds its way into tender cakes on a bed of apple slaw, and halibut is prepared with morels, local ramps, and spring herbs. Order up some heavenly potato purée, or handmade spaetzle with English peas and pearl onions on the side. Whether it's a hazelnut napoleon with dulce de leche mousse or a butterscotch sundae for dessert, the presentation is exceptional. With a deep collection of fine wines, house-made cocktails, including a daily punch, and experimentally chic environs, you'll have no question: the place is quite "Urban." **COME HERE FOR A GOOD STEAK UNDER THE STARS AND OUT OF THE RAIN.** *$$–$$$; AE, DC, MC, V; no checks; breakfast Mon–Fri, lunch, dinner every day, brunch Sat–Sun; reservations recommended; www.urbanfarmerrestaurant.com; valet parking; map:I3.* &

Veritable Quandary / ★★★

1220 SW 1ST AVE, DOWNTOWN; 503/227-7342

Peppered with such local ingredients as Cattail Creek lamb, VQ's market-driven menu is a swell representation of what the Northwest can bring to the table. That wasn't always the case at this cozy, 38-year-old mainstay, once a mere tavern. But since chef Annie Cuggino entered the kitchen, she's been replacing the pub fare with the likes of bacon-wrapped dates stuffed with Marcona almonds, and fork-tender duck confit with a contrasting crispy skin. When available, the must-have appetizer is Gruyère–and–Granny Smith beignets, weightless fritters oozing melted cheese and sweet-tart apple pieces. For the main course, try one of the fresh fish specials, such as red snapper and sweet crab paired with piquant kumquat slices. The narrow, high-ceilinged dining rooms are quieter, but true intimacy can be found on the meticulously landscaped patio during fair weather. VQ's approach to wine is as original as the food. It boasts an extensive by-the-glass list of about 40 wines and a smart cellar with plenty of bottles in the $20–$30 range. **COME HERE FOR OSSO BUCO AND WINE IN A CLASSIC TAVERN SETTING.** *$$–$$$; AE, DC, DIS, MC, V; no checks; lunch Mon–Fri, dinner every day, brunch Sat–Sun; full bar; reservations recommended; www.vqpdx.com; street parking; map:F4.*

Vindalho / ★★

2038 SE CLINTON ST, CLINTON; 503/467-4550

Channeling Indian spice route influences and history, Vindalho shows Portlanders are ready for vibrant spices and intensely layered regional specialties, from the tender naan breads of Muslim-inhabited north India to the creamy coconut curries and seafoods of the southern Goan seaboard. Premier

Portland restaurateur David Machado (see Lauro Kitchen review in this chapter) understands that Oregon's seasonal bounty only enhances this fusion: his local summer melon *chaat* salad is sprinkled with chiles and mint, and his beet salad is enhanced with a cardamom yogurt dressing. Starters such as crispy, light samosas are heavenly pillows best enjoyed with one of the house-made chutneys. A real tandoori oven creates perfectly "barbecued" meats and seafoods, and there are plenty of satisfying vegetarian options, such as *matar paneer*, made with fresh cheese, shiitake mushrooms, and English peas in a tomato sauce. **COME HERE FOR CONTEMPORARY INDIAN FOOD.** *$$; AE, DC, DIS, MC, V; no checks; dinner Tues–Sat; full bar; reservations recommended; www.vindalho.com; street parking; map:II5.* &

Vista Spring Café / ★

2440 SW VISTA AVE, PORTLAND HEIGHTS; 503/222-2811
This hidden neighborhood institution is a hyperlocal hangout for families living in the curving West Hills. Yet the friendly service and comfortable atmosphere make everyone feel welcome with offerings of gourmet burgers, an old-fashioned meat loaf sandwich, and other upscale comfort food. Pizzas are really where Vista Spring shines, though; besides the standards, look for the Thai spiced chicken or the rich smoked-oyster version with bacon bits, onions, and cheddar cheese. Entrée-sized salads are fresh and inspired; the hearty classic Cobb or a Southwest chicken served with crunchy tortilla chips are big enough to stand as a meal on their own. Parents can enjoy one of the well-chosen wines or beers while the little ones nosh on their own menu of spaghetti, grilled cheese, or PB&J sandwiches, with nothing over $4. **COME HERE WITH THE KIDS.** *$; DIS, MC, V; no checks; lunch, dinner every day; beer and wine; no reservations; www.vistaspringcafe.com; street parking; map:HH7.* &

Wildwood / ★★★

1221 NW 21ST AVE, NORTHWEST; 503/248-9663
Wildwood's reputation as one of Portland's top restaurants is completely deserved. Founded by James Beard Award–winning chef Cory Schreiber, it never gets lazy in its quest to create explosively flavorful food. Driven by the seasons, the menu changes weekly but is always solidly Northwest, taking full advantage of local bounty. Wildwood lets quality ingredients do most of the work, building dishes around beautiful shell beans, Chioggia beets, abalone, crayfish, and leg of lamb. Wild mushroom ragout and tender asparagus make a wedge of grilled polenta sing, while red wine–braised lamb is complemented perfectly by a cardoon gratin. Beef would never be served with mashed potatoes and steamed broccoli here; instead, it's slow roasted, then plated with a wild nettle–potato galette and green garlic aioli. Classic cocktails, a pleasing wine list, and intense fruit desserts, such as a mascarpone cream tart with a lemon crumb crust and plump summer blueberries, further the delicious dining experience. Watching your dining budget? Check out the bar's Chalkboard Menu, a smart selection of uncomplicated pizzas, house-made naan, salads, and a burger. **COME HERE FOR EXCELLENT, MARKET-DRIVEN COOKING.** *$$–$$$;*

MC, V; no checks; lunch Mon–Sat, dinner every day; full bar; reservations recommended; www.wildwoodrestaurant.com; street parking; map:GG7. &

Wong's King Seafood Restaurant / ★★★

8733 SE DIVISION ST, SOUTHEAST; 503/788-8883

The crown jewel of Asian restaurants that adorn what's now called Portland's new Chinatown, Wong's King Seafood is bar none the best Chinese eatery in Portland and quite possibly in the Pacific Northwest. This gigantic banquet hall is even on par with the great dim sum dining halls of San Francisco and Vancouver BC. With an unsightly strip-mall address on 87th and Division, it hardly looks like a jewel; but after you've made the trek to deep Southeast Portland and endured a predictable 40-minute wait for a table, you'll quickly understand the hype. Such dim sum treats as shrimp or pork dumplings, pork buns, and pot stickers are deeply layered with delicious and contrasting flavors. Wong's has great congee, simply gorgeous sauce-lacquered pork barbecued ribs, and roasted duck with a skin that cracks like a crème brûlée. Tanks brimming with crab and lobster feed the masses, and any seafood treat at Wong's is going to be good. Weekday lunch specials barely break a 10-spot with tea and tip. **COME HERE FOR DIM SUM.** *$; AE, DIS, MC, V; no checks; lunch, dinner every day; full bar; reservations recommended; www.wongsking. com; self parking; map:II2.* &

Wu's Open Kitchen / ★

17773 SW LOWER BOONES FERRY RD, LAKE OSWEGO (AND BRANCHES); 503/636-8899

The flames leaping high behind the windows in the back of the restaurant are firing the large woks in the kitchen, and you can watch the cooks deftly preparing dishes while you wait for dinner. Chef Jimmy Wu's extended family helps run this place, serving a variety of spicy and not-so-spicy dishes from all over China. But the cooks reckon on the American palate; the hot dishes won't wilt too many tastebuds. Seafood is fresh, vegetables are crisp, sauces are light, and service is speedy and attentive. Prepare for a wait on weekends, though. Wu's is well known by locals—not only in Lake Oswego, but also at its two Tigard outposts. **COME HERE FOR THE MU-SHU PORK.** *$–$$; AE, DIS, MC, V; no checks; lunch, dinner every day; full bar; reservations recommended; www.wusopenkitchens.com; self parking; map:LL7.* &

Ya Hala / ★★☆

8005 SE STARK ST, MONTAVILLA; 503/256-4484

Ya hala means "welcome" in Lebanese, and owners Mirna and John Attar have welcomed lovers of exceptional Lebanese and Middle Eastern food for years as the Montavilla neighborhood revitalizes around them. The *moghrabieh*, a specialty, is served in two separate bowls: one with braised beef shank in a rich brothy sauce, the other with braised chicken accompanied by a dish of flavorful Lebanese-type (large grain) couscous and a big spoonful of thick whole-milk yogurt. The Veggie Mezza is a great deal at $9.95 and comes with hummus, baba ghanoush, falafel, grape leaves, *arnabeet* (cauliflower), and pita. Every dish is cooked to order and well worth the wait. The artichoke hearts are braised, sautéed, and stuffed with either ground beef and onions; pine nuts; or a delicious mélange of carrots, potatoes, squash, and onions. Choose a garlic cream sauce or the vegan version: the chef's fresh tomato-onion sauce. On a Friday, be prepared to wait: in spite of an expanded dining room, waiting to be seated can take up to 20 minutes. **COME HERE FOR EXCEPTIONAL MIDDLE EASTERN FOOD.** *$–$$; AE, DIS, MC, V; lunch, dinner every day; full bar; no reservations; www.yahalarestaurant.com; street parking; map:HH3.* &

Yakuza / ★

5411 NE 30TH AVE, CONCORDIA; 503/450-0893
Japanese inspired, locally focused. This beautifully designed space with modern wood panels, a fun bar, and one of the best patios in Portland adds an element of big-city modern sophistication to Portland's NE 30th. The Asian cocktails complement the food; refreshing choices include the Pink Pepper, with pink pepper Boodles gin, pink peppercorns, grapefruit, bitters, and lime; or the Wasabi, made with local Aviation gin, fresh grated wasabi root, lime, and cucumber. The sushi is of excellent quality and features such creative rolls as the Kampachi: apple, avocado, and sweet peppers with seared Hawaiian amberjack on top. Signature dishes are a nod to classic American and European dining with an Asian twist—the American Kobe beef burger comes dressed with chèvre and a heaping side of shoestring fries, while the shredded, filo-wrapped sea scallop tempura with nori and a spicy, creamy sauce is decadent. An excellent sake list (try a flight of three for $20) rounds out the offerings. **COME HERE FOR THE SAKE.** *$–$$; AE, DC, DIS, MC, V; checks OK; lunch, dinner Wed–Sun; full bar; no reservations; www.yakuzalounge. com; street parking; map:EE5.*

Yoko's Japanese Restaurant and Sushi Bar / ★

2878 SE GLADSTONE ST, SOUTHEAST; 503/736-9228
More Okinawa surfer hangout than Tokyo temple, this low-key destination is a popular local spot for Japanese dinner standards and some surprisingly serious sushi. With only 7 tables and 10 counter seats, waits can be long and service haphazard, but those who stick it out will be rewarded with glistening fresh cuts of fish and creative rolls that pack a punch for the dollar. Traditionalists will be happy with buttery fresh *hamachi* (yellowtail) and melt-in-your-mouth *unagi* (eel), while others will delight in Yoko's signature Taka's Tuna—a scoop of spicy tuna and sliced avocado on a fried rice cake, eaten like an open-faced sandwich. The Smokin' roll is a crispy treat: snapper, salmon, and shrimp with broccoli and onion in a flash-fried tempura batter. Hawaiian marinated tuna poke, bright seaweed salads, and excellent udon and ramen noodle soups round out the offerings. Large portions and low prices pack 'em in; terrific food in fun surroundings keeps 'em coming back. **COME HERE FOR THE YELLOWTAIL.** *$–$$; MC, V; no checks; dinner every day; beer and wine; no reservations; street parking; map:NN4.* &

Zell's: An American Café / ★★

1300 SE MORRISON ST, BUCKMAN; 503/239-0196

Many restaurants pride themselves on their seasonally changing menus, but how many alter their breakfasts? At Zell's, the market-driven menu can produce the likes of pumpkin pancakes in the fall or daring German pancakes with rhubarb in the summer, all of which are skillfully executed. Simply put, Zell's serves one of the best breakfasts in this time zone. The brilliance of the hot-from-the-griddle specialties (try the ginger pancakes when available) is matched by a medley of inspired egg dishes. The trademark chorizo-and-peppers omelet is joined by a worthy brie-and-tomato effort. If you prefer scrambles, you won't be disappointed by the gently mixed eggs with smoked salmon, Gruyère, and green onions. Lunchtime brings an entirely different set of delights, including meat loaf, vegetarian sandwiches, and a chicken cordon bleu sandwich, but it's hard to compete with the expert breakfasts. The catch, especially on weekend mornings, is a long wait for a table, but owners Mike and Nancy offer coffee while you wait and a chance to chat with the locals. **COME HERE FOR A BRILLIANT BREAKFAST.** *$; AE, DIS, MC, V; no checks; breakfast, lunch every day; full bar; no reservations; street parking; map:HH5.*

Vancouver, Washington

Beaches Restaurant & Bar / ★★☆

1919 SE COLUMBIA RIVER DR; 360/699-1592

Think Seaside during spring break: youth culture, hibiscus-splattered shirts, footprints in the sand, high-decibel acoustics. With its undisturbed views high above the Columbia River, the beach here is more wishful than actual, but who cares? Not the Match-dot-commers flocking to happy hour, parents chaperoning kids who like wood-fired pepperoni pizza and a s'mores-style dessert, or the business crowd lunching affordably. Preparation styles follow beach cooking, mostly by grill or wood-fired oven; the menu has an expanded, trendier steak-house style minus pretension. The crowds sometimes overwhelm the kitchen and create slowdowns, but there's pretty good Caesar salad, famous Jack Daniels flaming wings, rib-eye steaks, garlic mashers, cilantro-lime chicken pasta, Black Angus burgers, and wood oven–baked fruit crisps. **COME HERE FOR A CONVIVIAL CROWD.** *$$; AE, DIS, MC, V; checks OK; lunch, dinner every day; full bar; no reservations; www.beaches restaurantandbar.com; self parking; map:CC6.* ㊐

Cactus Ya Ya / ★

15704 SE MILL PLAIN BLVD; 360/944-9292

This popular Southwestern-style cafe bundles enthusiasm and contagious camaraderie into a colorful package of great service, tons of fun, and surprisingly good food. Margaritas flow like the Rio Grande, their energy well suited to beer-battered halibut tacos with shredded cabbage, pico de gallo, and cilantro sauce. Enchiladas, fajitas, and jalapeño poppers join playful hybrids such as a turkey Reuben, and seasonings may speak up when least expected. That velvety white sauce over the mashed potatoes? Potent garlic cream sauce. The burrito tastes Asian? It's the peanut sauce. Many menu choices can be ordered in large or small sizes or à la carte. Owners Jim and Cheryl Rettig wished for a place to hang out with friends, and that's what they have. **COME HERE FOR FUN AND FULL FLAVORS.** *$; AE, MC, V; no checks; lunch, dinner every day; full bar; no reservations; self parking; map:CC1.* &

Fa Fa Gourmet / ★★☆

11712 NE 4TH PLAIN BLVD; 360/260-1378
Fa fa means "prosper," a wish extended by the hospitable Chia family to its customers. In a metro region where outstanding Thai and Vietnamese restaurants outnumber Chinese, it's worth crossing the Columbia and traveling to the northeast nether reaches of Vancouver to find this gourmet oasis of Hunan and Szechuan cuisine in Evergreen Plaza. Search the extensive menu beyond the familiar choices (cashew chicken, spring rolls) to discover unique house specials. Consider crisply fried prawns with honey-roasted walnuts in deep-red chile sauce or the yin-yang of beef in a spicy ginger sauce paired with chicken and snow peas in light wine sauce. The partially open kitchen oversees a Northwest-flavored dining room where regional wines and beers highlight the drink menu. **COME HERE FOR THE BEST CHINESE FOOD IN VANCOUVER.** *$–$$; MC, V; no checks; lunch, dinner every day; full bar; reservations recommended; self parking; map:AA3.* &

Hudson's Bar & Grill / ★★★

7805 NE GREENWOOD DR (HEATHMAN LODGE); 360/816-6100
The dramatic log-and-stone Heathman Lodge (see review in the Lodgings chapter), Hudson's hotel home, looks like it should be nestled in old-growth firs rather than standing beside a busy state highway opposite Vancouver Mall. Inside, grand WPA-style hand-hewn wood beams; a massive slate fireplace; a real dugout canoe; plush, rugged comfort; and an open, red-tiled kitchen set the scene. In the morning, there's a custardy bread-pudding French toast with candied pears and a delicious smoked-salmon Benedict. Midday, lobster ricotta ravioli and fresh Dungeness crab cakes with saffron aioli are superb. In the evening, oven-roasted venison with sweet-potato hash or a succulent steak from Washington-raised beef illustrate respect for local seasonal ingredients. Delectable house-made pastries change daily. **COME HERE FOR GOURMET LODGE-STYLE DINING.** *$$$; AE, DC, DIS, JCB, MC, V; local checks only; breakfast, lunch, dinner every day; full bar; reservations recommended; www.hudsonsbarandgrill.com; self parking; map:AA3.* &

Little Italy's Trattoria / ★

901 WASHINGTON ST; 360/737-2363
204 SE PARK PLAZA DR (CASCADE PARK); 360/883-1325

In the spirit of grandma's kitchen, this friendly trattoria still dares to dress in red-and-white-checked tablecloths while other Italian restaurants have changed to linens. These family-owned restaurants trace their roots to Naples, where chicken cacciatore and clams in white wine with linguine are recipes passed through the generations. Without fuss or pretension, but dosed with Italian pride, the kitchen sticks close to tradition: cheese-filled ravioli baked with marinara sauce and topped with mozzarella, ziti with crumbled meatballs and tomato sauce, pizza, and soft garlic bread. **COME HERE FOR PASTA AND RED SAUCE.** *$$; AE, DIS, MC, V; no checks; lunch, dinner every day; beer and wine; reservations recommended; www.littleitalystrattoria.com; self parking; map:CC6; map:CC2.* &

The Restaurant at the Historic Reserve / ★

1101 OFFICERS ROW, FORT VANCOUVER
NATIONAL HISTORIC PARK; 360/906-1101

General Ulysses S. Grant, hero of the Civil War and later a U.S. president, made this building his home and command headquarters when he was stationed at Fort Vancouver in the 1850s. Today you can almost feel his ghost brushing past your shoulder in the handsome dining room, on the wraparound deck, or in the elegant Commander's Whisky and Wine Bar. There's nothing particularly remarkable about the menu—wild salmon risotto with English peas and cherry jus or a grilled flatiron steak atop garlic and herb french fries and sautéed mushrooms—but it's solid, well-prepared cuisine. And besides, you came to create a mood. Not surprisingly, this is a very popular location for weddings and rehearsal dinners. **COME HERE FOR A LITTLE HISTORIC FLAIR.** *$$; AE, MC, V; no checks; lunch Sun–Fri, dinner every day; full bar; reservations recommended; www.restauranthr.com; self parking; map:CC6.*

Roots / ★★

19215 SE 34TH ST, CAMAS; 360/260-3001

Chef Brad Root had quite a pedigree when he opened his restaurant in 2007 just over the city line from Vancouver. He had cut his culinary teeth at three of Portland's finest restaurants: the Heathman, Higgins, and Wildwood. His handsome new eatery, at the edge of an edgy strip mall, looks very Frank Lloyd Wright–inspired. The menu has a similar sense of creativity and a local flair with such dishes as Puget Sound mussels with garlic, shallots, white wine, and olive oil, and grilled salmon salad with artichokes, olives, fennel, and herb vinaigrette. Root uses Pacific Northwest produce and purveyors almost exclusively, underscoring the theme that as a chef he has, indeed, gone back to his roots. **COME HERE FOR CREATIVE CUISINE IN THE PROVINCES.** *$$$; AE, DIS, MC, V; no checks; lunch Mon–Sat, dinner every day, brunch Sun; full bar; reservations recommended; www.rootsrestaurantandbar.com; self parking.*

Oregon Wine Country

Dundee Bistro / ★★

100 SW 7TH ST (AT HWY 99), DUNDEE; 503/554-1650

Wine pioneers Nancy and Dick Ponzi, founders of acclaimed Ponzi Vineyards, have never acknowledged limitations. After founding the vineyard, these industry leaders and advocates not only founded Oregon's first microbrewery (BridgePort, in 1984), but they also built the Dundee Bistro and Ponzi Wine Bar complex as a wine-and-food destination on the road through the heart of Yamhill County's lush vineyards. Cuisine focuses on Willamette Valley organic and sustainable agricultural products—and, of course, an indepth wine list with ample by-the-glass selections. Chef-partner Jason Stoller Smith's ambitious menu includes a starter of Dungeness crab *arancini* with grapefruit fennel salad, Fuji apples, and a creamy pink peppercorn vinaigrette, and SuDan Farms shaved leg of lamb on ciabatta with roasted red peppers, Montchevré cheese, and tapenade as a main. The bistro also serves wood-fired pizzas. For dessert, the dark chocolate soufflé cake with housemade vanilla ice cream is dreamy, and it's especially delightful served in the courtyard on a warm day. **COME HERE FOR HALIBUT FISH-AND-CHIPS AND PONZI WINE.** *$$$; AE, MC, V; local checks only; lunch, dinner every day; full bar; reservations recommended; www.dundeebistro.com; self parking.* &

The Joel Palmer House / ★★★☆

600 FERRY ST, DAYTON; 503/864-2995

Jack and Heidi Czarnecki came to Oregon in 1996 to find the perfect marriage of wild mushrooms and civilized pinot noir, and they've created a restaurant that no gastronome will want to miss. A mushroom scholar, hunter, author, and award-winning chef, Jack forages in secret locations for hat-shaped morels and trumpet-shaped black chanterelles, two of the many wild mushrooms that define his menu. The restaurant occupies the lovingly restored, white-pillared Palmer House, built in 1857 by pioneer Joel Palmer. European service—each server does every job—governs two small, elegant dining rooms. Not all dishes are built around wild mushrooms and wine, but Heidi's three-mushroom tart has graced the menu from the start and is a regionwide, glamorous classic. The Czarneckis call their cooking "freestyle," as it applies global inspiration to local ingredients, organic when possible. Heidi fashions desserts such as apricotwalnut bread pudding and rhubarb napoleon. A fantastic wine list offers pairings specially selected for the menu. It's a 45-minute drive from Portland, but worth it—and then some. **COME HERE FOR A FEAST OF WILD MUSHROOMS.** *$$$; AE, DIS, MC, V; checks OK; dinner Tues–Sat; full bar; reservations recommended; www.joelpalmerhouse.com; self parking.* &

Kame / ★★

211 NE 3RD ST, MCMINNVILLE; 503/434-4326

Authentic Japanese sushi has found its way to the Oregon Wine Country. Get started with gyoza before you move onto a delicious rice bowl or an entrée such as breaded chicken breast over shredded cabbage served with miso soup, pickled cabbage salad, or noodles. The sushi rolls here are also quite good and fresh. Try the Kame roll with snow crab, spicy tuna, lettuce, and roe, or choose from a variety of sashimis. **COME HERE FOR SUSHI IN WINE COUNTRY.** *$$; MC, V; checks OK; dinner Tues–Sun; beer and wine; no reservations; self parking.* &

Nick's Italian Café / ★★★

521 NE 3RD ST, MCMINNVILLE; 503/434-4471
Back in 1977, long before Yamhill County became Oregon's wine mecca, charismatic Nick Peirano was entertaining local winemakers with fine, prix-fixe Italian dinners. The historic downtown McMinnville storefront still has the feel of a North Beach haunt, reflecting Nick's childhood in San Francisco's Italian community. A wine list deep in Oregon vintages complements house-made pasta offerings that, like the menu, change regularly. And now following closely in her father's footsteps, chef Carmen Peirano and her husband, chef Eric Ferguson, are carrying on the tradition with a classic five-course nightly menu in addition to wonderfully crisp wood-fired pizzas. Desserts change daily and might include chocolate brandy hazelnut tortes or a berry crisp. Each dish is prepared with a wine pairing in mind, and Nick still can be found in the dining room, where he chats with loyal customers, celebrates a successful harvest with winemakers, and ensures that each guest enjoys a gracious visit. **COME HERE FOR GRANDMA'S PESTO MINESTRONE SOUP.** *$$$; AE, MC, V; checks OK; dinner Tues–Sun; beer and wine; reservations recommended; www.nicksitaliancafe.com; street parking.* &

Red Hills Provincial Dining / ★★☆

276 HWY 99W, DUNDEE; 503/538-8224
Nestled snugly in a 1912 Craftsman-style house, Red Hills deserves a healthy share of the attention directed to its higher-profile wine-country neighbors. For years it has quietly and unpretentiously lavished exceptional service, reliable European country cuisine, and a strong, award-winning wine list upon devoted patrons. Dinner is served on the deck and in the cozy living and dining rooms, which are personalized with souvenir plates on the walls and wine bottles displayed on a high encircling shelf. Changing its menu by season, the kitchen leans to such solid preparations as oysters with a sesame-seed crust, hand-cut organic beef fillet, veal osso buco, sautéed sole with corn-arugula salsa, and wild-mushroom pasta with sherry-rum cream sauce. A perfectly accomplished salad of field greens couples toasted hazelnuts, Parmigiano-Reggiano, and balsamic vinaigrette. Desserts made in-house include white-chocolate crème brûlée, espresso-chocolate torte, ice creams, and sorbets. **COME HERE FOR GREAT FOOD WITHOUT PRETENSION.** *$$; AE, MC, V; checks OK; dinner every day; full bar; reservations recommended; self parking.* &

Tina's / ★★☆

760 HWY 99W, DUNDEE; 503/538-8880

A tiny jewel, this modest single-story home with an emerald-and-garnet palette hides culinary treasures coveted by savvy Oregonians. Tina Landfried and husband David Bergen share ownership and chef responsibilities in two elegant dining rooms, divided by a fireplace. They offer warm hospitality, excellent service, and exemplary cuisine: clean, classic French techniques with impeccably fresh local ingredients, including herbs raised in the front garden and a few fruits and vegetables grown at home. The limited menu, which adds an occasional dash of Asian inspiration, delights diners with salmon spring rolls accompanied by hazelnut dipping sauce; fresh Pacific halibut steamed with fennel, leeks, and tomatoes; braised rabbit in duck stock and white wine, finished with a fresh apricot mustard and served with garlic mashed potatoes; and buttermilk-almond cake with fresh strawberries and cream. Full-flavored, house-made sourdough baguettes use a 13-year-old wild yeast starter built from local chardonnay grapes. Don't be surprised if you share the dining room with winery owners—many of whose vintages are carried on Tina's beverage list—and workers fresh from the fields. **COME HERE FOR SEASONAL SOUPS, BAGUETTES, AND WINE.** *$$$; DIS, MC, V; checks OK; lunch Tues–Fri, dinner every day; full bar; reservations recommended; www. tinasdundee.com; self parking.* ♿

LODGINGS

LODGINGS

Lodgings by Star Rating

★★★★
The Heathman Hotel

★★★★☆
The Benson Hotel
the Nines
Timberline Lodge

★★★
The Governor Hotel
Heathman Lodge
Hotel deLuxe
Hotel Lucia
Hotel Monaco Portland
Portland's White House

★★★☆
Heron Haus Bed
and Breakfast

Hotel Modera
Hotel Vintage Plaza
The Lion and the Rose
The Paramount Hotel

★★
Aloft
Avalon Hotel & Spa
Hotel Fifty
Inn @ Northrup Station
The Resort at the
Mountain
RiverPlace Hotel

★★☆
Ace Hotel
Collins Lake Resort
Edgefield

Jupiter Hotel
The Kennedy School
The Mark Spencer Hotel

★
Bluebird Guesthouse
Blue Plum Inn
Crowne Plaza Portland–
Lake Oswego
The Georgian House
Bed and Breakfast
Hostelling International–
Portland, Hawthorne
District
Hostelling International–
Portland, Northwest
Lakeshore Inn
Park Lane Suites

Downtown/Southwest Portland

Ace Hotel / ★★☆

1022 SW STARK ST; DOWNTOWN; 503/228-2277
Opened in early 2007 after a head-to-toe renovation of a 1912 hotel listed on the National Historic Register, the Ace couples artsy minimalism with practicality in all of its 79 guest rooms. They range from top- (fourth-) floor deluxe suites with restored roll-top claw-foot tubs to less expensive rooms with shared baths, including three "band rooms" with bunks for touring musicians. Do expect flat-screen TVs, DVD players, and natural latex foam mattresses; do not expect bell service (there isn't any). Guests are invited to relax and experience the very Portland-esque lobby scene while lingering over joe from adjoining Stumptown Coffee. Pets are welcome. Clyde Common restaurant (see review in the Restaurants chapter), named for the building's previous occupant, the Clyde Hotel, is also off the lobby and is certainly one of Portland's best. *$$; AE, DIS, MC, V; no checks; amenities include record players in some rooms, flat-screen TVs, DVD players, free wi-fi, on-site restaurant; www.acehotel.com; street parking; map:J2.* &

Avalon Hotel & Spa / ★★

0455 SW HAMILTON CT, JOHNS LANDING;
503/802-5800 OR 888/556-4402

An oasis of relaxation a short hop from downtown, the Avalon overlooks the Willamette River from the Johns Landing district off Macadam Avenue (Route 43). The hotel's design has an Asian flair, with floor-to-ceiling windows and contemporary wood furnishings. Seventy-eight of the Avalon's 99 rooms, including all 18 fireplace suites, have riverview balconies. If you're headed downtown, leave your car parked here and take the complimentary town-car service to the Avalon's sister property, the Governor Hotel (see review in this chapter). The beautiful, 9,000-square-foot Spa Chakra offers traditional Asian shiatsu treatments. The adjacent Aquariva restaurant offers fine Italian-style dining and an excellent wine bar. *$$$; AE, DC, DIS, MC, V; no checks; amenities include balconies, marble bath/showers, hair dryers, ironing boards, in-room safes, minibars, cable TV, free wi-fi, iPod docks, on-site restaurant; www.avalonhotelandspa.com; valet and self parking; map:JJ6.* &

The Benson Hotel / ★★★½

309 SW BROADWAY, DOWNTOWN; 503/228-2000 OR 888/523-6766

The Benson, open since 1913, remains the grande dame of the downtown luxury hotels. Many locals who want to spend a night downtown opt for the Benson, and it's still the first choice for politicos and film stars; with 287 rooms, there's space for everyone. Guest rooms are dignified and sophisticated, with modern furnishings in conservative blacks and beiges; every sitting president beginning with Harry S. Truman has stayed in the presidential suite. The hotel takes pets with an additional fee. The London Grill caters to an old-fashioned dining crowd; the El Gaucho steak house (see review in the Restaurants chapter) is also quite formal but draws a hip, younger crowd. *$$$–$$$$; AE, CB, DC, DIS, JCB, MC, V; checks OK; amenities include honor bar, cable TV, free wi-fi, fitness center, on-site restaurant; www.bensonhotel. com; valet parking; map:J3.* &

The Governor Hotel / ★★★

614 SW 11TH AVE, DOWNTOWN; 503/224-3400 OR 800/554-3456

This classic hotel, opened in the heady days following Portland's 1905 Lewis and Clark Exposition, celebrated its 100th birthday in 2009. The decor emulates the spirit of the Northwest with a bright, contemporary, stately elegance. The 100 spacious guest rooms are decorated in earth tones and hung with early photos of Northwest Indian tribes, circa 1900; all have standard furnishings and upscale amenities. Some also have whirlpool tubs, while suites feature gas-burning fireplaces, wet bars, and balconies. A recent remodel improved access to rooms in the west wing (the 1923 Princeton Building), whose upper-floor rooms sport the best city views. Guests in this well-appointed nonsmoking hotel will be staying in the heart of downtown. For dinner, stop in at Jake's Grill (see review in the Restaurants chapter). *$$$; AE,*

DC, DIS, JCB, MC, V; no checks; amenities include 24-hour room and house-keeping service, free wi-fi, business center and fitness room, on-site restaurant; www.governorhotel.com; valet and street parking; map:I2. &

The Heathman Hotel / ★★★★

**1001 SW BROADWAY, DOWNTOWN; 503/241-4100
OR 800/551-0011**

One of Condé Nast *Traveler*'s "World's Best Places to Stay," the Heathman Hotel has revolutionized check-in by providing personal concierges for each guest—a single point of contact for anything needed, be it in advance of arrival, theater tickets, room service, or even a tour guide. Located in the city's cultural heart, the Heathman shares a breezeway with the Arlene Schnitzer Concert Hall and is a mere block from the Portland Center for the Performing Arts, Portland Art Museum, and Oregon Historical Society museum. It has an extensive art collection of its own, including 10 signed Andy Warhol lithographs. The elegant Tea Room is a favorite during the holidays, and the library, one of the only hotel-catalogued libraries in the country, features over 3,000 signed books by authors, all of whom have spent the night. As well, the Heathman has completed a 99 percent landfill-free renovation of its 155 rooms with a commitment to high standards of sustainability and energy efficiency. And you're just steps (or room service) away from the Heathman Restaurant and Bar (see review in the Restaurants chapter), certainly one of the city's finest restaurants. $$$–$$$$; AE, DC, DIS, JCB, MC, V; checks OK; amenities include bed menu with European feather beds, HDTV on-demand video library, MP3-compatible sound systems, complimentary DSL connectivity; www.heathmanhotel.com; valet or street parking; map:G2. &

Hotel deLuxe / ★★★

**729 SW 15TH AVE, DOWNTOWN; 503/219-2094
OR 866/895-2094**

Hotel deLuxe, conveniently located on the MAX line, breathes new life into old Hollywood glamour with original 1940s crystal chandeliers and updated Art Deco–inspired furnishings. In the rooms, halls, and lobby, the hotel features an impressive collection of photographs from classic film sets, including shots of Ginger Rogers, Federico Fellini, and Bing Crosby. Rooms feature elegant yet comfortable decor with buttery yellow leather upholstery and peacock accents. The deLuxe goes above and beyond with all the modern amenities you could hope for, including a pillow menu and a spiritual menu from which guests may choose reading material about the religion of their choice, as well as an MP3 menu. Visitors can enjoy a cocktail and 1950s charm in the Driftwood Room or exceptional fare in Gracie's restaurant, a throwback to classic Hollywood dining rooms. Pets are welcome with an additional fee. $$–$$$; AE, DC, DIS, MC, V; no checks; amenities include 24-hour room service, pillow menu, HDTV, MP3 docking stations, free wi-fi, 24-hour fitness and business centers; www.hoteldeluxeportland.com; valet parking; map:I0. &

Hotel Fifty / ★★

50 SW MORRISON ST, DOWNTOWN; 503/221-0711 OR 877/505-7220
Located across the street from Gov. Tom McCall Waterfront Park, the Hotel
Fifty offers access to one of Portland's most scenic walks. Many of the hotel's
rooms face the park, and beyond it the Willamette River, and they're also a
short jaunt from the city's center. Because it's close to the park, it's a great
place for families, as well as an ideal location for the business traveler. Hotel
Fifty's rooms come with luxurious linens and sleek glass-and-marble bathrooms. Guests receive complimentary passes to the nearby Bally gym. Pets
under 50 pounds are welcome with an additional fee. *$$–$$$; AE, DC, DIS,
MC, V; no checks; amenities include flat-screen TVs, clocks with iPod and MP3
connectivity, free wi-fi, 24-hour business center; www.hotelfifty.com; self parking; map:H5.* &

Hotel Lucia / ★★★

400 SW BROADWAY, DOWNTOWN; 503/225-1717 OR 877/225-1717
The 127 well-appointed rooms in the Hotel Lucia offer luxury in a Euro-
efficient style. Suites are palatial, and what most rooms lack in size, they make
up in appeal. Plush bedding, clean lined furnishings in dark wood tones, and
tiled bathrooms with chrome and stainless steel fixtures make for very comfortable accommodations. The hotel's downtown location and exceptional
art collection—including an extensive assortment of Pulitzer Prize winner
David Hume Kennerly's photos—add to its sophistication. As well, each
room has a "get it now" button for your every wish, as well as 24-hour room
service providing Thai and American cuisine from Typhoon! restaurant on
the ground floor. The hotel also takes pets with an additional fee. *$$$; AE,
DC, DIS, MC, V; no checks; amenities include pillow menu, flat-screen TVs,
iPod docking stations, free wi-fi, 24-hour business center; www.hotellucia.com;
valet or street parking; map:J3.* &

Hotel Modera / ★★★

515 SW CLAY ST, DOWNTOWN; 503/484-1084 OR 877/484-1084
Hotel Modera offers a boutique hotel experience true to the spirit of Port-
land with beautiful style and simplicity. Rooms and suites have excellent
views of downtown, the West Hills, or the hotel's private courtyard with its
fire pits and living wall of ferns. Carefully selected art fleshes out the sleek
and comfortable lobby so you'll feel welcomed and right at home when you
come through the doors. The hotel is adjacent to the MAX light-rail, close to
the heart of downtown, but, with its excellent on-site meeting and banquet
rooms, as well as the adjacent Nel Centro restaurant (see review in the Res-
taurants chapter), the business traveler may never have to leave the premises.
Guests receive daily membership to 24 Hour Fitness. *$$–$$$; AE, CB, DC,
DIS, MC, V; amenities include luxury linens, pillow-top mattresses, down
comforters, free wi-fi, iPod docking stations, 24-hour business center; www.
hotelmodera.com; valet and self parking; map:F3.* &

Hotel Monaco Portland / ★★★

**506 SW WASHINGTON ST, DOWNTOWN; 503/222-0001
OR 800/711-2971**

Originally built in 1912 and formerly the 5th Avenue Suites, this 10-story hotel was renamed Monaco after a 2006 makeover with a focus on local art. Nearly two-thirds of the 221 rooms are spacious suites with two sets of French doors. The property has been recently renovated to uphold high environmental standards, has won awards for its recycling program, and offers a "Carless Vacation" package, which includes bike rentals and reimburses travelers for using MAX light-rail. The staff is gracious, and the bellhops are extremely attentive; the Monaco also welcomes pets. The lobby features a large corner fireplace, where you'll find complimentary coffee and newspapers in the morning and wine tastings come evening. Don't be surprised if you see some very tall people, as the hotel features extra-long beds and is known to accommodate visiting athletes. The Red Star Tavern & Roast House is a very good bistro (see review in the Restaurants chapter), and you'll find an art gallery and a day spa on the ground floor. *$$$; AE, DC, DIS, JCB, MC, V; no checks; amenities include ironing boards, hair dryers, flat-screen TVs, free wi-fi, 24-hour fitness room, on-site restaurant; www.monaco-portland.com; valet parking; map:I4.* &

Hotel Vintage Plaza / ★★☆

422 SW BROADWAY, DOWNTOWN; 503/228-1212 OR 800/243-0555

Oregon has some of the nation's finest wine country, and the 107-room Vintage Plaza celebrates that heritage with rooms named for Oregon vineyards or popular Oregon wine events. Lodged in a restored 1894 National Historic Register building, the 10-story hotel has a gracious staff and a charming lobby. The recently renovated rooms all feature luxurious earth-toned linens and furnishings. The top-floor Starlight Rooms are particularly delightful, with angled, greenhouse-style windows for romantic bedtime planet viewing, and below are nine two-story townhouse units. Pets are welcome (the desk staff even serve "treats"). Pazzo Ristorante on the main floor serves excellent Northern Italian cuisine, and next-door Pazzoria sells pastries, crusty Italian breads, and panini to take out or eat in (see reviews of both in the Restaurants chapter). *$$$; AE, DC, DIS, JCB, MC, V; no checks; amenities include mini-bars, free wi-fi, 24-hour business and fitness centers, on-site restaurant; www.vintageplaza.com; valet parking; map:J4.* &

The Mark Spencer Hotel / ★★☆

409 SW 11TH AVE, DOWNTOWN; 503/224-3293 OR 800/548-3934

Powell's has dubbed the Mark Spencer its "official" hotel. Stay here and you might find touring authors making a home-away-from-home in the 101 modestly priced rooms and suites of this low-key, European-style, nonsmoking inn. Every room is nicely but not ostentatiously decorated, with a fully equipped kitchen and a sofa sleeper. The pet-friendly property rises around an entry courtyard that leads out to a hip area of downtown, just a hop, skip, and a jump to Kenny & Zuke's Delicatessen (see review in the Restaurants chapter), and Stumptown Coffee, and a stone's throw to the Pearl District. *$$; AE, DC, DIS, MC, V; no checks; amenities include guest laundry, complimentary continental breakfast and afternoon tea, copy of the* New York Times, *library, rooftop garden; www.markspencer.com; self parking; map:J1.* ♿

the Nines / ★★★☆

525 SW MORRISON ST, DOWNTOWN; 877/229-9995
You'll find exquisite accommodations at the Nines, located on the top nine floors of the old Meier & Frank Building, once the home of the Meier & Frank department store and now Macy's. From the opulent turquoise velvet upholstery to the taupe brocade wall coverings and generous bathrooms, luxury is everywhere. Some rooms have fantastic views of downtown Pioneer Square, and others enjoy gorgeous cityscapes or balconies with views into the atrium—home to Urban Farmer restaurant (see review in the Restaurants chapter), which has an exceptional steak menu. On the rooftop, you'll find Departure, which serves some of the best pan-Asian cuisine in Portland. The Nines allows as many as two dogs, up to 80 pounds each. *$$$; AE, DC, DIS, JCB, MC, V; no checks; amenities include 24-hour room service, flat-screen TVs, in-room movies, iPod docking stations, free wi-fi; www.thenines.com; valet parking; map:I3.* ♿

The Paramount Hotel / ★★★☆

808 SW TAYLOR ST, DOWNTOWN; 503/223-9900 OR 800/663-1144
Built on a reputation of sophistication, the Paramount is steps away from downtown theaters and shopping. Elevators rise to 154 guest rooms, each one simply yet impressively decorated with Biedermeier furnishings and a granite-finished bathroom. The spacious Executive Rooms have the feel of an elegant lounge with refined furnishings and desks. A handful of rooms have corner views and jetted bathtubs. *$$$–$$$$; AE, CB, DC, DIS, JCB, MC, V; checks OK; amenities include two telephones, hair dryers, personal refrigerators, free w-ifi, fitness and business centers, on-site restaurant; www.portland paramount.com; valet parking; map:H3.* ♿

RiverPlace Hotel / ★★

1510 SW HARBOR WY, DOWNTOWN; 503/228-3233 OR 800/227-1333
Facing directly upon the busy Willamette River, this casually elegant hotel is lovely. The best rooms among 74 kings, doubles, and suites face the water or look north across park lawns to the downtown cityscape. The fully nonsmoking hotel has a wood-and-stone decor with a Craftsman appeal. Ten adjacent private condominiums—with dining and living rooms and wood-burning fireplaces—are also available. The hotel takes pets with an additional fee. Massage and spa treatments are available by appointment. While guests have access to the adjacent RiverPlace Athletic Club (including an indoor pool and running track), on nice days there's plenty of opportunity for outdoor exercise on the esplanade in adjacent Gov. Tom McCall Waterfront Park. *$$$–$$$$; AE, DC, DIS, JCB, MC, V; checks OK; amenities include turndown service, DVD and CD*

STUNNING COLLECTIONS

Art lovers will find hundreds of world-class paintings, photographs, sculptures, and mixed-media works available for viewing in downtown Portland hotels. From vibrant Andy Warhol prints to Pulitzer Prize–winning photographs, these curated collections showcase internationally known and Northwest artists. You can discover these Portland treasures on a self-guided art walk to four hotels within 12 blocks on and off SW Broadway.

Start at the **HOTEL LUCIA** at SW Broadway and Stark. Known for its contemporary style, the lobby rooms unfold to showcase a dramatic and eclectic collection. The centerpiece is the compendium of 680 black-and-white photographs by Pulitzer Prize–winning political photographer David Hume Kennerly. The images cover the wall at the far end of the lobby and are on display throughout the hotel. From historic photos of five American presidents standing together or Richard Nixon bidding farewell after his resignation to whimsical portraits of such cultural icons as a young Jodie Foster (1987) and a playful Ansel Adams (1979) in the hotel elevators, the collection shines a light on events of the day.

Be sure to walk up to the interactive cast-bronze sculpture *Composition with the Head of Mercury*, by John Buck, at the center of the lobby. You can spin the piece on its base to view it from different angles. Buck intends the intriguing artwork to marry a classical female nude with contemporary sculptural forms and uses random images such as the head of Mercury and a globe floating above the body in place of a female head. Nearby is a life-sized, glossy blue-and-beige-striped form of a crouching man by J. D. Perkin, an artist inspired by poses in yoga and meditation. Another of Perkin's pieces, a ceramic-and-steel tower of men in

libraries, fresh cookies and apples in the lobby, 24-hour business center, on-site restaurant; www.riverplacehotel.com; valet or self parking; map:E5. &

Northwest Portland/Nob Hill

Heron Haus Bed and Breakfast / ★★★

2545 NW WESTOVER RD, NORTHWEST; 503/274-1846
From the original oak-parquet floors of the elegant parlor to the mahogany paneling of the library, this spacious 1904 English Tudor home at the foot of the West Hills is a peaceful getaway just four blocks from NW 23rd Street. Listed on the National Historic Register, this casual yet elegant property has a conservatory that overlooks a lovely fountain patio, a mahogany library, and a peaceful backyard patio. Each of the six guest rooms has a king- or queen-size bed, private bath, and fireplace. The Kulia Room features an elevated

similar stances, each nearly a foot and a half tall, also reflects the artist's interest in the human form. And take a look downstairs to view an extensive collection of stark female portraits by Gregory Grenon, known for his bold, powerful view of women.

Next, stop at **THE NINES**, where former Andy Warhol confidante and art consultant Paige Powell commissioned original works from local artists for the hotel's stunning 419-piece collection. Notice above the valet desk the multidimensional, ethereal work *Pearl Moon* by Hap Tivey: in his words, "a surface of light and a luminous space." Take the elevator to the 8th floor lobby and, as the doors open, you'll be greeted by Storm Tharp's *Tie Salesman (Clark Gable)*. To learn more about Tharp and other artists whose work is featured in the collection, stop by the concierge desk for a printed art guide with comments by artists.

Some other highlights around the soaring atrium space include Ellen George's six vertical glass panels behind the reception desk, fabricated at Bullseye Glass, an internationally celebrated local company. The light plays with the white-based panels at different times of day, showing the blues, grays, and magentas of the spherical forms. And don't miss Melody Owen's dramatic *Bird Song Chandelier* in the grand stairwell: 11 strands of 35-foot-long lighted blown glass beads represent the songs of Northwest birds. The icy blue strands have the appearance of giant yet delicate spindles.

From the Nines, walk over to **HOTEL MODERA**, one of the city's newest boutique hotels. Studio Art Direct commissioned local artists to create the 364-piece collection here, emphasizing curves and the female form to contrast with the masculine lines of this modern hotel. The simple, graceful granite sculptures

spa tub with a city view and deluxe bathing accoutrements. Pam Walker, the proprietor, offers a full breakfast and is an avid baker who passes cookies and the occasional cupcake in the afternoon. *$$$; MC, V; checks OK; amenities include air-conditioning, fireplace, free wi-fi; www.heronhaus.com; street parking; map:GG7.*

Hostelling International–Portland, Northwest / ★

425 NW 18TH AVE, NORTHWEST; 503/241-2783 OR 888/777-0067
Frequent hostellers know that one drawback to this budget-lodging system is having to share a dormitory room with a dozen or more fellow travelers. That's not the case here. Located in a pair of restored circa-1900 houses two blocks from McMenamins' Mission Theater, this hostel's dorms—most separated by gender, some of them coed—have four to eight beds; seven private rooms may be reserved by couples or families. Except for three of

by Michihiro Kosuge (which predate the hotel art project) glisten in the sun as you walk through the courtyard with its living plant wall. *Venus*, by Tyler Marchus, a nearly wall-high, encaustic earth-toned portrait of a winsome young woman, is the focal point of the lobby. *The White Album*, a white-on-white acrylic-on-canvas abstract by William Park near the reception desk, echoes the concentric circles of the hotel's logo.

For your final stop, head a block over to Broadway, turn right, and walk three and a half blocks to **THE HEATHMAN HOTEL**. This historic 1927 landmark has long been celebrated as an art hotel with an extensive collection. The hotel owns 10 signed prints from "The Endangered Species" series of animals by Andy Warhol. Ask for the 20-minute audio tour of some of the 250 pieces in the collection or a guide to view the private Warhol collection. Wander through the richly wood-paneled Tea Court, past the wall-length canvases by 18th-century French landscape artist Claude Lorrain, up to the mezzanine. The local **ELIZABETH LEACH GALLERY** (see review in the Arts chapter) rotates art (for sale) each quarter on this floor. Be sure to peek through the skylight above the library to view the fanciful and colorful mural with its birds, botanicals, and abstract themes by Northwest artist Henk Pander, commissioned by the hotel in 1994. You can end your art walk with a meal in the award-winning Heathman Restaurant and Bar, afternoon tea, or a drink at the bar.

Visiting hotels may seem like an unconventional way to discover art, but in Portland it's an opportunity not to be missed.

—Joan Cirillo

the private rooms, bathrooms are shared, as are a coin-op laundry and community kitchen and dining area. A courtesy phone is available in the lounge, which features a coffee bar. Rooms are not available to anyone residing in the Greater Portland area. *$; DIS, JCB, MC, V; no checks; amenities include community kitchen, laundry room, free wi-fi; www.2oregonhostels.com; street parking; map:HH7.*

Inn @ Northrup Station / ★★

2025 NW NORTHRUP ST, NORTHWEST; 503/224-0543 OR 800/224-1180

The Inn @ Northrup Station is, beyond a doubt, the city's most eclectic in decor: industrial chic with nods to Art Deco and '70s retro. This all-suite boutique hotel startles the newcomer with colors the hotel defines as "energetic": lime green, lemon yellow, plum purple. All rooms have marble bathrooms and full furnished kitchens. Parking is free, and there's a streetcar stop (the "station") outside the front door. Several of Portland's finest restaurants are just around the corner on 21st Street. *$$–$$$; AE, DC, DIS, MC, V; checks OK; amenities include private balconies or patios, safe deposit boxes, free wi-fi, business center; www.northrupstation.com; self parking; map:HH7.* &

Park Lane Suites / ★

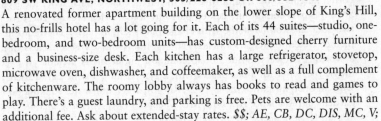

809 SW KING AVE, NORTHWEST; 503/226-6288 OR 800/532-9543

A renovated former apartment building on the lower slope of King's Hill, this no-frills hotel has a lot going for it. Each of its 44 suites—studio, one-bedroom, and two-bedroom units—has custom-designed cherry furniture and a business-size desk. Each kitchen has a large refrigerator, stovetop, microwave oven, dishwasher, and coffeemaker, as well as a full complement of kitchenware. The roomy lobby always has books to read and games to play. There's a guest laundry, and parking is free. Pets are welcome with an additional fee. Ask about extended-stay rates. *$$; AE, CB, DC, DIS, MC, V; checks OK; amenities include kitchens, oversized towels, two-line phones, data ports, free wi-fi; www.parklanesuites.com; street parking; map:HH7.* &

Northeast Portland

Blue Plum Inn / ★

2026 NE 15TH AVE, IRVINGTON; 503/288-3848 OR 877/288-3844

In their century-old Victorian home, hosts Suzanne and Jonathan Hansche specialize in gourmet breakfasts featuring Oregon produce. Meals are served in a pleasant dining room adjacent to a library. Four guest rooms all have private baths. The Iris and Tulip rooms feature antique furnishings and queen beds; the Hydrangea Suite can be reserved as a one- or two-bedroom suite with a full bath, double sinks, and a sitting room. The nonsmoking inn has a beautiful living room filled with afternoon sun. The Hansches make every effort to compost, reduce, reuse, and recycle, and the Blue Plum is affiliated with Sustainable Travel International. *$$; DIS, MC, V; no checks; amenities include free wi-fi; www.bluepluminn.com; street parking; map:GG6.*

The Georgian House Bed and Breakfast / ★

1823 NE SISKIYOU ST, IRVINGTON; 503/281-2250 OR 888/282-2250

With its lovely grounds and quiet neighborhood, this handsome 1922 brick B&B in historic Irvington—for architecture buffs, one of three true Georgian Colonials in Portland—combines the respite of a rural getaway with a convenient location: downtown is about 10 minutes away by car. Of the four guest rooms, the three upstairs are all air-conditioned. We like the East Lake for its private veranda and the Lovejoy Suite for its claw-foot bathtub. Willie Canning, the likable host, has guests sign up for breakfast times. *$–$$; MC, V; checks OK; amenities include personal refrigerators, private baths, TVs, VCRs; www.thegeorgianhouse.com; self parking; map:GG5.*

The Kennedy School / ★★☆

5736 NE 33RD AVE, CONCORDIA; 503/249-3983 OR 888/249-3983
If you're not familiar with the McMenamin brothers' brewpub–movie theater–B&B enterprises, you may find this place perplexing, but you're bound to like the Kennedy School. Located in a former public-school building in the Concordia neighborhood, built in 1915 in Italian Renaissance style, the Kennedy School is part community center, part fun house. It features 35 guest rooms—two to a classroom—some with chalkboards still in place. The requisite bars include Detention (cigars and jazz) and Honors (smoke-free and classical), plus a working brewery. Some not-so-common public areas include an excellent movie theater (with a bar of its own), a gymnasium, a wine bar–dessert room with an open-air patio (the Cypress Room), and a hot-water soaking pool in a garden courtyard. *$$; AE, DIS, MC, V; checks OK; amenities include free theater admission, access to the soaking pool, free wi-fi, on-site restaurant; www. mcmenamins.com; self parking; map:FF5.* &

The Lion and the Rose / ★★★☆

1810 NE 15TH AVE, IRVINGTON; 503/287-9245 OR 800/955-1647
Occupying the 1906 Freiwald House, a Queen Anne mansion with Craftsman flair in the historic Irvington district, the Lion and the Rose maintains its status as one of Portland's finest B&Bs. Genial hosts Steve Unger and Dustin Carsey let few details go unchecked: from handmade soaps (in the shapes of lions and roses), to beverages in the refrigerator, to extra blankets upon request. Of the six guest rooms, we recommend the Joseph, the Starina, and the Lavonna, with a spacious reading nook in the turret. A lavish breakfast is served in the formal dining room, while light refreshments and snacks are available 24/7. Those set on relaxing will appreciate the two elegant living rooms and the porch swing (roofed to guard against rain). *$$–$$$; AE, DC, DIS, MC, V; checks OK; amenities include telephones with free domestic calls, a guest computer, free wi-fi; www.lionrose.com; self parking; map:GG5.*

Portland's White House / ★★★

1914 NE 22ND AVE, IRVINGTON; 503/287-7131
Owners Lanning Blanks and Steve Holden hired a historian to help with the restoration of this stately old home, built in 1911 of solid Honduran mahogany and oak. On the outside, Portland's White House looks a bit like its Washington, DC, namesake. In addition to three guest rooms in the carriage house, there are five more inside; all rooms have private baths. The Canopy Suite features a large canopied bed; the Baron's Suite boasts a Victorian clawfoot tub. The White House serves a full gourmet breakfast in the main dining room. Evenings, wander down to the parlor for a turn at the grand piano or a game of chess. The White House is a catering specialist, and it hosts numerous weddings and social gatherings in its garden. *$$–$$$; AE, DIS, MC, V; checks OK; amenities include climate control, private baths, data ports, free wi-fi; www.portlandswhitehouse.com; self parking; map:GG5.*

Near the Airport

Aloft / ★★

9920 NE CASCADES PARKWAY; 503/200-5678 OR 866/716-8143

Aloft offers hip, trendy, affordable luxury a hop, skip, and a very short MAX ride from the Portland Airport. The loft-inspired, modern rooms look out on the Columbia River Slough and at incoming air traffic. They feature ergonomically designed desk chairs and famously comfortable beds with down comforters. *$$; AE, CB, DC, DIS, MC, V; amenities include personal refrigerators, flat-screen TVs, jack packs with cables for laptop connectivity, iPods or game systems, free cable Internet service; www.starwoodhotels/aloft.com; self parking; map:DD4.*

Southeast Portland

Bluebird Guesthouse / ★

3517 SE DIVISION ST, SOUTHEAST; 503/238-4333 OR 866/717-4333

Opened in 2006 by a former youth-hostel manager, the Bluebird offers budget lodging and a terrific central location near the Hawthorne, Belmont, and Clinton neighborhoods. The simple 1910 Arts and Crafts house has seven guest rooms, all but two of which share baths; each room is named for a noted author, including Oregonians Ken Kesey and Beverly Cleary. It's a great place to enjoy a book with no TVs to distract you. Guests may cook their own meals in the full kitchen, although a continental breakfast, with fruit and baked goods, is provided each morning at no additional charge. *$; MC, V; no checks; amenities include free local phone calls, free wi-fi; www.bluebird guesthouse.com; street parking; map:II5.*

Hostelling International–Portland, Hawthorne District / ★

3031 SE HAWTHORNE BLVD, HAWTHORNE;
503/236-3380 OR 866/447-3031

This hostel, in a charming early-20th-century house, couldn't be better located for budget travelers; within blocks are great used bookstores, good eats, and plentiful coffee and microbrew hangouts. This place will seem familiar to those who know hostels: bunk beds with blankets (clean linens are available), shared bathrooms with showers, a kitchen, and two small living areas—plus all-you-can-eat pancakes come morning. Check in by 10pm and enjoy 24-hour access with a security code. The hostel has a couple of private rooms, good for families. Bikes are available for daily rental. Hostelling International membership is not required but lessens the price; you can buy a membership ($28 for the year) when you arrive. *$; MC, V; no checks; amenities include free bagels, on-site lockers and laundry machines, free wi-fi; www.portlandhostel.org; street parking; map:GG4.*

Jupiter Hotel / ★★☆

800 E BURNSIDE AVE, SOUTHEAST; 503/230-9200 OR 877/800-0004

If there's such a thing as a rock-and-roll hotel in Portland, that distinction must go to the Jupiter. Located in the hip Lower Burnside district, the Jupiter wraps itself around one of the city's most popular nightclubs—the Doug Fir Restaurant and Lounge. Minimalist design characterizes the 80 guest rooms, which feature simple, low platform beds with down comforters. Some rooms have full-wall mirrors, others floor-to-ceiling mirrors; sage-green shag carpets and pillows hearken to the '60s. There is limited free basement parking. Bamboo gardens hide outdoor courtyards, including one with a communal fire pit, where guests are encouraged to mingle. *$$; AE, DIS, MC, V; no checks; amenities include down comforters and pillows, rental guest bicycles, free wi-fi, on-site restaurant, salon, tattoo parlor; www.jupiterhotel.com; limited self parking and street parking; map:HH6.* &

Lake Oswego

Crowne Plaza Portland–Lake Oswego / ★

14811 KRUSE OAKS BLVD, SOUTHWOOD; 503/624-8400 OR 877/424-4225

An atmospheric business hotel, the Crowne Plaza—sitting right off I-5—has a six-story waterfall cascading into a fountain in its central atrium. The 161 rooms, including 12 suites, are fairly standard, or you may request one of the posh sixth-floor rooms on the concierge level. All guests receive free van service within 5 miles (downtown Portland is 7). Pets are welcomed. Basil's Kitchen serves Mediterranean-style meals and cocktails. *$$; AE, DC, DIS, MC, V; checks OK; amenities include CD player–clock radios, indoor-outdoor pool, sauna, whirlpool, fitness center, laundry, free wi-fi, business center, on-site restaurant; www.cplakeoswego.com; self parking; map:MM8.* &

Lakeshore Inn / ★

210 N STATE ST, DOWNTOWN LAKE OSWEGO;
503/636-9679 OR 800/215-6431

From the street or parking lot, this four-story motor hotel might look like any other lodging located on a main thoroughfare, but this one is on the lakefront, right next door to the new and impressive Millennium Plaza Park and Lake View Village. All 33 rooms have windows on the lake, and the view is uncannily rural and picturesque. Although the one- and two-bedroom suites offer more room, the studios allow guests to view the water without getting out of bed. Every room is nonsmoking and has a kitchenette. During seasonal weather, guests have use of the outdoor pool perched over the lake; lakeside rooms have private sun decks. *$$; AE, DC, DIS, MC, V; checks OK; amenities include TVs and DVD players, free wi-fi; www.thelakeshoreinn.com; self parking; map:MM6.* &

Troutdale

Edgefield / ★★

2126 SW HALSEY ST; 503/669-8610 OR 800/669-8610
The McMenamin brothers of microbrew fame did a terrific job of turning the former Multnomah County Poor Farm into a quirky but winning place conveniently near the airport. There's the brewpub, also a movie theater, a winery, a distillery, the respectable Black Rabbit Restaurant and Bar, the Power Station pub, an amphitheater (which draws some big-name bands in the summer), an 18-hole par-3 golf course, meeting and party sites, and 114 guest rooms spread throughout three buildings. All rooms are furnished with antiques and cozy linens; most share a bath, although the 13 suites have private baths. Because Edgefield is billed as a European-style bed-and-breakfast, the first meal of the day is included in the room rate; as well, glasses and pitchers are readily available for fetching beer. There is also a men's and women's hostel, a great alternative for the budget traveler, as well as family rooms that sleep up to six. Wi-fi is in all public spaces, but may be spotty in some rooms. Hallways are lined with unique murals and wall paintings by an unconventional variety of artists. *$–$$; AE, DIS, MC, V; checks OK; amenities include free wi-fi; www.mcmenamins.com; self parking.* ⚹

Mount Hood Highway

Collins Lake Resort / ★★

E CREEK RIDGE RD AT GOVERNMENT CAMP LOOP,
GOVERNMENT CAMP; 503/272-3051
Government Camp was once a tiny enclave on the Mount Hood highway pass. Today it's booming as a resort destination, and Collins Lake Resort is at the heart of the new development. Built around a small artificial lake on a mountain stream are 151 privately owned chalet units available for nightly rental. They are mainly two- and three-bedroom homes, each with a ground-floor garage; second-story living quarters, including a spacious kitchen, dining room, and living room; and bedrooms on the top floor, with plenty of room for a family of six. The newest additions include the North Building, which houses 32 residences, and the South Building, with another 16. The resort is the hub of a proposed aerial gondola that would link Government Camp to Timberline Lodge. Winter packages include lift tickets for the adjacent Skibowl ski area (see the Recreation chapter). *$$$; AE, DIS, MC, V; no checks; amenities include fitness center, guest shuttle, chalets share pool and hot tub; www.collinslakeresort.com; self parking.*

The Resort at the Mountain / ★★

68010 E FAIRWAY AVE, WELCHES; 503/622-3101 OR 800/733-0800
A little piece of Scotland has been transplanted to the village of Welches, 45 miles east of Portland and about a dozen miles west of Government Camp.

It's not just the three nine-hole golf courses that remind some duffers of St Andrews, nor the Scottish Shoppe, nor the clubby atmosphere of the Tartans Pub. With 160 rooms, it's all those things and more. The croquet and lawn-bowling greens are championship quality; the resort also offers tennis, volleyball, and badminton, and it has a swimming pool and fitness center. The Highlands restaurant features Pacific Northwest–style fine dining. *$$–$$$; AE, DC, DIS, MC, V; no checks; amenities include private patios or decks, fireplaces, free wi-fi; www.theresort.com; self parking.* &

Timberline Lodge / ★★★⯪

GOVERNMENT CAMP; 503/231-5400 OR 800/547-1406
Nestled on the southern slope of Mount Hood, a winding 6-mile drive uphill from Highway 26 at Government Camp, Oregon's most famous hotel looks across the Cascade Range from 6,000 feet elevation. The National Historic Landmark was built in 1936–37 by the federal Work Projects Administration. Memorably used as the set of the classic horror movie *The Shining*, the lodge has a huge main lobby with a 98-foot-high fireplace of volcanic rock and giant Douglas fir pillars supporting the ceiling. The cozy but comfortable rooms have feather beds; some have small fireplaces. From the fine-dining restaurant to the Rams Head bar, Timberline Lodge is a living museum of Civilian Conservation Corps memorabilia, regional American Indian history, and the early Pacific Northwest ski industry. It sees nearly 2 million visitors a year, many of whom come in winter to ski on 11,245-foot Mount Hood, which looms high above the lodge. *$$–$$$; AE, DC, DIS, JCB, MC, V; no checks; amenities include hair dryers, modem ports, DSL Internet connection, on-site restaurant; www.timberlinelodge.com; self parking.*

Vancouver, Washington

Heathman Lodge / ★★★

7801 NE GREENWOOD DR; 360/254-3100 OR 888/475-3100
Vancouver's first luxury hotel—run by the pros who until recently owned Portland's venerable Heathman Hotel—looks like a national-park lodge, with its huge timbers and a carved cedar totem pole, and is set squarely in a Clark County suburb, near a shopping mall and high-tech office space. The striking lobby has a basalt fireplace; a range of suites and guest rooms are attractively furnished in Northwest-style. Take a dip in the pool or have a wonderful meal at Hudson's Bar & Grill (see review in the Restaurants chapter). The lodge is unlikely to become a destination in itself because of the surrounding neighborhood, but it should be the pick for those travelers making Vancouver their destination. *$$$; AE, DC, DIS, MC, V; no checks; amenities include microwaves, personal refrigerators, data ports, free wi-fi, fitness room; www.heathmanlodge.com; self parking; map:AA3.* &

EXPLORING

EXPLORING

Top 20 Attractions

1) WASHINGTON PARK

BETWEEN SW CANYON RD (HWY 26) AND W BURNSIDE RD, 3 BLOCKS WEST (UPHILL) OF VISTA AVE VIA SW PARK PL; 503/823-2223

The 129½-acre plot, originally purchased by Portland's founders in 1871, is the home of several different gardens, including the well-kept trails of the **HOYT ARBORETUM** (see no. 13 in this section) and its inspiring **OREGON VIETNAM VETERANS' LIVING MEMORIAL** (4000 SW Canyon Blvd).

Whether you want to obtain a blossom-framed snapshot of Mount Hood or scrutinize a new hybrid, the **INTERNATIONAL ROSE TEST GARDEN** (400 SW Kingston Ave; 503/823-3636) is an obligatory stop for any visitor to the City of Roses. The garden (established in 1917) is the oldest continually operating testing program in the country. With more than 7,000 plants (more than 600 varieties) and a knockout setting overlooking downtown Portland, it's an unmatched display of the genus *Rosa*. The garden's 4½ acres are a riot of blooms from June through October, from dainty half-inch-wide miniatures to great, blowsy 8-inch beauties. And you'll find fragrant old-garden varieties on the east side of the Washington Park tennis courts. While you're here, check out the **ROSE GARDEN STORE** (850 SW Rose Garden Wy; 503/227-7033), which sells rose-themed merchandise, including rose-patterned tea sets and floral wreaths; proceeds from the store benefit these gardens and Portland parks youth programs.

Washington Park is also home to the elegant **JAPANESE GARDEN** (see no. 8 in this section) and the **OREGON ZOO** (see no. 6 in this section), famed for its successful breeding of Asian elephants.

In the vicinity of the zoo are the educational **WORLD FORESTRY CENTER DISCOVERY MUSEUM** and **PORTLAND CHILDREN'S MUSEUM** (see Museums section in this chapter). One-way roads wind through Washington Park, and in warm-weather months a narrow-gauge train runs through the zoo to the rose garden (see Train and Trolley Tours in this chapter). Other facilities include four lit tennis courts, a covered picnic area, an archery range, a playground, public restrooms, and an outdoor amphitheater that features free summer musical and stage performances (503/823-2223 for schedule). *www.portlandonline.com/parks; map:HH7.* &

2) CENTRAL DOWNTOWN, PIONEER COURTHOUSE SQUARE, AND SOUTH PARK BLOCKS

BORDERED BY I-405 ON THE WEST AND SOUTH, W BURNSIDE ST ON THE NORTH, AND THE WILLAMETTE RIVER ON THE EAST

Portland's history lives in its well-maintained historic structures and dramatic modern and postmodern edifices. These buildings reflect the economics of

PORTLAND'S TOP 20 ATTRACTIONS

1) Washington Park
2) Central Downtown, Pioneer Courthouse Square, and South Park Blocks
3) Gov. Tom McCall Waterfront Park and Vera Katz Eastbank Esplanade
4) Portland Art Museum (PAM)
5) Oregon Museum of Science and Industry (OMSI)
6) Oregon Zoo
7) Portland Classical Chinese Garden
8) Japanese Garden
9) Powell's City of Books
10) Pearl District
11) Northwest Portland/Nob Hill
12) Oregon History Center
13) Hoyt Arboretum
14) Sauvie Island
15) Breweries and Brewpubs
16) River Cruises on the Columbia and Willamette Rivers
17) Portland Aerial Tram
18) Pittock Mansion
19) Multnomah Falls and Crown Point
20) Saturday Market

their time, the sponsors who backed them, and the architects' visions. An afternoon tour of some of the more interesting architectural designs in the city core (see "A Mini Guide to Portland Architecture" in this chapter) requires little more than a sturdy umbrella, a durable pair of boots, a raincoat, a camera, and a strong sense of wonder.

During the mid- to late 1800s, Portland's business center ran alongside the west bank of the Willamette River. Here, streets were lined with cast-iron-fronted architecture. Portland's Front Avenue then looked very much like San Francisco's Montgomery Street—a study in masonry and cast-iron facades. After the San Francisco earthquake in 1906, Portland was left with the largest collection of cast-iron structures on the West Coast. These structures declined as the city center moved west. The area was largely demolished in the 1940s.

Today, **PIONEER COURTHOUSE SQUARE** (600 SW Morrison Ave; map: H3) is Portland's living room. Designed by Will Martin, the square features an amphitheater-like design well suited to people-watching. Here is *The Weather Machine*, a sculpture that delights with its quirkiness, as well as the J. Seward Johnson statue, *Allow Me*, of a man with an umbrella extending his hand. Elsewhere, there are bits of cast-iron fence from the grand hotel that once graced this spot, as well as a Starbucks to duck into out of the rain. Most of the square's 72,000 bricks bear the names of individual contributors who helped pay for the project, completed in 1984. The square hosts more than 300 events each year, including summer festivals, and during the Christmas season, a 75-foot Douglas fir is lit with great fanfare.

Before leaving Pioneer Courthouse Square, stop at the **VISITOR INFOR-MATION AND SERVICES CENTER** (701 SW 6th Ave; 503/275-8355; map: H3), on the lower west side, to pick up a city map and other information. If you take a wrong turn as you walk these pedestrian-friendly half-size blocks, keep an eye out for the green-jacketed **PORTLAND GUIDES**, employees of the Portland Business Alliance. They roam the downtown core in pairs just to answer questions about the city.

PIONEER COURTHOUSE (555 SW Yamhill St; map:H3) itself faces the square from the east. Built from 1869 to 1875 as the second-oldest federal building west of the Mississippi River, the three-story sandstone-walled structure persists today as the Court of Appeals for the Ninth Circuit. Restored to historic glory, it is also open for public tours. From the cupola windows, you get great views of the city. Detailed maps explain surrounding sites.

Numerous early-20th-century buildings surround the square. The 1912 **JACKSON TOWER** (806 SW Broadway; map:H3) provides a beautiful example of Portland's early "White City" look, reflected in banks, department stores, and government offices. The tower, built by Sam Jackson, founder of the *Oregon Journal*, stood an astonishing (at the time) 186 feet, from the ground floor to the flagpole base. The building that housed Jackson's competitor, the *Oregonian*, then rose only 138 feet. Jackson Tower once housed presses in its basement and the business of writing on its main floors; it shot newspapers out to boys on roller skates who made distribution swift.

Architecture often corresponds to the music of its time, and, that being the case, the 1902 **CHARLES F. BERG BUILDING** (615 SW Broadway; map: I3) is pure Jazz Age razzle-dazzle. Its Art Deco architecture is considered the finest in Portland. The joint just stuns the inner eye: the black facade is frosted with pounds of gilt; inset designs range from chevrons to peacocks, sunbursts to rain clouds. Built by an eccentric businessman, the building—which once housed his elaborate store for women's fine clothing—now provides space for a number of retailers.

The **MULTNOMAH COUNTY CENTRAL LIBRARY** (801 SW 10th Ave; map: I2) dates from a similar era: 1912–13. Beautifully restored in the mid-1990s at a cost of $24 million, this Georgian architectural gem is worth a visit even if you're not feeling bookish.

It isn't hard to find Portland's tallest building, the **UNICO US BANK TOWER** (555 SW Oak St; map:G4): just stand anywhere downtown and look up. This astonishing study in light, mass, and space takes on a different color and shape depending on the time of day and viewpoint. A sculptural skyscraper, the 1983 building affectionately known as "Big Pink" was designed by Skidmore, Owings, and Merrill, with Pietro Belluschi as consulting architect.

Belluschi's first big commission after World War II was the Equitable Building (1948), now known as the **COMMONWEALTH BUILDING** (421 SW 6th Ave; map:J4). It's an outstanding example of how existing patterns can be combined with new materials and structural systems to produce an elegantly proportioned building. It features a detailed aluminum and glass-curtain wall that was the first of its type in the United States.

THE PORTLAND BUILDING (1120 SW 5th Ave; map:G3) was one of architect Michael Graves's first major designs. Portlanders love it or hate it; mostly, they love to hate it. Flamboyantly blue, wrapped with a brown ribbon design, and fit with tiny windows, it reflects a reverence for both classicism and cubism. Built in 1982, this is the best example of Portland's flirtation with postmodernism. Close-up, the building loses much of its grandeur, due more to economically driven compromises on materials than a failure of artistic vision. Perhaps the most important legacy of this building is *Portlandia*, Raymond Kaskey's famous hammered-copper statue above the entrance, which has become one of the city's icons.

Closer to the river, the bold 1984 brick **KOIN CENTER** (222 SW Columbia St; map:E4), like a blue-tipped pen, has left its indelible mark on Portland's skyline. Across from that is the **KELLER AUDITORIUM** (SW 3rd Ave and Clay St; map:E4), where many local and traveling performers take the stage. Also check out the 1963 **STANDARD INSURANCE BUILDING** (1100 SW 6th Ave; map:G3), at once very subtle and exquisitely designed. Often described as an architect's building, it is a modernist glass box built to the highest standard.

A peaceful component of Portland's downtown is the elm-lined oasis known as the **SOUTH PARK BLOCKS**. If Pioneer Courthouse Square is the heart of the city, the Park Blocks are its green backbone; sandwiched between SW Park and Ninth avenues, the blocks are reserved almost entirely for public use. In 1852, a 25-block stretch running parallel to Broadway was set aside for a park. However, in 1871, 8 blocks ended up in private hands, and they continue to be developed.

The South Park Blocks (demarcated on street signs as the Cultural District) begin in a pedestrians-only zone on the Portland State University campus and continue north for 12 blocks, hedged neatly along the way with student apartments, upscale condominiums, and public institutions such as the **PORTLAND ART MUSEUM** (1219 SW Park Ave; map:G2) and the **OREGON HISTORY CENTER** (1200 SW Park Ave; map:G2), nos. 4 and 12, respectively, in this section. In summer months the **PORTLAND FARMERS MARKET** (www. portlandfarmersmarket.org) sells fresh produce in the South Park Blocks on Wednesdays and Saturdays (see "The Portland Growing Season" in the Shopping chapter).

Sculpture abounds in the South Park Blocks. Tipped-over granite monoliths adorn the three-church block between SW Columbia and Jefferson streets; Theodore Roosevelt and his horse guard the next block north; and a somber statue of Abe Lincoln stands outside the art museum's North Wing. At the **PORTLAND CENTER FOR THE PERFORMING ARTS** (1111 SW Park Ave; map:G2), be sure to view the Henk Pander mural *Portland Town* through the glass on the west side of the building. Just across SW Main Street (a block that's closed during concerts) is the larger **ARLENE SCHNITZER CONCERT HALL** (SW Broadway and Main St; map:I2), aka "the Schnitz"; this plush and ornate theater, built in 1928 to host vaudeville shows, is home to the Oregon Symphony and the Portland Arts and Lectures Series (see the Arts Scene chapter).

The Park Blocks seem to end on SW Salmon Street, but they pick up again at SW Washington Street and **O'BRYANT SQUARE** (named for Portland's first mayor, Hugh Donaldson O'Bryant), with its jet engine–like fountain encircled by brick steps—a good spot to catch noontime rays in summer. *Map:J6.*

3) GOV. TOM MCCALL WATERFRONT PARK AND VERA KATZ EASTBANK ESPLANADE

WEST AND EAST SIDES OF THE WILLAMETTE RIVER FROM HAWTHORNE BRIDGE NORTH TO STEEL BRIDGE; 503/823-2223

It's a rare city that has both the planning sense and the political will to reclaim territory taken over by the automobile, but that is precisely what Portland did at the river's edge of its downtown. In the early 1970s, Portlanders decided they didn't like the way the city had grown: an expressway called Harbor Drive impeded access to the otherwise scenic Willamette River. So the Portland Development Commission did what the locals asked: it took the road away and replaced it with a showcase riverfront park.

GOV. TOM MCCALL WATERFRONT PARK—named for the state leader (1967–75) credited with giving Oregon its reputation as a "green" state—has become indispensable. Its 73 acres of sweeping lawns are the hardest-working turf in the city, from Cinco de Mayo through Labor Day; it's rare to find a weekend when something (Rose Festival, Brewers Festival, Blues Festival) isn't going on here. The 1½-mile riverside promenade is shared by anglers, walkers, runners, in-line skaters, and cyclists, and in the summer, many adults join children cooling off with a dash through the **SALMON STREET SPRINGS** fountain (foot of SW Salmon St).

At **FRIENDSHIP CIRCLE** (west end of Steel Bridge), a sculpture that emits the sounds of a Japanese flute and drum honors the strong sister-city relationship between Portland and Sapporo, Japan. The walkway passes 100 Japanese cherry trees in the **JAPANESE AMERICAN HISTORICAL PLAZA**, which honors the Japanese Americans interned during World War II. Memorable quotes by captive Oregonians are set in boulders along the pathway.

WATERFRONT STORY GARDEN (just north of Burnside Bridge) is a whimsical sculptural tribute by artist Larry Kirkland to storytellers of all ages, complete with etchings in granite and cobblestone of animals, queries ("What do you remember?"), and "safe havens." The Burnside's buttresses offer their own safe haven to the bustling **SATURDAY MARKET** (see no. 20 in this section).

A ship's mast at the Battleship Oregon Memorial—built to honor the 1893 "Bulldog of the U.S. Navy"—is your clue to start looking for the **OREGON MARITIME MUSEUM** (see Museums in this chapter). Its main exhibit is the steam-powered stern-wheeler *Portland*, moored in the Willamette opposite the foot of SW Pine Street. Continuing past the Morrison Bridge, you'll need a keen eye to find **MILL ENDS PARK**, located in the SW Naito Parkway median at Taylor Street. In season, it's planted with colorful flowers. A plaque at the site tells how a hole for a lamppost became the smallest park in the nation—and, probably, the world. Despite the spot's size, weddings are occasionally held here. River cruises on the *Portland Spirit* (no. 16 in this section) depart daily from a nearby dock. An amphitheater south of the Hawthorne Bridge, a few blocks farther, is center stage for many of the park's festivals.

When Harbor Drive was demolished, Portland was left with 15 acres of undeveloped riverfront land between the Hawthorne and Marquam bridges, now known as **SOUTH WATERFRONT PARK** (1814-1816 SW River Pkwy). It is highlighted by **RIVERPLACE**, a multimillion-dollar development that includes two hotels, several restaurants, 480 condominium units, extensive office and specialty retail space, and a broad promenade tying all this together with a marina, beach, and fishing pier. The esplanade ends at the world headquarters for PG&E Gas Transmission Northwest—thus establishing an attractive and efficient mixed-use neighborhood.

In May 2001, the **EASTBANK ESPLANADE** (see "River Walk" in this chapter) brought the two riverbanks together, connecting the east and west sides of the city around its central feature—the Willamette River—giving pedestrians, cyclists, and skaters the ability to complete a loop between the Hawthorne and the Steel bridges that can be walked in an hour or less. *www. portlandonline.com/parks; map:C5–M7.* &

4) PORTLAND ART MUSEUM (PAM)

1219 SW PARK AVE, DOWNTOWN; 503/226-2811
PAM is the oldest art museum on the West Coast. Its southern wing has been a landmark building in the heart of downtown's cultural district on the South Park Blocks since 1932, when celebrated Portland architect Pietro Belluschi bucked tradition to build a modernist brick structure trimmed in Italian travertine.

The museum got its start in 1892, when Portland business leader and art connoisseur Henry Corbett paid $10,000 for a collection of Greek and Roman antiquities. The extraordinary sculptures are still part of the museum holdings. So, too, are 750 Japanese prints purchased in 1932, as well as Claude Monet's impressionistic *Water Lilies*, purchased in 1959.

Today the museum's diverse collection has grown to more than 45,000 objects and works of art—including Northwest and American Indian art, contemporary and classic American and European works, English silver, African art, sculpture, graphic arts, and photography. Visitors can travel through history and tour the world in special exhibitions and magnificent galleries that feature rotating selections from the permanent collection. In 2005 the museum completed a renovation of the adjacent 141,000-square-foot Mark Building, which houses the **JUBITZ CENTER FOR MODERN AND CONTEMPORARY ART**, an art study center and library. Browse the **MUSEUM SHOP** and enjoy a bite in the **CAFÉ**, which provides outdoor service in the warmer months.

The museum's Web site includes a schedule of events, lectures, tours, art classes, and family activities. Museum general admission is $10 for adults, $9 for students and seniors (over 55), and free for children under 17. Special exhibition prices may apply. *Tues–Wed 10am–5pm, Thurs–Fri 10am–8pm, Sat 10am–5pm, Sun noon–5pm; www.portlandartmuseum.org; map:G2.* ⅙

5) OREGON MUSEUM OF SCIENCE AND INDUSTRY (OMSI)

1945 SE WATER AVE, SOUTHEAST; 503/797-4000

With its knockout view of downtown from the east bank of the Willamette, OMSI is a delightful diversion no matter the weather—and not just for kids. The facility has five immense exhibit halls, a planetarium that doubles as a theater in the round, an OMNIMAX theater, a great science store (see review in the Shopping chapter), and a riverfront cafe. There's even a naval submarine, the USS *Blueback*, permanently docked for tours by those 4 years and older (admission is $5.50 extra).

You can't miss the museum, an angular brick showpiece capped with a copper dome, topped by a Ferrari-red smokestack and a glass pyramid atrium. The 18½-acre industrial location (formerly owned by Portland General Electric, which donated the land) is ideal for a museum where science and industry are the emphasis: the Marquam Bridge soars just above, and a PGE substation still operates at one corner of the property.

Inside, you can poke around an old turbine, stand on a platform and feel an earthquake, touch a tornado in the **EARTH SCIENCE HALL**, observe nutrient cycling in the **GREENWAY**, or cruise the Internet in the **VERNIER TECH HALL**. The numerous hands-on exhibits are popular with people of all ages, but for the very young—and their grateful parents—there's **SCIENCE PLAYGROUND**, and a tots' room with tennis balls to feed into a pneumatic tube, a Lego table, a supervised arts room, a giant clean sandbox, and a water-play area. The **KENDALL PLANETARIUM** features a state-of-the-art Digistar 3 projection system, an all-digital system that combines star projection, full-motion color video, digital surround sound, and the ability to interact with the audience (admission is $5.50 extra). Traveling exhibits—on robotics, for example, or early humans—are both educational and entertaining.

Museum admission is $11 for adults, $9 for seniors (63 and older) and for children 3–13; OMNIMAX admission is an additional $8.50 for adults, $6.50 for seniors and children. But ask about the $20 package admission if you'd like to see a little of everything. And from after Labor Day until mid-June, every Thursday after 2pm, OMSI offers two-for-the-price-of-one admission to all attractions. Evening laser-light extravaganzas in the planetarium cost $7.50. Memberships are available. *Tues–Sun 9:30am–5:30pm (after Labor Day–mid-June), every day 9:30am–7pm (mid-June–Labor Day), closed Thanksgiving and Christmas; www.omsi.edu; map:HH6.* ⅙

6) OREGON ZOO

4001 SW CANYON RD, WASHINGTON PARK; 503/226-1561

What began more than a century ago as a seaman-turned-pharmacist's menagerie on SW Third Avenue and Morrison Street has since grown into an outstanding 64-acre zoo, winning awards for exhibits showcasing the fauna of the Cascades as well as a colony of endangered Peruvian Humboldt penguins, well protected (and thriving) here.

Born in 1962, Packy—the first Asian elephant born in the Western Hemisphere in 44 years—blazed the trail for the zoo's pachyderm breeding program. Now, some two dozen newborns later, the elephant program continues apace, with excellent viewing opportunities no matter the weather. The unique **LILAH CALLEN HOLDEN ELEPHANT MUSEUM** not only documents Packy's story but also highlights elephants' historic role as workers and cultural icons while decrying illegal poaching by ivory hunters.

The zoo has a complex primate exhibit, featuring an arena architecturally designed in keeping with the natural behavior of chimpanzees and other apes. The African savanna exhibit has black rhinoceroses, giraffes, impalas, zebras, and birds; the African rain-forest exhibit features hourly rainstorms and more than two dozen animal species, including the naked mole rat.

In 2007 the **BLACK BEAR RIDGE** exhibit opened, completing the Great Northwest section of the zoo: a **CREST TO COAST ADVENTURE**, where visitors can journey through lush mountain forests and wild coastlines. Located on the north end of the zoo, it includes **CASCADE CREST**, where mountain goats roam a simulated rocky cliff face; **STELLER COVE**, home to Steller sea lions, sea otters, and a kelp forest; **EAGLE CANYON**; and the **TRILLIUM CREEK FAMILY FARM**, along with a breeding center for the highly endangered California condor. Black bears, cougars, bobcats, and other Northwest animals are featured in a 90-year-old forest.

Every month the zoo hosts a variety of events such as the zoo summer concert series, the **WORLD ANIMAL FESTIVAL** in the fall, and on the weekend before Halloween, kids' trick-or-treat at the **HOWLOWEEN PARTY**. In December, the **ZOO LIGHTS FESTIVAL** is an incandescent holiday tradition. A new exhibit, **PREDATORS OF THE SERENGETI**, opening in fall of 2009, will showcase lions, cheetahs, and African wild dogs.

The cafeteria-style **CASCADE GRILL** serves better-than-average zoo food; its carpet and metalwork chandeliers are commissioned art pieces that reflect the Pacific Northwest. During warm-weather months, a small steam train chugs through the zoo and down to the International Rose Test Garden (separate fee); spring through Labor Day and for special events, the train makes a shorter run around the zoo's perimeter.

The westside light-rail line, MAX (503/238-RIDE), stops at the zoo; take time to notice the geological time line on the walls of this 260-foot-deep train stop—the deepest underground transit station in North America (elevators take you up and down in 20 seconds). At the entrance to the aboveground plaza sits a sculpture made from columnar basalt and etched granite, telling the story of the light-rail tunnel's creation. Those who arrive at the zoo by car take the chance of having to use overflow parking, especially on the weekend. Visitors who take the bus or MAX light-rail line receive $1 off zoo admission.

On the second Tuesday of each month, zoo admission is $2; regular admission is $9.75 for adults, $8.25 for seniors, and $6.75 for kids 3–11. There is a $2 fee to park in the lot at the zoo. Memberships are available. *Gate hours every day 9am–6pm (Apr 15–Sept 15), 9am–4pm (Sept 16–Apr 14), closed Christmas, visitors can stay in the zoo 1 hour after gate closes; www.oregonzoo. com; map:HH7.* ⅋

7) PORTLAND CLASSICAL CHINESE GARDEN

239 NW EVERETT ST, CHINATOWN; 503/228-8131
Escape to an authentically designed Ming Dynasty scholar's garden. Practicing craftsmanship perfected centuries ago, artisans from Portland's sister city of Suzhou traveled here to build **LAN SU YUAN—the GARDEN OF AWAKENING ORCHIDS—**in 1999.

Designed to reveal itself throughout the seasons, the Chinese Garden will surprise you at each turn. The walled urban oasis embraces hundreds of plant species indigenous to Southeast China, along with pavilions, covered pathways, mosaic stonework, Taihu rock, and poetic couplets in a naturalistic landscape. Serpentine walkways lead through open colonnades, over a bridge across Zither Lake, and into serene courtyards and pavilions such as **PAINTED BOAT IN MISTY RAIN** and **CELESTIAL HOUSE OF PERMEATING FRAGRANCE**. Meticulous rock groupings, as well as Chinese and Northwest native trees and shrubs, create a landscape that stays fixed—even as the visitor's view, framed through windows, doors, and lattice screens, continually shifts. A rockery with waterfalls embodies the Chinese philosophy that a garden must embrace mountains and water. An 8,000-square-foot pond offers a focal point around which the elements of the garden radiate and harmonize. Located within the garden is the **TOWER OF COSMIC REFLECTIONS**, a teahouse that offers light snacks, peaceful views, and numerous varieties of tea.

Free docent-led tours are offered daily at noon and 1pm. Groups of 15 or more can reserve a private tour at the group rate of $6 per person if reservations are made two weeks in advance. General admission is $8.50, $7.50 for seniors 62 and over, $6.50 for students with ID, and free for children 5 and under. *Every day 10am–6pm (Apr–Oct), 10am–5pm (Nov–Mar), closed Thanksgiving, Christmas, and New Year's Day; www.portlandchinesegarden. org; map:L5.* ⅋

8) JAPANESE GARDEN

611 SW KINGSTON AVE, WASHINGTON PARK; 503/223-1321
The Japanese Garden is an oasis of greenery, winding paths, and tranquil ponds. In 1988, the Japanese ambassador to the United States pronounced it the most beautiful and authentic Japanese garden outside of Japan, and it continues to enthrall visitors today. The extraordinarily peaceful spot is comprised of five gardens: the traditional raked-sand **FLAT GARDEN**; the serene and flowing **STROLLING POND GARDEN** with its colorful koi; the **TEA GARDEN**, with a *cha-shitsu* (ceremonial teahouse); the stark **DRY LANDSCAPE GARDEN**, nearly devoid of foliage; and the **NATURAL GARDEN**, lush with moss and maples.

Flowering cherries and azaleas accent the grounds come spring; in summer, the Japanese irises bloom; in autumn, the lace-leaf maples glow orange and red. Eaves and posts of the Japanese pavilion frame the Flat Garden to the west and Mount Hood to the east.

The garden's gift store stocks books on such topics as the art of Japanese flower arrangement and traditional tea ceremonies. Guided public tours are available April through October.

Admission is $8 for adults, $6.75 for seniors and college students (with ID), $5.25 for youth 6–17, and free for children 5 and under. Memberships are available at several levels, and events are held year-round for members and the general public. *Tues–Sun 10am–4pm, Mon noon–4pm (Oct–Mar); Tues–Sun 10am–7pm, Mon noon–7pm (Apr–Sept); www.japanesegarden.com; map:HH7.*

9) POWELL'S CITY OF BOOKS

1005 W BURNSIDE ST, DOWNTOWN; 503/228-4651

Portland is a city of book lovers, and Powell's City of Books is in the heart of town. With more than a million volumes occupying 77,000 square feet and an entire city block, Powell's is a day trip you can take without leaving the city limits (see "A Literary Legacy" in this chapter). Plan to spend at least several hours browsing the nine color-coded rooms. Your self-guided tour is made easy thanks to the store map—if there were awards for maps, this would be a winner (take an extra one home as a souvenir). But isn't getting lost in a city of books a bibliophile's dream?

The largest independent bookstore in the country and one of the most successful dot-coms in the history of retail, Powell's began in 1971 in a derelict car dealership. On the beamed ceiling of the Blue Room you'll see the words "Used Car Dept."

In the Gold Room, check out the posts—one lists award-winning titles and another has signatures from science fiction authors. Stick around long enough and you're likely to see famous people, since everyone who's anyone visits Powell's when they're in town. The coffee shop offers some of the best people-watching from its windows at the corner of 11th and Burnside—especially on Friday and Saturday nights. In the Pearl Room visit the Rare Book Room, open 11am–7pm, or catch an author reading most weekday evenings in the **BASIL HALLWARD ART GALLERY**—named after what fictional painter? *Open every day 9am–11pm; www.powells.com; map:J2.* &

10) PEARL DISTRICT

W BURNSIDE ST NORTH TO THE WILLAMETTE RIVER, BETWEEN NW BROADWAY AND NW 16TH AVES

Since the mid-1980s, warehouses and wholesalers' storefronts in the aged industrial Northwest Triangle district have taken on new lives. Empty spaces have been turned into clean-lined art galleries, antiques showrooms, furniture stores, boutiques, bookstores, and lofts for upscale urban dwellers.

The Pearl is the place to gallery-browse, especially on the **FIRST THURSDAY** of each month, when galleries throw open their doors to show off their

A LITERARY LEGACY

POWELL'S CITY OF BOOKS is more than a bookstore; it's a literary mecca. In fact, one man's wish to be buried at Powell's was realized when his ashes were added to what became the sandstone sculpture at the Couch Street entrance.

The Powell's story began in 1971, when Walter Powell took over a derelict car dealership at 10th and Burnside. A retired painting contractor, he had spent a summer working in his son Michael's bookstore in Chicago and was inspired to open his own.

When Michael returned to Portland in 1979, he found a business with an unusual recipe for success; used books were shelved side by side with new ones. And the store was open 365 days a year, well into the late-night hours.

Staffed with book lovers represented by the International Longshore and Warehouse Union, each store section has its own lore. (Try to figure out what the rolling book carts in the Purple Room are named after.) And there really was a cat named Fup who lived at **POWELL'S TECHNICAL BOOKSTORE** (33 NW Park Ave) from 1988–2007.

There are now six metro-area Powell's locations (main store at 1005 W Burnside St, Downtown; 503/228-4651; www.powells.com; map:J2), and while other independent bookstores disappeared with the advent of the Internet, award-winning Powells.com flourished and now ships books worldwide. It's hard to know what Michael's daughter Emily can do to improve upon the family business when she takes over someday, but just keeping the flame will be enough to keep her busy.

—Dana Cuellar

collections (see Galleries in the Arts Scene chapter) and beautiful people stroll the sidewalks. If you're lucky enough to catch First Thursday on a warm evening, the show on the sidewalk may be the best: artists of all stripes come to hawk their wares, creating a vibrant street scene. Besides the fine-art galleries, the Pearl District is saturated with "functional art" galleries and avant-garde furniture stores. Wine bars, cocktail lounges, brewpubs, and fine-dining restaurants have sprung up throughout the district, offering respite to gallery-goers on every night of the month.

Start a stroll through the Pearl at **POWELL'S CITY OF BOOKS** (see no. 9 in this section), the country's largest independent bookstore. A visit to this literary institution is a tour in itself, with a full city block of new and used books.

The surrounding, redeveloped five-block neighborhood is known as the **BREWERY BLOCKS**; after the Blitz-Weinhard Brewery, established in 1864, closed in 1999, it underwent urban renewal to 1.7 million square feet of retail, office, and residential space. Among the refurbished buildings in this complex are the 1908 Tuscan-brick **BLITZ-WEINHARD BREWERY BUILDING** (1133 W Burnside St; map:K2); the 1929 **A. B. SMITH AUTOMOTIVE BUILDING** (1207 W Burnside St; map:K2), with cast-stone eagles and Art Deco ambience; and the fortresslike **PORTLAND ARMORY BUILDING** (NW 10th Ave between Couch and Davis sts; 503/445-3700; www.pcs.org; map:K2), built in 1891, site of the first professional hockey game in the United States in 1912. The armory has undergone a multimillion-dollar transformation into the **GERDING THEATER**, home of **PORTLAND CENTER STAGE**. It is the first historic rehabilitation on the National Historic Register—and the first performing arts venue—to achieve a LEED (Leadership in Energy & Environmental Design) Platinum rating.

The five-story 1910 Ice House, now the **WIEDEN+KENNEDY BUILDING** (224 NW 13th Ave; map:K1), was renovated to the tune of $36 million in 1999 and houses the major advertising agency, **BLUEHOUR** restaurant (see review in the Restaurants chapter), and a handful of other shops.

At NW 11th Avenue and Flanders Street is **THE GREGORY** (map:L2), a 12-story Art Deco–style monument completed in 2001. A prototype for other modern mixed-use developments in the Pearl, this full-city-block giant boasts such architectural features as curved corners and futuristic detailing. Similarly spectacular is the **REI BUILDING** (1405 NW Johnson St; map:N1), its climbing wall clearly visible behind a two-story glass facade (see review in the Shopping chapter).

JAMISON SQUARE, between NW Johnson and Kearney streets and between 10th and 11th avenues, is a charming neighborhood park with unique water features that keep families cool in summer months. Jamison Square also hosts a summer concert series on First Thursdays. Fresh produce is ripe for purchase at the **PEARL PORTLAND FARMERS MARKET**, which takes place in the **ECOTRUST** parking lot (NW Johnson St between 10th and 11th aves) on Thursdays from early June through late September, 3:30–7:30pm.

Farther northwest is the **BRIDGEPORT BREWING CO. BUILDING** (1313 NW Marshall St; map:O1), built in 1888 and one of Portland's oldest industrial edifices still in use (see review in the Nightlife chapter). Virginia creeper vines cover much of the rough-hewn structure, once a marine cordage company.

On the west, I-405 separates the Pearl District from Northwest Portland. On the east, the **NORTH PARK BLOCKS** create a division between the district and Chinatown/Old Town. Stretching from Burnside to Glisan streets, these five blocks are home to the **ART IN THE PEARL** celebration each Labor Day weekend. The 1901 **U.S. CUSTOM HOUSE** (220 NW 8th Ave; map:L4) faces the park between Davis and Everett streets; it's a majestic French Renaissance structure with a granite colonnade and fenced courtyard. Recently home to the Army Corps of Engineers, the building is now owned by **THE INTERNATIONAL SCHOOL**, a private primary school with an emphasis on foreign language, which has long-range plans to move into the building. *www.explore thepearl.com; map:K1,K2,K3–O1.*

11) NORTHWEST PORTLAND/NOB HILL

NORTH OF W BURNSIDE ST, CENTERED ON NW 21ST AND 23RD AVES

For thousands of Portlanders, "Northwest" means home, but for nonresidents it mostly means shopping and dining along two of the most bustling avenues in the city: lively, urbane NW 23rd and NW 21st avenues. Though somewhat more downscale, NW 21st is home to several of Portland's finest restaurants.

In block after block along NW 23rd Avenue, from Burnside to Thurman Street, there is a wealth of cosmopolitan attractions. Victorian homes have been remodeled into small retail enclaves, nestled alongside attractive new developments. "Trendy-third," as the street is affectionately known, draws an eclectic crowd. (Look for the lineup of Harleys parked every evening outside the local Starbucks.) It's easy to pass a day here. Parking can be tough; your best bet for spaces may be on the east-west cross streets. Many visitors prefer to take Tri-Met or the Portland Streetcar from downtown. (See Getting Around in the Lay of the City chapter.)

A good way to see **NOB HILL**, as the heart of this district is sometimes known, is to walk up NW 23rd Avenue and back down NW 21st Avenue. Start at the **UPTOWN SHOPPING CENTER** (W Burnside St and NW 24th Ave; map:HH7), then wander north up 23rd, past shops such as **MOONSTRUCK CHOCOLATIER** and the **LENA MEDOYEFF STUDIO** (see Shopping chapter) and restaurants including **KORNBLATT'S DELICATESSEN**, **PAPA HAYDN**, and Bruce Carey's **23 HOYT** (see reviews of all three in the Restaurants chapter). Turn the corner at Pettygrove Street, just past the Good Samaritan Hospital, and cut over to 21st, where the slew of fine-dining establishments includes **WILDWOOD** and Vitaly Paley's intimate **PALEY'S PLACE** (see reviews of both in the Restaurants chapter). The city's smallest bar, **M BAR** (see the Nightlife chapter), serves beer and wine daily. Two spots worthy of special note are **CITY MARKET NW**, where individual purveyors of the finest pasta, seafood, fruits, vegetables, and meats are gathered under one roof; and **CINEMA 21** (see the Arts Scene chapter), an old-fashioned movie house, where rocking chairs provide seating for art-house and foreign-film patrons.

Northwest's other cinema is the McMenamins' **MISSION THEATER** (1624 NW Glisan St; 503/223-4031; map:M1). Built in 1912 and formerly a Swedish evangelical mission for four decades, the space was later occupied by the Longshoremen's Union. Three blocks west, **TEMPLE BETH ISRAEL** (1931 NW Flanders St; map:HH7) is a unique find in Oregon—a distinctive, turreted Byzantine synagogue with a domed tower and sculpted bronze doors, completed in 1927. Twelve blocks north is **SAINT PATRICK'S ROMAN CATHOLIC CHURCH** (1635 NW 19th Ave; map:GG7) and its Renaissance Revival dome, built in 1891. *www.nobhillbiz.com.*

12) OREGON HISTORY CENTER

1200 SW PARK AVE, DOWNTOWN; 503/222-1741 OR 503/306-5198

An eight-story-high trompe l'oeil mural, overlooking the spacious outdoor plaza and glass facade of this museum and research library, is a landmark on

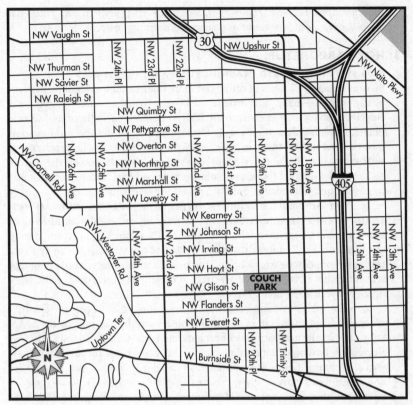

Northwest Portland

the South Park Blocks. Headquarters of the **OREGON HISTORICAL SOCIETY (OHS)** since 1966, the building reopened in fall 2003 after being closed a full year for renovation and expansion.

The **OREGON, MY OREGON** exhibit occupies an entire floor with more than 50 separate displays (several of them hands-on) interpreting state history—from ancient American Indians to modern corporate culture—through artifacts, documents, photographs, and videos. Other permanent exhibits depict Oregon's early maritime history as well as Northwest art. Future temporary exhibits will focus on sports, veterans, the arts, photography, and a one-of-a-kind Lincoln collection. Many collections are now geared toward families as well as avid history buffs.

The redesigned **OHS RESEARCH LIBRARY**, open to the public three days a week, contains 30,000 books, 25,000 maps, and more than 2.5 million photographs in its archives. There's also a fine **STORE** (SW Broadway and Madison St) with books and gift items. Museum admission is $11 for adults, $9 for students and seniors, $5 for youth, and free for children 5 and under.

Museum open Tues–Sat 10am–5pm, Sun noon–5pm, library open Thurs–Sat 1–5pm, both closed on major holidays; www.ohs.org; map:F2. &

13) HOYT ARBORETUM

4000 SW FAIRVIEW BLVD, WASHINGTON PARK; 503/865-8733

Sweeping views, 12 miles of trails, and more than 1,000 species of plants—all neatly labeled—make up Portland's 185-acre living museum located on a ridgeline 2 miles west of downtown. It's an international collection of woody plants, including the nation's largest assortment of conifer species. Blossoms dust the **MAGNOLIA TRAIL** in spring; pink and white flowers shower the **DOGWOOD TRAIL** in midsummer. Maps are available on racks outside the visitors center for self-guided tours, and volunteers are on hand during center hours to answer questions. Some trails are paved for wheelchair access.

In Hoyt Arboretum's southwest corner is the **OREGON VIETNAM VETERANS' LIVING MEMORIAL**, an inspiring outdoor cathedral built in 1987 to honor the 759 Oregonians who died, and the 32 still missing in action, during the Vietnam War. From the **GARDEN OF SOLACE** at its heart, a slowly rising trail spirals clockwise over a bridge and past six monuments, whose poignant text integrates news from the warfront with stories of day-to-day life back home between 1959 and 1976.

A place of beauty and serenity in all seasons, the arboretum is easily accessible from anywhere in the metropolitan area by car, bus, or the MAX light-rail. On the first Saturday of each month (Apr–Oct), Portland Parks and Recreation (www.portlandonline.com/parks) hosts tours through its **GREEN WALK** program. *Grounds open dawn to dusk, 365 days a year. Parking lot and access roads close at 10pm. Visitors Center open Mon–Fri 9am–4pm, Sat 9am–3pm, closed on major holidays; www.hoytarboretum.org; map:HH7.* &

14) SAUVIE ISLAND

VIA HWY 30, 10 MILES NORTHWEST OF PORTLAND, ACROSS SAUVIE ISLAND BRIDGE; 503/621-3488

For a quick trip into nature, you'll find something for everyone on Sauvie Island. Pick your own fruit and flowers along Gillihan or Sauvie Island roads—if you don't want to pick your own, **KRUGER'S** (17100 NW Sauvie Island Rd; 503/621-3489; www.krugersfarmmarket.com) or the **PUMPKIN PATCH** (16511 NW Gillihan Rd; 503/621-3874; www.thepumpkinpatch. com) are the two primary farm stores. Take in the sun at one of several beaches, or get serious about bird-watching on the 12,000-acre wildlife preserve (see Parks and Beaches in this chapter). Cyclists can ride Tri-Met bus #17 and take the popular 12-mile loop around the island. **WARRIOR ROCK LIGHTHOUSE** is a 3-mile hike from the north unit parking facility.

Spend an afternoon or an entire day (see the Sauvie Island section in the Day Trips chapter). Parking permits are $3.50 per day, $11 per year, available at **CRACKER BARREL GROCERY STORE** (15005 NW Sauvie Island Rd; 503/621-3960) on your left immediately as you cross over the bridge onto the island. Wildlife areas are open to the public April through September. Call **METRO REGIONAL PARKS & GREEN SPACES** (503/797-1850) for information. *www.sauvieisland.org; map:AA9.*

15) BREWERIES AND BREWPUBS

VARIOUS LOCATIONS

More than a century has passed since Henry Weinhard proposed pumping beer through the Skidmore Fountain. But even before that, Portlanders loved beer. Today, although Weinhard's beer is brewed elsewhere (and the former brewery has been developed into housing and retail space), the city has almost as many places to drink beer as it does coffee.

More than 40 craft breweries and brewpubs call Portland home, more per capita than any other American city (check out www.oregonbeer.com for a listing). The Northwest in general—and Portland in particular—is the national center for craft breweries: small, independent companies that turn out specialty beers, generally in small batches and according to traditional methods. Aficionados argue that Northwest brews are distinctly different from even the best imports. They claim that the Western barley, hops from the Willamette and Yakima valleys, and Cascades water give local concoctions their particular character.

One place to get a free tour of the brewing process is the **WIDMER BREWING COMPANY**, which produces the city's favorite hefeweizen in its facility on an industrial byway in North Portland. Tours (with beer sampling) are available Fridays at 3pm and Saturdays at 11am and 12:30pm—call 503/281-2437 for reservations Mon–Fri, 8am–6pm. Next door is the attractive **GASTHAUS PUB** (955 N Russell St, Albina; 503/281-3333; www.widmer. com; map:GG6), a fine place to sample Widmer suds with a plate of sausage and kraut or a pretzel (see review in the Nightlife chapter).

Head to the waterfront along the RiverPlace esplanade for **FULL SAIL BREWING COMPANY**'s Portland brewery (0307 SW Montgomery St; 503/222-5343; www.fullsailbrewing.com; map:C5). Tours are by appointment only, but you can see the works from the adjoining **HARBORSIDE** Pilsner Room (503/220-1865) and sample 12 beers, including Full Sail's best-selling Amber Ale, Golden Ale, and Nut Brown Ale.

One brewery that's garnered attention on the international level is **HAIR OF THE DOG** (4509 SE 23rd Ave; 503/232-6585; www.hairofthedog.com; map: HH5), which produces sublime, strong, "bottle-conditioned" (it improves with age) beer. British beer writer Michael Jackson picked the brewery as one of the best in the country, and its Adam beer is a favorite. It's a small operation, but the beermakers there are happy to give tours (call ahead).

While strolling in the Pearl District, stop for an India Pale Ale or a Black Strap Stout at the lofty **BRIDGEPORT BREWERY** (1313 NW Marshall St; 503/241-3612; www.bridgeportbrew.com; map:O1). Brewery tours are on Saturdays at 1pm, 3pm, and 5pm and weekdays by appointment.

You can learn about more than a dozen pubs offering custom-brewed suds in the Nightlife chapter. But one easy way to sample brews from about

70 different craft breweries is to head down to Gov. Tom McCall Waterfront Park during the last full weekend in July for the **OREGON BREWERS FESTIVAL** (503/778-5917; www.oregonbrewfest.com).

16) RIVER CRUISES ON THE COLUMBIA AND WILLAMETTE RIVERS
VARIOUS LOCATIONS

Before the arrival of railroads and paved roads, people could hail a steamboat just about anywhere between Portland and Eugene, Astoria, and The Dalles. Stern-wheelers still navigate the waters of the Columbia and Willamette rivers, offering some relief from today's crowded highways. But more importantly, they give patrons an opportunity to see the region from a riverine viewpoint.

PORTLAND SPIRIT (503/224-3900) and her sister vessels, the *Willamette Star* and *Crystal Dolphin*, offer fine-dining, sightseeing, and specialty cruises up and down the Willamette River. The *Spirit* leaves from its berth near the Salmon Street Springs in **GOV. TOM MCCALL WATERFRONT PARK**; catch the *Willamette Star* and *Crystal Dolphin* at **CARUTHERS LANDING** (near OMSI). The cost of the dinner cruise is $68, a midday lunch tour costs $38, and the Sunday champagne brunch cruise is $48 (all prices are lower for seniors and children). Two less expensive options are available without dining: sightseeing tours cost $28 for adults ($18 for children), and "Friday Early Escapes" (July–Sept) cost $22 for everyone. *www.portlandspirit.com.* &

WILLAMETTE JETBOAT EXCURSIONS (503/231-1532) offer perhaps the most exciting way to experience the Willamette River on a public boat, if you don't mind the possibility of getting splashed. The open-air jet boats ride close to the water and take sightseers upriver, past riverfront homes—the spectacular and the modest—all the way to Willamette Falls in Oregon City and downriver to Portland's cargo docks and shipyards. Two-hour 32-mile tours depart from OMSI every day from May 1 to early October. Cost is $33 for adults, $21 for children 4–11, and free for kids 3 and under. One-hour tours are also available. *www.willamettejet.com.*

THE STERN-WHEELER ROSE (503/286-7673), a 92-foot stern-wheeler replica, also sails from the OMSI dock on the east side of the Willamette. The downriver trip has an industrial view, passing shipyards, grain terminals, 7 of Portland's 12 bridges, and one of the world's largest dry docks. Upriver is more scenic, passing Johns Landing, Oaks Park, Sellwood, and gracious old homes on the bluffs overlooking the Willamette. Dinner cruises on the 120-passenger double-deck boat run $57.25 per person; $46.50 for brunch. *www.sternwheelerrose.com.*

From its base at **MARINE PARK** in Cascade Locks, about 45 minutes east of Portland (exit 44 from I-84), the **COLUMBIA GORGE STERNWHEELER** (800/224-3901), a triple-deck paddle wheeler, voyages through the dramatic Columbia River Gorge. In winter, the 147-foot vessel docks in Portland and takes guests up and down the Willamette River on dinner, lunch, brunch, and holiday cruises. Fares range from $18 to $68. *www.sternwheeler.com.* &

17) PORTLAND AERIAL TRAM

3303 SW BOND AVE, SOUTH WATERFRONT; 503/494-8283
Portland's newest public transportation link is a $57 million aerial tramway that connects the South Waterfront district with the top of Marquam Hill, home of **OREGON HEALTH AND SCIENCE UNIVERSITY (OHSU)**. Linking OHSU's main campus with its Center for Health and Healing, the Swiss-made modular tram cabins, lined with windows, slowly and steadily climb and descend the 3,300-foot cables. For a $4 round-trip fare—paid by credit card or change at automated ticket booths—the 3-minute ride gives you a bird's-eye view of the city and its architectural skyline, various bustling arteries, main waterway, and surrounding mountainous topography (you can see Mount Hood and Mount St. Helens on a clear day). At a small outdoor sitting area at the top, you can further enjoy the impressive vista. The tram cabins depart every 5 minutes; the base can be accessed by Portland Streetcar. *Mon–Fri 5:30am–9:30pm, Sat 9am–5pm; www.portlandtram.org; map:II6.* &

18) PITTOCK MANSION

3229 NW PITTOCK DR, PITTOCK ACRE; 503/823-3623
Henry Pittock (1835–1919) had the advantage of watching over Portland from two perspectives: from behind the founder's desk at the daily *Oregonian* and, in his later years, from this home 1,000 feet above the city. Built between 1909 and 1914 by San Francisco architect Edward T. Foulkes, the stately, 16,000-square-foot mansion stands on 46 acres that look across North Portland to Mount Hood. A fortresslike chateau of French Renaissance style, it boasts sandstone-faced walls and a red-tiled roof featuring turrets and dormer windows. It stayed in the Pittock family until 1964, when the property—in poor repair and threatened by the wrecking ball—was sold to the City of Portland for $225,000.

The house has two main wings that meet in a central drawing room. A graceful marble staircase sweeps from the basement to the second story; another, less conspicuous stairway leads to the servants' quarters on the top floor. The 22 rooms, furnished with antiques, include an oval parlor and a Turkish smoking room. Everywhere, it seems, are crystal chandeliers and beautiful wood paneling.

Regular tours are conducted in the afternoon, and the manicured grounds around the mansion and Pittock Acres (with numerous hiking trails) are open to the public until dark. The historic **GATE LODGE**, home to the steward of the mansion and his family, has been restored and is also open for viewing. Admission to the mansion is $7 for adults, $6 for seniors, $4 for kids 6–18, and free for children under 6. *Every day 11am–4pm (Feb–June, Sept–Dec), 10am–4pm (July–Aug), closed Jan; www.pittockmansion.org; map:HH8.* &

19) MULTNOMAH FALLS AND CROWN POINT

I-84 TO CORBETT (EXIT 22)

For travelers heading east on I-84, exit 22 links up with Hwy 30, the Historic Columbia River Hwy. This highway is no straight shot. Constructed between 1913 and 1922, it was designed not only to provide east-west transportation, but also to take full advantage of every natural aspect, scenic feature, water-fall, viewpoint, and panorama. Follow the road to **VISTA HOUSE AT CROWN POINT** for an unbeatable view of the Columbia River Gorge in either direction. Within the next 12 miles, you can choose from eight different waterfalls, all within a mile or less of the nearest parking area. Most visitors stop at famed **MULTNOMAH FALLS** (easily accessible from I-84), complete with visitors center and gift shop in the historic **MULTNOMAH FALLS LODGE**, where dining reservations are accepted (503/695-2376). The second-tallest year-round waterfall in the nation, Multnomah Falls is visible from the roadway, but for a closer look, the lower falls are only a quarter mile up, and the upper falls, only a mile. **BENSON STATE RECREATION AREA** is less than a mile away, should a picnic be in order. For a full day trip through this area, known as the **JOHN B. YEON SCENIC CORRIDOR**, start at exit 37 and wend your way back to Corbett, ending at Crown Point (see the Columbia River Gorge, Oregon section in the Day Trips chapter). *www.oregonstateparks.org.*

20) SATURDAY MARKET

108 W BURNSIDE ST, UNDER BURNSIDE BRIDGE
BETWEEN SW 1ST AND FRONT AVES; 503/222-6072

In 1974 a group of Portland artists assembled the beginnings of what may today be the largest continuously operating outdoor craft market in the country. This is no occasional street fair: every weekend for 10 months and during the week before Christmas (known as the "Festival of the Last Minute"), more than 350 craft and food vendors cluster under the Burnside Bridge and beyond to peddle handmade items ranging from stained glass to huckleberry jam, wool sweaters, and silver earrings. On any given weekend (and especially around holidays or during summer), musicians, jugglers, magicians, face painters, and clowns entertain the crowd. A main stage with scheduled entertainment is at the hub of the food court, where the bites are usually beyond what you'd expect from a cart.

Tri-Met buses and the MAX light-rail serve the market in Fareless Square; disembark at Skidmore Fountain, under the Burnside Bridge. Street parking is free on Sundays, but with a $25 purchase at the market, you can get either free bus tickets or two hours of free parking at the SmartPark garage on NW Davis Street and Naito Parkway.

While you're in the area, wander through the year-round stalls in the nearby **NEW MARKET VILLAGE** and the **SKIDMORE FOUNTAIN BUILDINGS** (see Old Town/Skidmore/Chinatown in the Neighborhoods section of this chapter). *Sat 10am–5pm, Sun 11am–4:30pm (Mar–Dec), every day 11am–6pm (Dec 18–Dec 24); www.portlandsaturdaymarket.com; map:J6.* ᕮ

Neighborhoods

To get a sense of the overall social landscape of Portland, you'll want to visit its numerous and diverse neighborhoods, each with its own distinct culture. Check out www.portlandneighborhood.com for more information about each neighborhood.

ALAMEDA/BEAUMONT VILLAGE

NE FREMONT ST BETWEEN 33RD AND 51ST AVES

In the heart of the Alameda neighborhood, a beautiful residential district developed between 1910 and 1940, is the portion of NE Fremont Street known as **BEAUMONT VILLAGE**. The quaint shops and refurbished homes have created a place where Northeast Portlanders like to shop, eat, and browse. The **BEAUMONT MARKET** (4130 NE Fremont St; 503/284-3032) has the sensibility of an old-time general store; next door, the unique **DUTCH VILLAGE** building (NE 41st Ave and Fremont St) houses several shops.

Strolling along Fremont Street you'll encounter numerous specialty shops, including the creative custom-clothing shop **SOFADA** (4623 NE Fremont St; 503/445-2006). Slide into the tall booths at the **ALAMEDA BREWHOUSE** (4765 NE Fremont St; 503/460-9025) for a microbrew and delicious lunch, or if you have Fido with you, stop in at the **GREEN DOG PET SUPPLY** (4605 NE Fremont St; 503/528-1800) for a range of healthy organic treats that are good for your dog and the earth. In the same building, you can also enjoy a fabulous gelato at **PARISI'S** (503/287-7444) or kick your feet up at **FOXFIRE TEAS** (503/288-6869) over a cup of specialty tea and a savory scone. In the spring and summer months, dine outside on the amazing patio at **THE BLUE OLIVE** (4627 NE Fremont St; 503/528-2822), while enjoying some of Portland's best Mediterranean food.

KLICKITAT STREET parallels Fremont just one block to the south. If you're a fan of author Beverly Cleary and her children's novels, you'll want to visit the neighborhood where Ramona ("the Pest") Quimby lived. Then check out the statues of Ramona, Ribsy, and Henry Huggins in **GRANT PARK**, about six blocks south of Fremont via 33rd Avenue. *www.bwna.org; map:FF4–5.*

ALBERTA

NE ALBERTA ST BETWEEN 10TH AND 31ST AVES

The best time to visit multicultural and arty NE Alberta Street is on the last Thursday evening of the month: galleries and shops come alive in a happy bustle of art, food, and bodies known as **LAST THURSDAY** (www.artonalberta.org)—not to be confused with First Thursday in the Pearl District and downtown. Street vendors sell their arts and crafts, and galleries are open late. The scene is quieter the rest of the time, but no less intriguing.

NE Alberta is rapidly becoming not only a commercial success story but also an ever-unwinding ribbon of community that ties together several residential neighborhoods (King, Vernon, Concordia, and Sabin). In order to satisfy hunger pains, Alberta hosts all manner of restaurants, such as Cajun-spiced **BERNIE'S SOUTHERN BISTRO** (2904 NE Alberta St; 503/282-9864), the swanky Thai restaurant **SIAM SOCIETY** (2703 NE Alberta St; 503/922-3675), Spanish tapas restaurant **LOLO** (2940 NE Alberta St; 503/288-3400), and the popular breakfast spot **TIN SHED GARDEN CAFE** (1438 NE Alberta St; 503/288-6966). See reviews for all in the Restaurants chapter.

For more aesthetic cravings, numerous studios and art galleries line the street, including **THE TALISMAN GALLERY** (1476 NE Alberta St; 503/284-8800; see Arts Scene chapter), **GUARDINO GALLERY** (2939 NE Alberta St; 503/281-9048; see Arts Scene chapter), and **ONDA ARTE LATINA** (2215 NE Alberta St; 503/493-1909). Lively retail shops sell custom-made clothing, including **GARNISH** (1524 NE Alberta St; 503/282-3200); shoes, including **PEDX SHOE SHANGRILA** (2230 NE Alberta St; 503/460-0760); and musical instruments, including **PORTLAND FRET WORKS** (3039 NE Alberta St; 503/249-3737). You won't find a Starbucks, but you can sip lattes at **RANDOM ORDER COFFEEHOUSE** (1800 NE Alberta St; 503/331-1420) and munch on a sweet or savory slice of pie. For 20-plus blocks, with everything from murals and Mexican grocers in between, Alberta Street is a burst of local color whichever way you look. A short jaunt up 30th Avenue to **KILLINGSWORTH STREET** and you'll find another enclave featuring **HAIL MARY**, the shop of artist Mary Tapogna, known for tile and glass mosaics. From there, it's a short walk to the **MCMENAMINS' KENNEDY SCHOOL** on 33rd Avenue (see Lodgings chapter) where you can soak in the hot pool or take in a second-run movie—and see more of Mary Tapogna's work on permanent display. *Map:FF5.*

CENTRAL DOWNTOWN
See no. 2 in Top 20 Attractions.

DIVISION/CLINTON
SE DIVISION AND CLINTON STS FROM 20TH TO 26TH AVES AND DIVISION UP TO 36TH AVE
In the 1970s, the City of Portland planned to tear down the housing and businesses along Clinton and neighboring streets to put in an eight-lane freeway and turn Division into a frontage road. The city purchased and emptied properties and the area deteriorated. The residents and businesses rose in active rebellion, and eventually the city cancelled the project, using the funds to build a light-rail system on the west side of the Willamette River.

A neighborhood in renaissance since the early 1980s, Division and Clinton streets continue to thrust up new shops and restaurants, refurbishing existing buildings and reinvigorating old haunts. With such popular restaurants as **POK POK**, **LAURO KITCHEN**, and **VINDALHO** (see reviews in the Restaurants chapter), visitors to the area won't have to venture beyond this understated southeast neighborhood for a fantastic dining experience. Coffee shops and bars dot this urban landscape, and a plethora of resale stores such as **VILLAGE MERCHANTS** (3360 SE Division St) will satisfy even hard-core second-hand shoppers. If it's sustainable shopping you're into, try **MIRADOR COMMUNITY**

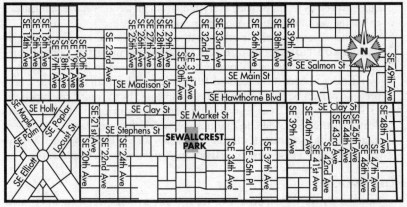

Hawthorne District

STORE (2106 SE Division St), or pick up some organic groceries at **NEW SEA-SONS** or **PEOPLE'S FOOD CO-OP** (see reviews in the Shopping chapter). You'll be shopping locally no matter where you stop. *www.divisionclinton.com*

HAWTHORNE DISTRICT

SE HAWTHORNE BLVD FROM SE 32ND TO 50TH AVES

Hawthorne Boulevard is one of Portland's most colorful and diverse neighborhoods, with a fun and eclectic mix of unique shopping and entertainment venues. The area has evolved from its tie-dyed past into a weird and wonderful area that has unbeatable people-watching from any one of its many sidewalk tables. With plenty of free parking and more Thai restaurants than you can shake a stick at, this whimsical and family-friendly street demands that you get out of the car and walk.

The hub of Hawthorne is McMenamins' brightly colored **BAGDAD THE-ATER AND PUB** (3702 SE Hawthorne Blvd; 503/236-9234; map:HH5). Built in 1927 with financing from Universal Studios, the Mediterranean-style building with the neon Middle Eastern marquee still packs in patrons for pizza, beer and wine, and celluloid. The remarkable interior flaunts barreled arches, ornate wrought-iron fixtures, brilliantly colored mosaic work, and painted and stenciled Mediterranean designs and mythical characters.

For blocks in either direction from the Bagdad are brewpubs, bakeries, taquerias, bars, coffee shops, and wonderfully idiosyncratic dining establishments such as the **BREAD AND INK CAFE** (3610 SE Hawthorne Blvd; 503/239-4756), which serves up a Yiddish brunch with great blintzes, and **3 DOORS DOWN CAFÉ** (1429 SE 37th Ave; 503/236-6886), which offers Mediterranean-inspired dinners in a warm, bistro-style setting (see reviews in the Restaurants chapter). A couple of unique bookstores between SE 31st and 37th avenues include the off-beat **MURDER BY THE BOOK** (3210 SE Hawthorne Blvd; 503/232-9995; see Shopping chapter), and a variety of quirky specialty shops provide everything from midcentury modern furniture to unique perfumes to goth accoutrements.

At its west end, the Hawthorne district brushes the northern edge of **LADD'S ADDITION** (between SE 12th and 20th aves; map:HH5), one of Portland's most intriguing neighborhoods. Extending south to Division Street, it was developed between 1903 and 1925 on the earlier plan of pioneer entrepreneur William S. Ladd, who had been impressed by the radial street pattern of Washington, D.C. Get lost circumnavigating the main streets in this residential district, SE Ladd and Elliott avenues, which form a large X and meet in a central park, **LADD'S CIRCLE**; secondary streets come together at four diamond-shaped rose gardens. *www.thinkhawthorne.com; map:HH4–5.*

HOLLYWOOD

FRAMED BY NE THOMPSON AND NE HALSEY STS BETWEEN NE 37TH AND NE 47TH AVES

Easily accessible by MAX, the Hollywood district, centered on Sandy Boulevard between 39th and 47th avenues, is largely residential, but has the feel of a bustling village, with a bunch of shops and the beautiful and historic **HOLLYWOOD THEATRE** (4122 NE Sandy Blvd; 503/281-4215; map:GG4) at its center. The theater shows art, foreign, and independent flicks daily, whenever it isn't hosting one of a dozen annual film festivals and special events. A brilliant neon-and-steel Hollywood sign stands in front of the whimsical, sculpted facade of this multicolored terra-cotta building. Built in 1926, when it had an eight-piece orchestra to accompany silent films, the Hollywood Theatre has been through many transformations. Film Action Oregon bought the theater in 1997 and gave it a thorough makeover; today, this community treasure thrives. Scores of arts and community organizations use it for performances, concerts, lectures, fund-raising events, and other gatherings, and the theater has hosted more than 400 premieres for Oregon filmmakers since 1998. Normal admission is $6.50 for adults, $4.50 for seniors 65-plus and children 4–12; Monday night, all shows are just $4. *www.hollywoodtheatre.org.* &

If you have time to browse or want to grab a meal before the film, you'll do well to check out the **HOLLYWOOD BURGER BAR** (4211 NE Sandy Blvd; 503/288-8965). Formerly a trolley station, this round little soda fountain has been in business—with the same owners—since 1954. There are several vintage/retro and antique shops along 42nd Avenue, between Hancock and Tillamook streets worth a good browse, as well. **MOON AND SIXPENCE** (2014 NE 42nd Ave; 503/288-7802), a British-style pub serving pub food, 20 craft and import beers on tap, plus over 80 more in bottles, has one of the largest outdoor patios in town. All of these businesses are locally owned, but the addition of a Whole Foods market is anticipated later in 2010 and will come with 53 condos built in the building above it, and additional neighborhood parking.

Irvington

IRVINGTON

FRAMED BY NE 7TH AND 26TH AVES, BROADWAY AND FREMONT STS

One of Portland's oldest eastside neighborhoods, Irvington was initially the 1851 land claim of Scottish Captain William Irving. Purchased by the Prospect Park Company in the late 1880s and developed as an exclusive residential enclave, it was built up between 1905 and 1930 with a variety of Arts and Crafts bungalows, Victorian houses, and (toward Broadway) apartment buildings. Today an easy mile-and-a-quarter stroll down Irvington's wide sidewalks reveals beautiful large homes (several of them now bed-and-breakfast inns) and attractive gardens, as well as a hip shopping district.

From Broadway, walk a block north on NE 15th to the **GUSTAV FREIWALD HOUSE** (1810 NE 15th Ave), now a B&B called **THE LION AND THE ROSE** (see review in the Lodgings chapter). The turreted Queen Anne Victorian was built in 1906 for an early microbrewer. The Gothic **WESTMINSTER PRESBYTERIAN CHURCH** (1624 NE Hancock St), another block north and east, was built from 1912–14 and trimmed with black basalt.

Turn east on Thompson to see the 1909 **MARCUS DELAHUNT HOUSE** (1617 NE Thompson St), a beautiful Prairie-style home with oversize porch, eaves, and support pillars. The architect, John Bennes, had been an office boy for Frank Lloyd Wright. Pass the **IRVINGTON CLUB** (2131 NE Thompson St), a tennis and swimming club established in 1898; its two-story

175

Craftsman-style home was built in 1912 by member Ellis Lawrence, founder of the School of Architecture at the University of Oregon in Eugene. The large 1910 **WILLIAM KENNARD HOUSE** (2230 NE Thompson St) is also in the Craftsman style; architect Raymond Hockenberry, best known for Oregon's Crater Lake Lodge, used concrete blocks to imitate natural stone. Just around the corner stands **PORTLAND'S FIRST ARTS AND CRAFTS HOME** (2210 NE 23rd Ave), also designed by Ellis Lawrence.

Turn south again to **PORTLAND'S WHITE HOUSE** (1914 NE 22nd Ave), the 1911 estate of timber baron Robert F. Lytle. Now a luxurious bed-and-breakfast inn (see review in the Lodgings chapter), the oak-and-Honduran-mahogany house does resemble the president's mansion with its pillared portico and circular drive. A block west is Pietro Belluschi's **CENTRAL LUTHERAN CHURCH** (2104 NE Hancock St), built from 1948–51. An architectural rebel best known for the Portland Art Museum, Belluschi designed a Scandinavian-style church with a Japanese gateway. The interior displays Northwest simplicity in its use of wood and stained glass.

On the neighborhood's south end, small stores, boutiques, restaurants, and coffee shops line NE Broadway and Weidler Street, a block farther south. The shop **TRADE ROOTS** (1831 NE Broadway; 503/281-5335) specializes in fair-trade goods; independent bookstore **BROADWAY BOOKS** (1714 NE Broadway; 503/284-1726) has been owned and operated by the same two friends for 17 years (see reviews in the Shopping chapter). Restaurants such as **COLOSSO** (1932 NE Broadway; 503/288-3333) and **MILO'S CITY CAFE** (1325 NE Broadway; 503/288-6456) have a strong local following.

One Sunday in mid-May, the Irvington Community Association sponsors an **OPEN HOUSE TOUR** ($20) of the neighborhood's historic homes. Year-round, its Web site provides a wealth of detailed information. *www.irvingtonhometour.com; map:GG5.*

LAKE OSWEGO

8 MILES SOUTH OF PORTLAND ON THE WEST BANK OF THE WILLAMETTE RIVER; 503/636-3634

Before white settlement, American Indians fished for abundant salmon in narrow, 3½-mile-long Lake Oswego, which they called Waluga for the wild swans that gathered there. Settlers first came in 1846, and a thriving iron industry (1865–94) gave the newly established town early prosperity. As the iron industry declined, the 405-acre lake became a popular recreation area, and the city grew around the lake, becoming an upscale community now rife with trendy shops and restaurants.

Lake Oswego is an 8-mile drive south from downtown Portland via the leafy corridor of SW Macadam Avenue (Hwy 43); the road first becomes Riverside Drive and then State Street, when you cross into Clackamas County. Or take the **WILLAMETTE SHORE TROLLEY** (503/697-7436) from RiverPlace along the Willamette River into Lake Oswego (see Train and Trolley Tours in this chapter).

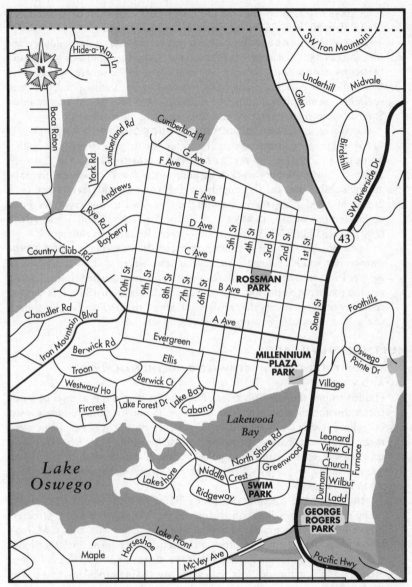

Lake Oswego

In downtown Lake Oswego, lettered avenues run perpendicular to the west of State Street. Numbered streets run north/south, parallel to State. More than two dozen public sculptures—in bronze, marble, stainless steel, and other media—have been placed along both sides of broad A Avenue and some cross streets. Stop in at the **LAKE OSWEGO CHAMBER OF COMMERCE** (242 B Ave; 503/636-3634) for a map of the local sights.

LAKE VIEW VILLAGE (A Ave between State and 1st sts), a six-building complex, boasts 84,000 square feet of restaurants, shops, and offices beside **MILLENNIUM PLAZA PARK** (200 1st St), an inviting public square with a lovely lake vista. The park has a charming fountain and reflecting pond, benches, sculpture, picnic tables, and public restrooms; it is also the site of a summer Saturday farmers market, concerts, and numerous other events.

Elsewhere downtown, **GOURMET PRODUCTIONS** (39 B Ave; 503/697-7355) will prepare a tasty take-out lunch for you to bring to the park (with a bottle of Oregon wine). Stores like **DIPINTO A MANO** (425 2nd St; 503/636-9940), a colorful pottery workshop, address the town's creativity. To make an anglophile's day, the thoroughly English **LADY DI BRITISH STORE** (425 2nd St; 503/635-7298) serves tea with finger sandwiches and crumpets. Fine-dining options include **CLARKE'S** (455 2nd St; 503/636-2667) and **TUCCI** (220 A Ave; 503/697-3383); see reviews in the Restaurants chapter.

Some of Lake Oswego's earliest homes can still be seen in the **OLD TOWN** district, just south of downtown, east of State Street, and north of George Rogers Park. In particular, look for the 42-foot iron-smelter chimney stack (on the riverfront at the foot of Furnace St); dating from 1866, it is the last reminder of a community that settlers had hoped to turn into the "Pittsburgh of the West." *www.lake-oswego.com; map:MM6.*

MULTNOMAH VILLAGE

SW CAPITOL HWY FROM 30TH AVE TO MULTNOMAH BLVD, AND VICINITY

Hidden among the hills and vales of Southwest Portland is a jewel of a district known to most as Multnomah Village. (Some longtime residents insist on calling it simply "Multnomah," its name when it was an independent town.) No doubt, part of its quaint, laid-back charm comes from the Capitol Highway, which winds through the district like an English country road. Antique shops, art galleries, bookstores, and specialty shops make the village a window shopper's delight.

MARCO'S CAFÉ & ESPRESSO BAR (7910 SW 35th Ave; 503/245-0199) occupies a 1913 building constructed as the Thomas Bungalow Grocery; it later served as the town's post office and as a dance hall. Today, Marco's serves breakfast all day and offers an eclectic dinner menu. Another long-established village favorite is the **FAT CITY CAFÉ** (7820 SW Capitol Hwy; 503/245-5457), a historic diner, with walls covered in traffic signs, that boasts the best hash browns in the state. It also has an honorable mention in local history books: the cafe once played a key role in civic politics. See reviews in the Restaurants chapter.

A few blocks east, in the old Multnomah School, is a multipurpose neighborhood treasure: the **MULTNOMAH ART CENTER** (7688 SW Capitol Hwy; 503/823-ARTS; www.multnomahartscenter.org). Any time of year, you'll find a variety of cultural events and community classes offered here. Across the

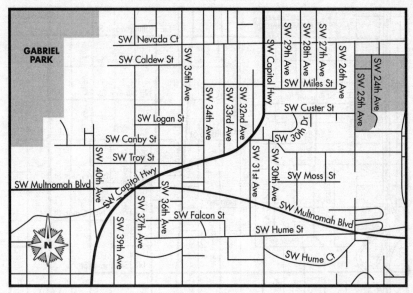

Multnomah Village

street, a vintage Masonic meeting hall now houses the brewpub **LUCKY LABRADOR PUBLIC HOUSE** (7675 SW Capitol Hwy; 503/244-2537). *www. multnomahvillage.com; map:JJ7.*

NORTH MISSISSIPPI

NORTH MISSISSIPPI AVE BETWEEN FREMONT AND MASON STS

The North Mississippi neighborhood is hip: plain and simple. A dynamic revival of the area has created an interesting scene that blends boutiques and brewpubs without any brouhaha. The short blocks of the Mississippi commercial area are family- and dog-friendly and enjoyable to walk, sprinkled as they are with interesting, funky stores; tasty restaurants (most with outdoor seating); and great coffee shops and cocktail lounges.

THE REBUILDING CENTER (3625 N Mississippi Ave; 503/331-1877; see Shopping chapter) reflects Portland's penchant for "green" living: this non-profit carries the region's largest volume of used building and remodeling materials. Stores to peruse include **BRIDGE CITY COMICS** (3725 N Mississippi Ave; 503/282-5484; see Shopping chapter), which has all sorts of rare comic books on its shelves, and **PISTIL'S NURSERY** (3811 N Mississippi Ave; 503/288-4889), which stocks luscious-looking, locally grown, and sustainable plants. Several clothing shops flaunt funky floral dresses in the windows. The street also has a used bookstore, a quaint antique store, and a bustling bike shop.

THE FRESH POT (4001 N Mississippi Ave; 503/284-8928) anchors the Mississippi neighborhood, offering the ever-important caffeine fix. Located in a historic Rexall Drugs location (its original neon sign remains intact), the

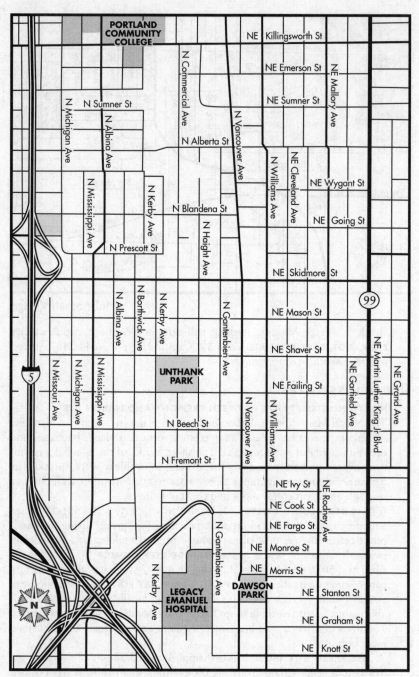

North Mississippi

shop serves up a mean cup of locally roasted Stumptown coffee. Reminiscent of a funky roadside stand, trailer-turned-juice-bar **MOXIE RX** (N Mississippi Ave at Shaver St; 503/285-0701) serves various juices and smoothies, plus it has an outdoor seating area for noshing on specialty sandwiches. Notable restaurants include the **MISSISSIPPI PIZZA PUB** (3552 N Mississippi Ave; 503/288-3231), which offers slices that are, some say, the best in town, as well as live music nightly. **POR QUE NO** (3525 N Mississippi Ave; 503/954-4149) fills its tacos with local meats or line-caught fish. **LOVELY HULA HANDS** (4057 N Mississippi Ave; 503/445-9910) offers a mix of delectable entrées such as steaks and pasta in a cozy atmosphere (see Restaurants chapter). **AMNESIA BREWING** (832 N Beech St; 503/281-7708), where you can wash down a delicious German-style sausage with a cold beer, has a laid-back, down-home feel (see Nightlife chapter). *Map:FF6.*

NORTHWEST PORTLAND/NOB HILL

See no. 11 in Top 20 Attractions.

OLD TOWN/SKIDMORE/CHINATOWN

NORTH OF W BURNSIDE ST TO NW HOYT ST AND 8TH AVE, SOUTH OF W BURNSIDE TO SW OAK ST AND 4TH AVE

Once the heart of the city's commercial core, the Skidmore and Old Town districts (Skidmore to the south of Burnside, Old Town to the north) have undergone major revitalizations since the mid-1970s. Today this is known as a multicultural neighborhood sporting people from all walks of life; it abounds with good restaurants, nightclubs, art galleries, and incubator businesses. Chinatown, with its magnificent gate on Fourth Avenue and W Burnside, is a relatively small area highlighted by the new classical Chinese garden. Overall, these districts contain one of the largest collections of restored brick and Italianate cast-iron buildings in the country, making the neighborhoods popular with film producers for period movie sets.

Start an exploration at the **SKIDMORE FOUNTAIN** (SW 1st Ave and Ankeny St; map:J6), the city's oldest and most gracious fountain, in cobblestoned Ankeny Square. Built in 1888 for the estate of city councilman Stephen Skidmore, the cast-iron fountain features two handmaidens dispensing water through lion-head spouts into drinking troughs earmarked "for horses, men and dogs."

Across the square, the **SKIDMORE FOUNTAIN BUILDING** has been remodeled as a mall with tourist-oriented shops. At the east end of the square, the **JEFF MORRIS MEMORIAL FIRE MUSEUM** (35 SW Ash St; map:J6) provides what is basically a window view of vintage fire engines; take a peek. West of Ankeny Square is a courtyard with tables for eateries inside the **NEW MARKET THEATER** (120 SW Ankeny St; map:J6). This magnificent brick and terracotta building in Victorian Renaissance style was considered the finest theater north of San Francisco after it opened (with *Rip Van Winkle*) in 1875. In fact, the 1,200-seat theater was on the second and third floors; a fresh-produce market with 28 marble stalls occupied the first floor. It was restored in 1984 to a jewel-like standard. Nearby, the **SATURDAY MARKET** (see no. 20 in Top 20 Attractions) bustles beneath the Burnside Bridge.

One of Portland's grandest buildings in the early 20th century was the Multnomah Hotel, now the **EMBASSY SUITES HOTEL**. A mammoth brick structure that occupies a full city block, the 1912 hotel has hosted celebrities from Charles Lindbergh to Elvis Presley to John F. Kennedy. Its enormous lobby, with 24 decorated marble columns, impresses visitors even today.

Notable restaurants in these precincts include **DAN AND LOUIS' OYSTER BAR** (208 SW Ankeny St; 503/227-5906; see Restaurants chapter), an institution since 1907, and **KELLS IRISH RESTAURANT & PUB** (112 SW 2nd Ave; 503/227-4057), ensconced in the last cast-iron building (with Art Nouveau touches) constructed in Portland: the 1889 Glisan Building.

Down the middle of SW First Avenue runs the MAX light-rail line. Follow it north, under the Burnside Bridge, to the carefully restored historic district of Old Town. As in the Skidmore district, you'll see all manner of Italianate cast-iron architectural treasures, including the 1888 **SKIDMORE BLOCK** (32 NW 1st Ave; map:J6), which now houses an antiques market. Many of the buildings here now provide office or warehouse space. On the exterior of the modern (1983) **ONE PACIFIC SQUARE** building (between NW 1st and 2nd aves, Davis and Everett sts; map:L6), find a plaque that indicates the high-water mark of the Willamette River flood of June 7, 1894: 3 feet above the present sidewalk level.

From the 1920s until the onset of World War II, when Americans of Japanese ancestry were moved to internment camps, the area between SW Ankeny and NW Glisan streets, and between First and Sixth avenues, was known as Japantown. The bustling community had more than 100 businesses concentrated especially between NW Second and Fourth avenues. Today the **OREGON NIKKEI LEGACY CENTER** (121 NW 2nd Ave; 503/224-1458; www.oregonnikkei.org; map:K6) preserves the heritage and offers walking maps of Japantown (see Museums in this chapter).

Portland's diminutive **CHINATOWN** blends into Old Town at about NW Third Avenue, but the serpent-adorned Chinatown Gate stands on NW Fourth Avenue at Burnside Street. Yu Tang Wang's 40-foot portal, dedicated in 1986, supports five roofs and 64 dragons. Although Portland's original Chinatown in the late 1800s was focused five blocks south of here, around Alder Street, the Chinese population slowly moved north. This area was designated a National Historic District in 1989; it's small enough that fiery red-and-yellow lampposts are needed to remind you of your whereabouts.

The highlight of Chinatown is the **PORTLAND CLASSICAL CHINESE GARDEN** (no. 7 in Top 20 Attractions). The largest of its kind in the United States, this Garden of the Awakening Orchid opened in 2000, the result of a friendship between Portland and its Chinese sister city, Suzhou.

The Old Town/Chinatown neighborhood extends north to **UNION STATION** (800 NW 6th Ave; map:N4), eight blocks north of Burnside. A city landmark with its 150-foot, red-brick, Tuscan-style clock tower, at the foot of the Broadway Bridge, the handsome Renaissance structure was built between

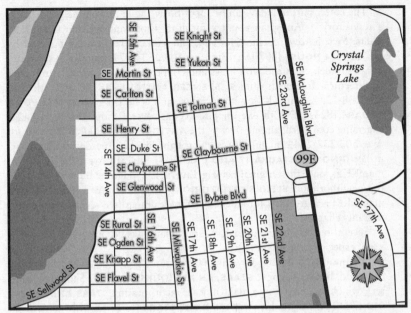

Sellwood/Westmoreland

1890 and 1896. Pietro Belluschi remodeled the interior in the 1930s, and the building underwent a full restoration in the late 1990s. It remains a transportation hub today. *www.oldtownchinatown.net; map:J6–N4.*

PEARL DISTRICT

See no. 10 in Top 20 Attractions.

SELLWOOD/WESTMORELAND

SE 13TH AVE FROM MALDEN TO UMATILLA STS, SE MILWAUKIE AVE FROM KNIGHT TO MALDEN STS

At the east end of the Sellwood Bridge, these two adjacent neighborhoods are a perfect blend of the old and new: one of Portland's best areas to go shopping for antiques and collectibles, alongside numerous newer restaurants and shops.

Sellwood, for six years a separate town on the east bank of the Willamette, was annexed to Portland in 1893. Proud of its past, shop owners have placed signs on their buildings identifying the structures' original uses and construction dates. One of the oldest buildings is the 1851 **OAKS PIONEER CHURCH** (455 SE Spokane St; www.oakspioneerchurch.org; map:KK6), a popular wedding site, but it is not a Sellwood original: built upriver in Milwaukie as Saint John's Episcopal Church by pioneer shipbuilder Lot Whitcomb, it was barged here in 1961.

The better part of a day can be spent browsing in this old neighborhood, a repository of American country furniture (both antique and new), lace, quilts, toys, hardware, china, jewelry, and trinkets. Particularly noteworthy are the **1874 HOUSE** (8070 SE 13th Ave; 503/233-1874; map:KK5; see Shopping chapter), crammed with brass and copper hardware, light fixtures, and architectural fragments, and **R. SPENCER ANTIQUES** (8130 SE 13th Ave; 503/238-1737; map:KK5), with furniture and collectibles. **OLD SELLWOOD SQUARE** (8235 SE 13th Ave; map:KK5) has several shops that surround a charming courtyard; among them is the **ANTIQUE ROW CAFÉ** (8235 SE 13th Ave; 503/232-2244; map:KK6), serving light lunches Tuesday through Saturday. **GINO'S RESTAURANT AND BAR** (8051 SE 13th Ave; 503/233-4613; map:KK5), once the Original Leipzig Tavern, is a longtime Italian favorite in this neighborhood; **ELENI'S ESTIATORIO** (7712 SE 13th Ave; 503/230-2165; map:KK6) is a great bet for a delicious Greek dinner (see reviews in the Restaurants chapter).

Several blocks north and east, Westmoreland has become a destination in itself, especially for foodies.

Westmoreland doesn't have as many antique stores as does neighboring Sellwood, but it does have **STARS, AN ANTIQUES MALL** (see Shopping chapter), which is actually two malls in one, incorporating **STARS AND SPLENDID** (7030 SE Milwaukie Ave) and **MORE STARS** (6717 SE Milwaukie Ave). Nearby independent bookstore **WALLACE BOOKS** (7241 SE Milwaukie Ave; 503/235-7350) offers a houseful of new and used books, and staff will help you track down that out-of-print volume.

The western fringe of this dual neighborhood is marked by the Willamette River and its newly extended **SPRINGWATER CORRIDOR** walking and biking trail, stretching south 3 miles from OMSI. The corridor slices past **OAKS PARK** (503/233-5777; www.oakspark.com; map:KK5), one of the oldest operating amusement parks in the country, famous for its huge roller rink and 1921 carousel, and transits the **OAKS BOTTOM WILDLIFE REFUGE** (www.portlandparks.org; map:KK5), a 160-acre woodland haven for bird-watchers (see the Recreation chapter for details). *Map:KK5–6.*

Museums

Architectural Heritage Center

701 SE GRAND AVE, BUCKMAN; 503/231-7264
With engaging gallery exhibits drawn from a renowned collection of architectural artifacts—one of the largest in the United States—the Architectural Heritage Center is a showcase for historic preservation, chronicling the history of building crafts in Portland and the Pacific Northwest. Exhibits at this nonprofit resource center include anything ever attached to a historic building: antique hardware, stained-glass windows, vintage doors, carved mantels, terra-cotta moldings, cast-iron building facades, period light fixtures, and architectural drawings. *Wed–Sat 10am–4:30pm; www.visitahc.org; map:HH5.* &

The Hat Museum

1928 SE LADD AVE, LADD'S ADDITION; 503/232-0433

Christian Dior once said, "Without hats, we would have no civilization." The Hat Museum couldn't agree more. Your tour guide—a milliner dressed in period costume—directs groups through a collection that includes more than 1,000 artfully arranged hats—the oldest dating back to the 1860s. This is the largest hat museum in the United States—if you want to see more hats, you'll have to go to Europe. Located in the historic Ladd-Reingold House, just minutes from downtown. Admission is $10. Tours daily—by appointment only. *10am–6pm; www.thehatmuseum.com; map:HH5.*

Oregon History Center

1200 SW PARK AVE, DOWNTOWN; 503/222-1741

See no. 12 in Top 20 Attractions.

Oregon Jewish Museum

310 NW DAVIS ST, OLD TOWN; 503/226-3600

The Oregon Jewish Museum—the only Jewish museum in the Northwest—was founded to preserve the rich cultural heritage of one of this state's earliest immigrant groups. It hosts four exhibits each year and maintains a library and archive with photographs, records, and ephemeral material dating from 1850 to the present. The largest collection of documents of Oregon Jews in existence, it is widely used by researchers, scholars, and students. The Oregon Jewish Museum also offers a variety of educational programs, as well as special lectures and collaborative programs with other institutions. The museum artifact collection includes small but significant holdings by regional Jewish artists, ritual Judaica, and family and business collections. Admission is $3. *Tues–Fri 10:30am–3pm, Sun 1–4pm, closed for Passover; no wheelchair access to restroom; www.ojm.org; map:K6.*

Oregon Maritime Museum

GOV. TOM MCCALL WATERFRONT PARK AT SW PINE ST; 503/224-7724

When Portland was founded in the early 1840s on the banks of the Willamette River, the town thrived because of its deep harbor: any ship that could come into the mouth of the Columbia could go all the way to Portland, and shipping was by far the cheapest way to move cargo. The Maritime Museum celebrates this history aboard *The Portland*, the last steam-powered sternwheeler tugboat built in the country (in 1947). Here you can see the engine room and then climb up to the Pilot House, 32 feet above the water, for a great view. Many of the exhibits once housed in a nearby museum building have been moved onto the ship; they include model sailing ships, photographs from Portland's shipbuilding heritage, and other maritime artifacts. Admission is $5 for adults, $4 for seniors, $3 for youth 6–17, and free for children under 6. *Wed–Sun 11am–4pm; www.oregonmaritimemuseum.org; map:I7.*

Oregon Museum of Science and Industry (OMSI)

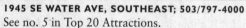

1945 SE WATER AVE, SOUTHEAST; 503/797-4000
See no. 5 in Top 20 Attractions.

Oregon Nikkei Legacy Center

121 NW 2ND AVE, OLD TOWN; 503/224-1458
This small museum in the heart of what was once Portland's Japantown
serves as a focal point for understanding Oregon's Japanese citizens and pre-
serving their history—from the arrival of the first immigrants in the 1880s
to their thriving communities in the 1930s to their displacement in World
War II internment camps and their postwar resettlement. The center provides
public education through its rotating exhibits, resource library of books
and videotapes, educational programs and speakers, and live performances.
Admission is $3. *Tues–Sat 11am–3pm, Sun noon–3pm; www.oregonnikkei.
org; map:K6.* &

Portland Art Museum (PAM)

1219 SW PARK AVE, DOWNTOWN; 503/226-2811
See no. 4 in Top 20 Attractions.

Portland Children's Museum

4105 SW CANYON RD, WASHINGTON PARK; 503/223-6500
Located directly opposite the Oregon Zoo, this is a museum that's not really
a museum: it's a play and learning center for children, from babies to 10-
year-olds. The "please touch" exhibits include a child-size grocery store and
cafe, complete with shopping baskets, a checkout line, and a cash register
where kids can ring up groceries. Other attractions include Water Works,
featuring a 12-foot waterfall and conveyor belt with everyday objects moving through water, which continues to delight children of all ages. The Play It
Again Theater gives the ham in everyone a chance to dress up, work the sound
and lights, move the curtain, and direct a play. Older children love the drop-
in clay studio, where they can make a sculpture to be fired and glazed, and
the Garage, where they can build frames and mobiles from recycled objects.
Museum educators are always on hand to help. Various craft and music
activities, special visiting performers, costume parades, and other events are
scheduled daily. Admission is $8. *Mon–Sat 9am–5pm, Sun 11am–5pm; www.
portlandcm.org; map:HH7.*

Portland Police Officer Museum

1111 SW 2ND AVE, DOWNTOWN; 503/823-0019
Whether you're a history buff, interested in law enforcement, or just want to
hop on a Harley Davidson police motorcycle for a photo op, going through
security at the Portland Police Officer Museum will be worth it. The museum
details Portland's history of law enforcement through exhibits showcasing
uniforms, arrest-record books, weapons, and other artifacts. One room is
dedicated to the memory of Portland's fallen officers. A gift shop sells apparel,

hats, patches, and more. Parking is located across the street. If you're over the age of 18, you will need a form of identification to show at the front desk, as this building is part of the Police Bureau. Admission is free; call in advance. *Tues–Fri 10am–3pm; www.portlandpolicemuseum.com; map:F4.*

Rice Northwest Museum of Rocks and Minerals

26385 NW GROVELAND DR, HILLSBORO; 503/647-2418

One of the top mineral museums in the nation has a vast collection of exquisite minerals, crystals, meteorites, fossils, and fluorescent rocks. Focusing on minerals found in the Northwest, the collection is housed in the first ranch-style home to be nominated for the National Register of Historic Places, in suburban Hillsboro, 16 miles west of Portland. Admission is $7 for adults, $6 for seniors (60 and over), $5 for students 5–17, and free for children under 5. *Wed–Sun 1–5pm; www.ricenwmuseum.org.*

Velveteria: The Museum of Velvet Paintings

2448 E BURNSIDE, KERNS; 503/233-5100

A self-proclaimed "Epicenter of Art," this museum of velvet paintings opened in December 2005 after curators Caren Anderson and Carl Baldwin spent eight years collecting velvet paintings from Tucson, Arizona, to Cuzco, Peru. This quirky museum displays 200 velvet paintings, rotating on and off exhibit from a collection of more than 1,500 paintings, and counting. Admission is $5. *Fri–Sun noon–5pm and by appointment; www.velveteria. com; map:GG4.* &

Wells Fargo History Museum

1300 SW FIFTH AVE, DOWNTOWN; 503/886-1102

At this second-story bank museum, you can explore the role of Wells Fargo in the pioneer history of Oregon and the West. A variety of displays include a Concord stagecoach, a hands-on telegraph, and other unique artifacts from events such as the gold rush of the early 1850s. Call ahead for a guided tour; admission is free. *Mon–Fri 9am–5pm; www.wellsfargohistory.com; map:F3.* &

World Forestry Center Discovery Museum

4033 SW CANYON RD, WASHINGTON PARK; 503/228-1367

Have you ever rafted in whitewater rapids without getting wet or smoke jumped without feeling the flames of a forest fire? How about getting strapped in and lifted 50 feet into the forest canopy to see life above the trees? You can try any of these activities at the World Forestry Center Discovery Museum. In here, traveling is a breeze: take a virtual trip to Russia, China, South Africa, and Brazil to see their amazing forests. More than a museum, the 20,000-square-foot facility, extensively renovated in 2005, is also home to the World Forest Institute and demonstration tree farms. It will change the way you look at trees—and that's the idea. Museum admission is $8 for adults, $7 for seniors, and $5 for children 3–18. *Every day 10am–5pm, closed Thanksgiving, Christmas Eve, Christmas Day; www.worldforestry.org; map:HH7.* &

Gardens

Portland has been called the gardening capital of the United States. That may or may not be true, but there's no disputing the fact that it's a fantastic place to get your hands dirty. The Willamette Valley's mild climate makes for a long growing season that supports a variety of plant life about which most American gardeners only fantasize, and the diversity, expertise, and wild enthusiasm of the local green thumbs make it fertile ground in more ways than one.

Accomplished Portland gardeners are not a recent phenomenon. In 1889, the nation's first rose society was established here, soon followed by the first primrose and rhododendron societies. By the 1920s, Portland boasted more garden clubs than any other city in the nation; they now total more than 20.

This predilection for plant life means that visitors will encounter gardens in unexpected places. A small bamboo garden, for example, is tucked between exhibits at the **OREGON ZOO** (see no. 6 in Top 20 Attractions). There are more than 101 named varieties of camellias on the **UNIVERSITY OF PORTLAND CAMPUS** (5000 N Willamette Blvd, North Portland; map:EE8). April through May, Metro Regional Government (www.oregonmetro.gov) sponsors tours of private gardens.

Since 1975, The **COMMUNITY GARDENS PROGRAM** (503/823-1612) rents 20x20 plots in over 32 neighborhoods; some gardens have waiting lists. For those who want to learn more, the **FRIENDS OF PORTLAND COMMUNITY GARDENS** has established a compost demonstration site at **FULTON GARDEN** (SW 3rd Ave and Barbur Blvd; map:A2). A backyard wildlife habitat cozies up to the **CLINTON GARDEN** (SE 18th Ave and Clinton St; map:II5), and a demonstration orchard spreads its limbs next to the **GABRIEL GARDEN** (SW 41st Ave and Canby St; map:JJ8).

The following gardens are among the city's horticultural highlights. All are free and open daily, unless otherwise noted.

Audubon Society of Portland

5151 NW CORNELL RD, WEST HILLS; 503/292-6855

Nestled against Forest Park, five minutes from downtown, is the Audubon Society's 143-acre wildlife sanctuary, showcasing native flora and fauna. More than 4 miles of forested hiking trails wind through a mixed conifer forest along gurgling Balch Creek. A stand of old-growth Douglas firs is a testament to Oregon's gentle giants, once prolific throughout the Pacific Northwest. The Audubon Center also has a small pavilion overlooking a pond—a lovely stop for lunch or bird-watching. *Trails open every day dawn to dusk; www.audubonportland.org; map:GG8.*

The Berry Botanic Garden

11505 SW SUMMERVILLE AVE, RIVERDALE; 503/636-4112

The Berry Botanic Garden's half-acre rock garden is more than an extraordinary accumulation of alpine plants; it's also part of Berry's nationally recognized effort to preserve endangered plant species of the Pacific Northwest in their native habitats. Three other plant groups—primulas, rhododendrons, and Northwest natives—are featured on the 6¼-acre estate of Mrs. Rae Selling Berry (1881–1976), famed patroness of plant expeditions. Located just south of Lewis & Clark College, Berry Botanic Garden is a national historic site. Groups may schedule tours with volunteer guides by calling at least two weeks in advance. Admission is $5 for adult nonmembers, free for members and children under 12. *Garden open every day during daylight hours by appointment, visitors center open Mon–Fri 9am–4:30pm; www.berrybot.org; map:LL6.* &

Crystal Springs Rhododendron Garden

SE 28TH AVE, I BLOCK NORTH OF SE WOODSTOCK BLVD, WOODSTOCK; 503/771-8386

Kodachrome was invented for places like this nationally acclaimed garden near Reed College, a peaceful retreat for bird-watchers and neighborhood strollers most of the year. In April, May, and June, however, it becomes an irresistible magnet for color-happy camera and video buffs, as some 2,500 rhododendrons, azaleas, and companion plants blaze on the 7-acre grounds. Japanese maples, sourwood trees, and fothergillas paint the garden in fall, and the spring-fed lake, home to a sizable colony of waterfowl, is a year-round attraction. The annual plant sale and show is held on Mother's Day, when loads of Portlanders traditionally promenade through at peak bloom, and Crystal Springs is the perfect spot for a spring wedding. The garden is open year-round from dawn to dusk. Admission is free Labor Day through February; $3 admission from 10am–6pm March through Labor Day on Thurs–Mon, free Tues–Wed and for children under 12. *Open every day dawn to dusk; www.portlandonline.com/parks; map:JJ5.*

The Elk Rock Gardens of the Bishop's Close

11800 SW MILITARY LN, DUNTHORPE; 503/636-5613

This 13-acre estate at the edge of the exclusive Dunthorpe neighborhood— 2 miles north of Lake Oswego—serves as the headquarters of the Episcopal Diocese of Oregon, which explains the name: "close" is a British term for an enclosed place or garden around a church or other sacred place for quiet and meditation, where monks used to stroll in peace. This garden's genesis, however, dates back to 1914 when its owner, Scottish grain merchant Peter Kerr, collaborated with New York landscape architect John Olmsted (son of Central Park designer Frederick Law Olmsted). Together, they created an exquisite terraced garden facing Mount Hood and overlooking pristine Elk Rock in the Willamette River. Both native and rare plants are featured, including a multitude of madrones and 70 varieties of magnolia. Other highlights are lily ponds, a landscaped watercourse fed by a natural spring, a large rock garden, a formal boxwood-hedged terrace, and some of the finest specimens of wisteria you're likely ever to see. *Every day 8am–5pm, closed some holidays; www.diocese-oregon.org/theclose; map:LL5.*

The Grotto

NE 85TH AVE AND SANDY BLVD, NORTHEAST; 503/254-7371

Out-of-towners sometimes introduce longtime Portlanders to the National Sanctuary of Our Sorrowful Mother, commonly known as the Grotto. Tended by Friars of the Order of the Servants of Mary (the Servites), the Grotto is both a religious shrine and a lovely woodland garden. Mass is held daily year-round in the chapel; from May to September, Sunday Mass faces the Grotto itself, a fern-lined niche in the 110-foot-tall cliff, which houses a marble replica of Michelangelo's *Pietà*. Throughout the 62-acre grounds, rhododendrons, camellias, azaleas, and ferns shelter religious statuary, providing both the prayerful and the plant lover with ample material for contemplation, while giant sequoias tower above. Upper-level gardens and a panoramic view of the Cascades and the Columbia River (seen from floor-to-ceiling windows in the Meditation Chapel as well as from the gardens) are reached via a 10-story elevator ride ($3.50 for adults, $2.50 for seniors and children 6–11, free for kids under 6). In December, the Grotto radiates with its spectacular Festival of Lights. *Open every day at 9am (call for seasonal closing times), closed Thanksgiving, Christmas; www.thegrotto.org; map:FF3.*

Hoyt Arboretum

4000 SW FAIRVIEW BLVD, WASHINGTON PARK; 503/865-8733

See no. 13 in Top 20 Attractions.

International Rose Test Garden

400 SW KINGSTON AVE, WASHINGTON PARK; 503/823-3636

See no. 1 in Top 20 Attractions.

Japanese Garden

611 SW KINGSTON AVE, WASHINGTON PARK; 503/223-1321

See no. 8 in Top 20 Attractions.

John Inskeep Environmental Learning Center (ELC)

19600 S MOLALLA AVE, OREGON CITY; 503/657-6958 EXT 2644

What was once an 8-acre plot of ravaged land—the wastewater lagoons and parking lots of a berry-processing plant—is now home to shady paths, ponds, and wildlife habitat in an urban setting. The learning center at Clackamas Community College demonstrates environmentally sound solutions to landscape problems, incorporating recycled plastic "logs" in footbridges and utilizing solar- and compost-heated greenhouses in the nursery. Kids flock to the ponds, home to three kinds of turtles—red-eared sliders, western pond, and painted—as well as ducks; parents appreciate the more delicate butterfly garden.

The ELC is the home of the **HAGGART ASTRONOMICAL OBSERVATORY** (www.depts.clackamas.cc.or.us/haggart) as well. This public observatory is operated by volunteer amateur astronomers and is open by appointment. A

$2 donation is suggested. *Every day dawn to dusk; www.clackamas.edu/elc; map:QQ3.*

Adjacent to the ELC, the **HOME ORCHARD SOCIETY ARBORETUM** has a dazzling assortment of fruit-bearing plants, including dwarf fruit trees and terrific samplings of apple and pear varieties. If you've wanted to add a blueberry bush to your yard—or a kiwi vine, persimmon, pawpaw, or plum-apricot (plucot) cross—this is the place to decide on the variety. *Tues and Sat 9am–3pm; www.homeorchardsociety.org; map:QQ3.*

Leach Botanical Garden

6704 SE 122ND AVE, SOUTHEAST; 503/761-9503

The emphasis on native Northwest plants in this garden is fitting: one of the garden's creators discovered 2 genera and 11 species in Northwest wildernesses. Well-known amateur botanist Lilla Leach and her husband, John, began their 5-acre garden along Johnson Creek in the early 1930s; today, its 15 acres are home to 2,000 species and cultivars of both native and nonnative plants, as well as a variety of different habitats, including a sunny rock garden; a cool, shady riparian area; and a xeric plant display. The Leaches' 1930s manor can be rented for weddings, receptions, and meetings. *Tues–Sat 9am–4pm, Sun 1–4pm, tours Sat 10am Feb–Nov; www.leachgarden.org; map:JJ2.*

Portland Classical Chinese Garden

239 NW EVERETT ST, CHINATOWN; 503/228-8131

See no. 7 in Top 20 Attractions.

Parks and Beaches

Portland is a city of parks: there are some 280 green spaces in the city. At more than 5,100 acres, **FOREST PARK** is by far the most sprawling and primitive, while the 24-square-inch **MILL ENDS PARK** is decidedly the city's smallest. And lovely **WASHINGTON PARK** may well be the most civilized. For a complete list of city parks, contact **PORTLAND PARKS AND RECREATION** (1120 SW 5th Ave, Rm 1302, Downtown; 503/823-7529; map:F3). A wide variety of naturalist-led excursions are also available in many of the region's parks, green spaces, and waterways, including hikes, walks, bicycle rides, bird-watching trips, and kayaking and rafting trips. The department also offers numerous opportunities to visit historical sites and architectural treasures in the city and beyond. Visit www.portlandonline.com/parks and click "Recreation." Or call the Outdoor Recreation office: 503/823-5127.

Blue Lake Park

BLUE LAKE RD AT N MARINE DR AND 223RD AVE,
TROUTDALE; 503/665-4995

Although there is a 5-acre natural wetlands area here, most of Blue Lake Park's 185 acres are unabashedly developed, with plenty of parking, swimming,

RIVER WALK

Prior to 2001, if you wanted to take a stroll along the Willamette River in downtown Portland, you did so only on the west bank, along **GOV. TOM MCCALL WATERFRONT PARK**. The east bank of the river was seen only from a distance. Now you can complete a loop on foot or by bike over the **HAWTHORNE AND STEEL BRIDGES**. This vantage point offers the best views of downtown, and often you'll see bride-and-groom photo sessions taking place from these vistas.

Ample parking is available on the east side, under or near the Hawthorne Bridge. Near the fire station sits a life-sized bronze statue of the **EASTBANK ESPLANADE**'s namesake, former mayor Vera Katz. This $30 million project was many years in the making: city planners had it in their 1998 city plan. The Esplanade is a demonstration project for improved fish and wildlife habitat and riverbank restoration; as such, construction was timed around the fish migration seasons.

boat rentals, volleyball courts, paved paths, playfields, and other facilities. In 2006, the park added an interactive water playground for kids to splash and spray with a variety of nozzles, buckets, and gadgets. Admission is $5 per car, $7 per bus, free for walkers and cyclists; no pets. *Every day 8am–sunset; www.metro-region.org; map:FF1.* &

Council Crest Park

TOP OF MARQUAM HILL; FROM DOWNTOWN TAKE SW BROADWAY, TURN LEFT ON SW GREENWAY
Set atop one of the tallest peaks in the Tualatin Mountains, which is thought to be Portland's highest point, Council Crest Park, a 10-minute drive southwest of downtown, is valued for its nearly panoramic views of the Coast Range and the Cascades. The Marquam Hill Trail crosses through the Douglas fir and maple forest on the northwest side of the hill. *Every day 5am–midnight, closed to vehicles at 9pm; map:II7.*

Elk Rock Island/Spring Park

SE 19TH AVE AND SPARROW ST, MILWAUKIE
Each spring, high waters on the Willamette impede access to this pristine island, but at other times you can step from Milwaukie's Spring Park across the gravel-scrubbed bedrock to the island. Great blue herons feed in the little bay between the island and Spring Park. Migrating Canada geese graze on the shelf of grass on the island's west side. A sublime natural rock formation cascades out of the oak forest on the northwest end, while the deepest waters of the Willamette (home to many sturgeon) slice by. Local lore attributes the name to American Indians driving elk over the bluff and floating them to the

Northward, you pass underneath I-5—which can be loud, but serves to remind you that you are where you'd rather be: on foot instead of on the freeway. Where the land once made this journey impassable, architects devised a 1,200-foot floating walkway to get you across—the longest of its kind in the country. These cement pathways are on pillars, and when a boat passes by or if the wind is up, you'll notice you're floating. Take in the sea-level view from one of the many benches, or venture out on the boat dock and cast a fishing pole. Continue north from here to connect to the **OREGON CONVENTION CENTER**, or head over the now pedestrian-friendly Steel Bridge alongside a train track where you'll often see cargo ships docked nearby.

With four art pieces tastefully embedded in the landscape and 13 urban markers indicating the eastside city grid, the esplanade is a 1½-mile triumph of city planning and engineering, and a testament to "the city that works."

—Dana Cuellar

island for processing. Watch for poison oak if you have a notion to wander into the woods. *Every day dawn to dusk; map:LL5.*

Forest Park

NW 29TH AVE AND UPSHUR ST TO NEWBERRY RD, NORTHWEST; 503/223-5449
In 1947, after more than 40 years of citizen effort, 4,200 acres of forestland an easy 10-minute drive from downtown were formally designated Forest Park. The land had survived logging, wildfire burns, subdivision into private lots, and an aborted scenic-road project. Now expanded to more than 5,100 acres, Forest Park is the largest city park in the nation. The forest wilderness includes 50 miles of trails and 30 miles of gated roadways for mountain biking along northwest Portland's Tualatin Mountains. Leif Erikson Drive, an 11-mile gravel road that stretches from NW Thurman Street to Germantown Road, is all that remains of an ambitious real-estate agent's 1914 plans for a subdivision. Now closed to cars, the popular hiking, running, and mountain-biking lane is bumpy in spots but affords good views north; it parallels the Wildwood Trail. An indispensable reference to the park is Marcy Cottrell Houle's *One City's Wilderness: Portland's Forest Park*, which includes maps, park history, and flora and fauna check lists. *Every day 5am–10pm; map:DD9–GG8.*

Gov. Tom McCall Waterfront Park

WEST SIDE OF THE WILLAMETTE RIVER FROM MARQUAM BRIDGE NORTH TO STEEL BRIDGE, DOWNTOWN; 503/823-2223
See no. 3 in Top 20 Attractions.

Hoyt Arboretum

4000 SW FAIRVIEW BLVD, WASHINGTON PARK; 503/865-8733
See no. 13 in Top 20 Attractions.

Kelley Point Park

N MARINE DR AND N LOMBARD ST, SAINT JOHNS
This isolated park is across the channel from Sauvie Island at the confluence of the Willamette and Columbia rivers. Biking, hiking, and wildlife viewing are best in the spring and fall; in the summer, Kelley Point is inundated with picnickers and sunbathers. Despite abundant wildlife, the slow-moving waters are polluted, and water experts advise against swimming and fishing. As in all urban-area parks, leave your valuables at home and lock your car. *Every day 6am–9pm; map:BB9.* &

Mary S. Young State Park

HWY 43, WEST LINN; 503/557-4700
Along the Willamette River, this suburban refuge is stalwartly defending itself from surrounding development. A favorite of urban birders, the 160-acre park has baseball diamonds, soccer fields, picnic spots, 5–8 miles of forest trails, a half-mile bike path, and restrooms. The state maintains it in as close to its original natural condition as possible. *Every day dawn to dusk; www.oregonstateparks.org/park_141.php; map:OO4.* &

Mill Ends Park

SW NAITO PKWY AND TAYLOR ST, DOWNTOWN
Portland is home to the world's smallest dedicated park, at 24 square inches: it is located in the median of this downtown intersection. The story goes that a journalist decided to plant some flowers in a pothole located below his office window. The pothole-turned-park is now maintained by the city's work crews. *Map:G5.*

Oxbow Regional Park

8 MILES EAST OF GRESHAM VIA SE DIVISION ST AND OXBOW PKWY; 503/663-4708 OR 503/797-1850
In the oxbow bends of the Sandy River Gorge, old-growth forests and wildlife thrive—in part because no dogs are allowed, not even on a leash. The park formally covers more than 1,000 acres, but the ecosystem appears to extend upstream to the Sandy River Preserve (owned by the Nature Conservancy) and downstream to the YMCA camp. The Sandy River is part of the National Wild and Scenic River system; evidence exists that American Indians lived here 9,000 years ago. The second weekend in October every year, the park hosts its annual Salmon Festival, focusing on the spawning salmon. About 15 miles of hiking trails follow the river and climb the ridges, and some are open to horses. The park includes 45 campsites, probably the closest public campground to Portland proper. Year-round interpretive hikes, programs,

films, and lectures are available; call for reservations. Admission is $5 per car, $7 per bus. *Every day 6:30am–dusk.* &

Peninsula Park

700 N ROSA PARKS WY, NORTH PORTLAND; 503/823-7529

This park has as much history as it does beauty. With a bond measure in 1909, for $60,000 the city became the owner of Peninsula Park, a former roadhouse and racetrack for quarter-mile horse racing. Planned by renowned Oregon architects Ellis Lawrence and Ormond R. Bean, the park was swept up into Portland's 1912 "City Beautiful" movement and completed in 1913. Many of the original features remain, including lantern-style streetlights, stone pillars, vast brickwork, and the nearly 100-year-old fountain in the center of the rose garden. Peninsula Park is home to the first public rose garden, a 2-acre parcel with over 8,900 plantings. The garden entrance is located on Albina Avenue, between Ainsworth Street and Rosa Parks Way. Bordering the steps that lead to the sunken rose garden, a magnificent palate of 65 rose varieties greets visitors. The official Portland rose, named 'Mme. Caroline Testout,' is maintained in the garden. The octagonal bandstand overlooking the rose garden, constructed in 1913, was designated a Portland Historic Landmark in 1973. Formerly used for World War I patriotic demonstrations, it's now the backdrop for many summer weddings and concerts. The first community center was established in a handsome Italian villa–style building on the grounds. The **PENINSULA PARK COMMUNITY CENTER AND POOL** (700 N Rosa Parks Wy; 503/823-3620) offers an expansive, oval-shaped outdoor pool as well as indoor basketball courts and a gymnasium (call for hours and admission fees). In 1957, the city zoo, lacking the proper facilities, temporarily housed its Humboldt penguins from Antarctica in the center's pool—many Portlanders still remember calling it Penguin Park. *Every day 5am–midnight; www. portlandonline.com/parks; map:EE6.* &

Powell Butte

SE POWELL BLVD AND 162ND AVE, SOUTHEAST

Plenty of horseback riders, mountain bikers, and hikers share the trails of this Gresham-area park, which on sunny days can be downright crowded. From the meadows at the 630-foot summit, you can see north to Mount St. Helens and south to Mount Jefferson. A 2-mile loop circles the volcanic mound on the way to the top. Watch out for poison oak. There's a designated off-leash dog area in the southeast corner of the park. *Every day 5am–10pm with restricted parking lot hours; map:II1.*

Rooster Rock State Park

I-84 EAST TO EXIT 25, COLUMBIA GORGE; 503/695-2661

On a warm weekend, all 1,800 parking spaces for this mile-long sandy beach are full. There's a logged-off swimming hole in the Columbia River, a boat launch, docks for boaters and anglers, and two Frisbee golf courses. On the far east end, a separate beach is designated "clothing optional." When the east wind is blowing, windsurfers crowd the beaches. There is a designated off-leash area for dogs, as they are not allowed on the beach. Admission is $3 per car. *Every day dawn to dusk; www.oregonstateparks.org/park_175.php.*

Sauvie Island Wildlife Area

AT THE CONFLUENCE OF THE WILLAMETTE AND COLUMBIA RIVERS VIA HWY 30, ON THE NORTH END OF SAUVIE ISLAND; 503/621-3488
The hinterlands of Sauvie Island, 10 miles northwest of Portland, offer great birding opportunities. The Oregon Fish and Wildlife Commission charges for car-park permits for this 12,000-acre state wildlife preserve. Walton Beach, one of the few sandy beaches on the Columbia (and open for swimming), is located at the end of the paved portion of NW Reeder Road. Warrior Rock Lighthouse is a 3-mile hike from the north unit parking facility. Non-wildlife-related activity is discouraged; open fires are prohibited, and there are no picnic facilities. Parking permits are $3.50 per day, $11 per year. *Open year-round are the road to Warrior Rock Lighthouse, bird-watching areas at Coon Pt and NW Reeder Rd, Columbia River beaches, and eastside viewing platform; rest of park closed Oct–Apr 15; www.sauvieisland.org; map:AA9.*

Smith and Bybee Wetlands Natural Area

ON MARINE DR BETWEEN EXPO CENTER AND KELLEY POINT PARK; 503/797-1850
Nearly 2,000 acres hidden in industrial North Portland, this is the largest protected wetlands within an American city. The bird blinds (camouflaged viewing spots) offer a good place to spy on wildlife, especially blue herons in the slough. Another great view is from kayak or canoe. *Every day dawn to dusk; www.oregonmetro.gov; map:CC8.*

Springwater Corridor

SE IVON ST TO TOWN OF BORING
See descriptions under Bicycling and Hiking in the Recreation chapter.

Tryon Creek State Park

11321 SW TERWILLIGER BLVD, LAKE OSWEGO; 503/636-9886 OR 503/636-4398
Like Forest Park, the Tryon Creek canyon was threatened with a housing project. Thanks to the Friends of Tryon Creek State Park, a citizens' group organized to raise money to buy the land, it's now a park consisting of 645 protected acres between Lewis & Clark College and Lake Oswego, 1 mile off Hwy 43. Among 8 miles of hiking trails and 3½ miles of horse trails are the paved half-mile Trillium Trail (the first all-abilities trail in an Oregon state park) and a 3-mile bike trail along the park's border with Terwilliger Boulevard. The Nature Center features a bookstore, exhibits, and a meeting room. The Trillium Festival is hosted in early spring, when these delicate flowers blossom. *Park open every day dawn to dusk, Nature Center open Mon–Fri 9am–5pm, Sat noon–4pm, Sun 9am–4pm; www.tryonfriends.org; map:LL6.* ঌ

Organized Tours

MOTOR TOURS

The Cultural Bus (aka Tri-Met bus 63)

503/238-7433

Bus 63 hits all the city's cultural hot spots: the Portland Art Museum, Oregon History Center, OMSI, and the Oregon Zoo, to name a few. Board at most attractions or in the Downtown Transit Mall (see Getting Around in the Lay of the City chapter). Prices are the same as for all Tri-Met buses.

Eco Tours of Oregon

3127 SE 23RD AVE, POWELL PARK; 503/245-1428

You don't have to be politically correct to book a tour with these folks, but if you consider yourself progressive, you'll definitely want to check out their tours. As its name implies, this tour company specializes in environmentally and culturally conscious tours, including an American Indians cultural tour to the Warm Springs Indian Reservation in central Oregon, where participants are guests of a tribal member; rafting in white or calm water; or whale-watching from Newport on the Oregon Coast. You can decide whether or not to be active on the tours, with options to visit the northern Oregon Coast, the Columbia Gorge, and Mount St. Helens volcano; there's even an evening Microbrewery Tour and a full-day Winery Tour. Or custom-design your own tour. Prices range from $45 (microbreweries) up to $78 (whale-watching). *www.ecotours-of-oregon.com.*

VanGo Transportation and Tours

503/292-2085 OR 888/292-2085

Like other minivan tour companies, VanGo will take you just about anywhere you want to go around Portland and northern Oregon: half-day city trips, half-day Columbia Gorge tours, full-day Mount Hood Loop and St. Helens trips, full-day Oregon Coast tours, and even lengthier charter trips. Call for details. *www.vangotransportation.com.*

WALKING TOURS

Peter's Walking Tours

503/704-7900

Former elementary schoolteacher Peter Chausse offers walking tours of downtown Portland, any day of the week. A knowledgeable and enthusiastic guide, Chausse focuses on the city's art, architecture, parks, fountains, and history, emphasizing his points with hands-on activities such as making sidewalk rubbings and using magnets to see whether a building is made of cast iron. A three-hour, 1-mile tour costs $15 for adults, $7 for teens, free for children 12 and under with a paying adult. Call to reserve a time. *www. walkportland.com.*

A MINI GUIDE TO PORTLAND ARCHITECTURE

Though notable architecture exists throughout the city, the majority of Portland's landmark buildings are found in the city's compact downtown core. And thanks to a penchant for historic preservation, many of Portland's greatest buildings remain intact. Because of this, and the city's diminutive city blocks, Portland offers a wonderful pedestrian experience and quaint streetscape more reminiscent of a European city than one in the United States. Portland is internationally known for city planning accomplishments, and **PIONEER COURT-HOUSE SQUARE** (600 SW Morrison) is the city's pièce de résistance: any tour of Portland's built environment must commence here. Once home to the showcase Queen Anne–style Portland Hotel built in 1890, the site was rendered an eyesore when the magnificent hotel was razed in 1951 to make way for a parking structure. Thirty years later, the city transformed the lot into the brick-clad European-style town that locals have come to call "Portland's living room." Though the busy square now hosts 300 public events annually, it pays homage to its past with an original archway from the hotel's entrance anchoring the square's southern entrance along Morrison Street.

Portland's most pioneering architect, A. E. Doyle, designed many downtown buildings. His style was firmly rooted in the Beaux-Arts tradition, embodying a fondness for buildings with classical proportions and ornate details, and two fine examples of his work are visible from Pioneer Courthouse Square. Look toward the river: to the right is the **PACIFIC BUILDING** (520 SW Yamhill St), a 10-story Italianate structure capped by an iconic Florentine-style red tile roof. To the left is the 1909 **MEIER & FRANK BUILDING** (621 SW 5th Ave), a 15-story towering edifice glazed in gleaming white terra-cotta. The building was renovated in 2008

Portland Public Art Walking Tour

503/823-5111

Request the map for this self-guided route at the Regional Arts and Culture Council (620 SW Main St, Ste 420, Downtown), the Oregon Convention Center (NE Martin Luther King Jr Blvd and Holladay St, Rose Quarter), the main lobby of the Portland Building (1120 SW 5th Ave, Downtown), or the Visitor Information and Services Center (Pioneer Courthouse Square, Downtown). See Art in Public Places in the Arts Scene chapter for more information on public art and architecture.

and now houses the Macy's department store and the Nines, a luxury hotel.

Doyle had other legacies. He designed the so-called **BENSON BUBBLERS**, the four-headed bronze drinking fountains found throughout the central city. He also mentored Portland's most transformational modern architect, Pietro Belluschi.

To locals, Belluschi's most loved building is the **PORTLAND ART MUSEUM** (1219 SW Park Ave) on the northwest corner of Ninth Avenue and Jefferson Street. Built in 1931, the simple but elegant brick building is an excellent example of classical modernism, borrowing from the scale of the classic buildings that surround it but eschewing their ornate detail in favor of clean lines and minimal adornment. Several blocks north on SW Sixth Avenue and Oak Street is Belluschi's **COMMONWEALTH BUILDING** (421 SW 6th Ave). Among his most famous works, it's considered one of the world's first stainless steel–clad skyscrapers. Though also of classical proportions, the Commonwealth is a textbook example of stripped-down modernism, which defined great mid-20th-century urban architecture. Built in 1948, it was decades ahead of its time.

Portland's most internationally famous building is undoubtedly the postmodern **PORTLAND BUILDING** (1120 SW 5th Ave), a 15-story municipal building on SW Fourth Avenue and Main Street. Designed by architect Michael Graves, the Portland Building's beribboned multicolored facade is almost universally abhorred by locals. In fact, some claim it to be the reason Portland has shied away from landmark buildings designed by big-name architects ever since its 1982 completion.

North of Burnside Street between Broadway and I-405 is the Pearl District, home to many converted warehouse buildings and modern condominium towers. Starting in 2000, developers Gerding Edlen converted five blocks formerly occupied by the Blitz-Weinhard Brewery into the **BREWERY BLOCKS**, a

Portland Underground Tours

503/622-4798

Operated by the Cascade Geographic Society, these tours tell true stories of subterranean Portland, focusing on the notorious network of Shanghai Tunnels that underlie much of downtown Portland. Between 1850 and the start of World War II, tens of thousands of men became "able-bodied seamen" here virtually overnight: they were kidnapped and held in filthy cells until they were sold to unscrupulous ship captains in search of trans-Pacific crews. *By appointment only; www.shanghaitunnels.info.*

landmark mixed-used hub for office, retail, high-rise condominiums, and the development's crown jewel: the **GERDING THEATER** (see the Arts Scene chapter). Built in 1891 as an armory for the National Guard, the 20,000-square-foot brick structure was reinvented in 2006 as a 600-seat theater and home to the local Portland Center Stage. Along with its giant wooden trusses and exposed brick, the Gerding Theater employs enough green features to earn the highly coveted LEED-Platinum status.

Just east of the Pearl District lies Portland's **OLD TOWN**, a historic district that boasts one of the most impressive collections of cast-iron-facade 19th-century buildings in the United States. After decades of decline, Old Town's unique architecture received a spark in 2008 when the University of Oregon moved its Portland operations into the **WHITE STAG BLOCK** (70 NW Couch St), a trio of LEED-certified historic brick-and-cast-iron buildings restored to their original 19th- and early 20th-century splendor. The centerpiece 1883 **BICKEL BUILDING** (70 NW Couch St), at NW Naito Parkway and Couch, is an immaculately restored edifice that embodies the best of the cast-iron era, with ornate columns, elaborate cornices, and giant windows. Truly unique, the block has added a spark to the long-neglected district, where, after years of decline, many planned renovations are under way.

—Mike Thelin

Portland Walking Tours

503/774-4522

These walking tours appeal to culture fiends, architecture buffs, wine lovers, and foodies. In the Best of Portland tour, patrons explore the city's art and architecture, as well as issues of livability, transit, and Portland culture; every day, 10am. The Underground Portland tour winds through Old Town, exposing the sordid side of this fair city, with a glimpse into the legendary Shanghai Tunnels; every day, 2pm. The Epicurean Excursion is a culinary journey through the Pearl District, leading walkers behind the scenes to taste, sip, and savor some of Portland's finest flavors; cost is $59; 21 and over, Fri–Sat, 10am. All tours begin at the Visitor Information Center in Pioneer Courthouse Square, Downtown. The Beyond Bizarre supernatural tour has a later version for 18 and over only and costs $29. Most tours are $19 for adults. Advance ticket purchase is strongly recommended. *www.portland walkingtours.com*.

Urban Tour Group (UTG)

503/227-5780

For more than 25 years, schoolchildren and adults alike have learned Portland history from UTG volunteers. You can choose one of four stock tours or have one custom made. Tours cost $5 per person ($25 minimum); school groups are free (teachers, round up the kids); reservations are a must. *www.urbantourgroup.org/index.htm.*

Waterfront Bridge Walks

503/222-5535

Few cities offer such diverse bridgework as Portland, and fewer yet feature tours by such a lively and devoted guide as Sharon Wood Wortman. Besides hosting tours through Portland Parks and Recreation, Wood Wortman also offers private tours. Her new tour, the Portland Circle Tour, begins in Chinatown/Old Town and includes rides on the city's newest transportation options: the Portland Aerial Tram and the Portland Streetcar. Enjoy an authentic Cantonese lunch in Chinatown and walk across the 660-foot Veterans Hospital Skybridge, the longest air-conditioned pedestrian bridge in the United States. Call for dates and other information. *www.bridgestories.com.*

BOAT TOURS

See no. 16 in Top 20 Attractions.

TRAIN AND TROLLEY TOURS

Molalla Miniature Train–Pacific Northwest Live Steamers

31803 S SHADY DELL DR, MOLALLA; 503/829-6866

All-volunteer hobbyists drive these miniature trains along a 0.7-mile route southeast of Portland. Passengers can bring their own lunches and relax in the shaded picnic area, admiring the fine, detailed antique trains. *Sun and major Mon holidays noon–5pm May–Oct; www.pnls.org.*

Mount Hood Railroad

110 RAILROAD AVE, HOOD RIVER; 541/386-3556 OR 800/872-4661

The restored Pullman cars of the Mount Hood Railroad chug through the beautiful Hood River Valley, 60 miles east of Portland via I-84, to the towns of Odell and Parkdale on two-hour and four-hour rail tours. A 1910 steam engine powers the historic Excursion Train, whose spring run gives rail riders spectacular views of blossoming orchards. Tickets are $25 for adults, $23 for seniors, $15 for children ages 2–12. There's also a Saturday Murder Mystery Dinner Train ($80) and a Sunday Brunch Train ($58), both pulled by diesel engines. Special events include art and music festivals, Western train robberies, Thomas the Tank Engine, and Peanuts! The Great Pumpkin Patch Express. In December, Christmas Tree Trains invite riders to join Santa and Christmas carolers and to buy a tree, which is then loaded onto the train. *Closed Jan–March; www.mthoodrr.com.*

Portland Vintage Trolleys

503/323-7363

Four oak-paneled and brass-belled trolleys—replicas of the city's old Council Crest trolley—follow the MAX route (catch the trolley at any light-rail station) from Lloyd Center to the downtown turnaround at SW 11th Avenue and back (Sun noon–6pm). Top speed is 35 mph, and the round-trip takes about 40 minutes. The trolley also runs on the Portland Streetcar route, Sat–Sun 10am–6pm. Both trips are free. *www.vintagetrolleys.com.*

Washington Park and Zoo Railway

OREGON ZOO, 4001 SW CANYON RD, WASHINGTON PARK;
503/226-1561

The zoo railway boasts the only surviving railroad post office in the country, so snail-mailing a postcard while you're on board is a must. On the round-trip ride from the zoo to the rose garden, you'll get a dose of history and some nice scenery along the 35-minute loop, which runs in warm-weather months; in spring the route is shorter. Tickets cost $5 (in addition to zoo admission). *www.oregonzoo.org/AboutZoo/train.htm; map:HH7.*

Willamette Shore Trolley

311 N STATE ST, LAKE OSWEGO; 503/697-7436

The Willamette Shore Trolley has been running the 6-mile stretch along the river from downtown Portland's South Waterfront district (corner of Moody and Bancroft sts) to the State Street terminal in Lake Oswego since 1990. The trolley, built in 1932, is available for charter runs as well as special events, such as the December Christmas boat-watching tour (additional fare) and the Fourth of July trip to watch fireworks (reservations required). Round-trip tickets are $10 for adults, $9 for seniors (55 and over), $6 for children 3–12, free for children 2 and under. Call for current schedule. *www.oregonelectric railway.org.*

SHOPPING

SHOPPING

When it comes to fashion, Portlanders no longer subscribe to outfitting themselves in Eddie Bauer castoffs, circa 1994. We are a stylish people, but trends are few and far between. We wear what is comfortable and practical (fleece and rain boots, at times), what is dear and loved (vintage, always), and what is local (as you'll see, the list of the city's designers and boutiques is lengthy).

Portland has flipped fashion on its head with an "anything goes" attitude, and the result is an unencumbered free-for-all of ideas and designs. The humble, intimate fashion orb that has surfaced within Portland's uniquely supportive creative class is a host of locals, transplants, and internationally trained designers who feed off each other's grassroots energy, aesthetic, and talent. With Portland's Fashion Week in its third year, celebrated local designers such as Leanne Marshall succeeding in competitions like *Project Runway*, and much press coverage of our fair city's growing, tight-knit design community, Stumptown is on its way to making a fashionable name for itself.

Downtown and Surrounding Neighborhoods

Portland's bustling downtown is surrounded by a cluster of neighborhoods, each with its own distinct character and notable shops to visit. Locals are loyal to independently owned businesses and are intensely proud of the city's devotion to sound urban planning and community building. As a result, cookie-cutter strip malls and big-box megaretailers have been banished to the outskirts—thankfully perpetuating the city's homegrown atmosphere.

DOWNTOWN PORTLAND

Continued investment by community and business has made **PORTLAND'S DOWNTOWN** a model for revitalizing urban areas across the nation. Buses, light-rail, and a fine streetcar system crisscross the city center, making it increasingly easy to maneuver through Portland's pockets of local flavor. Downtown packs in a handful of large department stores, including **NORDSTROM** (710 SW Broadway; 503/224-6666; map:I3), **MACY'S** (621 SW 5th Ave; 503/223-0512; map:I4), and **SAKS FIFTH AVENUE** (850 SW 5th Ave; 503/226-3200; map:H4), which, along with the **PIONEER PLACE MALL**—a glass-roofed, two-building complex full of chain retailers, on SW Fifth Avenue between Morrison and Taylor streets—dominate the downtown grid. Also tucked into downtown are upscale fashion spots such as **MERCANTILE** and **MARIO'S**. The **BREWERY BLOCKS**, a massive mixed-use redevelopment project just northwest of the city core in the Pearl District, encompasses a balanced mix of national retailers (Whole Foods, Anthropologie, Diesel) and tried-and-true local boutiques and restaurants (Cargo, Moulé, In Good Taste). The Brewery Blocks link downtown Portland with the Pearl District, a former industrial area–turned–gallery scene that has rapidly shape-shifted into a chic shopping district, sprinkled with of-the-minute fashions and housewares.

NW 23RD AVENUE

Portland's most frequented shopping neighborhood is **NW 23RD AVENUE** (from W Burnside St north to NW Thurman St; map:GG7), fondly dubbed "trendy-third," where stores such as **LENA MEDOYEFF STUDIO, SOUCHI**, and **KITCHEN KABOODLE** stock stylish apparel, gifts, housewares, and funky odds and ends. The street is littered with coffee shops and outdoor seating and caters to a slightly more upscale clientele—perfect for an afternoon spent shopping and people-watching.

PEARL DISTRICT

The **PEARL DISTRICT** (north of W Burnside and west of North Park Blocks; map:K3–P1), dominated by gentrified warehouses inhabited by lofts and art galleries, and home to a thriving First Thursday scene, offers various upscale restaurants, furniture retailers, and apparel shops. Check out the **ORCHID EXCHANGE** to see the exotic selection, the fine stationery at **OBLATION PAPERS AND PRESS**, **CARGO** for eclectic imports, and **NOLITA** for current men's and women's fashions.

SKIDMORE/OLD TOWN

East, toward the Willamette River, you'll find the restored **SKIDMORE/OLD TOWN** (between Naito Pkwy and 4th Ave from SW Oak to NW Glisan sts; map:H5–L5), which has a growing number of exclusive shops and galleries, some of them (closer to Portland's tiny Chinatown) with an Asian-inspired edge. On weekends, Skidmore perks up with the **SATURDAY MARKET**, a food-and-crafts fair with original homespun items from the studios and homes of artsy Portlanders (see Top 20 Attractions in the Exploring chapter).

MULTNOMAH VILLAGE

Southwest of town is charming **MULTNOMAH VILLAGE** (just off SW Multnomah Blvd on SW Capitol Hwy; map:JJ7), with a quaint, small-town personality revolving around several eateries, a few artsy shops, and about a dozen antique stores. Second only to Powell's Books, **ANNIE BLOOM'S BOOKS** has a wonderful selection, and **THINKER TOYS** has long been a favorite of Portland kids.

SOUTHEAST PORTLAND

Across the quaint Sellwood Bridge, in the city's southeast corner, are **SELLWOOD** (SE Tacoma St and 13th Ave; map:KK5), which is saturated with stores that hawk antiques, such as the inimitable **STARS, AN ANTIQUES MALL**, and **WESTMORELAND** (7027 SE Milwaukee Ave; 503/235-5990; map: JJ5), where there are a number of fun shops, primarily family oriented, such as the children's shoe store **HAGGIS MCBAGGIS**. Stop in to **STE. MAINE** for both fresh and classic decorating ideas.

    HAWTHORNE (SE Hawthorne Blvd between SE 20th and 49th aves; map:HH5) and **BELMONT** (SE Belmont St between SE 30th and 39th aves;

map:HH5) are two colorful neighborhood arterials with great thrift shopping and a funky, artsy vibe. (Think of an inspired, modern-day Haight-Ashbury.) Browsers can spend hours checking out secondhand record shops and vintage clothiers such as **HOUSE OF VINTAGE**. For trendier fashion, **LOCAL35** is a favorite, and **IMELDA'S** is a must for the shoe lover. Belmont boasts funky shops with hard-to-find vintage housewares, such as **NOUN: A PERSON'S PLACE FOR THINGS**; pick up a cupcake in the back from **SAINT CUPCAKE**, or browse through old vinyl for a long-lost favorite record at **SONIC RECOLLECTIONS**. Farther south, the up-and-coming **DIVISION/CLINTON** area (SE Division and Clinton sts near SE 25th Ave; map:II5) is chock-full of unconventional cafes and boutiques, such as **XTABAY**, where you'll surely get a deal on a vintage dress.

NORTHEAST PORTLAND

To the north, **NE BROADWAY** (east from NE 7th Ave; map:GG5), bordering Irvington and the Lloyd Center, has a freshly minted elegance, with clothing and shoe shops such as **HALO**, **ANTIQUE ALLEY** for the home, and a lot of other shops selling kitchenware and books. There's also a great wine shop called **GREAT WINE BUYS**, outdoor gear at **THE MOUNTAIN SHOP**, and several worthwhile restaurants.

The **ALAMEDA-BEAUMONT** neighborhood, spread along NE Fremont Street (especially between 41st and 47th aves), is home to numerous small restaurants, upscale boutiques and home-decor shops, and children's stores. North of there, the multicultural **ALBERTA** district (NE Alberta St between 14th and 30th aves) has carved a name for itself with its Last Thursday art walks, which swarm with decidedly unconventional art lovers. In addition to cafes and galleries, Alberta has several excellent clothing shops, such as **TUMBLEWEED** (with locally designed frocks), and eclectic stores such as **THE OFFICE**, which sells handmade clocks, notebooks, and local art. For an exceptional wine selection, stop in at **CORK**.

Similarly, **MISSISSIPPI** (N Mississippi Ave from Fremont to Skidmore sts) is an emerging neighborhood with a variety of boutique and antique home-decor shops to go along with bustling outdoor cafes and a top recording studio.

Clothing Stores and Boutiques

Portlanders have increasingly become more fashion conscious, but most still prefer to support local creatives rather than big-name brands. Thus, designers' boutiques like **ADAM ARNOLD** and **LIZA RIETZ AND EMILY RYAN** have found a dedicated following. Portlanders know how to chill out, and their sensibility shows in the cutting edge–casual aesthetic found in most of the city's shops. The following section begins with Men's and Women's Clothing; Men's and Women's Shoes; and then moves on to Children's Clothing, Accessories, and Shoes; and finally Vintage and Consignment.

MEN'S AND WOMEN'S CLOTHING

Adam Arnold

727 SE MORRISON ST, SOUTHEAST; 503/234-1376

Portland's quirkiest, yet most admired trailblazing independent designer, Adam Arnold, tailors ensembles to perfection in his Southeast studio. Although he draws from unexpected inspirations, his contemporary silhouettes and painstaking construction—not to mention his seasonal sample sales—are always anticipated. *Every day and by appointment; www.adam-arnold.com; map:G9.*

adidas Originals Store

1039 NW COUCH ST, PEARL DISTRICT; 503/223-3109

With the adidas headquarters in Portland, it comes as no surprise that the Pearl's adidas Originals Store is one of the best. The friendly yet chic shop, designed with clean, modern lines, exhibits retro remakes of early sneaker designs and hip track jackets from soccer clubs around the world, fusing adidas's authenticity and global street style. It suits the Pearl District's urban landscape, where athleticism and fashion savvy share the sidewalk. *Every day; www.adidas.com/originals; map:K3.*

Anthropologie

1125 NW COUCH ST, PEARL DISTRICT; 503/274-0293
203 SW BRIDGEPORT RD, TIGARD; 503/620-0682

This conceptual, oversize boutique links whimsical, travel-inspired housewares and apparel with a fine mix of detail and girlish sophistication. Find bold prints, traditional silhouettes, and a slew of European-primitive found objects among the eccentric cookbooks, quirky kitchen gadgets, and fragrant soy candles. *Every day; www.anthropologie.com; map:K2.*

Blue

3753 N MISSISSIPPI AVE, NORTHEAST; 503/542-0888

Blue packs wonderfully hip, retro-inspired skater clothes at affordable prices: screen-printed T-shirts, dresses from chic to funky for girls, and a great selection of jeans for guys. Hats, jewelry, and other accessories will send you on your way looking cool, with enough dough left in your pocket to grab some lunch. It's a great place for school shopping for the kids. *Every day; map:FF5.*

Brooks Brothers

921 SW MORRISON ST, DOWNTOWN; 503/224-2199

Home to the country club pink polo and the all-American plaid sports coat, Brooks Brothers is one of downtown Portland's latest retail openings. Wide panoramic windows give way to smart ensembles dashed with pastels, traditional silhouettes, and preppy distinction. Expect nothing less from the oldest surviving men's clothier in the United States. *Every day; www.brooksbrothers. com; map:I2.*

Bubble Boutique

1100 NW GLISAN ST, PEARL DISTRICT; 503/219-0098
Offering refined details for designer junkies, Bubble Boutique vends pricey labels such as Manoush, Dolan, Paul & Joe, and the Parisian BillTornade. A variety of shoes, handmade jewelry, and satchels will leave you feeling big-city chic without ever leaving the Pearl. *Every day; bubbleboutique.biz; map:K2.*

Changes—Designs to Wear

927 SW YAMHILL ST, DOWNTOWN; 503/223-3737
An extension of the Real Mother Goose (see review under Jewelry and Accessories in this chapter), this shop carries clothing designed by regional and national artists. There are often new and wonderful surprises: blocked silk shirts, tooled-leather purses, burned-velvet scarves, handwoven suits cut to flatter real women's bodies. Earthy and unusual jewelry complements it all. *Mon–Sat; map:I2.*

COMPOUND

107 NW 5TH AVE, OLD TOWN; 503/796-2733
With fashions from brands such as adidas and Stussy, a large selection of art-inspired T-shirts, plus a wide selection of vinyl toys, anime, and cutting-edge contemporary art prints, COMPOUND carries unique styles for the younger set. Good music and bright colors contribute to the squeaky-clean urban atmosphere. After finding the perfect pair of shoes, stop by the upstairs gallery and check out some cool, street-inspired, local art. *Every day; www. compoundgallery.com; map:K4.*

The English Dept.

1124 SW ALDER ST; 503/224-0724; DOWNTOWN
This closet-sized shop in the downtown bustle is expertly edited with modern-day girlyness in mind; poppy prints by independent designers and standout bridal gowns sidle coquettish designs from owner Elizabeth Dye's eponymous line. *Tues–Sun; www.theenglishdept.com; map:J2.*

Finn

132 NW 12TH AVE, PEARL DISTRICT; 503/467-4660
The menswear collection at Finn combines classic elegance and sophistication with the ever-appreciated quality of comfort and approachability that Portlanders cherish. Lines are chosen with attention to detail, from sports coats and sweaters to finely tailored trousers. They have an extensive selection of European shirts cut from the finest fabrics. Also find Lacoste, Ray Ban sunglasses, and sophisticated shoes for most occasions. *Every day; www. finnclothing.com; map:K2.*

Gazelle Natural Fiber Clothing

4100 NE FREMONT ST, BEAUMONT VILLAGE; 503/288-3422
This oasis of fun, colorful clothing for women offers comfortable natural fibers in timeless styles. Other attractions include some nice shirts for men, jewelry and accessories for women, delightful toys, housewares, curios, and the new Full Circle Resale by Gazelle next door. *Every day; map:FF4.*

Girlfriends

904 NW 23RD AVE, NORTHWEST; 503/294-0488
This shop carries a solid collection of cotton T-shirts, chic dresses, sweaters, comfy pants, pajamas, and stockings (not to mention soaps, scents, and candles). Think of it as slumber-party wear—and then some. The savvy owners provide treats like lemonade in the summer and see to it that even shoppers' companions can enjoy lounging in the shop. *Every day; www.girlfriends boutique.com; map:GG7.*

Jane's Vanity

521 SW BROADWAY, DOWNTOWN; 503/241-3860
An elegant lingerie boutique owned by Jane Adams, Vanity features the best in European bras, panties, garter belts, nightwear, and accessories by the likes of Eres, John Galliano, Christian LaCroix, and Chantal Thomass. Acquired every January in Paris, elegant bits of silk and lace are displayed on racks, in glass cases, and across the walls. *Every day; www.janesvanity.com; map:I3.*

La Paloma

6316 SW CAPITOL HWY, HILLSDALE SHOPPING CENTER; 503/246-3417
Kim Osgood and Mike Roach oversee one of the city's best finds for relaxed, contemporary women's natural-fiber clothing. The emphasis is on easy-care pieces that pack well, a must for well-dressed travelers. Brands such as Flax, Cut Loose, and Mishi mean breezy linens as well as separates and sweaters in cotton or rayon. There's also Indonesian batik and ikat clothing and silver jewelry from Southeast Asia. *Every day; www.palomaclothing.com; map:JJ7.*

Lena Medoyeff Studio
Lena Medoyeff Bridal

710 NW 23RD AVE, NORTHWEST; 503/227-0011
805 NW 23RD AVE, NORTHWEST; 503/223-4929
Portland dress designer Lynn Medoff learned her craft in a small town in Guatemala during a stint in the Peace Corps—not exactly your average fashion schooling. Her luxurious creations are equally extraordinary. She uses exquisite silks, imported from a small mill in India, and hand-stitched, ornate textiles in feminine dresses, skirts, blouses, and jackets. In the bridal shop, brides-to-be may purchase directly off the rack or place a special order for a one-of-a-kind dress. (This takes six weeks, depending upon the fabric chosen.) Medoyeff's sales team delivers excellent service with infectious enthusiasm. *Every day; www.lenadress.com; map:GG7.*

Liza Rietz and Emily Ryan

2305 NW SAVIER ST, NORTHWEST; 503/459-4292

Two of Portland's great designers under one roof make this working studio-cum-boutique a pleasure to visit. Maybe you'll catch Emily Ryan fashioning an otherworldly silhouette or Liza Rietz fitting a custom-made frock. Either way, you have a distinct selection to choose from, and you just may get a glimpse of the creative construction before the pieces hit the rack. *Tues–Sat; www.lizarietz.com; map:GG7.*

Local35

3556 SE HAWTHORNE BLVD, SOUTHEAST; 503/963-8200

This artful urban boutique continues to reign as one of Portland's best independent, local shops. Highly esteemed by mags such as *GQ*, Local35 hawks a well-curated, high-low blend of local, international, and independent designers: Anzevino & Florence, A.P.C., In God We Trust, RVCA, property of . . . , and Orthodox, to name a few. Second Thursday art exhibits make it a one-stop shop for no-nonsense fashion and culture. *Wed–Mon; www.local35.com; map:HH5.*

Mario's

833 SW BROADWAY, DOWNTOWN; 503/227-3477

For more than six decades, men demanding the best in designer fashion have shopped at Mario's. Armani, Vestimenta, Hugo Boss, Canali, and Zegna suits keep elegant company here with fine sweaters, top-notch cotton shirts, and tasteful Friday casual wear. *Every day; www.marios.com; map:I2.*

The Mercantile

729 SW ALDER ST, DOWNTOWN; 503/223-6649

Owners Victoria Taylor and Dottie Johnson love fashion, and their store seems at once a gallery of their favorite up-to-the-minute styles and an elegant, comfortable shopping destination. Clothing here suits mature women looking for tailored, upscale style, as well as young professionals seeking sophisticated, contemporary fashion. The sprawling space houses evening and sportswear by designers such as Nicole Miller and Eileen Fisher, with a smattering of sleepwear, eclectic accessories, and household objects. *Every day; www.mercantile.citysearch.com; map:I3.*

Michael Allen's Clothier

811 SW MORRISON ST, DOWNTOWN; 503/221-9963

Michael Allen stocks business wear from suits to shoes and casual sportswear for men from designers such as Lacoste and Tommy Bahama. Though Michael Allen's is really an oasis for men's shopping, it also carries sporty and sophisticated women's lines. Michael Fredrickson and his knowledgeable staff help clients create custom clothing from casual wear to gowns and tuxedos: choose a fabric and a style, sit back with a glass of wine, pet the store's dogs, and relax. *Mon–Sat; www.michaelallensstyle.com; map:H2.*

210

Monkey Wear

811 NW 23RD AVE, NORTHWEST; 503/222-5160

Monkey Wear is jam-packed with contemporary dresses, tops, tanks, jackets, purses, and other accessories for the teen and twenty-something set. The selection is hip, but the prices are more reasonable than other boutiques in the area. Shoppers peruse both floors for slinky evening wear, wild lingerie, tiaras, a wide selection of costume jewelry, wigs, and hats. The environment is playful, and you can find great gifts for girly occasions. *Every day; map:GG7.*

Moulé

1225 NW EVERETT ST, PEARL DISTRICT; 503/227-8530

Run by Canadian-born local fashion designer Rachel Gorenstein, Moulé is a store in two parts: the front section houses animated trinkets, toys, and coffee-table tomes, and the back gives way to sophisticated apparel collections for both men and women. Find metro looks for the boys and runway flair for the girls, including Gorenstein's own line, Rachel Mara. *Every day; www.moulestores.com; map:L2.*

Nolita

923 NW 10TH AVE, PEARL DISTRICT; 503/274-7114

Nolita caters to fashion-savvy men and women, with lines that are both ahead of the curve and accessible: Helmut Lang, Mike & Chris, Prairie Underground, and more than 20 lines of denim jeans. The shop picks up organic sustainable lines with a focus on quality, comfort, and knock-your-socks-off cool. The staff is dedicated to helping every person who comes through the door find a great-fitting pair of jeans, whatever their size or shape. And Nolita is a great store for men and women who want to shop together. *Every day; www.nolitaonline.com; map:N2.*

Odessa

410 SW 13TH AVE, DOWNTOWN; 503/223-1998

At Odessa the fashion lies ahead of most local offerings, and the space feels like a SoHo gallery. Shop here for coveted items spied in the latest magazines—not the high-end couture lines, but the more affordable, hip styles from young designers. Browse the racks for sumptuous evening wear or the sweater you won't find anywhere else for six months (if ever). The latest footwear and imported Indian bedding add to the appeal. *Every day; map:J2.*

Phlox

3962 N MISSISSIPPI AVE, NORTH PORTLAND; 503/890-0715

Phlox has a host of fun, graphic prints by designers such as Linda Loudermilk, Relais, and Corey Lynn Calter, but if simple separates are what you're after, you'll find essentials by Splendid and Three Dots here as well. *Every day; www.phloxpdx.com; map:FF6.*

Pinkham Millinery

515 SW BROADWAY, DOWNTOWN; 503/796-9385
Always distinctive and avant-garde, Dayna Pinkham's felt berets and fedoras, traditional cloches and exceptional feathered headdresses all carry her stylish mark. These toppers are steeped in either vintage or contemporary glamour, giving each one a tasteful, romantic finish. You can spot Pinkham hats at the Kentucky Derby and European weddings; both tennis stars Serena Williams and Maria Sharapova have commissioned these stylish chapeaus. *Appointments Tues–Sat; www.pinkhammillinery.com; map:I3.*

Pin Me Apparel

3705 N MISSISSIPPI AVE, NORTHEAST; 503/281-1572
This small north Portland boutique stocks a mixture of current apparel, from undiscovered new designers to small international brands and better-known contemporary lines. Providing a range of prices and sizes, Pin Me strives to outfit women to suit their individual styles. Find lovely dresses, hoodies, jeans, and original jewelry designs. *Every day; www.pin-me-apparel.com; map:FF5.*

Popina Swimwear

4831 NE 42ND AVE, NORTHEAST; 503/282-5159
Here's to a swimsuit that flatters the female form! Owner and designer Pamela Levenson brings back the retro low-cut boy short, the one-piece halter, and the modern strapless bathing suit with her custom designs, bright patterns, and genuinely accommodating manner. *Tues–Sun; www.popina swimwear.com; map:FF5.*

The Portland Pendleton Shop

900 SW 5TH AVE, DOWNTOWN; 503/242-0037
A passing knowledge of Pendleton's wool products—and at least one well-worn button-down shirt—is vital to being an Oregonian. The Portland shop, in the Standard Insurance Building, offers the most complete collection of Pendleton clothing anywhere in Oregon, including petite sizes, skirt-and-shirt matchables, and summer silk and rayon combinations. Of course, it wouldn't be Pendleton without the wool chemises and blankets, endearingly familiar to nearly every Northwesterner. *Every day; www.pendleton-usa.com; map:H3.*

Savvy Plus

3204 SE HAWTHORNE BLVD, HAWTHORNE; 503/231-7116
Plans to close were thwarted by a clamor from longtime customers, and this plus-size boutique is as vital and popular as ever. Women's resale clothing, sizes 12 and up, is offered in a comfy atmosphere by a supportive sales staff. Recognizing that women who wear larger sizes shouldn't have to sacrifice style, the store has loads of pretty jewel-toned tops, stretchy skirts, feminine knits, and dresses. As many women fluctuate a size or two, the buy-and-sell policy makes it possible to maintain a fashionable wardrobe that always fits. *Tues–Sun; map:HH5.*

Seaplane

827 NW 23RD AVE, NORTHWEST; 503/234-2409

This boutique carries more than 30 different, mostly local, emerging designers who create artsy frocks and jewelry. Its new owner, Tacee Webb, showcases the deconstructed, romantic collections of previous owners Holly Stalder and Kate Towers, among other inventive local designers. Most of the pieces are one of a kind. The shop has drawn national attention for its cutting-edge position in the exploding fashion-design scene. Many of the store's designers are featured in seasonal, highly anticipated fashion shows. *Every day; www. e-seaplane.com; map:GG7.*

Souchi

807 NW 23RD AVENUE, NOB HILL; 503/221-1200

With collections varying from classic cardigans to cashmere knit bikinis, owner Suzi Johnson's hand-loomed and hand-finished knits are a luxurious, worthy splurge. Funky accessories and brazen separates by Ports 1961 and Bruce give a little edge to the shop's lovely soft spots. *Every day; www.souchi. com; map:GG7.*

Spartacus Leathers

300 SW 12TH AVE, DOWNTOWN; 503/224-2604

A longtime downtown denizen, Spartacus has downplayed its seedy sex-shop origins in favor of a streetwise, slightly left-of-center collection of novelty lingerie and accessories. The selection is huge and, to the store's credit, not all geared toward the fetish crowd. Racks of sexy, elegant nighties and robes, nice bras and panties, and a wide range of men's underwear can be paired with accoutrements if you need them for your most adventurous fantasies. *Every day; www.spartacusleathers.com; map:J2.*

Stand Up Comedy

811 E BURNSIDE ST, EASTSIDE; 503/233-3382

Unisex in taste, strong in presence and experimentation, this place is a conglomeration of mixed media (including independent book projects) and apparel. A sort of minimalist, gallery-ish boutique, Stand Up Comedy takes style and flips it on its head, selling sculptural wares as works of art from lines such as Slow and Steady Wins the Race and Staerk. *Tues–Sun; www. shopstandingup.us; map:HH5.*

Tumbleweed

1812 NE ALBERTA ST, ALBERTA; 503/335-3100

Local designer Kara Larson opened this delightful store in the flourishing and eclectic Alberta Street neighborhood to showcase her rustic, prairie-inspired Kara-Line clothing. The timeless, sizeless dresses and separates are romantic and feminine, yet comfortable and cowboy boot–worthy. Wild Carrots gingham jumpers for the toddler set, beautiful beaded jewelry, novel wallets and journals, and dresses and separates by Kara's favorite designers are also charmingly displayed here. *Every day; www.tumbleweedboutique.com, www. kara-line.com; map:FF5.*

Una

2802 SE ANKENY ST, SOUTHEAST; 503/235-2326
Truly distinctive in her buys, owner Giovanna Parolari brings an international breadth of designers to Portland with her colorful, offbeat taste. Romantic frills designed by Crea and Coven share space with brilliant tops by Sunshine & Shadow. Local designs by Linea round out the gracefully stylish mix of separates, trinkets, hand-crafted jewelry, and one-of-a-kind rarities, all finding harmony in this small space, bursting with curiosity. *Tues–Sun; www. una-myheartisfull.com; map:HH5.*

Upper Playground

23 NW 5TH AVE, OLD TOWN; 503/548-4835
Upper Playground sells primarily urban chic T-shirts and hoodies for men and women, but the Old Town establishment also carries some housewares, limited-edition posters, New Era ball caps, books, and DVDs. Upper Playground caters to a wide-ranging clientele: skaters, rockers, hip-hoppers, designers, graffiti writers, fashionistas, punks, and hip urbanites, young and old, fresh and seasoned. Check out the adjacent gallery featuring some of the world's best graffiti-inspired contemporary artists. *Every day; www. upperplayground.com; map:K5.*

MEN'S AND WOMEN'S SHOES

Al's Shoes & Boots for Men

5811 SE 82ND AVE, SOUTHEAST; 503/771-2130
Third-generation owners continue the tradition—started in 1947—of supplying Portland's men and boys with handsome soles in time-tested styles. Work, cowboy, and hiking boots are plentiful, but Al's also offers a range of popular sneakers and other street shoes. This is where firefighters shop for indestructible Wesco Smoke Jumper boots, but a hipster seeking the perfect black slip-on will be treated with equal respect by the friendly and knowledgeable staff. *Every day; map:JJ3.*

Halo

1425 NE BROADWAY, NORTHEAST; 503/331-0366
This intimate shoetique on NE Broadway's bustling stretch of shops stocks incredibly rich leather styles, many of them from Europe. They carry ultra-feminine heeled sandals and other classic styles by the likes of Moma, CoSTUME NATIONAL, Dries Van Noten, and CYDWOQ. There is a thoughtful men's selection as well, including exclusive styles from Timberland Boot Company. *Every day; map:GG5.*

Imelda's Designer Shoes

3426 SE 37TH AVE, HAWTHORNE; 503/233-7476
935 NW EVERETT ST, PEARL DISTRICT; 503/595-4970

Imelda's has one of the best selections of shoes, sneakers, and boots in town, with a lot of imports from South America and Europe. You can find unique styles and colors in designs that are elegant, hip, or functional but always fashionable. New styles come in daily and are typically marked below 10 percent of the recommended retail price. The men's selection is not as vast as the women's, but lots of styles dress up or down easily. *Every day; map:HH5.*

Johnny Sole

815 SW ALDER ST, DOWNTOWN; 503/225-1241

Owner John Plummer's got sole. He keeps a close watch on the fashion trend meter and stocks his once-tiny shoe boutique—now a two-story shoe-hound heaven—accordingly. You'll find Italian and Spanish imports, steel-toed work boots, sexy women's flats and heels, beloved Fryes, Corso Como, and Jeffrey Campbell. (The funkiest stuff is upstairs.) With so much space, there's no excuse not to take your favorite pairs for a test stroll. *Every day; map:I3.*

Oddball

1639 NW MARSHALL ST, NORTHWEST; 503/525-2202

Here you'll find hip shoes for big feet, specializing in men's sizes 13–20. They carry popular brands in modern styles from Vans, PUMA, PF Flyers, J Shoes, Diesel, and more. Also find '80s retro arcade games like Donkey Kong and Popeye. *Every day; www.oddball.com; map:GG7.*

CHILDREN'S CLOTHING, ACCESSORIES, AND SHOES

Bambini's Children's Boutique

16353 SW BRYANT RD, LAKE OSWEGO; 503/635-7661

Little-girl glamour abounds at this dress-up paradise, from sassy striped pants, iridescent puffy coats, and gossamer party gowns to hundreds of hair bows and shelves of glittery kid-cosmetics. Bambini's has added a preteen boutique called Che Bella, making the sweet and smart clothes (often kid versions of trendy adult items like Petit Bateau and Three Dots T-shirts) available in a greater size range. *Mon–Sat; map:NN8.*

Black Wagon

3964 N MISSISSIPPI AVE, NORTHEAST; 503/916-0000 OR 866/916-0004

Is your kid cool? Maybe you aren't sure yet, because the little one can't talk. Don't fret: Black Wagon gives tots a head start. Find tiny Vans sneakers, a bitty silk-screened T-shirt, and Onesies imprinted with images of Stevie Wonder or Johnny Cash. You can order Haight-Ashbury–inspired concert posters featuring your little rebel's photo. If you're considering getting your newborn a skateboard or a guitar just to get him used to it, run (don't walk) to Black Wagon. *Every day; www.blackwagon.com; map:FF5.*

Duck Duck Goose

517 NW 23RD AVE, NORTHWEST; 503/916-0636

Duck Duck Goose has the very best of children's clothing from European and domestic lines: labels such as Petit Bateau and Lilly Pulitzer. The store stocks tasteful dresses in crisp cottons and beautiful candy-colored designs. For boys, find sports coats and short pants. Here's everything you need to dress kids up for such special occasions as weddings and christenings, as well as a nice selection of casual items. But be prepared to open your pocketbook; the irresistible frocks come at a premium, and it's hard to say no. *Every day; map:GG7.*

Generations

4029 SE HAWTHORNE BLVD, HAWTHORNE; 503/233-8130

A new generation now patronizes this reliable favorite, founded in 1981, for natural-fiber children's and maternity clothing. The store focuses on all-cotton basics for outerwear, sleepwear, and play clothes, with sweet, nature-inspired prints on T-shirts and dresses. A well-stocked resale rack in the store makes gently worn all-cotton kids' clothing available in sizes from newborn to 6X. *Mon–Sat; map:HH4.*

haggis mcBaggis

6802 SE MILWAUKIE AVE, WESTMORELAND; 503/234-0849

This store's delightful interior is a wild playhouse, complete with enough toys, slides, and brightly colored murals to divert any shop-weary little one. Parents will be pleased with the selection of kids' all-weather gear, dominated by functional but stylish shoes (Robeez infant slippers are reported to thwart your baby's desire to pull off his shoes). Service is helpful and personalized. And if there were an award for Best Changing Room in the Universe, this shop would win—hands down, bottoms up. *Every day; map:JJ5.*

Hanna Andersson

327 NW 10TH AVE, PEARL DISTRICT; 503/321-5275

7 MONROE PKWY, LAKE OSWEGO; 503/697-1953

Well known around the country for its catalog of Swedish-style cotton clothing for kids (and moms and dads, too), Hanna Andersson is one of Portland's brighter retail success stories. With colors this vivid and fabric this sturdy, could it be anything but? The quality of Hanna's goods is high, and the styles are irresistible. And for the family who likes to dress alike, there are pj's, T-shirts, and sweatshirts in every size. Buy discounted irregulars and last season's stock at the spacious outlet store in Oswego Town Square. *Every day; www.hannaandersson.com; map:L2; map:LL7.*

Mako

732 NW 23RD AVE, NORTHWEST; 503/274-9081

Colorful sweaters, vests, and hats hand-knit by Mako and her sister are one of the biggest draws in this shop under the stairs. There's also practical rain gear, bright bathrobes, flashy underwear, a fanciful sock collection, and shelves of toys, puzzles, and bath accessories for kids. Everywhere you look, it's lots of cotton—a great selection of rainbow-hued leggings and T-shirts—at everyday prices. *Every day; map:GG7.*

Second to None

6308 SW CAPITOL HWY, HILLSDALE SHOPPING CENTER; 503/244-0071
Tucked into a strip mall, this children's shop features a good selection of used clothing (often name brands like Guess, Gap, and Hanna Andersson) and colorful new cottonwear and polar-fleece jackets. Unfinished and hand-painted wooden toy chests and child-size chairs, American Girl clothes and accessories (some custom made), dress-up costumes, and used goods such as car seats and toys in good condition set this store apart from other consignment shops. *Mon–Sat; map:JJ7.*

VINTAGE AND CONSIGNMENT

Avalon Antiques

410 SW OAK ST, DOWNTOWN; 503/224-7156
Avalon is one-stop shopping, especially for men. It's easy to walk out of this well-stocked vintage emporium with a dashing suit, dress shirt, shoes, fedora, watch, and tie. From Victorian to '50s-era wear, the selection for both men's and women's clothing is outstanding. Those who adore '20s styles will be especially pleased. Antique lockets, scarves, and other accents are quite impressive, and the staff is knowledgeable and friendly. *Every day; map:J3.*

Bombshell Vintage

811 E BURNSIDE ST, BUCKMAN; 503/239-1073
Sharp fedoras, pristine retro '60s minis, paisley prints, and knee-high leather boots abound at this Eastside staple. Dudes will have a hell of a time choosing among the rock tees and authentic vintage workwear. *Every day; www. bombshellvintageclothing.com; map:GG5.*

Buffalo Exchange

1420 SE 37TH AVE, HAWTHORNE; 503/234-1302
1036 W BURNSIDE ST, DOWNTOWN; 503/222-3418
Buy, sell, or trade in your wardrobe: this Arizona-based resale chain carries mostly used, current styles of clothes and shoes. There are jeans for both sexes, trendy new bags, belts, and jewelry on the cheap. The vintage racks offer an occasional treasure, but customers are more likely to walk out with a J.Crew sweater or a Gap shirt than anything truly retro. The downtown location is opposite Powell's Books. *Every day; www.buffaloexchange.com; map:HH5; map:K2.*

Decades Vintage Company

328 SW STARK ST, DOWNTOWN; 503/223-1177

Specializing in men's and women's vintage fashions from the '30s to the '70s, Decades offers impeccable quality: items are spotless and often still have their original tags. The men's selection is especially dashing—think charcoal tweed jackets and hand-painted ties from the '40s. Vintage eyeglass frames, '50s cocktail frocks, costume jewelry, and deco bar collectibles also await shoppers who value workmanship and condition. *Every day; www.decadesvintage. com; map:I5.*

Hattie's Vintage

729 E BURNSIDE ST, BUCKMAN; 503/238-1938

Since moving into an outlet on East Burnside's "vintage strip," 18-year vintage veteran Hattie Shindler has expanded her offering of crisp dresses, satin jackets, and go-go boots. Finds include dead-stock Jantzen beach sarongs, gloves, and jewelry, and those in-demand men's Western shirts. Prices are affordable, and you can often find extraordinary pieces—like Italian-made wedge heels from the '50s—tucked amid the usual retro flotsam. *Every day; map:HH6.*

House of Vintage

3315 SE HAWTHORNE BLVD, HAWTHORNE; 503/236-1991

Unearth antique dress forms, shaggy sofa sleepers, retro blazers, and enamel kitchenware in this vast maze of vintage finds. Dealers pick their lucky spot and square footage, then start packing in the goods. This place is loaded with hidden gems for those who like the thrill of the hunt. *Every day; map:HH5.*

Ray's Ragtime

1001 SW MORRISON ST, DOWNTOWN; 503/226-2616

If you're a fan of Gus Van Sant films, you may have seen some of Ray's finest duds onscreen in *Drugstore Cowboy* or *My Own Private Idaho* (both filmed in Portland). Hundreds of gowns and glittery party dresses hang chronologically inside the store, with the valuable pieces out of reach. If you see something you fancy, Ray will gladly fetch it for a closer look. *Every day, closed Sun Nov–Dec; www.raysragtime.com; map:I2.*

Red Light Clothing Exchange

3590 SE HAWTHORNE BLVD, HAWTHORNE; 503/963-8888

This buy-sell-trade clothing boutique is a great place to build a one-of-a-kind costume, to shop for wild party clothes, or to score that perfect ancient Mötley Crüe T-shirt. The "clothes bought and sold" policy means inventory changes daily and is always surprising. Prices are affordable, and the men's selection rivals the women's in volume and variety. *Every day; www.redlight vintage.com; map:HH5.*

Seams to Fit

2264 NW RALEIGH ST, NORTHWEST; 503/224-7884
Seams to Fit stocks designer seconds from Chanel shoes to True Religion jeans, Louis Vuitton handbags, and everything in between. They also have a great selection of resale jewelry. Owner Sherry Linder and her daughters only buy used clothing in top condition to stock two levels of packed racks. You'll find excellent values on upscale brands without dropping a mint. *Mon–Sat; map:GG7.*

Village Merchants

3360 SE DIVISION ST, SOUTHEAST; 503/234-6343
Village Merchants is like your grandma's hallway closet, your mother's kitchen, and your hippie kid sister's fashion taste all wrapped into one clutter-filled treasure trove. Buy-sell-trade is the drill, and with a whole lot of patience, you're sure to leave with a lifetime of tchotchkes. *Every day; map:II5.*

Xtabay

2515 SE CLINTON ST, CLINTON; 503/230-2899
Fabulous and full of fun, Xtabay was born when Liz Gross left Lady Luck to open her own boutique. Peruse the racks for high-end women's vintage and bridal evening gowns and an inspiring range of funky, one-of-a-kind finds in this small neighborhood shop. Don't miss the cheap rack out front or the cases near the register, which hold enough ritzy-looking costume jewelry to sink a cruise ship. *Every day; map:II5.*

Home Design and Repair

Because we sometimes experience more than our fair share of indoor weather, and because we are individualists, generally, Portland boasts a load of shops with unique accoutrements for bolstering the home. To find things easily, we've divided this category as follows: Furniture, Antiques and Collectibles, Imports, Kitchenware, Hardware, and Decor.

FURNITURE

Design Within Reach

1200 NW EVERETT ST, PEARL DISTRICT; 503/220-0200
Perhaps the work of the classic furniture designers of the 20th century is indeed within reach—but it comes at a price. Names like Eames, Aalto, Breuer, Le Corbusier, and Jacobsen share center stage with such current designers as Phillipe Starck, Ron Arad, Enrico Franzolini, and Michael Goldin. This San Francisco–based gallery devotes itself to delivering products of quality workmanship, so don't expect knockoff prices. *Every day; www.dwr.com; map:L2.*

East West Fusion

408 NW IITH AVE, PEARL DISTRICT; 503/248-6806

East West Fusion markets carefully considered contemporary pieces and high-quality antiques from China, acquired on buying trips to find authentic individual pieces in good condition. The shop also carries contemporary Chinese crafts and art chosen with an eye toward complementing most decors. In addition, the shop sells exquisitely hand-painted Fortuny lamps. *Tues–Sat; www.eastwestfusion.biz; map:L2.*

EWF Modern

1122 NW GLISAN ST, PEARL DISTRICT; 503/295-7336

EWF Modern selects furniture with clean design lines, interesting textures, and an eco-friendly bent. This "environment furniture" is made with reclaimed or sustainably harvested woods. Chic and inviting Nicoletti leather chairs and sofas, in over 200 colors, use environmentally safe foam cushioning. *Every day; www.ewfmodern.com; map:M2.*

Goodnight Room

1517 NE BROADWAY, IRVINGTON; 503/281-5516

This is the place to shop for a child's "home." This colorful store houses almost everything to outfit, or at least to decorate, a child's nursery or bedroom: furniture, linens, hand-painted mirrors, lamps, and pint-size rocking chairs. If you don't have a grand to spend on a Maine Cottage dresser or bunk bed, at least stop by for one of the less expensive items: Groovy Girl dolls, bath toys, towels, whimsical bibs, hand puppets, books, games. *Tues–Sun; map:GG5.*

H.I.P.

1829 NW 25TH AVE, NORTHWEST; 503/225-5017

This is not your grandmother's furniture store. H.I.P. sets an urbane stage for modern living with streamlined furniture buffed to a fare-thee-well. Sofas, chairs, dining sets, and entertaining systems come in modern combinations of steel, wood and glass, leather, and contemporary upholstery fabrics. *Every day; www.ubhip.com; map:GG7.*

J. D. Madison Rug & Home Co.

1301 NW GLISAN ST, PEARL DISTRICT; 503/827-6037

One of Portland's top sources for classic contemporary furnishings of high quality, J. D. Madison has a look of maximum minimalism. Custom upholstery, sofas and chairs, tables, and cabinetry of elegant simplicity are displayed in a sophisticated living room–size showroom. Handcrafted rugs and carpeting provide a virtual couture line of floor coverings. *Every day; www. jdmadison.com; map:M1.*

The Joinery

4804 SE WOODSTOCK BLVD, WOODSTOCK; 503/788-8547

For many years a fine place for custom-made Mission- and Shaker-style furniture, the Joinery has expanded its style vocabulary to include wooden French country– and Pacific Asian–style designs. The shop also carries a selection of well-hewn wooden accessories—table lamps, mirrors, boxes, spinning tops—from all over the world, offering two floors of showroom. *Mon–Sat; www.thejoinery.com; map:JJ4.*

Kinion Furniture Company

1979 COLVIN CT, MCMINNVILLE; 503/434-5448

Kinion Furniture, located 40 miles southwest of Portland in the city of McMinnville, produces a stunning line of pieces crafted with meticulous detail in a Shaker style. The inventory is all contemporary, but it has the placid simplicity of Shaker antiques, using traditional methods with attention to joining and articulation. Find tables, chairs, desks, and beds: Kinion has pieces of the highest quality, solid enough to last generations. *Mon–Sat; www.kinionfurniture.com.*

P. H. Reed Furniture

1101 NW GLISAN ST, PEARL DISTRICT; 503/274-7080

Upscale upholstered furniture and sophisticated Italian lighting dazzle the eye at this gallerylike furniture boutique. Owner Pieter Reed represents local artists and designers, so expect one-of-a-kind cast-glass side tables, hand-loomed carpets, and incredible lamps. Its expansion also includes a luxurious selection of bed and bedding accessories. *Every day; map:M2.*

Rejuvenation House Parts

1100 SE GRAND AVE, BUCKMAN; 503/238-1900

This store has built a national reputation (and a booming catalog business) around superior reproductions of Craftsman-style lighting fixtures and Mission-style furniture. You'll also find salvaged doors, windows, tubs, and kitchen sinks. Powell's Books supplies interior-design and DIY building books for this home refinishers' hangout. In the store's southwest corner is the Daily Cafe (see review in the Restaurants chapter), a delicious place to break for coffee or lunch. *Every day; www.rejuvenation.com; map:F9.*

Simon Toney and Fischer

105 SE TAYLOR ST, INNER SOUTHEAST; 503/721-0392

Cabinetmakers David Simon and Bill Toney and designer Susan Fischer create wood furniture of astonishing beauty. Each piece is a custom-designed, one-of-a-kind work of artisanship for the client. The central eastside showroom features a broad sample of their work. This comfortable, unfussy furniture exhibits Mission and Arts and Crafts influences. Rarely used woods (walnut, pear, yew, and chinquapin) dominate the collection, and each board is handpicked. Luminous finishes and color kick up the luxe quotient. *Tues–Sat; map:F9.*

ANTIQUES AND COLLECTIBLES

Antique Alley

2000 NE 42ND AVE, HOLLYWOOD; 503/287-9848

Antique Alley, in the basement of the 42nd Street Station, is a fun place to find funky collectibles. There's not much in the way of authentic antiques, but it's a good place to rummage for neat things from the 1930s, '40s, and '50s, including ashtrays and cigarette boxes, Hawaiian shirts, art prints, and World War II memorabilia. *Every day; map:GG4.*

Bella Norte Antiques

3978 N MISSISSIPPI AVE, NORTHEAST; 503/288-8823

Bella Norte offers a lovely selection of American and European furniture from the 19th and early 20th centuries. The store takes pride in exceptionally reasonable prices and excellent quality. It is committed to selling only pieces that are ready to go into your home, with no loose joints or unfinished surfaces. The shop also offers repair services for pieces from home that might need attention. *Every day; map:FF5.*

Bernadette Breu Experience

1338 SE 6TH AVE, SOUTHEAST; 503/226-6565

Be prepared for a surprise when you enter this highly personal shop. Vintage bureaus, desks, and tables overflow with decorative items. Owner Breu applies her eye for whimsy and her talent for dramatic tableaux to this big gallery space with the look and feel of old-world Europe. All goods— including vintage jewelry and an impressive collection of Bakelite jewelry— were collected from local estate sales. *Wed–Sun; www.bernadettebreuantiques. com; map:L2.*

Fred Squire III Antiques

340 1ST ST, LAKE OSWEGO; 503/675-9002

An institution since 1960, Fred Squire carries some of the Portland area's most beautiful antiques. The awe-inspiring inventory is now in 4,000 square feet of retail space in Lake Oswego. Squire has a well-trained eye and carries gorgeous period furniture—Victorian, Georgian, French, Oriental, and Early American—as well as paintings, silver, china, and folk art. Customers flock from all over the country, and stock is in constant rotation. *Tues–Sat; map:LL7.*

Hollywood Antiques

1969 NE 42ND AVE, HOLLYWOOD; 503/288-1051

More than 50 dealers and 10,000 square feet of floor space make this a star-quality antique mall. On the main level are collectibles, from Depression-era glass to jewelry, while handsome vintage furniture and home accessories are found in the basement. *Every day; map:GG4.*

Jerry Lamb Interiors and Antiques

2304 NW SAVIER ST, NORTHWEST; 503/227-6077
Interior designer Lamb showcases an outstanding collection of Asian antiques and English and American antique furniture, silver, and porcelain. Take note, too, of the fine embroidery and woodblock prints from China and Japan, and the wide selection of porcelain—Imari, blue-and-white Canton, celadon, and Rose Medallion—from the Far East. *Tues–Fri; map:GG7.*

Stars, an Antiques Mall

7027 SE MILWAUKIE AVE, SELLWOOD; 503/235-5990
Stars has two vintage-goods and antique malls directly across the street from one another in the *Wonder Years*–like neighborhood of Sellwood. With items ranging from country kitsch to Belleek china and Tiffany silver, these outlets encompass a diverse conglomeration of wares. You can spend an entire afternoon searching through the offerings of nearly 200 dealers. *Every day; www. starsantique.com; map:KK5.*

IMPORTS

Arthur W. Erikson Fine Arts

1030 SW TAYLOR ST, DOWNTOWN; 503/227-4710
This astonishing mélange of traditional tribal artifacts appeals to novice and experienced collectors alike. The focus is on American Indian and Eskimo arts and crafts. Roman glass and 12th-century Persian pottery are among the out-of-the-ordinary offerings. *Wed and by appointment; map:H1.*

Cargo

380 NW 13TH AVE, PEARL DISTRICT; 503/209-8349
Welcome to another world. Where else but in this 10,000-square-foot warehouse will you find all of the world's treasures under one roof? Big-ticket home-furnishing items include Chang-dynasty beds and Indonesian puppets. Folding iron chairs, seed baskets from Borneo, Indonesian hutches, Mexican pottery and glassware, and funky doodads from everywhere fill this eclectic store to its rafters. A shopping oasis for those who want to create a homespun Shangri-la. *Every day; www.cargoinc.com; map:N1.*

Scandia Imports

10020 SW BEAVERTON-HILLSDALE HWY, BEAVERTON; 503/643-2424
Finnish glassware, gleaming brown stoneware by Arabia, and heavy pewter candelabra from Denmark dazzle at surprisingly low prices. Homesick Scandinavians can buy birthday cards in their native languages, good Swedish mint pastilles, linens, and enough candles for a hundred Santa Lucia nights. *Mon–Sat; www.scandiaimports.com; map:II9.*

Signature Imports

920 NW 23RD AVE, NORTHWEST; 503/274-0217

Signature Imports runs a brisk business in South American imports, including colorful sweaters and jewelry. It carries rough-hewn furniture and gorgeous handblown glass from Mexico, handcrafted figures from Oaxaca, drums from Ghana, and masks from Bali. Signature supports its own knitting co-op in Bolivia, so craftspeople benefit directly from their labors. *Every day; map:GG7.*

Swahili

128 NW 12TH AVE, PEARL DISTRICT; 503/684-0688

This craft boutique imports authentic handmade artwork and artifacts from Africa, including colorful fabrics and hand-carved hardwood sculptures and statues. The helpful staff is educated about the merchandise and generous with their knowledge. Also find books and African music. *Every day; map:K1.*

Trade Roots

1831 NE BROADWAY, IRVINGTON; 503/281-5335

Folk art at this friendly shop includes brightly painted coconut-shell masks from Mexico, Peruvian amulets, and vibrant scarves from Nepal. Gauzy skirts, embroidered vests, batik dresses, and other colorful apparel (including Cut Loose, Loco Lindo and Nomadic Traders), plus lots of silver jewelry, are available at good prices. *Every day; www.traderootsinc.com; map:GG5.*

KITCHENWARE

In Good Taste

231 NW 11TH AVE, PEARL DISTRICT; 503/248-2015

This is a place for people who are passionate about food and wine. What began as a cooking school has grown into retail space for professional-quality kitchen utensils, from copper and stainless cookware to Laguiole knives. A wine shop carries an extensive selection from Oregon, Washington, and California, plus imports; the foodie in your life will love the Scharffen Berger chocolate. Cooking classes are taught by well-known local chefs and visiting professionals, and most are small enough (14 max) to allow for hands-on participation. *Every day; www.ingoodtastestore.com; map:K2.*

Kitchen Kaboodle

404 NW 23RD AVE, NOB HILL (AND BRANCHES); 503/241-4040

Top-of-the-line cookware, tons of gadgets, and beautiful, reasonably priced tableware make this a favorite haunt of food enthusiasts. Novelty accessories are complemented by purely practical tools, appliances, and furniture: cherry dressers, ash side tables, and custom-made couches. Kitchen Kaboodle's January sale draws cooks out of the kitchen and into the store. The locally owned company has expanded its original Beaverton location and now has five other shops in Greater Portland. *Every day; www.kitchenkaboodle.com; map:I4.*

Sur La Table

1102 NW COUCH ST, DOWNTOWN; 503/295-9685

Always a registry staple, this kitchen and cookware store leaves no tagine or table setting left behind, running the gamut of high-end (All-Clad, Le Creuset) to affordable (Chef's Choice, VillaWare). Almost-nightly cooking classes make this a one-stop shop for both the adventurous foodie and the meat-and-potatoes cook. *Every day; www.surlatable.com; map:K2.*

HARDWARE

Ecohaus

819 SE TAYLOR ST, BUCKMAN; 503/222-3881

Ecohaus has three criteria for its products: they must be natural, low in toxicity, and renewable or recyclable. With that mission, this eastside store offers a wide range of hard-to-find floor coverings and finishes, cabinets and countertops, paint and plumbing supplies, all safe for the home and easy on the environment. You'll find sustainable hardwoods, wool carpets from New Zealand, and linoleum from Holland. Other locations are in Seattle and Bellevue, WA. *Every day; www.ecohaus.com; map:N1.*

1874 House

8070 SE 13TH AVE, SELLWOOD; 503/233-1874

Local architectural remnants that homeowners ripped out and discarded decades ago have found a new home at the 1874 House. An organized jumble of high-quality light shades and fixtures, antique as well as reproduction hardware, windows, shutters, and mantels all wait to be reinstalled in the bungalow of your dreams. A tad bit younger than most of its contents, this place has been around for nearly four decades. *Tues–Sat; map:KK5.*

Hippo Hardware and Trading Co.

1040 E BURNSIDE ST, BUCKMAN; 503/231-1444

This huge place can hook you up with a kitchen sink and just about every other house part you can think of. Built on a foundation of buy, sell, and trade, Hippo is always on the prowl for architectural elements—doors, windows, molding, and trim—as well as hardware from the 1800s through the 1940s. Pre-1970s lighting fixtures and specialized plumbing fixtures are also sought after. Hippo has a wonderfully quirky staff who'll keep you smiling as you sort through design treasures and organized bins of clutter. If you can't find something, ask; if they don't have it, they just might be able to splice, dice, or file something to fit. *Every day; www.hippohardware.com; map:HH6.*

Pearl Hardware

1621 NW GLISAN ST, NORTHWEST; 503/228-5135

This place has everything you ever, ever wanted in a hardware store, and then some. From paint to pots, bolts to barbecue grills, Pearl Hardware has it, and the staff is so friendly and knowledgeable you'll feel right at home. It also has a key-cutting facility, extensive housewares, and plenty of parking. *Every day; map:M1.*

The ReBuilding Center

3625 N MISSISSIPPI AVE, NORTHEAST; 503/331-1877

The ReBuilding Center will impress you, even before you walk in, with its facade of recycled window frames assembled into a contemporary skylight creation. Inside, the inventory of reclaimed, recycled doors and windows, right down to hardware, will blow your mind. Even if you don't need anything, looking through the different styles is like being in a museum. *Every day; www.rebuildingcenter.org; map:FF5.*

Winks Hardware

200 SE STARK ST, BUCKMAN; 503/227-5536

With everything from 1,000 sizes of springs to hundreds of styles of hinges, Winks is a full house for your home. Carrying an impressive array of hard-to-find, unusual, and useful items, Winks caters to the trade (hence the weekday-only hours), but experienced clerks happily share advice with do-it-yourselfers. This is about as old-fashioned a hardware store as it gets these days. *Mon–Fri; www.winkshardware.com; map:I9.*

Woodcrafters

212 NE 6TH AVE, BUCKMAN; 503/231-0226

This is where Portland's builders and woodworkers spend their fun money: a friendly warehouse filled with tools, wood stains, and high-quality lumber, mill ends, and hardwood carving blocks. An enormous book section (with back issues of *Fine Homebuilding*) serves as an unofficial library for do-it-yourselfers and craftspeople, making this the logical destination after an episode of *This Old House*. Free demonstrations of wood turning and other specialized skills are offered most Saturdays. *Every day, closed Sun June–Sept; map:HH6.*

DECOR

The Arrangement

4210 NE FREMONT ST, BEAUMONT; 503/287-4440

This friendly shop in the Alameda/Beaumont neighborhood beckons with an ever-changing flow of decorative items. Around holiday time, the winter-wonderland quality of the shop is as inviting as a cup of hot cocoa on a blustery day, and the helpful staff will assist you in designing just the right wreath or table arrangement. Like a mini department store with tons more personality, the Arrangement boasts casual clothing and jewelry, housewarming decor, and stationery. *Every day; map:FF4.*

Canoe

1136 SW ALDER ST, DOWNTOWN; 503/889-8545

This minimalist, ultramodern office/housewares boutique focuses solely on cultured international, national, and local design. Splurge on richly colored and crafted serving bowls by Heath Ceramics, distinguished business card holders, candy-colored birdhouses, and a collection of design-oriented coffee-table pleasure reading. *Every day; www.canoeonline.net; map:II2.*

Flutter

3948 N MISSISSIPPI AVE, NORTH PORTLAND; 503/288-1649

Whimsically inspired by Art Nouveau decadence, this shop houses beauty aplenty. Embellished chandeliers, gilded frames, antique birdcages, paper goods, and French-milled soaps fill every square inch. Flutter has now joined forces with a handful of local designers, including Frocky Jack Morgan, who reconstructs vintage couture garments into one-of-a-kind silhouettes. *Every day; www.flutterclutter.com; map:FF6.*

French Quarter

1313 NW GLISAN ST, PEARL DISTRICT; 503/282-8200

"Crème de la crème" describes this boutique, which caters to Francophiles who don't want to use up their frequent-flier miles in search of a gift but still want to wrap themselves in Parisian panache. Every square inch of the French Quarter is filled with something to lust after: plush bath mats, unbelievably soft flannel sheets (100 percent cotton, unbleached and undyed), aromatic candles, fancy French soaps and bath salts, colorful towels, downy bathrobes, and dreamy pajamas. *Every day; www.frenchquarterlinens.com; map:M1.*

hunt & Gather

1302 NW HOYT ST, PEARL DISTRICT; 503/227-3400

Treasures from around the globe make for an interesting mix of home accessories at this Pearl District favorite. Beyond global goodies for the table, hunt & Gather features custom-made, decadent down sofas and chairs sure to be the focus of any elegant home. Check out the nifty candle selection, too. *Tues–Sun; www.huntgather.com; map:M1.*

Michael Allen's Home

915 SW 9TH AVE, DOWNTOWN; 503/222-6535

Michael Allen Clothiers (811 SW Morrison St, 503/221-9963) has expanded, boosting its knack for style by introducing this store. In the spirit of traditional, refined living, homes are styled with small furnishings, fabulous fabrics, and gift goods for the discerning. *Every day; map:H2.*

Noun: A Person's Place for Things

3300 SE BELMONT ST, SOUTHEAST; 503/235-0078

Oh, the curious sweetness of this shop! Not only does it dole out boxed to-go treats from Saint Cupcakes in its back room, but it also carries unique flea

227

market/estate/garage sale finds. Prices are reasonable, and goods are added often. Local art sidles antique woodblock print letters, wire hat stands, and primitive furniture. *Every day; www.shopnoun.com; map:HH4.*

Office

2204 NE ALBERTA ST, NORTHEAST; 503/282-7200
With a contemporary take on retro-themed office supplies, Office sells russell+hazel organizers and accessories, cool trash cans, and presentation portfolios and laptop bags by local Acme Made and NYC's Jack Spade, making the otherwise 9–5 drag a stylish endeavor. The store's monthly free design/art events are a who's who of Portland's creative scene and a definite plus. *Every day; www.officepdx.com; map:FF5.*

Pendleton Woolen Mills Store

8500 SE MCLOUGHLIN BLVD, MILWAUKIE; 503/535-5786
This is the drop-off spot for products from the research and development department of Pendleton Woolen Mills, an Oregon pioneer. Prototypes for new products—from theme blankets to wool-upholstered furniture—are offered at discount prices. *Every day; www.pendleton-usa.com; map:KK5.*

Pratt & Larson Tile Co.

1201 SE 3RD AVE, INNER SOUTHEAST; 503/231-9464
With what seems to be tile by the mile—it lines every surface—this is one of the country's largest custom tile manufacturers. The shop is like a large working studio, with examples of kitchen and bathroom treatments that use both imported tiles and one-of-a-kind work by potter Michael Pratt and fabric artist Reta Larson. For bargains, check out their seconds room, where mistakes are practically given away. *Mon–Sat; www.prattandlarson.com; map:E9.*

Relish

415 NW LOVEJOY ST, NOB HILL; 503/227-3779
Relish's ultramodern aesthetic is apparent in its eclectic collection of beautifully made tableware, including wood vessels from Costa Rica; ceramic dishware from Italy, London, and Japan; and kitchen utensils from Denmark and Germany. Relish also features artsy jewelry of silver, enamel, and feathers, plus steel and acrylic jewelry from Ann Brumby of Portland. *Tues–Sat; www.shoprelish.com; map:L2.*

Ste. Maine

1626 SE BYBEE BLVD, WESTMORELAND; 503/232-1880
This exquisite design and housewares boutique carries objets d'art; home furnishings, including sofas; lighting; original artwork; and eccentric decor with travel-inspired flair. *Every day; www.saintmaine.com; map:KK5.*

Versailles

904 NW HOYT ST, PEARL DISTRICT; 503/222-2387

To get your hands on authentic Provençal French country style that looks cozy in a rustic farmhouse and stunning in grander châteaus, you must visit Versailles—the Pearl District shop, that is. It's like a mini trip to France. You'll find carved wood details and printed toile fabrics, woven rush chairs, rough plaster walls, and natural stone floors. The friendly staff will help you develop decorating ideas that you can apply in your own Versailles. *Every day; map:M3.*

The Whole 9 Yards

1820 E BURNSIDE ST, SOUTHEAST; 503/223-2880

The Oregonian calls this gem, relocated from the Pearl District, "one of the nation's top interior fabric stores." One step inside reveals why: seamsters come here in droves for the luxurious silks, velvets, and jacquards, but also for ideas and inspiration. Need a second opinion? The gracious staff double as design consultants. A custom furniture line and classes on making curtains and pillows are added bonuses. *Mon–Sat; www.w9yards.com; map:M2.*

Books and Magazines

Portlanders love to read, and our bookstores show it. Getting the title you want in Portland is generally not a problem, as Portlanders buy more books per capita than any other city in the country, and Multnomah County has the second-highest library circulation numbers of any county in the nation. Read on!

Annie Bloom's Books

7834 SW CAPITOL HWY, MULTNOMAH VILLAGE; 503/246-0053

Readers from all over the city are drawn to this independent bookstore. Staff recommendations pepper the extensive selection of fiction, parenting, and children's literature, the last of which surrounds a colorful play area at the back of the store. The Judaica section is quite strong, and special orders are no problem. The shop presents readings from local fiction and poetry writers. Cushy armchairs and complimentary tea make you feel right at home. *Every day; www.annieblooms.com; map:JJ7.*

Bridge City Comics

3725 N MISSISSIPPI AVE, NORTHEAST; 503/282-5484

Portland's love for comic books (the number of publishers and professionals living here is second only to New York City) is apparent at Bridge City Comics. Here you'll find a wide selection of new comics, new and used graphic novels, collecting supplies, and apparel. This isn't your run-of-the-mill comic shop! With thousands of graphic novels and a well-stocked Portland-authors section, Bridge City Comics is an oasis for the hard-core collector and the casual reader alike—and it's very tidy. *Every day; www.bridgecitycomics.com; map:FF5.*

Broadway Books

1714 NE BROADWAY, IRVINGTON; 503/284-1726
Together, Gloria Borg Olds and Roberta Dyer have been in the book biz in Portland for some 35 years, and they provide personal, educated service. There's a sizable selection of biographies and memoirs, the shop's specialty, but also fiction, Judaica, and contemporary fiction. Any book not already in stock can be special-ordered. *Every day; map:GG5.*

Cameron's Books

336 SW 3RD AVE, DOWNTOWN; 503/228-2391
Cameron's Books is Portland's oldest used-books shop, established in 1938. It stocks used hardbacks, paperbacks, and myriad used periodicals dating to the late 19th century; vintage *Life* magazines are the most popular seller. Cameron's also stocks old *Saturday Evening Post* and *Look* magazines, as well as vintage hobby mags on such subjects as cars, trains, aviation, and stage magic. *Every day; www.cameronsbooks.com; map:I5.*

A Children's Place

4807 NE FREMONT ST, BEAUMONT; 503/284-8294
This adorable store goes beyond being the neighborhood book nook. Toys, puzzles, and kid-friendly music complement an extensive selection of books for you and your pint-size bookworm. The selection varies from bedtime classics (*Goodnight Moon* and the *Madeline* series) to kids' reference books and survival guides for parents. And it's an excellent resource for educators, who receive a 20 percent discount. *Every day; www.achildrensplacebooks. com; map:FF4.*

Daedalus Books

2074 NW FLANDERS ST, NORTHWEST; 503/274-7742
If you love poetry, don't miss Daedalus, considered by some the best poetry bookstore in the world. This voluminous yet well-organized store stocks hard-to-find books, specializing in poetry. The staff is extremely attentive to customers and regularly sponsors poetry events. It's tucked away behind Ken's Bakery on 21st Avenue. *Mon–Sat; www.abebooks.com/home/daedalus; map:GG7.*

Future Dreams

1847 E BURNSIDE ST, BUCKMAN; 503/231-8311
Future Dreams is one part sci-fi bookstore and one part comics-art store. New and used magazines, books, and comics range from classic favorites to esoteric, hard-to-find titles. There's also a good selection of back issues and a reservation service for new volumes. *Every day; fdb@hevanet.com; map:HH5.*

The Great Northwest Book Store

3314 SW 1ST AVE, LAIR HILL; 503/223-8098
From its location in an 1895 church—in the Lair Hill neighborhood off Barbur Boulevard south of downtown—the Great Northwest Book Store

specializes in used books with an emphasis on Americana and western literature. First-edition modern and older literature and sports are particularly strong. The shop offers an appraisal service and a rare-book room; book buying is by appointment. *Every day; www.greatnorthwestbooks.com; map:II6.*

Hawthorne Boulevard Books

3129 SE HAWTHORNE BLVD, HAWTHORNE; 503/236-3211
Roger and Ilse Roberts invite the public into their Hawthorne home to browse their used and antiquarian books. They're particularly fond of classic literature and American history. A fireplace makes it difficult to leave in the chilly months. *Tues–Sat; hbb@teleport.com; map:HH5.*

In Other Words

8 NE KILLINGSWORTH ST, NORTHEAST; 503/232-6003
Here you'll find herstory written by womyn. This nonprofit store provides a repository of feminist, women-centered, lesbian, and holistic literature not available at mainstream retail venues, as well as "women-positive" videos to rent. The children's section is an excellent source for nonsexist literature. In Other Words has expanded with a gallery for local women artists. *Mon–Sat; www.inotherwords.org; map:FF5.*

Laughing Horse Books

12 NE 10TH AVE, NORTHEAST; 503/236-2893
Activists, heretics, and visionaries run this politically progressive and environmentally sensitive bookstore/collective. The schedule of events features discussion groups, speakers, and community potlucks that focus on social change. Sections on U.S. and world politics and economic globalization are strong. *Mon–Sat; map:HH5.*

Longfellow's Books

1401 SE DIVISION ST, LADD'S ADDITION; 503/239-5222
Tucked between a school and a residential neighborhood, this gem of a used bookstore will delight the dedicated book browser. Jon Hagen has run Longfellow's for more than two decades, and now that his son, Nile, is a partner, they are both quick to help new customers find their area of interest. Jon has a special focus on Oregon- and Portland-specific books, collectible periodicals, and books he remembers from childhood. *Mon–Sat; www.longfellowspdx. com; map:II5.*

Looking Glass Bookstore

7983 SE 13TH AVE, SELLWOOD; 503/227-4760
Relocated from downtown to Southeast Portland, this beautiful shop specializes in contemporary literature, political science, history, philosophy, biographies, and poetry. Established in the 1970s, it has become a mainstay for voracious readers in the Sellwood neighborhood. For anyone who has, knows, or was a child, there is a children's section irresistibly nestled in an

old caboose. With a lovely garden atrium, Looking Glass provides an atmosphere ripe for intellectual discovery. *Every day; lookingglassbook@quest. net; map:H4.*

Murder by the Book

3210 SE HAWTHORNE BLVD, HAWTHORNE; 503/232-9995
Mystery lovers and all fans of thriller and spy fiction adore this shop. An expanded selection of imported British books has introduced readers to many interesting but lesser-known European writers, as well as volumes out of print in this country. Friendly, knowledgeable staff offer new and used books to buy, sell—and even die for. *Every day; www.mbtb.com; map:HH5.*

New Renaissance Bookshop

1338 NW 23RD AVE, NORTHWEST; 503/224-4929
Two adjacent Victorians house some 15,000 titles and a varied selection of accoutrements to help you take your next spiritual step—whether it be recovery, growth, business prosperity, metaphysical knowledge, or self-transformation. Lectures, tarot readings, and discussions are also part of this harmonic convergence, as are chimes, rainbow crystals, videos, and a wide selection of DVDs. A play area has holograms, science toys, fairy costumes, and books on children's spirituality. *Every day; map:GG7.*

Oregon History Center Museum Store

1200 SW PARK AVE, DOWNTOWN; 503/306-5230
See no. 12 in Top 20 Attractions in the Exploring chapter.

Periodicals and Books Paradise

1928 NE 42ND AVE, HOLLYWOOD; 503/234-6003
You can't go wrong at Periodicals Paradise, with its vast selection of mysteries, used DVDs and videos, and the largest selection of periodicals in Portland. The myriad vintage volumes are in the back, so if you're looking for a specific edition, just ask. You can also e-mail ahead of time to see if the edition you want is available. Also in the store you'll find art, gifts, jewelry, and even some antiques for sale. *Every day; mookeymags@aol.com; map:GG4.*

Powell's City of Books

1005 W BURNSIDE ST, DOWNTOWN (AND BRANCHES);
503/228-4651
See no. 9 in Top 20 Attractions in the Exploring chapter.

Rich's Cigar Store

820 SW ALDER ST, DOWNTOWN; 503/228-1700
706 NW 23RD AVE, NORTHWEST; 503/227-6907
922 NW FLANDERS ST, PEARL DISTRICT; 503/595-5556
With the best magazine selection in Portland, as well as a humidor full of domestic and imported cigars, tobacco, and cigarettes, Rich's has the charm

of a throwback but is teeming with periodicals on the cutting edge. Find everything from *People* to top-notch literary journals. Also find a broad selection of foreign publications, pipes, and stylish lighters. The helpful staff can assist you in choosing literary or smoking-related accoutrements and gifts. *Every day; www.richscigar.com; map:I3; map:GG7; map:L3.*

Title Wave Bookstore

216 NE KNOTT ST, ALBINA; 503/988-5021
Ever wonder where old library books end up? More than 20,000 volumes from the Multnomah County Library sell for bargain prices here at the old Albina Library, a 1912 Spanish Renaissance Revival–style Carnegie Library building. Volunteers organize the books by—what else?—the Dewey decimal system. There are also magazines, CDs, books on tape, and videos. Prices start at $1 for hardbacks. *Mon–Sat; map:GG6.*

CDs and Vinyl

Portland has a rich heritage by which appreciators of music and musicians alike have lived in harmony, and by which albums old and new fly off the racks. While tapes for the most part have fallen through the cracks, records are still loved and revered, and Portland has a contingent of vinyl collectors and a good list of record stores that facilitate the frenzy.

Crossroads

3130-B SE HAWTHORNE BLVD, HAWTHORNE; 503/232-1767
This cooperative of 35 vendors in a storefront is modeled much like an antique mall. That makes sense, considering that they specialize in collectibles and hard-to-find records—they even offer a computerized record-search service. If you need *Meet the Beatles* on the black label, green label, red label, or Apple label to complete your collection, pay this place a visit. It will definitely be worth the trip. *Every day; www.xro.com; map:HH5.*

Everyday Music

**1313 W BURNSIDE ST, PEARL DISTRICT (AND BRANCHES);
503/274-0961**
Combined with a little browsing at nearby Powell's City of Books, a leisurely visit to Everyday Music makes for a fine afternoon—or evening (they're open till midnight). The huge space is stocked with new and preloved CDs, cassettes, and LPs from the worlds of rock, jazz, and dance music. The next-door annex has a great classical selection. Try before you buy at one of the listening stations. Other branches are in Northeast Portland (1931 NE Sandy Blvd, Buckman; 503/239-7610; map:HH5) and Beaverton (3290 SW Cedar Hills Blvd; 503/350-0907; map:II9). *Every day (including Christmas); www. everydaymusic.com; map:K1.*

Jackpot Records

203 SW 9TH AVE, DOWNTOWN; 503/222-0990
3574 SE HAWTHORNE BLVD, HAWTHORNE; 503/239-7561
Owner Isaac Slusarenko provides what mega music vendors can't: a cross-genre wealth of knowledge and a hands-on approach to selling music. Come here if you're seeking obscure reggae, rare vinyl, esoteric local artists, or an incredible array of independent rock and punk music. Just don't come looking for Jonas Brothers or Taylor Swift. *Every day; www.jackpot records.com; map:HH5.*

Mississippi Records

4007 N MISSISSIPPI AVE, NORTHEAST; 503/282-2990
Mississippi Records stocks old, hard-to-find vinyl and turntables on the main drag in the Mississippi neighborhood. Buy, sell, or trade. It also showcases community in-store events and boasts its own record label. *Every day; map:FF5.*

Music Millennium

3158 E BURNSIDE ST, LAURELHURST; 503/231-8926
Since 1969, the independently owned Music Millennium has stayed competitive with larger record chains. Its stock is truly impressive: an amazing variety of rock CDs plus separate areas for oldies, rap, jazz, blues, reggae, country, New Age, and a classical music annex. *Every day; www.musicmillennium. com; map:HH5.*

Platinum Records

104 SW 2ND AVE, OLD TOWN; 503/222-9166
This DJ-centric shop is the place to go for dance music and hard-to-find musical genres. The stock is mostly LPs—not surprising, as DJs don't mix with cassettes or CDs. There's also a good selection of DJ equipment, including mixers, PA systems, and a few glittering disco balls. *Every day; www. platinum-records.com; map:J6.*

2nd Avenue Records

400 SW 2ND AVE, DOWNTOWN; 503/222-3783
Definitely not a grab-and-go music shop, 2nd Avenue is a shrine to the record-hunting experience. Stacks of collectible and imported vinyl share scant store space with CDs; unfortunately, these are kept behind glass, which requires requesting them from the sales staff. All genres—including hip-hop, punk, ska, and rock—are represented, but selection is on a try-your-luck basis. *Every day; map:I5.*

Sonic Recollections

2701 SE BELMONT ST, BELMONT; 503/236-3050
Come here for an incredible selection of hard-to-find music on vinyl and reel-to-reel, as well as DVDs. Look for music like the soundtrack from *Goldfinger*, old Dylan, Stones, David Bowie, Nina Simone, or John Coltrane—you name

it. The selection is extensive and high quality, and the shop is very organized. *Tues–Sat; www.sonicrec.com; map:HH5.*

Gifts and Accessories

Because Portland likes to embrace the eclectic, myriad unique gifts can be found throughout the city. This section begins with a list of miscellaneous shops that feature items that would make great gifts. Following this initial list are the categories Florists and Nurseries, Jewelry and Watches, Cards and Stationery, and last but not least, Toys.

Dazzle
704 NW 23RD AVE, NORTHWEST; 503/224-1294
From the spotted pony mascot outside to an interior that looks as though it was decorated by Salvador Dali, Dazzle's chaotic collection of whimsical collectibles lives up to its name. It's an ideal place to find the perfect gift for someone who needs a little whimsy in their life, whether jewelry or a chandelier. *Every day; map:GG7.*

Escential Lotions & Oils
3638 SE HAWTHORNE BLVD, HAWTHORNE; 503/236-7976
This earth-friendly boutique invites customers to select mood-enhancing fragrances to infuse unscented lotions, massage oils, and body shampoos. Emily Mann runs the business begun by her mother in 1979. This is the perfect place to put together a gift basket for someone who loves luxurious baths and essential oil–scented skin treats. Classic shaving supplies, cosmetics, and incense round out the selection. *Every day; www.escential.net; map:HH4.*

Friends Library Store
801 SW 10TH AVE, DOWNTOWN; 503/988-5911
Multnomah County's Central Library gift shop is a quaint little nook of a shop with everything bookish. Operated by the Friends of the Multnomah County Library, this niche-filled haven offers literary-inspired bookends, small book lights, and writing implements (costly and not)—plus children's gifts, jewelry, and watches with the likes of Shakespeare and Che Guevara on their faces. Also find silk ties, T-shirts, and a small assortment of specialized books for sale. *Mon–Sat during library hours; www.friends-library.org/store; map:I2.*

The Gallery at the Museum of Contemporary Craft
724 NW DAVIS ST, PEARL DISTRICT; 503/223-2654
The Gallery at the Museum of Contemporary Craft, on the North Park Blocks, has a wide selection of beautiful handcrafted gifts perfect for weddings, birthdays, or any special occasion. The jewelry selection begins under $10, and there are hand-thrown mugs and teapots and handblown glass bowls. *Tues–Sat; www.contemporarycrafts.org; map:K4.*

235

Greg's

3707 SE HAWTHORNE BLVD, HAWTHORNE; 503/235-1257
A treasure of the Hawthorne District, Greg Klaus's shop offers an abundance of goodness. Portland-based candles by Pacifica, irreverent cards by Uncooked, and prints by local artist Ryan Berkley all round out the mix. Rub shoulders in the smallish space with other similar-minded shoppers on a Saturday afternoon, or stop in during the week for a more serene walk-through. *Every day; map:HH5.*

Made in Oregon

600 SW MORRISON ST (THE GALLERIA), DOWNTOWN (AND BRANCHES); 503/241-3630 OR 800/828-9673 FOR A CATALOG
If it's made, caught, or grown in this state, it's sold at Made in Oregon. Visitor essentials include smoked salmon, berry jams, chocolate, and hazelnuts that can be packed for traveling, along with souvenir wooden slugs, myrtlewood, and warm, cozy Pendleton blankets. There are 10 stores around the state, including 5 others in Greater Portland: at the airport, in Old Town, at Lloyd Center, at Clackamas Town Center, and at Washington Square. *Every day; www.madeinoregon.com; map:I2.*

The Nature Store at Portland Audubon Society

5151 NW CORNELL RD, NORTHWEST; 503/292-9453
Going bird-watching in Belize? Before you take flight, be sure to swoop down to this resource center and gift shop on the edge of Forest Park within the Audubon sanctuary. Inside, there's a treasure trove for naturalists: worldwide field guides, natural-history books, binoculars, bird feeders, and more. About one-third of the inventory is children's books; there are also stuffed animals, model insects, and jigsaw puzzles. *Every day; www.audubonportland.org; map:GG8.*

The Perfume House

3328 SE HAWTHORNE BLVD, HAWTHORNE; 503/234-5375
Chris Tsefelas's Perfume House has been praised as the ultimate source of rare authentic scents from abroad, from hard-to-come-by Russian perfumes to Corina (from the Patrician House), introduced at the 1962 Seattle World's Fair. *Mon–Sat June–Aug, Tues–Sat Sept–May, every day in Dec; www.the perfumehouse.com; map:HH5.*

Topanien

7832 SW CAPITOL HWY, MULTNOMAH VILLAGE; 503/244-9683
This world-friendly shop brings global treasures to the comfy confines of Multnomah Village. Find a colorful stock of soapstone from Kenya, woven baskets from Ghana, purses from Guatemala, and other educational gifts from all over the world. And for the home, there's a collection of decorative tablecloths, pillows, vases, and frames. *Every day; map:JJ7.*

Twist

30 NW 23RD PL, NORTHWEST; 503/224-0334

700 SW 5TH AVE (PIONEER PLACE), DOWNTOWN; 503/222-3137

Twist playfully displays some of the world's top jewelry designers beside unique American Arts and Crafts artifacts. The gallery focuses on exclusive designers, delicate glassware, hand-painted ceramics, crafts, and a smattering of furniture. While the Pioneer Place shop is geared for the traveler, it maintains the same level of quality merchandise and mystique. *Every day; www. twistonline.com; map:HH7; map:H4.*

FLORISTS AND NURSERIES

The Bovees Nursery

1737 SW CORONADO ST, SOUTHWEST; 503/244-9341

This specialty nursery features hundreds of types of neatly labeled rhododendrons in the display garden. The star rhodies and deciduous azaleas bloom nearly six months of the year; but trees, hardy perennials, and Northwest natives are no less visible. Catalog on request. *Every day; www.bovees.com; map:LL6.*

Cornell Farm

8212 SW BARNES RD, WEST SLOPE; 503/292-9895

A 1926 Dutch Colonial house, with a towering monkey-puzzle tree and lovely flower gardens, is the centerpiece of this 5-acre nursery. Owners Ed Blatter and Deby Barnhart grow more than 700 varieties of perennials and 150 types of annuals on the former goat and strawberry farm. Growing beds, open to the public, are across the road from the nearby Oregon College of Art and Craft. *Every day; map:HH9.*

Geranium Lake Flowers

555 SW OAK ST, DOWNTOWN; 503/228-1920

Painter and floral artist Kim Foren has built an oasis of blooms in the middle of the U.S. Bancorp Tower. The brightly colored space specializing in whimsical artistry caters to those looking for a hip edge in floral display. You won't find any baby's breath here. *Mon–Sat; www.geraniumlake.com; map:J4.*

Gifford-Doving Florists

1224 SW BROADWAY, DOWNTOWN; 503/222-9193

200 SW MARKET ST, DOWNTOWN; 503/222-5029

Family-owned since 1938, Gifford-Doving stocks one of the better selections of cut flowers in town. In the late afternoon, it's one of Portland's busiest florists. Several kinds of greens are on hand at both shops, making this a favorite of do-it-yourself arrangers. *Mon–Sat; www.giffordsflowers.com; map:F2; map:E4.*

The Meadow

3731 N MISSISSIPPI AVE, NORTHEAST; 503/288-4633
Somehow flowers look fresher and more vibrant at the Meadow. With a seasonally changing inventory, the store's arrangements are especially creative and beautiful. The Meadow delivers flowers within Portland and is available for weddings and special events. *Every day; www.atthemeadow.com; map:FF5.*

The Orchid Exchange

404 NW 12TH AVE, PEARL DISTRICT; 503/295-6899
Satisfy your craving for exotic blossoms at this exquisite floral shop. Reasonably priced potted orchids start at $25; rare exotics can range up to $500. Owner Matt White keeps you coming back for more: any plant can be exchanged for a discount on your next purchase. At any one time, around 100 orchids are in bloom in the store—some of them fragrant, some not. The shop also features Adam's sculptural wall pieces. *Every day; map:L2.*

Portland Nursery

5050 SE STARK ST, SOUTHEAST; 503/231-5050
9000 SE DIVISION ST, SOUTHEAST; 503/788-9000
A venerated landmark spread over 5 acres, Portland Nursery supplies city gardeners with a great variety of annuals, perennials, bushes, shrubs, and trees. A weekend visit is a cultural outing. An easy-to-follow layout takes you directly to the type of greenery you want, whether it be ground cover or climbing vine. The store's reputation owes much to its knowledgeable and helpful staff. This is also a good source for basic yard and deck furnishings, trellises, garden globes, and more. A second branch on Division Street specializes in ponds and houseplants. *Every day; www.portlandnursery.com; map:HH4; map:II3.*

Sammy's Flowers

2120 NW GLISAN ST, NORTHWEST; 503/222-9759
A choice of more than 50 varieties of cut flowers, plus a larger selection of tropicals, makes Sammy's a Northwest institution. A mixed bouquet can cost as little as $15. The shop keeps later hours than most (open until 8pm every night), and it offers delivery. *Every day; map:HH7.*

Tommy Luke Flowers

2335 NW 23RD PL, NORTHWEST; 503/228-3140
Established in Portland over 100 years ago, Tommy Luke has moved to an environmentally sound building with a massive water-filtration system that decreases water waste through hydroponic filtration. Luke carries gorgeous flowers, as always, with creative and traditional arrangements. The store is now moving toward more organic and local inventory when available. It also carries giftware, potted plants, pottery, and vases. *Mon–Sat; map:GG7.*

JEWELRY AND WATCHES

Carl Greve

640 SW BROADWAY, DOWNTOWN; 503/223-7121
Exclusive representation of the world's top jewelry designers is the specialty at fourth-generation, family-owned Carl Greve. Like the jewels and gems, much of it is exclusive to this chic Portland establishment. *Mon–Sat; www.carlgreve.com; map:I3.*

Gary Swank Jewelers

1309 SW BROADWAY, DOWNTOWN; 503/223-8940
Custom designer Gary Swank does on-the-spot creations, from bold earrings to necklaces that could have come from an Egyptian tomb. And he'll set anything from a diamond to a scarab. *Tues–Sat; www.garyswank.com; map:H3.*

Gilt

720 NW 23RD AVE, NORTHWEST; 503/226-0629
An eclectic collection of contemporary local designs and vintage Americana jewelry mingles with work from such faraway places as India and China. Jewels arrive weekly from trusted sources, adding to the ever-changing selection of precious, semiprecious, and costume pieces. Standouts include contemporary rings with unusual stones and settings. *Tues–Sun; map:GG7.*

Goldmark

1000 SW TAYLOR ST, DOWNTOWN; 503/224-3743
Cal Brockman, Goldmark's owner, loves working with customers to create one-of-a-kind jewelry designs. Endlessly fascinated with the variety of colored gemstones, he has been designing, updating, and restyling jewelry for more than 25 years. *Tues–Sat and by appointment; map:H2.*

Maloy's Jewelry Workshop

717 SW 10TH AVE, DOWNTOWN; 503/223-4720
In Maloy's you will find a cornucopia of fabulous pieces of vintage jewelry—from antique Rolex and Lord Elgin watches to Victorian emerald pendants, classic diamond engagement sets, and high-quality American Indian pieces. The staff is exceptionally knowledgeable. Maloys has a repair shop, too, where you can have your precious treasures fixed. *Mon–Sat; www.maloys.com; map:I2.*

Margulis Jewelers

800 SW BROADWAY, DOWNTOWN; 503/227-1153
Many of David Margulis's fetching designs—in 18- and 22-karat gold as well as platinum—are inspired by classical themes. You'll find Heracles-knot bracelets, Celtic-style rings adorned with granulation, and elegant pearl earrings. Established in 1932, this family-owned business was the first to sell estate jewelry in Portland. *Mon–Sat; www.margulis.com; map:H3.*

Marx Jewelers Ltd.

511 SW BROADWAY, DOWNTOWN; 503/228-5090

For more than a century, Portlanders and visitors have been buying from Oregon's oldest jewelry store. Clean-lined jewelry, gorgeous colored stones and diamonds, and the staff's quiet politeness set the tone. Eighteen-karat gold and platinum are showcased throughout this immaculate little family-owned shop, full of small and delicate treasures. *Mon–Sat; map:I3.*

The Real Mother Goose

901 SW YAMHILL ST, DOWNTOWN (AND BRANCHES); 503/223-9510

Since 1971, this fairy-tale shop—an American Craft Gallery of the Year award winner—has showcased the finest of Northwest designers. A jeweler and goldsmith create wedding rings and other custom pieces, while holiday shoppers and travelers find choice gifts that reflect the region's spirit. The downtown furniture gallery carries contemporary pieces in creative blends of fine (and sometimes exotic) woods, and you can buy distinctive Northwest gifts at the airport branch (7000 NE Airport Wy, Northeast; 503/284-9929; map:EE3) on your way out of town. Also in Washington Square (9300 SW Washington Square Rd, Tigard; 503/620-2243; map:KK9). *Mon–Sat; map:I2.*

Something Silver

700 SW 5TH AVE (PIONEER PLACE), DOWNTOWN; 503/248-0221

While most mall-bound jewelry stores leave something to be desired, this one offers a surprisingly whimsical collection of sparkling silver earrings, bracelets, pendants, and the like. Celebrate baby's arrival with a silver spoon or baby cup—or commemorate that all-important silver anniversary (25 years!) with something special. *Every day; www.somethingsilver.com; map:H4.*

Zell Bros.

723 SW SALMON ST, DOWNTOWN; 503/227-8471

More than three floors of jewelry, watches, sterling silver, china, and crystal mark the Zell brothers' legacy. Since 1912, when Julius and Harry Zell opened a small jewelry store near Union Station, the Zell family has offered the finest in jewelry and other precious items. *Mon–Sat; map:I3.*

CARDS AND STATIONERY

In the Bag

708 NW 23RD AVE, NORTHWEST; 503/223-3262

Like a well-packed suitcase, this shop makes the most of its precious real estate. A wide selection of bright, festive gift wrap creates a bubbly atmosphere—you might start searching for occasions and excuses to buy the beautiful papers. You'll also find colorful cards, address books, and journals, many of them all the way from London. Fancy gift bags, ribbon, and paper turn any present into a fabulous feast for the eyes. Wrapping service is complimentary when you buy the materials. *Every day; map:GG7.*

Oblation Papers and Press

516 NW 12TH AVE, PEARL DISTRICT; 503/223-1093

There's no other place in town like this when it comes to buying paper. Oblation has a rich inventory of artistic greeting cards, single-sheet wrapping paper from around the world, French stationery, and an extensive selection of fountain pens. Most notable are eight antique letterpress machines, all of them 75 to 100 years old. In its paper-making studio, Oblation makes all of the paper for its invitations and announcements. The shop employs four printers who run the presses; you can watch them in action behind the abundant retail space in this working urban paper mill. *Every day; www.oblationpapers.com; map:M2.*

Present Perfect

318 SW WASHINGTON ST, DOWNTOWN; 503/228-9727

This downtown destination for gift wrapping offers cheery papers sold by the sheet, gift bags galore, bows, and ribbons. Gifts and collectibles from Mary Engelbreit to Winnie the Pooh are ready to wrap. There's also a wide selection of stationery and a mammoth selection of cards (some of them exquisite handmade works of art). *Every day; map:H4.*

Presents of Mind

3633 SE HAWTHORNE BLVD, HAWTHORNE; 503/230-7740

Here, shopping for a birthday is as much an occasion as the celebration itself. Find a gem among the well-rounded and frequently rotated selection of cards. Picture frames, candles, photo albums, blank books, jewelry, and scarves make special gifts. Just for fun, toss in a glow-in-the-dark insect, plastic fish, candy necklace, or rubber stamp. *Every day; www.presentsofmind.tv; map:HH5.*

TOYS

Compound

107 NW 5TH AVE, OLD TOWN; 503/796-2733

Find manga- and anime-inspired toys and figurines from Japan and the United States at this refreshingly modern and cool store, which may seem to resemble a bit of a toy museum. A few of the toys in the anime style are geared toward collectors and may have a mature theme, but a number of offbeat robots and imaginary creatures are conceived with awe-inspiring creativity. Find street-chic clothes and jewelry in the complex, too. *Every day; www. compoundgallery.com; map:K4.*

Finnegan's Toys and Gifts

922 SW YAMHILL ST, DOWNTOWN; 503/221-0306

Portland's independently owned toy-shopping institution is the biggest and best in town. Finnegan's can keep you and your child enthralled for the better part of an afternoon. There's plenty of room for test drives of windup cars, building blocks, and whatnot. Look for Playmobil gear, dollhouses, craft

241

supplies, board games, dress-up clothes (including a number of amusing animal snouts), and a great selection of puppets and stuffed animals. *Every day; www.finneganstoys.com; map:I2.*

Grasshopper

1816 NE ALBERTA ST, ALBERTA; 503/335-3131

Here are toys as they should be: handmade amusements, soft or wooden, and handcrafted mobiles with a good selection for all ages. You'll also find books and clothes. The staff is friendly and happy, the prices excellent. If you have kids, it's a must-stop if you're checking out the up-and-coming Alberta neighborhood. *Every day; www.grasshopperstore.com; map:FF5.*

Kids at Heart

3445 SE HAWTHORNE BLVD, HAWTHORNE; 503/231-2954

It's playtime all the time at Kids at Heart, and the smiley, enthusiastic staff will help you make the most of it. Highlights include Playmobil toys, dollhouses and furnishings, dress-up wings and fairy garlands, glow-in-the-dark soccer balls, puzzles, and stuffed animals. A quick stop on the way to a birthday party yields the perfect less-than-$10 gift: craft kits, finger puppets, harmonicas, maracas, and cards, too. *Every day; map:HH5.*

Oregon Museum of Science and Industry Science Store

1945 SE WATER AVE, INNER SOUTHEAST; 503/797-4626

In addition to a great selection of thought-provoking, fun, science-oriented toys, games, puzzles, and project kits, the OMSI store boasts an awesome selection of science books. Virtually every major category is here, from astronomy to zoology, with books for readers of every age and knowledge level. *Tues–Sun; www.omsi.org; map:HH6.*

Tammie's Hobbies

12024 SW CANYON RD, BEAVERTON; 503/644-4535

A budding engineer's dream store and the Northwest's largest hobby store, Tammie's is packed floor-to-ceiling with plane and boat kits, radio-controlled cars, rockets, and model trains. The exhaustive inventory of model-building accessories and paint supplies thoroughly outfits the home hobbyist. *Every day; www.tammieshobbies.com; map:II9.*

Thinker Toys

7784 SW CAPITOL HWY, MULTNOMAH VILLAGE; 503/245-3936

Tye and Joan Steinbach, two science teachers who founded Thinker Toys in 1994, have christened their expanded 3,500-square-foot shop "Portland's most hands-on toy store"—and with good reason. An in-house fairy cottage and pirate ship, activity tables, and train sets provide ample diversion for kids, while plush armchairs await fatigued parents. Merchandise focuses on tactility, learning, and fun: find games from Klutz and Think as well as dress-up clothing and puzzles. *Every day; www.thinkertoysoregon.com; map:JJ7.*

Outdoor Gear

With access to some of the greatest terrain in the country for hiking, skiing, biking, kayaking, and surfing, you'll see outdoor enthusiasts everywhere in Portland. Bicyclists commute in droves at peak traffic hours and drift along residential streets at leisure. Serious adventurers get out of town daily. You'll therefore find no shortage of suppliers for every possible accoutrement for your adventure of choice.

Alder Creek Kayak and Canoe

250 NE TOMAHAWK ISLAND DR, JANTZEN BEACH; 503/285-0464

If it floats and you paddle it, Alder Creek probably sells it—whether it's a canoe, sea kayak, or river kayak. Demos in the nearby Columbia River are free (this is a great way to find out how much you're willing to lug around on the dock). The store carries an extensive line of gear, books, and videos, and emphasizes group and private instruction and guided tours. *Every day; www. aldercreek.com; map:CC6.*

Andy & Bax Sporting Goods

324 SE GRAND AVE, BUCKMAN; 503/234-7538

This is ground zero for sports lovers, campers, or people who just like to dress like them. Huge helpings of personality are split three ways between rafting and whitewater equipment, piles of Army/Navy surplus, and family camping and cold-weather gear. From commercial inflatables to information on guides and beginner classes, Andy & Bax is one of Portland's better rafting and whitewater resources. Prices are reasonable, and there are some awesome bargains (such as European army surplus blankets for cheapie cheap). *Mon–Sat; www.andyandbax.com; map:GG5.*

Bicycle Repair Collective

4438 SE BELMONT ST, BELMONT; 503/233-0564

The Bicycle Repair Collective has only a handful of peers nationwide. It sells parts and accessories, repairs bikes, and gives personal assistance in a rental work space. For $10 an hour, cyclists can self-tune their bikes and adjust their chains. *Tues–Sat; map:HH4.*

The Bike Gallery

**5329 NE SANDY BLVD, HOLLYWOOD (AND BRANCHES);
503/281-9800**

The Bike Gallery is to cycles what Saks is to clothing. With humble origins as a small, family-run shop, it's now one of the country's finest bike dealers. All sales are guaranteed, whether you buy a bicycle (road, mountain, crossover, tandem, child's, or adult), Burley rain gear, or a jogging stroller. Branches are in downtown (1001 SW Salmon St; 503/222-3821; map:H2), Lake Oswego (200 B Ave; 503/636-1600; map:MM6), Southeast (10950 SE Division St; 503/254-2663) and Beaverton (3645 SW Hall Blvd; 503/641-2580). *Every day; www.bikegallery.com; map:GG4.*

Columbia Sportswear

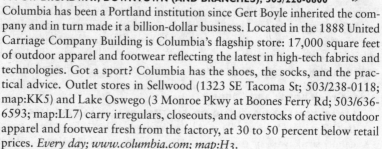

911 SW BROADWAY, DOWNTOWN (AND BRANCHES); 503/226-6800

Columbia has been a Portland institution since Gert Boyle inherited the company and in turn made it a billion-dollar business. Located in the 1888 United Carriage Company Building is Columbia's flagship store: 17,000 square feet of outdoor apparel and footwear reflecting the latest in high-tech fabrics and technologies. Got a sport? Columbia has the shoes, the socks, and the practical advice. Outlet stores in Sellwood (1323 SE Tacoma St; 503/238-0118; map:KK5) and Lake Oswego (3 Monroe Pkwy at Boones Ferry Rd; 503/636-6593; map:LL7) carry irregulars, closeouts, and overstocks of active outdoor apparel and footwear fresh from the factory, at 30 to 50 percent below retail prices. *Every day; www.columbia.com; map:H3.*

Exit Real World

206 NW 23RD AVE, NORTHWEST; 503/226-3948

Bored? Grab a board. Established in Salem in 1993, this is the ultimate shop for the new generation of snowboarders and skateboarders. Boards, bindings, boots, and cold-weather attire are all here or at Exit's mountain shop on Mount Hood (in Government Camp). Skateboarders find everything from wheels and bearings to decks and fashions. And Exit's demonstration teams offer expert instruction. *Every day; www.exitrealworld.com; map:HH7.*

Fat Tire Farm

2714 NW THURMAN ST, NORTHWEST; 503/222-3276

This shop has the advantage of immediate access to the nation's largest municipal playground: Forest Park. Novice mountain bikers can rent a bike and helmet here, load up on equipment, grab a water bottle and a fistful of Power Bars, and tour the park with a map and expert advice. Bikes and accessories, clothes, and literature are sold by a friendly, informed staff. *Every day; www.fattirefarm.com; map:GG7.*

Kaufmann's Streamborn Inc.

11960 SW PACIFIC HWY, TIGARD; 503/639-6400

Kaufmann's has been Portland's consummate fly shop since 1970. The knowledgeable staff can outfit you for fishing on the Clackamas River or equip you for specialty trips. Along with one of the finer selections of flies in the country, Kaufmann's offers fishing classes, guided tours, and fly-tying materials. Its free catalog has made the store world famous. *Mon–Sat; www.kman.com; map:MM9.*

The Mountain Shop

628 NE BROADWAY, NORTHEAST; 503/288-6768

Established in 1937, this store near Lloyd Center may well be the area's best one-stop shopping center for downhill and backcountry ski gear, both Nordic and tidemark. It's certainly the most unabashed, with three floors of skis, boards, and accessories to help you refine your technique—and a full line of footwear and apparel to help you perfect your style. The shop also outfits backpackers and four-season climbers who would rather go up and down the mountain without skis. Summer and winter rental packages are available. *Every day; www.mountainshop.net; map:GG6.*

Oregon Mountain Community

2975 NE SANDY BLVD, NORTHEAST; 503/227-1038
OMC is a four-season outfitter. As winter approaches, patrons of this popular store come for backcountry ski equipment; in spring and summer, they look for packs, tents, sleeping bags, and rock-climbing equipment. All manner of outdoor equipment, as well as men's and women's clothing, are sold year-round by an active and experienced sales staff. And a travel desk helps you plan that long-awaited backpacking trip to destinations such as New Zealand. *Every day; www.e-omc.com; map:K6.*

Pace Setter Athletic

4306 SE WOODSTOCK BLVD, WOODSTOCK; 503/777-3214
Wear your old running shoes to this store, and the staff will check them out, then recommend—based upon tread-wear patterns—an appropriate new pair from the 10 dozen models it stocks. The casual, friendly salespeople include some of the area's better competitive runners (several of them on Pace Setter's own race team), so the merchandise reflects a slightly more technical bias than at a typical running store. Students get discounts. *Every day; www.pace setterathletic.com; map:JJ4.*

Portland Niketown

930 SW 6TH AVE, DOWNTOWN (AND BRANCHES); 503/221-6453
This state-of-the-art showcase store displays all the latest from the entire Nike line. Fans come not only to buy but also to gawk at this sports enthusiasts' love fest. The young and fit clerks—athletes one and all—know what they're talking about. And, though you'll rarely find stuff on sale, there's plenty to purchase no matter what your budget. For less show and better prices, shop at the Nike Factory Store (2650 NE Martin Luther King Jr Blvd, Northeast; 503/281-5901; map:FF5). The Nike store on the mini retail row at Portland International Airport (503/284-3558) packs as much as it can into a small space. *Every day; http://niketown.nike.com; map:G3.*

The Portland Running Company

800 SE GRAND AVE, BUCKMAN; 503/232-8077
11355 SW SCHOLLS FERRY RD, BEAVERTON; 503/524-7570
Since the mid-1960s, when University of Oregon track coach Bill Bowerman and athlete Phil Knight germinated the seed that became the Nike corporation, the Willamette Valley has been a focus for runners. Sales staff fit shoes based upon a careful analysis of running or walking style and injury history; many customers are referred by their doctors. But this is more than a shoe and apparel store: it's a complete running service providing route maps, event

information, and training and nutritional tips. *Every day; www.portland runningcompany.com; map:KK9.*

Recreational Equipment Inc. (REI)

1405 NW JOHNSON ST, PEARL DISTRICT (AND BRANCHES); 503/221-1938
A spectacular Pearl District store, upon opening in early 2004 with a free-standing climbing pinnacle behind a two-story glass facade, solidified REI's longtime Portland presence. The 35,000-square-foot store stocks REI's full line of clothing and gear for hiking, camping, climbing, skiing, cycling, and water sports—and offers test areas for hiking boots, camp stoves, and water filters. A onetime Lifetime Membership $20 fee earns roughly 10 percent cash back on nonsale purchases. REI also has stores in Tualatin (7410 SW Bridgeport Rd; 503/624-8600; map:NN9) and Hillsboro (2235 NW Allie Ave; 503/617-6072). *Every day; www.rei.com; map:N1.*

River City Bicycles

706 SE MARTIN LUTHER KING JR BLVD, INNER SOUTHEAST; 503/233-5973
Open since 1994, this bike shop is among the finest wheel winders in town. With an 11,000-square-foot showroom, including a slow-speed indoor test track, it's certainly the largest. The friendly experts who run River City stock the store with all kinds of riding gear: tricycles, tandems, mountain and road bikes, helmets, shoes, a huge clothing section—you name it. This is a great place to outfit the family. *Every day; www.rivercitybicycles.com; map:H9.*

Running Outfitters

2337 SW 6TH AVE, LAIR HILL; 503/248-9820
At the foot of the popular Terwilliger Boulevard running route, two blocks from Duniway Park's track, is the city's oldest running-only store: smaller than your garage, but well stocked. Owner Jim Davis is, of course, an avid runner, and his store has a local cult following. *Mon–Sat; map:II6.*

21st Avenue Bikes

916 NW 21ST AVE, NORTHWEST; 503/222-2851
A household name in the Nob Hill neighborhood, this shop pleases loyal customers with excellent service. The staff is helpful, friendly, generous with their knowledge, and skilled with repairs. They happily give personal attention to customers whether they be serious commuters or 9-year-olds. *Every day; map:GG7.*

Spas and Salons

Since being pampered trumps playing in the rain some days, Portland has a wonderful selection of spas and salons. Each spa has a unique menu of services, and high-quality salons are more reasonably priced here than in larger cities. If you're inclined to indulge at some point while you're in our city, with these options, you sure won't regret it.

Aequis Spa

422 NW 13TH AVE, PEARL DISTRICT; 503/223-7847
Aequis Spa is a luxurious indulgence from beginning to end. The Eastern-inspired ambience is at once stunning and enchantingly calming. Every aspect of your experience here is designed to treat you with the utmost care and relaxation, from the gracious, professional staff to the varied services offered. Don't deny yourself the pleasure of a Therapeutic Fusion Massage, Warm Mud Purifying Body Wrap, or Ayurvedic Facial—but make no plans for the rest of your day. There is absolutely no rush to leave. *Every day; www. aequisspa.com; map:M2.*

Aveda Training Institute

325 NW 13TH AVE, PEARL DISTRICT; 503/294-6000
If you have a solid amount of patience, and cheap services are what you're after, this is the place for a walk-in. The bright-eyed beauty school students are here to practice on you, whether it be a cut, color, mani, pedi, or Brazilian. Discounted prices make up for the wait time (each student needs to check in with his/her professor before and after each service). *Tues–Sat; www. avedapdx.com; map:M1.*

Bishops

3742 SE HAWTHORNE BLVD, SOUTHEAST; 503/238-9600
210 NE 28TH AVE, NORTHEAST; 503/235-2770
326 NW 21ST AVE, NOB HILL; 503/274-4100
Known as Portland's "rock and roll barbershop," this local chain provides cheap, à la carte services, including styling, shampoo, blow-dry, cut, and color. Highly influenced by Portland's rockabilly, hipster set, trendy styles abound. Sit back and enjoy your complimentary Miller High Life. *Everyday; www.bishopsbarbershop.com; map:L2.*

The Dragontree

2768 NW THURMAN ST, NOB HILL; 503/221-4123
The spa services at this intimate sanctuary are as peaceful as its staff is knowledgeable in Ayurvedic wellness and counseling rituals. The Bliss Therapies are not to be missed. Check Dragontree's Web site for upcoming events and monthly specials. *Every day; www.thedragontree.com; map:GG7.*

Ethereal Day Spa

211 NE 28TH AVE, NORTHEAST; 503/245-5993
This results-driven spa provides facials using Yon-Ka and Jan Marini products. It also features top-of-the-line diamond microdermabrasion, anti-aging boosters, and treatments for challenged skin. Ethereal has a great menu of body wraps, scrubs, and glows, and its massage services include deep tissue, Swedish, hot stone, and prenatal. A retail space offers skin-care and hair-care products, locally crafted jewelry, and Aunt Sadie candles. *Every day; www. etherealspa.com; map:HH5.*

Faces Unlimited

25 NW 23RD PL, STE 7, NORTHWEST; 503/227-7366
Former model Pat Warren began this business in the 1970s, offering a full line of body-care treatments—from polishing scrubs and moisturizing wraps to bikini and brow waxing, manicures, pedicures, and (of course) facials. Now a Portland skin-care institution, Faces keeps an ample supply of European body-care products in stock, including Payot, Murad, and T. LeClerc, among others. *Mon–Sat; www.facesunlimited.com; map:HH7.*

Löyly

2713 SE 21ST AVE, HAWTHORNE; 503/236-6850
Portland's sole ode to Scandinavian spa amenities is a modern blend of steam and sauna with traditional deep-tissue massage methods. Soak up Swedish relaxation in the sauna and steam rooms (per-hour rates; check Web site for co-ed, men-only, and women-only schedule), or indulge in an aromatherapy massage. *Tues–Sat; www.loyly.net; map:HH5.*

Pharmaca Integrative Pharmacy

13 NW 23RD PL, NORTHWEST; 503/226-6213
In addition to being a traditional pharmacy, Pharmaca has a wide selection of natural skin-care lines, including brands like Astara, Dr. Hauschka, and Zia. Licensed aestheticians provide complimentary skin-care consultations. Mini facials, eye and scalp treatments, and make-up applications are available at reasonable rates. You can pick up myriad supplements to support good skin health, as well as brushes, toothpaste, and a wonderful selection of soaps for yourself or as a gift. *Every day; www.pharmaca.com; map:HH7.*

Rudy's

212 NW 13TH AVE, PEARL DISTRICT; 503/525-2900
3015 SE DIVISION ST, SOUTHEAST; 503/232-3850
If there's such a thing as a stylish barbershop, this is it. Rudy's is perfectly art-directed; old-school fonts combined with cutting-edge artists' showcases make for winning press in such magazines as *Women's Wear Daily* and *Paper*. And even better, they have the skills to back it up. *Every day; www.rudys barbershop.com; map:M1.*

Spa Chakra

455 SW HAMILTON CT, SOUTH WATERFRONT; 503/802-5900
Located in the Avalon Hotel, this convenient stop for visitors and locals alike offers treatments with delicious ingredients, from green tea and cucumber body washes to papaya purifying enzyme masks and lemon sugar body polishes. *Every day; www.spachakra.com; map:KK6.*

Trade Secret

700 SW 5TH AVE (PIONEER PLACE), DOWNTOWN (AND BRANCHES); 503/228-4488

It's OK to play with your hair at Trade Secret. In fact, it's encouraged. Stock up on products from KMS, Sebastian, Back to Basics, and other well-known brands. Promotions and sales encourage you to shop often and spend the bucks you save on your next haircut. Other area locations are at Clackamas Town Center, Jantzen Beach, Lake Oswego, Lloyd Center, Tanasbourne, and Washington Square. *Every day; www.tradesecret.com; map:H4.*

Urbaca

120 NW 9TH AVE, #101, PEARL DISTRICT; 503/241-5030

This chichi salon and spa is no-nonsense when it comes to facials. Spot treatments, deep pore cleanses, and peel treatments are just the start to repairing and renewing. Makeup artistry, body treatments, and waxing are equally as pleasing, and that's not even getting started on the hair services. *Every day; www.urbacahairsalon.com; map:K3.*

Ziva Salon-Store

610 NW 23RD AVE, NORTHWEST; 503/221-6990

Don't be surprised by the professional-quality hair and cosmetics lines in this vast body-care emporium. Ziva stocks an astounding selection of products for locks and skin, as well as pro tweezers, styling tools, and heavy-duty metal cases to tote your goods. Such product lines as Bumble and bumble, Dermalogica, and Portland-based von Natur (100 percent vegan) are just the tip of the iceberg. Salon and spa services are available in back. *Every day; www.zivanet.com; map:GG7.*

Food Shops

Portland is a city of foodies, which is reflected in restaurants that regularly catch the attention of the national media. As well, there's an exceptionally rich selection of stores stocked with good foodstuffs to take home to your own kitchen. This section begins with Bakeries, before tackling Candy and Chocolate, Coffee and Tea, Ethnic and Specialty Foods, Health Food Stores, Meats and Seafood, and finally, Wine, Beer, and Spirits.

BAKERIES

Beaverton Bakery

12375 SW BROADWAY, BEAVERTON; 503/646-7136
16857 SW 65TH AVE (SOUTHLAKE CENTER), LAKE OSWEGO; 503/639-8900

Elaborately decked wedding and birthday cakes are what this bakery is best known for, but the crusty breads and frosted seasonal shortbread cookies (pumpkins in October, baby chicks in April) are equally pleasing. It's part of the experience to take a number from the old-fashioned dispenser and wait in line, but impatient shoppers can visit the less-crowded Lake Oswego location. *Every day; map:II9; map:NN8.*

The German Bakery

10534 NE SANDY BLVD, PARKROSE; 503/252-1881
Atmosphere isn't everything—especially when you're a completely authentic bakery that turns out Bavarian landbrot, jägerbrot, and other German varieties from your ovens every day. The marzipan and sugar-dusted sweets, loaves of rye, and spongy rolls are comforting even if you don't have a single drop of German blood. If you do, the array of curious pickles available up front may have extra appeal. *Tues–Sat; map:FF1.*

Grand Central Baking Company

2230 SE HAWTHORNE BLVD, HAWTHORNE; 503/232-0575
3425 SW MULTNOMAH BLVD, MULTNOMAH VILLAGE; 503/445-1600
7987 SE 13TH AVE, SELLWOOD; 503/546-3036
714 NE FREMONT ST, NORTHEAST; 503/546-5311
1444 NE WEIDLER ST, IRVINGTON; 503/288-1614
2249 NW YORK ST, NORTHWEST; 503/232-0575
See review in the Restaurants chapter.

Great Harvest Bread Company

810 SW 2ND AVE, DOWNTOWN; 503/224-8583
Healthy, fundamental, fresh—this is bread of the "staff of life" variety. This bakery chain, based in Montana, grinds its own wheat—a practice compared to grinding one's own coffee for freshness and flavor. Here you can snag a just-baked sandwich loaf that will take you through the week, although the fruit-bread varieties and baked sweets are equally tempting. There's another branch southeast of Portland in Clackamas (8926 SE Sunnyside Rd; 503/659-5392; map:LL3). *Mon–Sat; map:H4.*

JaCiva's Chocolates and Pastries

4733 SE HAWTHORNE BLVD, HAWTHORNE; 503/234-8115
This delectable pastry and chocolate shop has specialized in European-style sweets—"a necessary indulgence"—since 1986. Under the burgundy-and-white awning, you'll find bakery, chocolate factory, retail, and wholesale operations. Everything's delicious, but the cakes are legendary. There's even a room where brides and grooms can sample wedding cakes (pictures and "dummy cakes" help you decide). *Mon–Sat; www.jacivas.com; map:HH4.*

Ken's Artisan Bakery & Café

338 NW 21ST AVE, NORTHWEST; 503/248-2202
See review in the Restaurants chapter.

Pearl Bakery

102 NW 9TH AVE, PEARL DISTRICT; 503/827-0910

Testament to Pearl Bakery's floury artistry comes in the form of lunchtime hordes—and the appearance of the blue paper–wrapped loaves in fine markets all over town. The irresistible pastries and breads are leavened by traditional methods, hand-formed, and baked before your very eyes in massive ovens. For lunch there's a delicious selection of sandwiches: eggplant on ciabatta, pears and gorgonzola on walnut levain, even an elegant PB&J. *Every day; www.pearlbakery.com; map:K3.*

Pix Patisserie

3402 SE DIVISION ST, SOUTHEAST; 503/232-4407
3901 N WILLIAMS AVE, NORTH PORTLAND; 503/282-6539

French-trained pastry maker Cheryl Wakerhauser used to wow dessert lovers with her incredible concoctions at the Portland Farmers Market. Now her charming bakeries are ground zero for sweet inventions with names like Cocoa Chanel and Amelie. The Royale with Cheese is a mind-blowing bombe of chocolate mousse, hazelnut cream, and rich triple-crème cheese on the side. Beautiful presentation and unexpected flavors—pears and rosemary, orange crème brûlée, and gold dust—make each dessert a treasure. Stay and enjoy yours with a dessert wine or a steaming cup of café au lait, or take a box of goodies home. You'll also find savory snacks such as grilled-cheese sandwiches on brioche. *Every day; www.pixpatisserie.com; map:II5.*

Saint Cupcake

407 NW 17TH AVE, NORTHWEST; 503/473-8760

The frosting on these cupcakes is like nothing you've ever tasted before—guaranteed—and it sits on top of light and luscious cake that you'll come back for. Choose from flavors such as pistachio, banana–chocolate chip, red velvet, and coconut. Yum! Every day the shop features a few different flavors of vegan cupcakes, too. Also, find a Saint Cupcake to-go outpost nestled in the back of Noun: A Person's Place for Things (see review under Decor in this chapter). *Tues–Sun; www.saintcupcake.com; map:GG6.*

St. Honoré Boulangerie

2335 NW THURMAN ST, NORTHWEST; 503/445-4342
315 1ST ST, LAKE OSWEGO; 503/445-1379

A neighborhood bakery and cafe, St. Honoré features handcrafted French breads and pastries, as well as sandwiches, salads, soups, and quiche. The bakery's decor and menu reflect owner Dominique Geulin's French roots and his passion for using the highest-quality ingredients, including flour locally produced with sustainable farming techniques. The massive stone bread oven, shipped from France, pairs European atmosphere with authentic flavors. It's like taking a trip to Paris. *Every day; www.sainthonorebakery.com; map:GG7; map:LL6.*

CANDY AND CHOCOLATE

Alma Chocolates

140 NE 28TH AVE, NORTHEAST; 503/517-0262
Owner Sarah Hart crafts beautiful Mexican chocolate truffles; bonbons accented with hints of habanero, lemon basil, lavender, or espresso; and trademark iconic chocolate figures and symbols hand-gilded with 23-karat edible gold leaf. A laughing Buddha, the elephant god Ganesha, and a Hamsa hand are all special-occasion favorites. *Every day; www.almachocolate.com; map:HH5.*

Cacao

414 SW 13TH AVE, DOWNTOWN; 503/241-0656
712 SW SALMON ST, DOWNTOWN; 503/274-9510
Cacao's new intimate location in the historic Heathman Hotel is a cozy spot for breaking from the day and sipping on its extremely rich, velvety drinking chocolates. The extensive selection of chocolate bars and handmade chocolates are hand-picked from all over the world and do not disappoint. *Every day; www.cacaodrinkchocolate.com; map:J1.*

Moonstruck Chocolate Cafe

608 SW ALDER ST, DOWNTOWN; 503/241-0955
700 SW 5TH AVE (PIONEER PLACE), DOWNTOWN (AND BRANCHES); 503/219-9118
Moonstruck offers a full line of handmade artisan chocolates. Choose a single truffle, pick up a hand-packed box, or personally pick out your selection. The cafes serve espresso and chocolate drinks, including great milkshakes and coffee-based beverages with Moonstruck's signature chocolate blend. Check out the fresh pastries and decadent desserts. The atmosphere is warm and fun: this is a great place to sit and have a treat! Others shops are in Northwest Portland (526 NW 23rd Ave; 503/542-3400; map:GG7), Lake Oswego (45 S State St, Village Shopping Center; 503/697-7097), and Beaverton (11705 SW Beaverton-Hillsdale Hwy, Beaverton Town Square; 503/352-0835). *Every day; www.moonstruckchocolate.com; map:I3.*

Sahagun Chocolates

10 NW 16TH AVE, NORTHWEST; 503/274-7065
This tiny place may be off the beaten path, but it has incredible chocolate drinks and truffles to die for. Every handcrafted masterpiece emanates love, whether it's sprinkled with shiny gold dust or powdery cocoa. *Mon–Sat; www.sahagunchocolates.com; map:K1.*

Sweets, Etc.

7828 SW CAPITOL HWY, MULTNOMAH VILLAGE; 503/293-0088
Look for a good mix of old and new: hard candies, saltwater taffy, malt balls, chocolate turtles, penguin gummies, truffles. If you want to sit for a spell with

an ice-cream cone or Italian soda, you'll find a couple of seats. Of special note are sugar-free and kosher candy. *Every day; map:JJ7.*

Teuscher Chocolates of Switzerland

531 SW BROADWAY, DOWNTOWN; 503/827-0587
First concocted by Dolf Teuscher in a small Alpine village in the 1940s, these Swiss-made chocolates contain the most costly all-natural cocoa, marzipan, fruits, and nuts available. Air-shipped from the Zurich factory to this tiny, ribbon-festooned boutique, the truffles and pralines arrive fresh and beautifully packaged. Toothsome wedding favors are a specialty of this shop. *Every day; www.teuscherportland.com; map:I3.*

Verdun Fine Chocolates

421 NW 10TH AVE, PEARL DISTRICT; 503/525-9400
Specializing in candies, chocolates, and confections imported from Lebanon, this little shop displays its wares like fine jewels—in beds of excelsior and glass-topped cases. The chocolate base is *gianduja* (cocoa, cocoa butter, and emulsified hazelnut), which makes for a rich flavor that's sweet but not cloying. Foil-wrapped dragée (chocolate- or candy-coated almonds) make popular gifts and wedding favors, and the shop also sells silver platters—to more elegantly display the chocolate, naturally. *Every day; www.verdunchocolates. com; map:L3.*

COFFEE AND TEA

Peet's Coffee & Tea

1441 NE BROADWAY, NORTHEAST (AND BRANCHES); 503/493-0192
Berkeley-born Peet's Coffee & Tea has brought its signature dark-roasted style north. The opening day of its NE Broadway store near Lloyd Center lived up to its anticipatory buzz, with droves of curious coffee hounds snatching up pounds of beans. Peet's wasted no time in opening a second location, this time downtown (508 SW Broadway; 503/973-5540). Now there are two other Portland stores (1144 NW Couch St, Pearl District; 971/244-0452; and 3646 SE Hawthorne Blvd, Hawthorne; 971/244-9920), and Peet's has expanded to suburban Lake Oswego, Tigard, and Vancouver, WA. Whichever side of the river you're on, you'll find consistent coffee, knowledgeable employees, and a respectable selection of coffee and tea accessories. *Every day; www.peets.com; map:GG5.*

Stash Tea

7250 SW DURHAM RD, TIGARD; 503/684-4482 OR 503/603-9905
Stash Tea, one of the largest specialty tea providers in the United States, has a retail store featuring the largest number of loose-leaf teas—around 200— available in the Portland area. They're sold by a friendly and enthusiastic staff that love to talk about, well, tea. *Tues–Sun; www.stashtea.com; map:LL9.*

THE PORTLAND GROWING SEASON

Strategically located in the beating heart of the agriculturally prolific Willamette Valley, Portland welcomes the return of growers' produce to the city every spring; most markets run through mid-October. Shoppers can find not only unbelievably fresh corn, carrots, and spinach at the city's open-air markets but also exotic and niche produce like Asian greens and long beans, heirloom tomatoes, edible nasturtium blossoms, and lobster mushrooms in vivid orange bloom.

Though prices at these markets are often higher than at grocery stores, the caliber of produce—much of it organically grown—makes up for the extra nickels and dimes. And there's an added benefit in supporting small family and community farms rather than the agribusinesses that supply large grocery chains; such support brings vitality to rural areas and new generations to farming, guaranteeing this quality will persist. Many farmers drive long distances to set up their booths in the heart of the city.

The city's most heavily attended market is the **PORTLAND FARMERS MAR-KET** (503/705-2460; www.portlandfarmersmarket.org), which runs from March through December in the South Park Blocks. It sets up Saturdays, 8:30am–2pm, Mar–Dec, on the Portland State campus (SW Park Ave and Montgomery St; map: E1) and Wednesdays, 10am–2pm, April through October, by the Arlene Schnitzer Concert Hall (SW Park Ave and Salmon St; map:H2). Though nowhere near the biggest, the Portland Farmers Market is one of the oldest, established in 1992 by the Albers Mill grain elevators on the Willamette River; its central location and twice-a-week schedule make it a prominent part of city life. Besides superstar vegetables, fruits, and nuts, this market boasts baked and dairy goods, organically raised meat and seafood, salsas and sauces, herbs, cut flowers, and live plants. Market-day events include cooking demonstrations, soil-management lectures,

Stumptown Coffee Roasters

128 SW 3RD AVE, OLD TOWN (AND BRANCHES); 503/295-6144

Since opening its airy Soho-style Old Town cafe, the legend of Stumptown's signature superstrong brew has spread to the city's four corners—if not the world. The original Southeast Portland location (4525 SE Division St; 503/230-7702; map:II4) has a garage door that opens on nice, breezy days; Belmont (3356 SE Belmont St; 503/232-8889; map:HH5) is packed with neighborhood hipsters. A new location is downtown at the Ace Hotel (1026 SW Stark St; 503/224-9060). Beans are sold by the pound in familiar and exotic roasts, including several organic varieties. You can also find Stumptown and live music, as well as a dozen or so stalls that serve up ready-to-eat fare such as Pine State Biscuits or Molly's Tamales.

Another popular market is the **BEAVERTON FARMERS MARKET** (SW Hall Blvd between 3rd and 5th aves; 503/643-5345; map:Il9), the state's largest agriculture-only market (there are no crafts sellers here). During peak season (Sat 8am–1:30pm May–Oct; also Wed, July–Sept), as many as 10,000 people descend upon 100 vendors for things as prosaic as snap peas or as special as wedding flowers. Fetzer's German deli has a sausage booth that welcomes long queues hungry for grilled bratwurst and kraut.

Other thriving farmers markets are in the **PEARL DISTRICT** (Ecotrust Building parking lot, NW 10th Ave and Johnson St; map:N2), Thursdays, June through September; **GRESHAM** (Miller St at 3rd St; www.greshamfarmersmarket.com) Saturdays, May through October; **HILLSBORO** (Courthouse Square, NE 2nd Ave and Main St; 503/844-6685; map:I11), Saturdays, May through October; **THURSDAY MARKET AT EAST BANK** (SE 20th Ave at Salmon between Belmont and Hawthorne in Hinson Baptist Church parking lot; www.portlandfarmersmarket.org; map:HH6), Thursdays, May through September; and **LENTS INTERNATIONAL FARMERS MARKET** (SE 91st Ave and Foster Rd; www.localharvest.org; map: JJ3), Sundays, June through October. There's even an all-organic market every Wednesday (2–7pm) outside the **PEOPLE'S FOOD CO-OP** (3029 SE 21st Ave, Brooklyn; 503/232-9051; map:Il5). The U.S. Department of Agriculture publishes a current Web directory (www.usda.gov/farmersmarkets/states/oregon.htm) of markets; check for times before you venture out, as some change locations and others have irregular (i.e., non-Saturday) schedules.

One caveat: In peak season, it's not surprising to see the best of the produce sell out long before 10am. Set that alarm clock if you want the best selection.

—Elizabeth Dye

coffee sold at many local coffee shops. (See review in the Nightlife chapter.) *Every day; www.stumptowncoffee.com; map:J5.*

The Tao of Tea

3430 SE BELMONT ST, BELMONT (AND BRANCHES); 503/736-0198
A serene, stone-lined enclave bedecked with colorful cushions, the Tao of Tea offers sweet respite from the clamor of modern life. Here, an encyclopedic range of teas is served in cups unique to each tea's character. In the adjacent Leaf Room, you can purchase leaves from the Tao's impressive range and choose from a wide selection of tea ware, from Yixing pots to yerba maté gourds. Newer teahouses are in Northwest Portland (2112 NW Hoyt St;

503/223-3563; map:GG7) and at the Classical Chinese Garden (239 NW Everett St, Chinatown; 503/224-8455; map:L5), the latter with occasional formal tea ceremonies (see review in the Nightlife chapter). *Every day (Belmont and Chinatown), Wed–Sun (Northwest); www.taooftea.com; map:HH5.*

The TeaZone

510 NW 11TH AVE, PEARL DISTRICT; 503/221-2130

More than 120 loose-leaf teas are offered at this soothing European-style tea salon. Enthusiastic owners Jhanne Jasmine and Grant Cull are happy to tell you even more about each variety than you can read on the detailed menu. A full food menu, including appetizers, desserts, and snacks, is also offered, in addition to cocktails. While you sip, let your eyes drift over the elaborate selection of teapots and tea accessories from around the world. *Every day; www.teazone.com; map:M2.*

World Cup Coffee & Tea

1740 NW GLISAN ST, NORTHWEST (AND BRANCHES); 503/228-4152

Beginning as a small shop in 1993, World Cup has grown to be a nationally recognized roaster with three homey cafes. Beans from all over the world end up here; emphasis is on shade-grown, organic, and fair-trade varieties. The popular house blend is a warm, full-bodied mix of Indonesian, Central American, and South American coffees. On the tea side, World Cup offers about 15 loose-leaf varieties, as well as wonderful pastries, desserts, and grilled sandwiches. World Cup is also in Powell's Books (1005 W Burnside St, Downtown; 503/228-4651; map:K2). *Every day; www.worldcupcoffee.com; map:GG6.*

ETHNIC AND SPECIALTY FOODS

Bashen's International Grocery

3022 NE GLISAN ST, LAURELHURST (AND BRANCHES); 503/234-7785

Here you're greeted by a friendly *Hola!* and the strains of Latin pop music. Disappear into aisles stocking all manner of Mexican, Salvadoran, Spanish, and South American foods and cooking supplies: cellophane cones of *chicharones*, packets of dried tamarind and chiles, tortilla presses, cast-aluminum cookware from Colombia, votive candles, frozen banana leaves, and cheese from Acajutla. You can also buy CDs of that music you're hearing. Other branches are on E Burnside and N Lombard streets. *Every day; map:HH5.*

Elephants Delicatessen
Flying Elephants at Fox Tower
Flying Elephants at Kruse Way

115 NW 22ND AVE, NORTHWEST; 503/224-3955
812 SW PARK AVE, DOWNTOWN; 503/546-3166
5885 SW MEADOWS RD, LAKE OSWEGO; 503/620-2444

Elephants features made-to-order or prewrapped fresh sandwiches, homemade soups from scratch, salads, and side dishes, as well as irresistible baked treats, all to be eaten in or taken out. If your purchase is $75 or more and you order by 10am, they'll deliver by noon in the downtown area, using all-recycled-fiber, biodegradable packaging. Flying Elephants, the downtown shop in the Fox Tower, provides an oasis for shoppers and office workers who want "fast, fabulous food for people on the fly." (See also review in the Restaurants chapter.) *Every day; www.elephantsdeli.com; map:HH7; map:H2; map:MM7.*

Foster & Dobbs

2518 NE 15TH AVE, IRVINGTON; 503/284-1157
With a deep history in Oregon (the Foster family settled here in 1910 and have been beekeepers for seven generations, and the Dobbs side features a mix of restaurateurs, ranchers, and coffee farmers), this intimate market filled to the brim with artisanal foods from family farms and products from small producers is a testament to locally grown, high-quality food. *Every day; www.fosteranddobbs.com; map:GG6.*

Hiroshi's Anzen

736 NE MARTIN LUTHER KING JR BLVD, NORTHEAST; 503/233-5111
For all things Japanese—fish and nori for sushi, pickled ginger, fresh yellowfin tuna, and octopus—Anzen is the place. The stock goes well beyond just food: you'll find lacquered dishes, rice cookers, and Japanese books and magazines. The inventory of more than 10,000 items includes prepared deli foods such as sushi and bento boxes, packaged and canned goods (including shelves of various soy sauces), and a large selection of sake and Asian beers. *Every day; map:N9.*

Martinotti's Café & Delicatessen

404 SW 10TH AVE, DOWNTOWN; 503/224-9028
Once upon a time, Martinotti's was Portland's only Italian foods shop, with one of the first espresso machines in town. Even though the city is now saturated with venues offering Italian flavor, there's still a place for what the Martinotti family has to offer: a solidly Italian grocery of good tastes, good smells, and good products—including towers of boxed panettone at Christmas. The wine selection is rich in Italian varietals as well as French wines and port. For everyday shopping, there are dried pastas and sundry other imports such as Italian tomatoes, olive oil, meats, cheeses, chocolate, and cookies. *Mon–Sat; map:J2.*

Pastaworks

3735 SE HAWTHORNE BLVD, HAWTHORNE; 503/232-1010
735 NW 21ST AVE (CITY MARKET NW), NORTHWEST; 503/221-3002
4212 N MISSISSIPPI AVE, NORTH PORTLAND; 503/445-1303
Pastaworks is all things Italian: fresh pastas, pesto and mushroom sauces, dozens of olive oils, herbed and aged vinegars, whole-bean coffees, delectable desserts, exotic cheeses, aged prosciutto—and the best Italian wine section in town. Don't hesitate to ask the staff for help when choosing that Brunello or

Barolo. The inventory of kitchenware has been expanded to include Reidel glassware, Spanish pottery, wooden salad bowls and cutting boards, and top-notch cooking utensils. *Every day; www.pastaworks.com; map:HH5; map: GG7; map:GG6.*

Sheridan Fruit Co.

409 SE MARTIN LUTHER KING JR BLVD, INNER SOUTHEAST; 503/235-9353
The lower eastside industrial area has become something of a neighborhood, and Sheridan Fruit Co. is its grocery store. Founded in 1916, this is one of the last remnants of the city's old Produce Row. You'll still find hints of its former glory as a bulk supplier of nature's bounty—oversize sacks of roasted nuts, dried fruit and honey, boxed pasta, and bins of lentils. But the store has also become a full-service supermarket with a meat counter, a bakery, and a respectable wine section. Stop for ethnic items like Israeli couscous and curry sauces; if you ever need a 5-pound bag of sun-dried tomatoes or an industrial-size can of artichoke hearts, check here first. *Every day; map:I9.*

Uwajimaya

10500 SW BEAVERTON-HILLSDALE HWY, BEAVERTON; 503/643-4512
This is no pint-size Asian specialty shop, but an American-style supermarket packed with imported canned foods, exotic fruits and vegetables, and sashimi-grade ahi and other fresh seafood—some of it still swimming. Kaffir lime leaves, daikon, and lemongrass are as prolific as apples in the stunning produce department. Grocery offerings are dominated by Japanese foods, but Southeast Asian, Indian, and Chinese goods are mixed in. You will also find the largest sake selection available in Oregon. A housewares section is as pleasurable as it is functional. A branch of the Japanese bookstore chain Kinokuniya is on the premises, as well as the Japanese restaurant Hakatamon (specializing in house-made udon noodles), a Shiseido Cosmetics boutique, and Azumano Travel Agency. *Every day; www.uwajimaya.com; map:II9.*

Zupan's Market

**2340 W BURNSIDE ST, PORTLAND HEIGHTS (AND BRANCHES);
503/497-1088**
Zupan's strives for full service with its deli, bakery, meat counter, and wine section. The produce section is hard to beat: fresh water chestnuts, starfruit, ugli fruit, and boutique salad greens are laid out in freshly misted, parsley-garnished heaps. Zupan's also has specialty food items, an excellent meat section, and an in-house coffee shop. Prices can be a little steep, but watch for seasonal produce sales. Look for branches in Belmont and Corbett. *Every day; www.zupans.com; map:HH7.*

HEALTH FOOD STORES

Food Front

2375 NW THURMAN ST, NORTHWEST; 503/222-5658

Stocking a large selection of fresh organic produce and the best prices on fall apples, Food Front also carries what may be the city's best crop of vegan and vegetarian groceries. You'll also find no-cruelty body-care products, vitamins and homeopathic remedies, bulk foods, coffee, and fresh juices. A fantastic deli (the dynamite sandwiches come wrapped with a delectable honey candy on top) makes a midday stop a pleasure. Also find delectable baked goods and a wide variety of breads. Discounts and rebates are offered to co-op members (a lifetime membership costs $150, a year is $25). *Every day; map:GG7.*

New Seasons

1214 SE TACOMA ST, SELLWOOD; 503/230-4949

5320 NE 33RD AVE, NORTHEAST; 503/288-3838

1954 SE DIVISION ST, SOUTHEAST; 503/445-2888

7300 SW BEAVERTON-HILLSDALE HWY, RALEIGH HILLS; 503/292-6838

This store was established by former Nature's Fresh Northwest employees when the national health-food chain Wild Oats took over the former market. There's an abundance of fresh local produce and meats here, as well as a good deli section and bakery. New Seasons also offers lots of prepackaged, middle-brow stuff, so you don't have to slink off guiltily to Safeway for Oreos. *Every day; www.newseasonsmarket.com; map:KK5; map:FF5; map:II5; map:II8.*

People's Food Co-op

3029 SE 21ST AVE, BROOKLYN; 503/232-9051

Once a pokey neighborhood natural-foods grocery with cramped aisles and a spotty selection, the little co-op that could blossomed into a full-service market. An elaborate and ecologically conscious remodel expanded the space to include such necessities as toilet paper and laundry soap. Buy a share for $180 (or $30 per year over 6 years). Be sure to check out their year-round farmers market on Wednesdays. *Every day; www.peoples.coop; map:II5.*

Whole Foods

1210 NW COUCH ST, PEARL DISTRICT; 503/525-4343

3535 NE 15TH AVE, IRVINGTON; 503/288-3414

2825 E BURNSIDE ST, EAST BURNSIDE; 503/232-6601

Located on the downtown edge of the Pearl District, Whole Foods has almost everything you'd want from a natural-foods store. There's a vast and beautiful selection of organic produce, very good seafood, a meat section, cheeses from all over the world, a wine section, bulk food, natural cosmetics, a salad and dessert bar, a bakery, and an in-house coffee and tea counter. A seating area pleases those who want to eat from the salad and hot bar before heading down to the parking lot (free with a purchase of $15 or more). *Every day; www.wholefoodsmarket.com; map:K2.*

MEATS AND SEAFOOD

Chop Butchery

735 NW 21ST AVE (CITY MARKET NW), NORTHWEST; 503/221-3012
Formerly known as Viande and renowned for fresh cuts and prepared meat items, new ownership finds Chop equally as successful with its emphasis on local produce and high-quality exotics (like Kobe beef). All the deli meats and sausages are house-made by a staff of former restaurant chefs. Chop carries five or six handmade pâtés at a time; they change regularly and include unusual ingredients like bourbon and fruit. Charcuterie is an art here, and the chefs who prepare the duck confit, stuffed quail with figs and polenta, and country breakfast sausage take pride in their work. *Every day; map:GG7.*

Edelweiss Sausage & Delicatessen

3119 SE 12TH AVE, BROOKLYN; 503/238-4411
Even if you can resist the aromas of house-made sausage, smoked ham hocks, and exotic wursts drifting from the cases in back, you'll be hard pressed to leave this tiny wonderland without sinking your teeth into something. The deli serves incredible sandwiches made from a dazzling array of German-style meats (almost everything is prepared on-site), as well as house-made potato salad. Groceries from spaetzle and grainy mustards to imported beers join diverting odds and ends—German magazines, lovely European candies—for an immersive Fatherland experience. (See also review in the Restaurants chapter.) *Mon–Sat; map:II5.*

Gartner's Country Meat Market

7450 NE KILLINGSWORTH ST, NORTHEAST; 503/252-7801
This is a no-flourishes, serious-about-meat store. Busy but ever-pleasant counter people staff a large, open preparation area. Roasts, steaks, chops, and house-smoked hams and bacons fill the L-shaped meat case. Aromas spice the air, and meat saws whir in the background. *Tues–Sun; map:FF3.*

Laurelhurst Market

3155 E BURNSIDE ST, LAURELHURST; 503/206-3099, 503/206-3097
This newly minted steakhouse restaurant and butcher shop was opened by the founders of the renowned Simpatica and Viande Meats and Sausage, and sits at the gates of Laurelhurst Park. Kudos go to the mussels frites with saffron crème and the extensive list of all-natural, house-cured meats, pâtés, rillettes, and duck confit. (See also review in the Restaurants chapter.) *Butcher open every day, restaurant Wed–Mon; www.laurelhurstmarket.com; map:HH4.*

Newman's Fish Co.

735 NW 21ST AVE (CITY MARKET NW), NORTHWEST; 503/227-2700
Hands down, fins up, Newman's is the best place in town to buy fresh fish; it's been in business since 1890. The staff is knowledgeable, energetic, and pleasant; helping customers learn to buy and prepare fish is a priority of the

owners (who also have a thriving wholesale business). The variety is notewor-thy: Pacific oysters, Manila clams, Mediterranean Blue mussels, and colossal scampi are joined by a fine array of house-smoked fish, such as Alaskan sock-eye lox and Columbia River sturgeon. Peer into the tanks to pick live Maine lobsters or Dungeness crabs. *Every day; map:GG7.*

Otto's Sausage Kitchen and Meat Market

4138 SE WOODSTOCK BLVD, WOODSTOCK; 503/771-6714
The deli gets crowded with loyal neighborhood customers at lunchtime, but this good-natured and unpretentious store is famed for its smoked meats and house-made sausages, ground and stuffed in the back room. There's a German flavor here, but you'll find meats in dozens of European styles: pep-peroni and pastrami, Black Forest ham, Portuguese linguica, and good ol' British bangers. A small but decent wine selection emphasizes vintages from the Northwest, Germany, and France. Check out the generous jars of Ger-man mustard and cornichons. (See also review in the Restaurants chapter.) *Mon–Sun; www.ottossausagekitchen.com; map:JJ4.*

Phil's Uptown Meat Market

17 NW 23RD PL, NORTHWEST; 503/224-9541
If there was such a thing as a "meat boutique," this would be it. Located in the Uptown Shopping Center off Westover Road, this black-and-white-tiled shop with white porcelain display cases, butcher blocks, and fan-type scales marries old-time butcher-shop atmosphere with up-to-the-minute freshness. Cuts of lamb, pork, beef, and poultry are of the highest quality, and there's a small seafood selection. Passersby have trouble resisting the skewers of chicken grilled out front. *Tues–Sat; map:HH7.*

White's Country Meats

1206 SE ORIENT DR, GRESHAM; 503/666-0967
Residents of the eastern suburb of Gresham recommend this straightfor-ward meat store with its own smokehouse and processing facilities. Expect fresh, honestly trimmed, good-quality meats at reasonable prices. A variety of roasts, steaks, and ground meats are available; the poultry and pork look better than at many other meat counters. *Mon–Sat.*

WINE, BEER, AND SPIRITS

Clear Creek Distillery

2389 NW WILSON ST, NORTHWEST; 503/248-9470
With a gorgeous copper still, fruit from his family's Hood River orchards, and other local ingredients, Stephen McCarthy crafts impeccable versions of classic European liqueurs. He is best known for his pear brandy, a colorless ambrosia that's available with or without a pear in the bottle, but his range extends from a Calvados-style apple brandy to grappa to Oregon's first single-malt whiskey. McCarthy also makes framboise (raspberry eau-de-vie),

kirschwasser (cherry brandy), and slivovitz (plum brandy). Clear Creek is open every day except Sunday, but it's best to call ahead and let them know you're coming. *Mon–Sat; www.clearcreekdistillery.com; map:GG7.*

Cork

2901 NE ALBERTA ST, ALBERTA; 503/281-2675
1715 NW LOVEJOY ST, NORTHWEST; 503/501-5028
This establishment supplies a great selection of wines in the up-and-coming Alberta neighborhood. Cork features hand-selected, quality wines from around the world, including 100 different wines for under $20. The shop also exhibits talented painters, offers an exquisite selection of chocolates, and carries olive oils, vinegars, and spices. *Every day; www.corkwineshop.com; map:FF5.*

E&R Wine Shop

6141 SW MACADAM AVE, JOHNS LANDING; 503/246-6101
Ed ("E") Paladino and Richard ("R") Elden play starring roles in the growing vitality and sophistication of Portland's wine scene. Besides offering many hard-to-find (and—gulp—hard-to-afford) elite selections, they feature a large inventory of lovely, moderately priced vintages. The shop's frequent (and often free) events and tastings are a great opportunity to learn more about, say, Italian whites or prosecco. Also offered are books, accessories, and foodstuffs. *Tues–Sat (every day in Dec); www.erwines.citysearch.com; map:JJ6.*

Great Wine Buys

1515 NE BROADWAY, IRVINGTON; 503/287-2897
Founded in 1985, this neighborhood shop was bought by employee John Kennedy in 1999, forever banishing the image of the wine-shop owner as grizzled sage. Young Kennedy—a would-be PhD in French literature—has thrown his heart into making this store a folksy, friendly place, with cozy armchairs and marble-topped tables surrounded by open cases of affordable vintages. The huge Northwest selection is augmented by bottles from the Rhône Valley, and special attention is paid to German and Alsatian Rieslings. Kennedy takes groups of customers on insider wine trips to Europe; patrons now ask about the next excursion. *Every day; www.greatwinebuys.com; map:GG5.*

Liner & Elsen Wine Merchants

2222 NW QUIMBY ST, NORTHWEST; 503/241-9463
The display of empty wine bottles from the '60s and '70s should clue you in to Liner & Elsen's lineage as one of Portland's most venerable wine suppliers. Dimly lit and hushed as a library, this shop is comprehensive, with hundreds of labels from France lining the walls and glamorous vintage ports kept under lock and key. Despite the intimidating vibe, the helpful and approachable staff will point you to a Web site or another wine shop if they don't stock what you're looking for. *Mon–Sat; www.linerandelsen.com; map:GG7.*

Mount Tabor Fine Wines

4316 SE HAWTHORNE BLVD, HAWTHORNE; 503/235-4444
This low-key, tastefully appointed shop caters to both penurious and plush oenophiles with equal grace. There's something for everyone here, from Oregon pinot noirs to Italian rosés, and wines are displayed democratically (a $90 Château-Figeac St. Emilion looks right at home next to that $14 Spanish table wine). A monthly broadsheet advertises a selection of reasonably priced wines, and the front of the store is stacked with open cases of colorfully described cheap hits. The crowds at Friday tastings nibble baguettes and sample wines of the world for a nominal fee. *Tues–Sat; www.mttabor finewines.com; map:HH4.*

Oregon Wines on Broadway

515 SW BROADWAY, DOWNTOWN; 503/228-4655
The name says it all, although there are a few bottles of Washington red here among the ranks of outstanding regional wines. Located in Morgan's Alley, an elegant downtown shopping arcade, the narrow street-facing shop has a woody, classic ambience that suits the garnet-colored nectar available for tasting by the glass. There are over 30 pinot noirs offered by taste or glass and more than 30 to purchase. *Mon–Sat; map:I3.*

Vino Paradiso

417 NW 10TH AVE, PEARL DISTRICT; 503/295-9536
Vino Paradiso sits right on the streetcar line in the Pearl District, so drink up and take public transport home. If you want to take home a couple of bottles from the extensive selection, retail price is a whopping 50 percent off. Also check out the excellent dinner menu and hip retro atmosphere where everyone is made to feel at home. *Tues–Sun; www.vinoparadiso.com; map:L2.*

Vinopolis

1025 SW WASHINGTON ST, DOWNTOWN; 503/248-2247
Vinopolis has the largest selection of retail wines in Oregon. It makes buying wine easy at its downtown location or online. Vinopolis also has monthly discounts, as deep as 15 percent, on selected wines. You can also get discounts with the purchase of multiple bottles. *Every day; www.vinopoliswineshop. com; map:J2.*

Wizer's Lake Oswego Foods

330 1ST ST, LAKE OSWEGO; 503/636-1414
What looks like an average suburban supermarket houses one of the biggest retail cellars in Greater Portland. This wine department has a wide array of domestic and imported wines. Ask to explore the cellar, with bottles from places as far-flung as Hungary and South Africa and years as distant as the 1930s. *Every day; www.wizers.com; map:MM6.*

Woodstock Wine and Deli

4030 SE WOODSTOCK BLVD, WOODSTOCK; 503/777-2208
The Fujino family's shop and restaurant—which they've operated near Reed College for 23 years—may not be the fanciest, but it has plenty to brag about. It has one of the largest and most affordable selections of wines in town, including kosher wines and sake, and an encyclopedic inventory of Oregon and Northwest specialties like pinot noir and merlot. Dozens of tables sit amid the cases and bottles (ranging in price from $7 to $150); diners can enjoy a glass of wine with hearty soups, sandwiches, meats, and cheeses, or purchase a bottle and enjoy it on-site. *Mon–Sat; www.woodstockwineanddeli. com; map:JJ4.*

THE ARTS SCENE

THE ARTS SCENE

Not only does the city of Portland offer a bounty of historic public sculptures, murals, and architecture, but it also seems every pocket is home to an emerging or legendary artist, filmmaker, or author. Prolific film director Gus Van Sant; celebrated architect Pietro Belluschi; indie musicians James Mercer (The Shins), Isaac Brock (Modest Mouse), and Carrie Brownstein and Corin Tucker (Sleater-Kinney); as well as *Fight Club* author Chuck Palahniuk have all made Portland their home base. On any given day, one neighborhood or another is hosting some sort of artistic event, whether it be gathering an onslaught of talented crafters all in one room at Crafty Wonderland (the second Sunday of every month at the Doug Fir Lounge) or setting up artists' receptions at boutiques, such as Local35's progressive, monthlong solo shows featuring anything from painting and photography to sculpture and video art. And best of all, true to Portland's resourceful, DIY nature, most of these celebratory events are dirt cheap, if not free. Portland's welcoming, tight-knit community has a no-nonsense, "everyone's invited" atmosphere, which makes for a creative crowd of newcomers, visitors, and locals alike, all up for the same thing: a new, inspired, artistic experience.

Fine Arts

THE MUSEUM OF CONTEMPORARY CRAFT

The Museum of Contemporary Craft (724 NW Davis St; 503/223-2654; www.museumofcontemporarycraft.org; map:K3), once called the Contemporary Crafts Museum and Gallery, re-branded itself when it moved to its new location on the North Park Blocks in 2007. The museum strives to inspire dialog about craft in artistic capacities and in its role in modern American culture with exhibits that feature national and international artists. It's also open to the public by voluntary donation. See "An Artistic Confluence" for more details.

PORTLAND ART MUSEUM (PAM)

The pride of the city's art community is the venerable Portland Art Museum (1219 SW Park Ave, Downtown; 503/226-2811; www.portlandartmuseum.org; map:G2), the Northwest's first art museum, founded in 1892. Its collection of 32,000 pieces spans 35 centuries. In 2005 the museum completed a renovation of the adjacent 141,000-square-foot Mark Building, which houses the Jubitz Center for Modern and Contemporary Art, an art study center and library, and the headquarters of the NW Film Center. See Top 20 Attractions in the Exploring chapter for more details.

GALLERIES

Portland has become a destination for artists and designers looking for an opportunity to produce and show their best work. An older echelon of established artists put Portland on the map; they included George Johanson (a painter, printmaker, and portraitist) as well as Jay Backstrand, Louis Bunce, Sally Haley, Lee Kelly, Jack McLarty, Henk Pander, Michele Russo, and Harry Widman. Their energy, and that of early gallery owners (particularly William Jamison), have expanded the city's creative scene and produced a flourishing business for the gallery culture.

The streets of the Pearl District and adjacent central downtown come alive each month on **FIRST THURSDAY** (www.firstthursday.org), when galleries feature their best and newest work. Roaming visitors jam the streets and crowd the galleries, becoming visions themselves for people-watchers. Even on the rainiest days, the turnout of sturdy, dedicated gallery-goers is impressive.

Galleries can be found in every corner of the city and its suburbs, but many cluster in three areas: downtown, the Pearl District, and Alberta Street. Alberta, a newly gentrifying stretch of Northeast Portland, opens the last Thursday of every month instead of the first for its **ART CRAWL** (6–9pm); it has developed its own following of mostly young and chic patrons.

The Art Gym

MARYLHURST UNIVERSITY, 17600 HWY 43, LAKE OSWEGO; 503/699-6243

Once a gymnasium, this 3,000-square-foot space on the third floor of the Marylhurst University administration building (10 miles south of Portland) is a well-respected showcase and testing ground for work by the Northwest's rising stars and established artists. Lucinda Parker, Tad Savinar, and Mel Katz have all shown here. As this is an educational institute, lectures and panel discussions accompany show openings. *Tues–Sun; www.marylhurst. edu/artgym; map:NN5.*

Augen Gallery

716 NW DAVIS ST, PEARL DISTRICT; 503/546-5056
817 SW 2ND AVE, DOWNTOWN; 503/224-8182

As one of the largest and most comprehensive galleries in Portland, Augen caters to the tastes and budgets of a diverse clientele with a variety of art— from prints by Robert Motherwell and Jim Dine to paintings by regional artists. Monthly exhibits occupy the central space on the main floor. *Mon–Sat; www.augengallery.com; map:G5; map:K4.*

beppu wiarda gallery

319 NW 9TH AVE, PEARL DISTRICT; 503/241-6460

Established in late 2005, the beppu wiarda gallery has carved out a vibrant place for itself in the Portland art scene. Featuring both emerging and established artists, its shows generally feature contemporary works that favor a pleasant aesthetic. *Wed–Sun; www.beppugallery.com; map:L3.*

THE JUBITZ CENTER FOR MODERN AND CONTEMPORARY ART

THE JUBITZ CENTER in the **PORTLAND ART MUSEUM (PAM)** has fast become one of the best art spaces in Portland. The museum opened up over 30,000 square feet of new gallery space in October 2005 to house its modern and contemporary collections. After purchasing the Mark Building in 1992, PAM commissioned Boston firm Ann Beha Architects to convert the tired, old, practically windowless Masonic temple into a modern venue sleek enough to house internationally recognized contemporary art. The firm successfully created the Jubitz Center with high ceilings and open galleries to complement the modern collection.

The dynamic new space includes six levels of large windows that pull in great light, even on the rainiest days. Transparent flights of floating stairs move through the levels, giving new perspectives to works exhibited above and below. On the ground level, the contemporary wing is connected to the main museum by an outdoor sculpture court, including which features a giant Roy Lichtenstein piece from his "Brushstroke" series, and underground galleries join the two wings inside. The building also includes administrative offices; glass penthouses for special events are on the upper levels.

The contemporary collection includes works from the likes of Mark Rothko (a Portland native), Marcel Duchamp, Alexander Calder, Andy Warhol, and Barnett Newman. The museum added 150 pieces when it acquired the collection of New York art critic Clement Greenberg. Newer acquisitions include Robert Rauschenberg's *Patrician Barnacle* and Robert Colescott's *Beauty Is in the Eye of the Beholder*. The collection in the Jubitz Center breathes new energy into the Portland Art Museum and celebrates the Portland art scene's love of creative boundary pushing.

—Elizabeth Lopeman

Blackfish Gallery

420 NW 9TH AVE, PEARL DISTRICT; 503/224-2634
Housed at the sign of the wooden fish, Blackfish is the country's oldest artists' cooperative, primarily displaying the latest work of its 30-plus members in monthly shows. Over the years, 117 artists have hit the Blackfish roster, their work chosen for an openness to innovation. Media, as varied as the members' styles, run from figurative sculpture and weaving to abstract painting. *Tues–Sat; www.blackfish.com; map:L3.*

Blue Sky Gallery and Nine Gallery

122 NW 8TH AVE, PEARL DISTRICT; 503/225-0210
Blue Sky, which opened in 1975, displays outstanding contemporary photography. The contemporary selections often show considerable wit, in distinct contrast to the seriousness of more traditional photography shows. The Nine Gallery, in an adjoining room, is a cooperative run by 12 local artists who take turns dreaming up installations. *Tues–Sun; www.blueskygallery. org; map:*M2.

Bonnie Kahn's Wild West Gallery

1524 NW 23RD AVE, NORTHWEST; 503/293-9414
Kahn specializes in authentic American Indian and Western art and antiques. The gallery has a wide selection of kachinas, art, jewelry, paintings, baskets, pottery, historic photos, and rugs. Kahn is available for curating and consulting services; she has extensive experience assembling collections. She can masterfully track down rare artifacts for discerning collectors, with whom she has established long-term relationships. She also provides authentication services and is frequently asked to trace pieces back to their artist. *Tues–Sat; www.bonniekahngallery.com; map:*GG6.

Bullseye Gallery

300 NW 13TH AVE, PEARL DISTRICT; 503/227-0222
Thanks to the presence of Bullseye, Portland is now known for exceptional glasswork: the gallery's collection boggles the mind. Bullseye shows contemporary kiln-formed glass and related works. Artists in residence show their work in a stunning, industrial space in the Pearl District. *Tues–Sat; www. bullseyegallery.com; map:*L1.

Butters Gallery

520 NW DAVIS ST, CHINATOWN; 503/248-9378
This beautiful gallery features monthly exhibits by such nationally known artists as sculptor Ming Fay and painters David Geiser and Frank Hyder, as well as Portland painter Ted Katz. Highlights include glass exhibits by West Coast artists. *Tues–Sat; www.buttersgallery.com; map:*L4.

Charles A. Hartman Fine Art

134 NW 8TH AVE, PEARL DISTRICT; 503/287-3886
With an exquisite and extensive collection of fine photography that spans a century, Hartman has one of the best camera-work galleries in the Northwest. It features local, regional, national, and internationally acclaimed photographers, including Ansel Adams and Imogen Cunningham, as well as other artists. The gallery also sometimes features other media. It is located in the new DeSoto arts complex. *Tues–Sat; www.hartmanfineart.net; map:*K3.

Elizabeth Leach Gallery

417 NW 9TH AVE, PEARL DISTRICT; 503/224-0521
This airy space in the historic Femco Building is well suited to large-scale sculpture. But exhibits here are equally strong in two-dimensional works, including Northwest, national, and international contemporary painting and photography. You'll find work by such artists as Christopher Rauschenberg, Robert Lyons, Stephen Hayes, Judy Cooke, and Dinh Q. Le. *Tues–Sat; www.elizabethleach.com; map:J6.*

Fifty 24 PDX Gallery

23 NW 5TH AVE, OLD TOWN; 503/548-4835
Fifty 24 exhibits cutting-edge, often graffiti-inspired work from all over the world. The vibe is fresh, young, and generally spun out of urban popular culture, sometimes with manga or street themes. Fifty 24 frequently features internationally recognized and award-winning artists and photographers. *Every day; www.upperplayground.com; map:K4.*

Froelick Adelhart Gallery

714 NW DAVIS ST, PEARL DISTRICT; 503/222-1142
An attractive, long space, the Froelick Adelhart Gallery exhibits and represents contemporary Northwest artists in sculpture and on canvas, as well as national and international painters and printmakers. *Tues–Sat; www.froelickgallery.com; map:G5.*

The Gallery at Museum of Contemporary Craft

724 NW DAVIS ST, DESOTO PROJECT, PEARL DISTRICT; 503/223-2654
The Museum of Contemporary Craft, formerly the Contemporary Crafts Museum and Gallery, is located in the progressive DeSoto Project on the North Park Blocks. The museum's gallery features an exquisite selection of craft-based art, from handblown glass masterpieces to jeweled baubles, from artisans featured in the free museum. The gallery strives to make crafts accessible to everyone. In a world of mass production, this gallery, with its handmade treasures, is an oasis. *Tues–Sat; www.museumofcontemporarycraft.org; map:K3.*

Guardino Gallery

2939 NE ALBERTA ST, ALBERTA; 503/281-9048
Since 1997 the Guardino has changed its shows monthly, always presenting the finest contemporary art from the Pacific Northwest. Paintings, sculpture, and photography are curated by Sal and Donna Guardino. A great time to visit is on the last Thursday of every month during the Alberta Street Art Crawl. *Tues–Sun; www.guardinogallery.com; map:FF5.*

Hoffman Gallery

OREGON COLLEGE OF ART AND CRAFT, 8245 SW BARNES RD, WEST SLOPE; 503/297-5544

There's eye-pleasing detail and design in every corner of this college and its grounds. Enter the Hoffman Gallery through a gate of elaborate, swirling wrought iron to see work in wood, metal, glass, fiber, photography, drawing, painting, and ceramics; student art is sometimes featured. Buy handcrafted gifts in an adjacent gallery, and stop for a bite at the Hands On Café (see review in the Restaurants chapter). *Every day; www.ocac.edu; map:HH9.*

Interstate Firehouse Cultural Center (IFCC)

5340 N INTERSTATE AVE, PATTON SQUARE, NORTH PORTLAND; 503/823-4322

A performance space, gallery, and workshop make up the body of this multi-faceted arts showcase, housed in a refurbished 1910 firehouse. The emphasis is on the work of the city's artists from all heritages, and often the IFCC scores with shows not likely to be seen at other venues. The Kwanzaa celebration in December is a major event. *Tues–Sat; www.ifccarts.org; map:GG6.*

Laura Russo Gallery

805 NW 21ST AVE, NORTHWEST; 503/226-2754

Laura Russo maintains a strong commitment to contemporary Northwest artists and represents many of the most respected ones. Russo does not shy away from the contemporary and experimental; her artists show paintings, sculpture, works on paper, and fine-art prints, with a scope ranging from landscape to abstract expressionism. The handsome gallery is one of a handful with space enough for large-scale works. *Tues–Sat; www.laurarusso.com; map:GG7.*

Lawrence Gallery

903 NW DAVIS ST, PEARL DISTRICT; 503/228-1776

Northwest landscape painters Charles Palmer and Hans Schiebold are among the 150-plus premier artists represented by this outstanding gallery. It was originally established in 1977 in Oregon's Wine Country and is now the state's largest. Inside, you'll find photography, mixed-media creations, bronze sculptures, porcelain, pottery, and works on canvas; outside, a sculpture garden (facing 9th Ave) displays fountains, wood art, and metal landscaping accents. The Lawrence is renowned for encouraging young artists such as Amanda Dunbar, a university student whose work sells for $75,000 and up. Additional galleries are in Sheridan and Salishan. *Every day; www.lawrence gallery.net; map:L3.*

AN ARTISTIC CONFLUENCE

THE MUSEUM OF CONTEMPORARY CRAFT (724 Northwest Davis St, 503/223-2654; www.museumofcontemporarycraft.org) and the **PACIFIC NORTH-WEST COLLEGE OF ART** (1241 NW Johnson St, 503/226-4391; www.pnca.edu) recently joined forces to create a highly interactive relationship between two of Portland's most progressive, culturally rich institutions.

Founded in 1937, the Museum of Contemporary Craft and curator Namita Gupta Wiggers consistently brings in high-caliber exhibitions and installations that exceed expectations and playfully challenge the history of craft. The shows usually highlight how modern craft has pushed the boundaries and become indispensable to modern art. The museum inhabits 4,500 square feet of exhibition space, a venue with a solid emphasis on physical interaction with objects, discovery of new ideas and thoughts behind construction and process.

Like the Museum of Contemporary Craft, Pacific Northwest College of Art has long been renowned for its influence on Portland's artistic landscape. In 1891 a collective of bright minds created the burgeoning arts community as a place to pursue and represent their work. In 1909 PNCA was finally established as an arts college and has been a champion of artistic voice and talent in Portland ever since. At 100 years old, the college has cemented itself as one of Portland's most established arts and learning institutions.

In late 2008, PNCA paired with the **OREGON COLLEGE OF ART AND CRAFT** (8245 SW Barnes Rd, 503/297-5544; www.ocac.edu), creating a joint MFA in Applied Craft and Design. Now, with its partnership with the Museum of Contemporary Craft, significant strides have been made in the artistic momentum of the Portland arts community.

Curatorial and educational programming adds a vibrant backbone to PNCA's mission of student programming, while the museum continues to advocate and engage visitors with thought-provoking exhibits, hands-on classes, artist demonstrations, and panel discussions and lectures. It's an exciting new era in Portland for arts and craft.

—Elianna Bar-El

Littman Gallery and White Gallery

SMITH MEMORIAL CENTER, PORTLAND STATE UNIVERSITY, DOWNTOWN; 503/725-5656

The Littman has an excellent regional reputation for its engaging photographic exhibits. The White features paintings and sculptures, often hosting such touring exhibits as the Harlem Renaissance display, which showcased

20 artists, including Jacob Lawrence. *Mon–Fri; www.portlandstateart galleries.com; map:E1.*

Manuel Izquierdo Gallery and the Philip Feldman Gallery

PACIFIC NORTHWEST COLLEGE OF ART, 1241 NW JOHNSON ST, PEARL DISTRICT; 503/226-4391

This huge space is broken into two galleries: the Manuel Izquierdo Gallery and the Philip Feldman Gallery. There's always something interesting going on, whether it be a retrospective of Oregon printmaker Gordon Gilkey, a new-media exhibit, or an open-studio show of student work. *Every day; www.pnca.edu; map:N2.*

New American Art Union

922 SE ANKENY ST, SOUTHEAST; 503/231-8294

The Art Union's mission is to expand the appreciation of art in the Northwest. The privately funded union presents contemporary installations and exhibits from a wide array of media and artists. *Thurs–Sun; www.newamerican artunion.com; map:HH5.*

Ogle

310 NW BROADWAY, DOWNTOWN; 503/227-4333

This delightfully curious gallery hosts consistently stunning work, from detailed, large-scale installations to provocative paintings. And it even does one better with its offering of high-end, artful eyewear for sale. *Tues–Sat; www.ogleinc.com; map:L4.*

PDX Gallery

925 NW FLANDERS ST, PEARL DISTRICT; 503/222-0063

Critically acclaimed nationally, this tiny pearl of the Pearl represents highly original American Indian painter James Lavadour and more than two dozen up-and-coming artists. Intellectually driven pieces by Ellen George, Joe Macca, Storm Tharp, Marie Watt, and others are exhibited. *Tues–Sat; www. pdxcontemporaryart.com; map:M2.*

Pulliam Deffenbaugh Gallery

929 NW FLANDERS ST, PEARL DISTRICT; 503/228-6665

The diversity and quality of this gallery's contemporary art selections are often stimulating and rewarding. Once focused on figurative pieces, the gallery has switched its viewpoint toward abstract and expressionistic works. Noted artists include Laurie Reid, Jeffrey Mitchell, and Hildur Bjarnadóttir. *Tues–Sat; www.pulliamgallery.com; map:M2.*

Quintana Gallery

120 NW 9TH AVE, PEARL DISTRICT; 503/223-1729

The only Portland gallery dedicated to Inuit and Northwest Coast American Indian arts, this establishment features contemporary and antique works:

sculptures, carved masks, and totems from such tribes as the Haida, Inupiat, Kwakiutl, and Tlingit. Some Southwest Indian and Mexican pieces are displayed as well. *Tues–Sat; www.quintanagalleries.com; map:K3.*

The Talisman Gallery
1476 NE ALBERTA ST, ALBERTA; 503/284-8800
This cooperative gallery in the heart of Alberta displays the diverse work of 22 member painters and sculptors. "We let people work from their heart and their spirit," says artist Serena Barton. "What we get is work with a contemporary edge." *Fri–Sun; www.talismangallery.com; map:FF5.*

Art in Public Places

Public art is everywhere in Portland, thanks to the patronage of its citizens and a program that requires all new, large-scale commercial and public building construction to include public art in the budget. Every City of Portland office building, lobby, and park boasts a signature mural, sculpture, painting, relief, or fountain. With artwork spread out across the city, you needn't try to cram a tour into an afternoon. Choose a few arty blocks, stop for a soda along the way, and enjoy.

Start at **TRAVEL PORTLAND** (701 SW 6th Ave at Morrison St, Downtown; 503/275-8355 or 877/678-5263; www.pova.com; map:H3), located on the lower west side of Pioneer Courthouse Square. Pick up a free map indicating the location of public art works. Then begin looking around Pioneer Courthouse Square. Just before noon the **WEATHER MACHINE**, a shiny sphere atop a 25-foot pole, plays a musical fanfare and sends forth one of three creatures, depending on the day's weather. When it's clear, you'll see the sun figure Helia; on stormy days, a dragon; and on gray, drizzly days, a great blue heron. Equally popular is the bronze sculpture by J. Seward Johnson, **ALLOW ME**, a life-size replica of a businessman with an umbrella. On either side of the historic Pioneer Courthouse building (on SW 6th Ave at Yamhill and Morrison sts; map:H3), look for Georgia Gerber's delightful bronze bears, beavers, ducks, and deer wandering down the sidewalk and playing in small pools of water.

On SW Yamhill Street between Third and Fourth avenues (map:H4), the **SIDEWALK** speaks, thanks to author/artists Katherine Dunn and Bill Will. Engraved in the right-of-way are thought-provoking phrases and quotes, ranging from a Pablo Picasso quip to "Step on a crack, break your mother's back." Across the parking lot to the north is Gary Hirsch's **UPSTREAM DOWNTOWN**, 18 colorful aluminum fish that decorate the south side of the parking structure at SW Third and Alder Street. Backtrack a bit to catch John Young's **SOARING STONES** on SW Fifth Avenue between Yamhill and Taylor streets.

One of the city's most familiar landmarks is the bronze **ELK** by Roland Perry, set in the fountain on SW Main Street between Third and Fourth avenues (map: G4). The **JUSTICE CENTER** (between SW 2nd and 3rd aves and SW Madison and Main sts; map:F4) houses a fine 19th-century Kwakiutl carving of an eagle and an array of contemporary pieces. At the entrance are Walter Dusenbery's untitled travertine sculptures representing the various paths to justice. Near them is a wall of stained-glass windows by Ed Carpenter.

The famous **PORTLAND BUILDING** (1120 SW 5th Ave; map:G3) is a provocative landmark. The first major work by architect Michael Graves, it has been described with adjectives ranging from brilliant to hideous. Kneeling above its entrance on SW Fifth Avenue is Raymond Kaskey's monumental **PORTLANDIA**. Inside the Portland Building, on the second floor, find a detailed history behind the statue. In 1985, locals cheered as the nation's second-largest hammered-copper sculpture (only the Statue of Liberty is larger) was barged down the Willamette River, trucked through downtown, and hoisted to a ledge three stories up. Most Portlanders have forgotten that *Portlandia* is fashioned after Lady Commerce, the figure on the city seal.

Directly across the street from *Portlandia* is Don Wilson's abstract limestone sculpture **INTERLOCKING FORMS**. Nearby is **CITY HALL** (1220 SW 5th Ave; map:F3), erected in 1890, whose east courtyard contains the oldest of Portland's artworks: petroglyphs carved into basalt rock near Wallula, Washington, some 15,000 years ago. Inside City Hall are numerous interesting pieces of art, including Jim Blashfield and Carol Sherman's **EVOLUTION OF A CITY**, a photographic tour through time.

The **TRANSIT MALL** on SW Fifth and Sixth avenues (map:E2–G3) is lined with sculptures, including Kathleen McCullough's **CAT IN REPOSE** (a children's favorite) and Norman Taylor's **KVINNEAKT**, the notorious nude that Portlanders know as former mayor Bud Clark's accomplice in an "Expose Yourself to Art" poster. At the southern end of the transit mall, Portland State University has created a city-block-size plaza at the heart of its **COLLEGE OF URBAN AND PUBLIC AFFAIRS** (between SW 5th and 6th aves and SW Montgomery and Mill sts; map:E2), with a variety of attractive stone sculptures and stair-stepping fountains.

North of PSU, facing the South Park Blocks, are two of the city's cultural institutions. The inviting **SCULPTURE GARDEN** on the north side of the Portland Art Museum (1219 SW Park Ave; map:G2) features rotating exhibits of historic and contemporary sculpture from the museum's collection. Across the Park Blocks, cast a lingering eye at a modern application of trompe l'oeil effects on the south and west walls of the **OREGON HISTORY CENTER** (1200 SW Park Ave; map:G2). The Richard Haas murals depict figures from Oregon history: Lewis and Clark, Sacagawea, fur traders, and pioneers who journeyed westward on the Oregon Trail. For another rendering of the Lewis and Clark expedition, visit the lobby of **JAKE'S GRILL** (611 SW 10th Ave; map:I2), where Melinda Morey's sepia-toned murals cover the south wall.

Some of Portland's best privately financed artwork is set inside the **PACIFIC FIRST FEDERAL CENTER** (SW Broadway between Taylor and Yamhill sts; map: H3): Larry Kirkland's suspended woven panels cascade into the lobby, catching the changing light throughout the day. More of Kirkland's work, including an intricately carved staircase and an enormous golden light fixture on the second floor, can be found in the **MULTNOMAH COUNTY CENTRAL LIBRARY** (801 SW 10th Ave; map:I2).

WASHINGTON PARK (see Top 20 Attractions in the Exploring chapter) also has some of the city's finest public sculpture. At the entrance to the park, off SW Park Place, an impressive memorial dedicated to Lewis and Clark hovers above an awe-inspiring view of the city. Down the west-facing hill is a fountain designed for Portland in 1891 by a Swiss woodcarver, Hans Staehli. North of it is a sculpture of Sacagawea, Lewis and Clark's Shoshone guide. Herman A. McNeil's **THE COMING OF THE WHITE MAN** sculpture features two larger-than-life American Indian men looking to the east. Also nearby is the **OREGON HOLOCAUST MEMORIAL**, paying tribute to those killed in the WWII Holocaust, with grounds and sculptures designed by artists Tad Savinar and Paul Sutinen and landscape architect Marianne Zarkin.

Fountains abound in central Portland. The smallest are the ornamental bronze drinking fountains found all around the downtown core, called **BENSON BUBBLERS** after lumberman and civic leader Simon Benson; he gave them to the city in 1917 hoping people would drink water instead of whiskey. The city's most popular fountain may be the ever-changing **SALMON STREET SPRINGS**, in Gov. Tom McCall Waterfront Park, where SW Salmon Street meets Naito Parkway (Downtown; map:F5). To the southwest, in front of Keller Auditorium (SW 3rd Ave between Market and Clay sts, Downtown; map:E3), is the **IRA KELLER FOUNTAIN**, also known as the Forecourt Fountain. It's a cool resting place in the middle of downtown, a full city block of waterfalls and pools built specifically with splashing in mind. Less well known but equally playful is the **LOVEJOY FOUNTAIN** (between SW 3rd and 4th aves on Hall St, Downtown; map:C2), built to resemble a cascading mountain stream. In Old Town stands Portland's first piece of public art, the 1888 cast-iron **SKIDMORE FOUNTAIN** (SW 1st Ave and Ankeny St; map: J6); two handmaidens hold an overflowing bowl above their heads.

William Wegman's **PORTLAND DOG BOWL** is a functioning bronze water fountain for pets in the North Park Blocks, north of Burnside Street between NW Eighth and Park avenues (Downtown; map:L3). This whimsical take on a dog's water bowl, an homage to Portland's Benson Bubblers, sits atop a floor reminiscent of kitchen linoleum. The revitalized Pearl District has added color and vibrancy to **JAMISON SQUARE** (NW 11th Ave and Johnson St; map:N2) with Kenny Scharf's **TIKITOTEMONKI** totems, selected in 2002 by *Art in America* magazine as one of the top 10 examples of new public art in the United States.

For a different perspective on Portland's public art, take a MAX ride across the river. The **OREGON CONVENTION CENTER** (NE Martin Luther King Jr Blvd and Holladay St, Northeast; map:N9) is home to one of the state's most impressive public art collections. From the **SOUND GARDEN**, created with bronze bells and chimes donated by Portland's Pacific Rim sister cities, to local artist Lucinda Parker's painting *River Song*, the works at the convention center define the spirit of the state's people. The vision is universal, as seen in Kristin Jones and Andrew Ginzel's **PRINCIPIA**—a pendulum hanging in the north tower above a 30-foot halo of suspended rays and a circular blue terrazzo floor inlaid with brass and stones. The vision is also provincial, as in a series of 30 etched and color-filled plaques noting key events and figures in Oregon history by Terrence O'Donnell, Dennis Cunningham, and John Laursen. And it's witty, as in Elizabeth Mapelli's enameled-glass panels of Oregon waterfalls, installed above men's-room urinals. Particularly telling and provocative is Seattle artist Buster Simpson's outdoor installation facing NE Martin Luther King Jr Boulevard—a nurse log pulled from Bull Run Reservoir; seedlings sprout from the irrigated, decaying wood, generating a bit of forest in the middle of the city.

While in Northeast Portland, don't miss the works scattered around the **LLOYD CENTER** mall, including Larry Kirkland's fountain, **CAPITALISM**. Outside the **ROSE GARDEN** stadium, children love **ESSENTIAL FORCES**, a computerized water feature: the fountain was a gift to the city from high-tech tycoon Paul Allen, owner of the Trail Blazers. Farther east, at **GRANT PARK** (NE 33rd Ave between Knott St and Broadway; map:GG5), children's books come alive in the **BEVERLY CLEARY SCULPTURE GARDEN FOR CHILDREN,** as cast-bronze statues of Ramona Quimby, Henry Huggins, and Henry's dog Ribsy cavort through a fountain, inviting real kids to join them.

Literature

Portland is a city of many loves, but it loves nothing more than a good book. Thanks to **POWELL'S CITY OF BOOKS** (1005 W Burnside St, Pearl District; 503/228-4651; www.powells.com; map:K2), Portlanders get the opportunity to not only track down their most adored published works (including those that are out of print) but also attend weekly readings of today's most renowned writers. With its multiple floors and gigantic collection—open 14 hours a day, 365 days a year—Powell's is the nation's largest independent bookstore and, indeed, one of the city's Top 20 Attractions (see the Exploring chapter).

The large national bookstore chains like Barnes & Noble and Borders have arrived in Portland full force. As well, smaller stores equipped with espresso bars, deep reading chairs, and great lighting dot the city. There are dozens of independent new-book shops and probably just as many, if not more, dealers in used and rare books (see Books and Magazines in the Shopping chapter). And the **FRIENDS OF THE MULTNOMAH COUNTY LIBRARY** (503/248-5439) each fall conduct an enormous used-book sale that raises as much as $150,000 for the library.

Many shops host touring authors to discuss their books and the writing life, and open-house readings are regularly scheduled at coffeehouses on both sides of the river; check the calendar listings in local newspapers. Book clubs, meanwhile, are prolific; members meet in libraries and small shops.

Among the best-known **PORTLAND-AREA WRITERS** are Jean Auel (*The Clan of the Cave Bear*), Larry Colton (*Goat Brothers*), Charles D'Ambrosio (*The Point, The Dead Fish Museum, Orphans*), Monica Drake (*Clown Girl*), Katherine Dunn (*Geek Love*), Matt Groening (*The Simpsons*), Diana Abu-Jaber (*Crescent*), Ursula K. LeGuin (*The Left Hand of Darkness*), Phillip Margolin (*Wild Justice*), Blake Nelson (*Paranoid Park, Destroy All Cars*), Chuck Palahniuk (*Fight Club*), Tom Spanbauer (*The Man Who Fell in Love with the Moon*), and the most recent literary sensation, Chelsea Cain, whose thrillers (*Heartsick, Sweetheart, Evil at Heart*) have made the *New York Times* bestseller list.

Since 2005, Portland has hosted the largest book and literary festival in the Pacific Northwest. Known as **WORDSTOCK**, the annual event-packed, storytelling fete has presented more than 550 writers to date, 10 author stages (including children's lit), and a book fair boasting 150 exhibitors, in addition to a series of writers' workshops. Wordstock also serves as a nonprofit organization that works to promote writing in the classroom. Visit its Web site (www.wordstockfestival.com) for specific event information and author bios.

One of the most revered literary journals in the country, **TIN HOUSE** (800/786-3424; www.tinhouse.com), spearheads the Portland literary scene each summer with a writers' workshop. For a week in July, such well-known writers as Charles D'Ambrosio, Whitney Otto, and Denis Johnson converge on Portland's Reed College for readings and book signings. Established in 1999, Tin House occupies an old zinc-sided Victorian house in Northwest Portland. The company has begun publishing books of "lively, engaging work from established, underappreciated, and emerging writers of our day."

Portland is one of the few cities in the country to have its own nonprofit literary organization. **LITERARY ARTS** (503/227-2583; www.literary-arts.org) enriches readers and writers through fellowships, book awards, and the hugely popular **PORTLAND ARTS AND LECTURE SERIES**. Created in 1984, the series, which runs September to May, surprises even the nation's best-known authors with the enthusiasm of its audience. Readers from Salman Rushdie to Gore Vidal, Sandra Cisneros to David Guterson, take the stage to read from their work, discuss the writing process, and answer audience questions.

After more than 30 years, the **MOUNTAIN WRITERS SERIES** (www.mountain-writers.org) has become one of the largest poetry-reading series in the United States, offering readings, workshops, and lectures by distinguished writers. MWS works with more than 90 literary sponsors around the Northwest to bring great writers to local communities. The series maintains the **MOUNTAIN WRITERS CENTER** (3624 SE Milwaukie Ave, Brooklyn; 503/236-4854; map:II5), where you can hear readings, read a literary journal, take a class or workshop, and chat up an accomplished writer or poet.

You need not be a full-time student to take advantage of Lewis & Clark College's **NORTHWEST WRITING INSTITUTE** (0615 SW Palatine Hill Rd, Riverdale; 503/768-7745; www.lclark.edu/dept/nwi; map:JJ6), headed by poet-writer and local literary stalwart Kim Stafford, with its ever-evolving list of courses and workshops.

Theater

The theater scene in Portland offers something for everyone; big-box productions à la *Wicked* are equally as entertaining as one-act plays, and much of the deserved thanks goes to the talent both on and off the stage. Portland Center Stage's **GERDING THEATER** at the Armory has upped the ante citywide, and every company has risen to the challenge with stunning productions. Smaller companies like **HAND 2MOUTH** and **MIRACLE THEATRE GROUP** always lend an intimate, provocative perspective and display a whole lot of heart.

Artists Repertory Theatre (ART)

1516 SW ALDER ST, DOWNTOWN; 503/241-1278
One of Portland's best small theaters, ART features acclaimed local actors and directors overseen by artistic director Allen Nause. Occasionally, actor William Hurt, Nause's good friend, appears in ART productions. The company focuses on cutting-edge American plays juxtaposed with relevant classics. A sparkling black-box theater built in 1998 has given ART a dream space in which to work: Portland's small theaters often appear in makeshift settings, but here, the stage and seating—which can be reconfigured as needed—are gems. *www.artistsrep.org; map:J1.*

Broadway in Portland

211 SE CARUTHERS ST, SOUTHEAST; 503/241-1802
This is the big shot in Portland's theater scene, importing extravagant touring blockbusters such as *Stomp*, *Chicago*, and *Wicked* for presentation on the local stage—most often, the Keller Auditorium (222 SW Clay St, Downtown; map:E3). Tickets are sold through the Portland Opera. *www.portlandopera. org/broadway.php; map:HH6.*

CoHo Productions

2257 NW RALEIGH ST, NORTHWEST; 503/220-2646
Coho Productions produces plays by local playwrights and theater artists. It has received 12 local Drammy awards since its inception in 1995. Because the company is cooperative—all participants are treated as partners—the productions are packed with the energy of its players' personal investment. One of its most notable shows yet, "The 24 Hour Plays," is a production that spans a 24-hour period with patrons able to come and go at their leisure. *www.cohoproductions.org; map:GG7.*

Imago Theatre

17 SE 18TH AVE, BUCKMAN; 503/231-9581
With its blend of mask, mime, and vaudeville, this whimsical, movement-based company astonishes young and old alike. From a skit with comical penguins in a game of musical chairs to a play based on the male ego and cloning, Imago captures the human spirit and melds it with the spirit of the times. *www.imagotheatre.com; map:HH5.*

Many Hats Collaboration

VARIOUS LOCATIONS; 503/952-6646
Founded by three women, Many Hats delivers stellar performances and frequently visits issues loaded with taboos such as race, addiction, and gender. With their exquisite execution, the shows resonate strongly with their audiences. The company frequently chooses creative venues to stage its productions—a restroom in the Gerding Theater, for example, for a production of *Restroom*. Many Hats is a solid company with an emerging presence in Portland. *www.manyhatscollaboration.com.*

Miracle Theatre Group

425 SE 6TH AVE, BUCKMAN; 503/236-7253

"Teatro Milagro" tours internationally, crafting current global issues into cutting-edge drama infused with Latino culture, Spanish language (with supertitles), and original music. But since its inception in 1985, it has evolved into more than a performing arts group: El Centro Milagro is now a regional cultural center for Portland's large Hispanic community, and its Bellas Artes division stages a variety of music festivals and other events. *www.milagro. org; map:HH6.*

Northwest Children's Theater

1819 NW EVERETT ST, NORTHWEST; 503/222-4480

This theater presents a variety of plays each year, from *Jack and the Beanstalk* to *Arabian Nights*. Its 450-seat theater and theater school for Portland's youngest thespians are lodged in the Northwest Neighborhood Cultural Center. *www.nwcts.org; map:HH7.*

Oregon Children's Theatre

600 SW 10TH AVE, DOWNTOWN; 503/228-9571

Children's favorite stories—from *The Chronicles of Narnia* to *The Velveteen Rabbit*—come to life in an annual handful of engaging works. They are presented at the Portland Center for the Performing Arts' Keller Auditorium (222 SW Clay St, Downtown; map:E3) and Newmark Theatre (1111 SW Broadway, Downtown; map:G2). *www.octc.org; map:I2.*

Portland Center Stage at the Gerding Theater and Armory

128 NW 11TH AVE, PEARL DISTRICT; 503/274-6588

Portland's leading professional theater company is one of the best regional theaters in the country. Its move to the gorgeous, remodeled armory building in the Pearl District has raised the bar for companies throughout Portland. Chris Coleman, company director since 2000, has a distaste for complacency; he has upgraded every element of Portland Center Stage, bringing in seasoned actors and plays that illuminate. Coleman twists even the most conventional plays with energy and wit: expect to be surprised. *www.pcs.org; map:G2.*

Tears of Joy Puppet Theatre

323 NE WYGANT ST, NORTHEAST; 503/248-0557

Founded in 1972, Tears of Joy always awes the family. The award-winning company thrills with over-the-top, puppet-enhanced retellings of classic tales and original works like *Pinocchio* and *Rumpelstiltskin*, as well as classic Greek epics. Each year, Tears of Joy mounts 100 performances of six productions at the Winningstad Theatre (1111 SW Broadway, Downtown; map:G2) and in Vancouver, Washington's Royal Durst Theatre (3101 Main St; map: CC6). Its outreach programs extend throughout the West. This company is a local treasure; everything it does is a class act. *www.tojt.com; map:FF6.*

Theatre Vertigo

3430 SE BELMONT ST, BELMONT; 503/306-0870
With a fulfilled ideal of "live storytelling," Theater Vertigo produces edgy, often hilarious ensemble works, occasionally in collaboration with other local companies. Plays by writers like Oscar Wilde, Henrik Ibsen, and Paula Vogel deliver an acute understanding of the human experience. *www. theatrevertigo.org; map:II5.*

Third Rail Repertory Theater

5340 N INTERSTATE AVE, NORTH PORTLAND; 503/235-1101
Performances at the Interstate Firehouse Cultural Center are moving audiences and critics citywide. In its first full year, 2006–07, Third Rail garnered six Drammy awards, catapulting it to a position as a Portland drama darling. *www.thirdrailrep.org; map:EE5.*

Classical Music and Opera

During the symphony season, Portland audiences have many opportunities to listen to classical music, both by the powerful **OREGON SYMPHONY ORCHESTRA** and by smaller orchestras, ensembles, and choral groups. The highlight of the year, however, comes midsummer with **CHAMBER MUSIC NORTHWEST**—a five-week celebration that is among the finest festivals of its type in the nation. If you're in town during July, investigate ticket availability. The rest of the year, look to local newspapers for a schedule of the best performances in Portland.

Chamber Music Northwest

CATLIN GABEL SCHOOL, 8825 SW BARNES RD, WEST SLOPE
REED COLLEGE, 3203 SE WOODSTOCK BLVD, WOODSTOCK;
503/294-6400
A talented group of musicians, recruited from New York's Chamber Music Society of Lincoln Center and other Big Apple ensembles, puts the annual summer festival (late June–mid-July) in an elite class. Longtime artistic director David Shifrin is committed to a wide-ranging repertoire from duos and trios to large ensembles, baroque and classical masterpieces to world and West Coast premieres. More than two dozen concerts, held at Reed College or the Catlin Gabel School, range from solo recitals to evenings for small orchestras, from Bach to Bartók, and from chamber music staples (Brahms, Schubert, Beethoven) to surprises. Between October and April, the company presents a concert series (often featuring touring chamber groups) at venues around the city; watch local media or call for information. Keep an eye out for Portland's own Florestan Trio, an internationally acclaimed violin-cello-piano group. *www.cmnw.org; map:HH9; map:JJ5.*

Oregon Repertory Singers

909 SW WASHINGTON ST, DOWNTOWN; 503/230-0652

More than 30 years of innovative concerts have given Gilbert Seeley's 65-voice adult ensemble a reputation for creative programming. In four shows from October to May, Seeley specializes in new commissions and neglected classics; he is also a gifted orchestral conductor. Collaborations with other ensembles on works by Haydn, Bach, Mozart, and Handel are high-quality repertoire staples. Most performances are in area churches; call for locations. A youth choir mounts three productions a year. *www.oregonrepsingers.org; map:GG5.*

Oregon Symphony Orchestra

ARLENE SCHNITZER CONCERT HALL, 1037 SW BROADWAY, DOWNTOWN; 503/228-1353

One of the largest arts organizations in the Northwest and a Portland institution since 1896, the Oregon Symphony is one of the major orchestras in the United States. Legendary conductor James DePreist (who remains as laureate music director) has transferred his baton to Carlos Kalmar, who plans a return to a core orchestral repertoire. An all-star roster of guest artists joins him; over the years they have included Aaron Copland, Maurice Ravel, Igor Stravinsky, Wynton Marsalis, and Yo-Yo Ma. The Portland Symphonic Choir chimes in a couple of times a year. Pops and youth series fill out the 39-week calendar. *www.oregonsymphony.org; map:G2.*

Portland Baroque Orchestra

1020 SW TAYLOR ST, STE 275, DOWNTOWN; 503/222-6000

The Baroque Orchestra has gained enormous stature since 1995 under the baton of English superstar violinist Monica Huggett. The Portland early-instrument specialists tackle music written between 1600 and 1825 in performances designed to re-create the sound of period ensembles. Visiting soloists on trumpet, cello, violin, harpsichord, and recorder, plus a crack 24-voice chorus, conspire in brisk versions of Bach, Handel, Vivaldi, Mozart, Haydn, and Beethoven. From October to April, Friday- and Saturday-night concerts are at the First Baptist Church (909 SW 11th Ave, Downtown; map:F2); most Sunday matinees are in Reed College's Kaul Auditorium (3203 SE Woodstock Blvd, Woodstock; map:JJ5). *www.pbo.org; map:H2.*

Portland Opera

KELLER AUDITORIUM, 222 SW CLAY ST, DOWNTOWN; 503/241-1802

With productions of Mozart's *The Magic Flute* and Verdi's *Macbeth*, Christopher Mattaliano's artistic stage direction has brought the Portland Opera to new heights. Spectacular voices accompany world-class scores as the company strives to make opera available to a diverse clientele, touting itself as "never stuffy." The costumes and set design reflect the high aesthetic expected by Portlanders. The Portland Opera includes the Portland Opera Chorus and the Portland Opera Orchestra. *www.portlandopera.org; map:E3.*

Third Angle New Music Ensemble

VARIOUS LOCATIONS; 503/203-2836

This ensemble—eight permanent members and a revolving roster of guest artists—specializes in 20th-century chamber music by American composers, refreshingly not just those of European descent. You might hear a commissioned piece by Ghanaian master drummer Obo Addy (who makes Portland his home), a concert devoted entirely to tango, or the work of New Romantic composers. Four to six polished, provocative programs are presented each year at locales that vary from Reed College (3203 SE Woodstock Blvd, Woodstock; map:JJ5) to Winningstad Theatre (1111 SW Broadway, Downtown; map:G2) and the Arlene Schnitzer Concert Hall (1037 SW Broadway, Downtown; map:G2). *www.thirdangle.org.*

Dance

Portland's dance explosion can be readily traced to a single event: the creation, in 1997, of **WHITE BIRD**. This nonprofit organization has brought a wealth of national and international performers to the city, from Mikhail Baryshnikov and Alvin Ailey to Paul Taylor, Twyla Tharp, and Urban Bush Women. Reviewers have described White Bird's works as "diamond-edged dancing" and "a world where madness waltzes with grace." Numerous other dance companies make their home in Portland, chief among them the much-celebrated **OREGON BALLET THEATRE**. For both local and national appearances, keep an eye on newspaper listings.

BodyVox

1300 NW NORTHRUP ST, PEARL DISTRICT; 503/229-0627

Launched almost coincidentally with White Bird, this high-energy contemporary dance theater operates out of a studio loft above the BridgePort Brewpub. Choreographers/founders Jamey Hampton and Ashley Roland bring a bold athleticism and inherent theatrical spirit to their troupe. Dynamic and emotional, the touring company has won rave international reviews. *www.bodyvox.com; map:O1.*

Do Jump! Extremely Physical Theater

1515 SE 37TH AVE, HAWTHORNE; 503/231-1232

These tremendously energetic dancers fuse acrobatics with athletics using props from hand trucks to ladders, breaking down the boundary between audience and performers. Over three decades, director Robin Lane has created 16 full-length works. Do Jump! is the resident company of the Echo Theatre, where the Dance Cartel (503/972-7709) also performs its showcase work. *www.dojump.org; map:HH5.*

The Northwest Afrikan American Ballet
77 NE KNOTT ST, ALBINA; 503/287-8852
The first traditional African dance company in the Northwest, this 16-member troupe has been inspired for 20 years by drummer/dancer/director Bruce Smith. Performing indigenous dances of Senegal, Gambia, Mali, and Guinea to the insistent beat of a virtuoso drum contingent and clad in the gorgeous fabrics of those West African nations, the athletic troupe re-creates village festivals that celebrate marriage, coming of age, harvest time, and the passing of seasons. An annual Rose Festival fixture, the company appears in schools and other locations up and down the West Coast. *Map:GG6.*

Oregon Ballet Theatre
818 SE 6TH AVE, BUCKMAN; 503/222-5538
This energetic company of talented dancers wowed critics in New York with its strong blend of classical and modern ballet when it toured in 2000. A wellspring of youth and daring, the troupe satisfies both the cravings of Portland's traditional ballet fans and the appetites of the MTV generation. Director Christopher Stowell celebrates the evolution of ballet through a series of works inspired both by the great masters and by the hottest young talents. OBT's obligatory holiday *Nutcracker* is pure guilty joy, with a dance narrative set in czarist Saint Petersburg and superb costumes and sets. Performances are in Keller Auditorium (222 SW Clay St, Downtown; map:E3) and the Newmark Theatre (1111 SW Broadway, Downtown; map:G2). *www.obt.org; map:HH6.*

Oslund + Company/Dance
918 SW YAMHILL ST, 4TH FLOOR, DOWNTOWN; 503/221-5857
Artistic director and choreographer Mary Oslund stages a concert when the spirit moves her: several times a year. Noted for erratic, gestural movement, she combines modern dance and live, newly composed music with excellent scenery and lighting, giving her shows a spirit both postmodern and avant-garde. The efforts of musicians, poets, visual artists, and filmmakers put Oslund in the best tradition of collaborative art. Usually at home in the cozy Conduit Contemporary Dance Studio, above the MAX tracks downtown, Oslund also performs at the larger Imago Theatre (17 SE 18th Ave, Buckman; map:HH5). *www.oslundandco.org; map:I2.*

Performance Works NorthWest
4625 SE 67TH ST, SOUTHEAST; 503/777-1907
Founded in 1999 by dancer/choreographer Linda Austin and technical director Jeff Forbes, this company—ensconced in a former Romanian Orthodox church off Foster Road—both produces its own imaginative works and performs that of other artists. Austin herself emcees the off-the-wall Cabaret Boris & Natasha, an occasional tongue-in-cheek mix of dance, music, theater, and performance art, and Holy Goats!, an almost-monthly Sunday-afternoon improv session. *www.performanceworksnw.org; map:II3.*

White Bird

PO BOX 99, PORTLAND; 503/245-1600

Established in 1997 by East Coast entrepreneurs Walter Jaffe and Paul King, White Bird has hosted more than four dozen dance companies in 10 years. Named for a white cockatoo whose passion is for flight and fancy, White Bird seeks out and delivers dancers who make the soul soar. The company regularly collaborates with local arts and dance schools, public schools, and private colleges. Performances run monthly (Oct–May); cost is $12–$25, with a half-price student rush special. *www.whitebird.org.*

Film

Since 1999, more than four dozen feature films have been shot in Oregon. More and more film companies—small independent filmmakers as well as big Hollywood conglomerates—are using Oregon's landscape as a backdrop for their stories. Films such as *Wendy and Lucy* (2008), *Twilight* (2008), *Into the Wild* (2007), *What the #$*! Do We (K)now!?* (2004), *The Hunted* (2003), *The Ring* (2002), *Pay It Forward* (2000), and *Men of Honor* (2000) were filmed, in part, in the Portland area. Not to mention Portland's own animation studio, LAIKA, which strongly debuted with *Coraline* (2009).

Cutting-edge filmmaker **GUS VAN SANT** moved to Portland from New York in the late 1980s. In his own new backyard, he directed Matt Dillon and Kelly Lynch in *Drugstore Cowboy* (1989) and Keanu Reeves and River Phoenix in *My Own Private Idaho* (1991). *Paranoid Park* (2007), also shot in Portland, features loads of scenes in the city. In 2003 Van Sant won the top prize at the Cannes Film Festival for *Elephant*, a film he shot in North Portland, casting real high-school students. He also garnered a Best Director Oscar nomination for *Milk* in 2009.

By the time Van Sant scored box-office gold with *Good Will Hunting* (1997), other international-caliber artists had followed him to Portland. Among them is director **TODD HAYNES**, acclaimed for *I'm Not There* (2007), *Far From Heaven* (2002), and *Velvet Goldmine* (1998).

Portland has quite a love affair with going to the movies. Our first thoughts would attribute it to the weather and the chance to be indoors and escape the day-to-day for a while, but it most definitely comes down to the sheer variety of offerings this town presents on a weekly basis: first-run flicks, art-house films, and local, independent festivals showing everything from shorts to foreign films to animation. For complete movie listings, check out the entertainment section of the *Oregonian* (www.oregonlive.com), *Portland Tribune* (www.portlandtribune. com), or *Willamette Week* (www.wweek.com).

Broadway Metroplex

1000 SW BROADWAY, DOWNTOWN; 800/326-3264

This is a multiplex, true—but it's in central downtown, and its coffee bar serves first-rate mochas and quality chocolates. Enjoy the old Portland theater marquees hanging in the lower lobby and the continuous classic film footage that entertains you as you wait in line for tickets. *www.regalcinemas.com; map:H3.*

CineMagic

2021 SE HAWTHORNE BLVD, HAWTHORNE; 503/231-7919

This independently owned rep house serves up the classics as well as near-first-run faves. You might see *My Fair Lady* one week and a recent feature the next—or even an East Indian film. Seats are soft and comfy, and the ambience is calm and pretty. Popcorn is drenched in real butter, and regular admission is $4.50 for showings before 6pm. *Map:HH5.*

Cinema 21

616 NW 21ST AVE, NORTHWEST; 503/223-4515

Portland's best movie house is one of a dying breed: the single-screen neighborhood theater. Spacious and clean, it still has a roomy balcony and rocking-chair seats, and it features a crying room for troubled tots. Films range from way-left documentaries to art-house intrigues to premieres. Watch for the annual festival of animation. *www.cinema21.com; map:GG7.*

Fox Tower 10

SW PARK AVE AND TAYLOR ST, DOWNTOWN; 800/326-3264

Tall escalators deliver patrons from the street into this huge 10-auditorium theater in the central shopping district. Cozy individual theaters feature tiered seating, retractable armrests for snuggling (or arm wrestling) with your popcorn partner, and digital everything. Look for both major Hollywood releases and alternative fare. *www.regalcinemas.com; map:H2.*

Hollywood Theater

4122 NE SANDY BLVD, HOLLYWOOD; 503/281-4215

A brilliant neon-and-steel "Hollywood" sign stands in front of the whimsical sculpted facade of this multicolored terra-cotta building. Built in 1926, when it had an eight-piece orchestra to accompany silent films, the theater was purchased by Film Action Oregon in 1997 and given a thorough makeover. Today, it is a nonprofit theater serving classic, family, and second-run fare to frequently sold-out audiences. This is also a site for film festivals, concerts, lectures, live performances, and other public events. Concessions include fat-free, sugar-free, and vegan options. And on Monday nights, all shows are just $4. *www.hollywoodtheater.org; map:GG4.*

Laurelhurst Theater and Pub

2735 E BURNSIDE ST, LAURELHURST; 503/232-5511

It doesn't get much better than this: $3 admission, a slice of Pizzicato pizza, and a draft microbrew or a glass of wine. Get comfy in the wide seats at this friendly neighborhood cinema, a 1923 Art Deco classic. Set your snacks on the tables between seats in each of the four theaters, and take in a classic

PIFF: THE PORTLAND INTERNATIONAL FILM FESTIVAL

Opening with Orson Welles's *F for Fake* in 1977, the Portland International Film Festival has brought thousands of films from all over the world to Portland screens. In doing so, it has drawn hundreds of thousands of eager Northwest moviegoers. PIFF provides one of the most culturally diverse experiences in the region, opening a window into the expansive talent in acting and storytelling captured by film the world over.

The highlight of the 2009 festival was the much-anticipated premier screening of *Coraline* based on Neil Gaiman's popular children's book. The animated film was created in the Portland-based LAIKA studios and was created with the help of a lot of local staff and artists. It was exciting to see the film finally come to life!

Since its inception, PIFF has delivered world-class cinematic events. Held in the cold and rainy season of February, the festival brightens screens for more than two weeks of films in the cloisters of a handful of Portland theaters. Each year, about 100 films from 30 countries are chosen for presentation, each conveying stories rich in setting and circumstances, illuminating the human experience common to all.

—Elizabeth Lopeman

or recent first-run film. No one under 21 is admitted after 4pm. *www.laurelhursttheater.com; map:HH5.*

Living Room Theaters

341 SW 10TH AVE, DOWNTOWN; 971/222-2010

You can enjoy an indie or foreign film with a cocktail at this casual complex near Powell's City of Books. The lobby has a full bar, an espresso bar, and a kitchen: order your movie with fries. Excellent happy-hour specials are offered (3–6pm and 10pm–closing). In the morning, stop by for coffee, a croissant, and the morning news on the big screen. You can get wireless Internet, the seats are large and cushy, and the staff is delightful. *www.livingroomtheaters.com; map:J2.*

Lloyd Center and Lloyd Cinemas

1510 NE MULTNOMAH BLVD, LLOYD CENTER;
503/225-5555, EXT 4601 AND 4600

With 10 screens in the mall and 10 across the street, this is the biggest movie site in the city. Both theaters are owned by the Regal Cinemas chain, so films are traditional, first-run Hollywood fare. The Lloyd Cinemas building features a long, neon-lit interior corridor and an espresso bar. *www.regalcinemas.com; map:GG5.*

McMenamins Theater Pubs

VARIOUS LOCATIONS; 503/225-5555, EXT 8830

What may well be Portland's favorite movie-theater chain is actually a group of brewpubs that show movies: not only can you enjoy a handcrafted beer while catching a flick, but admission is a mere $3; children are allowed during matinees. There are six options: the Mission (1624 NW Glisan St, Northwest; map:HH7), the Bagdad (3710 SW Hawthorne Blvd, Hawthorne; map:HH5), the St. Johns (8203 N Ivanhoe St, Saint Johns; map:EE9), the Kennedy School (5736 NE 33rd Ave, Northeast; map:FF5), the Edgefield (2126 SW Hawley, Troutdale), and the Grand Lodge (3505 Pacific Ave, Forest Grove). *www.mcmenamins.com.*

Northwest Film Center

1219 SW PARK AVE, DOWNTOWN; 503/221-1156

A steady menu of art films, independent features, and documentaries appear here, as do guest filmmakers presenting their recent work. This nonprofit organization, a branch of the Portland Art Museum, also presents several annual festivals: the Portland International Film Festival screens international indie films over two weeks in February; the Northwest Film & Video Festival highlights work by regional artists in November; and the Young People's Film & Video Festival honors school-age filmmakers in July. *www.nwfilm.org; map:G2.*

Pioneer Place Stadium Six Cinemas

700 SW 5TH AVE, DOWNTOWN; 800/326-3264

At the top of the escalator in Pioneer Place's downtown mall is Portland's most modern theater experience. With six screens showing the most current Hollywood blockbusters, the stadium-style theaters are well maintained, clean, comfortable, and air-conditioned. Located in the heart of downtown, this cinema is within walking distance of many of the best shops and restaurants. *www.pioneerplace.com; map:H4.*

Roseway Theater

7229 NE SANDY BLVD, ROSEWAY; 503/287-8119

This classic, family-owned neighborhood theater—a throwback to days of yore—has high ceilings, wide aisles, comfortable seats with spacious leg room, an elegant lobby, and great attitude. Theater here is a gift to the community. Quality second-run films are presented with pleasure and flair. *www.rosewaytheater.com; map:FF3.*

NIGHTLIFE

NIGHTLIFE

Nightlife by Neighborhood

ALBERTA
Bye and Bye
The Know Microtheater
    and Bar
Townshend's
Zilla Saké House

ALBINA
820 Lounge at Mint
White Eagle Rock 'n' Roll
    Hotel (McMenamins)
Widmer Brewing
    and Gasthaus

BEAUMONT VILLAGE
Alameda Brewhouse

BELMONT
Aalto Lounge
Horse Brass Pub
The Pied Cow
Stumptown Cof-
    fee Roasters
The Tao of Tea

BROOKLYN
Aladdin Theater
C Bar
Pub at the End of
    the Universe

BUCKMAN
Crush
Holocene
Rimsky-Korsakoffee
    House

CHINATOWN
Backspace
East Chinatown Lounge
Ground Kontrol
Harvey's Comedy Club
Roseland Theater
The Tao of Tea

CLINTON/DIVISION
Bar Avignon
Dots Cafe
Pix Patisserie

DOWNTOWN
The Benson Hotel
    Palm Court
Boxxes/Red Cap Garage
Cassidy's
Clyde Common
The Crystal Ballroom
The Driftwood Room
Fez Ballroom
The Heathman Hotel
Huber's
Jake's Grill
Living Room Theaters
Market Street Pub
    (McMenamins)
Mary's Club
Rialto Poolroom
    Bar & Cafe
Ringler's (McMenamins)
Ringler's Annex
    (McMenamins)
Satyricon
Saucebox

Stumptown Coffee
    Roasters
The Tugboat Brewery
Veritable Quandary
Virginia Cafe
World Cup at Powell's
    City of Books

GOOSE HOLLOW
Goose Hollow Inn

HAWTHORNE
Bagdad Theater and
    Pub (McMenamins)
Bar of the Gods
Fresh Pot
Greater Trumps
    (McMenamins)
Sapphire Hotel
Space Room/Brite Spot

HOLLYWOOD
Laurelwood Brew-
    ing Company
Sam's Hollywood Billiards

INNER SOUTHEAST/ LOWER BURNSIDE
Doug Fir Lounge
Kir
My Father's Place
Produce Row Cafe
rontoms

IRVINGTON
Secret Society Lounge
Wonder Ballroom

LADD'S ADDITION
Palio Dessert &
  Espresso House

LAURELHURST
Beulahland
Chopsticks Express II
The Goodfoot Pub
  & Lounge
LaurelThirst Public House
Navarre
Staccato Gelato
Wine Down

MULTNOMAH VILLAGE
Lucky Labrador Brewing
  Company

NEAR LLOYD CENTER
Windows Lounge
  Skyroom & Terrace

NORTHEAST
Amnesia Brewing
Biddy McGraw's
Billy Ray's Neighborhood
  Dive
Fresh Pot
Kennedy School
  (McMenamins)
Moloko Plus
Spare Room
Voodoo Doughnut

NORTH PORTLAND
The Alibi
Chopsticks Express III
Pix Patisserie
Ponderosa Lounge at
  Jubitz Truck Stop
Saraveza

NORTHWEST
Anna Bannanas
  Coffee House
The Bitter End Pub
Blue Moon Tavern and
  Grill (McMenamins)
Coffee Time
Crackerjacks Pub
  and Eatery
The Gypsy
Laurelwood Brewing
  Company
Lucky Labrador Brewing
  Company
M Bar
MacTarnahan's Taproom
The Matador
Mission Theater and
  Pub (McMenamins)
The New Old Lompoc
Rams Head
  (McMenamins)
Slabtown
The Tao of Tea
Uptown Billiards Club
Vivace Coffee House
  & Crêperie
World Cup at
  Powell's City of Books

OLD TOWN
Ash Street Saloon
Berbati's Pan
Dante's
Darcelle XV Showplace
Shanghai Tunnel
Stumptown
  Coffee Roasters
Tube
Voodoo Doughnut

PEARL DISTRICT
Bluehour
BridgePort Brewpub
Jimmy Mak's
Rogue Ales Public House
Vino Paradiso
World Cup at Powell's
  City of Books

RIVER DISTRICT
Wilf's Restaurant and Bar

RIVERPLACE
Harborside Restaurant
  & Pilsner Room
Thirst Wine Bar & Bistro

SAINT JOHNS
Anna Bannanas
  Coffee House
St. Johns Theater and
  Pub (McMenamins)

SELLWOOD
Staccato Gelato

SOUTHEAST
Barley Mill Pub
  (McMenamins)
The Egyptian Club
Hopworks Urban
  Brewery
Lucky Labrador Brewing
  Company
Pix Patisserie
Stumptown
  Coffee Roasters
The Victory

SOUTHWEST
Fulton Pub and Brewery
  (McMenamins)

TROUTDALE
Edgefield (McMenamins)

Nightlife by Feature

ALL AGES
Aladdin Theater
All coffeehouses
BridgePort Brewpub
Ground Kontrol
Hopworks Urban
    Brewery
Huber's
Laurelwood Brewing
    Company
Lucky Labrador Brewing
    Company
MacTarnahan's Taproom
Roseland Theater
Satyricon
Wonder Ballroom

BILLIARDS AND OTHER GAMES
Berbati's Pan
Billy Ray's Neighborhood
    Dive
The Bitter End Pub
C Bar
Crackerjacks Pub
    and Eatery
The Egyptian Club
The Goodfoot Pub
    & Lounge
Ground Kontrol
Horse Brass Pub
LaurelThirst Public House
The Matador
Palio Dessert &
    Espresso House
Ponderosa Lounge at
    Jubitz Truck Stop
Pub at the End of
    the Universe
Rialto Poolroom
    Bar & Cafe

Ringler's (McMenamins)
Rogue Ales Public House
Sam's Hollywood Billiards
Shanghai Tunnel
Slabtown
Uptown Billiards Club

BLUES, FOLK, AND ACOUSTIC MUSIC
Aladdin Theater
Ash Street Saloon
Biddy McGraw's
Billy Ray's Neighborhood
    Dive
The Bitter End Pub
LaurelThirst Public House
Produce Row Cafe
Roseland Theater
Spare Room
St. Johns Theater and
    Pub (McMenamins)
The Tugboat Brewery
Wine Down

CABARET
Berbati's Pan
Boxxes/Red Cap Garage
Dante's
Darcelle XV Showplace
Mary's Club

CIGARS
Greater Trumps
    (McMenamins)

COMEDY
Ash Street Saloon
Dante's
Harvey's Comedy Club

COUNTRY
Ponderosa Lounge at
    Jubitz Truck Stop

DANCE FLOORS
Berbati's Pan
Boxxes/Red Cap Garage
Crush
The Crystal Ballroom
The Egyptian Club
Fez Ballroom
The Goodfoot Pub
    & Lounge
Holocene
LaurelThirst Public House
Ponderosa Lounge at
    Jubitz Truck Stop
Ringler's (McMenamins)
Roseland Theater
Spare Room
Wonder Ballroom

DIVE BARS
Billy Ray's Neighborhood
    Dive
Chopsticks Express II/III
Crackerjacks Pub
    and Eatery
The Matador
My Father's Place
Slabtown
Space Room/Brite Spot
Virginia Cafe

EDITORS' CHOICE
Amnesia Brewing
Bluehour
Dots Cafe
Driftwood Room
The Heathman Hotel
Jake's Grill
Jimmy Mak's
LaurelThirst Public House
Lucky Labrador Brewing
    Company

Mary's Club
Moloko Plus
Pix Patisserie
Ringler's
Satyricon
Stumptown Coffee
  Roasters
Townshend's
Voodoo Doughnut
World Cup at Powell's
  City of Books

FAMILY

Anna Bannanas
  Coffee House
Hopworks Urban
  Brewery
LaurelThirst Public House
Laurelwood Brewing
  Company
Townshend's
World Cup at Powell's
  City of Books

GAY/LESBIAN

Boxxes/Red Cap Garage
Crush
Darcelle XV Showplace
The Egyptian Club
Holocene

GOOD VALUE

Aalto Lounge
Crackerjacks Pub
  and Eatery
Harborside Restaurant
  & Pilsner Room
The Matador
Uptown Billiards
Vivace Coffeehouse
  & Creperie
Voodoo Doughnut

**HAPPY HOUR/
LATE-NIGHT GRUB**

The Alibi
Bye and Bye
Cassidy's
Dante's
The Driftwood Room
Harborside Restaurant
  & Pilsner Room
Mary's Club
Moloko Plus
Saucebox
Thirst Wine Bar & Bistro
Tube
Veritable Quandary
Voodoo Doughnut

HIP-HOP

Boxxes/Red Cap Garage
The Crystal Ballroom
East Chinatown Lounge
Fez Ballroom
Holocene
Roseland Theater
Wonder Ballroom

JAZZ

The Goodfoot Pub
  & Lounge
The Heathman Hotel
Jimmy Mak's
The Know Microtheater
  and Bar
Living Room Theaters
Produce Row Cafe
Sapphire Hotel
Saucebox
The Tugboat Brewery
Wilf's Restaurant and Bar

KARAOKE

The Alibi
Boxxes/Red Cap Garage
Chopsticks Express II/III

Dante's
The Egyptian Club
The Gypsy

**MARTINIS AND
SPECIALTY
COCKTAILS**

Aalto Lounge
The Benson Hotel
  Palm Court
Bluehour
Clyde Common
Crush
Doug Fir Lounge
The Driftwood Room
East Chinatown Lounge
820 Lounge at Mint
The Heathman Hotel
Holocene
Jake's Grill
Living Room Theaters
Moloko Plus
rontoms
Sapphire Hotel
Saucebox
Secret Society Lounge
The Victory
Wilf's Restaurant and Bar
Zilla Saké House

**PIANO BAR/
CLASSICAL MUSIC**

The Heathman Hotel
Rimsky-Korsakoffee
  House
Wilf's Restaurant and Bar

POETRY (LIVE)

Coffee Time

**PUBS AND
ALEHOUSES**

Alameda Brewhouse
Amnesia Brewing

Beulahland
Biddy McGraw's
The Bitter End Pub
BridgePort Brewpub
Crackerjacks Pub
and Eatery
The Goodfoot Pub
& Lounge
Goose Hollow Inn
Hopworks Urban
Brewery
Horse Brass Pub
LaurelThirst Public House
Laurelwood Brew-
ing Company
Lucky Labrador Brewing
Company
McMenamins pubs
The New Old Lompoc
Produce Row Cafe
Pub at the End of
the Universe
Rogue Ales Public House
The Tugboat Brewery
Widmer Brewing
and Gasthaus

PUNK
Aladdin Theater
Dante's
East Chinatown Lounge
Satyricon
Slabtown
Wonder Ballroom

REGGAE AND WORLD BEAT
Aladdin Theater
The Crystal Ballroom
Fez Ballroom

Roseland Theater
Wonder Ballroom

RETRO
The Alibi
Bar of the Gods
Beulahland
The Crystal Ballroom
The Driftwood Room
Dots Cafe
The Gypsy
Huber's
Space Room/Brite Spot
Spare Room
Wilf's Restaurant and Bar
Wonder Ballroom

ROCK
Aladdin Theater
Backspace
Berbati's Pan
The Crystal Ballroom
Doug Fir Lounge
Holocene
LaurelThirst Public House
Roseland Theater
Slabtown
Spare Room
St. Johns Theater and
Pub (McMenamins)
White Eagle Rock 'n' Roll
Hotel (McMenamins)
Wonder Ballroom

ROMANTIC
The Benson Hotel
Palm Court
The Driftwood Room
820 Lounge at Mint
The Heathman Hotel

Kir
Noble Rot
Palio Dessert &
Espresso House
Safire Hotel

TECHNO AND ELECTRONICA
Boxxes/Red Cap Garage
The Crystal Ballroom
Fez Ballroom
Holocene
Saucebox
Tube
Wonder Ballroom

VIEW
Harborside Restaurant
& Pilsner Room
Noble Rot
Ringler's Annex
(McMenamins)
Thirst Wine Bar & Bistro
Vino Paradiso
Windows Lounge
Skyroom & Terrace

WINE BARS
Bar Avignon
Kir
M Bar
Navarre
Noble Rot
Thirst Wine Bar & Bistro
Vino Paradiso
Wine Down

NIGHTLIFE

Because Portland's nightlife has so much to offer, you might want to make a plan before going out. The majority of venues and bars are located downtown and in the Pearl District, including the area on Stark Street between SW 9th and 14th avenues, where many of Portland's gay bars are located. The mod hipsters continue to reign over SE Belmont and lower Burnside, and over on SE Hawthorne, a host of clubs and bars cater to a more rootsy, hippie-oriented crowd. The remaining fourth (and fifth) quadrants of the city—Northeast and North Portland—are constantly in flux, with new hot spots opening and dive bars gaining in popularity, especially on Alberta and Mississippi. The city is quite spread out, so if you want to hit more than one event per night, be sure to do a little research first.

Music, Clubs, and Lounges

Aalto Lounge

3356 SE BELMONT ST, BELMONT; 503/235-6041

This supersleek bar neighboring Stumptown Coffee is an urbanite's paradise, with a simple wine list and excellent cocktails in a comforting price range. DJ decks, built right into the bar, cook up tasteful mixes for Portland's famed creative class. Be prepared for a pop quiz flashback to high school biology if you head to the XX/XY-labeled bathrooms. *MC, V; no checks; every day; full bar; map:HH5.* &

Aladdin Theater

3017 SE MILWAUKIE AVE, BROOKLYN; 503/234-9694

The Aladdin began as a venue for vaudeville acts (including Jack Benny), evolved into a family movie theater, and landed a 20-year stint as a notorious porn house (*Deep Throat* played here). Today it features a choice selection of musical acts as diverse as its beginnings. Popular bluegrass, acoustic, rock, R&B, even indie and art-punk bands have filled these old wooden seats. After the show, stop by the adjoining bar (The Lamp) where you just may have the chance to sidle up and throw one back with the evening's performers. *DIS, MC, V; checks OK; open during events only; beer and wine; www.aladdin-theater. com; map:II5.* &

The Alibi

4024 N INTERSTATE AVE, NORTH PORTLAND; 503/287-5335

Lured here by the hypnotic, Route 66–like pageantry of neon that throws a glow over Interstate Avenue, you don't need an alibi to go to the Alibi. It's simply one of Portland's best blasts from the past, an authentic tiki lounge where the servers efficiently deliver big platters of "Macho Nachos." Friendly karaoke hosts lead a wholesome lung-powered and exotic-drink-fueled jamboree, starting at 9pm, seven nights a week. A complimentary midnight buffet makes Saturdays really busy, so if you're itching to bust a move, try the Thursday-night fest. *AE, DIS, MC, V; no checks; every day; full bar; map:FF6.*

Ash Street Saloon

225 SW ASH ST, OLD TOWN; 503/226-0430

This grimy neighborhood bar has musical acts hitting the stage seven nights a week with the occasional dose of stand-up comedy. High-backed booths and an outdoor patio make it a comfortable spot to catch a show or just ogle the many tattooed bike messengers who, in a way, represent the real heart of Portland. Try the famous "Kick Your Ash" burger. *AE, MC, V; no checks; every day; full bar; www.ashstreetsaloon.com; map:J6.* &

The Benson Hotel Palm Court

309 SW BROADWAY, DOWNTOWN; 503/228-2000

It's always fun to have a drink in a nice hotel. You can even pretend you're from some foreign port, in town for the weekend. The classy lounge oozes ambience with its beautiful new glazed windows streaming natural light on the imported Russian walnut trim. Sit back in comfortable chairs and allow your culinary senses to be pampered. *AE, DC, DIS, MC, V; no checks; every day; full bar; www.bensonhotel.com; map:J4.* &

Berbati's Pan

10 SW 3RD AVE, OLD TOWN; 503/226-2122

This popular club was an afterthought to the adjoining Greek restaurant, but it has grown considerably in size and prominence. Featuring a long bar, large dance floor, and separate cafe and game room, the club showcases acts that range from burlesque cabarets to eclectic DJ nights, local bands, and national touring acts. Because the schedule is always full, Berbati's is a favored destination for live-music lovers. *AE, MC, V; no checks; every day; full bar; www. berbati.com; map:J6.* &

Biddy McGraw's

6000 NE GLISAN ST, NORTHEAST; 503/233-1178

If a sweaty, jigging joint fits the bill, Biddy's is your place. You'll swoon to hear half the patrons using a brogue straight from the land o' the green. And, along with the good times, these folks have brought their politics from the old country: the whitewashed walls are decked with posters urging sentiments such as all-party peace talks. You can get Guinness as well as a full spectrum of drafts, hard cider, and whiskeys—of course. Celtic, Irish, and rock musicians ignite the crowd into a toe-to-the-sky frenzy. *MC, V; no checks; every day; full bar; www.biddymcgraws.com; map:HH4.* &

Bluehour

250 NW 13TH AVE, PEARL DISTRICT; 503/226-3394

In the glossy Pearl District, Bluehour offers a place both chill and swank to linger over an original cocktail. This longtime Portland fixture has a delectable bar menu and top-shelf cocktails such as the refreshing Bluehour Gimlet (house-infused lavender gin with loads of fresh lime). Indulge in the artisanal three-cheese flight—presented tableside by a helpful *fromager*. Weekend nights can see a splash more rollick than the rest of the week. *AE, DC, MC, V; no checks; every day; full bar; www.bluehouronline.com; map:L2.* &

Boxxes/Red Cap Garage

330 SW STARK ST, DOWNTOWN; 503/226-4171

The dynamic duo of the Portland queer dance halls, these bumpin' clubs form a giant gay-plex that can accommodate most nights of debauchery. With fierce dancing five nights a week and insane drink specials, there's no telling what can happen. Head to the Boxxes section on Wednesday nights for onstage karaoke. Tuesdays and Thursdays are dollar drink nights. And don't forget Tuesday-night go-go boys. *AE, DIS, MC, V; no checks; Tues–Sun; full bar; www.boxxes.com; www.redcapgarage.com; map:I5.* &

Chopsticks Express II

2651 E BURNSIDE ST, LAURELHURST; 503/234-6171

This divey lounge in the back of a fast-food Chinese restaurant is a popular hub for Portland karaoke fanatics. This place can pack quickly, especially on the weekends, so it's best to go early. Karaoke starts at 8pm on the weekends and 8:30pm all other nights. If you don't want to share the spotlight with so many others, check out Chopsticks III (535 NE Columbia Blvd, North Portland; 503/283-3900; map:HH5), a little off the beaten path but just as divey and fun. *MC, V; no checks; every day; full bar; www.chopstickskaraoke. com; map:HH5.*

Crush

1400 SE MORRISON ST, BUCKMAN; 503/235-8150

Crush started off life as a wine bar but in recent years has morphed into a cocktail lounge that pairs hand-shaken martinis with serious booty-shaking on the weekends. Three rooms marked by carefree glitz offer comfy harbors for dancing and dining. DJs spin nearly every night, taking a break each Wednesday for Crush's unique version of game show bingo—hosted by charming drag queens. Saturday and Sunday brunch offers a chance to explore Crush during the light of day. *MC, V; no checks; Tues–Sun; full bar; www.crushbar.com; map:HH5.* &

The Crystal Ballroom

1332 W BURNSIDE ST, DOWNTOWN; 503/225-0047

The chandelier-bedecked icing on the McMenamin brothers' entertainment cake, this refurbished dance parlor/rock club/whatever is a sensory experience to sink your feet into. The floating dance floor can make you feel slightly seasick during a raucous rock show but light on your feet during a ballroom dance soiree. Note the artistic motifs on the walls, re-creating the room's past incarnations as a soul shack and hippie hangout. The offerings are eclectic:

PORTLAND'S EVOLVING MUSIC CULTURE

Portland is known as a magnet for beer guzzlers and tree huggers, but it's also turning into a major destination for musicians and music lovers—and not just the punk and indie rockers that have historically been identified with the Rose City.

A few decades ago, there were only a handful of music venues catering to rock music in Portland. The most notable, **SATYRICON** (see review in Music, Clubs, and Lounges in this chapter), where Kurt Cobain and Courtney Love purportedly first met, provided a gritty environment for local punk bands such as The Wipers and Poison Idea.

In the early '90s, as the punk scene wilted, grunge music started taking off in Seattle. The resulting Northwest music environment influenced such Portland bands as Sleater-Kinney and Hazel, as well as tragic singer-songwriter Elliott Smith. These musicians were mainstays of small, bygone music outlets like the X-Ray Cafe, La Luna, EJ's, and Meow Meow, and laid the groundwork for a new wave of musicians whose international success has boosted Portland's status as a music haven teeming with creativity and talent.

Sizable festivals such as **PDX POP NOW!** (www.pdxpopnow.com) in late July and **MUSICFEST NORTHWEST** (www.musicfestnw.org) in late September showcase the impressive volume and diversity of Portland musicians. Fans turn out in droves, taking pride in homegrown acts and transplants: The Decemberists, The Thermals, Menomena, Viva Voce, M.Ward, The Shins, Blitzen Trapper, The Shaky Hands, Strategy, Yacht, and Starfucker, among others. While these seminal indie rockers—and corresponding indie record labels such as **KILL ROCK STARS**, **HUSH**, and **AUDIO DREGS**—have come to define the local music scene,

---

indie rock, jam bands, electronica, hip-hop—even plain-old rock. Don't miss '80s night every Friday at Lola's Room (on the second floor), where costumes and bad dancing are encouraged. *AE, DIS, MC, V; no checks; open during events only; full bar; www.danceonair.com; map:K1.* &

Dante's

350 W BURNSIDE ST, OLD TOWN; 503/226-6630

This steamy hangout is dark and red enough to make you assume everyone here is gorgeous. An open oil-drum fire blazes near the windows; a naughty stage flirts through its rich, red-velvet curtains; and a glowing red bar smolders with anticipation of your imminent cocktail. It's the perfect ambience for a mélange of cabaret-style performances, live bands, and such special events as theme parties, go-go girls, and Karaoke from Hell, where you sing with a live band. *MC, V; no checks; every day; full bar; www.danteslive.com; map:K5.* &

Portland also has countless options for different styles of music.

Though the once-thriving strip of jazz clubs in North Portland and the beloved Jazz De Opus are no longer, other venues—**JIMMY MAK'S** (see review in Music, Clubs, and Lounges in this chapter), **CANDLELIGHT CAFÉ & BAR** (2032 SW 5th Ave, Downtown; 503/222-3378), and more recently **THE BLUE MONK** (3341 SE Belmont St, Belmont; www.thebluemonk.com; 503/595-0575)—continue to provide a home for local jazz favorites **DAN BALMER**, **THE MEL BROWN QUARTET**, and others. For true devotees, Portland has an all-jazz/blues radio station, **KMHD 89.1** (www.kmhd.org); a yearly **JAZZ FESTIVAL** (held in February to coincide with Black History Month); and a huge **BLUES FESTIVAL** that takes place on the waterfront each summer.

Enduring emcee **COOL NUTZ** has kept the Portland hip-hop scene vital over the years, while the soulful group **LIFESAVAS** serve as ambassadors of Portland hip-hop worldwide. DJs **KEZ**, **REV. SHINES**, **OHMEGA WATTS**, **DUNDIGGY**, and **MR. MATT NELKIN** run the hip-hop scene in town, routinely packing **THE FIX** (Thursdays at Someday Lounge) and **ROCKBOX** (third Fridays at Holocene; see review in Music, Clubs, and Lounges in this chapter).

With so many artistic people living in Portland, discovering anything from a raucous rock show to an enlightening evening at the symphony is no problem. The easiest way to find what you're looking for is to pick up a local weekly paper—*Willamette Week* and the *Portland Mercury* offer complete listings of all upcoming concerts and club nights. Also check the *Oregonian*'s "A&E" section, the *Tribune*'s "Weekend Life," and Pdxpipeline.com.

—Ava Hegedus

Darcelle XV Showplace

208 NW 3RD AVE, OLD TOWN; 503/222-5338
Portland's only long-running drag house has been purveying glitz since 1967, thanks to the sharp and teasing, blonde-wigged, false-eyelashed Darcelle herself. The Queen Mother of Portland, Ms. Darcelle is also involved in city politics and holds special shows on voting days, along with a cornucopia of ongoing banquets, drag coronations, and New Year's extravaganzas worthy of champagne and feather boas. Dinner reservations are recommended. *AE, DIS, MC, V; no checks; Wed–Sat; full bar; www.darcellexv.com; map:L5*.

Doug Fir Lounge

830 E BURNSIDE ST, INNER SOUTHEAST/LOWER BURNSIDE; 503/231-9663
The reigning champ of Portland's renowned indie-chic, Doug Fir continues to receive considerable national attention not only for the innovative design of

its lounge and belowground venue, but also for the hot musical acts it draws. Like a log cabin dropped on the Sunset Strip, Doug Fir is an elegant, comfy spot to enjoy a cocktail or gourmet diner food. Partnered with the Jupiter Motel (see review in the Lodgings chapter), these trendy twins form a hot spot not to be missed. *AE, DIS, MC, V; no checks; every day; full bar; www. dougfirlounge.com; map:HH5.*

The Driftwood Room

729 SW 15TH AVE, DOWNTOWN; 503/219-2094

Walking into the 1950s-era Driftwood Room is like taking a very comfortable, sophisticated step back in time. The buttery-soft yellow leather bar stools are the perfect place to enjoy an expertly concocted champagne cocktail during one of the happiest happy hours in town. Life just seems better after an Elizabeth Taylor (crème de violette and champagne) and a slice of savory gorgonzola cheesecake. *AE, DIS, MC, V; no checks; every day; full bar; www.hoteldeluxeportland.com; map:I0.* &

East Chinatown Lounge

322 NW EVERETT ST, CHINATOWN; 503/226-1569

East Chinatown Lounge (more commonly known as just "East") is smaller than it looks; it's dark, and if you're not careful, you might run into one of its mirrored walls. The bar's sleek, expensive, modern interior attracts a bevy of upper-crust hipsters and aspiring graphic designers; its selection of DJs spinning great New Wave and hip-hop (always cover-free) attracts everyone else. *AE, MC, V; no checks; Tues–Sat; full bar; www.eastchinatownlounge. com; map:L5.* &

The Egyptian Club

3701 SE DIVISION ST, SOUTHEAST; 503/236-8689

This sapphic social club comes complete with DJ dancing Thursday through Saturday, Texas Hold 'Em every Monday and Wednesday, and free pool all day on Tuesdays. What's more, there's an ever-changing roster of special events (open mic, karaoke, dances), singer-songwriters, and Portland's cutest lesbians. *AE, DIS, MC, V; no checks; every day; full bar; www.eroompdx. com; map:II5.* &

820 Lounge at Mint

820 N RUSSELL ST, ALBINA; 503/284-5518

The lounge adjoining Mint (see review in the Restaurants chapter) has a dark interior that lends a sense of mystery, but the drinks dreamed up by nationally acclaimed mixologist Lucy Brennan are überfresh and inventive, so you feel more like you're on a night train to Paris than hanging out in a cave. *AE, MC, V; no checks; every day; full bar; www.mintand820.com; map:GG6.* &

Fez Ballroom

316 SW 11TH AVE, DOWNTOWN; 503/221-7262

A dark ballroom with a distinctly Middle Eastern ambience (and up three flights of stairs), the Fez is a classy yet laid-back venue with a good variety of music, from live hip-hop to *desi* (South Asian) parties hosted by bhangra DJs playing Punjabi dance music. It's a great place to escape, especially on the last Saturday of every month, when DJ Anjali heats it up with a Bollywood-style dance party. *AE, DIS, MC, V; no checks; open during events only; full bar; www.fezballroom.com; map:J2.* &

The Goodfoot Pub & Lounge

2845 SE STARK ST, LAURELHURST; 503/239-9292

This unpretentious, bilevel Southeast hangout comes equipped with an upstairs haven of pool tables, but downstairs is where it's really at. The basement bar showcases a range of jazz and funk (with tendencies toward the hippie); on Friday nights, shake a tail feather to Soul Stew, a popular weekly soul night that attracts neighborhood denizens and Portland break-dancers alike. *AE, MC, V; no checks; every day; beer and wine; www.thegoodfoot. com; map:HH5.*

Harvey's Comedy Club

436 NW 6TH AVE, CHINATOWN; 503/241-0338

The sole continuous comedy-only club in Portland or any of the surrounding areas, Harvey's has all the intimacy of an auditorium, but the comedy can be first-rate, often including big national names. Purchase a ticket the old-fashioned way, or sign up for their promotional mailing list to score free tickets to shows—there's a two-purchase minimum for the "free" tickets, so you'll have to laugh yourself over to a plate of mozzarella sticks or a thirst-quenching beverage. *MC, V; no checks; open during events only; full bar; www. harveyscomedyclub.com; map:M4.* &

Holocene

1001 SE MORRISON ST, BUCKMAN; 503/239-7639

Holocene is a hip mecca for DJs, dancers, and diners, pairing some of the world's most creative electronic music with a unique, reasonably priced selection of drinks, an intriguing menu, and a gaping concrete dance floor. Electro, house, techno, hip-hop, New Wave—you name it, they spin it. Check the calendar for surprisingly big-name indie bands that keep the place open during off-weekdays. The bimonthly Saturday queer dance parties—Gaycation and Double Down—are some of Holocene's reliably best nights. *AE, DIS, MC, V; no checks; Wed–Sat; full bar; www.holocene.org; map:G9.* &

Jimmy Mak's

221 NW 10TH AVE, PEARL DISTRICT; 503/295-6542

Jimmy Mak's is nationally renowned as a classy, great place to hear jazz, and with good reason. Legendary jazz drummer Mel Brown (who has worked with Marvin Gaye, Stevie Wonder, and The Temptations) plays with his band in this beautiful venue every Tuesday and Wednesday; top regional guitarist Dan Balmer plays Mondays; and a host of cool cats from around the globe fill in the rest. *DIS, MC, V; no checks; Mon–Sat; full bar; www.jimmymaks. com; map:L3.* &

The Know Microtheater and Bar

2026 NE ALBERTA ST, ALBERTA; 503/473-8729
Portland has a long-standing tradition of underground art spaces, basement parties, do-it-yourself venues, and makeshift bike-in theaters. The Know is a continuous venue that truly captures the eclectic feel of Portland's grassroots arts and music scenes. Events range from live jazz to experimental and noise music; local mini film festivals in the adjacent microtheater to online zine-publishing classes and quirky art exhibitions. *DIS, MC, V; no checks; every day; beer and wine; www.theknowbar.com; map:FF5.* &

LaurelThirst Public House

2958 NE GLISAN ST, LAURELHURST; 503/232-1504
Tavern by night, cafe by day, the LaurelThirst always has someone hanging out—either munching on a late breakfast, playing pool with a pitcher of brew, or taking in live local music. A beautiful antique bar and comfy leather booths add to the zero-pretension atmosphere. On the billiards side, you can cram around a small table and catch up on gossip. In the main section, live bands— blues, rock, acoustic—keep the karma flowing and get people dancing. *MC, V; no checks; every day; full bar; www.laurelthirst.com; map:HH5.* &

Living Room Theaters

341 SW STARK ST, DOWNTOWN; 971/222-2010
Taking a note from successful theater-brewpubs in the area, this stylish institution has taken a new direction. Combining the cinephile's lust for independent film with the foodie's desire for great fare, this is the ultimate dining-and-cinema experience. Watch groundbreaking films (Mondays and Tuesdays all shows are just $5) while sampling good food and wine. The lounge offers live jazz every Friday and Saturday. *MC, V; no checks; every day; full bar; www.livingroomtheaters.com; map:J2.*

Mary's Club

129 SW BROADWAY, DOWNTOWN; 503/227-3023
Mary's has been a Portland institution for more than 50 years and is now one of the city's pride and joys. The all-female-run strip club is welcoming to all genders and has a great jukebox. Under control by three generations of jolly matrons, the club is about as idiosyncratic as Portland itself. Mexican food is available until 2am, and there is a measly $2 cover charge on Fridays and Saturdays. *DIS, MC, V; no checks; every day; full bar; www.marysclub. com; map:J3.*

Moloko Plus

3967 N MISSISSIPPI AVE, NORTHEAST; 503/288-6272
The name of this bar references a highly intoxicating and illegal drink from the movie *A Clockwork Orange*. However, since no outside sign designates this hipster hot spot, it's simply known to many as "The White Bar" for the interior's holier-than-thou color scheme. Also reverence-worthy are the 30 different creative liquor infusions, from beet or chamomile vodka to jalapeño-lime tequila. Besides the drinks, the crowd flocks to DJs spinning most nights of the week, a long happy hour, and a heated outdoor patio. *MC, V; no checks; every day; full bar; map:FF6.* &

Ponderosa Lounge at Jubitz Truck Stop

10350 N VANCOUVER WY, NORTH PORTLAND; 503/345-0300, EXT 4459
There's possibly more testosterone pumping through this truck stop, near East Delta Park, than on a battlefield. Live country-western bands play on Friday and Saturday nights, and the dance floor at the Ponderosa Lounge—lined with lit-up tailgates—offers burly drivers, cowboys, and spectators an outlet for their hormones and relief from highway stress. You'll find pool tables and video games, and next door there's a motel and weigh station. *AE, DIS, MC, V; no checks; every day; full bar; www.ponderosalounge.com; map:DD6.*

Roseland Theater

8 NW 6TH AVE, CHINATOWN; 503/224-2038
Once a two-story Apostolic Faith church, Roseland is now a comfortable midsize concert hall for mostly out-of-town acts. It's boozy and noisy with metal, rock, hip-hop, and folk music (some shows are all ages). Whether you dance or not, be prepared to sweat, especially in the balcony, which commands an excellent view of the stage. Roseland also has a full restaurant and bar, with a separate stage downstairs. *Cash only; open during events only; full bar; www.doubletee.com; map:K4.* &

Sapphire Hotel

5008 SE HAWTHORNE ST, HAWTHORNE; 503/232-6333
"Eat, drink, kiss" is the flirty motto for this intimate and fun bar in the shadow of Mount Tabor. Though the name and motifs conjure up a bygone Asian seaport hotel, the only thing this spot doesn't offer is a place to lay your head. Everything else—inventive cocktails, quality wine, and tasty cuisine—is alive and well in this neighborhood hangout. Try a Room Service or a Going Up? while listening to live jazz on Sunday nights, and perhaps you'll set the mood to converse with one of your fellow "travelers." *AE, MC, V; no checks; every day; full bar; www.thesapphirehotel.com; map:HH4.* &

Saucebox

214 SW BROADWAY, DOWNTOWN; 503/241-3393
Saucebox's artfully appointed interior is awash with well-coiffed up-and-comers—and occasional visiting celebrities like Vince Vaughn and Benicio del

Toro—enjoying expensive but perfect cocktails alongside the incredible tapioca dumplings. Dinner may stop at 10, but the late-night menu keeps the beat of DJs who turn up the hot wax, including house, electro, down-tempo, and nu-jazz. Exceptionally attractive staff accept the moony stares of a devoted public as their due. (See also review in the Restaurants chapter.) *AE, MC, V; local checks only; Tues–Sat; full bar; www.saucebox.com; map:J4.*

Satyricon

125 NW 6TH AVE, DOWNTOWN; 503/227-0999

Once the centerpiece of Portland's punk scene, Satyricon gave rise to bands such as Poison Idea and The Wipers. It has hosted bands from all over the Northwest, including Nirvana, and is purported to be where Courtney Love met Kurt Cobain. Since it closed and reopened, this historic venue has been cleaned up and puts on shows for a new generation of metal, hardcore, and punk-rock fans. It now allows all ages and is still the place to see the region's best local and touring hardcore shows. *AE, MC, V; no checks; every day; full bar; www.myspace.com/satyriconpdx; map:K4.*

Secret Society Lounge

116 NE RUSSELL ST, IRVINGTON; 503/493-3600

A nightcap at the Secret Society—located above Toro Bravo (see review in the Restaurants chapter) and next door to the Wonder Ballroom—completes an evening's perfect trilogy of food, music, and the art of the cocktail. The small, pleasantly dark bar is filled with classy individuals, creatively dressed to complement the old-fashioned cocktails they sip, such as the Moscow Mule. The Portland absinthe craze is also taken seriously here, with an extensive selection and beautiful, traditional presentation. *AE, MC, V; no checks; every day; full bar; www.secretsociety.net; map:GG6.*

Slabtown

1033 NW 16TH ST, NORTHWEST; 503/223-0099

Just a freeway-width across I-405 from the Pearl District, this great dive-lounge near the streetcar depot offers regular gigs leaning toward the punk-rock side, as well as the occasional Guitar Hero video-game jam session, open to any who dare play in front of a crowd. Ping-Pong, pool, and pinball are available in the game room. Street-side sliding windows open up to let in the night air and out the bar funk. *MC, V; no checks; every day; full bar; map:O1.* &

Spare Room

4830 NE 42ND AVE, NORTHEAST; 503/287-5800

This twinkle-lit, mirror-walled bar is packed with regulars (septuagenarians and hipsters alike) tearing it up to swing, rock, and blues on the dance floor of this former bowling alley. Charming audiences a couple of times a month, Teri and Larry—an adorable husband-and-wife cover band—make cute-cheesy "married couple" jokes and take pop/rock requests. If you need a breather, you can take a load off at one of the couches in the back or refuel in the dining room. *AE, MC, V; no checks; every day; full bar; map:FF4.* &

Tube

18 NW 3RD AVE, OLD TOWN; 503/241-8823
The convex walls make this place quite literally a tube, so this small bar can get crowded with its limited space, but it's worth it for the turntable masters who tear up the decks. With one of the longest happy hours in the city, there is plenty of time to try a tasty vegan treat, like the (faux) ham-and-cheese on an English muffin. There is likely to be a plethora of friendly mustaches behind the bar and some psychedelic-rabbit artwork to get you geared up to dance. *MC, V; no checks; every day; full bar; map:K5.*

Wilf's Restaurant and Bar

800 NW 6TH AVE (UNION STATION), RIVER DISTRICT; 503/223-0070
This piano bar in the train station has certainly rolled with the times but still retains its old-fashioned nightclub feel. Sink deep into an insanely high-backed red-velvet chair and enjoy some of Portland's best—and most intimate—jazz acts every Wednesday through Saturday. The bar makes an excellent martini, served in its own beaker and nested in a bowl of ice, and the restaurant offers delicious, sophisticated fare. *AE, MC, V; no checks; Mon–Sat; full bar; www. wilfsrestaurant.com; map:N4.* &

Wonder Ballroom

123 NE RUSSELL ST, IRVINGTON; 503/284-8686
A perfect eastside counterpart to the Crystal Ballroom, this cavernous venue built in 1914 for the Ancient Order of Hibernians was refurbished in 2004. It's now a registered historical landmark and a great place to catch a show. Situate yourself by the balcony bar and enjoy top local groups and interesting acts from around the world. The venue's Under Wonder Lounge offers cheap (nothing over $10!) and cheerful fare. *Cash only (ballroom), MC, V (lounge); no checks; open during events only; full bar; www.wonderballroom. com; map:GG6.*

Bars, Pubs, and Taverns

Bar of the Gods

4801 SE HAWTHORNE BLVD, HAWTHORNE; 503/232-2037
From its name, you might expect an exalted temple of insobriety, but instead you'll find a small, dark, very personable, well-populated hole-in-the-wall. Nods to its sobriquet are given in various depictions of the Bacchae, in the grapevine-wrapped beams, and in the regular mixing of an eclectic crowd that spans Portland's social strata. *MC, V; no checks; every day; full bar; map:HH4.* &

Beulahland

118 NE 28TH AVE, LAURELHURST; 503/235-2794

A museum-quality assortment of quirky old restaurant and bar fixtures and vintage advertising paraphernalia has been hauled out of retirement and placed into service at Beulahland, creating an atmosphere rich in Mayberry-esque character. In keeping with the Southern-fried atmosphere, it tends to get steamy rather quickly in here. But respite from the heat can be taken on the charming back patio. *AE, MC, V; no checks; every day; full bar; www. beulahlandpdx.com; map:HH5.* &

Billy Ray's Neighborhood Dive

2216 NE MARTIN LUTHER KING JR BLVD, NORTHEAST; 503/287-7254

Housed in a rickety A-frame that looks like a barn fallen from the sky, Billy Ray's is most definitely a dive. But it's friendly and charming, and miniature booths-for-two provide the perfect spot for a cheap date. An outdoor Ping-Pong table, six pinball machines, and a pleasant patio keep your thirst up for those 22-ounce mugs. *Cash only; every day; full bar; map:GG6.* &

The Bitter End Pub

1981 W BURNSIDE ST, NORTHWEST; 971/222-2000

The busy lanes of West Burnside don't offer much in the way of neighborhood pubs; luckily, the Bitter End comes to the rescue. Of course, you don't have to live in the neighborhood to enjoy the 21 beers on draft or the laid-back banter of the friendly bartenders. If you're feeling competitive, stop by on Tuesdays for a free Trivia Night, scope out the foosball table, or root on the Portland Timbers. *AE, DIS, MC, V; no checks; every day; full bar; www. thebitterendpub.com; map:HH7.* &

Bye and Bye

1011 NE ALBERTA ST, ALBERTA, 503/281-0537

What may seem at first glance to be a hipster haven actually draws a more eclectic crowd—even the wee ones are allowed till the clock strikes eight. The Bye and Bye anchors the western end of the Alberta Arts district and serves Southern-inspired food all night long. Owner-operated by six friends, it's likely one of them will be the bartender mixing up Rebel Yell Bourbon with spicy Blenheim, a hard-to-find South Carolina ginger ale. For the sweeter-toothed, try their namesake drink, which fills up a mason jar and transports easily to the sunny patio. *MC, V; no checks; every day; full bar; map:FF6.* &

Cassidy's

1331 SW WASHINGTON ST, DOWNTOWN; 503/223-0054

Cassidy's dim, circa-1900 environs are conducive to heavy thoughts and heavier conversation. In this night-owl place, you can knock 'em back until 2:30am in the company of personable staff and off-duty barkeeps from surrounding establishments. Keep an eye on the windows, as the entertaining antics of Cassidy's colorful neighbors often transpire within full view of the bar. For an affordable late-night meal—perhaps a grilled romaine salad or the chicken-fried pork belly—it doesn't get much better than this. *AE, DIS, MC, V; no checks; every day; full bar; www.cassidysrestaurant.com; map:J1.* �&

Clyde Common

1014 SW STARK ST, DOWNTOWN; 503/228-3333
Perhaps the fact that all of Clyde's employees are listed on the menu—an unprecedented symbol of respect—gives them that extra incentive to keep a sweet smile while wriggling their way through the late-night crowd. The airy open kitchen and family-style seating invite a loud, happy dinner-party-like atmosphere. Join the soiree with an old-school classic cocktail and the best burger in town. After checking out of Clyde, slip next door and capture the spirit of the evening at the Ace's black-and-white-photo booth. (See also review in the Restaurants chapter.) *AE, DIS, MC, V; no checks; every day; full bar; www.clydecommon.com; map:J2.* �&

Crackerjacks Pub and Eatery

2788 NW THURMAN ST, NORTHWEST; 503/222-9069
CJ's, as some call it, is the perfect place to stop for a few beers and a burger or pizza after a long hike or ride through Forest Park. The neighborhood dive has a superfriendly, cute staff who can shoot a mean game of pool and always coax you into just one more pint. They offer micros on tap or by the bottle and some stiff mixed drinks. Outdoor seating and a comfortable indoor space make just about everyone feel at home. *AE, DIS, MC, V; no checks; Mon–Sat; full bar; map:GG7.*

Dots Cafe

2521 SE CLINTON ST, CLINTON; 503/235-0203
Manhandling the black-velvet wallpaper at Dots may be an acquired taste, but the kitschy, dark digs and creative, affordable offerings are universally appreciated. Vegans, vegetarians, and carnivores coexist harmoniously, and microbrews and PBR flow readily on tap. On the menu the common language is grease—the fries with spicy tofu sauce are always a hit. Enjoy gazing at a healthy cross section of Portland hipsters. (See also review in the Restaurants chapter.) *No credit cards; checks OK; every day; full bar; map:II5.* �&

Goose Hollow Inn

1927 SW JEFFERSON ST, GOOSE HOLLOW; 503/228-7010
For decades, the Goose was a hotbed of political debate and discussion. Not surprisingly, it remains a social institution, owned by former Portland mayor J. E. "Bud" Clark, the JFK of city politics. Join the hundreds who came before you and carve your initials into a dark wooden booth. The thick Reuben sandwiches have made this place as much a classic as the proudly displayed "Expose Yourself to Art" poster, featuring Clark flashing one of Portland's street sculptures. *AE, DIS, MC, V; checks OK; every day; beer and wine; www. goosehollowinn.com; map:HH7.* �&

Ground Kontrol

511 NW COUCH ST, CHINATOWN; 503/796-9364

Yet another time machine in Portland, this arcade and bar offers the best of
'80s and '90s arcade games and a host of pinball machines upstairs. It's the
perfect spot to indulge your inner geek or just take a break from clubbing one
night. From the Arkanoid to Ms. Pac-Man and Galaxians, all the machines
are in great working order. After 7pm, the time machine gets woozy and
serves up 12 different bottled beers. *MC, V; no checks; every day; beer and
wine; www.groundkontrol.com; map:K5.*

The Gypsy

625 NW 21ST AVE, NORTHWEST; 503/796-1859

The Gypsy ought to hand out vintage bathing trunks with every order, because
you can practically swim in their gigantic, yummy drinks. The excellent
collection of pinball art, Sputnik-style space-age fixtures, and extra-comfy
booths are more slick than kitsch for that retro-NASA vibe, but without all
of the mildew. Thursday through Saturday there's karaoke at 9pm. *AE, DIS,
MC, V; no checks; every day; full bar; www.cegportland.com/venues_gypsy.
html; map:HH7.* ⅃

Harborside Pilsner Room

0309 SW MONTGOMERY ST, RIVERPLACE; 503/220-1865

The lounge at McCormick & Schmick's RiverPlace restaurant (see review in
the Restaurants chapter) is perhaps the best waterfront drinking-with-a-view
spot in Portland. The crowd tends toward yuppie elders in business casual,
but the beer selection is large—Full Sail is brewed right next door—and you
can get a decent mixed drink as well. Park yourself near one of the floor-to-
ceiling windows and look out onto the esplanade and the Willamette beyond.
From 3 to 6pm and 9pm to closing, killer happy-hour specials are about $3
a plate with a $3-minimum drink. *AE, DC, DIS, MC, V; no checks; every day;
full bar; www.mccormickandschmicks.com; map:C5.* ⅃

The Heathman Hotel

1001 SW BROADWAY, DOWNTOWN; 503/241-4100

The bar in the Heathman is one of Portland's swankiest. There's the cool
ambience of the Marble Bar, where symphony crowds rendezvous around
the grand piano after a performance and executives convene for lunch. The
high-ceilinged Mezzanine and Tea Court is as formal as a Tudor drawing
room, with a fire blazing in the hearth. The Tea Court serves tea and drinks
in the afternoons and has jazz every Wednesday through Saturday, 7pm to
midnight. During the holiday season reservations can be made for a traditional English tea service in the Tea Court. For a delicious light meal, both
the Marble Bar and the Tea Court offer a gourmet menu from the bar. (See
also review in the Restaurants chapter.) *AE, DC, DIS, MC, V; no checks; every
day; full bar; www.heathmanhotel.com; map:G2.* ⅃

Horse Brass Pub

4534 SE BELMONT ST, BELMONT; 503/232-2202
Truly a slice of merrie olde England, the Horse Brass is a magnet for British expats and Portland Anglophiles alike. It's also a favorite of beer fanatics, with more than 50 microbrews, imports, and cask-conditioned ales. The convivial staff will guide you to the perfect pint or toward the extensive selection of Scotch and other whiskeys. Enjoy your brew over a hot game of darts on one of the four highly competitive boards. One of the best fish-and-chips in town, along with other English pub fare, is served well into the evening. *AE, DIS, MC, V; no checks; every day; full bar; www.horsebrass.com; map:HH4.* &

Huber's

411 SW 3RD AVE, DOWNTOWN; 503/228-5686
Said to be Portland's oldest extant bar (it opened in 1879), Huber's is a fabulous rendezvous spot for famous, flaming Spanish coffees and turkey sandwiches—two great tastes that actually go well together. Its Gothic architecture and old-world panache add to the flair of the tableside service. Although the menu has more bird dishes than a post-Thanksgiving weekend, it's the passing sidewalk show that lures regulars and tourists alike. (See also review in the Restaurants chapter.) *AE, DC, DIS, MC, V; no checks; every day; full bar; www.hubers.com; map:I5.* &

Jake's Grill

611 SW 10TH AVE (GOVERNOR HOTEL), DOWNTOWN; 503/241-2100
Career dress dominates at the Grill, located in the exquisitely refurbished Governor Hotel. But all walks of Portland life gravitate here after work to see the original 1909 mosaic-tiled floor, slow-turning fans, gold-framed mirrors, and big-game heads staring down at the plates of onion rings on the bar. Jake's Grill serves excellent classic cocktails in addition to a great selection of beer and wine. The Grill's parent establishment, Jake's Famous Crawfish (401 SW 12th Ave, Downtown; 503/226-1419; map: J2), is much the same, but with a little less elbow room. (See reviews in the Restaurants chapter.) *AE, DC, DIS, JCB, MC, V; no checks; every day; full bar; map:I2.*

The Matador

1967 W BURNSIDE ST, NORTHWEST; 503/222-5822
Every town worth its salt has at least one perfect dive bar, and Portland is no exception. The Matador has all the essentials: an old jukebox loaded with esoteric classics, cheap drinks that'll put hair on your chest, a couple of well-used pool tables, lots of booths, and plenty of seedy patrons to keep the adrenaline flowing. *MC, V; no checks; every day; full bar; www.thematadorbar. com; map:HH7.* &

My Father's Place

523 SE GRAND AVE, INNER SOUTHEAST; 503/235-5494

Almost as rowdy for brunch as it is at night, this eastside institution fills up fast with tattooed regulars and future punk-rock stars. Even a brief glimpse at the dusty relics that line the walls and ceiling shows just how much this place has remained the same over the years. The boozy coziness lends itself to booth-hopping and strange meetings. A mammoth menu of greasy-spoon fare will banish any hangover. *MC, V; no checks; every day; full bar; map:HH5.*

Produce Row Cafe

204 SE OAK ST, INNER SOUTHEAST; 503/232-8355

Hunker down at a rough-hewn table on the Produce Row patio and contemplate a selection of 25 bottled beers, 21 drafts, and fresh cider. Much loved since it opened in the early '70s, the Row is a friendly spot to mix with a mélange of Portlanders as freight trains whistle past the gritty warehouses. Monday nights feature jazz. In summer, the back deck is filled with imbibers enjoying an open sky framed by the neighborhood's industrial walls. *AE, MC, V; no checks; Mon–Sat; full bar; www.producerowcafe.com; map:I9.* &

Pub at the End of the Universe

4107 SE 28TH AVE, BROOKLYN; 503/235-0969

Reed students frequent this hard-to-find pub and yuk it up with locals, shooting pool, avoiding being bull's-eyed by the continuous dart games going down, and drinkin' 'em down in this lounge-away-from-home. At least one of the 23 microbrews on tap should loosen you up for the weekly (Monday) open mic night. *MC, V; no checks; every day; beer and wine; map:II5.* &

Rialto Poolroom Bar & Cafe

529 SW 4TH AVE, DOWNTOWN; 503/228-7605

A hustler's paradise, this pool hall also boasts video poker, a great jukebox (essential to any shark's game), and a basement wonderland of off-track betting. Fifteen pool tables usually ensure a weekday game, but big booths abound if you've gotta wait your turn. Not only are the drinks generous and reasonably priced, but also the fries are to die for. *AE, MC, V; no checks; every day; full bar; www.rialtopoolroom.com; map:I5.* &

rontoms

600 E BURNSIDE ST, INNER SOUTHEAST; 503/236-4536

This expansive space on E Burnside is so modern there's not even a sign out front, but you'll know you've arrived when you see sunken conversation pits, a wood-burning stove, and minimalist decor. Fondue pots are a kitchen favorite, along with delicious stuffed cremini mushrooms. You may be over your Vespa-driving, angst-waxing, Buddy-Holly-glasses-wearing era, but don't let that stop you from drinking a dry martini in an Eames-chair style. *MC, V; no checks; every day; full bar; www.rontoms.net; map:HH5.* &

Sam's Hollywood Billiards

1845 NE 41ST AVE, HOLLYWOOD; 503/282-8266

A mural on an outside wall—of men immersed in a billiards game—tips off
visitors that pool sharks may lurk within. But it's not just Minnesota Fats types
who find joy here. All sorts gather at Sam's on weekends to test their hand-eye
coordination on 10 regulation-size (plus a few snooker) tables. The first Sunday of every month features a tournament that heats up the action. *DIS, MC,
V; no checks; every day; full bar; www.samsbilliards.com; map:GG4.*

Saraveza

1004 N KILLINGSWORTH ST, NORTH PORTLAND; 503/206-4252

Everyone is welcome at this gem owned by a Wisconsin native; however,
noncheeseheads who want to participate in the rowdy Wisconsin trivia nights
better do some preparation. More than 200 American and Belgian craft beers
are available, along with an eclectic menu that includes house-made soups,
rotating pastries, and pickled deviled eggs. The spacious red leather booths
are bottle-cap-bedecked and perfect for enjoying the company of friends—or
Packers, Brewers, and Blazers games. Saraveza also sells bottles to go at a 20
percent discount. *AE, MC, V; no checks; Wed–Mon; beer and wine; www.
saraveza.com; map:FF6.* &

Shanghai Tunnel

211 SW ANKENY ST, OLD TOWN; 503/220-4001

Portland sits atop a maze of tunnels just below its blacktop, leftovers from the
days when "Puddletown" was a port of call for sailors and smugglers. Most
of the passageways were bricked up long ago—a defense, perhaps, against the
ghosts rumored to reside there. But at this subterranean hipster oasis, you can
enjoy a PBR or Spanish coffee, a game of pool, or a yummy bowl of noodles
while you're waiting for your "spirited" captain to reassign you. *AE, MC, V;
no checks; every day; full bar; www.shanghaitunnel.com; map:J6.* &

Space Room/Brite Spot

4800 SE HAWTHORNE BLVD, HAWTHORNE; 503/235-8303

Divey, tacky, and oh-so-'80s—so much so that even *Wonder Years* cherub
Fred Savage has been sighted here—the Space Room's Saturn lamps and
glowing murals of Portland (downtown on the south wall, Mount Tabor on
the north) beckon Southeast hipsters and old-school regulars alike. Watch
out for the inexpensive yet dramatically strong cocktails: a lone mai tai could
blast you to Neptune. *MC, V; no checks; every day; full bar; map:HH4.* &

Uptown Billiards Club

120 NW 23RD AVE, NORTHWEST; 503/226-6909

Uptown Billiards is a find for pool aficionados who want to quench their
appetites with more than greasy fries or burgers. The club's refreshingly
original happy hour is one of the best in town—don't miss the five-course,
seasonally focused tasting menu for an incredible $10 (make it $20 to add

wine pairings). With 10 immaculate replicas of French-style billiards tables, exposed brick walls, and a liberal supply of pool stools, this posh hall is a great place to shoot some serious stick. *AE, MC, V; no checks; Tues–Sat; full bar; www.uptownbilliards.com; map:HH7.*

Veritable Quandary

1220 SW 1ST AVE, DOWNTOWN; 503/227-7342

The narrow, galleylike shape of this exposed-brick and dark-wood bar encourages body contact. By day, you rub up against corporate types and politicos who come for the efficient business lunches. After dark, a dressy crowd moves in and transforms the VQ into a sultry late-night spot with outdoor seating that invites you to kiss your date under the moonlight. (See also review in the Restaurants chapter.) *AE, DC, DIS, MC, V; no checks; every day; full bar; www.vqpdx.com; map:F4.* &

The Victory

3652 SE DIVISION ST, SOUTHEAST; 503/236-8755

This low-key and unpretentious bar, across from the Egyptian Club, is for winners. You may feel initially daunted by the extensive beer, wine, and specialty cocktail selections—but rest assured, any path you follow will lead to a fabulous destination. Special touches, like the house-made cinnamon bitters in the New-Fashioned cocktail, add that little something extra. Celebrate your beverage choice with the criminally cheesy and delicious baked spaetzle. *MC, V; no checks; every day; full bar; www.thevictorybar.com; map:HH5.*

Virginia Cafe

820 SW 10TH AVE, DOWNTOWN; 503/227-0033

This mainstay twice survived fire and flood—but never famine, as the bar food is hearty and moderately priced. The cafe moved from its home of 93 years on Park Avenue to its current location in early 2008, but it brought its history and regular patrons with it. Classic photos of Portland adorn the walls, and all sorts of urbanites stop in for a drink before catching a film or a show nearby. *MC, V; no checks; every day; full bar; map:I3.* &

Windows Lounge Skyroom & Terrace

1021 NE GRAND AVE (RED LION), NEAR LLOYD CENTER; 503/235-2100

With all of Portland's glamorous hotel bars, it seems unlikely that one of the best is in a Red Lion. Yet nesting at the very top of the chain hotel near the Convention Center sits Windows Skyroom. Its vantage point, from just across the river, affords the best view of downtown in the whole city. Drinks are expensive at hotel prices, but the excellent vista—from an outdoor patio terrace—is worth the extra expense. *AE, DIS, MC, V; no checks; every day; full bar; map:GG6.* &

Zilla Saké House

1806 NE ALBERTA ST, ALBERTA; 503/288-8372
Marked with a string of red paper lanterns outside, Zilla Saké House is a sophisticated celebration of the Japanese elixir. Offering moderately priced flights of sake and a host of accompanying delicious plates and fresh sushi, the unpretentious but enthusiastic staff give patient advice on their massive selection. Beautiful, locally made decor adds to the neighborhood charm. *MC, V; checks OK; every day; full bar; www.zillasakehouse.com; map:FF5.*

Brewpubs

Alameda Brewhouse

4765 NE FREMONT ST, BEAUMONT VILLAGE; 503/460-9025
This modern brewpub boasts huge fiberglass partitions, lofty ceilings, and a long, sinuous bar to complement its tasty selection of handcrafted ales—made distinct with ingredients such as sage, juniper, and Willamette Valley fruit. Above-average pub fare includes such classics as fish-and-chips and burgers with big leafy salads; it also ventures into less-standard territory, with tahini-soy tiger prawns, salmon gyros, and whiskey barbecue baby-back ribs, augmenting the Alameda's one-of-a-kind feel. *AE, DIS, MC, V; no checks; every day; full bar; www.alamedabrewhouse.com; map:FF4.* &

Amnesia Brewing

832 N BEECH ST, NORTHEAST; 503/281-7708
The brewmasters at Amnesia recognize their audience—successfully entering distinct, mature creations into an astute marketplace. A converted metal shed displays a rotating selection of local artists; the young, laid-back staff aims to please the crowd of neighborhood yupsters; and the barbecued sausages and burgers are a nice complement to one of the best house-made IPAs in the city. The big outdoor patio is where the action is, and it's both dog- and people-friendly. Expect to share a table with your fellow imbibers. *MC, V; no checks; every day; beer and wine; map:FF5.* &

BridgePort Brewpub

1313 NW MARSHALL ST, PEARL DISTRICT; 503/241-3612
The Ponzi family's vision of producing beer as good and as complex as their Oregon wines was realized in 1984 with the opening of this self-contained brewery and pizza pub. After several expansions and a change in ownership, this former cordage factory (with gargantuan wooden rafters) remains a favorite nightspot for 20-ounce pints of thick, creamy Black Strap Stout or floral India Pale Ale. *AE, MC, V; no checks; every day; full bar; www. bridgeportbrew.com; map:O1.* &

Hopworks Urban Brewery

2944 SE POWELL BLVD, SOUTHEAST; 503/232-4677

This eco-brewpub is perhaps the most quintessentially "Portland" of all the numerous local breweries. The recycled and bike-friendly motif is ubiquitous without being obtrusive: old bike rims dangle the lights down to the tables, and a portion of the leftover barley malt is used to make the (excellent) pizza crusts. The bar is a great place to pop in after work for a stellar organic IPA. Lots of large booths cater to the child-oriented crowd as well. *AE, MC, V; no checks; every day; beer and wine; www.hopworksbeer.com; map:HH5.* &

Laurelwood Brewing Company

1728 NE 40TH AVE, HOLLYWOOD; 503/282-0622
5115 NE SANDY BLVD, HOLLYWOOD; 503/282-0622
2327 NW KEARNEY ST, NORTHWEST; 503/228-5553

Bright neighborhood pubs with delicious organic beer, these are places where brewskis and kidskis mix harmoniously—on NE 40th, in fact, children run wild in an adjoining play area. It is friendly to moms and pops looking to relax in adult ambience without having to leave the kids behind. And the food meets the challenge: the rosemary-porter steak salad and generous hummus plate complement a long list of burgers and other sandwiches. *AE, DIS, MC, V; no checks; every day; full bar; www.laurelwoodbrewpub.com; map:GG4; map:GG7.* &

Lucky Labrador Brewing Company

915 SE HAWTHORNE BLVD, SOUTHEAST; 503/236-3555
7675 SW CAPITOL HWY, MULTNOMAH VILLAGE; 503/244-2537
1945 NW QUIMBY ST, NORTHWEST; 503/517-4352

Opened by a band of BridgePort defectors, the eastside hangout has an easy-going atmosphere; flavorful, British-inspired brews; and top-notch pizza. A vast covered patio, with nearly three dozen picnic tables, welcomes your favorite canine. Several brews are named after dogs—Black Lab Stout, Dog Day India Pale Ale, Top Dog Extra Special Ale—and if you're the owner of a Lab, you can bring a photo for wall-hanging. The Multnomah Village location occupies a vintage Masonic meeting house, and the airy Northwest spot has indoor bike parking. *MC, V; no checks; every day; beer and wine; www.luckylab.com; map:HH6; map:JJ7; map:GG7.* &

MacTarnahan's Taproom

2730 NW 31ST AVE, NORTHWEST; 503/228-5269

Founded in 1986, Portland Brewing has survived financial turmoil and a glutted, cutthroat microbrew market. After selling its Pearl District pub, it tightened its belt and refocused on what it does best: making affable specialty beers and running a convivial in-house restaurant. The flagship MacTarnahan's Amber Ale is its Scottish beacon of light, while seasonal brews, such as a German-style Oktoberfest, are equally robust and drink-able. The Taproom is highlighted by two large copper kettles and a menu that features garlic rosemary fries with beer ketchup and grilled wild salmon with citrus-ginger butter. *AE, MC, V; no checks; every day; beer and wine; www.macsbeer.com; map:GG8.* &

McMenamins

MULTIPLE LOCATIONS; 503/669-8610

Like the old Roman Empire, the McMenamins' pub chain (spawned in 1983 when Mike and Brian McMenamin opened the Barley Mill Pub) continues to expand into all corners of the Northwest: north to Seattle, south to Roseburg, and east to Bend. Its center is the **CRYSTAL BALLROOM** (see Music, Clubs, and Lounges in this chapter), a renovated entertainment venue glowing with so much history that the founders commissioned an entire book to be written about it. Beneath the ballroom sits **RINGLER'S** (1332 W Burnside St, Downtown; 503/225-0627; full bar; map:K1), a youthful hot spot to shoot pool and practice pickup lines. Perhaps the hippest of the pubs is **RINGLER'S ANNEX** (1223 SW Stark St, Downtown; 503/525-0520; full bar; map:J2), an old radio station wedged into a pie-cut corner and redesigned into a three-level den of revelry. The dank basement bar is moody and intriguing, decorated like a French Resistance hideout, while the top seating area offers an interesting spot for people-watching at the corner of Stark Street and Burnside Street.

From this epicenter, all roads lead out to other McMenamins. While each pub has its own quirky traits, all maintain a few sacred characteristics—namely, great beer and wine (produced at the McMenamins' local brewery and winery, of course), crispy fries and juicy burgers, and an unobtrusive hippie-meets-yuppie ambience.

At the **MISSION THEATER AND PUB** (1624 NW Glisan St, Northwest; 503/223-4527; beer and wine; map:M1), where McMenamins once had its head offices, you can sink into a comfy couch and sip on a trademark intoxicant while enjoying a second-run film—or a Blazers game on a screen of movie-epic proportions. Similarly, the **BAGDAD THEATER AND PUB** (3702 SE Hawthorne Blvd, Hawthorne; 503/236-9234; full bar; map:HH5) offers cheap films in a cavernous (and haunted!) big-screen environment reminiscent of cinema's halcyon days. Neighborhood residents gather at outdoor tables at the adjacent pub to gawk at passing tourists. The McMenamins' signature mosaic design and recurrent court jester theme mark both the Mission and Bagdad theaters. Around the corner from the Bagdad lies **GREATER TRUMPS** (1520 SE 37th Ave, Hawthorne; 503/235-4530; full bar; map:HH5), a smoky yet alluring cigar-and-whiskey room. **ST. JOHNS THEATER AND PUB** (8203 N Ivanhoe St, Saint Johns; 503/283-8520; full bar; map:EE9) has a nice pub feel and a beautiful historic dome in which to catch second-run films and selected sporting events on a big screen.

Less cinematic and more pragmatic is the **FULTON PUB AND BREWERY** (0618 SW Nebraska St, Southwest; 503/246-9530; full bar; map:II6), a compact eatery south of downtown with a functional and friendly flower-trimmed beer garden out back. The **BLUE MOON TAVERN AND GRILL** (432 NW 21st

PORTLAND MICRODISTILLERIES: A SPIRITED BUNCH

In a part of the country already well known for its sophisticated reincarnations of coffee, wine, and beer, the explosion of the craft spirit scene completes the fourth cornerstone of locally produced beverage perfection. The newly formed **OREGON DISTILLERS GUILD** is the first artisan distillers guild in the nation, and its very existence confirms the huge impact that regional distilleries are making. No other city can boast as many microdistilleries as Portland, but riding on the buzz of sheer quantity alone would be quite contrary to the heart of the matter. It's quality that counts when pure Pacific Northwest flavor and creative experimentation are the rules of the game.

The new wave of craft distillers is cresting in a little pocket of industrial SE Portland known casually as **DISTILLERY ROW** (around SE 7th Ave and Hawthorne Blvd). Welcome yourself to the neighborhood with a visit to **HOUSE SPIRITS** (2025 SE 7th Ave; 503/235-3174; www.housespirits.com), where founders Christian Krogstad and Lee Medoff have already successfully given life to Aviation Gin, Medoyeff Vodka, and Krogstad Aquavit. House Spirits has a delightful apothecary-style tasting boutique where you can sample and purchase the aforementioned and more.

Back before there was House Spirits (or other distillery row denizens: **INTEGRITY**, **ARTISAN**, and **NEW DEAL**) there was **CLEAR CREEK DISTILLERY** (2389 NW Wilson St, Northwest; 503/248-9470; www.clearcreekdistillery.com)—the first artisan distillery in the Pacific Northwest. Twenty-five years later, owner

Ave, Northwest; 503/223-3184; full bar; map:HH7) and the **BARLEY MILL PUB** (1629 SE Hawthorne Blvd, Southeast; 503/231-1492; full bar; map: HH5) are casual lunch and dinner neighborhood joints with sidewalk seating. The **MARKET STREET PUB** (1526 SW 10th St, Downtown; 503/497-0160; full bar; map:F1) caters to urbanites and Portland State students alike. Equally upscale is **RAMS HEAD** (2282 NW Hoyt St, Northwest; 503/221-0098; full bar; map:GG7), fronting bustling NW 23rd Avenue.

McMenamins operates three other notable historic properties in Greater Portland. The **WHITE EAGLE ROCK 'N' ROLL HOTEL** (836 N Russell St, Albina; 503/282-6810; full bar; map:GG6), a circa-1905 former brothel and opium den in the North Portland industrial district, has live bands seven nights a week and European-style sleeping rooms on the second floor. **THE KENNEDY SCHOOL** (see also review in the Lodgings chapter; 5736 NE 33rd Ave, Northeast; 503/249-3983; full bar; map:FF5) is a really pleasing pub, performance space, movie theater, outdoor soaking pool, and bed-and-breakfast-style inn housed in a charming old elementary school that the

Stephen McCarthy and Clear Creek are still going strong, as one of the world's most respected producers of high-quality eau-de-vie, grappa, fruit liqueur, and small-batch whiskey. Clear Creek's value is directly related to the impressive amounts of pure Hood River Valley fruit that it uses—30 pounds of pears produce just one bottle of McCarthy's famous pear brandy. Tours are available on Saturdays, and the tasting room (open six days a week) showcases such unlikely creations as Douglas Fir buds in drinkable form. (See also review in the Shopping chapter.)

After a nearly 100-year absence, the "green fairy," absinthe, is the notable newcomer on the shelves of many restaurants and bars around town. **INTEGRITY SPIRITS** (909 SE Yamhill St, Southeast; 503/729-9794; www.integrityspirits.com) produces one of Portland's first offerings, the spot-on Trillium Absinthe Supérieure. If you're in the distillery district, a perfect bar pit stop for absinthe and more would be the brand-new, spirit-centric **BEAKER AND FLASK** (727 SE Washington St, Inner Southeast; 503/235-8180; www.beakerandflask.com).

In the same vein as farm-to-table, the distillery-to-goblet mind-set is captivating throngs of faithful followers. The drink lists and specialty cocktail menus at many of Portland's most visit-worthy restaurants (**CLYDE COMMON** or **TEN 01**, for example) highlight a revival of the classic cocktail (with a local twist), and spotlight the intersection between spirits and cuisine.

Be sure to check the Web sites of all the distilleries to keep up on expanded tours and tasting rooms, as well as special events and new concoctions.

—Mollie Firestone

brothers rescued from bulldozers. **EDGEFIELD** (see also review in the Lodgings chapter; 2126 SW Halsey St, Troutdale; 503/669-8610; full bar) is a rambling former poor farm located at the gateway to the Columbia Gorge. It combines multiple pubs and restaurants with a working vineyard and winery, a distillery, a live stage, a movie theater, and an inn. *AE, DIS, MC, V; no checks; every day; www.mcmenamins.com.*

The New Old Lompoc
1616 NW 23RD AVE, NORTHWEST; 503/225-1855
Taking its name from a W. C. Fields film, this small brewpub sits in a ramshackle little house that proudly sags at the end of 23rd Avenue. It's a great place to pound some LSD—that is, Lompoc Strong Draft. Though the establishment opened in 2000, the Lompoc Brewery has been crafting ales and lagers since 1996. The company also runs the **HEDGE HOUSE** (3412 SE Division St, Richmond; 503/235-2215), the **5TH QUADRANT** (3901-B N Williams St, North Portland; 503/288-3996), and **OAKS BOTTOM** (1621 SE Bybee St,

Sellwood; 503/232-1728). *AE, MC, V; no checks; every day; full bar; www. newoldlompoc.com; map:GG7.*

Rogue Ales Public House

1339 NW FLANDERS ST, PEARL DISTRICT; 503/222-5910
Originating in Ashland, Oregon, in 1988 and now based in Newport on the Oregon Coast, the cheeky Rogue Nation populates the Pearl at a homey pub: a "micro meeting hall," as it calls itself. With pub food, a Lego table, a full bar, and the ever-popular Dead Guy Ale, the Rogue pub is every bit an easy hangout. Its location makes it a busy superdestination on First Thursday, when it fills with parched, famished art crawlers. *AE, DIS, MC, V; no checks; every day; full bar; www.rogue.com; map:L1.* &

The Tugboat Brewery

711 SW ANKENY ST, DOWNTOWN; 503/226-2508
Producing only a few barrels of various malted elixirs each week, this most microscopic of microbreweries serves up its delicious homebrew in a library-like space lined with books and staffed by the owner's gregarious relatives. The pints and nightly jazz music attract a wide swath of Portlanders, though not too many at a time since the bar only seats 50. *Cash only; Mon–Sat; beer and wine; www.d2m.com/Tugwebsite; map:J4.* &

Widmer Gasthaus Pub

955 N RUSSELL ST, ALBINA; 503/281-3333
Lovers of flavorful, light beer, unite: the Widmer Brothers produce Oregon's top-selling microbrew, a delicious hefeweizen that goes great with a lemon wedge. You can sample the ever-evolving seasonal beers at the Gasthaus adjacent to the brewery, where a German-centric menu—sauerkrauts, wursts, fondue, pretzels—awaits the masses. Widmer celebrated its 25th anniversary in 2009 with a "Prost" heard round the city. *AE, DC, MC, V; no checks; every day; beer and wine; www.widmer.com; map:GG6.* &

Wine Bars

Bar Avignon

2138 SE DIVISION ST, CLINTON/DIVISION; 503/517-0808
Big windows let in the late-afternoon light, and candles keep it cozy as the evening descends into darkness. Approachable staff will help you find the perfect wine or, for the vino-phobic, guide you through a similarly worthy selection of beer, spirits, and specialty drinks. Opt for the "choose your own adventure" meat and cheese plate, or something less decision intensive—like the salt cod brandade with crostini. If you prefer to try before you buy, then stop in for a free wine tasting (Saturday afternoons), where themes range across countries and styles. *AE, MC, V; no checks; full bar; every day; www. baravignon.com; map:II5.* &

C Bar

2880 SE GLADSTONE ST, BROOKLYN; 503/230-8808

In recent years C Bar has expanded and evolved into a comfortable neighborhood gastropub, no longer just the place to get a drink before hitting up the popular sushi spot next door. Striking a near-perfect balance between fashion and function, painted in mauve with a large marble bar, it feels comfortable and hip. A solid bet for a night out when a game of pool and good conversation are on the itinerary. *AE, MC, V; no checks; every day; full bar; www.cbarpdx.com; map:II5.*

Kir

22 NE 7TH AVE, LOWER BURNSIDE; 503/232-3063

If owner Amalie Roberts has her way, you'll be having a love affair with the long-neglected rosé before the evening is up. Not one to be exclusive however, she'll also happily set you up with sparkling vino, reds, and whites as she shares her love of good wine with her patrons, who are made to feel immediately welcome in this tiny, lovely spot. Small plates such as *fromage blanc* with prosciutto and fig compote, or house-made pickles and bread, combine equal parts invention and simplicity. The pink-chalked wine list on the large blackboard adds to the rosy ambience. *MC, V; no checks; Tues–Sat; beer and wine; www.kirwinebar.com; map:HH5.* &

M Bar

417 NW 21ST AVE, NORTHWEST; 503/228-6614

If you're in the mood for good conversation and a reasonably priced glass of beer or wine, squeeze yourself into what is certainly the tiniest bar in town. The bar itself seats only five people (uncomfortably), but with all walls practically within reach and the few tables easily within earshot, everyone weighs in on the topic at hand. There is sidewalk seating for the claustrophobic. *Cash only; every day; beer and wine; map:HH7.*

Navarre

10 NE 28TH AVE, LAURELHURST; 503/232-3555

Navarre occupies a delicious gray area between being a small-plate restaurant with great wine and a wine bar with great small plates. Over 50 wines are served by the glass in this intimate and subtly homey charmer. (See also review in the Restaurants chapter.) *AE, MC, V; checks OK; every day; beer and wine; www.navarreportland.blogspot.com; map:HH5.* &

Noble Rot

1111 E BURNSIDE ST, 4TH FLOOR, INNER SOUTHEAST; 503/233-1999

Enjoy an inexpensive glass of the house wine in this classy bar. Or get a taste of everything, with moderately priced flights that complement a rotating menu of smartly crafted dishes. Noble Rot's new location on Burnside dazzles with a fourth-floor view of the city. Twinkling lights outside coexist perfectly with the interior's gentle glow of candles, illuminated bar, and oversized white leather booths that can comfortably hold large groups of imbibers. (See also review in the Restaurants chapter.) *AE, MC, V; local checks only; Mon–Sat; full bar; www.noblerotpdx.com; map:HH5.* &

Thirst Wine Bar & Bistro

315 SW MONTGOMERY ST, STE 340, RIVERPLACE; 503/295-2747
If you need another reason to stroll down the RiverPlace Esplanade, this busy little wine bar makes it worth your journey. Sip on fine local wines and soak in the view of the Willamette River from an outside table, or situate yourself near the vast indoor windows. Special events occur twice weekly from 5–8pm: there are $15 wine-and-cheese pairings on Tuesdays, and complimentary wine tastings on Thursdays. Don't miss the divine house-made truffles such as the King, a playful creation involving candied bacon. *AE, DIS, MC, V; no checks; Tues–Sun; full bar; www.thirstbistro.com; map:C5.* &

Vino Paradiso

417 NW 10TH AVE, PEARL DISTRICT; 503/295-9536
The temperature-regulated wine cellar at Vino Paradiso is floor level, encased in glass, and silently insistent on being the center of attention. A fresh and locally focused menu beautifully complements the lengthy, oft-changing wine list. This Pearl District spot attracts a healthy clientele of nouveau riche and hip entrepreneurs, but bright orange walls and midcentury modern decor keep the atmosphere friendly and accessible. *AE, DIS, MC, V; no checks; Tues–Sun; full bar; www.vinoparadiso.com; map:L2.* &

Wine Down

126 NE 28TH ST, LAURELHURST; 503/236-9463
Wine Down's initial environment is intimate—a few oak tables and chairs, a counter, a dessert case—but an adjacent lounge sprawls out to several more tables and offers occasional live acoustic music. It's an informal, breezy space with more family than date ambience, if that can be said about a wine bar. Northwest cuisine with a Mediterranean influence complements fine Oregon and other wines. Don't miss the impressive selection of ports. *AE, MC, V; checks OK; every day; beer and wine; www.winedownpdx.com; map:HH5.* &

Coffee, Tea, and Dessert

Anna Bannanas Coffee House

8716 N LOMBARD ST, SAINT JOHNS; 503/286-2030
1214 NW 21ST ST, NORTHWEST; 503/274-2559
The laid-back and welcoming neighborhood spot in North Portland is an extension of the original, more bohemian landmark in Northwest Portland's Knob Hill, but with a few extra perks. Outdoor seating, a separate play area for the kids, and plenty of craft brews and wine prove there can be life after

parenting. A long list of specialty coffees and a promise to "ice anything" make this a year-round destination. *MC, V; no checks; every day; beer and wine; www.annabannanascoffee.com; map:DD8; map:GG7.*

Backspace

115 NW 5TH AVE, CHINATOWN; 503/248-2900
Despite Backspace's exposed brick walls and concrete floors, smart Portlanders recognize its unique home-away-from-home potential: there's hot Stumptown coffee, vegetarian food, and the fastest Internet in town. Billing itself as a modern arcade "techni-playground," Backspace houses ten computers and is best known for its top-notch computer-gaming capabilities and high-quality, diverse musical acts. Featured art exhibitions come and go in turn with First Thursday art nights, save for one notable exception: the uninhabitable treehouse stubbornly parked in the center of the room. *AE, DIS, MC, V; no checks; every day; beer and wine; www.backspace.bz; map:K5.* &

Coffee Time

712 NW 21ST AVE, NORTHWEST; 503/497-1090
Just in case you simply can't wait till morning for your daily caffeine fix, Coffee Time is open till 2:30am. If you think there's absolutely no reason to be drinking coffee in the wee hours of the morning, think again. Any time of day or night, you'll find buzzing yuppies, mellow hippies, and newly existentialist teenagers all bonding over their love of java. Perhaps you can write a poem about the mixed crowd and join one of Coffee Time's semiregular performance nights. *DIS, MC, V; no checks; every day; no alcohol; www. portlandcoffeetime.com; map:GG7.* &

The Fresh Pot

4001 N MISSISSIPPI AVE, NORTHEAST; 503/284-8928
3729 SE HAWTHORNE ST, HAWTHORNE; 503/232-8928
It began with the coffee shop inside Powell's bookstore on Hawthorne, but when Fresh Pot's owners branched out into the promising North Mississippi area, they almost single-handedly jump-started that neighborhood's now-bustling renaissance. In this former Rexall pharmacy, you can now enjoy the medicinal healing power of a cup of Stumptown coffee or a locally baked vegan cookie. For later-night brew, the Hawthorne location is where it's at. *MC, V; checks OK; every day; no alcohol; www.thefreshpot.com; map:GG5; map:HH4.* &

Palio Dessert & Espresso House

1996 SE LADD AVE, LADD'S ADDITION; 503/232-9412
Situated in the quaint Ladd's Addition neighborhood between Division and Hawthorne streets in Southeast Portland, Palio is friendly and cozy: candles and dim lights warmly illuminate this den; and lest you get bored, there are toys, games, and books galore. The desserts change often, but they're always decadently sweet, and you're sure to find a luscious chocolate cake of some

sort. *AE, DIS, MC, V; no checks; every day; no alcohol; www.palio-in-ladds. com; map:HH5.* &

The Pied Cow

3244 SE BELMONT ST, BELMONT; 503/230-4866
A bay window, beads, lace curtains, and low couches leave this colorful hangout aglow in Victoriana, but the candlelit backyard-soiree ambience of its patio ensures its place as a hip spot in Belmont. This is the ultimate coffeehouse: the food is cheap, the cappuccinos are delicious, and there's always a goopy-sweet chocolate dessert on hand to enrich the coffee drinks. *MC, V; no checks; every day; beer and wine; map:HH5.*

Pix Patisserie

3901 N WILLIAMS AVE, NORTH PORTLAND; 503/282-6595
3402 SE DIVISION ST, SOUTHEAST; 503/232-4407
At petite Pix, chocolate and drinks go hand in hand: pair a *fleur de sel* macaroon with a glass of wine, or go the more direct route and try the beer float (chocolate stout and mocha ice cream) or the Chambord Chanel, an adult version of decadent hot chocolate. There's a yearly Bastille Day celebration and frequent movie, music, and gastronomical trivia nights—as if you needed more excuses to come. *MC, V; no checks, every day; full bar; www.pix patisserie.com; map:FF5; map:II5.* &

Rimsky-Korsakoffee House

707 SE 12TH AVE, BUCKMAN; 503/232-2640
Laughter and music from the resident piano greet the ear at the threshold of this grand old Victorian mansion befitting its Russian composer namesake. The place is nearly always filled with young lovers sharing ice-cream sundaes or a decadent mocha fudge cake. The Cafe Borgias are exceptional: coffee, chocolate, and orange harmoniously mingle in one cup. You might drive right by this place—there's no sign marking its presence—but once you're inside, with a string trio or classical guitarist providing entertainment and a proper cup of coffee to sip, you may not want to leave. *No credit cards; checks OK; every day; no alcohol; map:HH5.*

Staccato Gelato

232 NE 28TH AVE, LAURELHURST; 503/231-7100
1540 SE BYBEE ST, SELLWOOD, 503/517-8957
This charming ice-cream and coffee joint is generally brighter and less formal than its Italian counterparts, but its creamy product is just as authentic. Eighteen changing flavors are offered daily—ranging from fig to peppermint stick to straight-up vanilla—along with house-made doughnuts on the weekends. Don't miss out on the Gelato Affogato, a shot of espresso poured over two scoops of gelato: the most decadent concoction this side of Italy. *DIS, MC, V; no checks; every day; beer and wine (Sellwood location only); www.staccato gelato.com; map:HH5; map:KK6.*

Stumptown Coffee Roasters

128 SW 3RD AVE, OLD TOWN (AND BRANCHES); 503/295-6144
Five locations and a roastery have turned this local company into one of Portland's definitive establishments. Stumptown roasts the richest, deepest cup in town: it's so good that many local restaurants hang signs boasting "Proudly Serving Stumptown Coffee." And owner Duane Sorenson hires some of the most attractive and talented baristas this side of *Friends'* Central Perk. The downtown location serves beer and wine, along with the Ace Hotel spot (1022 SW Stark St, Downtown; 503/224-9060; map:J2), which stays open until 11pm. The Southeast (4525 SE Division St; 503/230-7702; map: II4), Belmont (3356 SE Belmont St; 503/232-8889; map:HH5), and Annex (3352 SE Belmont St; 503/467-4123) locations close earlier in the evening. (See also review in the Shopping chapter.) *MC, V; local checks only; every day; beer and wine; www.stumptowncoffee.com; map:J5.* &

The Tao of Tea

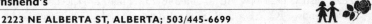

3430 SE BELMONT ST, BELMONT (AND BRANCHES); 503/736-0198
Enter the Tao of Tea, and the trickling water, meditative music, exotic teapots, and feng shui-ed decor will instantly draw you into another world. The tea selection features more than 180 types, with the finest varieties of oolong, green, white, red, and black teas, as well as fruit and herbal infusions. The eclectic vegetarian menu is designed to complement the teas; the green tea, bean curd, and mango ice-cream assortment will complement your palate. Branches in Northwest Portland (2212 NW Hoyt St; 503/223-3563; map: GG7) and at the Classical Chinese Garden (239 NW Everett St, Chinatown; 503/224-8455; map:L5). (See also review in the Shopping chapter.) *AE, DIS, MC, V; checks OK; every day; no alcohol; www.taooftea.com; map:HH5.* &

Townshend's

2223 NE ALBERTA ST, ALBERTA; 503/445-6699
This Alberta Street teahouse has more of a social coffee-shop vibe than other mellow tea houses, without at all sacrificing quality or its unique version of zen. There are over 100 different kinds of tea, including an exceptional selection of chai "latte" blends, and velvety green couches on which to enjoy your selection. A candle-burning teapot warmer will keep your 20-ounce pot toasty for as long as you want to stay. You'll find just as many people hanging out here during Alberta's Last Thursday celebrations as you will at any neighborhood bar—only they'll be sipping on a house-brewed kombucha or deciding whether they want aloe pearls in their bubble tea. *AE, DIS, MC, V; no checks; every day; no alcohol; www.townshendsteas.com; map:FF5.* &

Vivace Coffee House & Crêperie

2287 NW PETTYGROVE ST, NORTHWEST; 503/228-3667
This well-situated crêperie on the corner of 23rd Avenue has a friendly staff and an indisputable knack for delicious, generous, savory and sweet crepes. Located in one of the upscale strip's many converted Victorians, Vivace

provides plenty of room to sprawl with its two floors and ample patio close to the street action. The skilled baristas do wonderful things with Stumptown beans. Best of all, Vivace won't break the bank. *MC, V; no checks; every day; beer and wine; map:GG7.*

Voodoo Doughnut

22 SW 3RD AVE, OLD TOWN; 503/241-4704
1501 NE DAVIS ST, NORTHEAST; 503/235-2666

In the tradition of Portland's late, lamented 24-Hour Church of Elvis, you can tie the nuptial knot in this tiny downtown doughnut stop. Effectively a walk-up counter adjacent to Berbati's Pan (see Music, Clubs, and Lounges in this chapter), the 24-hour shop takes Krispy Kreme to task with a wide assortment of flavors most doughnut lovers would never dream of. Some—like Maple Bacon, Pepto-Bismol, and Froot Loops—are surprisingly delicious. Voodoo's popularity recently warranted the opening of a second location. *Cash only; every day; no alcohol; www.voodoodoughnut.com; map: J5; map:GG5.* &

World Cup at Powell's City of Books

1005 W BURNSIDE ST, DOWNTOWN (AND BRANCHES);
503/228-4651

After you orient yourself in the byzantine empire that is Powell's City of Books, meander through the Blue and Yellow rooms into World Cup, where you can peruse books and magazines over a latte, tea, or pastry. It's usually crowded; with windows overlooking Burnside, it's also a great place to people-watch. But visitors observe an informal, librarylike quiet out of respect for readers. The beans are roasted nearby at their Northwest shop (1740 NW Glisan St; 503/228-4152; map:GG7), and the Ecotrust shop in the Pearl District (721 NW 9th St; 503/546-7377; map:L3) specializes in sustainable blends. *MC, V; checks OK; every day; no alcohol; www.worldcupcoffee. com/cafes/powells; map:K2.* &

DAY TRIPS

DAY TRIPS

Situated at the foot of the Willamette River Valley, an easy two-hour drive from both the Pacific Coast and the Cascade Mountains, Portland is a great hub for planning one- to three-day trips. The famed Columbia River Gorge National Scenic Area is just east of the city. Mount Hood, the Oregon Wine Country, the spectacular coast, and other attractions are nearby.

Sauvie Island

Pastoral Sauvie Island, with its farms, orchards, produce stands, waterways, and wildlife—just 20 minutes from downtown Portland via westbound US Hwy 30—is a quick escape for bicyclists, bird-watchers, anglers, and boaters.

Located at the confluence of the Willamette and Columbia rivers, where both salmon and the edible wapatoo root were found in abundance, the island became the Multnomah Indians' summer and fall home. You too can enjoy the island's bounty at in-season U-pick farms or local produce markets, such as **SAUVIE ISLAND FARMS** (503/621-3988) or the **PUMPKIN PATCH** (503/621-3874). Be forewarned: On rainy days, the island's broad, golden fields turn into mud farms, so take your rubber boots if you're going to pick.

There's only one access route to Sauvie Island: a bridge at its south end, well marked off Hwy 30. In the fall, when the pumpkins get big and the last of the berries are ready to pick, this route gets pretty congested, but the trip is worth the hassle. To see the island by bike, park your car at the east end of the bridge (you can't miss the lot), and from there take the 12-mile biking loop. At the halfway point, if you're feeling energetic, a 5-mile loop that branches down to the Columbia offers several bird-watching turnouts.

The northern half of the island is a game refuge—one that is open to duck hunters October through January, which means this is no time for either you or the birds to hang around. At other times, the marshes and open fields make a fine playground for enjoying the bountiful wildlife. Look for red foxes, black-tailed deer, great blue herons, geese, ducks, bald eagles, and migrating sandhill cranes. Reeder Road extends to the northern shore's sanctioned **COLLINS BEACH CLOTHING-OPTIONAL AREA** and other short, sandy beaches that freighters and small pleasure craft pass by. The western branch of the road follows the dike of the **MULTNOMAH CHANNEL**, passing the historic Bybee-Howell House, humble houseboats, rickety marinas, and the old site of the Hudson's Bay Company's Fort William (abandoned in 1836; nothing remains) before the road eventually dead-ends. You'll want to purchase a parking permit (daily or yearly) if you plan to venture to the refuge or beaches; permits are available at the grocery on your left immediately as you cross over the bridge onto the island.

The **BYBEE-HOWELL HOUSE**, in Howell Territorial Park, was built in 1858 by James F. Bybee on a donation land claim and was sold to neighbor Benjamin Howell in 1860. The Classical Revival–style two-story house has nine rooms and six fireplaces. Unfortunately, it is not currently open to the public. In the adjacent

Pioneer Orchard are more than 115 varieties of apple trees (many unknown to modern orchardists) brought here by early settlers. Call **METRO REGIONAL PARKS & GREEN SPACES** (503/797-1850) for information.

Columbia River Gorge (Oregon)

The federally designated **COLUMBIA RIVER GORGE NATIONAL SCENIC AREA** preserves what is among the most impressive riverscapes in North America. You'll want to explore it by taking I-84 east from Portland. On your return to the city, you can choose one of two routes: either back down the Washington side of the gorge, or a loop around Mount Hood.

In 1792, Boston trader Robert Gray and his crew were the first nonnatives to sail on a strip of then-wild water that flowed into the Pacific Ocean. Gray named it the Columbia, after his ship, and proclaimed it a "noble river." After a week or so, the crew sailed out to sea without much of a second thought; Gray barely acknowledged his find when he returned to Massachusetts. Historians note that Gray sailed on rather hastily because he didn't find any sea otter pelts to buy from the native people on the banks of the river. Would he have lingered a bit if he'd sailed the *Columbia Rediviva* as far east as the majestic Columbia River Gorge? This landscape, with its magnificent waterfalls, dramatic cliffs, and rock formations cut by the river, is enough to make nature lovers want to explore every crevice.

In decades past, when the gorge highway was narrow and winding, driving here was not for the queasy. These days, most of the traffic travels down I-84, leaving the beautiful old **HISTORIC COLUMBIA RIVER HIGHWAY** (Hwy 30) for unhurried wanderers. This engineering marvel originally went from Portland to Mosier (just past Hood River), continuing to The Dalles; today the old highway can still be followed for 22 miles from Troutdale to Ainsworth State Park (exit 35). In addition, portions near Bonneville Dam and Hood River have been restored for hikers and cyclists; call the **OREGON DEPARTMENT OF TRANSPORTATION** (503/731-8200; www.oregon.gov/ODOT) for details and maps, and also see the Hood River section.

Start your exploring in charming **TROUTDALE**—home of the McMenamins' unique **EDGEFIELD** complex at a former poor farm (see review in the Lodgings chapter). Merchants have renovated a four-block stretch of the Historic Columbia River Highway (between exits 16 and 17 off I-84) as **HISTORIC OLD TOWN TROUTDALE**, with various antique shops, art galleries, and specialty shops. Peek into the **TROUTDALE GENERAL STORE** (289 E Historic Columbia River Hwy; 503/492-7912) for a look at an early-1900s soda fountain and confectionary. For a full meal, continue across the Sandy River Bridge to **TAD'S CHICKEN 'N DUMPLINS** (1325 E Historic Columbia River Hwy; 503/666-5337), a riverside dinner destination since the 1930s.

You enter the national scenic area just past Tad's, and popular viewpoints and attractions become numerous. **CROWN POINT**, 733 feet above the river, features a stone visitors center—the **1917 VISTA HOUSE**—with gorgeous views and,

---

MOUNT ST. HELENS NATIONAL VOLCANIC MONUMENT

Flat-topped Mount St. Helens in Washington, about an hour's drive north of Portland and east of I-5, enthralls visitors. On a clear day, it is well worth the trip to see the 8,365-foot remains of the volcano, as well as the vegetation that's sprouted since its incredible eruption of May 18, 1980 (it's 1,300 feet shorter than it was before the blast). There are two areas to explore, and each is reached by a different highway. One area covers the south and east sides of the volcano, where climbers ascend and where there are caves to brave; the other is on the west side, where a string of visitors centers provide information about the blast and the area's regrowth. All visitors must display a **MONUMENT PASS** (360/449-7800 for national monument headquarters) at developed recreation sites; these can be purchased at visitors centers and information stations throughout the area ($10 per person for three days, $5 for seniors, free for children under 15).

West Side

Most visitors take the **SPIRIT LAKE MEMORIAL HIGHWAY** (State Hwy 504) east from Castle Rock, about 40 minutes north of Portland via I-5. About 5 miles east of I-5, on your way up to the volcano, sits the oldest of the visitors centers in the Mount St. Helens area: the wood-and-glass center at **SILVER LAKE** (360/274-2100; June 15–Dec. 1). Built shortly after the eruption, this center commemorates the blast with excellent exhibits, a walk-through volcano, hundreds of historical and modern photos, geological and anthropological surveys, and a film documenting the area's destruction and rebirth.

The **JOHNSTON RIDGE OBSERVATORY** (360/274-2143; closed in winter) is located at the end of Spirit Lake Memorial Highway, about 8 miles beyond Coldwater Ridge. This futuristic-looking structure, within 5 miles of the crater, offers the best views of the steaming lava dome inside the crater—unless, of course, you climb the volcano.

---

sometimes, tremendous winds. **ROOSTER ROCK** is at the heart of a state park flanked by sandy swimming beaches. Nearby, look for **LARCH MOUNTAIN ROAD**, which leads 14 miles uphill to one of the best sunset-watching spots in western Oregon (unless you're atop Mount Hood). A short road's-end trail leads to **SHERRARD POINT**, a rocky promontory at Larch Mountain's summit with spectacular 360-degree views that take in Mount Hood, Mount Adams, Mount St. Helens, Mount Jefferson, the Columbia River Gorge, and all of Portland.

Driving east from Troutdale, the route passes numerous waterfalls; if you stop at only one, make it **MULTNOMAH FALLS** (exit 31 off I-84), whose two-step drop

Two visitors centers can be visited without the monument pass: Cowlitz County's **HOFFSTADT BLUFF CENTER** (milepost 27 on Spirit Lake Memorial Hwy; 360/274-5200), which explores the lives and deaths of those most directly affected by the blast, and Weyerhaeuser's **FOREST LEARNING CENTER** (milepost 33½; 360/414-3439), which focuses on the land's recovery in the wake of the eruption.

South and East Sides

State Hwy 503 east from Woodland or north from Battle Ground, less than 20 minutes' drive north of Portland, will take you past Yale Lake to these areas of the national monument. En route, check out the map at visitors centers in Woodland or Amboy; the St. Helens area has a confusing range of attractions, and it may help to orient yourself at the beginning of your trip.

There are two possibilities for spelunking at the **APE CAVES** (on Forest Service Road 8303, an hour from Woodland): the moderately difficult lower cave, three-quarters of a mile long, and the more challenging 1½-mile upper cave. This lava tube, the longest in the continental United States, was formed 1,900 years ago in a St. Helens blast. Rent lanterns and gather more information at the **APES HEADQUARTERS** (open every day mid-May–Sept). For a dramatic view of a vast pumice plain, travel east and north another hour and 45 minutes to the **WINDY RIDGE VIEWPOINT**, situated within 4 miles of the volcano's crater.

For information on climbing St. Helens, call the **CLIMBING INFORMATION LINE** (360/247-3961). You'll need to buy a climbing permit ($15 per person); a few are available on a daily basis, but it's best to reserve in advance. Most climbers take one of two trails (Butte Camp or Monitor Ridge) up the south face. It's more of a rugged hike than real alpine climbing, but an ice ax is still recommended. The all-day climb (8 miles round-trip) is ideal for novice alpinists; the only big dangers are some loose-rock cliffs and the unstable edge around the crater. In winter, you can ski back down.

of 620 feet makes it the second-highest waterfall in the country. The wood-and-stone **MULTNOMAH FALLS LODGE** at the foot of the falls was designed in 1925 by architect Albert E. Doyle (of Portland's Benson Hotel fame); now a National Historic Landmark, the lodge houses a naturalists and visitors center. The large restaurant (503/695-2376) serves good breakfasts (brunch on Sunday), lunch, and dinner, but the lodge does not have overnight facilities. A few more miles upriver, **ONEONTA GORGE** is a narrow, dramatic cleft through which a slippery half-mile trail winds through a streambed to secluded Oneonta Falls; the quite rugged trail is suitable only for the adventurous.

You'll rejoin I-84 at exit 35. Five miles on, stop to visit the **BONNEVILLE DAM** (541/374-8820), the first federal dam on the Columbia. Here you can take tours of the dam itself, the fish ladders (seen through underwater viewing windows), and the shipping locks. You can also tour the adjacent **BONNEVILLE FISH HATCHERY** (541/374-8393) year-round, but the best time is September to November, when the chinook salmon are spawning. Be sure also to visit the outdoor pond, where 10-foot sturgeon reside.

THE BRIDGE OF THE GODS, in the old river town of Cascade Locks, is now steel, but at the site is a fine little museum that recounts the Indian myth about the original, legendary arching-rock bridge that collapsed into the Columbia River eons ago. The locks that the town is named for are themselves a sight worth seeing: the stonework is beautiful and the scale awesome, accentuated by the small figures of the people who fish off the walls. The **PORTLAND SPIRIT STERN-WHEELER COLUMBIA GORGE** (503/224-3900; www.sternwheeler.com) departs on two-hour tours every day, May through October (call for exact times), from Marine Park at the locks (narrated tour, $20); the boat also offers nightly dinner cruises ($68) and weekend champagne brunch trips ($48). The "Landmarks of the Gorge" cruise ($84) takes you by the most impressive sites in the gorge and runs only on Wednesdays.

HOOD RIVER

Fruit orchards are everywhere near the bustling town of **HOOD RIVER**, an hour's drive east of Portland via I-84. Sunny weather combines with substantial moisture (about 31 inches of rain annually) to create a climate perfect for cultivating pears, apples, and plums. It's pastoral indeed, but there's drama, too: 30 miles to the south, 11,235-foot Mount Hood looms, and from the town itself, the stunning views are of Washington's 12,326-foot Mount Adams.

In summer you can't miss the brilliant sails of windsurfers dotting the river and the influx of wind chasers who lend the town a distinctly touristy feel. They've come since the 1980s because of the roaring winds that blow opposite the Columbia River current, making Hood River one of the world's top three **WINDSURFING** destinations (the other two are in Hawaii and Australia). More recently, **KITEBOARDING** has also caught the attention of river-sports lovers. While Hood River reaps all the reputation, the waters on the Oregon side of the Columbia are reportedly tame compared with those off the Washington banks, where boardheads claim the wind "really pulls." Hence, the best sailors circumvent rocky shores and industrial areas to surf off points on the river's north bank, such as Swell City and Doug's Beach. Tune in to radio station KMCQ-104 FM for the local wind report.

Two fine spectator spots are located right in Hood River. The **HOOD RIVER WATERFRONT CENTER EVENT SITE** (from I-84, follow signs to the visitors center) is a grassy park with a small sandy beach and unrestricted access to the Columbia. Sailing is somewhat easier at the **COLUMBIA GORGE SAILPARK** at Port Marina Park, which features a marina, rental shop, and cafe with an enclosed porch. (After all, who wants to dine in the wind?) For lessons or for information on wind conditions, rentals, or launching spots, investigate a multitude of sailboard equipment shops such as **BIG WINDS** (207 Front St; 541/386-6086; www.bigwinds.com) or **REAL WIND** (216 Cascade St; 541/386-3693; www.realwind.com). **BRIAN'S WINDSURFING AND KITESURFING** (from I-84, take exit 63 and follow signs to events site; 541/490-2047; www.brianswindsurfing.com) also provides lessons; meet at the Hood River event site—call first.

DOUG'S SPORTS (101 Oak St; 541/386-5787; www.dougsports.com) carries a wide selection of clothing and activewear for the whole family, as well as boards of all kinds. **MELIKA** (316 Oak St; 541/387-4400; www. melika.com) makes colorful and practical activewear, including bathing suits for women and children. Down the street, **PARTS + LABOUR** (209 Oak St; 541/387-2787; www.parts-labour.com) sells probably the most stylish onshore clothing in town, at boutique prices.

As longtime Hood River residents attest, while acknowledging the economic boost the windsurfers have provided, there was life in this town of 6,000 before the modern-day sailors arrived. You can learn its story at the **HOOD RIVER COUNTY HISTORY MUSEUM** (300 E Port Marina Dr; 541/386-6772; every day Apr–Oct). The local **VISITORS INFORMATION CENTER**, tucked inside the **HOOD RIVER EXPO BUILDING** (405 Portway Ave; 800/366-3530), is a friendly place to get informed. If it's closed (as it sometimes is on winter weekends), you can find reading material at the **WAU-COMA BOOKSTORE** (212 Oak St; 541/386-5353; www.waucomabookstore. com), a notable independent bookseller. **PUBLIC RESTROOMS** are located at Second and State streets, on the ground floor of the city hall. **LIBRARY PARK**, above the intersection of Fifth and Oak streets, offers a great view of both town and river.

Hood River's grandest structure is the **COLUMBIA GORGE HOTEL** (4000 Westcliff Dr; 541/386-5566 or 800/345-1921; www.columbiagorgehotel. com). Built just west of town by lumber baron Simon Benson in 1922 to crown the opening of the old gorge highway, it also boasts Hood River's fanciest dining spot, **SIMON'S**. In the heart of the city, the restored 1913 **HOOD RIVER HOTEL** (102 Oak St; 541/386-1900 or 800/386-1859; www. hoodriverhotel.com) is a simple but intimate country hotel with 41 rooms, including 9 kitchen suites, and a fine in-house restaurant called the Cornerstone Cuisine.

You can enjoy light meals with handcrafted ales at the employee-owned **FULL SAIL TASTING ROOM AND PUB** (506 Columbia St; 541/386-2247; www.fullsailbrewing.com). The outdoor deck (with live music on weekends) is an apt place for tired board sailors to unwind while keeping the river in sight. Another popular spot for brews—as well as steaks, fish, pastas, and house-made desserts—is **BRIAN'S POURHOUSE** (606 Oak St; 541/387-4344; www.brianspourhouse.com). Choices for more-substantial dining include **NORTH OAK BRASSERIE** (113 3rd St; 541/387-2310; www.hoodriver restaurants.com/restaurant_no.html) for classic Italian, **CELILO** (16 Oak St; 541/386-5710; www.celilorestaurant.com) for creative Pacific Northwest cuisine, **NORA'S TABLE** (110 5th St; 541/387-4000; www.norastable.com)

for seafood, and the **6TH STREET BISTRO AND LOFT** (509 Cascade Ave; 541/386-5737; www.sixthstreetbistro.com) for an eclectic international menu. **BETTE'S PLACE** (416 Oak St; 541/386-1880) is a local diner that's been serving almost the same breakfast-and-lunch menu for 30-odd years. Charming **STONEHEDGE GARDENS** (3405 Cascade Ave; 541/386-3940; www.hoodriverrestaurants.com/restaurant_sg.html) has some of the best food in town, a Northwest bistro menu with continental flair.

The region's bountiful orchards and beautiful landscape are celebrated during the wonderful small-town **BLOSSOM FESTIVAL**, held annually in mid-April. The **MOUNT HOOD RAILROAD** (800/872-4661; www.mthoodrr.com) makes two- or four-hour round-trips—and dinner-train excursions—from the quaint Hood River Depot into the heart of orchard country; call for the schedule. You can buy the fruit of the orchards at the **FRUIT COMPANY** (2900 Van Horn Dr; 541/387-4116), at **RIVER BEND FARM & COUNTRY STORE** (2363 Tucker Rd; 541/386-8766), or at one of the many fruit stands that dot the valley. **RASMUSSEN FARMS** (3020 Thomsen Rd, 1 mile off State Hwy 35; 541/386-4622; www.rasmussenfarms.com), in addition to selling seasonal fruit, also has a pumpkin patch and U-pick flower fields. The **CATHEDRAL RIDGE WINERY** (4200 Post Canyon Dr; 541/386-2882; www.cathedralridgewinery.com) was honored as Oregon's winery of the year in 2007; its pinot gris and zinfandel are outstanding.

If you're returning to Portland via the Mount Hood Loop route, this is where you turn south on Hwy 35. If you're continuing east toward The Dalles, another 20 minutes' drive, be sure to exit I-84 at Mosier (5 miles east of Hood River) and climb to the **ROWENA CREST VIEWPOINT** on old Hwy 30. The grandstand Columbia River view is complemented by a wildflower show in the **TOM MCCALL PRESERVE**, maintained by the Nature Conservancy.

The area's newest hiking and biking option is the 6½-mile restored section of the Historic Columbia River Highway connecting Hood River to Mosier. The highway was decommissioned in 1953, and the Twin Tunnels were plugged with gravel to keep the curious out. A lengthy and expensive effort reopened (and reinforced) the **TWIN TUNNEL TRAIL** in 2000. To reach this spectacular trail, follow the signs to the parking lots from I-84's Hwy 35 exit in Hood River or from exit 69 in Mosier. You'll need $3 in correct change for the parking-fee machine.

THE DALLES

A couple of miles west of The Dalles on Crates Point is the excellent **COLUMBIA GORGE DISCOVERY CENTER/WASCO COUNTY HISTORICAL MUSEUM** (5000 Discovery Dr; 541/296-8600; www.gorgediscovery.org), the official interpretive center for the national scenic area. Split into two wings, the center recounts the natural and human history of the Columbia Gorge and Wasco County—which extended all the way to the Rocky Mountains when it was created in 1854. Multimedia exhibits focus on the life and uses, past and present, of this stretch of the Columbia, from American Indian culture to the river's current recreational popularity. The location is stunning and the architecture noteworthy; even the cafe is above average.

Twenty minutes east of Hood River is The Dalles, a small city of about 12,000 people. In the 1840s, the Oregon Trail ended here; goods from wagons were loaded onto barges for the final float to Portland or were taken around Mount Hood on the notorious Barlow Road. Later, Fort Dalles was here; today the **FORT DALLES MUSEUM** (500 W 15th St; 541/296-4547; www.historicthedalles.org/fort_dalles; admission $5) displays exceptional pioneer-era relics in its 1856 surgeon's house and 1880s homestead. Stop by **THE DALLES AREA CHAMBER OF COMMERCE** (404 W 2nd St; 541/296-2231; www.thedalleschamber.com) for a **HISTORIC WALKING TOURS** brochure of more than 100 historic sites, including numerous handsome buildings in Colonial, Gothic Revival, Italianate, and American Renaissance styles.

As befits a town of historical flavor, The Dalles has several charming bed-and-breakfast inns, including the Dutch Colonial **WINDRIDER INN** (200 W 4th St; 541/296-2607), whose amenities include sailboard storage. Dining options include the delightful 1876 **BALDWIN SALOON** (1st and Court sts; 541/296-5666; www.baldwinsaloon.com), once a steamboat navigational office, warehouse, coffin storage site, and saddle shop.

At **THE DALLES DAM** (exit 87 off I-84, 2 miles east of The Dalles; 541/296-9778), a visitors center has informative displays on Lewis and Clark and on the fishing industry. A free tour train makes stops at the dam, powerhouse, locks, fish ladders, and picnic area.

Columbia River Gorge (Washington)

To return to Portland from The Dalles, you could cross the Columbia River to the Washington side via US Hwy 197 and turn west on State Hwy 14. We recommend continuing east another 19 miles and crossing on US Hwy 97—at which point you may ask, "Where in the Sam Hill am I?"

You're in Sam Hill country, and the early-20th-century Seattle millionaire left two monuments here to his eccentricity. One of them is the eclectic **MARYHILL MUSEUM OF ART** (Hwy 14, Maryhill; 509/773-3733; www.maryhillmuseum.org; mid-Mar–mid-Nov; $7 for adults), a massive neoclassical edifice perched rather obtrusively upon the river's barren benchlands. In 1907 Hill bought 6,000 acres here with the intention of founding a Quaker agricultural community. When that failed to materialize, friends encouraged Hill to turn his mansion into an art museum. Art collector Alma Spreckels became Maryhill's principal benefactor, and Queen Marie of Romania (whom Hill met during their shared philanthropic work in Europe after World War I) offered Hill much of her royal and personal memorabilia and graced the dedication of the Maryhill Museum in 1926.

Today the museum boasts one of the world's largest collections of Rodin art (78 bronze and plaster sculptures and 28 watercolors), three floors of classic French and American paintings and glasswork, unique exhibitions such as chess sets and 19th-century royal Romanian furnishings, and splendid American Indian art.

Along with its permanent collection, the museum hosts many traveling collections, often featuring Northwest artists. A cafe serves espresso, pastries, and sandwiches; and dozens of peacocks roam the lovely landscaped grounds. Take time to explore the intriguing sculptural overlook on the east side of the museum.

Four miles east of the museum on Hwy 14, Hill built a full-scale replica of the inner third of Stonehenge, to honor the World War I veterans of Klickitat County. About 3 degrees off center, Hill's **STONEHENGE** (not stones but poured concrete) functions as an observatory. It embodies Hill's personal vision: a pacifist, he considered his monument a statement on the human sacrifices made to the god of war.

Hwy 14 will carry you all the way west to Vancouver, Washington—96 miles, which on this two-lane road will take well over two hours. We recommend you follow it at least 60 miles, at which point you can cross back over to I-84 at the **BRIDGE OF THE GODS** (Cascade Locks, $1 toll). En route, you'll pass through one of Washington's lesser-known wine-growing districts. The half-dozen or so wineries here are all open for tastings; we recommend **MARYHILL WINERY** (9774 Hwy 14, Maryhill; 877/627-9445; www.maryhill winery.com) and **SYNCLINE CELLARS** (307 W Humboldt St, Bingen; 509/365-4361; www.synclinewine.com). **VIENTO** (216 W Steuben St, Bingen; 509/493-0049) is a delightful bistro-style restaurant just around the corner from Syncline. For an overnight stay or dinner en route between Maryhill and Bingen, the **LYLE HOTEL** (100 7th St, Lyle; 509/365-5953; www.lylehotel.com) is a 10-room 1905 railroad hotel that has gained regional renown for its gourmet cuisine.

BINGEN, a railroad town, is on the Columbia; its twin community of **WHITE SALMON** sits on a hillside directly above it. Turn off Hwy 14 at Bingen and drive just a couple of miles on Hwy 141 to reach this charming town, whose main-street architecture hints at a German heritage. A good choice of accommodation here is the **INN OF THE WHITE SALMON** (172 W Jewett Blvd, White Salmon; 509/493-2335; www.innofthewhitesalmon.com), a fixture since the 1930s.

White Salmon is named for the river of the same name, regarded by watersports lovers as one of the outstanding white-water streams in the Northwest. Several outfitters offer one-day rafting trips, including **ZOLLER'S OUTDOOR ODYSSEYS** (1248 Hwy 141, White Salmon; 509/493-2641, 800/366-2004; www.zooraft.com). The charming **HUSUM HIGHLANDS BED & BREAKFAST** (70 Postgren Rd, Husum; 509/493-4503; www.husumhighlands.com) has a 20-acre hillside location overlooking the river.

For more than 100 years, people have come to **CARSON MINERAL HOT SPRINGS** (St Martin Springs Rd, Carson; 509/427-8292; www.carsonhotspring resort.com), 20 miles west of Bingen, to take the waters via mineral baths and massages. A recent upgrade and expansion, including a new lodge, restaurant, and golf course, are bringing this property into the 21st century, although the spa is still rather primitive. The women's side is much more crowded than the men's, so if your entourage is mixed, the men will finish sooner. It's wise to reserve massages in advance.

For a higher standard of accommodation, travel 15 minutes west to the **SKAMANIA LODGE** (1131 Skamania Lodge Wy, Stevenson; 509/427-7700 or

800/221-7117; www.skamania.com). The lodge was constructed in the early 1990s with the help of a $5 million grant to spur economic development on the Washington side of the river. Built in the style of the old Cascades lodges, with big timbers and river rock, it wasn't intended to be a four-star resort. But the common rooms are grand, the conference center works well, and the setting in the woods overlooking the river is pleasant indeed. The hotel has 254 rooms and numerous amenities: bar, restaurant, lap pool, saunas, outdoor hot tub, 18-hole public golf course, and an original art collection. The Forest Service's small room in the massive lobby offers maps, info on area recreation, and wildflower and geology books. A day pass ($10 for adults, $5 for kids) buys you entrance to the pool, hot tub, and workout center without having to be a hotel guest; anyone can hike the trails. Sunday brunch in the restaurant draws visitors from near and far for a spread that includes fresh crab, smoked salmon, omelets made to order while you watch, and miles of pastries and desserts.

The **COLUMBIA GORGE DISCOVERY CENTER** (5000 Discovery Dr, Stevenson; 541/296-8600; www.gorgediscovery.com; every day 9am–5pm, year-round; $8 for adults, $4 for kids), located just below the lodge on Hwy 14, displays the history of the gorge via a nine-projector slide show that re-creates the gorge's cataclysmic formation. The show also features American Indian fishing platforms and a 37-foot-high replica of a 19th-century fishing wheel. A 26,000-artifact collection includes a wealth of material from the Lewis and Clark Expedition of 1803–06.

BEACON ROCK STATE PARK, just east of Skamania, surrounds one of the world's largest monoliths, an 848-foot-high volcanic plug with a viewing platform at its summit. (A steep, railed, three-quarter-mile trail climbs the rock.) It was here that Lewis and Clark first detected the tidal influence of the Pacific Ocean.

Mount Hood Loop Highway

To return to Portland from Hood River via Mount Hood, turn south on State Hwy 35 at Hood River, passing the spectacular **PANORAMA POINT** viewpoint as you leave town. After 43 miles, turn west (right) on US Hwy 26; Portland is 55 miles away.

When British navigator Captain George Vancouver first spied **MOUNT HOOD** from the mouth of the Columbia River in 1792, he thought it must have been the highest mountain in the world. It is Oregon's tallest, but at just over 11,235 feet, Mount Hood is not even the highest in the volcanic Cascades Range (Washington's Mount Rainier, at 14,411 feet, holds that honor). Nonetheless, Hood's proximity to Portland, its beautiful asymmetry, and its relatively easily ascended terrain make it one of the busiest peaks in the country. According to geologists, Mount Hood still conceals hot magma and is bound to spew at some point. For now, though, all's peaceful in the towns scattered on its flanks.

About 20 miles south of Hood River, Hwy 35 enters **MOUNT HOOD NATIONAL FOREST.** Soon thereafter, a road climbs to the family-oriented **COOPER SPUR MOUNTAIN RESORT** (Cooper Spur Rd; 541/352-6692; www.cooperspur.com), with gentle slopes for child skiers and a rough-hewn inn with a fine steak house and cabins—with fireplaces and hot tubs. Climb this switchbacking Forest Service road another dozen or so miles to the 1889 **CLOUD CAP INN**, a log landmark at timberline on the north flank of Mount Hood. No longer a hotel, it's anchored to the mountain by cables, and the view alone is worth the detour. If the inn happens to be occupied by a search-and-rescue team (common in the summertime), ask if they have time to give you a tour. The lodge is also an access point for the **TIMBERLINE TRAIL**; call the ranger station in Hood River (541/352-6002) for information.

The largest of Mount Hood's five ski areas is **MOUNT HOOD MEADOWS**, off Hwy 35 about 5 miles north of the Hwy 26 junction. Just after the turn onto Hwy 26, you'll encounter the others: **GOVERNMENT CAMP** and **SKIBOWLS EAST AND WEST** are right off the highway, and a detour takes you to **TIMBERLINE**. Information on any of these ski areas, or any other Mount Hood activities, can be obtained from the **MOUNT HOOD INFORMATION CENTER** (503/622-4822; www.mthood.info).

The tiny hamlet of **GOVERNMENT CAMP**, named for an 1849 army equipment cache, is the hub—such as it is—of Mount Hood activities. From here, a 6-mile road twists its way to stunning **TIMBERLINE LODGE** (800/547-1406; www.timberlinelodge.com), at 6,000 feet elevation, with its impressive frontal views of Mount Hood's glaciers. The massive timber-and-stone lodge was constructed in the 1930s by government workers, who completed the monument in just 15 months. Throughout the building are structural and decorative pieces made by hand from native materials: the 100-foot-high chimney and enormous central fireplace were fashioned out of volcanic rocks from the mountain, the hand-wrought andirons were made from old railroad tracks, and the hardwood chairs and tables were hand-hewn from Oregon timber. The lodge's rooms with fireplaces get booked early, so call well in advance. The popular **CASCADE DINING ROOM** (503/622-0700) serves an array of notable Northwest fare; reservations are suggested. (Other, more modest dining options are also available.) For lodgers dying to shop, the **GALLERY** on the ground floor has locally made handicrafts and more images of Mount Hood than you can imagine. The Forest Service offers historical tours of the lodge at midday on weekends, and a self-starting movie of the lodge's history shows daily.

One of the best hiking trails in the area, the 40-mile **TIMBERLINE TRAIL**, leads 4½ miles west from Timberline Lodge to flower-studded **PARADISE PARK**. The Timberline Trail is a circuit of the entire peak that traverses snowfields as well as ancient forests. The lower parts can blaze with rhododendrons (peaking in June) and wildflowers (peaking in July); all are easily reachable from trails that branch out from the lodge.

Mid-May to mid-July is the prime time for **CLIMBING MOUNT HOOD**, a peak that looks deceptively easy, although its last 1,500 feet involve very steep snow climbing. **TIMBERLINE MOUNTAIN GUIDES** (541/312-9242; www.timberlinemountainguides.com) in the ski area's Wy'east Day Lodge equips and conducts groups of climbers to the summit. The climb starts early in the morning; allow four to six hours to go up and two or three to come down.

For those looking for an easier route up the mountain, the **MAGIC MILE SKY RIDE** chairlift hoists the brave and curious to the 7,000-foot level year-round, weather permitting (503/222-2211 for weather conditions; www.timberlinelodge. com). All they ask is that you buy a ticket, wear sturdy shoes, and (no matter how warm you feel in the parking lot) bring a jacket. At the top of the lift you can buy a barbecue lunch, look through the powerful telescope, or find your favorite vantage point for a magnificent view. You may see skiers and snowboarders here even in the middle of summer: Timberline is the only year-round ski area in North America.

The nearby **SILCOX HUT** (503/219-3192; www.timberlinelodge.com) has been gutted and restored to its original stone-and-timber glory. Six cubicles off the large central room provide sleeping quarters for 22. Organize a dozen or more of your best friends: in winter you can ride up on a Sno-Cat, have dinner, stay overnight, wake up to breakfast, and then ski down to the lodge ($125–$150 per person, $15 less if you bring your own sleeping bag).

The village of Government Camp itself has been undergoing a renaissance of sorts, spurred by the development of the new **COLLINS LAKE RESORT** complex (E Creek Ridge Rd at Government Camp Loop; 503/272-3051; www.collinslake resort.com). Built around a small lake, it presently has 199 condominium and lodge units. Construction of the **COLLINS LAKE VILLAGE CENTER**, with another 200 units, retail shops, restaurants, an ice rink, and more, is currently underway, but completion won't be for a few years. By 2012, its owner hopes that the center, named for a small, man-made lake on Camp Creek, which flows through the property, will draw comparisons to Rocky Mountain resort communities.

Collins Lake is being developed by Kirk Hanna, the owner of the Skibowl winter-sports complex. Hanna also is proceeding with plans to build an aerial gondola, more than a mile long, from Collins Lake to Timberline Lodge, linking across Hwy 26 to Skibowl. Visitors would then be able to avoid the meandering 6-mile road to Timberline. Exhibits at the **MOUNT HOOD CULTURAL CENTER AND MUSEUM** (Government Camp Loop; 503/272-3301; www.mthoodmuseum. org) show that in the 1950s, a passenger bus that was ungainly rigged as a gondola actually plied this route on an aerial cable for three years.

In summer, Skibowl becomes the **MT HOOD ADVENTURE PARK AT SKIBOWL** (800/234-6288; www.skibowl.com; every day Memorial Day–Labor Day, weekends in Sept). Mount Hood National Forest is a willing partner, giving its blessing to such attractions as scenic horseback rides, a mountain-biking park, a dual alpine slide, and hayrides on the federally owned ski slopes. Down in the parking lots, meanwhile, you can tumble off the 100-foot free-fall bungee tower. If that's not enough, go for an 80-foot fling on the reverse rapid-riser bungee jump. Indy karts, kiddy jeeps, trampolines, miniature and Frisbee golf, Velcro fly trap, body Nerfing, batting cages, and a 40-by-60-foot play zone offer fun for all ages. The mountain bike park has 40 miles of trail and is served by two chairlifts. Scenic helicopter rides take off from the parking lot for a bird's-eye view of Mount Hood.

From Government Camp, the 50-mile, 90-minute drive to Portland—downhill all the way—passes through a series of small resort villages with names including Rhododendron, Zigzag, and Brightwood. A fine restaurant en route is the **RENDEZVOUS GRILL** (67149 E Hwy 26, Welches; 503/622-6837; www.rendezvousgrill.net), with creative continental cuisine at moderate prices. Nearby, the beautiful **RESORT AT THE MOUNTAIN** (68010 E Fairway Ave, Welches; 503/622-3101; www.theresort.com) is a slice of the Scottish Highlands an hour south of Hwy 26 (see review in the Lodgings chapter).

Nineteen miles from Portland, the town of **SANDY**—named for the nearby river—makes a nice stop with its century-old buildings, weekend country market, and fruit stands. Here you'll find **ORAL HULL PARK** (503/668-6194; www.oralhull. org), designed for the blind but a pleasure for the sighted as well, with splashing water and plants to smell and feel. You'll need permission to walk through the garden unless you're a guest at the conference lodge here. If you're headed up to the snow from Portland, several ski shops can provide equipment and information—including busy **OTTO'S CROSS COUNTRY SKI SHOP** (38716 Pioneer Blvd; 503/668-5947), next to the historic Good Shepherd Episcopal Church.

Oregon Wine Country

Oregon's rolling hills—with their good sunlight exposure, soil composition, and drainage—are choice locations for vineyards. Winemakers are at work in this state as far south as Ashland and as far east as Milton-Freewater, but the majority are clustered west and southwest of Portland in the northern Willamette Valley. State Hwy 99W, through the heart of Yamhill County, is an avenue to the greatest concentration of wineries in the state, which has developed a worldwide reputation for its fine **PINOT NOIR** and **PINOT GRIS** grapes.

The wineries themselves are delightful to visit for those with even a passing interest in wine. In all seasons, there is much to take in, from misty hills reminiscent of a Japanese woodcut to flaming fall colors to the harvesting of the small, intensely flavored grapes. Almost all wineries have tasting rooms staffed by either winery owners or workers with intimate knowledge of the wines and production methods. Facility tours are often offered, and, of course, there are wines to sample, which may include vintages not available elsewhere or small lots from grapes in scarce supply. Do take along bread, cheese, and other wine-friendly foods to enjoy, or stop into one of a handful of eateries in **DUNDEE** or **MCMINNVILLE**. Calling in advance is always recommended; some wineries are closed in January.

Start your wine tour by making an advance dinner reservation at one of the fine restaurants in this region such as **TINA'S**, **NICK'S**, or **DUNDEE BISTRO** (see reviews of all three in the Restaurants chapter). Then enjoy the drive along Hwy 99W, Oregon's official wine road. Local produce stands dot the roadside in summer, and the wineries, antique shops, and galleries will give you many options to follow your whims as you pass through these lush green hills. Between Dundee and McMinnville, you might drop in at the former **LAFAYETTE SCHOOLHOUSE** (Hwy 99W, Lafayette; 503/864-2720), now a 100-dealer antique mall.

Because Oregon has more than 350 wineries, it can be hard for the traveler to know where to stop. These are a few of our favorites, all of them located on or near Hwy 99W in Yamhill County (listed from north to south), all with tasting rooms open year-round.

REX HILL VINEYARDS (30835 N Hwy 99W, Newberg; 503/538-0666; www. rexhill.com) occupies a restored 1920s fruit-and-nut-drying plant. Founder Paul Hart's winery has produced numerous vineyard-designated pinot noirs that have received critical attention. Rex Hill's location is splendid, with perennials in bloom even when the grapevines are not, making this one of the state's best visitor facilities.

DUCK POND CELLARS (23145 Hwy 99W, Dundee; 503/538-3199; www. duckpondcellars.com) gets wide commercial exposure for the various wines it produces here from Washington vineyards (mainly Columbia Valley merlots and chardonnays) as well as Oregon pinots. A gourmet food and gift market is on-site.

ARGYLE WINERY (691 Hwy 99W, Dundee; 503/538-8520; www.argylewinery. com) is producing some of the best sparkling wines in the region as well as fine chardonnays and pinot noirs. Argyle has a tasting room ensconced in a restored Victorian farmhouse.

ERATH VINEYARDS (9409 NE Worden Hill Rd, Dundee; 503/538-3318; www. erath.com), one of the pioneer Oregon wineries, is noted for wonderful pinots and late-harvest Rieslings. Dick Erath's wines are a good value, and his winery is in a beautiful setting uphill from Crabtree Park—nice for picnics.

SOKOL BLOSSER WINERY (5000 Sokol Blosser Ln, Dundee; 503/864-2282; www.sokolblosser.com), high on a hill overlooking the Yamhill Valley, offers visitors a self-guided vineyard tour showcasing grape varieties and seasonal changes. The winery is renowned for its pinot noirs and its unique underground barrel-aging cellar, winner of environmental design awards.

CHATEAU BENOIT WINERY (6580 NE Mineral Springs Rd, Carlton; 503/864-2991; www.chateaubenoint.com) is best known for pinots, chardonnays, and German-style white wines. With a marvelous hilltop view, it's popular with picnickers.

LAUREL RIDGE WINERY (13301 NE Kuehne Rd, Carlton; 503/852-7050; www. laurelridgewinery.com) has a location in the WillaKenzie district where you can taste excellent sparkling wine and award-winning sauvignon blanc and pinot noir.

Many other wineries are open to the public only on Thanksgiving and Memorial Day weekends or by appointment. Most offer case discounts over the holiday weekends. For a complete guide to the state's wineries, contact the **OREGON WINE ADVISORY BOARD** (1200 NW Naito Pkwy, Ste 400, Portland; 503/228-8336; www.oregonwine.org). For an organized tour of the wine country, contact **OREGON WINE TOURS** (2200 SE 45th Ave, Hillsboro; 503/681-9463; www. orwinetours.com). To take a bicycle tour of wine country, contact **PEDAL BIKE TOURS** (503/916-9704; www.pedalbiketours.com).

If you're inclined to overnight in the wine country, the **BLACK WALNUT INN & VINEYARD** (9600 NE Worden Hill Rd, Dundee; 866/429-4114; www.black walnut-inn.com) offers Tuscan-style luxury in the heart of the Yamhill Valley.

MCMINNVILLE

With about 30,000 residents, McMinnville is decidedly the population center of Oregon's Wine Country. At the **CHAMBER OF COMMERCE** (417 NW Adams St; 503/472-6196; www.mcminnville.org), pick up a walking-tour map of the **DOWNTOWN HISTORIC DISTRICT**; it points out many late-19th- and early-20th-century buildings up and down Third Street.

Then drop by the **EVERGREEN AVIATION MUSEUM** (3685 NE Cumulus Ave, at McMinnville airport; 503/472-9361; www.sprucegoose.org). Howard Hughes's famous "flying boat," the Spruce Goose, is the star attraction here. The largest aircraft in the world, it was built to carry 750 men into World War II battle. The plane has a 335-foot wingspan and took so long to build that the war ended before the plane was completed. The institute also has a '40s-style cafe, a movie theater, and 40 other planes on display.

Another McMinnville attraction is the McMenamins' **HOTEL OREGON** (310 NE Evans St; 503/472-8427; www.mcmenamins.com), 100 years old in 2005. The refurbished four-story hotel has 42 rooms and a popular pub for dining and drinking.

Conclude your Yamhill County wine touring with a visit to the **LAWRENCE GALLERY** (19700 SW Hwy 18, Sheridan; 503/843-3633; www.lawrence gallery.net), about 10 minutes' drive southwest of McMinnville. You can picnic among the sculptures in the outdoor garden, and indoor displays include paintings, jewelry, prints, and pottery by some 200 artists. (Ask to see the tonalist wine country landscapes of local painter Ramona Youngquist.) Within the gallery is the **OREGON WINE TASTING ROOM** (503/843-3787), where you can sample wines from more than 50 different wineries—including a long and impressive roster of Oregon pinot noirs. Put your new wine knowledge to good use as you order lunch at **FRESH PALATE** (503/843-4400), above the gallery. Eating on the deck feels like dining in the treetops; Northwest cuisine, crab cakes, and sandwiches are all made from scratch.

WASHINGTON COUNTY WINERIES

Even closer to Portland than the Yamhill County wineries are the dozen or so of Washington County's Tualatin Valley. It's easy to pack a picnic lunch and take a short afternoon drive west of the metropolis. Each of the following recommended wineries (listed from east to west) has a three-decade reputation, and each welcomes visitors daily year-round.

PONZI VINEYARDS (14665 SW Winery Ln, Beaverton; 503/628-1227; www.ponziwines.com), designed by Dick and Nancy Ponzi, is now in the hands of their three children. Bottlings of pinot noir, pinot gris, and chardonnay are first rate. The Ponzis also own and operate the charming **DUNDEE BISTRO** (see review in the Restaurants chapter).

Founded in 1970 by the Vuylsteke family, **OAK KNOLL WINERY** (29700 SW Burkhalter Rd, Hillsboro; 503/648-8198; www.oakknollwinery.com) produces notable fruit and berry wines (including a raspberry framboise), plus award-winning pinot noir and pinot gris. Its picnic grounds are very popular.

SHAFER VINEYARD CELLARS (6200 NW Gates Creek Rd, Forest Grove; 503/357-6604; www.shafervineyardcellars.com; open weekends only in Jan), at its tasting room overlooking the Gates Creek Valley, shares an unusually wide range of wines: sparkling wines, pinot noir, pinot gris, chardonnay, Riesling, and German-style whites (gewürztraminer and Müller-Thurgau).

Two additional wineries worth your attention are **MONTINORE ESTATE** (3663 SW Dilley Rd, Forest Grove; 503/359-5012; www.montinore.com) and **KRAMER VINEYARDS** (26830 NW Olson Rd, Gaston; 503/662-4545; www.kramerwine.com).

Champoeg-Aurora

A pair of old pioneer communities on opposite sides of the Willamette River, about 20 miles south of Portland via I-5, Champoeg and Aurora can make an interesting half-day trip for the history-minded traveler.

Before fur traders and settlers arrived in the early 1800s, **CHAMPOEG** (pronounced "sham-POO-ey") was home to Calapooya Indians. Today the town's history is remembered at the **CHAMPOEG STATE HERITAGE AREA** (8239 Champoeg Rd NE, St Paul; 503/678-1251; www.oregonstateparks.org/park_113.php; $3 per vehicle), a 568-acre park on the banks of the Willamette. The excellent visitors center describes how, in 1843, local settlers voted to form the first provisional government of the Oregon Country. The heritage area allows picnicking, bicycling, Frisbee, and volleyball on summer weekends. In **THE PIONEER MOTHERS MEMORIAL CABIN** (www.newellhouse.com/pioneercabin; open Mon and Fri–Sat; $2 adults, $1 children), an original log cabin maintained by the Daughters of the American Revolution, kids can knead bread dough, card wool, and make fires using flint and steel—just as pioneer children did.

Just west of the park entrance is the **NEWELL HOUSE** (503/678-5537; call for hours, closed Nov–Feb; $4 adults, $2 children), a replica of the 1852 original, which serves as a museum of American Indian and pioneer artifacts. On the grounds are the Butteville Jail (1850) and a pioneer schoolhouse.

The town of **AURORA**, midway between Portland and Salem on the east bank of the Willamette, is a well-preserved turn-of-the-20th-century village that's been put on the National Register of Historic Places. It's also a well-known antique center. About two dozen clapboard and Victorian houses line a mile-long stretch of Hwy 99E, and more than half of them have been made into antique shops (most closed Mon). An outstanding restaurant, the popular **CHEZ MOUSTACHE** (21527 Hwy 99E; 503/678-1866), has for many years served French continental cuisine.

In 1856, Prussian immigrant Dr. William Keil led a group of Pennsylvania Germans here to establish a communal settlement of Harmonites; Aurora is named for Keil's daughter. Property, labor, and profits were shared, and the society prospered under his strong rule. Farming sustained the economy, but outsiders knew the colony for the excellence of its handicrafts: furniture, clothing, tools, embroidered goods, baskets, and clarinet reeds. After a smallpox epidemic in 1862 and the coming of the railroad in 1870, the colony gradually weakened.

The **OLD AURORA COLONY MUSEUM** (15018 2nd Ave; 503/678-5754; www.auroracolony.org; call for days open, which vary annually; $6 adults, $2 children) recounts the history of the town with five buildings: the ox barn, the Karus home, the Steinbach log cabin, the communal washhouse, and the farm-equipment shed. Among its annual events, **COLONY DAYS** in August and a quilt show in October are standouts.

Northern Oregon Coast

It won't take you much more than 90 minutes, if that, to drive to the Oregon Coast from Portland. Once you've arrived, however, chances are you'll want to stay for longer than a day. Technically, it's no problem driving this 300-mile loop—Portland west to Astoria, south down US Hwy 101 to Lincoln City, then east and north back to Portland—in a single day. Practically speaking, you may want to take three days.

Therefore, we've broken the northern Oregon Coast section into three parts: **ASTORIA TO SEASIDE** (between US Hwys 30 and 26), **CANNON BEACH TO TILLAMOOK** (US Hwy 26 and State Hwy 6), and **TILLAMOOK TO LINCOLN CITY** (State Hwys 6 and 18). Any one of these loops provides you quick access to and from Portland, in case you must cut your journey short.

ASTORIA TO SEASIDE

Situated on the tip of a peninsula where the Columbia River reaches the Pacific Ocean, **ASTORIA** has a unique, edge-of-the-world flavor. Its Victorian architecture, natural beauty, and rich American Indian and immigrant history offer much to the visitor.

Take Hwy 30 west from I-405; it's 107 miles from Portland to Astoria. Your first stop might be the **ASTORIA COLUMN**, atop Coxcomb Hill, Astoria's highest point. The 164-step climb to the top is well worth it, affording a seemingly endless panorama of the harbor, the Columbia estuary, and the distant headlands of the Pacific. Spiral murals of the region's history wrap around the outside of the column. To get there, drive up to the top of 16th Street and follow the signs.

The history of U.S. exploration and settlement here begins with Captain Robert Gray, who sailed up the river in 1792, naming it after his ship, the *Columbia Rediviva*—which saw only 10 miles of the river before turning back to sea. In 1805–06, Lewis and Clark spent a miserably rainy winter at Fort Clatsop, now restored as the **FORT CLATSOP NATIONAL MEMORIAL** (6 miles SW of Astoria; 503/861-2471; www.nps.gov/lewi/planyourvisit/fortclatsop. htm). The cabin was destroyed by an arson fire in 2004 but has since been rebuilt. Besides audiovisuals and exhibits in the visitors center, there are living-history demonstrations of musket firing, candle making, and the like during the summer.

In 1810 New York fur trader John Jacob Astor sent to the Northwest the fur-trading company that founded **FORT ASTORIA** (at 15th and Exchange sts). The fort had all but disappeared by the mid-19th century but now has been partially reconstructed.

The city of Astoria really dates from the late 1840s, when it began to thrive as a customhouse town and shipping center. The well-maintained Victorians lining the harbor hillside at Franklin and Grand avenues provide glimpses of that era. Astoria today is a museum without walls, an unstirred mix of the old and new that find common ground along the busy waterfront—once the site of canneries and river steamers, now an active port for oceangoing vessels and Russian fish-processing ships. Salmon- and bottom-fishing trips leave from here.

SIXTH STREET RIVER PARK, with its always-open, covered observation tower, provides the best vantage point for viewing river commerce, observing river pilots as they board tankers and freighters, and watching seals and sea lions search for a free lunch. Just down the waterfront is the **COLUMBIA RIVER MARITIME MUSEUM** (1792 Marine Dr; 503/325-2323; www.crmm. org; every day 9:30am–5pm, year-round; $10 adults), the finest museum of its type in the Northwest. The 1951 Coast Guard lightship *Columbia* is moored outside, and inside are restored small craft and thematic galleries depicting the region's maritime heritage: fishing and whaling, fur trading, navigation, and shipwrecks.

Three other museums devoted to Astoria's history are operated by the **CLATSOP COUNTY HISTORICAL SOCIETY** (503/325-2203; www.cumtux. org). The **CLATSOP COUNTY HERITAGE MUSEUM** (16th and Exchange sts; 503/338-4849; www.ohwy.com/or/h/herimuse.htm; every day 10am–5pm May–Sept) is in the 1904 city hall building. **THE FLAVEL HOUSE** (8th and Duane sts; every day 9:30am–5:30pm May–Sept; $5 for adults, $4 for seniors, $2 for kids), built by the Columbia River's first steamship pilot, Captain George Flavel, is the city's best example of ornate Queen Anne architecture. The **UPPERTOWN FIREFIGHTERS MUSEUM** (2986 Marine Dr) houses an extensive collection of fire-fighting equipment dating back to 1879.

An unpretentious town of about 10,000 residents, Astoria all but shuts down on Sundays. Downtown, art galleries are tucked in next to the fishermen's bars and mom-and-pop cafes, and there are a few notable restaurants as well. If there's a gathering place for the town's intelligentsia, it's **GODFATHER'S BOOKS AND ESPRESSO** (1108 Commercial St; 503/325-8143; godfathers.mosaicglobe.com).

The leading accommodation in Astoria is the newly renovated **CANNERY PIER HOTEL** (10 Basin St; 503/325-4996; www.cannerypierhotel.com), a luxury boutique property extending atop a pier into the Columbia River on the site of a former fish cannery. Amenities include a full-service spa and a private yacht. Bed-and-breakfasts have proliferated, particularly in the lovely Victorian homes on the steep hillsides overlooking the river. The **BENJAMIN YOUNG INN** (3652 Duane St; 503/325-6172 or 800/201-1286; www. benjaminyounginn.com) has five lavishly decorated guest rooms and stellar views of the Columbia River. The Finnish innkeepers at the **ROSE RIVER INN** (1510 Franklin Ave; 503/325-7175 or 888/876-0028; www.roseriverinn. com) bring European flair to their lodging; ask about the sauna paneled in Alaska yellow cedar. The reasonably priced and rambling **ROSEBRIAR INN**

(636 14th St; 503/325-7427; www.rosebriar.net) has 11 rooms, each with a private bath.

For upscale creative dining, visit the **SILVER SALMON GRILLE** (1185 Commercial St; 503/338-6640; www.silversalmongrille.com) or the **URBAN CAFE** (1119 Commercial St; 503/338-5133). The **RIO CAFE** (125 9th St; 503/325-2409) offers inspired south-of-the-border cuisine. But the place to go in this fishermen's town for Sunday brunch and the catch of the day is the **CANNERY CAFE** (foot of 6th St; 503/325-8642), which sits on pilings right over the water. Buy fresh seafood at **UNIONTOWN FISH MARKET** (229 W Marine Dr; 503/325-9592; www.uniontownfishmarket.com) or at **JOSEPH-SON'S SMOKEHOUSE** (106 Marine Dr; 503/325-2190; www.josephsons. com), whose superb hot-smoked and cold-smoked seafood includes salmon, tuna, and sturgeon.

Astoria is a natural starting point for excursions to the Oregon and Washington coasts. Get panoramic views of both from the **SOUTH JETTY LOOKOUT TOWER**, Oregon's northwesternmost point. **FORT STEVENS STATE PARK AND HISTORICAL SITE** (Pacific Dr, Hammond), 20 minutes west of Astoria off Hwy 101, preserves a military reservation built at the mouth of the Columbia during the Civil War as part of Oregon's coastal defense. Fired upon in June 1942 by a Japanese submarine, it was the only fort in the continental United States to see action during World War II. Today Fort Stevens is a 3,500-acre park offering 604 campsites, 7 miles of bike paths, uncrowded beaches, and Mongolian yurts (rigid-walled domed tents) for rent. (Yurts in Oregon state parks have light, heat, and sleeping space for eight people. For reservations and information, call Reservations Northwest, 800/452-5687.) Walk the beach to see the rusted hulk of the British schooner *Peter Iredale*, wrecked in 1906.

Fifteen miles south of Astoria, **SEASIDE** is a horse of a very different color. Just past the charming, almost-bohemian seaside village of **GEARHART**, which lures visitors to its **PACIFIC WAY BAKERY & CAFE** (601 Pacific Wy; 503/738-0245), Seaside is a mini Atlantic City, minus the casinos.

Established at the turn of the 20th century as a summer resort for Portlanders, the town today spreads north and south along Hwy 101, flanking both sides of the tidal Necanicum River. Broadway, its main drag, is lined with souvenir shops, seafood houses, and youth-oriented amusement centers. From the vehicle turnaround at its seaward end, a broad, paved pedestrian walk—known as **NORTH PROM** and **SOUTH PROM**—extends for 1½ miles along the shore, sometimes shielded from the waves by bunchgrass.

Seaside's premier attraction is its historic **SEASIDE AQUARIUM** (200 N Prom; 503/738-6211; www.seasideaquarium.com; every day 9am–close; $7.50 for adults, $6.25 for seniors; $3.75 for children 6–13, free for children under 5), Oregon's original (1937) marine-life center, though its importance has long since been eclipsed by Newport's Oregon Coast Aquarium. The **SEASIDE HISTORICAL SOCIETY MUSEUM** (570 Necanicum Dr; 503/738-7065; www.seasidemuseum.org; hours vary; $3 for adults, $2 for seniors, $1 for students, free for children under 6) encompasses the 1912 Butterfield

Beach Cottage. On the south side of town, you can view a circa-1900 re-creation of a **SALT CAIRN** established at the site by the Lewis and Clark Expedition (the southernmost point they visited), a touching **UNKNOWN SAILOR'S GRAVE** ("Found on the Beach April 25 1865 Known Only to God"), and a popular cold-water surfing destination at the **COVE** (watch surfers from benches in Seltzer Park).

The **SEASIDE CHAMBER OF COMMERCE** (800/444-6740; www.seaside chamber.com) recommends 48 places to stay in town, including the unique **SEASIDE OCEANFRONT INN** (581 S Prom; 503/738-6403 or 888/772-7766; www.theseasideinn.com). For dining, consider the ever-popular **NORMA'S OCEAN DINER** (20 N Columbia St; 503/738-4331; normasoceandiner.com).

Four miles south of Seaside, Hwy 101 meets Hwy 26, the most direct route back to Portland from the coast. Cannon Beach is about 3 miles south of the intersection.

CANNON BEACH TO TILLAMOOK

CANNON BEACH relishes its reputation as the Carmel of the Northwest. This artsy community with a hip ambience has strict building codes that prohibit neon and ensure that only aesthetically pleasing structures of weathered cedar and other woods are built. In summer, the town explodes with visitors who come to browse local galleries and crafts shops on crowded Hemlock Street. Its main draw is the spectacular beach: wide, inviting, and among the prettiest anywhere. Dominating the long, sandy stretch is **HAYSTACK ROCK**, at 235 feet high, one of the world's largest coastal monoliths. It's impressive enough just to gaze at, but check it out at low tide to observe the rich marine life in the tidal pools.

ECOLA STATE PARK (on the north side of Seaside) has fine overlooks, picnic tables, and good hiking trails. If you climb to Tillamook Head, you can see the **TILLAMOOK ROCK LIGHT STATION**, a lighthouse built offshore under difficult conditions more than 100 years ago and abandoned in 1957. Today it is a columbarium (a facility for storing cremated remains) called "Eternity at Sea." No camping is allowed along the densely wooded trail, except for summer campsites atop the head.

Shopping is a favorite pastime in Cannon Beach, and there are enough shops and galleries along Hemlock Street, the main drag, to keep you busy until the tide goes out. Especially good ones are the **JEFFREY HULL GALLERY** (172 N Hemlock St in Sandpiper Square; 503/436-2600; www.hullgallery. com), with notable watercolors; **HAYSTACK GALLERY** (183 N Hemlock St in Cannon Beach Mall; 503/436-2547; www.haystackgallery.com), with prints and photographs; and **WHITEBIRD GALLERY** (251 N Hemlock St; 503/436-2681; www.whitebirdgallery.com), featuring a variety of arts and crafts.

The **COASTER THEATRE PLAYHOUSE** (108 N Hemlock St; 503/436-1242; www.coastertheatre.com) has a year-round schedule of mainly comedies and musicals. Its summer repertory theater includes the likes of Ken Ludwig's *Moon Over Buffalo*, George Stiles and Anthony Drewe's *Honk!* and Ira Levin's *Death Trap*. Portland State University's **HAYSTACK PROGRAM IN THE**

ARTS (503/725-8500; www.ohwy.com/or/r/r0248867.htm) conducts workshops for adult students at the Cannon Beach grade school.

There are several good restaurants in town. One of the very best is **NEWMAN'S AT 988** (988 S Hemlock St; 503/436-1151; www.newmansat988. com), which inhabits an unmistakable yellow house and is carefully looked over by John Newman, four-time champion at the Tillamook County Black Box competition, as well as winner of numerous other culinary awards. The **OCEANFRONT WAYFARER** (Oceanfront and Gower sts; 503/436-1108; www. wayfarer-restaurant.com) and **JP'S AT CANNON BEACH** (1116 S Hemlock St in Cannon Beach Hotel; 503/436-0908; www.jpsatcannonbeach.com) are renowned for their seafood. For something more artsy, in keeping with the community's ambience, consider the **BISTRO** (263 N Hemlock St; 503/436-2661): intimate and rustic, with Mediterranean-style chops, seafood, and pastas; or the **LAZY SUSAN** (126 N Hemlock St; 503/436-2816; www. lazy-susan-cafe.com), a casual restaurant beside the Coaster Theatre.

For accommodations, a centrally located choice is the clean and comfortable **ARGONAUTA INN** (188 W 2nd St; 503/436-2601 or 800/822-2468; www. thewavesmotel.com), in a series of early-20th-century Victorian beachside cottages, now operated by the Waves Motel. The nicely refurbished **CANNON BEACH HOTEL** (116 S Hemlock St; 503/436-1392; www.cannonbeachhotel. com) is on the main road through town, three blocks from the beach.

The south side of Cannon Beach is better suited for luxury lodgers. Side by side on a beautiful stretch of sand are two elegant properties. The well-known **STEPHANIE INN** (2740 S Pacific St; 503/436-2221 or 800/633-3466; www.stephanie-inn.com) has 46 rooms with ocean or mountain views and a renowned prix-fixe dining room with two seatings nightly (non-inn guests can also dine here). Its beautiful, pet-friendly next-door neighbor, the **OCEAN LODGE** (2864 S Pacific St; 503/436-2241 or 888/777-4047; www.theocean-lodge.com), has 45 rooms with fireplaces and eight beach bungalows.

TOLOVANA PARK, nestled on Cannon Beach's south side, is more laid-back and less crowded than the in-town beach. Leave your vehicle at the Tolovana Park Wayside (with parking and restrooms) and stroll the uncluttered beach. At low tide you can walk all the way to **ARCH CAPE**, 5 miles south, but take care: the incoming tide might block your return. **HUG POINT STATE PARK**, south of Arch Cape, is comprised of a rocky beach nestled between two headlands. Just south of here is **OSWALD WEST STATE PARK**, with one of the finest campgrounds on any coast in the world. You walk a half mile from the parking lot (where wheelbarrows are available to carry your gear) to tent sites among old-growth trees; the ocean, with a massive cove and tide pools, is just beyond. No reservations are accepted (open for camping Mar–Oct only), but the walk deters some of the crowds who might otherwise come.

Low-key **MANZANITA** is gaining popularity as a second home for in-the-know Portlanders. The attractions are obvious: the adjacent Nehalem Bay area is a windsurfing mecca, and **NEHALEM BAY STATE PARK**, just south of town, offers hiking and bike trails, miles of little-used beaches, and lodging in yurts. Overlooking it all is nearby **NEAHKAHNIE MOUNTAIN**, its steep, switchbacked trail leading to a 1,600-foot summit with the best viewpoints on Oregon's North Coast. Hundreds of miles of Coast Range logging roads offer unlimited mountain-biking thrills. The nearby, quaint river town of **NEHALEM**, just inland from Manzanita, is becoming a destination for kayakers, who find rental craft available here.

Besides a great beach, Manzanita has great food. The best pizza on the North Coast can be had at **MARZANO'S** (60 Laneda Ave; 503/368-3663; www.affordablewebhosting.com/marzanos.htm). For a pampered, adults-only retreat, try the **INN AT MANZANITA** (67 Laneda Ave; 503/368-6754; www.innatmanzanita.com).

A few miles south of Manzanita, at the head of Tillamook Bay, is the old fishing town of **GARIBALDI**, whose charms are all about fresh seafood. Head out to the fishermen's terminal to buy live crabs, steamer clams, oysters, and fresh fish, or take a table and order some finny delights at **TILLAMOOK BAY BOATHOUSE** (500 S Biak St; 503/322-3600; www.tillamookbayboathouse. com). Nearby **BAY CITY** is Oyster Central: watch the gritty mollusks harvested and shucked at the **PACIFIC OYSTER COMPANY** (5150 Oyster Dr; 503/377-2323); see them artistically rendered at the **ARTSPACE** gallery and bistro (Hwy 101 and 5th St; 503/377-2782); or stop for a bowl of chowder at **DOWNIE'S CAFE** (9320 5th St; 503/377-2220).

If you're planning to return to Portland, turn east on Hwy 6 in downtown Tillamook. The big city is a 78-mile drive away.

TILLAMOOK TO LINCOLN CITY

In Tillamook County alone, there are 198 dairy farms and 41,600 cows. So say the displays at the **TILLAMOOK COUNTY CREAMERY ASSOCIA-TION** (4175 Hwy 101N; 503/815-1300; www.tillamookcheese.com; every day)—better known as the Tillamook cheese factory. With an international reputation, this cheesery at the north end of town draws hordes of tourists for the self-guided tour (including big windows overlooking the factory floor) and for scoops of rich ice cream in waffle cones. For less kitsch—but no ice cream—you might drive another mile south on Hwy 101 to the **BLUE HERON FRENCH CHEESE COMPANY** (2001 Blue Heron Dr; 503/842-8281; www. blueheronoregon.com; every day), where you can sample a variety of cheeses and other Oregon-made specialty foods, including wine.

THE TILLAMOOK COUNTY PIONEER MUSEUM (2106 2nd St; 503/842-4553; www.tcpm.org) occupies three floors of Tillamook's 1905 county courthouse. Shipwreck buffs will be particularly interested in the artifacts (including huge chunks of beeswax with Spanish markings) from an unnamed 18th-century Spanish galleon that wrecked near the base of Neahkahnie Mountain. The **MUNSON FALLS NATURAL SITE** (Munson Creek Rd off Hwy 101), 7 miles south of Tillamook, features a 319-foot waterfall—Oregon's second tallest.

Tillamook lodgings are strictly of the franchise variety. For breakfast or lunch featuring Tillamook cheese, stop in at the **FARMHOUSE CAFÉ** (4175 Hwy 101N; 503/815-1300; www.tillamookcheese.com), located at the factory; for dinner you may want to backtrack to Manzanita or move on to Lincoln City.

Unless you're in a tremendous hurry to get to Lincoln City, plan to detour close to the water, following the 22-mile **THREE CAPES SCENIC DRIVE**. This is arguably Oregon's most beautiful stretch of coastline. The narrow, winding road skirts Tillamook Bay, climbs over **CAPE MEARES** (a state park with a working lighthouse), traverses the shores of **NETARTS BAY**, and runs over **CAPE LOOKOUT**, the westernmost headland on Oregon's North Coast. The trail from the parking lot at Cape Lookout's summit meanders through primeval forests of stately cedar and Sitka spruce. Camping facilities in the state park include yurts.

The lower side of the drive provides spectacular ocean vistas. Down at sea level, the desertlike dune landscape presents a stark contrast to Cape Lookout's densely forested slopes. The road to **PACIFIC CITY** and the route's third cape, **CAPE KIWANDA**, runs through lush, green dairy country. Pacific City is known for its hang gliders, which swoop off the slopes of the cape and land on the sandy expanses below. Kin to the one at Cannon Beach, another Haystack Rock sits a half mile offshore. Even if you've never visited before, this area may look familiar: the late Ray Atkeson, a nationally acclaimed Oregon photographer, made Cape Kiwanda the most photographed spot on the Oregon Coast.

ROBERT STRAUB STATE PARK at the south end of Pacific City occupies most of the Nestucca Beach sand spit. The Nestucca River flows idly to the sea right outside the **RIVERHOUSE RESTAURANT** (34450 Brooten Rd; 503/965-6722), a calming, apple-pie sort of place. Gargantuan cinnamon rolls and crusty bread and pizzas can be had nearby at the **GRATEFUL BREAD BAKERY** (34805 Brooten Rd; 503/965-7337; www.pacificcity.org/Grateful-Bread/home.html). At the secluded **EAGLE'S VIEW BED AND BREAKFAST** (37975 Brooten Rd; 503/965-7600), all five guest rooms have private baths. As you might guess, the panoramas are grand.

The Nestucca dairy land inland from here is some of the most fertile in the state. You can pick up Hwy 101 again in **CLOVERDALE**, a town that became famous for a 1986–87 battle with state officials over two roadside signs (featuring Clover the Cow) that violated a state signage law. Outside Cloverdale, in the middle of nowhere, is the historic 1906 **HUDSON HOUSE BED & BREAKFAST** (37700 Hwy 101S; 503/392-3533; www.hudsonhouse.com).

OTIS is barely more than a junction, but the busy **OTIS CAFE** (you can't miss it; 541/994-2813; http://otiscafe.tripod.com) and its down-home breakfasts, shakes, and homemade pies—good enough to have been touted in *The New York Times*—have put this tiny town on the map. Here's where Hwy 18 from Portland (a two-hour drive) joins Hwy 101, just north of Lincoln City.

If local business owners have their way, **LINCOLN CITY** may someday have a more "beachlike" (and thus more tourist-friendly) name. Most locals seem happy with the name as is, though, and it hasn't stopped hordes of Willamette Valley residents from converging on Lincoln City year-round. Whale watchers appreciate the nearby viewpoints; shoppers hunt for bargains at the huge outlet mall on the east side of Hwy 101; and others simply pass through before dispersing to quieter points north and south.

Outstanding lodgings are few and far between in Lincoln City, although the scene has slightly improved over the past few years. The upscale ocean-front **O'DYSIUS HOTEL** (120 NW Inlet Ct; 541/994-4121 or 800/869-8069; www.odysius.com) contains 30 sizable units outfitted with such amenities as fireplaces and whirlpool baths. The **INN AT SPANISH HEAD** (4009 SW Hwy 101; 541/996-2161 or 800/452-8127; www.spanishhead.com) is a 10-story, 120-room hotel with a large outdoor swimming pool and full kitchens in most rooms. If you happen to be here in December or January, take some time to search the Pacific horizon for **MIGRATING WHALES** that make their way south to Mexico to mate and give birth, or catch them on their way back March to June.

Consistently the finest place to dine is the **BAY HOUSE** (5911 SW Hwy 101; 541/996-3222; www.thebayhouse.org), where the food, like the view, is worth savoring. The **BLACKFISH CAFÉ** (2733 NW Hwy 101; 541/996-1007; www.blackfishcafe.com) has a bustling open kitchen that turns out exemplary clam chowder and much more. At the **LIGHTHOUSE BREW PUB** (4157 N Hwy 101; 541/994-7238; www.mcmenamins.com), expect the same pub grub as at any McMenamins establishment—and beer made on the premises.

Two good shopping stops are **BARNACLE BILL'S SEAFOOD MARKET** (2174 NE Hwy 101; 541/994-3022; www.barnaclebillsseafood.com), famous for fresh seafood and smoked fish—salmon, sturgeon, albacore tuna, and black cod—and **CATCH THE WIND KITE SHOP** (266 SE Hwy 101; 541/994-9500; www.catchthewind.com), headquarters for a coastal chain of excellent kite stores.

RECREATION

RECREATION

Outdoor Activities

Proud and protective of their parks and green spaces, Portlanders are never more than a few minutes from a quick getaway for bird-watching, kayaking, or cycling. A little farther afield, they have the magnificent scenery of the Pacific Coast, the snowy slopes of Mount Hood, and the dry air of the central Oregon desert. As the city continues to grow and freeways clog with newcomers and old-timers alike, harried drivers at least know that where the traffic jams end, the fun begins.

Outdoor Recreation, published four times a year by **PORTLAND PARKS AND RECREATION** (1120 SW 5th Ave, Rm 1302, Downtown; 503/823-5132; www.portlandonline.com/parks; map:F3), is a comprehensive guide to seasonal recreation programs. There's something in it for everyone: from cross-country ski trips and whale-watching in winter to hiking, paddling, biking, fly-fishing, tot walks, and historic bridge tours in summer. Pick it up free at libraries and outdoor stores. **METRO** (503/797-1850, ext 4; www.oregonmetro.gov) has a department of parks, trails, and green spaces that publishes *GreenScene*, another quarterly guide to the great outdoors, this one focused on wildlife habitats. Other suburban park districts have similar programs.

BICYCLING

In 2008 the League of American Bicyclists gave Portland a platinum level, one of only two cities in the country to achieve the highest level yet awarded. In 2007 the Census Bureau found that more people bike to work in Portland than in any other U.S. city. In 2006, in its most recent rating, *Bicycling* magazine named the City of Roses the most bike-friendly city in the country. Why does Portland love bicycles? The diverse topography—flat and breezy stretches on the east side, steep and breathless hills on the west—has something for every cyclist, and many streets have bike lanes. In Portland, a lot of people bike to work and shop, and urban messengers work on bikes, as do some of the downtown police patrols.

Want to know the quickest and safest bike route to your destination? Grab a copy of the 25th anniversary map *Bike There* ($6), published in 2007 by Metro and available at area cycle shops and some bookstores. You can take your bike on any Tri-Met bus or MAX train without a special pass, just paying the standard fare; buses and trains are outfitted with racks to make the going easy.

Cyclists looking for organized 30- to 100-mile rides at a touring pace should call the hotline for the **PORTLAND WHEELMEN TOURING CLUB** (503/257-7982; www.pwtc.com). As many as 120 people show up for group and nongroup rides—several each weekend and at least one nearly every day of the year—and you don't have to be a member to pedal along. **PEDAL BIKE TOURS** (503/916-9704; www.pedalbiketours.com) provides bikes and offers a variety of organized bike tours around Portland and through the Willamette Valley wine country. The **BEAVERTON BICYCLE CLUB** (www.bbcbike.com), which sponsors road, track, and criterium events, has a strong group of junior riders but no age limit. The **OREGON BICYCLE RACING ASSOCIATION** (www.obra.org) acts as a clearinghouse for race information for two dozen competitive clubs in Oregon. From May to late August, races are held at **PORTLAND INTERNATIONAL RACEWAY** (West Delta Park; 503/823-7223; map:DD7) on Monday and Tuesday nights and at the **ALPENROSE DAIRY VELODROME** on most weeknights (6149 SW Shattuck Rd, Raleigh Hills; 503/246-0330; map:II8). The velodrome, one of the shortest in the country (hence heroically steep), is situated next to a working dairy farm. Admission is free for spectators. Classes are offered on Wednesdays, and fixed-gear bikes are available to rent.

The annual **CYCLE OREGON** (800/292-5367; www.cycleoregon.com) is staged each year in different parts of the state. The weeklong early-September event usually fills its quota of 2,000 riders. It has added a three-day summer weekend ride.

In the interest of protecting environmentally sensitive areas, **MOUNTAIN BIKING** is restricted to a handful of marked trails in the metropolitan region, but the available choices are well managed and rewarding. Portland was named "Top Dog in the USA" in the International Mountain Biking Association's 2007 report card, while the state of Oregon also got an "A" grade. Trail maps are available from Portland Parks and Recreation for Forest Park, Powell Butte, and the Springwater Corridor. Fat-tire cyclists looking for like minds join the **NORTHWEST TRAIL ALLIANCE** (formerly Portland United Mountain Pedalers) (www.nw-trail.org), whose motto is "Mountain biking is not a crime," for organized year-round weekend rides (see also the Leif Erikson Drive listing in this chapter). Check with a bike store for the latest club contact information or check PUMP's Web site. Also check out **THE BIKE GALLERY** (1001 SW 10th Ave, Downtown, 503/222-3821, map:G2; 5329 NE Sandy Blvd, Northeast, 503/281-9800, map:FF4; plus four other locations), the biggest bike-shop network in the city.

Although one avid **CYCLO-CROSS** racer has described that sport as "ballet on wheels," a less biased observer might see it as a mud festival for people who just can't get off their bikes. (Cyclo-cross first gained popularity in Europe as a means of breaking up the winter doldrums between racing seasons.) The annual **RIVER CITY BICYCLES CROSS CRUSADE** (www.crosscrusade.com), which runs early October through December, has half a dozen races. A typical cyclo-cross course takes riders through mud bogs, over barriers, down sharp slopes, and up short, steep hills. Racers spend about 30 percent of the race running with their bikes slung by their sides or over their shoulders. For information on all things mountain biking, contact **FAT TIRE FARM MOUNTAIN BIKE COMPANY** (2714 NW Thurman St, Northwest; 503/222-3276; www.fattirefarm.com; map:GG7).

The following are our favorite mountain- and road-bike routes in the Portland area. For more rides and details, ask the resident experts at a local bike shop, or pick up a copy of any cycling guidebook.

Banks/Vernonia State Trail

25 MILES WEST OF PORTLAND ON HWY 26 TO MANNING TRAILHEAD; 800/551-6949

An old railroad has been converted to a 21-mile-long trail in the eastern foothills of the Coast Range in Washington and Columbia counties. Most of the trail is paved, and it is scheduled to be completed in 2010 when the missing half-mile link into Banks is completed. About 3 miles of the trail pass through the new L. L. Stub Stewart State Park, which has an ongoing trail building program that is adding to its 17-mile system.

Hagg Lake

7 MILES SOUTHWEST OF FOREST GROVE; 503/846-8715

From early spring to October, cyclists swarm the paved and single-track loops around man-made Henry Hagg Lake in Scoggins Valley Park. The loops climb gentle hills and pass through woods and fields for some 16 miles, with numerous picnic and swimming spots along the way. The mountain bike route is more difficult than you might expect, due to the many short but seemingly endless ups and downs. Ambitious cyclists can start in Forest Grove and take the Old Tualatin Valley Highway to Scoggins Valley Road. Search the Web for "Hagg Lake," or look through the county's site: www. co.washington.or.us.

Leif Erikson Drive

END OF NW THURMAN ST TO NW GERMANTOWN RD, FOREST PARK

This 11-mile gravel road twists along the park's north side. For the first 6 miles, the road threads in and out of gullies, offering occasional spectacular views of the Willamette River and North Portland; the last 5 miles are the most isolated and peaceful. Leif Erikson is rough going (but possible) on touring bikes. Although the fragile Wildwood Trail is off-limits to bikes, four other areas are open for mountain biking. Take the cutoff to NW Skyline Boulevard via Fire Lane 3 (just past the 3-mile marker), NW Saltzman Road (6 miles), Springville Road (9 miles), or NW Germantown Road (11 miles). Then loop back on the precariously busy Hwy 30, or continue to Bonneville Road and Fire Lanes 12 and 15. Fat Tire Farm Mountain Bike Company, located about a mile from the Leif Erikson gate into Forest Park, will rent you everything you need. PUMP organizes year-round, after-work rides; meet at the gate to Leif Erikson Drive at 5:30pm Wednesday evenings. *Map: DD9–GG7.*

Marine Drive

KELLEY POINT PARK, AT THE CONFLUENCE OF THE WILLAMETTE AND COLUMBIA RIVERS, TO THE EAST END OF N MARINE DR

Just across the Willamette from Sauvie Island, Kelley Point Park anchors a favorite ride that follows the Columbia east along the airplane-swept flats of N Marine Drive. Most riders take the river road, but you can also cross the Columbia River on I-205 into Washington and on the bike sidewalk alongside roaring I-5. Connect the freeway river crossings in Vancouver with bike paths south of the Evergreen Hwy and Columbia Way. The bike lane across the Columbia is part of the I-205 bike path, which extends 15 miles south to the Clackamas River in Gladstone. *Map:AA9–BB6.*

Sauvie Island

10 MILES NORTHWEST OF PORTLAND VIA HWY 30

On this ride, the ends justify the means. Endure 10 miles of pedaling alongside 18-wheelers through the mostly industrial section of Hwy 30 from Northwest Portland to Sauvie Island (or shuttle your bike on Tri-Met bus 17 or on your car, crossing the new bridge to the island), and you'll be rewarded. The island is a bicycle-friendly zone—as long as you ride single file. The standard 12-mile loop has many scenic offshoots. Forgo the head-down hammer for a chin-up view of farm animals, U-pick flower and vegetable farms, great blue herons, and more. Be sure to visit Howell Territorial Park, a 100-acre park rich in cultural and natural history, including the 1850s Bybee-Howell House (see the Day Trips chapter). Metro has added a new restroom building and interpretive displays that explain how some of Oregon's earliest pioneers lived. *Map:CC9.*

Skyline Boulevard

BETWEEN NW CORNELL AND ROCKY POINT RDS

This 17-mile loop requires pedaling an elevation gain of 1,400 feet, but Skyline Boulevard is truly the most scenic ridgetop road in town, offering broad views of the Willamette Valley. Begin in Portland or Beaverton (the climb is about the same either way). From Portland, turn off NW Cornell onto 53rd Drive or Thompson Road for a peaceful (albeit steep and winding) climb to Skyline. Pack a few dollars and plan to stop for microbrews and a view at the Skyline Tavern (8031 NW Skyline Blvd; 503/286-4788; map:FF9) or for burgers, fries, and malts at the Skyline Restaurant (1313 NW Skyline Blvd; 503/292-6727; map:GG8). *Map:DD9–GG7.*

Springwater Corridor

SE IVON ST, SOUTHEAST PORTLAND TO TOWN OF BORING; PORTLAND PARKS AND RECREATION; 503/823-2223

Since 1990, when the City of Portland acquired the land, 21 miles of abandoned rail line and new trail have been opened to bikers, hikers, and horseback riders. The trail is linked on the Portland end to riverfront paths on both sides of the Willamette River, with good bike crossings on the Hawthorne and Steel bridges. The wild and weathered railbed was replaced by a tamer, smooth surface called sandseal. While mountain bikes are still the best two-wheel bet in the corridor, narrow road-bike tires can also negotiate most parts of the trail. The hardened surface runs from the Hawthorne Bridge through Westmoreland east to Gresham. Trailheads and toilets are located at SE Johnson Creek Boulevard, SE Hogan Road, and the Main City Park in Gresham. For more information, search the Web for "Springwater Corridor," or use the Internet shortcut "tinyurl.com/msnpd." *Map:JJ1–JJ5.*

BIRD-WATCHING/WILDLIFE VIEWING

Water makes Portland a wildlife haven. The infamous rainfall results in lush vegetation; the confluence of the Columbia and Willamette rivers lures myriad waterfowl; and streams, lakes, and wetlands form an emerald necklace around the metropolitan area. There's a regional effort to protect these wildlife habitats and promote responsible use of natural areas. As mentioned at the start of this chapter, four times a year, at the beginning of each season, Metro's department of parks, trails, and green spaces publishes *GreenScene*, a guide to hikes, benefit concerts, history tours, biking, river trips, and other organized activities that increase awareness of local wildlife habitats.

From great blue herons to beavers, minks to muskrats, an impressive array of wildlife calls Portland home. Every glove compartment or bike pack should include a copy of *Wild in the City*, a guide to Portland's natural areas by Michael C. Houck and M. J. Cody. Many viewing sites are marked with state highway signs depicting binoculars. For nature unleashed, venture to Powell Butte, Sauvie Island Wildlife Management Area, or Kelley Point Park (see entry in the Exploring chapter). Here are a few other notable natural areas.

Beggars-Tick Wildlife Refuge

SE 111TH AVE AND FOSTER RD, SOUTHEAST; 503/797-1850
Named after a native sunflower, the Beggars-Tick Wildlife Refuge serves as a wintering habitat for a diversity of waterfowl: wood ducks, green-winged teals, and hooded mergansers, to name a few. The marsh dries up during summer, but it still provides a permanent residence for muskrats, raccoons, and other species. *Map:II5.*

Fernhill Wetlands

1399 FERNHILL RD, FOREST GROVE; 503/357-5890
Located near the confluence of Gales Creek with the Tualatin River, 1 mile southeast of Forest Grove, the wetland has no maintenance staff, but its active friends group has built two viewing shelters. From the gravel parking lot 200 feet south of a sewage treatment plant, visitors can walk more than 2 miles of trail on gravel paths on dikes at the edge of the bird-rich ponds and sloughs. The east viewing shelter is surrounded by water, with waterfowl abundant during migrating seasons on the 243 acres.

Heron Lakes Golf Course

3500 N VICTORY BLVD, NORTH PORTLAND; 503/289-1818
Built around wetlands, the course is home to great blue herons as well as other waterfowl. Ask for permission and directions at the pro shop and, once on the course, be sure to keep your eyes open for birdies of the round, white, dimpled sort. *Map:CC7.*

Jackson Bottom Wetland Preserve

2600 SW HILLSBORO HWY, HILLSBORO; 503/681-6206
The 725-acre wildlife preserve within the Hillsboro city limits harbors a diverse array of birds typical in the Willamette Valley. A big attraction in winter is the appearance of bald eagles. The preserve has more than 4 miles of trail, but during the wet season, flooding keeps most of it inaccessible. A 12,000-square-foot farm-style building serves as the Wetlands Education Center, where a display features a rarity: an intact bald eagles' nest—all 1,500 pounds of it.

Oaks Bottom Wildlife Refuge

SE 7TH AVE AND SELLWOOD BLVD, SELLWOOD PARK
These 141 acres of woods and wetlands form the first officially designated wildlife refuge in Portland. The walk, just short of 3 miles, begins in Sellwood Park, with another trailhead at SE Milwaukie Boulevard and Mitchell Street in Westmoreland. More than 140 species of birds have been spotted here, among them great blue herons, which feed on carp in the refuge. Others include pileated woodpeckers and warblers (spring) and green-backed herons (spring and summer). *Map:JJ5.*

Portland Audubon Society Sanctuary

5151 NW CORNELL RD, FOREST PARK; 503/292-6855
This 150-acre sanctuary is surrounded by the vast wildness of Forest Park and connects to the Wildwood and MacLeay Park trails. The trails wrap around a pond and follow the creek. The Audubon House features a nature-oriented store (503/292-9453) with a selection of excellent books, an interpretive area, and a viewing window overlooking the feeding platforms for local songbirds. Year-round, the Audubon Society sponsors free field trips to teach people about nature. During winter, spring, and summer vacations, the sanctuary offers educational nature classes for kids. To listen to the weekly updated Rare Bird Alert message, call and ask for extension 2. *Map:FF7.*

Ross Island

WILLAMETTE RIVER, JUST SOUTH OF ROSS ISLAND BRIDGE
The Willamette island south of downtown actually includes the complex of Ross, Hardtack, East, and Toe islands. All but one are owned by a gravel mining business, but the dredging permit has expired, and what's left of the islands is slowly being reclaimed by nature. The city has accepted a 45-acre donation, but public access will still be restricted except for special occasions.

The northwest side of privately owned Toe Island is a 50-nest great blue heron rookery in a black-cottonwood grove. The rookery can be viewed only by boat or with binoculars from the mainland. The best shoreside views (try for winter, when the trees are leafless) are from the Willamette Greenway, just north of Willamette Park. Look for belted kingfishers nesting on the island's steep banks, as well as beavers and red foxes. Bald eagles have also nested on the island in the past. The nearest boat ramp is in Willamette Park, but don't land on the island. *Map:II6.*

Rosse Posse Acres

32690 S MATHIAS RD, MOLALLA; 503/829-7107
A commercial elk farm, family-owned Rosse Posse Acres (the family name is Ross) is a fun place to visit to see majestic Rocky Mountain elk. Children also love the petting zoo, with its pygmy goats, chickens, miniature donkeys and horses, sheep, turkeys, dogs, and cats. The best time to view the bull elk is before their antlers are cut. The antlers usually come off in mid-August, so that the bulls don't injure themselves in the fenced enclosure. *www.rosseposse acres.com.*

Tualatin River National Wildlife Refuge

19255 SW PACIFIC HWY, TUALATIN; 503/625-5944
Located in the floodplain of the Tualatin River, the national wildlife refuge has been acquiring land since 1992, but only opened to the public in 2006. It has acquired about 1,400 of its targeted 3,000 acres. The refuge's 6,300-square-foot Wildlife Center, one of the showcase visitors centers at any Northwest refuge, opened in fall 2007. The refuge provides important habitat for wild things, including 200 species of birds, in a rapidly growing suburban area, while allowing humans a chance to get out into nature and go bird-watching near home. A 1-mile trail is open year-round, with another 3 miles available May through September. *www.fws.gov/tualatinriver.*

Wallace Park

NW 26TH AVE BETWEEN PETTYGROVE AND RALEIGH STS, NORTHWEST
If you loved Alfred Hitchcock's classic *The Birds,* you won't want to miss Wallace Park in late September and early October. For about two weeks during their migratory route south, Vaux's swifts have been known to roost in the several-story-tall chimney of Chapman School on the west side of the park. Each evening thousands of birds circle the chimney and then drop down inside, one by one, for the night; at sunrise they fly out just as dramatically. *Map:GG7.*

CAMPING

Portland residents who want to get away for a quiet weekend camping trip need not drive far. Visitors from outside the city also have the opportunity to explore the city sights, its restaurants, and other attractions while staying inexpensively in a nearby campground. Metro, the Portland area's regional government, has upgraded Oxbow Regional Park, the nearest publicly owned campground to the city. Other campgrounds less than an hour's drive from downtown are managed by the Oregon or Washington state park system or by Clackamas County. Campsite fees range from $12 to $24, depending on the season and the amenities.

OXBOW REGIONAL PARK (6 miles east of Gresham via SE Division St; 503/797-1850) has long been a favored spot for fishing on the Sandy River, hiking through old-growth forests, and studying nature (especially the fall chinook salmon run). Installation of a new water-pumping and treatment system allowed Metro to construct two new restroom buildings, complete with hot running water, showers, and flush toilets. The campground was expanded to include 67 campsites. It's open year-round but does not take reservations. Pets are not allowed in the 1,200-acre park.

The **OREGON PARKS AND RECREATION DEPARTMENT** (800/551-6949; www.oregonstateparks.org) manages four state parks close to Portland that have campsites. The new **L. L. STUB STEWART STATE PARK** (31 miles northwest of Portland) has 78 hook-up sites, 12 walk-in tent sites, 23 hike-to tent sites, 15 rustic cabins, and 14 equestrian sites. The park is in a second-growth Coast Range forest, not the most appealing of Oregon's environments, but the quality of its construction and closeness to the metro area makes it very popular. **MILO MCIVER STATE PARK** (4 miles west of Estacada) has 44 electrical sites and 9 primitive tent sites. The main attraction is the park's Clackamas River frontage and its trail system for hikers and equestrians. **CHAMPOEG STATE HERITAGE AREA** (30 miles south of Portland and 7 miles east of Newberg) has 12 full-service sites, 67 electrical sites, 6 cabins, 6 yurts, and 6 walk-in tent sites. The park preserves a historic settlement on the banks of the Willamette River (see the Day Trips chapter). **AINSWORTH STATE PARK** (37 miles east of Portland in the Columbia River Gorge) has 45 full-service sites and 6 walk-in tent sites. Only Stewart and Champoeg are open all year. Reservations are available at Stewart, McIver, and Champoeg (800/452-5687).

The **WASHINGTON STATE PARKS AND RECREATION COMMISSION** (360/902-8844; www.parks.wa.gov) has three parks with campgrounds within an easy drive of Portland. **PARADISE POINT STATE PARK** (on the east fork of the Lewis River 16 miles north of Vancouver) has 58 tent sites, 18 utility sites, and 2 yurts. **BEACON ROCK STATE PARK** (35 miles east of Vancouver in the Columbia River Gorge) has 28 sites. **BATTLE GROUND LAKE STATE PARK** (19 miles northeast of Vancouver) has 25 tent sites, 6 electrical sites, 4 cabins, and 15 walk-in tent sites. Battle Ground Lake is open for camping all year, but the other parks are seasonal, except for two winter tent sites at the Beacon Rock Columbia River moorage. Reservations are taken May through September for Battle Ground Lake and Paradise Point (888/226-7688).

CLACKAMAS COUNTY (503/742-4414; www.co.clackamas.or.us/parks) offers camping at **BARTON PARK** (9 miles west of Estacada on the Clackamas River), **METZLER PARK** (5 miles south of Estacada on Clear Creek), and **FEYRER PARK** (3 miles southeast of Molalla on the Molalla River). Barton is largest, with 98 sites. Camping season runs May through September.

BOATHOUSE BRINGS POWER TO THE PADDLE

Portland's disparate paddling and rowing clubs joined together about five years ago to solve a long-running problem. Spread widely along the river, club members had no place to call home where they could mingle with their ilk.

Thus, several of the main clubs joined forces, with a big boost from the Portland Development Commission, to lease space in a warehouse at the east end of the Hawthorne Bridge. The giant **PORTLAND BOATHOUSE** now shares space with private architecture and software design consultants in the same building and doesn't look a bit out of place with its high-tech neighbors.

The lower level of the boathouse is stacked with more rowing shells in one place than you're likely to see west of Boston's Charles River. The boats can be conveniently carried to trailers for towing or hand carried down to the Boathouse's nearby Willamette River dock.

Partners in the Boathouse include five rowing clubs, a paddle club, river advocate **WILLAMETTE RIVERKEEPER**, and **ALDER CREEK KAYAK AND CANOE**, which serves the public by renting craft at the boathouse. Individuals can also rent space and store their private boats. *1515 SE Water Ave, Inner Southeast; 503/223-6418; www.portlandboathouse.com; map: HH6.*

—Terry Richard

CANOEING/KAYAKING

Many rivers converge in the Portland area, joining the Columbia in its final push to the Pacific. Boaters paddle kayaks and canoes at a leisurely pace along the shores of the **WILLAMETTE, COLUMBIA, AND TUALATIN RIVERS**, watching for great blue herons, which nest along the banks. White-water kayakers surf the rapids of the **SANDY, CLACKAMAS, EAST FORK LEWIS, AND WASHOUGAL RIVERS.** Pick up a copy of *Oregon's Quiet Waters: A Guide to Lakes for Canoeists and Other Paddlers* by Cheryl McLean and Clint Brown; it includes more than a dozen lakes within two hours of Portland. Another must-read for Portland paddlers is the third edition of *Canoe and Kayak Routes of Northwest Oregon*, by Philip N. Jones. The **OREGON OCEAN PADDLING SOCIETY** (www.oopskayak.org), with 300 active members, also fills a niche.

South of downtown, canoe and kayak rentals are available on both sides of the Willamette. On the west side, book a rental or join an organized kayak tour at **PORTLAND KAYAK CO.** (6320 SW Macadam Ave, Lair Hill, 503/459-4050; www.portlandkayak.com: map:JJ6). They also lead tours from the dock at **RIVERPLACE MARINA** downtown. On the east side, there's the floating **SPORTCRAFT MARINA** (1701 Clackamette Dr, Oregon City; 503/656-6484; www.sportcraftmarina.com; map:OO4), which rents flat-water kayaks, canoes, and motorboats. The marina's history dates to the 1920s, when it was just a floating moorage. At the north edge of town, **ALDER CREEK KAYAK AND CANOE** (250 NE Tomahawk Island Dr, Jantzen Beach; 503/285-0464; www. aldercreek.com; map:CC6) rents and sells a variety of inflatable kayaks, touring canoes, and white-water and flat-water kayaks, and offers trips, tours, and classes. It also rents from its store in the **PORTLAND BOATHOUSE** (see "Boathouse Brings Power to the Paddle" in this chapter), for launching from the east side of the Hawthorne Bridge and on the Tualatin River during summer.

In recent years, the state, counties, federal agencies, and private interests have combined to establish the **WILLAMETTE RIVER WATER TRAIL** (www. willamettewatertrail.org), a signed river route from Eugene to Portland. Two detailed waterproof booklets describe public land and access points along segments of the river. Pick up the guides ($10 for one or $15 for two) at a paddle shop or at **WILLAMETTE RIVERKEEPER** (1515 SE Water Ave, Inner Southeast; 503/223-6418; willamette-riverkeeper.org; map:HH6). Travis Williams, head of Willamette Riverkeeper, published a new guidebook to the river in 2009, called *The Willamette River Field Guide*. He also leads the annual five-day, 96-mile Paddle Oregon trip on the Willamette.

CLIMBING

On July 19, 1894, aided by the complex carbohydrates of an old-fashioned bean bake, 193 persons climbed Mount Hood and initiated themselves as members of the **MAZAMAS** (Mazama Mountaineering Center, 527 SE 43rd Ave, Southeast; www.mazamas.org). Now 3,000 members strong, the Mazamas is Oregon's biggest climbing group. This safety-conscious organization is a superb resource, offering seasonal group climbs, weekly lectures at its clubhouse, midweek climbs, day hikes, and other adventurous activities around the Northwest.

Throughout the year, avid rock climbers—as well as those just starting out—hone their skills at local indoor climbing facilities. The **PORTLAND ROCK GYM** (21 NE 12th Ave, Lower Burnside; 503/232-8310; www. portlandrockgym.com; map:HH6) accommodates a 70-foot lead wall, including overhang; it has 12,000 square feet of climbing, 30 top ropes, and 12 lead anchors. **STONEWORKS CLIMBING GYM** (6775 SW 111th Ave, Beaverton; 503/644-3517; www.belay.com) features 13 roped sections of wall and a large bouldering area. **CLUBSPORT OREGON** (18120 SW Lower Boones Ferry Rd, Tigard; 503/968-4500; www.clubsports.com; map:NN9), a sports megastore that includes basketball and volleyball courts and a soccer/hockey field, has a 45-foot climbing wall and 11,500 square feet of climbing space.

OREGON MOUNTAIN COMMUNITY (2975 NE Sandy Blvd, Hollywood; 503/227-1038; www.e-omc.com; map:GG4) rents and sells alpine and ice-climbing gear as well as rock shoes. Check out the piles of adventure literature lining the entrance for info on classes and trips, and see the For Sale bulletin board for gear. **RECREATIONAL EQUIPMENT INC.** (1405 NW Johnson St, Pearl District; 503/221-1938; www.rei.com; map:N1)—better known as REI—rents rock shoes, sells climbing equipment, and occasionally holds classes. It also has stores in Tualatin, Clackamas, and Hillsboro. Portland Parks and Recreation hosts spring and summer events that include rock-climbing classes in Portland and at Smith Rock State Park in central Oregon, as well as mountaineering ascents of Mount Hood, Mount St. Helens, and other Cascade volcanoes. Free mountaineering slide shows and lectures are a regular feature of the Mazamas, REI, and the **MOUNTAIN SHOP** (628 NE Broadway, near Lloyd Center; 503/288-6768; www.mountainshop.net; map: FF6). A favorite among cutting-edge technical climbers is **CLIMB MAX MOUN-TAINEERING** (928 NE 28th Ave, Sullivans Gulch; 503/797-1991; www. climbmaxmountaineering.com; map:GG5).

The following are a few of the major climbs (alpine and rock) within three hours of Portland. For a more complete list, talk to the experts at one of the local rock gyms or outdoor stores.

Broughton's Bluff

LEWIS AND CLARK STATE PARK, OFF E HISTORIC COLUMBIA RIVER HWY, TROUTDALE, ABOVE THE EAST BANK OF THE SANDY RIVER
Broughton's Bluff is just 30 minutes from Portland and offers about 200 midrange to difficult climbs. A new trail was cut in 1990, and the rock is relatively clean. The southwestern exposure protects climbers from the chill winter winds of the Columbia River Gorge.

Horsethief Butte

2 MILES EAST OF THE DALLES BRIDGE, ON HWY 14 IN WASHINGTON
Here's a good practice spot 90 miles east of Portland, a basaltic rock mesa offering corridors of short climbs and top-rope challenges.

Mount Hood

50 MILES EAST OF PORTLAND; INFORMATION CENTER ON HWY 26 IN WELCHES; 503/622-4822
At just over 11,235 feet, Mount Hood is Oregon's highest mountain. Its beautiful asymmetry and relatively easy terrain to ascend make it one of the busiest peaks in the country for climbers. Still, unpredictable weather and very steep snow climbing (the last 1,500 feet) require either a skilled guide or solid mountaineering skills. During the spring climbing season, smart climbers start early, finishing before the heat of the day turns the snow to mush. By July, rockfall becomes a serious issue and the climbing season is pretty much over. **TIMBERLINE MOUNTAIN GUIDES** (541/312-9242) are based, during climbing season, at the Wy'east Day Lodge at Timberline. The primary guide service on Mount Hood and other Oregon volcanoes, this group teaches mountaineering, mountain-climbing, and ice-climbing courses; rock climbing is taught at Smith Rock State Park and in the Columbia Gorge. *www.fs.fed. us/r6/mthood.*

Mount St. Helens National Volcanic Monument

55 MILES NORTHEAST OF PORTLAND VIA HWY 503 IN WASHINGTON; 360/449-7800 HEADQUARTERS, OR 360/449-7861 CLIMBING HOTLINE
Flat-rimmed Mount St. Helens, about an hour's drive north of Portland and east of I-5, enthralls visitors. The 8,365-foot volcano's fame was established in its incredible eruption of May 18, 1980. Most climbers take one of two trails up the south face: Butte Camp or Monitor Ridge. These are more like rugged hikes than real alpine climbs, but an ice ax is still recommended. The all-day climb (8 miles round-trip) is ideal for novice alpinists; the only big dangers are some loose-rock cliffs and the unstable edge around the crater. A climbing permit is required ($15 per person, plus a $7 service charge); a few are available on a daily basis, but it's best to reserve in advance online at www.mshinstitute.org. In winter, backcountry adventurers can ski down. For more on Mount St. Helens, see the Day Trips chapter. *www.fs.fed.us/r6/ gpnf/mshnvm.*

Smith Rock State Park

9 MILES NORTHEAST OF REDMOND OFF HWY 97, 3 HOURS SOUTHEAST OF PORTLAND; 541/548-7501
Its extremely challenging routes (the welded-tuff volcanic rock is sometimes soft enough to tear off in your hand), stunning scenery, and arid climate have helped make Smith Rock a mecca for world-class climbers. The park is open year-round, but rock climbers are busiest March to May and September to November. There are more than 1,000 routes in the park (as well as great hiking trails and scenic vistas)—something for all abilities. The nationwide climbing consensus is that the "Just Do It" route is still one of the hardest in the country, although several other less famous but just as difficult routes have been put up in the park in recent years. Bivouac camping only (hike-in sites; showers available; no reservations) along the Crooked River. *Climber's Guide to Smith Rock* by Alan Watts will teach you the ropes. *www.smithrock.com.*

FISHING

To maintain a minimum number of spawning chinook salmon, the Oregon Department of Fish and Wildlife has issued quotas on Portland-area waters. Once, from February through June, fanatical anglers would line their boats from bank to bank across the Willamette River, wait for the river's monsters to bite, and be rewarded with 10- to 30-pound salmon. In recent years, quotas of 3,000 or 6,000 fish caught after April 1 have brought the season to a close by mid-May. Indeed, the fishing week has been limited to a few days in some instances.

Even so, there's a lot of fun to be had: industrious fishermen head for other nearby waters with an open season. Throughout the year, the **CLACKAMAS** and **SANDY RIVERS** lure a steady stream of anglers to their banks, with deep pools that hold spring chinook salmon and summer and winter steelhead.

The Willamette is a good place to catch warm-water species such as bass, bluegill, and crappies. **BLUE LAKE PARK** in the East Portland suburb of Fairview (off I-84) and **SMITH** and **BYBEE LAKES** in North Portland (off N Columbia Blvd) are also good bets.

For more info on the best places for local fishing, pick up a copy of *Fishing in Oregon* (10th edition), by Madelynne Sheehan, at a local outdoor store or bookstore. Hog liners and other anglers can find salmon and steelhead tag information at the **OREGON DEPARTMENT OF FISH AND WILDLIFE** (503/947-6200, press 2, a 24-hour automated number that provides answers to oft-asked questions; www.dfw.state.or.us); also, pick up the annual regulations at fishing-tackle stores. The state sponsors a free weekend of fishing on an early Saturday in June. The **OREGON STATE MARINE BOARD** (435 Commercial St NE, Ste 400, Salem OR 97310; 503/378-8587; www.oregon. gov/osmb) publishes a guide to the lower Columbia and Willamette rivers, as well as a statewide facilities guide that includes information on boat ramps, parking, and types of fishing available.

Guide services are numerous and easy to find under "Fishing Trips" in the Yellow Pages. For home-river specialists, try **JACK'S SNACKS AND TACKLE** (1208 E Historic Columbia River Hwy, Troutdale; *503/665-2257*), on the Sandy River, or **NORTHWEST FLYFISHING OUTFITTERS** (10910 NE Halsey St, Gateway; 503/252-1529; map:GG2).

Two local sport-fishing groups have been especially active in watchdogging area fish populations. The **ASSOCIATION OF NORTHWEST STEELHEADERS** (503/653-4176) promotes fishery enhancement and protection programs, river access, and improved sport-fishing. Since 1958, the **OREGON BASS AND PANFISH CLUB** (503/282-2852) has promoted preservation of, improvement of, and education about warm-water fishing in Oregon. Thanks to the club's efforts, access to warm-water fishing may be stabilizing after an increased amount of privately owned shoreline had been causing access points to diminish.

GOLFING

Portland has more golfers than greens, but additional courses are being built all the time. Currently, about 55 golf courses are less than an hour's drive from the city center, although half of them are private, including the older generation of spectacular courses: the **COLUMBIA EDGEWATER COUNTRY CLUB** (2200 NE Marine Dr, North Portland; 503/285-8354; map:DD5), **PORTLAND GOLF CLUB** (5900 SW Scholls Ferry Rd, Raleigh Hills; 503/292-2651; map:II8), **RIVERSIDE GOLF & COUNTRY CLUB** (8105 NE 33rd Dr, Sunderland; 503/288-6468; map:DD5), **PERSIMMON COUNTRY CLUB** (500 SE Butler Rd, Gresham; 503/667-7500), and **WAVERLEY COUNTRY CLUB** (1100 SE Waverly Dr, Sellwood; 503/654-9509; map:KK5). The following are among the best of the public courses in the Portland area.

Cedars Golf Club

15001 NE 181ST ST, BRUSH PRAIRIE WA; 360/687-4233

Just north of Vancouver, the Cedars offers a long, rolling challenge with a lot of water hazards. Clubhouse facilities are especially nice.

Eastmoreland Golf Course and Driving Range

2425 SE BYBEE BLVD, EASTMORELAND; 503/775-2900

Bordered by the Crystal Springs Rhododendron Garden and blessed with venerable trees and lovely landscaping, the second-oldest golf course in the state (founded in 1917) is a technically challenging championship course. In the early '90s Eastmoreland was named one of the top 25 public golf courses in the nation by *Golf Digest*, a rarity for a municipal course. *Map:II5.*

Heron Lakes Golf Course

3500 N VICTORY BLVD, NORTH PORTLAND; 503/289-1818

Designed by renowned golf-course architect Robert Trent Jones II, Heron Lakes is a championship-quality public golf facility with two 18-hole courses. Great Blue has been described as one of the hardest courses in the Northwest, thanks to water and sand on every hole. The Green Back is a bit less challenging and retains the old, economical rates. Located just 15 minutes from downtown, Heron Lakes is one of the busiest courses in the city. *Map:CC7.*

Pumpkin Ridge: Ghost Creek Course

12930 NW OLD PUMPKIN RIDGE RD, NORTH PLAINS (20 MILES WEST OF PORTLAND OFF HWY 26); 503/647-4747

Pumpkin Ridge's claims to fame have been hosting the 2006 U.S. Women's Amateur Championship, the 1997 and 2003 U.S. Women's Open, and the 1996 U.S. Men's Amateur Championship, which Tiger Woods won so easily that he had to turn professional in order to find a challenge. In 2003 *Golf Digest* rated it No. 39 on its list of top 100 places you can play. Designed by Robert E. Cupp, Pumpkin Ridge features natural areas and views of both the Cascades and the Coast Range. A second course at Pumpkin Ridge (Witch Hollow) is private.

The Reserve Vineyards and Golf Club

4805 SW 229TH AVE, ALOHA; 503/649-8191

Opened in 1997 west of Beaverton, the Reserve is a 36-hole, semiprivate golf facility with two courses, one designed by John Fought and the other by Robert E. Cupp. Fought's is a championship, traditional, 7,300-yard course with 114 bunkers; Cupp's is a slightly less difficult, open-design course with a lot of water and trees.

HIKING

Oregon offers superlative hiking. The cascading waterfalls of the Columbia River Gorge, the alpine lakes of the Cascades, majestic Mount Hood, and the rugged Oregon Coast are all within easy access of Portland. To really get away, however, you barely need to leave the city limits. A 30-mile hike on the **WILDWOOD TRAIL** begins in Northwest Portland in Forest Park; it's part of the **40 MILE LOOP** (www.40mileloop.org) hiking-biking-running system around the city. (The network's distance has actually now surpassed 140 miles.)

Looking for company? Metro's department of parks, trails, and green spaces publishes *GreenScene*, a seasonal guide to organized outdoor activities, including hikes.

For tramping farther afield, good maps of hikes in the Gorge and around Mount Hood can be found at the **FOREST SERVICE INFORMATION OFFICE** (800 NE Oregon St, Ste 177, near Lloyd Center; 503/872-2750; www. naturenw.org; map:GG6) and at local outdoor stores. Parking lots at some trailheads are subject to car prowls, so don't leave anything valuable behind. The following are a few of the better close-in hikes.

Columbia River Gorge

TROUTDALE (17 MILES EAST OF PORTLAND) TO DESCHUTES RIVER (100 MILES EAST) VIA I-84 IN OREGON AND HWY 14 IN WASHINGTON; COLUMBIA RIVER GORGE NATIONAL SCENIC AREA, HOOD RIVER; 541/308-1700

The Columbia's magnificent gorge has dozens of hiking trails. Its closeness to Portland and relatively mild weather make it a year-round destination. The east end, beyond Hood River, is especially beautiful when wildflowers bloom during spring. Trails in the midgorge ascend high enough to escape summer's heat; those at the west end are awesome during fall as the leaves change color. Favorite trails are Angels Rest at Bridal Veil, Larch Mountain at Multnomah Falls, McCord Creek at Warrendale, and Eagle Creek near Bonneville. Each spring, the **FRIENDS OF THE COLUMBIA GORGE** (503/241-3762; www. gorgefriends.org) leads hikes to lesser-known trails to follow the wildflower bloom. Also check out the book *Day Hike! Columbia Gorge*, by Seabury Blair Jr, for more than 50 recommended trails. For more on the Columbia Gorge, see the Day Trips chapter. *www.fs.fed.us/r6/columbia*.

Lower MacLeay Park

NW 29TH AVE AND UPSHUR ST, NORTHWEST

Balch Creek is one of the few streams that still flows unfettered down the heavily developed West Hills. Lower MacLeay Trail connects NW Upshur Street to Forest Park's long Wildwood Trail (see description in this section), but hikers can make a 2-mile loop up Balch Canyon by taking a right at the first trail intersection (at the stone hut), then right again at the second intersection (near an open meadow), ending up on NW Raleigh Street. A short northeasterly walk through the Willamette Heights neighborhood takes you to the Thurman Bridge above the park; take the stairs on the east side of the bridge back down to the starting point. *Map:FF7*.

Marquam Nature Park

SW SAM JACKSON PARK RD (JUST WEST OF CARNIVAL RESTAURANT)

A series of trails makes this one of the best hilly hiking areas in the city, with clever use of the Portland tram, light-rail, and street car allowing for interesting loops through the inner Southwest neighborhoods. From the parking lot and shelter off SW Sam Jackson Park Road, the trail to the right climbs 900 feet to Council Crest Park, where there's another trailhead. To walk to the Oregon Zoo, continue over the top to the intersection of SW Talbot and Patton roads; a short downhill trail leads to a Hwy 26 overpass. The trail to the left of the parking lot and shelter follows an old roadbed up and around Oregon Health Sciences University, crosses Marquam Hill Road, and comes out on SW Terwilliger Boulevard (another trailhead). At Terwilliger and SW Nebraska, the trail departs from the bike path and goes under Barbur Boulevard and I-5, coming out in Johns Landing, four blocks from Willamette Park. A third trail, a 1½-mile nature loop, also begins at the shelter and parking lot; follow the signs. The trails are all remarkably quiet and peaceful, but be forewarned: It's possible to round a corner and stumble upon folks making a temporary home in the woods. *Map:GG7.*

Oaks Bottom Wildlife Refuge

SE 7TH AVE AND SELLWOOD BLVD, SELLWOOD PARK

The nearly 3-mile trail begins in Sellwood Park, with another trailhead at SE Milwaukie Boulevard and Mitchell Street in Westmoreland. It can be damp at times—you're in a wetland, after all—but what an inner-city escape! See Bird-Watching/Wildlife Viewing in this chapter. *Map:HH5.*

Springwater Corridor

SE IVON ST, SOUTHEAST PORTLAND TO TOWN OF BORING; PORTLAND PARKS AND RECREATION, 503/823-2223

This is one of the region's best rails-to-trails hikes, 21 miles long. It's not urban chic every mile of the way, but the Springwater Corridor serves its purpose, connecting the downtown Hawthorne Bridge to suburban Boring. It also connects with the $30 million floating Willamette River boardwalk, the Vera Katz Eastbank Esplanade (named for a former mayor). While the trail has many highlights (among them the Oaks Bottom Wildlife Refuge and Powell Butte Park), it also has its share of lowlights (scruffy inner-city neighborhoods and industrial zones). The trail's "three bridges" project, completed late in 2006, spans the West Coast's major rail line, busy McLoughlin Boulevard and flood-prone Johnson Creek. The trail is used by bike commuters, athletes in training, mothers with strollers, bird-watchers, dog walkers, skaters, as well as walkers. It's a big hit with those who live nearby but also draws visitors from around the metro area. The corridor still has a few missing links where users are diverted to city streets in inner Southeast Portland. See Bicycling in this chapter. *Map:JJ1–JJ5.*

Wildwood Trail, Forest Park

WORLD FORESTRY CENTER, WASHINGTON PARK; 503/823-2223
One of the country's longer natural woodland trails winding through a city park, the Wildwood Trail is Portland's cherished refuge for hikers and runners. The shady route through groves of fir and aspen officially begins at the World Forestry Center (near the Oregon Zoo) and travels north, linking such attractions as the Hoyt Arboretum, Pittock Mansion, and Portland Audubon Society Sanctuary (at a trailhead on NW Cornell Road) before it plunges into the less-trodden territories of Forest Park. It ends some 30 miles later, at NW Newberry Street. Bring plenty of water, as there are no drinking fountains. Many spurs cross the trail, joining it to various neighborhoods and parks; trailheads are at a W Burnside Street gravel parking area and at Leif Erikson gate at the end of NW Thurman Street (hike Leif Erikson Dr up to Wild Cherry Trail, which climbs to Wildwood). The first 10 miles are well used; the last 10 miles (hike north from NW Germantown Rd to BPA Rd along Skyline Blvd) are good for solitude. The central 10 miles (NW Cornell Rd to NW Germantown Rd) have a few brutally steep sections in long, solitary stretches of rolling hills. Another trail begins across the Hwy 26 overpass and continues south, connecting the Wildwood Trail to panoramic Council Crest Park; a walk on this uncrowded mile-long trail is best when timed with the setting sun. Large, glass-encased maps of the entire trail are situated at convenient locations along the way. The Hoyt Arboretum Tree House has brochures and maps. The ultimate guide to the park's trails is *One City's Wilderness: Portland's Forest Park*, by Marcy Cottrell Houle. *Map:HH7*.

HORSEBACK RIDING

Although Oregon is about as far west as you can get, it's not the romantic Wild West of the Rocky Mountains. Still, look hard enough and you can find a horse to ride. Look under "Horse rentals and riding" in the Yellow Pages.

Flying M Ranch

10 MILES WEST OF YAMHILL ON HWY 99W (WATCH FOR SIGNS); 503/662-3222
Known for its Old West, down-home flavor, the Flying M is a great place to take the kids (ages 7 and up) riding, though the lodge has closed in recent years. The fee is $25 per hour per person, including a guide. Pony rides for the younger set are available. For more adventuresome travel, a handful of two-day overnight rides up Trask Mountain are scheduled each summer, including all meals, lodging, and singing cowboy's campfire songs at the top of the mountain. Flying M also takes private groups on overnight trail rides and has special steak-dinner, breakfast, daylong, and starlight rides. *www.flying-m-ranch.com*.

Hill Top Riding Stables

20490 SW FARMINGTON RD, BEAVERTON; 503/649-5497

The last public riding stable in the Portland metro area, Hill Top has 50 wooded acres, plus an indoor arena. Cost is $30 an hour; make your reservation on the day you want to ride. Once clients become known by the staff, they can rent horses and ride on their own.

ICE SKATING

Even in the deep of winter, you'd be hard pressed to find naturally occurring ice in the Portland area. Skaters settle for one of several indoor rinks.

Lloyd Center Ice Chalet

953 LLOYD CENTER MALL, NORTHEAST; 503/288-6073

For more than 30 years, only the Portland sky covered the ice rink at Lloyd Center, but in 1990, the rink and the mall went under cover. The facility includes a pro skate shop, where group and private lessons are available. Public skate admission (including skate rentals) is $9. *www.lloydcenterice. com; map:FF5.*

Mountain View Ice Arena

14313 SE MILL PLAIN BLVD, VANCOUVER WA; 360/896-8700

The star among the metro area's neighborhood ice rinks when it opened in 1998, Vancouver's ice rink has downsized from two to a single sheet of ice. Portland's junior hockey team, the Winter Hawks, uses it for practice. Frequent public skate sessions cost $7.50, plus $2.25 for skate rental. *www. mtviewice.com; map:CC1.*

Sherwood Ice Arena

20407 SW BORCHERS DR, SHERWOOD (SOUTHWEST OF PORTLAND); 503/625-5757

This rink opened in 2000 with one ice sheet, a pro shop, and a restaurant. Daily public skate sessions are $6.50, plus $2.50 skate rental. *www. sherwoodicearena.com.*

Valley Ice Arena

9250 SW BEAVERTON-HILLSDALE HWY (VALLEY PLAZA SHOPPING CENTER), BEAVERTON; 503/297-2521

The largest recreational skating rink on the Portland side of the Columbia River has been a fixture at the Valley Plaza Shopping Center for more than 40 years. Lessons are available, and skate rentals are free with $8 admission (children 6 and under skate free with a paid adult). There's public skating most weekday mornings, afternoons, and weekends. *www.valleyicearena. com; map:HH9.*

RECREATION

RIVER RAFTING

The local rafting season generally runs from April to October. Outfitters rent the necessary equipment to run the closest white-water rivers—Clackamas, Sandy, White Salmon, and Klickitat—as well as the Deschutes, the busiest of all. Since river conditions can change rapidly, inexperienced rafters should stick to **GUIDED TRIPS** (www.oregonwhitewater.com). For those who want to develop their own boating skills, a good place to start gathering equipment and information is **ANDY & BAX SPORTING GOODS** (324 SE Grand Ave, Inner Southeast; 503/234-7538; www.andyandbax.com; map:GG5), with its basement full of rafting gear.

Clackamas River

35 MILES FROM THREE LINKS TO CLACKAMETTE PARK (AT THE CONFLUENCE WITH THE WILLAMETTE RIVER IN OREGON CITY)
The upper Clackamas River is one of the most challenging runs so close to a major American city. The 13 miles from Three Links to North Fork Reservoir, just above Estacada, have Class IV water. Bob's Hole is a favorite play spot for kayakers. For a guided trip, arrange an excursion with **BLUE SKY WHITEWATER RAFTING** (800/898-6398; www.blueskyrafting.com) or **OREGON RIVER EXPERIENCES** (800/827-1358; www.oregonriver.com). The 22 miles of the lower Clackamas, from McIver State Park (near Estacada) to Clackamette Park, provide a good introduction for beginners; inner tubers placidly float it during summer, but cold water during spring runoff makes it potentially dangerous because of the risk of hypothermia. Shorten the trip by using Clackamas County boat facilities at the communities of Barton or Carver.

Deschutes River

100 MILES FROM WARM SPRINGS (ON HWY 26) TO THE COLUMBIA RIVER
Two hours southeast of Portland, the Deschutes is an extremely popular day trip, especially for the 10.4-mile "splash and giggle" day-use section on either side of Maupin (on Hwy 197). The river's lower 100 miles can also be run as a pair of three-day trips: 53 miles from Warm Springs to Sherars Falls (including the Maupin section) and another 42.4 miles to the Columbia River. The multiday float and fishing sections have a limited-use permit Friday through Sunday during the busy season. With some days seeing around 100,000 boaters each summer, the Deschutes has plenty of outfitters. Maupin's four big rental companies are **ALL STAR RAFTING AND KAYAKING** (800/909-7238; www.asrk.com), **DESCHUTES RIVER ADVENTURES** (800/723-8464; www. 800-rafting.com), **DESCHUTES U-BOAT** (866/468-2628), and **DESCHUTES WHITE WATER SERVICE** (888/324-8837).

Nobody does the Deschutes like the **IMPERIAL RIVER COMPANY** (800/395-3903; www.deschutesriver.com). The family-owned business has recently expanded its riverside lodge to 25 nicely appointed rooms. Because the outfitter is located riverside in Maupin, its trips start at a private launch (which beats the crowds that begin upriver), return to the lodge for lunch, then restart on the upper river after everyone else has left. The company's riverside

370

patio may have Oregon's finest outdoor restaurant seating during summer. *www.boaterpass.com.*

Sandy River

45 MILES FROM THE MOUNT HOOD NATIONAL FOREST BOUNDARY TO LEWIS AND CLARK STATE PARK (OFF I-84)
Most use is on the lower Sandy, a relatively calm 7½ miles from Oxbow Park to Lewis and Clark State Park, and a more challenging 8 miles from Dodge Park (near Bull Run) to Oxbow Park. A convenient rental outfitter, very busy on summer weekends, is **RIVER TRAILS CANOE AND RAFT RENTALS** (336 E Historic Columbia River Hwy, Troutdale; 503/667-1964); up to four people can float these sections for $55 per raft. In May and June, confident rafters and kayakers can run the longer section that starts at Sleepy Hollow near Brightwood. This passes the site of Marmot Dam, which underwent a planned breach in 2007 to let the Sandy again run free, and the Sandy Gorge. This section is designated an Oregon Scenic Waterway and features Class III rapids. The dam is still a de-construction site, so access is restricted, but boaters like the Class II water on the river at the old dam much better than the previous portage.

White Salmon River

The White Salmon River enters the Columbia River across from Hood River off Hwy 14, less than a two-hour drive east of Portland; Hwy 14 intersects I-5 at exit 1B in Vancouver and can be followed all the way to the river. The White Salmon, a federal Wild and Scenic River, is fed by springs; the river has Class II, III, and IV rapids. **ZOLLER'S OUTDOOR ODYSSEYS** (1248 Hwy 141, White Salmon WA; 509/593-2641, 800/366-2004; www.zooraft.com) offers guided day trips from April to October; the company makes up to five three-hour runs per day. Prices start at $65 per person. Another good resource for trips and supplies in the area is **WET PLANET** (860 Hwy 141, White Salmon WA; 877/390-9445; www.wetplanetwhitewater.com).

ROLLER AND IN-LINE SKATING/SKATEBOARDING

In Portland the best skate park is beneath the east side of the Burnside Bridge, which is pretty much maintained and monitored by those who skate there. Two park districts have also created places to ride. The **TUALATIN HILLS SKATEBOARD PARK** (50 NW 158th Ave, Beaverton) is part of the **TUALATIN HILLS PARK AND RECREATION DISTRICT** (503/645-6433). The **CITY OF TUALATIN SKATEBOARD PARK** (8535 SW Tualatin Rd; 503/691-3061; map: NN9) is part of the Tualatin Community Park. For up-to-date information on the best half-pipes, skate parks, and roller hockey leagues, try **CAL SKATE** (210 NW 6th Ave, Oldtown; 503/248-0495; map:K6); or look on www. skateoregon.com.

In-line skaters who long for open skies have a few options from which to choose in Portland: **GOV. TOM MCCALL WATERFRONT PARK** (see Top 20 Attractions in the Exploring chapter), **SPRINGWATER CORRIDOR**'s paved sections along the Willamette River and in Gresham (see Bicycling in this chapter), and the **BIKE PATHWAY** along I-205.

Oaks Amusement Park

7805 SE OAKS PARK WY, SELLWOOD; 503/233-5777

The Northwest's largest roller-skating rink stays open year-round: its floor is designed so that it can be cut away from the wall to float atop rainwater. A DJ rocks the rollers Friday and Saturday nights, and a giant Wurlitzer pipe organ entertains the rest of the time (the rink is closed most Mondays). A full session costs $5.75, plus skate rentals. The rink is available for private parties; call ahead. *www.oakspark.com; map:II5*.

Skate World

1220 NE KELLY AVE, GRESHAM; 503/667-6543
4395 SE WITCH HAZEL RD, HILLSBORO; 503/640-1333

Skate World describes itself as a "clean, family-oriented, modern skate center," and the rinks welcome all sorts of patrons and parties. Public skating costs $3.25 to $6.75, depending on the time of session.

ROWING

The Willamette is to Portland what the Charles is to Boston. When the weather is good, it's best to get on the water at sunrise; later in the day, barges and motorboats turn smooth water to chop. Most rowing takes place between the Sellwood and Fremont bridges. Boathouses on this stretch of water are at a premium, though the addition of the warehouse-size **PORTLAND BOATHOUSE**, near the east end of the Hawthorne Bridge, has helped tremendously. Check with **WILLAMETTE RIVERKEEPER** (1515 SE Water Ave, Inner Southeast; 503/223-6418; www.willametteriverkeeper.org) about renting space. **STATION L ROWING CLUB** (49 SE Clay St, Inner Southeast; www.stationlrowingclub.com) offers learning-to-row classes, as well as adult programs. For lessons, check with **LAKE OSWEGO COMMUNITY ROWING** (503/697-6503; www.lorowing.com); for sculling lessons, try **RIVERPLACE ATHLETIC CLUB** (503/221-1212, ext 776).

RUNNING/WALKING

Regardless of the weather, Portlanders like to run—a lot. This is, after all, the home of Nike. And those who don't run, walk. The **OREGON ROADRUNNERS CLUB** (4840 SW Western Ave, Ste 200, Beaverton; 503/646-7867; www.orrc. net) is the premier running/walking club in the Northwest with 1,300 active members ($30 per year for individuals, $40 per family). The club coordinates spring and summer running programs for youths, sponsors running clinics, and publishes a magazine and newsletter. The ORRC also puts on a dozen local races, including the Thanksgiving Turkey Trot at the Oregon Zoo. The annual **PORTLAND MARATHON** (www.portlandmarathon.org, www.teamoregon.com) is held each year in late September or early October.

Training clinics (free and fee-based) are held year-round, although the pace picks up in the spring and summer.

Council Crest Park

TOP OF MARQUAM HILL, SOUTHWEST

SW Hewett, Humphrey, and Fairmount boulevards form a figure eight to the west of this park, creating one of the more popular recreation paths in the city. People walk, run, cycle, even roller-ski here. The most heavily used portion is 3½ miles along SW Fairmount Boulevard, which circles Council Crest Park; this moderately hilly course on a clear day overlooks virtually everything from the Willamette Valley to Mount St. Helens. Take SW Hewett Boulevard to avoid the busier Humphrey Boulevard during rush hour—making, in fact, a figure nine. *Map:II7.*

Duniway Park and Terwilliger Boulevard

NORTH END OF SW TERWILLIGER BLVD TO BARBUR BLVD AND I-5

Runners have worn grooves into the lanes of the Duniway track, which now holds water like a drainage ditch. Up one terrace, however, is the quarter-mile sawdust track. The track has certain conveniences—the adjacent YMCA, an exercise and stretching area, public toilets—but parking is not one of them. Terwilliger continues all the way south to Lake Oswego, although few trot that far, due to the hills and hard asphalt surface. *Map:GG6–II6.*

Fanno Creek Greenway Trail

SW HALL BLVD AND GREENWAY ST, BEAVERTON

A suburban common, the Greenway along Fanno Creek is surrounded by modern commercial and residential developments. A 4-mile section follows the creek between SW Denney Road and SW Scholls Ferry Road, with another section between SW Oleson Road and upper SW Scholls Ferry Road. Long-range plans call for connecting it to the Willamette River. *Map:HH9.*

Glendoveer Golf Course

14015 NE GLISAN ST, GLENDOVEER; 503/253-7507

The sawdust trail around the circumference of this 36-hole golf course measures 2 miles and 95 feet, according to one coach who measured it for his team's workouts. The north and south sides border sometimes-busy streets, but the east-end trail curves through a miniature wildlife refuge in woods overrun with well-fed (and fearless) rabbits. *Open daylight hours; map:FF1.*

Gov. Tom McCall Waterfront Park and Willamette River Greenway

WEST BANK OF THE WILLAMETTE RIVER, 3¼ MILES SOUTH FROM BROAD-WAY BRIDGE

Noontime runners flock to the promenade in what's considered by many to be the city's front yard. It runs only 1¾ miles north from RiverPlace to the Steel Bridge; to the south, however (after a brief interruption), the path reappears along the river to Willamette Park, making a round-trip of 6½ miles. It also connects to the Vera Katz East Bank Esplanade, via the Hawthorne and Steel bridges, to make a 4-mile loop on both sides of the Willamette River downtown. *Map:A6–K6.*

Laurelhurst Park

SE 39TH AVE BETWEEN ANKENY AND OAK STS, LAURELHURST

Once a gully and swamp, Laurelhurst is now a lovely 25-acre parkland where paved and gravel trails crisscross under elegant shade trees, and a pond set amid manicured lawns holds ducks. The mile-long path rings the park—but pay attention to the kids on bikes and roller skates. *Map:FF4.*

Leif Erikson Drive in Forest Park

NW THURMAN ST TO GERMANTOWN RD

Runners share this road with hikers, dog walkers, and cyclists, but no motorized vehicles. See Bicycling or Hiking (Wildwood Trail) in this section. *Map: DD9–FF7.*

Mount Tabor Park

SE 60TH AVE AND SALMON ST, MOUNT TABOR

One of only two volcanoes within city limits in the contiguous 48 states (the other is in Bend, Oregon) has one of the better eastside views of Portland's West Hills and Mount Hood. Asphalt roads loop up the hill; the upper roads are for bikers and walkers only. Dirt trails stretch for 1 to 5 miles. The park has become a focal point for the city's dog-leash laws, leading to increased enforcement but also to more off-leash areas and hours throughout city parks. *Map:GG3.*

Powell Butte

SE POWELL BLVD AND 162ND AVE (UNMARKED STREET), SOUTHEAST

This is a hilly 2-mile run on an open butte. See Parks and Beaches in the Exploring chapter. *Map:II1.*

Tryon Creek State Natural Area

11321 SW TERWILLIGER BLVD (1 MILE OFF HWY 43), LAKE OSWEGO; 503/636-9886

There's lots of room to stretch out here, with 14 miles of trails. See Parks and Beaches in the Exploring chapter. *Map:KK6.*

Tualatin Hills Nature Park

15655 SW MILLIKAN BLVD, BEAVERTON; 503/629-6350

Fortunately, the Tualatin Hills Park and Recreation District has left Saint Mary's Woods virtually untouched since it purchased the 200 acres from the Catholic archdiocese of Portland in the mid-1980s. Deer trails work their way through the woods, but the path (clearly marked) makes a 1-mile loop on the west bank of Beaverton Creek. If it's wet out, the dirt trail is likely to be quite muddy. The Nature Park Interpretive Center is the focal point of the

1½-mile paved and 3-mile dirt trail system. Westside light-rail stops at the park's north entrance.

SAILING

Scores of speedboats chop the water on the Willamette River, making a simple summer Sunday sail a fight for survival, especially against the wakeboarders and personal watercraft in the stretch of river just upstream from downtown. And while sailing on the Columbia is certainly pleasant, windsurfing gets more attention on that river these days, mainly upstream from Portland in the Columbia River Gorge. Nevertheless, sailing is a business for the following organizations, which specialize in rentals and instructions.

Island Sailing Club

515 NE TOMAHAWK ISLAND DR NE, NO 103, JANTZEN BEACH; 503/285-7765
This members-only Columbia River club offers instruction for American Sailing Association certification and rentals (20- to 30-foot crafts) year-round. Members are also welcome at the club's two Washington locations. Charters are available. *www.islandsailingclub.com; map:CC6.*

Portland Sailing Center

3315 NE MARINE DR, NORTH PORTLAND; 503/281-6529
Primarily an American Sailing Association–certified school, the center allows students at all skill levels to practice the particulars of tacking and jibing on a range of boats (every day 10am–dusk). The center also rents to certified parties and offers brokered charters beyond the Columbia—to Baja or the San Juans, for example. *www.portlandsailing.com; map:CC4.*

Willamette Sailing Club and School

6336 SW BEAVER AVE, JOHNS LANDING; 503/246-5345
The club is a family affair, costing $500 to join and $42 per year. The club-owned school offers adult and youth classes. Most popular are the weekend and Thursday-evening classes from May into September and the weeklong youth session during the summer. *www.willamettesailingclub.com; map:JJ6.*

SKIING: CROSS-COUNTRY/SNOWSHOEING

The popularity of cross-country (or Nordic) skiing has outpaced the availability of new groomed trails, Sno-Parks (designated parking areas), and trail information. Many maps list the popular or marked trail systems, but Klindt Vielbig's guide, *Cross-Country Ski Routes of Oregon's Cascades*, offers a more comprehensive listing. So does Mike Bogar's *Best-Groomed Cross-Country Ski Trails in Oregon*. Portland has more than a dozen ski clubs that have banded together to form the **NORTHWEST SKI CLUB COUNCIL** (www.nwskiers.org).

Snowshoeing, which often uses the same locations as cross-country skiing, is booming at Mount Hood, as it is everywhere else with snow. Snowshoers are asked to walk alongside ski tracks in order to avoid obliterating them. Their best reference is *Snowshoe Routes: Oregon* by Shea Anderson.

Bend Ranger District

160 MILES SOUTHEAST OF PORTLAND VIA HWYS 26 AND 97 OR I-5 AND HWYS 22 AND 20; 541/383-4000

Fifteen miles west of Bend on the road to Mount Bachelor, the Forest Service's Swampy Lakes trail system has warming huts and exquisitely beautiful (if hilly) terrain. Six more miles up Century Drive is the Sno-Park for Dutchman Flat, a trail system that connects back to Swampy Lakes. Together, the systems are the best-planned web of trails in Oregon. The commercial **MOUNT BACHELOR NORDIC CENTER** (800/829-2442, ext 2909; www.mtbachelor. com) is the state's best, with 56 kilometers of groomed trails. Be aware of the mysterious workings of the Oregon State Park permit, sold at department of motor vehicle offices and ski areas. While you need the $3 daily permit to park at a Forest Service trailhead, you don't at the Mount Bachelor Nordic Center. If the state department of transportation plows the parking lot, you need a permit. If the resort manager plows the lot, you don't need a permit.

Mount Hood

50 MILES EAST OF PORTLAND VIA HWY 35 OR 26; SNOW CONDITIONS: 503/222-2211 TIMBERLINE, 503/227-SNOW MOUNT HOOD MEADOWS, OR 503/222-BOWL MOUNT HOOD SKIBOWL; ROAD CONDITIONS: 5-1-1 OR 800/977-6368

It takes more than a glance out the window to assess weather conditions at Mount Hood. Miserable rainy weather in Portland sometimes shrouds excellent Nordic conditions on the mountain. Snow reports can be dialed at each of the mountain's ski areas (the snow is rarely the same at all three). Of the major downhill ski areas, only **MOUNT HOOD MEADOWS** (off Hwy 35, watch for signs; 503/287-5438 Portland office, or 503/337-2222 mountain office; www. skihood.com) has a Nordic center, featuring 15 kilometers of cross-country and snowshoe trails; when the Nordic trails are groomed, the fee is about $10.

The Portland chapter of the **OREGON NORDIC CLUB** (www.onc.org) operates the popular weekend **NORDIC CENTER AT TEACUP LAKE**, on the east side of Hwy 35, across from the Mount Hood Meadows parking lot. A permanent lodge replaced a temporary trailer there. The 20 kilometers of groomed trails are open to the public for a small donation. The Nordic Club schedules year-round weekend activities, including hiking, backpacking, and cycling. **THE BENNETT PASS SNO-PARK** nearby has the highest elevation (4,800 feet) of any Nordic ski-trail system at Mount Hood.

South of Hwy 26, just past the Timberline Lodge turnoff (watch for signs), the **TRILLIUM LAKE BASIN** is especially popular. A local resident grooms the two main areas, Trillium Lake Road and Still Creek Campground Loop, as well as six other trails. For trail information and other Sno-Park areas, check with the **MOUNT HOOD ADVENTURE** (503/272-3062) at Government Camp, about 55 miles east of Portland.

Santiam Pass

90 MILES SOUTHEAST OF SALEM VIA HWY 20; 503/854-3366 DETROIT RANGER DISTRICT, OR 541/549-7700 SISTERS RANGER DISTRICT
The Forest Service trail system at Ray Benson Sno-Park near Hoodoo Ski Area is one of the most extensive in the state, with warming huts (and wood-stoves) at the trailhead and beyond.

Southwest Washington

76 MILES EAST OF PORTLAND, 26 MILES NORTH OF CARSON WA; 509/395-3400 MOUNT ADAMS RANGER DISTRICT, OR 360/449-7800 MOUNT ST HEL-ENS HEADQUARTERS
Oregon winter parking permits are valid, on Oregon-licensed vehicles, for Sno-Parks in Washington. Along the **UPPER WIND RIVER**, 20 miles of groomed, well-marked trails take you through generally rolling terrain, heavy clear-cuts, and forested areas (be sure to check whether the Forest Service road has been plowed). Two areas south of Mount St. Helens are both accessible from Forest Service Road 83. Recommended are the **MARBLE MOUNTAIN–MUDDY RIVER AREA** and the **APE CAVES–MCBRIDE LAKE–GOAT MARSH AREA**. Unmarked roads through gentle, wide-open areas offer extensive views of the volcano.

SNOWBOARDING AND DOWNHILL SKIING

Mount Bachelor

21 MILES WEST OF BEND, 180 MILES SOUTHEAST OF PORTLAND VIA HWYS 26 AND 97 OR I-5 AND HWYS 22 AND 20; 800/829-2442, OR 541/382-7888 SNOW REPORT
Oregon's premier winter-sports resort, as judged by size and services, is one of the most highly regarded in the country. The only thing that drops Portland's weekend getaway down the "best" lists is that there's no lodging at the ski area. Everyone stays less than a half hour away in Bend or Sunriver, which provides lots of lodging options, restaurants, and nightlife. Bachelor has runs for skiers of all abilities across nearly 3,700 acres of patrolled terrain. Panoramic views from the apex of the 9,065-foot volcanic peak ogle the Three Sisters Wilderness (thus the name "Bachelor") and, on a clear day, the entire range of the Southern Cascades from Mount Hood to California's Mount Shasta. Ten chairlifts serve skiers and riders from mid-November to late-May, and the mountain offers a 3,365-foot vertical drop. The U.S. Olympic team has trained on Bachelor's uppermost slopes in summer. Adult one-day tickets are in the $60 range, higher on peak days. *www.mtbachelor.com*.

Mount Hood Meadows

68 MILES EAST OF PORTLAND, OFF HWY 35; 503/287-5438 IN PORTLAND, OR 503/337-2222, 503/227-7669 SNOW REPORT
Meadows offers the most varied terrain of all Mount Hood ski areas, from wide-open slopes for beginners and novices to plenty of moguls and steep,

narrow chutes for the experts. This ski area is big: there are 85 runs, including one that goes on for 3 miles. Lift lines can be long on weekends for some lifts, but five high-speed express lifts and six double chairs get skiers up the mountain in a hurry. The vertical drop is 2,777 feet from a 7,300-foot summit; a Sno-Cat brings skiers even higher on good-weather days in spring. There are two day lodges, and night skiing is offered Wednesday through Sunday. Adult tickets are in the $55 range, higher on peak days. The resort has teamed with Hood River's many inns, making an attractive weekend outing. Meadows also operates Cooper Spur Mountain Resort, a family ski area with an overnight lodge and restaurant, on the northeast side of Mount Hood. *www.skihood.com.*

Mount Hood Skibowl

53 MILES EAST OF PORTLAND, OFF HWY 26 AT GOVERNMENT CAMP; 503/222-2695

With 210 acres under lights, Skibowl is one of America's largest night-skiing areas. It also is the state's lowest-elevation ski area (its base elevation is just 3,500 feet), which means it suffers during seasons with light or late snowfall. The lower bowl suits beginners and intermediates, while the upper bowl is challenging enough to host ski races and draws the region's best skiers for extreme, steep challenges. Also, a snowboard park includes an in-ground half-pipe. Facilities include four double chairs and five rope tows. Adult tickets are in the $35 range, higher on peak days. The ski area stays busy during summer with its Action Park and concerts. The ski area owner is also a principal investor in Collins Lake Resort, a development that is changing the face of Government Camp with more than 300 luxury condominium units. The town's first liquor store opened recently, inside the luxurious Lodge at Government Camp (affiliated with Timberline Lodge), with its upscale grocery store and high-rent hotel rooms upstairs. *www.skibowl.com.*

Timberline

58 MILES EAST OF PORTLAND VIA HWY 26, FOLLOW SIGNS 6 MILES FROM GOVERNMENT CAMP; 503/231-7979 FROM PORTLAND, OR 503/272-3311, 503-222-2211 SNOW REPORT

North America's only year-round ski area, with five high-speed quad lifts and triple and double chairs, is focused around the historic 1937 Timberline Lodge (see Mount Hood Loop Highway in the Day Trips chapter), situated at the mountain's 6,000-foot level. In summer, one lift carries die-hard skiers up to the Palmer Snowfield at 8,500 feet elevation right through Labor Day. After a brief break for maintenance, the season starts up again and continues, weather permitting, until snow flies for the new season. Night skiing got a major boost with the opening of a new chairlift in 2007 below the lodge. Timberline got a big boost in 2007 with the opening of the Jeff Flood high-speed lift, which tied the lift system together much better and offers more skiing down low when winds are howling up high. Adult tickets are in the $55 range, higher on peak days. On sunny spring days when all the lifts are running, there's a state-best 3,690-foot vertical drop. *www.timberlinelodge.com.*

SWIMMING

Water, water everywhere—but Portland Parks and Recreation discourages swimmers from plunging into the Willamette River. Though cleaner than it was half a century ago, the Willamette still has sewer-system overflows after rainstorms. The **COLUMBIA RIVER**, however, has two popular wading areas: at Rooster Rock State Park and at Walton Beach on Sauvie Island (see Parks and Beaches in the Exploring chapter). The **SANDY RIVER** at Troutdale and the **CLACKAMAS RIVER** at Gladstone draw crowds on hot summer days, but both are fed by chill mountain water and have been the settings for numerous drownings over the years.

The indoor public pools in the city are busy during the winter. Every year, thousands of children take swimming lessons at 13 pools through **PORTLAND PARKS AND RECREATION** (503/823-5130; www.portlandonline.com/parks); the **WILSON HIGH SCHOOL POOL** (1151 SW Vermont St, Multnomah Village; 503/823-3680) and the **SELLWOOD POOL** (7951 SE 7th Ave, Sellwood; 503/823-3679)—both outdoor pools—are among the more popular. The **EAST PORTLAND COMMUNITY CENTER**'s new pool, Portland Parks' showcase water venue, opened in 2009 (see "Pooling Energy Efficiency").

The largest indoor swim spot is **NORTH CLACKAMAS AQUATIC PARK** (7300 SE Harmony Rd, Milwaukie; 503/794-8080 hotline or 503/557-7873; www.clackamas.us/ncprd/aquatic; map:LL4), where there are attractions for all ages. Four-foot waves roll into one pool, and older kids can dare the twister and drop slides. There's a heart-shaped whirlpool for adults and an outdoor sand volleyball court. Admission is $9.99 for adults (less for district residents), $6.99 for ages 9–17, $4.99 for ages 3–8, free for children under age 3 (rates are less for the lap pool only). Lessons and aquatic exercise programs are available.

Most high schools have pools, but public access is usually limited to the summer months. Both the **MOUNT HOOD COMMUNITY COLLEGE** and **TUALATIN HILLS AQUATICS CENTERS** can handle many swimmers (see following listings). These are the better public indoor pools in the area.

Columbia Pool

7701 N CHAUTAUQUA BLVD, NORTH PORTLAND; 503/823-3669
One of Portland's largest indoor pools is actually two 25-yard pools side by side. The shallow one ranges from 1½ to 4 feet deep; the deep pool slopes to 7 feet. *$3.50 for adults 18 and over, $2 for children 3–17; map:DD7.* &

Harman Swim Center

7300 SW SCHOLLS FERRY RD, BEAVERTON; 503/629-6314
This is a hot spot in the Tualatin Hills Park and Recreation District's award-winning swim program; the water's 88 degrees make it noticeably 4 degrees warmer than most of the other pools in the district. Swimming instruction is

> ## POOLING ENERGY EFFICIENCY
>
> Portland Parks and Recreation likely ushered in a building blueprint for future recreation projects when it opened an indoor pool in 2009 at the **EAST PORT-LAND COMMUNITY CENTER AND POOL** (740 SE 106th Ave, Montavilla; 503/823-3450; www.portlandonline.com/parks; map:HH2).
>
> The $11 million project is a showcase of energy efficiency, water conservation, and other green features. It also has a playful shark made from recycled plastic, a three-loop waterslide, and enough pool space to keep hundreds of kids happy on a swim day during spring break.
>
> The 150,000-square-foot pool building uses windows and skylights to let in enough natural light to meet needs on all but the gloomiest of days, though an ever-watching sensor adds and adjusts artificial light when needed. The air inside is refreshed eight times hourly, and the water in the 4,500-square-foot leisure pool is constantly cycled through a four-step cleaning-treatment system, which means the addition of chlorine is kept to a minimum.
>
> The lockers were built with recycled plastic, and the showers are heated by solar energy. All in all, it's the cleanest, greenest pool in the business, at least for now.
>
> —Terry Richard

available for all ages. The pool runs the area's largest water-therapy program for disabled or physically limited individuals. *Out-of-district walk-in rates $9 for adults, $6.75 for teens and children; map:HH9.* &

Matt Dishman Pool

77 NE KNOTT ST, IRVINGTON; 503/823-3673
This indoor public pool's best feature is its 10-person whirlpool. *$3.25 for adults 18 and over, $2 for children 3–17; map:FF6.* &

Metro Family YMCA

2831 SW BARBUR BLVD, SOUTHWEST; 503/294-3366
Its location next to the Duniway Park track and running trail makes the Barbur YMCA extremely popular. (Avoid parking headaches and take one of the many buses that stop here.) The pool is available for lap swimming whenever the YMCA is open, except for a brief period on Tuesdays and Saturdays. A day pass ($13 for adults, $7 for 18 and under) entitles visitors to use the entire facility; members of the Southeast and Northeast YMCAs are welcome free anytime. Water step-aerobics and swim lessons are available to members. *Map:A2.* &

Mount Hood Community College

26000 SE STARK ST, GRESHAM; 503/491-7243
The Aquatics Center runs four pools: an outdoor 50-meter pool (Jun–early Oct) with morning, noon, and evening lap swims; an indoor 25-yard six-lane pool; a very warm (90–92°F) 4-foot-deep pool for the physically impaired; and an oft-used hydrotherapy pool. There is also a climbing wall. *$4 for adults, $3 for youths; annual memberships $305 for families, $230 for individuals; summer passes also available.* &

Mount Scott Community Center

5530 SE 72ND AVE, SOUTHEAST; 503/823-3183
A Portland Parks and Recreation facility, the community center has a 25-yard pool with six lanes. Another play pool has a slide, a lazy river, and a water vortex. *$4.50 for adults 18–59, $3.75 for teens and seniors, $3.25 for children, free for kids 2 and under. Map:KK4.* &

Oregon City Municipal Swimming Pool

1211 JACKSON ST, OREGON CITY; 503/657-8273
Lap swimming, swimming lessons, and water exercise classes are all available in this 25-meter, six-lane indoor pool. *Nonresident walk-in rates $4 for adults, $3.50 for youth and seniors; map:OO4.* &

Southwest Community Center

6820 SW 45TH AVE, MULTNOMAH VILLAGE; 503/823-2840
This attractive Portland Parks and Recreation facility in Gabriel Park has a 25-yard pool with six lanes. Children have their own pool with a slide and fountain structure. *$6.50 for adults 18–59, $4.75 for teens and seniors, $3.25 for children, free for tots 2 and under; map:II8.* &

Tualatin Hills Aquatic Center

15707 SW WALKER RD, BEAVERTON; 503/629-6310
At 50 meters long, this is Portland's largest enclosed public swimming pool. It's part of a large recreation complex in the Sunset Corridor, where the facilities include covered tennis courts, playing fields, and a running trail. The parks district operates an additional five indoor and two outdoor pools in Washington County. *$9 per session for adults, $6.75 for children; memberships and lessons are available.* &

TENNIS

Portland is well supplied with public tennis courts. **PORTLAND PARKS AND RECREATION** (503/823-2223) has 110 outdoor courts at 40 sites. Washington Park, which has six lit courts above the rose garden—and a waiting line on warm weekends—is a favorite. For a nominal fee, one-hour court reservations can be made May through September for individual outdoor courts at Grant, Portland Tennis Center, and Washington Park. Otherwise it's first come, first served—and free.

In addition, city parks owns two indoor tennis centers. The excellent **PORTLAND TENNIS CENTER** (324 NE 12th Ave, Buckman; 503/823-3189; www.pdx10s.com; map:GG5) has eight free outdoor courts and four indoor courts ($24 per 75-minute session). At **ST. JOHNS RACQUET CENTER** (7519 N Burlington St, Saint Johns; 503/823-3629; map:DD8), everything is under cover: three indoor tennis courts ($24 per 75-minute session) and three racquetball courts ($12 per hour). It closes June through August, when most tennis is played outside.

Other area indoor courts are open to the public, though some require more than a day's advance notice, and weekdays are a better deal: **GLENDOVEER TENNIS CENTER** (14015 NE Glisan St, Glendoveer; 503/253-7507; map: FF7), **H. M. TERPENNING RECREATION COMPLEX** (15707 SW Walker Rd, Beaverton; 503/645-6433), **LAKE OSWEGO INDOOR TENNIS CENTER** (2900 SW Diane Dr, Lake Oswego; 503/635-5550; map:KK6), and, across the Columbia, **VANCOUVER TENNIS & RACQUETBALL CENTER** (5300 E 18th St, Vancouver WA; 360/696-8123; www.vancouvertenniscenter.com; map:BB5). Here are a few of the better courts in the area.

West Side

GABRIEL PARK: SW 45th Ave and Vermont St, Multnomah Village; map:II8
HILLSIDE: 653 NW Culpepper Terrace, West Hills; map:GG7

Southeast

COLONEL SUMMERS: SE 17th Ave and Taylor St, Brooklyn; map:HH5
KENILWORTH: SE 34th Ave and Holgate Blvd, Brooklyn; map:HH4

Northeast

ARGAY: NE 141st Ave and Failing St, Northeast; map:FF1
GRANT: NE 33rd Ave and U.S. Grant Pl, Hollywood; map:FF5

WINDSURFING

See Columbia River Gorge (Oregon) in the Day Trips chapter.

YOGA AND MEDITATIVE HEALTH

With the myriad benefits of yoga, including fitness and beauty, its practice has been gaining popularity in the United States for years, and Portland is no stranger to the trend. More and more yoga mats seem to be popping up under people's arms, attached to backpacks, and on bicycle racks, and so it only makes sense that there are also a variety of yoga studios in Portland to choose from. Here are some of the most popular:

BIKRAM'S YOGA COLLEGE OF INDIA: 4831 NE Fremont St, Beaumont; 503/284-0555; www.bikramyogaportland.com; map:FF4.

COREPOWER YOGA: 2277 NW Quimby St, Northwest, 503/26-9642, map:GG7; 808 SE Morrison St, Buckman, 503/233-9642, www.corepower yoga.com, map:HH6.

GUDMESTAD YOGA STUDIO: 3903 SW Kelly St, Suite 210, Corbett; 503/223-8157; www.gudmestadyoga.com; map:II6.

HOLIDAY'S HEALTH AND FITNESS YOGA: 3942 SE Hawthorne Blvd, Sunnyside; 503/224-8611; www.holidaysyogacenter.com; map:HH4.

JULIE LAWRENCE YOGA CENTER: 1020 SW Taylor St, Ste 780, Downtown; 503/227-5524; www.jlyc.com; map:I2.

YOGAPADA: 1016 SE 12th Ave, Buckman; 503/963/9642; map:HH6.

YOGA PEARL: 925 NW Davis St, Pearl District; 503/525-9642; www.yogapearl.com; map:L3.

YOGA UNION: 2043 SE 50th Ave, Hawthorne; 503/235-9642.

Spectator Sports

Oregon Sports Authority

1888 SW MADISON ST, DOWNTOWN; 503/234-4500

This valuable resource for anyone interested in organizing or attending spectator sports in Portland and Oregon also has info on recreation. Look for the extensive event calendar on the Web site. *www.oregonsports.org; map:HH7.*

Oregon Sports Hall of Fame

8500 SE MCKOUGHLIN BLVD, SELLWOOD; 503/227-7466

The keeper of the flame for sports in Oregon, the hall is seeking a new location to display memorabilia from Oregon's best: Steve Prefontaine, Bill Walton, Mary Decker Slaney, Dale Murphy, Don Schollander, Rick Wise, Mac Wilkins, and the teams that won titles. *www.oregonsportshall.org.*

Portland Beavers

PGE PARK, 1844 SW MORRISON ST, DOWNTOWN; 503/553-5400 BUSINESS OFFICE, OR 503/224-4400 TICKETS

Portland rejoined the Triple A Pacific Coast League for the 2001 baseball season by buying and moving the Albuquerque Dukes as the cornerstone of its revitalization plans for long-established (1926) Civic Stadium, now known as PGE Park. In 2009, the city announced plans to turn PGE Park into a soccer stadium and build the Beavers a new home across the Willamette River in the Rose Quarter. The 140-game PCL schedule runs April through September. Last stop before players reach the major leagues, the Beavers are the top farm club of the National League's San Diego Padres. *www.portlandbeavers.com and www.pgepark.com; map:GG7.*

Portland International Raceway (PIR)

WEST DELTA PARK, 1940 N VICTORY BLVD, NORTH PORTLAND; 503/823-7223

The PIR hosts more than 400 events each year, for cars, motor bikes, bicycles, karts, and dragsters, but is trying to lure back a signature event after the Champ Car World Series withdrew. *www.portlandraceway.com; map:DD7.*

Portland Meadows

1001 N SCHMEER RD, NORTH PORTLAND; 503/285-9144
It's possible to catch live horse racing at the Meadows (October into March; call for a schedule), but if the timing isn't right, you can always watch simulcasts of greyhound and horse racing. *www.portlandmeadows.com; map: DD6.*

Portland Timbers

PGE PARK, 1844 SW MORRISON ST, DOWNTOWN; 503/553-5400 BUSINESS OFFICE, OR 503/224-4400 TICKETS
The Timbers play a 30-game United Soccer League schedule from late April into September, with plans to move up to Major League Soccer in 2011 with renovated PGE Park as a home. The city loves its soccer and routinely hosts world-caliber games and exhibitions. *www.portlandtimbers.com and www.pgepark.com; map:GG7.*

Portland Trail Blazers

ROSE GARDEN ARENA, 1 CENTER COURT, ROSE QUARTER; 503/234-9291 BUSINESS OFFICE, 503/797-9600 TICKETS, OR 503/321-3211 ROSE QUARTER EVENT HOTLINE
Owned by Paul Allen, one of the country's richest men and a self-avowed basketball nut, the Trail Blazers' long run of playoff appearances ended in 2004 but started again in 2009. They haven't won an NBA championship since 1977. Since 1995, the team has played the home half of its 82-game regular-season schedule in the beautiful 21,500-seat Rose Garden Arena. The season runs from mid-October into May or later, as playoff success permits. Recently, things have been looking up for the team: Allen has regained ownership of the Rose Garden and is building an exciting young team that features the 2006–07 NBA Rookie of the Year, Brandon Roy, and the No. 1 pick in the 2007 NBA draft, Greg Oden. *www.nba.com/blazers; map:O7.*

Portland Winter Hawks

MEMORIAL COLISEUM, 300 N WINNING WAY, ROSE QUARTER; 503/238-6366 BUSINESS OFFICE, OR 503/236-4295 TICKETS
Tomorrow's National Hockey League players compete today in the Western Hockey League. This developmental league grooms young hockey players for the big time, but the Winter Hawks already think their team is the best. The 72-match season runs from September through March. Some matches are held at the Rose Garden Arena. *www.winterhawks.com; map:O7.*

Index

A

385